The Freedom of Fantastic Things

Books by Clark Ashton Smith also Published by Hippocampus Press

The Black Diamonds (2002)
The Last Oblivion: Best Fantastic Poems (2003)
The Sword of Zagan (2004)
The Shadow of the Unattained: The Letters of George Sterling and Clark Ashton Smith (2005)

The Freedom of Fantastic Things

Selected Criticism on Clark Ashton Smith

Edited by Scott Connors

with maps by Tim Kirk

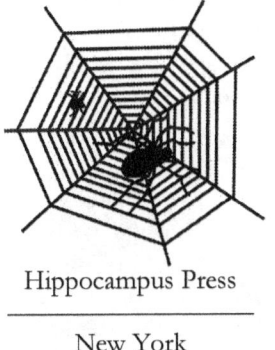

Hippocampus Press
New York

Copyright © 2006 by Hippocampus Press

Published by Hippocampus Press
P.O. Box 641, New York, NY 10156.
http://www.hippocampuspress.com

All rights reserved.
No part of this work may be reproduced in any form or by any means
without the written permission of the publisher.

Cover illustration "Resistance, or the Black Idol" (1903) by Franz Kupka © 2005
Artists Rights Society (ARS), New York / ADAGP, Paris.
Cover design by Barbara Briggs Silbert.
Hippocampus Press logo designed by Anastasia Damianakos.

First Edition
1 3 5 7 9 8 6 4 2

Hardcover: ISBN 0976159244
Paper: ISBN 0976159252

Contents

INTRODUCTION 7
Scott Connors

THE CENTAUR 11
Clark Ashton Smith

KLARKASH-TON AND "GREEK" 13
Donald Sidney-Fryer

CONTEMPORARY REVIEWS OF CLARK ASHTON SMITH 34

EBLIS IN BAKELITE 71
James Blish

JAMES BLISH VERSUS CLARK ASHTON SMITH;
TO WIT, THE YOUNG TURK SYNDROME 76
Donald Sidney-Fryer

THE LAST ROMANTIC 85
S. J. Sackett

COMMUNICABLE MYSTERIES: THE LAST TRUE SYMBOLIST 90
Fred Chappell

WHAT HAPPENS IN *THE HASHISH-EATER*? 99
S. T. Joshi

THE BABEL OF VISIONS: THE STRUCTURATION OF
CLARK ASHTON SMITH'S *THE HASHISH-EATER* 108
Dan Clore

CLARK ASHTON SMITH'S "NERO" 124
Carl Jay Buchanan

SATAN SPEAKS: A READING OF "SATAN UNREPENTANT" 132
Phillip A. Ellis

LANDS FORGOTTEN OR UNFOUND:
THE PROSE POETRY OF CLARK ASHTON SMITH 138
S. T. Joshi

OUTSIDE THE HUMAN AQUARIUM:
THE FANTASTIC IMAGINATION OF CLARK ASHTON SMITH 148
Brian Stableford

CLARK ASHTON SMITH: MASTER OF THE MACABRE 168
John Kipling Hitz

GESTURING TOWARD THE INFINITE:
CLARK ASHTON SMITH AND MODERNISM 180
Scott Connors

CLARK ASHTON SMITH: A NOTE ON THE AESTHETICS OF FANTASY 195
Charles K. Wolfe

FANTASY AND DECADENCE IN THE WORK OF CLARK ASHTON SMITH 200
Lauric Guillaud

HUMOR IN HYPERSPACE: SMITH'S USES OF SATIRE 221
John Kipling Hitz

SONG OF THE NECROMANCER:
"LOSS" IN CLARK ASHTON SMITH'S FICTION 229
Steve Behrends

BRAVE WORLD OLD AND NEW: THE ATLANTIS THEME IN THE
POETRY AND FICTION OF CLARK ASHTON SMITH 239
Donald Sidney-Fryer

COMING IN FROM THE COLD:
INCURSIONS OF "OUTSIDENESS" IN HYPERBOREA 259
Steven Tompkins

AS SHADOWS WAIT UPON THE SUN: CLARK ASHTON SMITH'S ZOTHIQUE 277
Jim Rockhill

INTO THE WOODS: THE HUMAN GEOGRAPHY OF AVEROIGNE 293
Stefan Dziemianowicz

SORCEROUS STYLE: CLARK ASHTON SMITH'S
THE DOUBLE SHADOW AND OTHER FANTASIES 305
Peter H. Goodrich

LOSS AND RECUPERATION:
A MODEL FOR READING CLARK ASHTON SMITH'S "XEETHRA" 318
Dan Clore

"LIFE, LOVE, AND THE CLEMENCY OF DEATH": A REEXAMINATION OF
CLARK ASHTON SMITH'S "THE ISLE OF THE TORTURERS" 324
Scott Connors

REGARDING THE PROVIDENCE POINT OF VIEW 334
Ronald S. Hilger

AN ANNOTATED CHRONOLOGY OF THE FICTION OF CLARK ASHTON SMITH 338
Steve Behrends

BIBLIOGRAPHY 347
CONTRIBUTORS 357
ACKNOWLEDGEMENTS 361
INDEX 363

Introduction

Scott Connors

The late L. Sprague de Camp was fond of referring to the "Three Musketeers" of *Weird Tales*, meaning H. P. Lovecraft, Robert E. Howard, and Clark Ashton Smith. Regardless of the merits or accuracy of this nomenclature, it does suggest the close connection that the three writers enjoy in the popular consciousness. While the first two writers have achieved popular success, and in Lovecraft's case even a measure of canonical recognition, Smith has remained, to use Benjamin De Casseres's phrase, the "Emperor of Shadows," often seeming about to breakthrough into a wider public consciousness, but never quite managing to do so. Why this is so is a source of constant frustration to the cognoscenti who consider Smith to be in many ways the most interesting of the three men most responsible for shaping American weird fiction since their time, but there it is.

There are of course as many theories about this state of affairs as there are readers. One school of thought attributes Smith's relative obscurity to the lack of a touchstone or "brand" with which the public might associate him. Lovecraft has the eldritch horrors of the so-called Cthulhu Mythos, and Howard's character Conan the Barbarian ranks with Sherlock Holmes and Tarzan of the Apes as one of the most recognized literary figures of all time. Both writers have spawned multitudes of imitators. Smith, on the other hand, created whole secondary worlds such as Zothique, Averoigne, and Hyperborea, but as distinctly Klarkash-Tonic as these worlds might be, it is what he does with them that makes them memorable, and not anything intrinsically notable about them *per se*. Another theory, first proposed by the late Robert Bloch, suggests that because he outlived his peers by almost three decades, and because he scrupulously protected his privacy, Smith did not become the focus of the sort of legendry that arose following the premature deaths of Howard and Lovecraft (*SS* xvi–xvii).

Part of Smith's distinctive flavor may be found in his cosmic perspective, which he shared to a large degree with Lovecraft. "Literature can be, and does, many things; and one of its most glorious prerogatives is the exercise of imagination on things that lie beyond human experience—the adventuring of fantasy into the awful, sublime and infinite cosmos outside the human aquarium" (*PD* 14). Many people, including Smith's friend and mentor George Sterling, mistook his intent: "It is art in unhuman, almost unearthly form—a deliberate evasion of reality" (*SU* 291).

This did not, and does not, do anything to enhance Smith's chances of making the best seller lists. As he remarked to an early reviewer, "work like mine, which is so far removed from the everyday interest of the immense bulk of mankind, stands in little danger of being overestimated in these days" (*SL* 18). However, the fact that the reviewer wrote his notice indicates that sympathetic and perceptive readers did indeed exist.

Even in his lifetime Smith was the subject of considerable attention, more than either of his two colleagues. First he was praised and damned extravagantly as a poet, one of the so-called "California Romantics," a pupil and protégé of George Sterling and a nine-day wonder as the "Boy Keats of the Sierras." He attracted the attention and praise of such figures as Ambrose Bierce, Edwin Markham, and Vachel Lindsay, and was widely reviewed on both coasts and in England. Much of what was written about him failed to understand him or his work properly, but much did. Many of the avant garde regarded his work, and especially *The Hashish-Eater*, as being a mere extension of Sterling's; Witter Bynner's half-joking references to "the Star Dust Twins" are typical. This did not prevent the publication of Smith's work in venues such as the *Yale Review*, *Poetry*, *Smart Set*, and *Laughing Horse*, and it was no stranger to popular anthologies and even school and college textbooks.

As a writer for *Weird Tales* and later Arkham House, Smith became the object of an enthusiastic following among the science fiction fan movement. Much of what was written about him in the "fanzines" was impressionistic, uncritical and superficial, but as fandom matured so too did the quality and sophistication of the writing for the 'zines. Smith singled out articles by Stanley Mullen ("Cartouche: Clark Ashton Smith," *Gorgon*, July 1947) and Richard Stockton ("An Appreciation of the Prose Works of Clark Ashton Smith," *Acolyte*, Spring 1946) for special attention, noting that the latter in particular "really showed some understanding of my work" (*SL* 366). Occasionally the larger literary world would take notice in the form of a rare review of one of his collections, or the avant garde would see in Smith and his fellow writers qualities with which they themselves identified, as when Robert Allerton Parker praised Smith and Lovecraft in the surrealist journal *VVV* ("Such Pulps as Dreams Are Made On," March 1943). The increasing respectability of Lovecraft sometimes reflected some light onto Smith, as when August Derleth sent a copy of *Out of Space and Time* to William Rose Benét after he made some favorable remarks about Lovecraft's *The Outsider and Others*, saying that Benét should also "know Clark Ashton Smith." In the October 10, 1942 issue of *Saturday Review of Literature*, Benét pointed out that he was already quite familiar with Smith from when he was part of Sterling's literary colony at Carmel, and praised Smith's "extraordinary rhetoric." Benét would later publish some of Smith's poems in the *Review*. The "hip" monologist, Brother Theodore, would pay him tribute when he performed a version of a Smith story in concert that was later recorded.

After Smith's death in 1961, his study for many years was largely the private preserve of one man, Donald Sidney-Fryer, who had actually visited Smith twice with a view to compiling a bibliography. Assisted by a few of Smith's friends and fans, Sidney-Fryer not only established the foundations for all future scholarship in this field, but he also wrote some of the most insightful and valuable evaluations of Smith's oeuvre ever written, culminating in his magnum opus, *Emperor of Dreams: A Clark Ashton Smith Bibliography*, published in 1978.

Interest in Clark Ashton Smith has ebbed and waned since his death, but he has retained both a core audience and a reputation that has led others to seek out his books on the second-hand market when they were temporarily out of print. The first paperback reprints of his work from Ballantine's Adult Fantasy Series and the adaptation of "The Return of the Sorcerer" for the television show "Rod Serling's Night Gallery" brought Smith to the attention of a new generation of readers. Reprints of his Arkham House collections in both hardcover and paperback in England and an increasing number of translations of his work into German, Italian, French, Spanish, Dutch, Greek, Japanese and Finnish made his reputation an international one. His stories have been adapted for graphic novels and role-playing games. Scholars such as Dennis Rickard, Charles K. Wolfe, Marvin R. Hiemstra, and especially Steve Behrends advanced our understanding of Smith's work through their own work and especially in the preparation of primary source material such as his letters to H. P. Lovecraft. There would be periodic episodes of drought when prospective readers had to search out Smith on the used book market, making him highly collectable, but then there would come an explosion of new editions of his work to satisfy the pent-up demand.

The quality of scholarship in the weird fiction genre has improved tremendously over the past couple of decades, with the rise of a type of independent scholar who has brought a new discipline to the study, and Smith has not escaped their attention. At the same time a new generation of writers has arisen who name Smith among their influences; as they become better known, their tide lifts Smith's boat.

It is going on half a century since he drew his last breath, and yet his volumes and his philtres yet abide. Smith will probably never achieve the type of phenomenal popularity achieved by either of his two pen-pals, yet he undoubtedly will endure. Smith loved to watch the skies above his home in northern California, and as Leonard Cline observed "By starlight some men work, hoping for their books not the success of a season, but the success which established by a few readers keeping them on their shelves dusted by loving use."[*] I think that it is safe to conclude that we have not seen the apex of interest in the Emperor of Dreams.

---

[*]Leonard Cline, "Logodaedaly," *Book Notes Illustrated* 6, No. 1 (October–November 1927): 13–19; in *The Dark Chamber* (Cold Spring Harbor, NY: Cold Spring Press, 2005), p. 258.

Abbreviations used in this work are as follows:

ALS	autograph letter, signed
AY	*The Abominations of Yondo* (1960)
BB	*The Black Book* (Sauk City, WI: Arkham House, 1979)
BH	*The Book of Hyperborea*, ed. Will Murray (West Warwick, RI: Necronomicon Press, 1996)
CAS	Clark Ashton Smith
CAS	Steve Behrends, *Clark Ashton Smith* (1990)
DC	*The Dark Chateau* (Sauk City, WI: Arkham House, 1951)
DN	*The Devil's Notebook* (Mercer Island, WA: Starmont House, 1990)
DS	*The Double Shadow and Other Fantasies* (Auburn, CA: Auburn Journal, 1933).
EC	*Ebony and Crystal* (Auburn, CA: Auburn Journal, 1922)
EOD	Donald Sidney-Fryer, *Emperor of Dreams* (West Kingston, RI: Donald M. Grant, 1978)
GL	*Genius Loci* (Sauk City, WI: Arkham House, 1948)
JHL	John Hay Library, Brown University (Providence, RI)
LL	*Letters to H. P. Lovecraft*. Ed. Steve Behrends (West Warwick, RI: Necronomicon Press, 1987)
LO	*The Last Oblivion: The Best Fantastic Poetry of Clark Ashton Smith*, ed. S. T. Joshi and David E. Schultz (New York: Hippocampus Press, 2002)
LW	*Lost Worlds* (Sauk City, WI: Arkham House, 1944)
NU	*Nostalgia of the Unknown: The Complete Prose Poetry of Clark Ashton Smith*, ed. Marc and Susan Michaud, Steve Behrends, and S. T. Joshi (1988)
OD	*Other Dimensions* (Sauk City, WI: Arkham House, 1970)
OST	*Out of Space and Time* (Sauk City, WI: Arkham House, 1942)
PD	*Planets and Dimensions* (Baltimore: Mirage Press, 1973)
RA	*A Rendezvous in Averoigne* (Sauk City, WI: Arkham House, 1988)
RWP	*Red World of Polaris* (San Francisco: Night Shade, 2003)
S	*Sandalwood* (Auburn, CA: Auburn Journal, 1925)
S&P	*Spells and Philtres* (Sauk City, WI: Arkham House, 1958)
SL	*Selected Letters of Clark Ashton Smith*, ed. David E. Schultz and Scott Connors (Sauk City, WI: Arkham House, 2003)
SP	*Selected Poems* (Sauk City, WI: Arkham House, 1971)
SS	*Strange Shadows: The Uncollected Fiction and Essays of Clark Ashton Smith*, ed. Steve Behrends (Westport, CT: Greenwood Press, 1989)
ST	*The Star-Treader and Other Poems* (San Francisco: A. M. Robertson, 1912)
SU	*The Shadow of the Unattained: The Letters of George Sterling and Clark Ashton Smith*. Edited by David E. Schultz and S. T. Joshi (New York: Hippocampus Press, 2005)
TSS	*Tales of Science and Sorcery* (Sauk City, WI: Arkham House, 1964)

The Centaur

Clark Ashton Smith

I belong to those manifold Existences
Once known, or once suspected,
That exist no more for man.

Was it not well to flee
Into the boundless realms of legend
Lest man should bridle me?

Sometimes I am glimpsed by poets
Whose eyes have not been blinded
By the hell-bright lamps of cities,
Who have not sent their souls
To be devoured by robot minotaurs
In the infamous Labyrinths of steel and mortar.

I know the freedom of fantastic things,
Ranging in fantasy.
I leap and bound and run
Below another sun.
Was it not well to flee
Long, long ago, lest man should bridle me?

Klarkash-Ton and "Greek"

Donald Sidney-Fryer

Preface

This commemorative essay is being written on the eve of the one hundred and tenth anniversary of Clark Ashton Smith's birth, 13 January 2003. On that occasion a group of friends and admirers will dedicate a monument to Smith's memory in Bicentennial Park in Old Auburn, California. This essay seeks to honor not only Smith as a great poet but also that other great poet without whom there might not have existed any Smith as poet at all: George Sterling.

It is important that, in conjunction with the life and career of Smith, we review those proper to Sterling himself. What Sterling accomplished, initially under the tutelage of Ambrose Bierce, led inexorably to what Smith in turn achieved. The group that we have labelled the California Romantics, and that flourished from c. 1890 to c. 1930, or slightly refigured, to c. 1960, included other significant figures, but with the one exception perhaps of Nora May French, Sterling and Smith remain two eagles flying high over flocks of sparrows.

As the leading California Romantic, Clark Ashton Smith—poet, storyteller, painter, and sculptor—inherited from George Sterling the figurative Cloak of Elijah bequeathed him by Ambrose Bierce. It is their shared and uncompromising vision, their vision of what they perceived as the truth—and the burning need to communicate it in the manner of the Biblical prophet Elijah, that is, with utter passion—that we commemorate in this essay.

George and Clark, Respectively

George Sterling emigrated to Oakland, California, from his birthplace Sag Harbor, New York, in 1890. While working, during the period 1890–1915, as personal secretary for his uncle, Frank C. Havens, his mother's brother, a wealthy real-estate operator in Oakland, Sterling met a variety of significant literary figures there during the mid-1890s, including Joaquin Miller, Ina Donna Coolbrith, Ambrose Bierce, and Jack London. London belonged to the same generation as Sterling, and the others represented an important survival from California's first "Golden Age" of literature that had also included Bret Harte, Mark Twain, and Robert Louis Stevenson, among many others. Sterling became good friends with each of his new acquaintances, but a special bond soon united Sterling and London. Kindred spirits in many respects, they became the closest of friends: truly, drinking buddies and boon companions. Whereas Sterling called London "Wolf," London called Sterling "Greek." Although London would go on to become one of the most popular authors of his time, Sterling's fame would remain restricted more or less to the United States, Britain, and especially California. Because Joaquin Miller and Bierce had established a sort of literary beach-head in Britain during the 1870s, this foothold had served as a special mode of communication between the London and San Francisco literary scenes, a conduit that benefited many California poets and writers from the 1870s on into the 1920s at least. It helped many littérateurs who would not otherwise have become known abroad. These figures would include both Sterling and Clark Ashton Smith in their turn.

Jack London admired Sterling enormously as person and poet. Later, in the novel *Martin Eden*, he painted a glamorous portrait of him as the elegant and cultured Russ Brissenden. Sterling for his part thought so highly of London's ability as storyteller that he volunteered to edit and proofread all London's books published from the late 1890s up to his death, apparently by suicide, in 1916. Later still, during the 1920s, after H. P. Lovecraft and Clark Ashton Smith (as Sterling's own chief protégé) became close friends, but only through correspondence, Lovecraft often addressed Smith as Klarkash-Ton. However, in their own correspondence and friendship that lasted from January 1911 until the elder poet died in November 1926, Sterling and Smith simply called each other George and Clark, respectively.

Today many admirers of Smith's highly imaginative stories know Sterling only through Smith, and it would seem that, just as Sterling "carried" Smith in a sense under his protective aegis (during 1911–26), so now it seems likely that, as time goes on, Smith will return the favor and increasingly will "carry" his long-term friend and mentor under the aegis of his own ever-expanding international reputation as a unique and inimitable author. Nevertheless, Sterling in his time created an extraordinary legend of his own as a poet, and as the popular ideal of a poet in his public persona.

George Sterling: Poet Laureate of the Far West

At some point during the 1890s George Sterling (born in 1869, and thus in his twenties at that time) began writing his first mature poetry under the direction more or less of the satirist and storyteller Ambrose Bierce, who had agreed to act as Sterling's poetic mentor. Poetically the two had much in common: a disdain for the then fashionable sentimentality and a preference for traditional meter, form, and rhyme. Very much the product of the *fin-de-siècle*, Sterling's first major poem (in two extended sections) emerged as *The Testimony of the Suns*, a striking and grandiose appraisal of the cosmos at large. The first section is dated December 1901, and the second February 1902. The poem became the dominant feature, as well as title poem, of Sterling's first collection, published by W. E. Wood of San Francisco in 1903. It remains an austere and very sober disquisition on the uncharted and star-strewn immensities of the cosmic-astronomic spaces, as well as the utter indifference of the cosmos at large to human beings and their concerns while residing and evolving on a small and inconspicuous planet circling around an insignificant sun located almost at the edge of the Milky Way, one galaxy among billions. This long, rather digressive, but certainly impressive poem still represents the strongest statement of cosmic pessimism or nihilism ever penned.

The poem and the collection, by the scope of the subject matter and the quality of the execution, established Sterling as the foremost poet of San Francisco and California, if not indeed on the entire west coast of the U.S.—although he did not become recognized as such until the publication (under Bierce's aegis) of his next major poem, "A Wine of Wizardry," in the *Cosmopolitan* during the summer of 1907. Meanwhile, changes were happening in Sterling's life, of a radical but positive nature. In 1905 his aunt, Mrs. Frank C. Havens, gave her nephew his "freedom money," and with this gift he left the San Francisco Bay Area to settle on the Monterey Peninsula. He purchased some land in the village of Carmel-by-the-Sea, built a house there (as well as a cabin farther back on his property), and proceeded to devote his time to writing, fishing for abalone, hunting small game, growing a vegetable garden, and fostering other forms of do-it-yourself husbandry. Soon other writers and artists, inspired by Sterling's example, came down from the Bay Area to set up a Bohemian existence in Carmel. The town owes its early development and character almost completely to Sterling as San Francisco's "King of Bohemia" (as the journalist Idwal Jones nicknamed him). Apart from occasional sojourns back in the City and elsewhere, Sterling's principal residence from 1905 until 1913 remained the developing town of Carmel.

Whatever reputation he may have won from *The Testimony of the Suns*, the young poet soon saw it eclipsed when, through Bierce's influence, the *Cosmopolitan* for September 1907 published "A Wine of Wizardry," a glittering and highly colored fantasy in sumptuous rhymed verse. Sterling's poetic mentor outrageously trumpeted the poem's praises in his accompanying essay. The poem and the poet, no less than the claims made for them by Bierce, aroused an astonishing and often inimical chorus of controversy from all over the U.S. But the controversy produced Bierce's desired effect: it established Sterling as the poet laureate of the Far West, even if uncrowned as such. It placed poem and poet solidly on the literary map of America. Among other connoisseurs of the weird and fantastic, the science fiction writer Fritz Leiber has judged "A Wine of Wizardry" equal in value to Coleridge's ineffable effusion "Kubla Khan," that Holy Writ of the high romantic imagination.

Meanwhile, the performance that same summer of Sterling's first verse drama, *The Triumph of Bohemia*, had proven eminently successful for what it was, a hastily composed although competent poetic drama of no great merit, but amusing and appropriate. It depicted with naive idealism the triumphant battle waged by the good forces of Nature against the evil strategems of Mammon, seeking to cut the Bohemian Grove itself down for mere filthy lucre. Sterling had written the play for the Bohemian Club of San Francisco (to which he belonged) for its annual revels, or High Jinks, that took place every summer at the Bohemian Grove on the Russian River up in Marin County north of the City. This was a small forest of giant redwoods and of great beauty. The Bohemian Club subsequently published the play in 1907 as the second of Sterling's books of poetry. The national notoriety deriving from the magazine publication of "A Wine of Wizardry," no less than the local fame generated anew by his Grove Play, produced another and very positive result. It brought Sterling to the attention of the eminent bookseller and publisher A. M. Robertson, who owned and operated a successful bookstore in San Francisco, a significant cultural institution of its type known throughout the Bay Area.

Living chiefly in Carmel and making occasional sojourns up to the City, Sterling himself was very little affected by the great earthquake and fire that devastated much of San Francisco during April 1906, although he did go up there at the time to lend what aid that he could to those dear and close to him. Like everyone and everything in the areas surrounding the City, whether near or far, he felt the shocks, which had proven of unprecedented severity within living memory.

Both the major new poem and his first verse play now made up the principal contents of Sterling's next collection, *A Wine of Wizardry*, brought out in 1909, the first of ten volumes of poetry published by A. M. Robertson. Their titles evoke not only the poet's lush and exotic romanticism but also (some of them) their *raison d'être* in contemporary places and events of San Francisco and California, no less than in the world at large: *The House of Orchids* (1911), one of his best single collections; *Beyond the Breakers* (1914); *Ode on the Opening of the Panama-Pacific International Exposition* (1915), actually celebrated in honor of the completion of the Panama Canal in 1914, and at the resplendent fair grounds in both San Francisco and San Diego; *The Evanescent City* (1915), a series of three connected poems detailing the building, then the animated existence, and finally the demolition of the San Francisco fair's grandiose but ephemeral structures; *Yosemite: An Ode* (1915), celebrating one of California's greatest natural wonders.

But now the Great War that raged in Europe during 1914–18 obtruded into the lives of Americans everywhere when, in part because of the sinking of the British liner *Lusitania* (with American citizens aboard) by German submarine action in May 1915, the U.S. entered the war in April 1917, staying the course until the Armistice in November 1918. As part of his new role as San Francisco's unofficial poet laureate, several books by Sterling at this time reflect the war and connected events, as was perhaps expected, even if it did not result in some of his best work: *The Caged Eagle* (1916) and *The Binding of the Beast* (1917), a collection of war sonnets. (Although both the last two volumes reflect the Great War in Europe, the latter title does so much more than the former.) A special mention must be made here of a rare volume not brought out by A. M. Robertson, and one of the few books of poetry ever published by the Book Club of California based in San Francisco: *Thirty-five Sonnets* (1917), honoring Sterling's acknowledged supremacy in this form, almost invariably of the Petrachan type. *Rosamund* (1920), another verse drama, and the collection *Sails and Mirage* (1921), one of his best, are the last volumes by Sterling published by A. M. Robertson. Most, if not all, of these ten books constitute elegant examples not only of Art Nouveau binding but above all excellent printing by various fine-art printers of San Francisco during the period of 1909–23.

A variety of publishers, located outside California with two exceptions, issued Sterling's remaining seven volumes during his lifetime or afterwards: *Selected Poems* (New York: Henry Holt, 1923), his single most important collection by its very nature; *Truth* (Chicago: The Bookfellows, 1923), another verse drama; *Truth* (San Francisco: The Bohemian Club, 1926), a revised version; *Robinson Jeffers: The Man and the Artist* (New York: Boni & Liveright, 1926). Finally there are three posthumous collections: *Sonnets to Craig* (New York: Albert and Charles Boni, 1928); *Poems to Vera* (New York: Oxford University Press, 1938); and *After Sunset* (San Francisco: Howell, 1939). Of Sterling's four verse dramas, only two have been produced and performed, and moreover successfully, *The Triumph of Bohemia* in 1907 and *Truth* in 1926, both by the Bohemian Club. Both *Rosamund* and *Lilith* (1919) appear eminently stageworthy in a practical sense, and it might make a fascinating experiment for the Bohemian Club or some other appropriate organization in San Francisco to produce and perform these plays.

Along with an occasional negative criticism (as usually caused by his perceived lack of modernism), many honors came to Sterling in the course of the years between 1907 and 1926, and most of them he richly deserved. Following his unsuccessful sojourn back east (mostly in New York City) from the spring of 1914 until the spring of 1915, he returned to San Francisco, welcomed back as its unofficial poet laureate, a role that he played to perfection until his death late in 1926. The architraves of the grandiose edifices erected on the fair grounds of the Panama-Pacific International Exposition presented (in carved or engraved form) apposite quotations not only from the poetry of Shakespeare, Milton, Dante, Firdausi, etc., but also from that of Sterling as San Francisco's own adopted son. Somewhat later the San Diego version of the same exposition (constructed in Balboa Park) honored him with a "George Sterling Day." Following the fair in Bagdad-by-the-Bay, the vast piece of real estate that had provided the fair grounds became the Marina District, the northernmost section of San Francisco southeast of the Golden Gate at its most narrow location. The land was mostly fill.

All these honors represented the greatest public accolades that Sterling was ever to receive. It happened coincidentally during early 1915 that the governor and legislature of the state proffered to Sterling the position of poet laureate of California, seemingly created expressly for him as the state's most visible poet as well as its most flamboyant public figure of a poet. This was a very great and unprecedented honor, indeed! However, with characteristic self-effacement and generosity he did that which most people in his position would never have done: he declined the honor, insisting instead that such should go by all poetic justice to Ina Donna Coolbrith, that now rare survivor from California's first "Golden Age" of literature. With deserved acclaim Coolbrith fulfilled this position from 1915 until her death in 1928, thus outliving Sterling himself by several years. But, let us remember and emphasize, she could not have done so without Sterling's fine gesture of self-sacrifice. Only he would have known of all the help and encouragement that she had given as librarian at the Oakland Free Library to so many emerging minds, such as Jack London and the dancer Isadora Duncan, guiding their adventurous reading among the great books inherited from the past. After all, Sterling had honors to spare, universally if unofficially acknowledged as he was as the poet laureate not just of San Francisco but of the Far West.

Having changed almost overnight from artistic revolutionary or outlaw (at least as perceived in 1907 because of "A Wine of Wizardry") to virtual civic institution, Sterling entered the final phase of his life and career from 1915 to 1926, thus recognized as the very spirit of the City's now long-lasting Bohemia. In this role he functioned as the on-site but unofficial ambassador or master of ceremonies for San Francisco, entertaining a great variety of celebrities literary and otherwise. Whether in person or through correspondence, whether before or after 1915—in fact, almost from the very start of his life in California and lasting until his death—Sterling maintained an enormous range and number of friendships and acquaintances, and as indulged by San Francisco's city fathers, he performed various picturesque pranks on occasion, such as the celebrated swimming in the nude in one or more ponds or lakes of Golden Gate Park in the company of some attractive lady friend, also nude.

The poet, it must be remarked, was tall, slender, well knit, and spectacularly handsome. Many people referred to him as an Apollo, and he had great charm. He was also athletic, an excellent boxer, swimmer, etc. At Carmel he seemed to be a veritable ocean deity, frequently diving for abalone and other shellfish, and performing the task with skill and panache. Given his looks and charming personality, it is not a surprise that many females found Sterling irresistibly attractive, and that, with no strings attached, he consummated relationships with an innumerable succession of willing and beautiful women. Almost throughout the entire period of his marriage to Carrie, from 1896 through 1913 (they had separated in 1911 and were divorced in early 1914), Sterling had made love with a great many other women besides his wife. Carrie committed suicide by poison in 1918.

During all this very busy life and career Sterling not only had had his poetry and prose very widely published in all manner of periodicals and collections nationally circulated, but as always he found the time and energy to help, encourage, and instruct innumerable poets, both men and women. Apparently he regarded this as a sacred obligation, the passing of the "sacred fire" of art from one generation to another, and it is the one thing that remains as a genuine credit, in a very personal sense, to his memory, and that possesses a real nobility and selflessness. Although he had others, his one outstanding protégé was Clark Ashton Smith, "The Bard of Auburn." In addition, as we have already indicated, Sterling was one of the first to "discover" Robinson Jeffers, and with his monograph on Jeffers (the very first ever dedicated to him) to play a pivotal role in establishing him as a major new poet.

Paradoxically, as he approached the end of his life and career, Sterling increasingly felt himself to be a failure, so much had poetic tastes changed since the *fin-de-siècle* when he had come of age. During the 1920s the whole trend of literary art, at least in English, was radically changing from the long-established romance tradition, that is, from the highly imaginative, to the disillusioned and ironic nitty-gritty of modern realism. In a bold and innovative fashion Sterling had specialized in creating highly imaginative poetry, but quite apart from his *manner*, his *matter* had presumably much less relevance and appeal to the young intellectuals taking over the emerging literary establishment.

Despite this radical and catastrophic shift in literary taste—catastrophic at least from the elder poet's perspective—Sterling nonetheless managed to leave behind him quite a substantial output, especially from the very last decade of his life: eight collections of lyrical poems, three volumes of occasional pieces, four or five verse dramas, one study of a fellow poet; and then between 1928 and 1939 three posthumous collections appeared. Sterling scholars rate his last three verse plays as ranking among his very best work, comparable to such early extended pieces as *The Testimony of the Suns* and "A Wine of Wizardry."

Just as important, perhaps, Sterling also left behind him one protégé and poet similar to himself in style and substance, but with far greater depth. This person would not only redeem Sterling's own type of make-believe, as the direct inheritance of the full-blown romantic tradition, but would also redeem—incidentally and in an indirect manner—Sterling's own substantial poetic output, and justify its existence despite the condition of half-oblivion into which it would lapse, leaving behind it a curious legend as of fabulous treasures but remotely known and unintentionally buried amid the shifting sands of time. This person was the still young "Bard of Auburn."

Clark Ashton Smith: Poet Laureate of the Otherworldly

Smith was in his early thirties when his great and good friend, patron, and poetic mentor died in San Francisco, whether by deliberate or accidental suicide, on 17 November 1926. Of course, his death proved an extraordinary loss to the younger poet, but it also occasioned, as was to be expected, near universal regret in much of northern California, and even to some extent in the southern part of the state, where Sterling had accomplished some script writing for Hollywood on a sporadic basis. We can gauge the depth of Smith's own loss by reading his first and most extended poem to Sterling's memory, which first appeared in the *Overland Monthly* for November 1927, and of which the first stanza reads as follows:

> Farewell, a late farewell! Tearless and unforgetting,
> Alone, aloof, I twine
> Cypress and golden rose, plucked at the chill sunsetting,
> Laurel, amaracus, and dark December vine
> Into a garland wove not too unworthily
> For thee who seekest now an asphodel divine.
> Though immaterial the leaf and blossom be,
> Haply they shall outlinger these the seasons bring,
> The seasons take, and tell of mortal monody
> Through many a mortal spring.
> —"A Valediction to George Sterling" (*SP* 258)

If Smith, thus left behind, would redeem the full-blown romantic tradition, with its complete appanage of imaginative efflorescence, as he had inherited it from the elder poet, he would achieve this, paradoxically, by doing it in the very manner which Sterling had counselled him overtly not to use. Noting the trend that Smith's creativity was taking, as observed in the twenty-nine poems in prose included in *Ebony and Crystal*—and even more recently in the two short stories (actually extended poems in prose), "Sadastor" and "The Abominations of Yondo," both composed in 1925—Sterling had sincerely advised his protégé to give up "this macabre prose." However, if Smith had done as counselled, the very avalanche of highly imaginative tales that he would produce from 1928 to 1938 for *Weird Tales*, *Wonder Stories*, and other pulp magazines of the period before World War II would never have materialized, and neither Smith nor Sterling would be as well known as they are today.

Although he had seemingly tended to disparage himself and his kind of imaginative poetry as he neared the end of his life and career, the truth is that Sterling did, of course, take himself quite seriously as an artist. It would seem that to some of his friends and correspondents the elder poet depreciated his own work, but he did not do so to all of them. As perceptively noted by Thomas E. Benediktsson in his excellent biography-cum-critical-study *George Sterling* (1980), Sterling's "correspondence with various literary figures is of great biographical and historical value" (174). It is much less in his letters to such well-known figures like Jack London and H. L. Mencken than it is much more in his letters to such lesser-known writers like Ambrose Bierce and Clark Ashton Smith that the true and serious artist reveals himself. As proof of this seriousness we may cite the three dramatic poems *Lilith* (1919), *Rosamund* (1920), and *Truth* (1923), which occupied much of Sterling's chief creative energy during his final decade. Poets and writers in general cannot produce great or outstanding work by taking the attitude that their output does not matter or has no value. It is this earnest aspect of Sterling's output to which Smith responded in depth, and which he continued as his own special inheritance from the elder poet.

After 1926 Smith continued it in a new mode, in prose, but he had already done so in verse for sixteen years, that is, for the period of his correspondence and friendship with Sterling, which began in early 1911. Two major discoveries had triggered Smith's development as a poet. In 1906, at the age of thirteen, he came upon the poems of Edgar Allan Poe, in the library of the grammar school in Auburn that he was attending. Taking the volume home in a veritable trance, he revelled for days in Poe's innovative meters and otherworldly melodies. Whatever poetry he may have experienced before, nothing impacted him as did the small but individual corpus of Poe's extant poems. In 1907, at the age of fifteen, Smith made another discovery, and this had an even greater impact on him and his poetic evolution. Twenty years later he described this discovery in "George Sterling—An Appreciation," published in the *Overland Monthly* for March 1927:

> Likewise memorable, and touched with more than the glamour of childhood dreams, was my first reading, two years later, of "A Wine of Wizardry," in the pages of the old *Cosmopolitan*. The poem with its necromantic music and splendours as of sunset on jewels and cathedral windows, was veritably all that its title implied; and—to pile marvel upon enchantment—there was the knowledge that it had been written in my own time, by someone who lived little more than a hundred miles away. In the ruck of magazine verse it was a fire-opal of the Titans in a potato-bin; and, after finding it, I ransacked all available contemporary periodicals for verse by George Sterling, to be rewarded, not too frequently, with some marmoreal sonnet or "molten golden" lyric. I am sure that I more than agreed, at the time, with the dictum of Ambrose Bierce, who placed "A Wine of Wizardry" with the best work of Keats, Poe and Coleridge; and I still hold, in the teeth of our new Didactic School, the protagonists of the "human" and the "vital," that Bierce's judgement will be the ultimate one regarding this poem, as well as Sterling's work in general. Bierce, whose own fine qualities as a poet are mentioned with singular infrequency, was an almost infallible critic. (*SU* 294)

This poem represented Smith's introduction to Sterling, and it would haunt and fructify the younger poet's mature work in verse and in prose from start to finish, and not just in the most obvious way. True, generically Sterling's poem anticipates, it is patent, Smith's later (and greater) compressed epic *The Hashish-Eater*, and many episodes in the latter poem anticipate some of Smith's later short stories; but by the same token Sterling's earlier poem not only prefigures Smith's own mature fiction of 1928–38, but at least one episode or passage, the one involving Satan and Lilith (not far from the poem's conclusion), directly anticipates one of Smith's very last stories, "Schizoid Creator."

At some point after his initial discovery of Sterling, Smith would have obtained the elder poet's first two collections *The Testimony of the Suns* and *A Wine of Wizardry*, and from *The House of Orchids* onward Sterling himself would have supplied Smith with copies of his own books as they came off the press. In January 1911 the two poets began their correspondence, the elder poet taking on the role of poetic mentor to the younger one and advising him during 1911 and 1912 not just concerning the first mature poems that Smith was creating at the age of eighteen and nineteen but just as much concerning which poems would constitute his first collection, *The Star-Treader,* brought out by Sterling's own publisher in November 1912. The subjects range from the cosmic-astronomic spaces and Graeco-Roman mythology to charming nature vignettes and little-known archaeological or mythic topics. Despite Sterling's obvious influence in terms of cosmic-astronomic subjects, this first book of poetry still remains very much Smith's own.

Meanwhile, during June and July 1912 poetic mentor and younger poet met in person when Sterling had Smith come down from Auburn to Carmel to spend an idyllic month of great happiness, during which the latter shared almost all aspects of the older poet's ideal Bohemian existence. It proved a major eye-opener for Smith, and in quite a positive way. It was the younger poet's first prolonged exposure to residing by the sea, and it left a lasting impression on him (as found among other instances in the gorgeous lyric in alexandrines "Sea-Memory," created at the same time as analogous lyrics included in *Ebony and Crystal*). Things now happened rapidly in Smith's ongoing literary career after he returned home to Auburn.

By means of San Francisco's half a dozen daily and weekly newspapers, a wealthy property owner in Placer County, Boutwell Dunlap, who had just discovered Smith and his poetry for himself, triggered in August 1912 the official public discovery of Smith as a youthful poetic genius. The resultant uproar of publicity thus prepared poetry lovers, as well as the general public in California and elsewhere, to receive both poet and first volume with heightened interest, and (just as important) actually moved them to purchase copies of that first volume, which at one hundred pages made up a substantial volume of solid poetry. All this alerted the east-coast critics to the presence of a significant new voice. Despite the inevitable negative reactions incited by all the publicity—relatively low-key and not amounting to much numerically—Clark Ashton Smith had made his entrance, and then some, on the American literary scene.

Interviewing the poet Witter Bynner in *Town Talk: The Pacific Weekly,* in the issue for Saturday, 7 September 1912, Edward F. O'Day (he and editor-in-chief Theodore Bonnet served as the weekly's principal literary critics) provides us with an amusing sidelight on Smith's new-found fame, and how he and Sterling became yoked as poetic partners in the public's collective mentality. This interview or profile appears in the department "Varied Types," invariably written by O'Day himself.

> Bynner and George Sterling are friends, such good friends that Bynner is not afraid to speak freely of Sterling's poetry.
>
> "It is too stellar for me," he says. "There's too much Aldebaran in it. It gives me cosmic indigestion. Somebody at the Bohemian jinks called Sterling and this young poet Clark Ashton Smith the Star Dust Twins. It is shocking to me to see such a young man write poetry which might be written by Sterling. In saying so

I'm not deprecating Sterling. The young poet has some prodigious lines. But as Harry Lafler says, two are less than one. I like Sterling best when he comes closest to earth. For that reason I was delighted with that little poem of his about the coyote. I regard that poem as a most hopeful sign in Sterling's development."

The poem about the coyote is "Father Coyote," later gathered by Sterling into his fourth major collection, *Beyond the Breakers*. Already recognized nationally, Witter Bynner would go on to have a very long life and career, outliving both Sterling and Smith. His patronizing remarks about Smith imitating Sterling, however, are typical of other such comments at the time as well as later. Also, how two are less than one is at best a moot point. To have written cosmic-astronomic poetry such as Smith wrote—with the same depth and power of emotion, insight, and imagination as the younger poet commanded—would have been impossible for Sterling, all evidence to the contrary. He wrote only one such poem, and it remains his greatest, *The Testimony of the Suns*, even if the general sensibility permeates his overall output. To judge from Bynner's remarks, the significance of Sterling's as well as Smith's greatest achievements in verse completely passed over Mr. Bynner's head.

Yet for all their poetic and even personal similarities the two figures and their respective bodies of work are noticeably distinct, even without the difference in age between them. On the one hand, whereas privately Sterling was a true artist who took his art quite seriously, he went out of his way publicly to disguise the fact that he had often to work hard at his poetry. In addition to the demands made on him by his own creativity, he increasingly had to play the role of a public figure as the most conspicuous poet in California, and hence as the poet laureate of the Far West. Here his Apollonian good looks, his great charm, his practiced ease in society helped him enormously in such a role. On the other hand, although very poor in a monetary sense most of his life, Smith managed to have the luxury of leading a more or less quiet private existence during which he could concentrate on his own creativity almost completely. Relative to the extraverted Sterling, Smith was almost painfully shy and ill at ease around groups.

If Sterling reigned as the poet laureate of the Far West for the period of 1903–26, then his protégé would soon reveal himself as the uncontested poet laureate of the otherworldly, as "the emperor of dreams," and moreover one who would reign as such for a termless while. Whereas Sterling's life seems at times rife with bustle and animation, Smith's uneventful existence appeared to come to life only when his ongoing creativity manifested itself externally from time to time in a book of poetry and later in a book of short stories, not to mention the rare exhibit of drawings and paintings, together with his small but fascinating sculptures (which he would begin during the spring of 1935 and continue the rest of his life). The external uneventfulness of Smith's existence compels us to concentrate on the products and events of his creativity almost exclusively as the source of the greatest excitement.

Meanwhile, as formerly, Sterling did not let up in his advocacy for Smith. During his brief period back on the east coast (mostly based in New York City), from spring 1914 to spring 1915, when invited to read aloud from his own output before a group of influential or wealthy littérateurs and other solid members of the arts community there, Sterling instead insisted on reading largely from Smith's works. Then, late in 1915, before the Panama-Pacific International Exposition closed up for the last time, Smith came down from Auburn to see the fair during a visit to San Francisco with Sterling as his cicerone. The exposition's exuberant and grandiose architecture impressed and pleased the young poet, but not the amusement zone. All this occurred while, from January 1911 onward, the two poets were exchanging letters as well as manuscripts of their new and old poems, no less than the occasional clipping from newspaper or periodical.

In the year following the publication of Sterling's own *Thirty-five Sonnets* (1917), the Book Club of California brought out a small selection of only fifteen pieces of Smith's poetry, under the title *Odes and Sonnets*. Like Sterling's own volume, this is one of the few books of poetry ever published by this book club, probably the oldest in the U.S. Just as Sterling had secured publication for Smith's very first book of poetry, by his very own publisher, the elder poet's advocacy without a doubt played a decisive part in the publication of *Odes and Sonnets* in a small but elegant Art Nouveau *édition de luxe* of only 300 copies. The volume has only thirty pages. Each page is surrounded by the same decorative design by Florence Lundborg of New York, a design featuring peacocks, grapes, and pomegranates.

Distributed only to the club's members, like all their editions, this choice volume did not appear for sale in bookstores. Much more than general advocacy, Sterling had provided the succinct and pithy foreword (dated "Bohemian Club, / April 17, 1918"). Among other cogent statements, the foreword maintained that, vis-à-vis the "devotees of [poetic] austerity" (that is, the adherents of non-traditional modern poetry), "an even partial use of the intelligence that is their one asset will cause them to shrink from the stern conclusions involved in some of the passages of this book—to turn from its terrible vistas. Clark Ashton Smith is unlikely to be afflicted with present-day popularity" (*SU* 289–90). If this statement emerged as a true prediction—and it did at that time—then such was the price to be paid by the poet who donned the figurative Cloak of Elijah in the manner of Ambrose Bierce.

Although a great honor to the young but evolving author, *Odes and Sonnets* at best served as a mere stopgap or update on his progress as a poet. Whatever he may have achieved with The *Star-Treader* in late 1912—a volume that had gained in sustaining power during the ten following years—it now paled before *Ebony and Crystal: Poems in Verse and Prose,* issued by Smith himself in December 1922 (printed by the *Auburn Journal* press)—one of the most remarkable volumes of pure poetry ever published in any language. Once again Sterling had continued his advocacy with another preface (dated "San Francisco, October 28, 1922"), making even more audacious claims than he had made on behalf of *Odes and Sonnets*. As it turned out, his claims were and are completely justified. We quote his first paragraph in full.

> Who of us care to be present at the *accouchement* of the immortal? I think that we so attend who are first to take this book in our hands. A bold assertion, truly, and one demonstrable only in years remote from these; and—dust wages no war with dust. But it is one of those things that I should most "like to come back and see." (*SU* 290)

Because Smith published his second major collection himself, the edition totalled only 500 copies, rather than the 2,000 that Robertson had brought out of *The Star-Treader* in 1912, this figure being the usual number of copies mandated for the collections by Sterling that Robertson issued. Because Smith had self-published, Sterling took it upon himself, in person or by mail, to distribute the review copies that Smith sent him, with most of them going to the San Francisco daily newspapers and other periodicals. With such copies distributed under Sterling's aegis, Smith's latest major production was virtually guaranteed critical attention.

At over 150 pages, with over 90 short to medium-length poems in verse, almost 30 poems in prose, and one very long poem (totalling almost 600 lines) positioned after the first third of the volume, *Ebony and Crystal* ran almost two-thirds longer than any collection by Sterling in actual material, with the exception of Sterling's *Selected Poems*. The one very long poem, *The Hashish-Eater*, could have better and more profitably appeared as a separate book. Printed as it was at almost forty lines per page, and filling sixteen very full pages, the format just avoids being too crowded for its typeset layout. Whereas *The Star-Treader* sold for $1.25 per copy, *Ebony and Crystal* went on sale at $2.00 per copy, an incredible bargain even for 1922, given the extremely high quality of the contents, no less than its overflowing abundance.

In general the book received excellent reviews wherever it managed to get them, and it managed to get them principally because of Sterling's assiduous and effectual ministrations. In addition to his general and long-term advocacy on behalf of Smith's poetry, Sterling in a direct manner had contributed to the physical welfare and maintenance of both Smith and his parents. Sometime during the 1910s the elder poet managed to get a pittance mailed to the Smiths on a regular basis from one of California's authentic multimillionaires. He had convinced "Old Man" Templeton Crocker to send the family the monthly sum of $10.00, which must have proven useful, and which still represented something of real value back in the second decade of the 1900s, however small it may seem to us today. Then, beginning sometime in the later 1910s or early 1920s, two well-known patrons of the arts mailed Smith a small quarterly allowance, one of them being the well-known bibliophile and *fin-de-siècle* Bohemian Albert M. Bender (actually a successful lawyer) and the other being James Duval Phelan, one of the U.S. senators from California.

Bender sent Smith the allowance from the later 1910s until sometime in the early to middle 1930s. Phelan sent Smith the allowance from the later 1910s or early 1920s until sometime in the later 1920s.

Despite all these positive developments in Smith's life and career, the still young poet (he was almost thirty when *Ebony and Crystal* made its appearance) had just committed two major tactical errors in his career, as it has now become apparent in hindsight. Although he had submitted the manuscript of his second major collection to at least one New York publisher (Knopf, which turned it down with no more ado than with the customary form letter of rejection), for some reason or other he did not want to submit it to A. M. Robertson, although Sterling encouraged him to do so. Smith stated that he did not like the manner in which Robertson had conducted business with Smith in regard to *The Star-Treader*. Possibly Smith felt cheated, but in his letters to Sterling he did not state that overtly. However, Robertson's books regularly received reviews, and generally good ones, on both the west and east coasts, he had perfectly adequate book distribution, and whatever the business part of the deals he struck with his authors may have involved, he promoted them and their books efficiently and effectively.

Had he accepted the manuscript of *Ebony and Crystal* for publication, Robertson probably would have suggested that *The Hashish-Eater* be detached from the main mass of the contents and brought out in a separate edition, printed in the same style as any of Sterling's collections, thus allowing about twenty lines of blank verse per page, and furnished with a short preface by Sterling or some other notable, not to mention a brief introduction about the poem and its purpose by the poet himself. Such an edition would have totalled somewhere around 35 to 40 pages on good rag paper, and Robertson could have issued it as a companion volume to *Ebony and Crystal*. The chief volume, presented in a similar format but with far more pages, probably would have totalled around 240 pages, quite a large book of poetry for that time. Whether he liked or disliked Robertson's mode of business, Smith could have achieved much, much more career-wise if the San Francisco bookseller-publisher had issued his latest major collection, in however many volumes it might have required. The poems in prose could easily have constituted their own separate volume, say, as in the manner of *The Hashish-Eater* suggested above. The young poet certainly missed out on what could have developed into a major chance not necessarily for fame and fortune but simply overall recognition for him as a major poet by the literary mainstream.

The second tactical error in his career that Smith had just made involved the *Smart Set*, and sending a copy of *Ebony and Crystal* to the magazine for review. Mencken himself would probably have reviewed it, and quite favorably. He had already published in the magazine a number of the poems in verse and in prose that Smith had included in *Ebony and Crystal*, he certainly knew the high regard in which Sterling held Smith and his poetry, and he probably shared something of the same high value that Sterling put on the poems of his protégé. Mencken, like Bierce, had quite a fondness for romantic poetry, especially when profound and intelligent thought might lie behind romantic effusions.

George Jean Nathan and H. L. Mencken edited the *Smart Set*, the distinguished precursor to the *New Yorker*, from 1914 to 1923, and Sterling in his letters to Smith had mentioned the possibility of sending a copy to Mencken to review. Smith decided not to do so, thinking that the book would not prove to Mencken's taste. Whatever else such a review might have been worth, Smith would not have lost anything even if the only thing he might have received at the hands of Mencken was a mere capsule review. Such a review published in a magazine of national circulation and acknowledged prestige might have accomplished much for Smith in terms of national recognition at this time in his career. But it was not to be. The decision would haunt the young poet into the early 1940s.

In 1923 the New York publisher Henry Holt brought out the definitive collection of Sterling's own *Selected Poems*, which gathered all his best work into one volume. Because they had appeared in published form within half a year or less of each other, Benjamin De Casseres reviewed both *Ebony and Crystal* and Sterling's own volume, a large one, together for the magazine *Arts and Decorations* in the issue for August 1923, in De Casseres' regular department "And a Little Book Shall Lead Them." Once again the two poets were yoked together as a team in the public's collective mentality. Although this critic gave the books a favorable reaction, he himself had apparently burned out on poetry in general around that time.

The printing and binding costs for the 500 copies of his own new collection had forced Smith to become indebted to B. A. Cassidy, the editor and owner of the *Auburn Journal* and its press. Although the edition was apparently selling well enough, the sales did not suffice in themselves to take care of Smith's indebtedness to Cassidy, who nevertheless offered the poet another way to handle it. He suggested that, if Smith contributed a column more or less for each weekly issue, as prorated over a period of a few years, this would repay the newspaper's owner-editor for having printed *Ebony and Crystal*.

The poet was free to make of his column what he wished, to feature poems or epigrams or whatever in it. Clearly this represented an exceptional deal, and Smith agreed. Thus it was that Smith became a journalist, and "Clark Ashton Smith's Column" came into being. The new department would now see some of the newest, as well as most remarkable, pure poetry, no less than some of the most adroit and profound epigrams and pensées, ever produced in America during the next three years.

During the first half of the 1920s the *Auburn Journal* published 101 installments of "Clark Ashton Smith's Column"—the first dated 5 April 1923, the last 7 January 1926. The columns highlighted both poems and epigrams, but mostly poems: overall, 81 poems (59 original ones and 22 translations from Baudelaire), plus 329 original, and 17 selected, epigrams, etc. To the *Journal* overall, Smith contributed 84 poems. Most of the poems in *Sandalwood*—that is, 49 of the total 61 poems in that collection (37 of the 42 original ones and 12 of the 19 translations from Baudelaire)—made their first appearance in this column or department. Although most of the poems first published in the *Journal* have since reappeared elsewhere, almost all of the 329, or 346, epigrams and pensées have not, that is, until recently, languishing uncollected in the files of Auburn's leading local newspaper for over half a century.

Some east-coast publisher tentatively considered publishing a selection of them (as made by Smith himself) during the early 1940s. The epigrams and pensées appeared in the *Journal* under the following titles: "Epigrams" (once), "Cocktails and Creme de Menthe," "Points for the Pious," "Unpopular Sayings" (once), "New Teeth for Old Saws" (once), "The Devil's Note-Book," and "Paradox and Persiflage." "The Devil's Note-Book," as a title, has obvious analogies with Ambrose Bierce's *The Devil's Dictionary*, originally named *The Cynic's Word-Book*. At long last, after sixty-five years of languishing uncollected and unpublished in book form, a complete collection of Smith's epigrams and apothegms, as published by Starmont House, came forth in December 1990, compiled by Donald Sidney-Fryer, and edited with an introduction and notes by Don Herron, and under the overall title *The Devil's Notebook*. This chapbook-sized and softbound booklet totalled almost 100 pages. Smith's epigrams and pensées have obvious affinities with Bierce's definitions in *The Devil's Dictionary*.

Because once more Smith published another major collection of poems himself—his third, under the title *Sandalwood*, in October 1925—the edition totalled only 250 copies (plus the usual extra ones), and thus only half of that for *Ebony and Crystal*. The book, dedicated to Sterling, is about the same size in terms of width and height, but is paperbound, rather than hardcover, and at about only fifty pages overall, totalling about only sixty poems, *Sandalwood* contains about only one-third the amount of material that had gone into the second major collection. The book went on sale at only $1.00 per copy, another incredible bargain, given the extremely high quality of the contents, even if much less abundant than those of the previous volume. Whereas much of *Ebony and Crystal* seems epic in subject matter and monumental in tone, the character and subject matter of the original poems in *Sandalwood* appear much more gossamer and evanescent.

Once again Sterling took it upon himself, both in person and through the post office, to distribute the review copies that Smith sent him, with most of them going to the San Francisco daily newspapers. However, this time a book of poems by Smith received less than half a dozen reviews, even though the critical reaction proved favorable in general wherever the collection managed to get it. Because of its less than widespread distribution in a limited edition, *Sandalwood* at first underwent the same fate as *Ebony and Crystal* of being little better than unknown, and in fact of being even more unknown than the former volume. Nevertheless, whether in terms of technique, inspiration, or new directions in an imaginative sense, the new volume is no less remarkable and innovative than the last one. In particular the twenty or so translations from *Les Fleurs du mal* of Baudelaire represent a real triumph on behalf of Smith's technical mastery, inasmuch as he had learned sufficient French to make his translations in something less than a year, no mean accomplishment. Fancifully speaking, perhaps we can perceive in his mastering a new language some possible evidence of "ancestral memory," descended as he was from Norman-French counts and barons on his mother's side, the Gaylords or Gaillards, who had fled to Britain from France when the Edict of Nantes was revoked.

Let us ponder some of the implications of Smith's creativity during 1911–25, and the various personal and poetic statistics, that we have cited. When he is eighteen and nineteen, during 1911–12, he composes his first mature poetry, resulting in *The Star-Treader*, published in late 1912. However, a long period of self-education and apprenticeship has preceded this, from 1906 to 1910, during which he writes his earliest or juvenile poetry, imitations of Poe's extant poetry, as well as of Edward FitzGerald's version of the *Rubaiyat* of Omar Khayyam, among other models. The greatest influence has derived from Poe and (even more) Sterling's own opus "A Wine of Wizardry." The five years of this apprentice work suddenly results in a period of rapid and fervent creativity, 1911–12, and his first book. A period of mature apprenticeship ensues during 1912–22, when everything slows down again as during 1906 to 1910. Then in early 1920 things pick up speed again when from mid-January to mid-February he creates his greatest and longest poem, *The Hashish-Eater*, finishing it on 20 February, and totalling almost 600 lines of highly imaginative blank verse, most of it the result of white-hot inspiration.

The whole decade of 1912–22 culminates in *Ebony and Crystal*, published in late 1922. However, following the decade in question, things do not slow down, but throughout 1923–26 Smith maintains the speed, facility, and high quality of his poetic productiveness, over eighty original poems at least and two dozen or more translations. Although his productiveness and speed lessen somewhat, possibly by as much as half, he remains quite prolific all during 1926–30. By the latter date fictioneering takes over almost exclusively until 1934, when he resumes creating poems in verse in some noticeable quantity. Obviously we are dealing here with a great or major poet, but rather strangely, following his greatest period of productiveness in poetry, say, 1911–25, there is no major mainstream recognition of Smith as the great poet that he has patently become, a great poet who has just produced a major body of work as represented in three major collections, published in 1912, 1922, and 1925, respectively. (The highly productive years of 1923–25 have culminated in *Sandalwood*, issued in late 1925.) Has his long and patient apprenticeship under the poetic tutelage or mentorship of George Sterling amounted to nothing more than three or four volumes acclaimed only by a small chorus of discerning voices in California and Britain? Thus it would appear. Something is gravely wrong in this configuration.

Let us look around at the national and international situation regarding poetry (at least in English), and see if we can find a clue as to what else may have conspired against Smith receiving his just recognition as a major poet. The year 1922 saw the beginning of the apotheosis for that modernist poet par excellence, T. S. Eliot. During that year he won the Dial Award of $2,000 for his 434-line poem *The Waste Land*, which (including the fascinating notes) he had carefully prepared for publication with the help and advice of Ezra Pound. The latter figure would reveal his own poetic vision in all its abundance a little later in his own major work *The Cantos*. These two great poems, along with works by other significant modern poets, anticipated or signalized in advance the major shift in taste and sensibility that was occurring early in the 1920s, and that gained critical momentum as the decade progressed. In the case of his own major poem Eliot, only in his mid-thirties at the time, had summed up, in a thoroughly novel and then modern manner, the disillusionment and the disenchantment that had become prevalent among the younger generation following the catastrophe of World War I.

The implications of the triumph attendant on Eliot's own success, and later that of Ezra Pound, along with other modernist figures, can only be imagined for those poetic masters whose work had been painstakingly cast in the traditional prosody, regardless of the grandeur of the vision and thought behind their verses. Right in the forefront of these traditionalist masters Sterling and Smith occupied a prominent place, for those cognoscenti who knew their work in depth. The two poets in their final exchange of letters during 1926 show themselves quite conscious of the major shift in poetic taste and sensibility that was occurring, and also sensitive to the implications for their own respective outputs. Whether by deliberate or accidental suicide Sterling as the poet laureate of the Far West, the foremost public defender of the classico-romantic tradition, died in late 1926. True, his death represented a great loss to that tradition, not to mention personally to Clark Ashton Smith, but Sterling had accomplished almost everything that he could have on behalf of traditionalist poetry in English, that is, as it had evolved up through the first quarter of the twentieth century.

Just what could Smith do now, stranded as he was, almost "in the teeth of our new Didactic School, the protagonists of the *human* and the *vital*," the newly triumphant masters of the modern mode in poetry? Left behind in the countryside of rolling hills near Auburn, a thousand feet above sea level, Smith as the poet laureate of the otherworldly continued to live with his parents from the mid-1920s to the mid-1930s; but now, thanks to the earnest encouragement of Smith's friend Genevieve K. Sully, who, during the summer of 1927 when they were visiting Crater (now Hyperboreal) Ridge, urged him to write fiction for the emerging pulp magazines, the young poet would ignore his former mentor's advice to give up "this macabre prose" and would produce between the late 1920s and late 1930s some 140 completed stories.

There is a certain irony here because, just as "A Wine of Wizardry" anticipates *The Hashish-Eater,* and the latter poem anticipates much of Smith's fantastic fiction of that decade (1928–38), so does "A Wine of Wizardry" clearly prefigure in a generic way the extremely picturesque or pictorial character of many of Smith's typical, far-ranging, and most polished fantasies, his extended poems in prose.

At least one episode in "A Wine of Wizardry," the one involving Satan and Lilith, lines 155–64, directly anticipates one of the details or episodes near the end of one of Smith's very last stories of any type whatsoever as published in the fantasy and science fiction magazines of the early 1950s.

> But Fancy still is fugitive, and turns
> To caverns where a demon altar burns,
> And Satan, yawning on his brazen seat,
> Fondles a screaming thing his fiends have flayed,
> Ere Lilith come his indolence to greet,
> Who leads from Hell his whitest queens, arrayed
> In chains so heated at their master's fire
> That one new-damned had thought their bright attire
> Indeed were coral, till the dazzling dance
> So terribly that brilliance shall enhance. (Sterling 150–51)

In its issue for November of 1953 the magazine *Fantasy Fiction* published a late and rather mordant story "Schizoid Creator." Near the end of the narrative one of his lieutenants, Bifrons, comes to report to Satan.

> He found that Master of that picturesque region occupied in caressing a half-flayed girl. The flaying had been done to render the caresses more intimate and more exquisitely agonizing.
> Satan listened gravely [. . .] His tapering artistic fingers, with long-pointed nails of polished jet, ceased their occupation; and a furrow appeared like a black triangle between his luminous brows.
> [. . .]
> When Bifrons departed, Satan summoned his chief lieutenants before him in the halls of Pandemonium.
> "I am going away for awhile," he told them. "There are certain obligations of a pressing nature that call me—and I must not neglect them too long. In my absence, I consign the management of Hell to your competent hands."
> [. . .]
> When they had gone, he descended from his globed throne and passed through many corridors and by upward-winding stairs to the small postern gate of Hell.
> The door swung open without touch of any visible hand. A long white robe seemed to weave itself from the air about Satan's form. His infernal attributes withered and dropped away. And the long white beard of the Elohim sprouted and flowed down over his bosom as he stepped across the sill into Heaven. (*TSS* 219–20)

But it is less in the specific passages and details of "A Wine of Wizardry," and more in the *manner* of envisioning any fantastic scene or tableau, and of shaping it into words, that we can trace the genuine continuity from the variegated contents of Sterling's second greatest poem to many scenes and settings in Smith's mature fiction of 1928–38. (The greatest influence on Smith's early or juvenile fiction seems to have been *The Arabian Nights*, coupled with the standard fairy tales.) However, it is beyond the scope of this essay to pursue this continuity from Sterling (and not just from "A Wine of Wizardry," but from his four earliest collections of poetry) to Smith in detail, apart from our one token example. The compressed or compact mode of presentation so typical of poetry, including "A Wine of Wizardry," obviously carries over to the clear but compact prose typical of Smith's best short stories, those which justify the designation of extended poems in prose.

It is precisely by the veritable flood or avalanche of Smith's often dark and mordant fantasies in prose, with their cosmic indifference (rather than pessimism or nihilism), that Sterling's protégé redeems not only Sterling's own type of make-believe (marked by his own profound cosmic pessimism), as the direct but very late inheritance of the full-blown romantic tradition, but redeems no less, even if indirectly, Sterling's own substantial poetic output. Without the latter there might not have existed any Smith at all whether as poet or as prosateur of fantasy, or of the uninhibited human imagination. This creative influence from the older poet to the younger one, like father to son, or older brother to younger one, will always remain as the greatest possible monument or homage to Sterling as a fructifying force of literature.

What of Sterling's bold assertion or prophecy that he made on behalf of Smith in late October 1922 while writing the foreword for *Ebony and Crystal*? "Who of us care to be present at the *accouchement* of the immortal? I think that we so attend who are first to take this book in our hands. A bold assertion, truly, and one demonstrable only in years remote from these; and—dust wages no war with dust." The first step to immortality for any author or poet is to have his output in whole or in part printed and then reprinted. Produced by Smith during 1944–49 as a manuscript, and published in November 1971 by Arkham House, the *Selected Poems,* totalling almost 425 pages, resurrects not only his first three major collections but makes available for the first time his later collections or cycles of poems, created in the later 1920s, the 1930s, and the 1940s, such as *The Jasmine Girdle, Incantations, The Hill of Dionysus,* and *Experiments in Haiku. Selected Poems* contains about 500 selections, and hence a major part of Smith's mature poetic output. Published in 1923, Sterling's own *Selected Poems* at over 230 pages contains his best work, but only one major portion of his overall output of poems. Sometime after 1970, a specialist publisher for libraries reprinted Sterling's own volume on acid-free paper in a facsimile edition by photolithography, the copies being sturdily bound in library-style hardcovers, made to withstand a great deal of handling. Thus the poems of both Smith and Sterling, at least in part, have managed to take the first important step on the way to immortality: their poetic output, or the best of it, has undergone reprinting. *Vivat liber!* Long live the book!

Postscript

Although probably interpreted by most readers as a mythic presentiment of a major new poetic voice, Sterling's sonnet "The Coming Singer" (first collected in *Beyond the Breakers* in 1914) was privately dedicated to Smith, but never in print. It remains the most ideal tribute ever paid to Klarkash-Ton.

> The Veil before the mystery of things
> Shall stir for him with iris and with light;
> Chaos shall have no terror in his sight
> Nor Earth a bond to chafe his urgent wings;
> With sandals beaten from the crowns of kings
> Shall he tread down the altars of their night,
> And stand with Silence on her breathless height,
> To hear what song the star of morning sings.
>
> With perished beauty in his hands as clay,
> Shall he restore futurity its dream.
> Behold! his feet shall take a heavenly way
> Of choric silver and of chanting fire,
> Till in his hands unshapen planets gleam,
> 'Mid murmurs from the Lion and the Lyre. (Sterling 171)

Works Cited

Benediktsson, Thomas E. *George Sterling*. Boston: Twayne, 1980.

Sterling, George. *The Thirst of Satan: Poems of Fantasy and Terror*. Edited by S. T. Joshi. New York: Hippocampus Press, 2003.

Contemporary Reviews of Clark Ashton Smith

I. *The Star-Treader and Other Poems*

Porter Garnett. "A Young Poet and True." *San Francisco Call* (1 December 1912): 6.[1]

The emergence of a true poet usually excites an interest which is more general than genuine. Clark Ashton Smith, whose book *The Star-Treader and Other Poems* has just been brought out by A. M. Robertson, is a true poet. He is a truer poet than we had any right to infer from the examples of his which have appeared in the news columns of the daily press in advance of their publication. Let one of Mr. Smith's most charming productions speak for itself:

CLOUD ISLANDS[2]

What islands marvellous are these,
    That gem the sunset's tides of light—
Opals aglow in saffron seas?
    How beautiful they lie, and bright,
Like some new-found Hesperides!

What varied, changing magic hues
    Tint gorgeously each shore and hill!
What blazing, vivid golds and blues
    Their seaward winding valleys fill!
What amethysts their peaks suffuse!

Close held by curving arms of land
    That out within the ocean reach,
I mark a faery city stand,
    Set high upon a sloping beach
That burns with fire of shimmering sand.

Of sunset-light is formed each wall;
    Each dome a rainbow-bubble seems;
And every spire that towers tall
    A ray of golden moonlight gleams;
Of opal-flame is every hall.

> Alas! how quickly dims their glow!
>   What veils their dreamy splendours mar!
> Like broken dreams the islands go,
>   As down from strands of cloud and star,
> The sinking tides of daylight flow.

Here is a poem of a rare and symmetrical beauty which does not falter unless one were to quarrel with the line,

> That out within the ocean reach.

If, however, its beauty seems too frail, let us turn to the splendid sonnet "Retrospect and Forecast," in which we meet the philosophic note. It is upon a poem such as this that Mr. Smith's reputation may most securely rest:

RETROSPECT AND FORECAST

> Turn round, O Life, and know with eyes aghast
>   The breast that fed thee—Death, disguiseless, stern;
>   Even now, within thy mouth, from tomb and urn,
> The dust is sweet. All nurture that thou hast
> Was once as thou, and fed with lips made fast
>   On Death, whose sateless mouth it fed in turn.
>   Kingdoms debased, and thrones that starward yearn,
> All are but ghouls that batten on the past.
>
> Monstrous and dread, must it fore'er abide,
>   This unescapable alternity?
>   Must loveliness find root within decay,
>   And night devour its flaming hues alway?
>   Sickening, will Life not turn eventually,
> Or ravenous Death at last be satisfied.

But these poems are not typical of Mr. Smith's muse. They are merely his best. They are the poems that he himself is likely to prefer in a few years. Here is another short poem of exquisite perfection. Two similar lyrics, "The Dream Bridge" and "A Live Oak Leaf" almost equal it:

PINE NEEDLES

> O little lances, dipped in grey,
>   And set in order straight and clean,
>   How delicately clear and keen
> Your points against the sapphire day!

* * * * *

> Attesting Nature's perfect art
> > Ye fringe the limpid firmament,
> > O little lances, keenly sent
> To pierce with beauty to the heart!

The following quatrain is a peculiarly happy expression of a form seldom handled so well.

The Price

> Behind each thing a shadow lies;
> > Beauty hath e'er its cost;
> Within the moonlight-flooded skies
> > How many stars are lost!

A careful examination of the contents of this little volume is productive of certain definite impressions. The first impression is drawn from the poems—"Nero," "The Star Treader," etc.—which have been placed at the beginning presumably because they are considered the poet's best. They are his most ambitious productions and in many ways they are remarkable. There is no denying their richness and power, but in the last analysis they fail to evoke the finer emotions which it is the function of poetry to excite. If one were to read these first poems only, the verdict could hardly be favorable. Indeed, it is probable that some critics, basing their judgments on these poems in seeing in them imperfections, will say things that are hasty and unkind.

It is unfortunate that in this first collection of Mr. Smith's poems the dates of production should not have been given. It would then be possible (and interesting) to mark the steps of what is patently a growing talent. It is perhaps unnecessary to add that all true talent must be in a fluid state of growth! The moment it becomes set it ceases to have constructive value. The more nearly it keeps apace with the forward movement of the art of which it is the expression, the greater its significance and the more enduring it will be.

Regarding these more ambitious poems of Mr. Smith's, the reader will find the poet's declaration of principles (from which in the poems already quoted he happily departs) in his "Ode on Imagination," which begins thus:

> Imagination's eyes
> Outreach and distance far
> The vision of the greatest star
> That measures instantaneously—
> Enisled therein as in a sea—
> Its cincture of the system-laden skies.
> Abysses closed about with night
> A tribute yield

> To her retardless sight;
> And Matter's gates disclose the candent ores
> Rock-held in furnaces of planet-cores.

As has already been shown, all of Mr. Smith's poetry is not erected upon the conception of imagination expressed in these lines and emphasized in the remainder of the poem. Much of it is. In many of his poems he projects his mind beyond the immediate and the human. His thoughts fly on the wings of Imagination to where

> She stands endued
> With supramundane crown, and vestitures
> Of emperies that include
> All under-worlds and over-worlds of dream—

In some of these poems he takes an external view of the material universe, looking in from space like a "curious god." In others he looks out upon space like an astronomer at the eyepiece of his telescope which lures his vision beyond the stars, yet does not permit him to see the forested hills about him nor the cottage nearby, where a child is being born. Now the poet whose imagination takes him in such wide courses addresses himself to our emotions in two ways only—either by an impelling and powerful diction which armors his thought, or by the creation through imagery of a high visual beauty. To those who do not react to powerful diction or who, considering it only a small part of art to be used sparingly, crave another evocation, he will have little to say. By the same token, he will have little to say to those who do not conceive beauty in terms of supramundane things. The fundamental difficulty with all poetry written in contemplation of infinitude is that the exalted nature of the object contemplated exalts language in the effort to express it; the truest poetry, however, is cast in language so passionate or so beautiful that it infuses passion or beauty into the thing of which it treats and which becomes thereby transfigured. The poet should be able to say, "I speak and my words make beautiful and vital whatsoever they touch." He should not say, "That is sublime, let me find adequate words to describe it."

But as we have endeavored to show in the poems quoted above, Mr. Smith does not always soar in spaces whither one may follow him without becoming dizzy. "The Cloud Islands" has to do with the sky, it is true, but it is of the earth. The poet deals with a simple subject and beautifies and makes it memorable by means of his art.

It will be seen that Mr. Smith's poetry falls into two major categories. In one his imagination transcends the limits of life and matter; in the other he clothes the things of earth with lyric beauty. There is, however, a third category in which fall such poems as "The Butterfly." In this he applies the method of the first category to the material of the second. The poem is as aloof as "The Star Treader."

Of the poems in the spatial and stellar vein "The Song of the Comet" is in many ways the best. It shows a freer rhythm and the pentasyllables and words of disturbing unusualness are comparatively infrequent.

It would be idle to allude to the influences detectable in Mr. Smith's work. They are sufficiently obvious. The really important thing is that, in spite of the derivative character of some of the poems—so inevitable in the work of a young poet as to call for no comment—there is abundant evidence that the poet has the independence of modernity in his blood. He shows it in the free rhythms of some of his poems and it is easy to fancy his being picked up by the great wave which has been sweeping poetry away from tradition with greater swiftness than it has ever moved since the beginning of English literature. It is the wave upon which Whitman the pioneer rode so mightily. It is the wave that bore Browning and Meredith and Henley. It is on the crest of this wave that Masefield rides today like one of his great and beautiful ships

> Whose tests are tempests and the sea that drowns

Others too—singers of the new voice—Davidson, Housman, Dowson, Symons, Bridges, Middleton, Bynner—have ridden on this wave that sweeps irresistibly onward.

Poets may escape the wave by scrambling up on the ancient peaks of song or by soaring into the empyrean, but both places are deserted and lonely and filed with death and the coldness of death. Even hell is cold in poetry, as it is in slang. Only life is hot. Nature is warm.

Regarding Mr. Smith's adherence or nonadherence to the traditions of prosody, it is only necessary to quote Edwin Bjorkman's words, "Rules are made for those who do not think." There is much that might be said about the mechanics of Mr. Smith's poetry, but let it suffice to call attention again to his rhythm. In many cases his sentence structure militates against rhythmical flow, and frequent polysyllables impair the music of his measures. Their absence from "The Song of the Comet" results in a superior rhythmical unity. How welcome, too, the two lines that emerge in agreeable monosyllabic rhythm from "Ode to the Abyss:"

> O thou whose hands pluck out the light of stars,
> Are worlds grown but as fruit for thee?

Save for the consonantal plexus in "worlds grown," the rhythm here shows a successful handling of a succession of monosyllables which is one of the ultimate tests of technique. A greater suavity of rhythm is achieved in the beautifully wrought octave of a sonnet entitled "A Dream of Beauty." Let our young and true poet speak once more and exquisitely:

> I dreamed that each most lovely, perfect thing
>   That Nature hath, of sound, and form, and hue—
>   The winds, the grass, the light-concentering dew,
> The gleam and swiftness of the sea-bird's wing;

Blueness of sea and sky, and gold of storm
    Transmuted by the sunset, and the flame
    Of autumn-colored leaves, before me came,
And, meeting, merged to one diviner form.

Incarnate Beauty 'twas, whose spirit thrills
Through glaucous ocean and the greener hills,
    And in the cloud-bewildered peaks is pent,
    Like some descended star she hovered o'er,
But as I gazed, in doubt and wonderment,
    Mine eyes were dazzled, and I saw no more.

[Anonymous.] "Clark Ashton Smith: California Boy-Poet, Whose Muse Gives Promise of Masterpieces of Melody." *Wasp* (23 November 1912): 16.

That the hand of the press agent dealt most unkindly with Clark Ashton Smith, the juvenile bard of Auburn, when booming him as a new Byron, and reincarnated Keats in the dailies some months ago, is evidenced by *The Star-Treader and Other Poems*, published by A. M. Robertson of this city. Speaking for himself in book form, Smith is infinitely more eloquent than those who introduced him in a manner, which, however fitting for a new vaudeville performer or a new line of liver pill, was in the worst taste for a poet, or rather one who will be a poet when the years have added a message to his melodic felicity. The boy was not to blame. He shrank nervously from the ordeal of hearing his verses read by a press agent to busy city editors, who had to interrupt the readings every few minutes with talks over the telephone to hotel or police reporters. If later on, he seemed to endure and even like it, that was only another crime on the shoulders of his self-advertising discoverer. However, it is pleasant to be able to say that the writer of this volume has a poetic quality, proof against even the absurd encomiums and grotesque comparisons, with which he made his unfortunate bow.

    The remarkable feature of the verse of Clark Ashton Smith is that while it recalls the mannerisms of various poets, it has yet a native daring and distinctiveness marking an original outlook on the problems of man and the mysteries of nature. Above all, he is singularly free of the literary vice of the age, that of subordinating everything to the startling phrase, or striking simile. The putting of words together that have never been introduced to each other is a mechanical accomplishment in which so many are proficient. It is of value only in advertisements, political and other articles, calling more for the sensational than the literary. Occasionally, as in "Nero," Smith vexes with "the eyeballs of posterity" and other bizarre expressions, and there is a tendency to overwork such words as "gyre," but in the main, his blemishes are insignificant.

As the first exercises of a youth, as yet innocent of the master passion, still looking "with wonder's wide and startled eye at common things of life and day," and minus the message of the poetical interpreter, they are laden with richest promise. When the breadth of Eros shall have touched his lyre, and when the inspiration shall have given him some central theory for his wonderings, then will come the melodies that may warrant the most daring comparisons.

Meanwhile, and dropping into the key of those who foolishly wrote of him as though he were the author of a best-seller and not of genuine poetry, it is safe to say that all who would come in on the ground floor of a great poet should buy this neatly printed volume of exquisite verse. If you have any doubt, read these lines from a boy of eighteen:

NIRVANA

Poised as a god whose lone, detachèd post,
    An eyrie, pends between the boundary-marks
    Of finite years, and those unvaried darks
That veil Eternity, I saw the host
Of worlds and suns, swept from the furthermost
    Of night—confusion as of dust with sparks—
    Whirl tow'rd the opposing brink; as one who harks
Some warning trumpet, Time, a withered ghost,
Fled with them; disunited orbs that late
    Were atoms of the universal frame,
    They passed to some eternal fragment-heap.
And, lo, the gods, from space discorporate,
    Who were its life and vital spirit, came,
    Drawn outward by the vampire-lips of Sleep!

G. R. Y. "Clark Ashton Smith and His Book of Verse."[3]

Along the path of friendship there has come a man with more than two generations behind him, and every year of his life has been filled with remarkable experiences and choice studies. He studied art before the American invasion of Parisian Bohemia and knew Whistler and De Maurier before either became famous; as a friend he listened to Wilde's retorts when that archer of epigram waged a merry war with literary foemen; he was the friend of Ruskin, Gladstone, and Fitzgerald. One thing puzzled him then, one thing puzzles him now: Where does genius come from?

Clark Ashton Smith is a poet. There are but few alive and in the catacombs of Immortality there are not many. But this boy, this stripling of the mountains, this youngster who knows nothing of our universities and could not name a half dozen metres by their correct names, writes with power and vividness and writes poetry.

It does not matter that he is too young to take part in selecting the village justice of the peace in that he has not arrived at those years of discretion necessary to mark a ballot correctly. Keats was dead at 26, and Chatterton never reached 20. It is not years that count. William Watson was born in 1858 and with heroic effort has labored in vain ever since to be a poet.

Like most proverbs, that one which says a prophet is not without honor save in his own country is false. Poets and prophets are honored by their countrymen and the proverb originated from a prophet who had exceptionally unappreciative countrymen, but since that time inferior and worthless poets and prophets have been quoting the proverb when they should have been busy working and doing something for which they might be appreciated. Clark Ashton Smith is not famous and will not be for many years. To begin with he has no press agent. A. M. Robertson, the book publisher of Union Square, San Francisco, has issued Smith's only volume of verse, *The Star-Treader,* and Mr. Robertson sells his books on their own merit—not on his ability to advertise them. But Smith is appreciated and is honored by his countrymen as well as by the critics of New York, and any time a critic of New York honors any one without being paid for it, it is a sure sign that the critics of that city have been maligned.

There is much of Smith's poetry that is better than the rest; there is some of it that almost anyone could have written, but what of that? Poets are the only people on earth that are judged by their worst work. Byron is disliked because he wrote love-sick trash, Browning is ignored because he wrote dramas that read like a jumbled abracadabra, Milton is tabooed because he is so heavy he makes people think—and so on. The poorest critics can find fault with the greatest poets. But as we do not judge an athlete by his lowest record so we should judge a poet by the best that he has done.

Smith has written:

> And were I a god,
> Exempt from this mortality which clogs
> Perception, and clear exercise of will,
> What raptures it would be, if but to watch
> Destruction crouching at the back of Time,
> The tongueless dooms which dog the traveling suns;
> The vampire Silence at the breast of worlds,
> Fire without light that gnaws the base of things,
> And Lethe's mounting tide, that rots the stone
> Of fundamental spheres.

—and that is poetry.

Most of his verse deals with the universe, chaos, destruction, death, immensity and other things that appeal mightily to the imagination of a melancholy youth. It is not a fault—but is a characteristic that it will undoubtedly be beneficial to outgrow. A poet by the name of Young once had a series of nightmares that he put into verse and called "Night Thoughts," and a poet was spoiled because he took too great a delight in feeling bad and telling other people about it.

But Smith can write other things than "Nero," who as the poet portrays him, is not satisfied with wanting to wring the single neck of all Rome, but would pluck out the eye of the universe and kick the stars and planets out of the heavens. Smith has a poem called "The Butterfly" that has so far not received much attention, but which is worthy of it. In the beginning the butterfly is called a "wonderful winged flower," and the man who first used that phrase, no matter if magazine editors would have refused manuscripts all of his life, would have written one line of perfect poetry.

From "The Butterfly" also comes:

> From out the web of former lives,
> The ancient catenated chain
> Of joy and sorrow, loss and gain,
> One certain truth my heart derives:—
> Though Beauty passes, this I know,
> From Change and death, this verity:
> Her spirit lives eternally—
> 'Tis but her forms that come and go.

Smith has a terrific imagination, and not unfrequently he allows it to lead him off into the horrible. The following is taken from "Medusa:"

> The land is claimed of Death: the daylight comes
> Half strangled in the changing webs of cloud
> That unseen spiders of bewildered winds
> Weave and unweave across the lurid sun
> In upper air.

That is word painting with a vengeance. If Dr. Young could have incorporated those lines into his midnight chronicles, he would have felt delighted enough to brood an hour longer than usual by some newly made grave.

Smith is a boy of our mountains; he is shy and studious and 19 years of age. Youth is the most melancholy period of life and it is natural that since he has the genius that he has that he should write as he does. But where, where does that genius come from? Perhaps it is

> "A gift divine, a wondrous sign from God
> Which proves to man that he is not a mere clod."

—who can say?

Sophie Treadwell. "Makers of Books and Some Recent Works." *San Francisco Evening Post* (23 November 1912): magazine section, p. 2.[4]

Clark Ashton Smith's little book of poems has proved a hard disappointment to me. I had heard so much, read so much of this young genius of the Sierras; this new-discovered greater-than-Keats, that I ventured into the promising looking book with awed expectancy. For me, there is little, nothing near to Keats. But there is something near to Sterling; the lesser part of Sterling.

Stars, suns, comets, abysses, moon, have been the strongest inspirer of the boy; and it is where he plunges into these vastnesses and voids that he is lost. Here is a characteristic bit from "The Lament of the Stars:"

> Beyond restrainless boundary-nights surpassing
> All luminous horizons limited,
> The substance and the light of her have fed
> Ruin and silence of the night's amassing:
> Abandoned worlds forever morningless;
> Suns without worlds in frory beamlessness
> Girt for the longer gyre funereal.

Or this from "Ode to the Abyss:"

> In aeon-implicating wars
> Thou tearest planets from their place;
> Worlds granite spined
> To thine erodents yield
> Their treasures centrally confined
> In crypts by continental pillars sealed.

Within a page and a half of this poem appear the words unhorizoned, undimensioned, unborn, unswerved, unconstrainable, undiscoverable, unstriving; and later, ungrasped, unsure, unfound, unexceeded.

The diction throughout is unusual. The lad shows a fondness for the more weighty forms of expression—what might be called "near Latin." He has a strong penchant for obsolete words, and words which apparently are of home brew. Consider that expression "frory beamlessness." Is that not delightfully reminiscent of Lewis Carroll, and "unescapable alternity, mystic immancence, cadences of threne, pits of infinite duress, mazeful gyres, star-dominated gyres, unswervable eclipse gyre-release unsphered restorelessly, murkiness, levins, cerementless, immingle, conterminate, malefice, clomb, discorporate," and many, many more. When these tread fast and furious one upon the other, the exhausted reader can but wonder why the publishers did not warn with a more definite title. Why not "The Unrevealed," or "The Mystic Meaning," or perhaps "The Shadow of Nightmare?"

One realizes that the boy has a genuine feeling for beauty, and, many times, its true expression. In "The Masque of the Forsaken Gods," Pan says:

> 'Man hath forgotten me:
> Yet seems it that my memory
> Saddens the wistful voices of the wood;
> Within each erst-frequented spot
> Echo forgets my music not,
> Nor Earth my tread where trampling years have stood.

The song to Oblivion is exquisite:

> Art thou more fair
> For all the beauty gathered up in thee,
> As gold and gems within some lightless sea?
> For light of flowers, and bloom of tinted air,
> Art thou more fair?
>
> Art thou more strong
> For powers that turn to thee as unto sleep?
> For world and star that find thy ways more deep
> Than light may tread, too wearisome for song.
> Art thou more fair?
>
> Nay! thou art bare
> For power and beauty on thine impotence
> Bestowed by fruitful Time's magnificence;
> For fruit of all things strong and bloom of fair.
> Thou art still bare

There are many charming bits in this very simple manner and mood:

PINE NEEDLES

> Oh, little lances, dipped in grey,
>   And set in order straight and clean,
>   How delicately clear and keen
> Your points against the sapphire day!
>
> Attesting Nature's perfect art
>   Ye fringe the limpid firmament,
>   Oh, little lances, keenly sent
> To pierce with beauty to the heart!

The publisher, A. M. Robertson, has made the collection into an exceptionally attractive book. The cover, of deep tan boards, is decorated by a narrow panel suggestive of the mountains and pines that have been the inspiration of much of the boy's verse.

> Out from its incunabula my spirit burst
> And wild-eyed fling its body-bonds aside,

Like to some snake that sloughs its freckled rind,
And zipped abroad in space.
Through darkness all unlit by any light—
Though all space loomed agloom
I heard and felt
With soul abhorrible,
The beat of alien things,
The while continuously crossed my ken
Planets wild-tressed, uncharted and unkempt.

Then waxed a febrile light and by its gloom
I saw about my feet strange griffous forms
That rising from a tas of molecules
Would upward in grim gyroscopic flight.
And with a strange dim prescience cardiac
I heard them wailing forth their lamentings,
"O thou who knowest us in long dead lives,
(In Oriental parlance, too-long time)
Grant us—oh grant—immunity from toll.
We are the poor dead words that bloomed
Athwart the white dawn of Chaucerian times
And died in peace when Spenser was a boy.
We did our work—why shoulds't thou resurrect
And start us o'er upon the weary round?
Grant us sureness, nor haul us from our tomb."

Then as these syllables
Engulphed themselves
In utter unintelligentibility
I heard an unrejoicing wail again
And saw
A long array of togad forms,
Majestic, emperant, with one that thundered out:
"How long, Oh poet, wilt abuse our patience?
Immortal gods, to what length shall he go
Wrestling us thus from meaning and e'en form?
Spirit of Archias! Maro's shade, defend!
Me miserum"—and sobbed aloud the rest
Upon the undelectant void of night
And my impenerable maze of mind.

At last howe'er the voidful darkness fled
And in its place reigned crimson-radiant hues,
And orange light and oleander tints,

> Cerise-bespattered while with mauve and taupe
> Commingled were soft tones of Alice blue,
> For as aloft I swung
> Borei-eyed, drenched with gloom,
> I heard soft cheering words
> That throbbed fair semitones and wizard sounds
> Reverberating on from orb to orb
> And waking kindred echoes in my soul—
> Sweet to me as my own words sterling ring!

A friend read "The Star-Treader" and was moved by Smith's peculiar muse to tear off the following:

> "Twas brillig, and the slithy toves
> Did gyre and gimble in the wabe:
> All mimsy were the borogroves,
> And the mome raths outgrabe."

John Jury. "The Star-Treader. A Book of Verse by Clark Ashton Smith—A Review." *San Jose Mercury and Herald* (8 December 1912): magazine section, p. 2.

In a state of such fertility as California it would certainly indicate a drought in the valleys or perhaps a slight snowfall in the mountains if a harvest of at least one poet a year were not produced. We are certainly near, if not actually at the threshold of our golden literary age. Very much surprisingly good work is being done in California just at present and especially by the younger generation of writers. The latest writer sprung, as it were, full-panoplied from the brain of Jove, is Clark Ashton Smith, a youth of about 19 years. This young man who lives near Auburn, a beautiful little city in the Sierra foothills, was heralded a few months ago by the newspapers as a writer of exceptional ability and promise. His little book, "The Star Treader," from the press of A. M. Robertson of San Francisco, is most certainly an extraordinary work for so young a man.

In looking into the book one is ever impressed with its maturity of thought and its opulence in language. The poet displays little, if any of the lyrical quality which characterizes most poetry, but this characteristic is due primarily to the fact that his subjects are cosmic in their scope and are too heavily charged with intellectualism and with a sort of scientific despair to lend themselves to lyrical quality. The dominant theme of the little book is drawn from a contemplation of the infinitudes of time and space and of the marvelous cycles of life and death. Passing for the time, consideration of the philosophy of the poet, if it is proper to so speak of his fundamental purpose or thought, I cannot refrain first from quoting a few lines that would seem by any test to prove Mr. Smith a true poet.

In "The Star Treader," the title poem is found this expression, certainly one of chaste and delicate beauty:

> One world I found, where souls abide
> Like winds that rest upon a rose.

And the following, revealing, it would seem, the faith of a devotee of the occult

> In unimagined spheres I found
> The sequence of my being's round—
> Some life where firstling meed of Song,
> The strange imperishable leaf,
> Was placed on brows that starry Grief
> Had crowned, and Pain anointed long.

Again, in the short dramatic poem, "The Masque of Forgotten Gods," at the conclusion we hear the gods lamenting in unison as follows:

> Our power is dead upon the earth
> With the first dews and dawns of time;
> But in the far and younger clime
> Of other worlds, it hath rebirth.
>
> * * * * * * *
>
> Fresh altars in a distant sphere
> Are keen with fragrance, bright with fire
> New hearths to warm us from the night,
> Till, banished thence, we pass in flight
> While all the flames of dream expire.

Certainly these are most remarkable lines from one so youthful. It would seem that in such precocity itself the advocates of the doctrine of Karma must find their most powerful arguments.

It is often said that genius is a law unto itself, and I suppose this is a necessary and fundamental principle among literary folk. Not to say that all workers in this branch of human activity are geniuses, there are, nevertheless, good reasons for holding the ordinary rules and regulations prescribed by rhetoricians and critics in healthy contempt. It cannot be said, however, that the spirit which defies all dogmas, forms, and ceremonials where such run counter to individual ideals is justified in its attitude unless based upon absolute verity in its interpretation of its theme. In respect to the view of life and nature taken by the author of "The Star-Treader," I must confess to a feeling of great disappointment. The thought is constantly borne in upon me in reading the lines that an undue and sinister emphasis is placed upon the thoughts of chaos, of indirection, of death. Adjectives depicting the hideous, the ghoulish, the destructive, and the seemingly brutal in nature are over-worked. In this respect, as well as in respect to a most frequent selection of the inappropriate or the obsolete word, I would say the work displays the faults most common to youthful writers.

For example, aside from consideration for the verity of the thought which may well be questioned, I can see no justification in poetry at least for speaking of the skies as "dumb, dead and passionless." And the omission of the adjective "fleshless" in the following it seems would not be objectionable:

> With hills
> That seem the fleshless earth's
> Outjutting ribs.

Because where ribs "outjut," the reader might well be permitted to exercise his own imagination as to their being "fleshless."

The same overuse of words is evident in such lines as:

> Dull Matter's tongueless mouth.

And in the following:

> Fuel of vision, brief embodiment
> Of wandering will and wastage of the strong
> Fierce ecstasy of one tremendous hour
> When ages piled on ages were a flame
> To all the years behind and years before.

It might be contended that the alliteration in the second line detracts from the beauty and strength of the expression and that the thought embodied in the words "brief" in the first line and the word, "fierce" in the third, are sufficiently suggested by the context. In the same poem, "Nero," we find the following powerful picture of the frenzy of a sateless ambition:

> And were I weary of the glare of these,
> I would tear out the eyes of light, and stand
> Above a chaos of extinguished suns
> That crowd and grind a shiver thunderously,
> Lending vast voice and motion, but no ray
> To the stretched silence of the blinded gulfs.
> Thus would I give my godhead space and speech
> For its assertion, and thus pleasure it,
> Hastening the feet of Time with casts of worlds
> Like careless pebbles, or with shattered suns
> Brightening the aspect of Eternity.

This poem illustrates what seems to be the poet's over-emphasis of the sinister in life, the diabolical and inimical in nature.

This from "Retrospect and Forecast" illustrates the author's same attitude, an attitude which so far as the reader is concerned is surcharged as with the spirit of complaint. I think the vice of the spirit animating the lines consists in its libel upon the nature of life which is given the character of a vampire.

Turn round, O Life, and know with eyes aghast,
. . . Even now within thy mouth, from tomb and urn
The dust is sweet. All nurture that thou hast
Was once as thou, and fed with lips made fast
On Death, whose sateless mouth it fed in turn.

I have been trying to analyze in my own mind the spirit of much of the present day which seems to invest the thought of the infinite extent of the physical universe with preeminence. It seems to me that the intrinsic values contained in the many and varied attributes of nature as reflected in the spirit have not been given their full and fair appraisement. I would say that the work of Mr. Smith is more potent with promise than achievement. That he is a young man of marvelous powers cannot be denied.

In concluding this review I submit that the following poem "To the Darkness," to me the best in the book in itself alone would justify the publication of any book of verse and afford a basis for predicting that our young poet will accomplish much in the years to come that will insure him a place of honor and permanency in California literature.

To the Darkness
by Clark Ashton Smith

Thou hast taken the light of many suns,
And they are sealed in the prison-house of gloom
Even as candle-flames
Hast thou taken the souls of men,
With winds from out a hollow place;
They are hid in the abyss as in a sea,
And the gulfs are over them,
As the weight of many peaks,
As the depth of many seas;
Thy shields are between them and the light:
They are past its burden and bitterness:
The spears of the day shall not touch them,
The chains of the sun shall not hale them forth.
Many men there were,
In the days that are now of thy realm.
That thou hast sealed with the seal of many deeps;
Their feet were as eagles' wings in the quest of Truth
Aye, mightily they desired her face,
Hunting her through the lands of life

As men in the blankness of the waste
That seek for a buried treasure-house of kings.
But against them were the veils
That hands may not rend nor sabers pierce;
And Truth was withheld from them,
As a water that is seen afar at dawn,
And at noon is lost in the sand
Before the feet of the traveller.
The world was a barrenness,
And the gardens were as the waste.
And they turned them to the adventure of the dark,
To the travelling of the land without roads,
To the sailing of the sea that hath no beacons.
Why have they not returned?
Their quest hath found end in thee,
Or surely they had fared
Once more to the place whence they came,
As men that have travelled to a fruitless land.
They have looked on thy face,
And to them it is the countenance of Truth.
Thy silence is sweeter to them than the voice of love,
Thine embrace more dear than the clasp of the beloved.
They are fed with the emptiness past the veil,
And their hunger is filled;
They have found the waters of peace,
And are athirst no more.
They know a rest that is deeper than the gulfs,
And whose seal is unbreakable as the seal of the void;
They sleep the sleep of the suns,
And the vast is a garment unto them.

Shamus O'Sheel. "A Young Poet. He has Quality, but Also the Faults of Youth." *New York Times Book Review* (26 January 1913): 38.

Clark Ashton Smith is as typically Californian as ever a Lake Poet was typically English. He is the latest note in that symphony of the arts which undoubtedly is taking form under the favorable skies, amid the caressing hills, of our Pacific empire. When it is understood that not "Mister," but "Master," is the title of our poet, his years being but eighteen, it will be the more leniently forgiven him that his verse has more than a faint echo of that somewhat laboriously titanic poet, George Sterling. He has drunk too deeply of the "Wine of Wizardry" for one of his tender years. The result is a book which is a bit uncanny in its persistent preoccupation with themes of mighty scope and deepest speculation, and more or less like a splendid wilderness in which we long for an occasional oasis with tiny rippling springs and small flowers. To become serious, this youth has become super-serious. He is overtrained. The efforts to produce such a book at such a time has been a bit too much for him. Hardly a note breathes of personal love or any such vivid adventurous life of the body and the blood as youth should have. So the book becomes monotonous. There are failures, too, in its chosen field. So "The Masque of Forsaken Gods" is another rehearsal of the original Olympian company in their classical stunt. Each deity steps forward and says a little bit about their former divinity, just as a thousand poets have made them do before. Alas, poor Pan, protesting too much that he is not dead. Gods were not killed by Christian priests, but by the poets who have fed upon their fame. There are moments of youthful hysteria in the presence of great themes, and instances of arid pseudo-mysticism which makes us hope that Mr. Smith will read the Celts and learn that true mysticism is a subtle and sudden and magic thing. But what makes us say that there is at last to be a poet by the name of Smith is, that the best poems in the book are astonishingly splendid and majestic treatments of cosmic themes, in a style of high and radiant rhetoric. We should like to quote from the title poem, from the "Song to Oblivion" and the "Ode to the Abyss," but we will let this splendid sonnet, in which rhetoric soars up into vision, stand for example; it is called "Nirvana:"

> Poised as a god whose lone, detached post,
> An eyrie, pends between the boundary-marks
> Of finite years, and those unvaried darks
> That veil eternity, I saw the host
> Of worlds and suns, swept from the furthermost
> Of night—confusion as of dust with sparks—
> Whirl tow'rd the opposing brink; as one who harks
> Some warning trumpet, Time, a withered ghost,
> Fled with them; disunited orbs that late
> Were atoms of the universal frame,
> They passed to some eternal fragment-heap
> And, lo the gods from space discorporate,
> Who were its life and vital spirit, came
> Drawn outward by the vampire-lips of sleep!

William Stanley Braithwaite. "Our Modern Poets." *Boston Evening Transcript* (2 April 1913): 24.[5]

From the New England tradition and atmosphere in the *Poems* of Frederic and Mary Palmer to the broad and awesome spaces of California in Clark Ashton Smith's *The Star-Treader and Other Poems* is a contrast more impressive in mental and spiritual qualities than for physical opposites in the formation and scale of nature.

Mr. Smith is a very young man, this collection of poems being to the credit of his nineteenth years. They show his youth, his as yet unrealized value of simple words and phrases. The imagination of childhood is still with him; he has glimpses of those presences which Wordsworth said lay about our infancy like an atmosphere. He shows in places a tolerable command of music, and now and then breaks out with a flaming characterization of mood, a haunting and a piercing epithet that cuts into mystery like a flashing gleam of a bird's wing darting in the sunlight. These successes are notable because they are rare in the midst of a heavy, rumbling, confused, piled-up succession of images. There is a lot of rough ore in this book, which time and practice on Mr. Smith's part might refine into very noble and beautiful poetry. The spell of those vast, towering mountain heights which tinge with sublimity the poets of California is upon this youth, and he appears helpless under their daring evocations. We are constantly confronted with such phrases as "intervital sleep,"[6] "systems triplicate,"[7] "anterior ones,"[8] "shuttles intricate of earth,"[9] "rapt in aural splendors ultimate,"[10] and "candent ores."[11] We find imitations of Keat's worst mannerisms in compound verbs, as in this example:

> It yours adown the sky
> And rears at the cliff of night
> Uppiled against the vast [sic][12]

But the substance of a very fine poet is in Mr. Smith. He has displayed in this book imagination enough to stock a good many poets, but where poets of infinitely less imagination are his masters as artists and seers, is in the focusing of the imaginative quality with the intensity that generates vision. The instinct of vision is lacking in this young poet; his imagination is without vision. What he yet may do is attested in this isolated gleam that burns in the dull metal of his chaotic ideas; this lines in which the one word "pinnacled" transforms the significance of an otherwise commonplace expression: "Great ideals pinnacled in thought."[13]

Harriet Monroe. "Recent Poetry." *Poetry: A Magazine of Verse* 2, No. 1 (April 1913): 31–32.[14]

This Californian has extreme youth in his favor, so it would be idle to complain that his subjects are chiefly astronomic. Life will bring him down to earth, no doubt, in her usual brusque manner, and will teach him something more intimate to write about than winds and stars and forsaken gods. Meantime he shows an unusual imaginative power of visualizing these remote splendors until they have the concrete definiteness of a personal experience. These lines *To the Sun* for example:

> Thy light is an eminence unto thee,
> And thou art upheld by the pillars of thy strength.
> Thy power is a foundation for the worlds;
> They are builded thereon as upon a lofty rock

> Whereto no enemy hath access.
> Thou puttest forth thy rays, and they uphold the sky
> As in the hollow of an immense hand.
> Thou erectest thy light as four walls
> And a roof with many beams and pillars.
> Thy flame is a stronghold based as a mountain;
> Its bastions are tall, and firm like stone.

In spite of the sophomoric quality in many of these poems we have here a rare spirit and the promise of poetic art.

II. *Ebony and Crystal*

[Frank] Morton Todd. "Clark Ashton Smith's New Volume. *Ebony and Crystal* Marks Another Stage in the Development of a California Genius." *Argonaut* (16 December 1922): 387–88.[15]

On a piece of ranch land above Auburn there dwells at peace with life one of the authentic poets of today; a self-educated man, who, under the blue school law of Oregon, would probably have been packed in a mental cannery and turned out a standardized mind with a state label. But because, like Herbert Spencer, he could not attend school, he was driven by the force of an unusual intellect to what is called in olden phrase omnivorous reading. And being ridden with the soul of a poet he has woven into exquisite verse the winnowings of years and of libraries, with more of his own creations, until he ranges into one sweep some of the power of Kipling, the imagery of Poe and Milton and Coleridge, the delicacy of Shelley, the verbal beauty of Keats. I do not think of claiming for him that he is any of these. On the contrary, he falls short of any of them. He may never develop the stark force of Kipling, he may never penetrate so deeply into things as to learn to lift the soul with beauty like Coleridge, or haunt it eternally with the enchantments of Poe. And yet, no one knows. Give him time, and he may stir us with something more musical than "Ulalume," more poignant in its love-and-death tragedy than "Annabel Lee," or the stanzas "To Annie." At present he seems to be delving from the surface of things into certain dark pits of sorcery too remote from our common emotional experience to get a real hold on us except through our perception of beauty and our admiration of his gorgeous, flaming visions. But that is much; in fact, tremendous. And so when George Sterling, who is his mentor and who mothers his growing genius, came into the office with a new volume of Clark Ashton Smith's verses, the book was hailed as an event in the literary history of California, and one worthily upholding the traditions of the state.

Smith's latest book is entitled *Ebony and Crystal*. In verse after verse, one stanza after another, it exerts that peculiar charm he finds in the beauty of *things*. If he made a catalogue of his nouns it would alone be enticing. He seems to have culled from all the objects in the world those that are beautiful, to weave the names of them into lines as delicate as bedewed gossamer. It is the "beauty of the visible"—yet not altogether satisfying, so he sets us this:

A Precept

With words of ivory,
Of bronze, of ebony,
Of alabaster, marble, steel, and gold,
The beauty of the visible is told.

But how with these express
The unseen Loveliness—
Splendour and light, and harmony, and sound.
The heart hath felt, the sense hath never found?

No shining words of stone—
Shadow and cloud alone—
These shall the poet seek eternally,
Whose lines would carve the mask of Mystery.

It seems to be required of a poet that he shall have a "philosophy," and perhaps Smith's is expounded in this crystal splinter:

Transcendence

To look on love with disappointed eyes;
To see with gaze relentless, rendered clear
Of hope or hatred, of desire and fear,
The insuperable nullity that lies
Behind the veils of various disguise
Which life or death may haply weave; to hear
Forevermore in flute and harp the mere
And all-resolving silence; recognize
The gules of autumn in the greening leaf,
And in the poppy-pod the poppy-flow'r—
This is to be the lord of love and grief,
O'er Time's illusion and thyself supreme,
As, half-aroused in some nocturnal hour,
The dreamer knows and dominates his dream.

It is not, however, in any philosophy that we find the best of this poet, but in the veritable poetic spell, conveyed in the vehicle of the great Keats himself: that of the beauty of thoughts, strengthened by that compelling philtre, the beauty of things. This example is probably as good as any, although the whole volume is pervaded with these qualities:

FLAMINGOES

On skies of tropic evening broad and beryl-green,
Above a tranquil sea of molten malachite,
With flare of scarlet wings, in long and level flight,
The soundless, fleet flamingoes pass to isles unseen.

They pass and disappear, where darkening palms indent
The horizon, underneath some high and tawny star—
Lost in the sunset gulfs of glowing cinnabar,
Where sinks the painted moon, with prows of orpiment.

There can be no question of workmanlike method and technique. This poet shirks nothing. He has not, in the latest fad, adopted free verse or other formlessness to save himself the proper poetic travail of rhyming and of metering. And there are no forced rhymes, but such as fall so naturally as to be a delight to the ear and the understanding at once. That calls not only for skill, but for craftsmanlike devotion, for soul-searching and self-discipline, and for conscience in execution, the lack of any trace of which in the submitted work of most amateurs is one of the things that makes editors go mad.

His titles show the attraction of many of the subtleties of life. And then there is the possible loss of identity in death, an idea that has laid its chill hand on the fancy of Bierce and many another. In these exquisite stanzas Smith deals with that frosty theme:

A FRAGMENT

Autumn far off in memory,
That saw the crisping myrtles fade! ****
Aeons agone, my tomb was made
Beside the moon-constrained sea.

Ah, wonderful its portals were!
With carven doors of chrysolite,
And wall of sombre syenite
They wrought mine olden sepulchre!

About the griffin-guarded plinth,
White blossoms crowned the scarlet vine;
And burning orchids opaline
Illumed the palm and terebinth.

On friezes of mine ancient fame,
The cypress wrought its writhen shade;
And through the boughs the ocean made
Moresques of blue and fretted flame.

Poet or prince, I may not know
My perished name, nor bring to mind
Years that are one with dust and wind,
Nor songless love, and tongueless woe—:

Only the tomb they made for me,
With carven doors of chrysolite,
And walls of sombre syenite,
Beside the moon-constrained sea.

Returning to the mundane, here is a song of camel trains in their endless processions, processions that have been part of the life of Asia for untold ages:

BEYOND THE GREAT WALL

Beyond the far Cathayan wall,
A thousand leagues athwart the sky,
The scarlet stars and morning die,
The gilded moons and sunsets fall.

Across the sulphur-colored sands
With bales of silk the camels fare,
Harnessed with vermil and with vair,
Into the blue and burning lands.

And, ah, the song the drivers sing,
To while the desert leagues away—
A song they sang in old Cathay,
Ere youth had left the eldest king,—

Ere love and beauty both grew old,
And wonder and romance were flown
On fiery wings to worlds unknown,
To stars of undiscovered gold.

And I their alien worlds would know,
And follow past the lonely Wall,
Where gilded moons and sunsets falls,
As in a song of long ago.

We find in these verses much diction of the rare, the precious, the obsolete, of terms of heraldry and ancient arts. Their strangeness does not greatly help, but if you have acquired such a vocabulary there is an undoubted temptation to use it. And artistically used it does help some—give a note of gems in embroidery, that is rich and Oriental. There are such words as queach, irrison, lote, wyvers, flaffling, eidolon, prore, terebinth, fulvous, levins, fulgor, vair, nenuphar. Of course, Intelligent Reader, you know all those; down to nenuphar. But do you know what a nenuphar is? Now, as Ingersoll used to plead with his audiences, be honest. Do you? When I first read of one in Smith's verses I thought it would be fine to have a little tame nenuphar running about the yard to welcome me when I came home, but when I consulted the dictionary to see what sort of dog-house to build for it I found it was a water lily. I never did have any luck with pets.[16]

Clark Ashton Smith is already one of the best working poets between the two oceans. It is not too much to put him in a class with Bliss Carman and William Rose Benèt, both of whom he excels in the quality of imaginative splendour, although his contacts with life are less, and he has not yet arrived at much realism in subject matter. Call him rather a master of abstract verse, or pure poetry, in the sense that it is that alone. And perhaps that is rather compliment than criticism, and I hope it is. One of the most exquisite poems in the language (Bierce thought it the most nearly perfect) is "Kubla Khan," which isn't "about" anything in particular that any one ever experienced—yet the damsel with a dulcimer, singing of Mount Abora, which probably has no existence, and certainly the damsel never did, haunts the mind like a vision of that Paradise with which the fragment ends. And there is the wizard spell of Keats, a spell which, if it once seizes you, you can never be shaken off, those "magic casements opening on the foam of perilous seas in faery lands forlorn." If you could hold Keats up about it and demand to know "What de yeh mean by it?" he would probably say he meant nothing at all except to create one of those things of beauty which are a joy forever; wherein he certainly succeeded, and so does Clark Ashton Smith. And yet that Keats line is totally irrelevant and immaterial and without legal force or effect. No, pure poetry does not have to be related to sociology, or investment banking, or glandotherapy, or the labor movement, or the petroleum output, or anything like that, and therein is its pricelessness. The spirit must be fed on the bread of beauty, or it dies. So let us thank Clark Ashton Smith for so featly purveying it.

The volume includes "The Hashish-Eater, or The Apocalypse of Evil," a *tour de force* of visualization and blazing imagery, running for several pages apace with that remarkable poem, "A Wine of Wizardry," by his friend, Sterling. With its "marble apes," and its "war of pygmies, met by night, with pitter of their drums of parrot's hide," it is supremely well done—if you like that sort of thing: the sort of thing which, in prose, made *Vathek*, and some part of the Arabian Nights. It is as splendid and as colorful as any Oriental weave. But to most of us earth-bound peoples it is a bit too far removed from any real experience to get a fast grip. It is a splendid gem, but it has in it neither sorrow nor joy nor dread nor pity—and still it is compelling for the brilliance of its fantasies.

These are the workings of a soul still somewhat apart; without the grasp of Edgar Lee Masters on the village scandals which by so many young philosophers are held to reveal "life." And Heaven be praised for it! Yet Clark Ashton Smith should, and I believe in time will, come into closer touch with real things, to move us even more deeply. It is his job. When he does it he may stand with Poe, and if he does that we shall owe him more, for of Poe there is too little, whereas Smith is industrious. Already he has to his credit *The Star-Treader*, including "Nero," which alone would be a good grist for so young a miller. He has several years between him and thirty.

Ebony and Crystal was printed by the Auburn *Journal*. It is limited to 500 copies and can be obtained, at present, for $2. If you love poetry, this is it.

[William Foster Elliot.] "A California Poet. Clark Ashton Smith of Auburn Reveals Unusual Talents in New Volume." *Sacramento Bee* (30 December 1922): 26.[17]

A volume has just been issued from the press of the Auburn Journal which makes two distinct demands upon the sympathies of western poetry lovers. First, and vastly the more important, is the quality of the verse which this book contains; but when that has been duly appraised it cannot fail to one's pleasure to know that the author is a Californian.

Clark Ashton Smith lives at present on a ranch near Auburn. He has already published one volume of verse, *The Star-Treader and Other Poems,* and his work is known to the discriminating. George Sterling stands godfather to the present volume with a preface in which he does not hesitate to use terms of the highest praise. There have been times when a similar combination of events would have turned many feet toward Auburn. Today one may hope that a few hearts may be inclined in that direction.

For the poetry of Clark Ashton Smith is authentic poetry, of which there is not enough in the world at any one time to permit one to regard an addition to the supply as an ordinary event. This young man (he is still under thirty) has had one love whom he has worshipped and one allegiance which he has served. He has condescended neither to the theories of revolutionists nor to the sentimentalities of the mediocre. Beauty has been his goddess; he has served her singly, with unbiased heart and unremitting ardor; and the result of this service lies in *Ebony and Crystal,* plain to be seen of eyes which have sought her also.

All classifications are important, but for some convenience some lines must be drawn, if for nothing else, to do away with the necessity for long winded description. Poetry may be roughly classified under three principal heads. There is the poetry of the heart, of the head, and of both. None of the three kinds is ever found quite pure except the third, and here there is seldom a perfect balance; but the poetry of Clark Ashton Smith is as nearly pure as things are apt to be in this heterogeneous world, and it is of the second kind.

He has, as Sterling has said in his gracious preface, "lent himself the more innocently to the whispers of his subconscious daemon." He is for the most part not of the world. He roams a strange world beneath the wan light of fleeing moons, beside dark pools where lilies gleam—a land where geography need not be more specifically cited than as lying somewhere between Saturn and the sun.

A sense of space is his, and its natural correlative, an enormous distaste for limitation. He cries out for vast prospects. He is at peace among the thunder of planets. Comets are his familiar spirits; on the far rim of space he sifts falling stardust for strange words of gold; he is intoxicated with the reel of nebulae, and in the cold fire of Sirius his mind finds a natural affinity.

It is the fate of most poetry today to revolt more or less madly against things as they are. This poetry is no exception; but the intensity of Smith's revolt has effaced all consciousness of itself and become pure creation, erecting a new cosmos with laws and beauties peculiar to itself. It is not a pose. The far-off, the fabulous, the exotic, are necessary to him; and though now and then one finds a trace of preciosity in his phrasing, the most notable fact in this poetry is its almost desperate sincerity.

Naturally enough, it has the defects of its qualities. No man may turn his back completely upon common things without loss. Earth takes her revenge. It was not in the mere fancy that the old Greeks pictured the giant with whom Hercules wrestled as gaining new vigor with each contact with the soil. Poetry is such a giant, and may also be conquered by removal from earth; but with the conquest goes an inevitable loss of sheer human vigor in the verse.

In the case of *Ebony and Crystal* the result of this alienation from life is a certain sterility even in the midst of its greatest beauty. The poet describes himself as having

> "—placed my wealth before thy fabled eyes
> Pallid and pure as jaspers from the moon."

And much of his verse is like the eyes of this goddess of Lemuria—fabled, pallid, pure, beautifully wrought with an almost flawless technique, but infinitely remote, a thin high music as of crystal bells beaten far off in the night.

But there are unforgettable pictures on almost every page, and in certain poems—notably in the sonnet "Transcendence" and the lyric "Solution"—there are definite traces of a broader comprehension and a richer harmony. It seems as if in these Clark Ashton Smith had set a foot over the borderline of pure imagination and breathed for a moment an atmosphere of sympathy which could fertilize his art and give it a far wider significance.

But one must not find too much fault with such work as this, and one would find none at all if it were not that the fineness of this poet's achievement leads one inevitably to hope for him, as time goes on, a conquest finer still.

He has had courage to avoid the sentimental, the obvious, the trite. He has withstood the much more subtle seductions of the Time-Spirit, which would make poetry out of street cars, hucksters, slum harlots, and the dregs and refuse of life. His life bears no date line; it is neither modern nor ancient; it is merely beautiful.

This, it may be repeated, is no small achievement. He has a vivid imagination, a copious and personal vocabulary, an unfailing sense for literary form. With some disciplining of the seductions of his own temperament, some warmer recognition of the beauty that also lies in loves and hates, struggles, failures and successes of the world that surges about the base of his ivory tower it would be hard to match him in the fold of present-day poetry.

III. *Sandalwood*

[Frank Morton Todd.] "The Bard of Auburn." *Argonaut* (14 November 1925): 9.

Clark Ashton Smith dedicates his latest volume of verse to George Sterling, and the dedication is significant for the reason that "Sandalwood" marks the author's emancipation from the Sterling influence. Not that it was a bad influence, but simply that it was something not the poet himself. Even more remarkable is the fact that although the collection includes nineteen translations from Baudelaire the original verse is far less in the mood of Baudelaire than was that in "Ebony and Crystal." By translation and dedication the poet pays his debt and burns the mortgage.

Smith now sings for himself in his own tones and in the key of his own emotion. He is singing out of life as he is living it, and not devising variations on the themes and moods of others. Others he might imitate when addressing nature, but not when appealing to human nature—to the woman or women of his inspiration. One would as soon offer a woman a second-hand engagement or marriage ring, as a second-hand simile or a shop-worn sentiment.

Though scarcely more than a boy when he began to write verse of great promise and some achievement, Smith has been slow of emotional development. Only now do we find him swayed by the passion without which pulsating poetry is not written. In earlier poems he spoke of love, but not as one absorbed by it. His tributes to Eros were carven of fine gold, but the carving almost concealed the precious metal. In other words, he was writing and not singing. All this has been changed. He now dips his pen in ink that has been "tempered with love's sighs." We find him singing:

> Queen, whose perilous bosom bare
> Was the field of Love's emprise,
> I would hush my weary sighs
> In the silence of thy hair.
>
> In my heart thy kisses wrought
> Raptures of the fabled faun;
> Seal my lids before the dawn
> With thy lips and lift them not.

The translations from Baudelaire are poems in themselves, as good translations of poetry ought to be. Of what value are mere literal versions if their very literalness necessitates loss of the original music?

IV. *Out of Space and Time*

Anthony Boucher. "Among the New Books." *San Francisco Chronicle* (15 November 1942): "The World," p. 31.[18]

Clark Ashton Smith is the sort of obscure and admirable artist that California has a way of producing. He was born in Long Valley in the '90's, has lived and worked around the State (in San Francisco for a while), and now lives in Auburn. He has been a fruit packer, a hardrock miner, a sculptor, a windlasser and a poet.

In the last role he has published four volumes, was a protege of George Sterling, and has been praised by William Rose Benèt. There his story might stop, and he would seem just another talented individual of chiefly local reputation. But in 1930 he took up another career—that of a pulp fantasy writer.

Pulp fantasy, best represented by the magazines *Weird Tales* (for which Smith does most of his work) and *Unknown Worlds,* is a unique and largely misunderstood genre. Fantasy of any sort, humorous or horrible, is frowned on by most markets. I remember an editor of the *Saturday Evening Post* telling me, "The *Post* has only three editorial tabus: Sex, religious controversy, and fantasy-except-by-Stephen-Vincent-Benèt."

But fantasy is an essential part of the tradition of the English short story—see any anthology for proof. It has its writers and its readers, and the general editorial opposition has driven them, the supercilious might say, underground, into a few pulps. Don't be too hasty to sneer at the word "pulp." These pulps provide the only market that would publish the work of a latter-day Bierce or Machen or Poe.

Outside of anthologies, these often excellent pulp stories have been unknown to the book-buying public until August Derleth, the Wisconsin Saroyan and himself a noted pulp practioneer, founded Arkham House for the express purpose of giving permanent form to the pick of the pulp crop. Arkham House has so far published a selected volume of Derleth and a titanic complete volume of the master, H. P. Lovecraft; now it offers this mouth-watering collection of the best of Clark Ashton Smith.

Smith's fantasy is possibly the purest now going, and for that very reason, sometimes less effective than it might be. Where Machen or Lovecraft makes you feel the world is a horrible and uncertain place, Smith transports you to horrible and uncertain worlds—Hyperborea before the ice age, the medieval French land of Averoigne, or Zothique, the last continent on earth. They are strange and beautiful, these worlds, but they do not impinge upon your own; there is rarely the later-than-you-think sensation of "This could happen to me."

Much of Smith, perhaps too much, is strongly under the influence of Lovecraft and Dunsany, adorned with the arabesques of his own fantastic and poetic prose. Where his originality shows most clearly is in a peculiar blend of horror and irony, a fantasy so extreme that you hang poised between the shudder and the smile. Such a memorable classic as "The Monster of the Prophecy" is pure Smith, and incomparable.

If you are an aficionado of pulp fantasy, you need no urging; *Out of Space and Time* is just what you've been waiting for. If the field is strange to you, this volume might well make a convert. Here is a poet singing dark and unmentionable horrors, while the ironic sparkle in his eye provides the one ray of light through such monstrous gloom.

V. *Genius Loci and Other Tales*

Arthur F. Hillman. "The Lure of Clark Ashton Smith." *Fantasy Review* 3, No. 1 (February–March 1949): 25–26.

When a critic cannot find major blemishes in a book he is reduced to seeking minor faults in order to flight his shafts of wit and pronounce his omniscient judgements. Therefore, it is with a tinge of malice that I point to the fact that this volume is five tales short of the contents originally proposed by the publishers. Doubtless rising costs are responsible for this lamentable curtailment; and only the promise of further collections of the Sage of Auburn's work will alleviate the disappointment of his followers.

Meanwhile, it must be admitted that this third assembly of Mr. Smith's tales is the equal of its predecessors; perhaps even better, since several of them belong to the realm of science fiction. In the beginning, the weird and fantastic provided the motifs for his colourful stories, but the gradual development of his work towards the sort of material he produced, in particular, for *Wonder Stories*, was all to the good. For his science fiction, despite its utter variance to modern trends in this field, will always stand as a superb example of imaginative writing.

For instance, the cosmic sweep and majesty of "The Eternal World" and its supramundane guardians, the Timeless Ones; the spell-binding mystery of ancient Mars wrapped in the eldritch despotism of "Vulthoom;" the inconceivable torture of the other-dimensional world of "The Visitors from Mlok" (now re-titled "A Star-Change"). The weird stories, too, ranging from the enchanting irony of "The Disinternment of Venus" to the powerful malignancy of "The Colossus of Ylourgne," are not only full of intriguing elements in themselves, but are presented in words of glowing fire and poetic imagery.

Clark Ashton Smith may be a Prophet of Doom, but he is robed in hues of gorgeous purple and gold. Although the fatalistic acceptance of the utter inhumanity of Fate and Death runs like a sombre thread through his tapestries, all are beautiful. His men and women are but puppets twitching to the strings suspended from alien talons but the puppets, stage and scenery are fashioned and contrived by a master craftsman. His devotion to beauty, the ultra-imaginative outlook which pervades his plots, and the avoidance of outworn stock situations and characters, place his tales in the highest level of fantastic literature.

Today, many writers have succumbed to the realistic or humanistic trend of science fiction; and there is a disturbing schism between their work and the science fiction in this book. Even in the past, there was a bitter struggle between the two schools of thought. But Mr. Smith has remained faithful to the views he expounded in 1932: "One of literatures most glorious prerogatives is the exercise of imagination on things that lie beyond human experience—the adventuring of fantasy into the awful, sublime and infinite cosmos outside the human aquarium. The real thrill comes from the description of ultrahuman events, forces and scenes which properly dwarf the terrene actors to comparative insignificance . . . Science fiction, at its best, is akin to sublime and exalted poetry in its evocation of tremendous non-anthropomorphic imageries" [*PD* 14–15].

To all the subscribers to such a doctrine this book will need no urging, for true delvers into the ultramundane will know what Mr. Smith has to offer. It is to the protagonists of the modern school that it throws down a challenge: whether they too, in spite of their inclinations, can resist the lure of Mr. Smith's kind of science fiction. I venture to suggest that if they once dip into these tales, they will find it as potent an attraction as the singing of the Lorelei to the sailors of old.

VI. Edwin Markham[19]

From *California the Wonderful.* New York: Hearst's International Library Co., 1914, p. 360.

Gossip on Parnassus

The wind of poesy bloweth where it listeth; poesy is a mystery deep as the world. She strikes her chords in unexpected places. Up in the leafy coverts in our Auburn hills, there is a young man who has felt the thrilling touch of her rushing wing; and not he has a gift of song that colleges cannot confer. This young man is Clark Ashton Smith.

His first volume of verse shows that his mind tends toward the vast, the remote, the mysterious. Shall I say that he exhorts Orion, instructs the Shadow, admonishes Demogorgon, explores the Abyss? He has some of the excess of youth—yes: yet how much nobler is the excess of youth than the poverty of age. Ashton Smith is a true poet: he has caught sight of the wonder behind the appearance of the world, the vision that forever allures and forever eludes.

From a letter to Smith from Albert M. Bender, undated but sometime after the publication of *Odes and Sonnets* in 1918 (CAS Papers, John Hay Library).

Dear Clark,
 I take great joy in passing on this compliment from Edwin Markham:
 "I was especially delighted to receive from your hand a copy of the poems of Clark Ashton Smith. For a long time I had been wanting a copy of his poems, for they have lines of unusual beauty, glints and gleams of true genius. There is something terrific in Smith as there was in John Martin, the illustrator of *Paradise Lost*. It cheers me to know that you Californians have honored yourselves in your honoring of this distinguished poet."[20]

From "The Judgment of Mr. Markham." *Literary Review (New York Evening Post)* (12 September 1925): 6.

 [. . .] Since I have already mentioned in The Literary Review (August 1) the fine lines of George Sterling, Louis Untermeyer and others, I will merely name them, as I have close with a hasty reference to Clark Ashton Smith of Auburn, Cal. Mrs. Chauncey Juday sends a line from his poems, but I like better this one:

> Were I God,
> What rapture it would be if but to watch
> Destruction crouching at the back of Time.

This seems to me to be one of the highest reaches of the wing of the imagination.

From "Clark Ashton Smith Publishes New Book. Late Poems and Translations Contained in New Work of Poet." *Auburn Journal* (5 November 1925): 3.

> West New Brighton, N.Y.
> September 20, 1925.

My dear Clark Ashton Smith:
 A few days ago I sent you a copy of The Literary Review of New York City, wherein I had the happiness to quote two or three of your remarkable lines of poetry. I fancy that my article will interest you as it touches upon the poetic realm to which you have dedicated your intellectual powers. I have already heard good reports of this summary of the great line symposium.[21]
 If I mistake not, you had the kindness to send me a copy of your book of poems a long time ago. I fear that I did not acknowledge it. If I failed in this matter, I wish you to know that the failure was not due to any lack of interest in your remarkable contribution to modern verse. No, it was due to the fact that much of my time has been in eagle-flights over the continent, lighting at times in the great cities to read from my own verse and to proclaim the gospel of poetry.

I now wish to express my keen admiration of some of your lines and passages, for there are moments when you rise to the high realms of the creative imagination. In these moments you stir our hearts with beauty and wonder.

I trust that you will have the strength and courage to go on with your noble devotion to the Muse. I can assure you that the circle of those who admire your distinguished work will continue to widen, for that circle will include all discriminating and intelligent readers who happen to come into contact with your poetry.

Ever cordially yours,
EDWIN MARKHAM

VII. Vachel Lindsay[22]

Letter to Clark Ashton Smith (22 April 1913).[23]

My dear Clark Ashton Smith:

Greeting and god speed to you. You have already done wonders. On the whole I think you have chosen the finest and most representative poem for your book title. For many reasons though, I prefer section III and section V of "The Butterfly" (though they could on the whole, more appropriately refer to Mount Shasta). There's not much Butterfly in your universe yet.

If I have any technical advice it would be to study Japanese prints and Whistler, and after that to read and re-read the *life*, not necessarily the works, of John Ruskin. Though Ruskin and Whistler were at war, I owe a debt to both.

But I suppose everyone is recommending their own patent medicine.

Please read my poem in the May American. That may perhaps show how the Ruskin and Whistler motives may be combined in a fashion. That poem is my whole gospel in rhyme.

But what is advice? My only advice to you is to be good, say your prayers, keep sacredly your health and follow the dream. When you reach the Dark Tower, blow your horn bravely and when you find the Grail, make the Pacific echo with your music.

And so, good morning. You have already done wonders.

Very sincerely,
Nicholas Vachel Lindsay

VIII. H. P. Lovecraft[24]

Yes—I certainly would like to meet Smith, who is in some ways the most unusual person I know. I have been a close correspondent of his since August 1922, when I was 'put next' to him by my friend Samuel Loveman (the "Harley Warren" of my "Statement of Randolph Carter"), who in turn got in touch with him through the late poet George Sterling. Smith was born in Auburn, California, in 1893, and has never been out of his native state. He lives with his parents in a cottage on a hill side somewhat outside Auburn village—within easy access of a rather weird type of mountain scenery (Crater Ridge etc.—cf. "The City of the Singing Flame") which has figured in some of his tales. His family has always been in very straitened circumstances, and his parents are now in the 80's—having married late in life. His father is a gentleman of a very ancient English Catholic family—born in England, and bearing the hyphenated name of Ashton-Smith. (C A S does not use the hyphen) The elder Smith in his youth was something of a soldier of fortune, and travelled in many odd corners of the earth, including the Amazon jungles of South America. Clark probably derives much of his exotic taste from the tales told him by his father when he was very small—he was especially impressed by accounts of the gorgeously plumed birds and bizarre tropical flowers of equatorial Brazil. On his mother's side Smith comes of American Southern blood—Huguenot and English. From childhood he was a poet, artist, and dreamer—obviously something of a boy wonder. He attended ordinary public schools and never went to a university, but has amassed an immense and curious erudition through private study. When 17 he published his first book of poetry—"The Star-Treader"—[...] and attracted the favourable attention of George Sterling. At the same time he conducted his original and untutored experiments in art—evolving a fantastic style of drawing and painting which is really ineffably powerful despite its lack of technical smoothness. When he had an exhibition of paintings at Berkeley many critics highly praised his work. Smith's tastes have always inclined toward the cosmic and the fantastic, and his poetry is mainly concerned with bizarre themes despite occasional excursions into more mundane lyrical fields. Much of his verse shows the influence of Sterling; whom he has visited many times, and who wrote prefaces for some of his books. At one period—when he was about 18—Smith wrote several stories . . . . in a vein somewhat less non-terrestrial than his present work . . . . but he did not keep up the practice. His present series of tales dates from 1925. Until lately he suffered from very poor health—including a now-vanished touch of tuberculosis. During his ill period he displayed the greatest disregard of health rules—exposing himself recklessly to all kinds of weather—but his rashness cured instead of killed him. I believe he was at one time inclined toward a touch of artistic "pose"—wearing a picturesque shock of hair and even growing a full beard—but that is all over now. Naturally, he is rather misunderstood and unappreciated by the provincial villagers among whom he lives, but as he gets into middle age this disturbs him less than it used to. I can see a perceptible mellowing and growth of geniality in him during the last five years. He no longer has the touch of active, cynical bitterness that he once had. At one period Smith conducted a column—largely verse—in his local paper, *The Auburn Journal*. At the age of 32 he took up the study of French—at home, and without a teacher—and in six months was writing French poems of marvellous power. He has since contributed verse to some of the leading Paris magazines—the editor of one of which wrote him that he could hardly believe he was not a Frenchman. And yet Smith has never known any French-speaking person, and could hardly *pronounce* the language intelligibly! His translations of Baudelaire—both free paraphrases in verse, and literal ones in prose—are the best I have ever seen, although they have not yet found a publisher. Smith has read the magazine W T [*Weird Tales*] from the start—and was the first to direct my attention to it. At that period he did not expect to contribute to it, but at my urging he sent in several poems—many of which were accepted. I kept urging the editors—first Edwin Baird and then Wright—to use his art work, but they were very slow to respond. Indeed, it was not till this year that any picture of his was accepted. His new period of fiction writing was very slow in developing. In 1925 he wrote "Sadastor" and "The Abominations of Yondo", but Wright rejected both. Not till about 1930 did he become prolific—and persistent in bombarding editors. Then his success as a fictionist began quite suddenly—both W T and the science-fiction magazines accepting his tales in unlimited quantity. This unfortunately caused him to write many cheap hack tales, but such pot-boiling has never spoiled his real style. When he sets out to write something really serious, he *does* it! His pictorial work would require a chapter in itself. Some of his hideous heads—proboscidian, semi-reptile, semi-insect—are classics of their kind, and no one excels him in drawing unearthly, abnormal, and poisonous *vegetation*. His large landscapes—scenes on Saturn, and on still remoter worlds—are full of a mysterious spell. If you'd like to see some of Smith's smaller drawings I'll gladly lend you those in my possession—as soon as their present borrower returns them. I have met two people who have seen Smith face to face—one friend of his in Auburn who visited the east last year, and one easterner (George Kirk) who visited him in California in 1921. He is very kindly and likeable, and incredibly brave in his lifelong struggle against illness, poverty, and misunderstanding. He has at times helped out his revenues by fruit-picking, but is always forced to struggle hard. His home is a very small one, with no running water—just a primitive well outside. He writes in the open a good deal—at a table in his front yard—and takes many walking trips in the picturesque mountains of his region. The responsibility of his aged parents (who are inclined to domineer a bit) has kept him chained rather closely at home—if it were not for them, he would probably manage to see more of the world. Perhaps, though, his localism has been a blessing in disguise—his limited acquaintance with this world (San Francisco being the only metropolis he knows) giving his imagination all the keener force in depicting other worlds and other universes!

Notes

1. Porter Garnett (1871–1951) was a librarian at the Bancroft Library from 1907 to 1912. He was also a printer of some note. He edited *The Grove Plays of the Bohemian Club* (3 vols., San Francisco, 1919), which lists "C. A. Smith" among the participants in the chorus (p. xxviii). He later taught at the Carnegie Institute of Technology in Pittsburgh.

2. Actually "The Cloud-Islands."

3. Uncredited newspaper clipping, A. M. Robertson Papers, Bancroft Library 2002/203c, Box 2 folder 2.

4. Sophie Treadwell (1885–1970) is today regarded as one of the foremost women playwrights of the twentieth century. She worked as a journalist while attending the University of California at Berkeley and was the only American reporter granted an interview with Pancho Villa after the Mexican Revolution.

5. CAS to GS, 12 April 1913: "The enclosed is Stanley Braithwaite's review of my book, in the Boston Transcript. The tag at the top doesn't mean that I'm subscribing to a cutting-bureau. The Komicke firm keeps sending me samples, along with an invitation to subscribe. This is the third or fourth that they've sent; and I think you admit that it's a prize. Think of getting a hundred such for only five dollars! (the subscription price) Don't return the thing" (*SU* 85). William Stanley Braithwaite (1878–1962) was a conservative critic and poet who exercised immense influence during this period, despite the fact that he was of African-American ancestry (something which he downplayed). As literary editor of the *Boston Evening Transcript,* he commissioned GS to write an "Ode on the Centenary of the Birth of Robert Browning," which won second prize in the *Lyric Year* contest for 1912. GS later fell out with Braithwaite concerning delays in responding to submissions, requests for "occasional" poems, and the general opinion he formed that Braithwaite was "opaque to pure poetry, that you miss 'the soul and inner light of song,' and fail to note when the baser rock passes into crystal. You care for assertions, optimisms, and pieties, and become art-brother to that absurd old hunker [William Lyon] Phelps, whose breath of life is platitudes and sanctimonies" (GS to Braithwaite, 8 April 1919). See Dalton Gross, "George Sterling's Letters to William Stanley Braithwaite: The Poet Versus the Editor," *American Book Collector* 24, No. 2 (November–December 1973): 18–20. GS contributed an article on "The Poets of the Pacific Coast" to Braithwaite's *Anthology of Magazine Verse for 1926;* the paragraph that discussed CAS's work was reprinted in the *Step-Ladder* for May 1927 (rpt. *SU* 291–92). For a discussion of Braithwaite's relationship with Lovecraft, see S. T. Joshi, *H. P. Lovecraft: A Life* (West Warwick, RI: Necronomicon Press, 1996), p. 200.

6. "The Star-Treader," IV.8.

7. "The Star-Treader," V.5.

8. "The Star-Treader," VII.1.

9. "The Star-Treader," VII.9.

10. "Ode to Music," l. 49.

11. "Ode on Imagination," l. 10.

12. "The Soul of the Sea," ll. 5–7, should read as follows:

> It pours adown the sky,
> And rears at the cliffs of night
> Uppiled against the vast.

13. "Ode to Music," l. 15.

14. Monroe (1860–1936) was founder of *Poetry: A Magazine of Verse.*

15. Frank Morton Todd was the author of *The Story of the Exposition: Being the Official History of the International Celebration Held at San Francisco in 1915 to Commemorate the Discovery of the Pacific Ocean and the Construction of the Panama Canal* (New York: G. P. Putnam's Sons, 1921). See CAS to GS, 17 December 1922: "I was delighted with the Argonaut review—I hadn't expect [*sic*] anything half so intelligent and sympathetic from a San Francisco reviewer" (*SU* 221).

16. See GS to CAS, 4 October 1912: "Thanks for the poems, one of which I return with a suggestion.... It's a beautiful thing, tho 'nenuphar' is a bit puzzling—I had to look it up in the dictionary" (*SU* 66).

17. CAS to GS, 3 January 1923: "Here's the latest review of my book. It appears simultaneously in the Fresno 'Bee' and the Sacramento 'Bee,' and was written by the assistant editor of the former, William Foster Elliot, who is also a poet and has written some uncommonly good stuff" (*SU* 225). GS to CAS, 16 January 1923: "I return the 'Bee' man's review, which is by much the most discerning and adequate of any you have (so far as I know) yet received. I could wish I'd written it for the preface of the book" (*SU* 225).

18. Anthony Boucher (1911–1968) was a founding editor of the *Magazine of Fantasy and Science Fiction*. He wrote book columns for the *San Francisco Chronicle*, the *Chicago Sun-Times*, and the *New York Times*. In another review of *Out of Space and Time* that Boucher published in *Unknown Worlds* for April 1945, he refers to CAS as "the outstanding disciple of H. P. Lovecraft, a disciple, in fact, who was not without his influence in turn upon the master," adding the following:

> The Lovecraft influence is perhaps fading now, with the rise of the newer school of fantasy exemplified by de Camp or Sturgeon or [Jane] Rice; but the best of the Lovecraft school remains incomparable for the creation of the dire extremities of horror. And Smith, because he is a poet and a craftsman, has produced by far the best work in the Lovecraft tradition.
>
> How much Smith himself has added to the field of fantasy is more difficult to estimate. In most of his work the echoes of Lovecraft and Dunsany drown out his own voice. Possibly two features, aside from the sometimes self-conscious, sometimes macabrely evocative poetic prose, are distinctively Smith.
>
> One, which is odd in a man experienced in so many workaday fields, is the absoluteness of his fantasy. Lovecraft wove his mythos into our everyday life until we were haunted by the suspicion that the world was a dark and uncertain place. Smith rather transports us to dark and uncertain worlds and relates their appalling histories. These are wonderful and horrible; but they happened long ago or are to happen long hence—they do not bring you up against the choking realization that it is darker than you think.
>
> The other, Smith's most important contribution, is a guignol irony—a gentle skill in telling that which is so inhumanely fabulous as to be neither horrible nor farcical, but balances on the razor edge between the shudder and the titter. Read "The Monster of the Prophecy," my favorite Smith story, or "The Testament of Athammaus," and try to analyze your reaction.
>
> The corpse of a strychnine victim wears on its face a sardonic smile. That smile is as exact an expression as any of the sensations evoked by these unique Smith grotesques.
>
> There is much else in this volume, almost four hundred pages of magnificent fantasy reading. There are three stories of Averoigne. There is the novelette, "The City of the Singing Flame," which is something akin to science-fiction, but transfigured by Smith's extraordinary visual imagination. There are stories of Zothique, including the nightmarish "The Dark Eidolon," and of Hyperborea, including possibly the most popular of Smith's works, "The Weird of Avoosl Wuthoqquan."

There is the interplanetary horror of "The Vaults of Yoh-Vombis," which gave me my first authentic shudder in some time, and there are two exquisitely melancholy prose poems never printed in popular magazines.

19. Edwin Markham (1852–1940) was a colleague of Ambrose Bierce and George GS who achieved national celebrity with "The Man with the Hoe" (1899), although Bierce, GS, and CAS did not care for that poem's didacticism.

20. Quoted in "Clark Ashton Smith Publishes Poems. 'Ebony and Crystal' is New Masterpiece of Auburn Genius," *Auburn Journal* (14 December 1922): 1.

21. Markham started a running symposium in the *Literary Review,* a supplement to the *New York Evening Post,* in the 1 August 1925 issue, "Searching for the Magic Line," in which he invited readers to send in their favorite lines of poetry. In a letter to GS dated 2 August 1925, CAS made his observations regarding its theme: "The symposium of great poetic lines is interesting; so many of the selections lean toward the didactic, which is just what one would expect! Personally, I am quite unable to select any particular line in English verse that seems more beautiful than all others. I think, however, that Keats is richer in fine lines than any other English poet. He was able to play on more than one string, too:—'Mid hushed, cool-rooted flowers fragrant-eyed;' 'Savour of brass and poisonous metal sick'; 'Her open eyes where he was mirrored small in paradise;' 'Aea's isle was wondering at the moon,' etc." (*SU* 254).

22. Nicholas Vachel Lindsay (1879–1931) achieved fame when "General William Booth Enters into Heaven" was published in the fourth issue of Harriet Monroe's *Poetry* (January 1913). It was set to music by Charles Ives in 1914. CAS's first book of poems was brought to Lindsay's attention by E. Olon James, a friend who taught at Mills College in Oakland, California. According to an interview with CAS published in the *Sacramento Union* for 21 December 1941, Lindsay initiated a correspondence with CAS after first reading his poetry; however, from the context and the wrong date given for Lindsay's death (1937, not 1931) it is clear that the interviewer, Eleanor Fait, was confusing Lindsay with H. P. Lovecraft ("Auburn Artist-Poet Utilizes Native Rock in Sculptures"; rpt. *Dark Eidolon* No. 2 [July 1989]: 27). In any event, no correspondence between CAS and Lindsay has come to light, save the following letter. Lindsay also mentions CAS, along with GS and Edwin Markham, in *Golden Whales of California* (New York: Macmillan, 1920): "If California has a shining soul, let her forget her seventeen year old melodramatics [Lindsay is referring to the infant motion picture industry], and turn to her poets who understand the heart beneath the glory. Edwin Markham, the dean of American singers, Clark Ashton Smith, the young star-treader, George Sterling . . . have, in their songs, seeds of better scenarios than California has sent us" (p. xviii).

23. Ms., Special Collections, University of Iowa Library.

24. Letter to F. Lee Baldwin, 27 March 1934; ALS, JHL. In *Lord of a Visible World,* Ed. S. T. Joshi and David E. Schultz (Athens: Ohio University Press, 2000), pp. 254–56.

Eblis in Bakelite

James Blish

with an addendum by Donald Sidney-Fryer

> The shaddow of that Body heer you find
> Which serves but as a case to hold his mind,
> His intellectual part be pleas'd to look
> In lively lines described in the Booke.
> —Thomas Cross: "In Effigem Nicholai
> Culpeper Equitis" (*A Physical Directory*, 1649)

Clark Ashton Smith has been called "the greatest American poet" by Edwin Markham, and while it is obvious from internal evidence that "The Man with the Hoe" was a fluke, it is possible for a man to be right twice in his life. Benjamin De Casseres, once a considerable figure in American letters before he took a job with one of Hearst's brothels, spoke for Smith in glowing terms; David Warren Ryder and George Sterling, as well as Samuel Loveman, may be added to the list of discerning people who have found things in Smith's work to admire. If one adds to this list the nearly endless columns written about Smith by fantasy fans from Lovecraft on down, it becomes evident that this one man has been one of the most extravagantly eulogized figures in American literary history—the sheer wordage concerning him nearly equals that written about Branch Cabell, a truly fantastic numeral if one attempts, as I have, to run most of it down.

In the attempt another fact soon becomes evident: except for one or two short articles, totaling perhaps 2000 words, no true criticism of Smith ever has appeared in professional or amateur print. I have sought nearly fruitlessly for paragraphs about the man which set forth a clear perception of the kind of work he does, its relationship to the rest of literature past and present, its antecedents and progeny; for any paragraph about him not crammed with sweeping dogmatic statements, false associations, bases of judgement that shift at the whim of the writer sometimes in the course of a line, report of estimates without documentation or demonstration, and emotional assessments which clearly indicate nothing save that their author likes fantasy no matter who writes it, or how badly. More: until last year, despite the fact that Smith has been active for more years than most fans can remember, there was no anthology of Smith's work, nor did any general anthology include a line of his much-lauded poetry—nor are any of the latter ever likely to do so now, since the Arkham bookbinders in their expected way have crammed every turkey egg Smith ever laid into print without the slightest discrimination, so that Smith in book form actually means less than Smith hidden from sight in pulp, amateur and private publications.

It would be interesting to compile a list of representative paragraphs from some of the best articles about this man with comments appended in the style of the Institute of Propaganda Analysis, but the space limitations of *Tumbrils* being what they are, a bibliography must serve. In the meantime, the pertinent question is: Does Smith deserve the damnation his admirers have visited upon him? And the business with which I concern myself is to answer this question in a milieu as remote as possible from the unselective happiness with which the average *Weird Tales* reader has greeted every tale of Zothique or Averoigne, upon the premise that such an estimate is grossly unfair to the poet and scholar which is Smith at his best.

For Smith at his best is a fine creative scholar. I know of no more impressive way to introduce Smith to a stranger than with "The Kingdom of the Worm," which was published in *The Fantasy Fan* many years ago. The episode was perfectly in the style of its ostensible period; it could have been slipped into *The Voyage and Travel of Sir John Mandeville, Knight* without the unwary reader's detecting it in his perusal of that recondite volume; as an entity in itself it held together beautifully, and preserved throughout that atmosphere of naive wonder mixed with uneasiness which is the literary signature of the great French liar—and a far more difficult thing to achieve than a mere parroting of stylistic tricks. Some time later, in R. H. Barlow's excellent mimeographed magazine *Leaves,* Smith addressed himself to the fragmentary narratives of the prisoners of Eblis which Beckford had planned for *Vathek* but never included. If anything, this performance was the more exacting of the two; *Vathek* anticipated the main course of literary development by a century in several ways, but in general Mandeville's way of doing things is much closer to what we know as the "Smith style" than Beckford's, since the last-named remained always an undoubted child of the Eighteenth Century, wherein neither Smith nor Lovecraft, despite the propaganda, could reasonably be expected to feel at home; but Smith carried it off with manifest ease and pleasure.

One of the consequences of these observations is to separate his poetry rather sharply from his prose, in a manner which will become clear in a moment. A study of the poetry will convince anyone seriously interested that its idiom is the product of a pyramid of influences—Poe and Wilde particularly, and then Shelley, Milton, James Thomson and a lengthening list of stragglers, who exert their effects not in concert but one at a time in the most marked fashion. "The Constellations of the Law,"* for instance, is "The Massacre at Piedmont" to the life; "Satan Unrepentant" advertises its parentage too loudly for me even to bother naming it; "Requiescat" is Wilde's,

---

*I.e., "The Ministers of the Law" [*EC*].

well-thumbed; and so on. It is not so easy to attach single names to individual prose stories of Smith's, though the influences are plain enough. (I am not counting, naturally, the prose-poems, though even there Lanier occasionally nibbles at the edge of the Baudelaire.) One expects poets, however, to be an ancestor-worshiping race, and if Smith appears to be more than a little overly sensitive to the decadent-Romantic universe of discourse, still and all such a pressure is not lightly to be shrugged off. In addition, the synthesis of the best of bygone poems, up to and including direct quotation, has become through "The Waste Land" and the "Cantos" a nearly standard Twentieth Century technique; and Smith has occasionally achieved some really moving effects with such eclectic material—witness the ending of "Medusa," or "In November," or even more markedly, in "Chant of Autumn" where the intoxication is no less magical for being the heritage of Swinburne. Occasionally the results are more unfortunate and Smith gushes forth a "Hashish-Eater"—"perilous nightmares of superterrestrial fairylands accursed," in Lovecraft's mashed-potato language,* but to the sober reader merely the sewage of a plastic-and-chromium Eblis. . . . The matter, it appears, is not entirely under Smith's control, and until he decides just *who* he is, we must be content to spear the effective poems like fishes as they float by.

In prose the matter *is* entirely under Smith's control. In the two works I have named above, and in one or two others, he has demonstrated conclusively that he has the sensibilities and the sensitivity to handle nearly any prose style that happens to appeal to him, excepting only the very tightest and sparest of modern idioms. The inevitable conclusion is that his characteristic prose manner, with its material drawn exclusively from the Poe horror story and the Wilde fairy tale, and its style from the glaucous logorrhea of Sir Thomas Browne's *Hydriotaphia,* is a conscious choice. And from almost any angle it is a bad one. It is incomprehensible and boring to the pulp readers whom he has—perhaps perforce—addressed most often. It is moribund and intolerably "arty" to a literate reader. The best he can hope from it is that it will please the very tiny segment of the reading public which is made up of men like Derleth and Lovecraft, who, incapable of distinguishing the artistic from the arty, can pass it through their digestive tracts and absorb from it the little nourishment that it contains.

As a product of irresistible influences and inclinations it might have been forgivable. As the conscious choice of a man who has shown that he can do better, it is funny. And tragic? Yes; if you think Smith could do *that* much better. When the laughter is over, it might also be counted as evidence for damnation, however; and probably it is better, in the long run, to let his admirers attend to that.

(Bibliography upon request.)

N. B. Because there is evidently no way to discover or obtain the "Bibliography upon request" mentioned at the end of Blish's essay, we have attempted here to reconstitute what may have been this listing of books and articles, at least relative

---

*Actually Samuel Loveman. [DSF]

to Smith's own life and career, or output, in the present addendum, but only in the order of appearance for the said books and articles as discussed by Blish in his critique. In this reconstitution we have used our own Clark Ashton Smith bio-bibliography *Emperor of Dreams* (West Kingston, RI: Donald M. Grant, 1978). We have also appended here and there any relevant comment where such appears to warrant it. A strategic detail concerning the general date of composition for "Eblis in Bakelite": although his essay appeared in June of 1945, it is clear that Blish apparently wrote it sometime in 1943, a fact that we deduce from the reference to what must be Smith's collection *Out of Space and Time*, published in August of 1942. The reference reads in part: "until last year . . . there was no anthology of Smith's work," and thus the statement cannot refer to the second Arkham House collection by Smith, *Lost Worlds*, published in October of 1944.

Benjamin De Casseres, "Clark Ashton Smith: Emperor of Shadows," a brief but incisive appreciation written c. August 1937, and published by The Futile Press (Lakeport, California), c. November 1937 (70 copies), evidently at Smith's own request, and evidently included with some copies of Smith's collection *Nero and Other Poems*, published by The Futile Press in May 1937 (c. 250 copies), along with the separate article "The Price of Poetry," by David Warren Ryder, published by the same press in June 1937 (reprinted from *Controversy* for 7 December 1934).

George Sterling, prefaces to Smith's two poetry collections *Odes and Sonnets* (published June 1918) and *Ebony and Crystal* (published December 1922).

Samuel Loveman, no known published source, but Smith dedicated *Ebony and Crystal* to this fine lyrical poet, who was also a friend to H. P. Lovecraft. Loveman's one and only major collection is *The Hermaphrodite and Other Poems*, published by The Caxton Printers (Caldwell, Idaho), 1936.

Clark Ashton Smith, *Out of Space and Time* (Sauk City, Wisconsin: Arkham House, August 1942), with an introduction by August Derleth and Donald Wandrei. The curious phrase "the Arkham bookbinders" undoubtedly refers to Derleth and Wandrei as the then owner-editors of Arkham House.

Smith, "The Kingdom of the Worm," first published in *The Fantasy Fan*, October 1933, and included in Smith's collection *Other Dimensions* (Arkham House, April 1970), but under his preferred and final title "A Tale of Sir John Maundeville."

Smith, "The Third Episode of Vathek: The Story of the Princess Zulkais and the Prince Kalilah," by William Beckford, first published in *Leaves*, issue "1" (Summer 1937). Conclusion only (c. 4000 words) written by Smith to this final episode deliberately left unfinished by the original author. Included in Smith's collection *The Abominations of Yondo* (published by Arkham House, February 1960), wherein the completed episode occupies pp. 177–222; Smith's conclusion occupies pp. 212–22 only.

Smith, *Ebony and Crystal: Poems in Verse and Prose*, published by Smith himself but printed by the press of *The Auburn Journal* (Auburn, California, December 1922). This collection contains nearly all the poems mentioned by Blish in his text. "Medusa" is either the sonnet "The Medusa of Despair" or the ode "Medusa" (first published in Smith's first collection *The Star-Treader and Other Poems*, November 1912, later republished in *Nero and Other Poems*).

Smith, *The Star-Treader and Other Poems*, A. M. Robertson (San Francisco); *Odes and Sonnets*, The Book Club of California (San Francisco); *Nero and Other Poems*, The Futile Press (Lakeport, California). For dates of publication and other data, see the entry above and also the entries under De Casseres and George Sterling. Blish may or may not have had copies of these three collections.

James Blish versus Clark Ashton Smith; to Wit, the Young Turk Syndrome

A RIPOSTE

Donald Sidney-Fryer

By an odd coincidence—and it surely must remain as no more than that—two of the strongest negative criticisms of Clark Ashton Smith and his writing appeared at almost the exact same time during the mid-1940s. These criticisms came to light in two different fanzines, or perhaps more accurately, perzines, or personal magazines. The first one appeared in the May 1945 issue of *Diablerie,* "Of Corsets and Flea-Traps," by one "Maliano" (otherwise unidentified). Of the two criticisms this is the less interesting, despite its piquant appellation. Its main item of attention remains the illustration chosen to accompany it: a rather charming caricature-portrait of Smith by Virgil Partch, of all people. No, Smith and Partch never met; instead, the artist worked from a photograph of Smith supplied him by Forrest J. Ackerman c. 1945. At that time Ackerman was the editor of the camp newspaper at the U.S. Army induction center Fort MacArthur near San Pedro (the port of Los Angeles located between Rancho Palos Verde to the northwest and Long Beach to the northeast). Partch was one of the staff artists on the newspaper and was officially assigned to do caricatures of the officers at that military base. However, between his official assignments, Ackerman would furnish him with photos of various fantasy and science fiction authors, from which Partch would create his caricatures. This was how the cartoonist-artist happened to make his caricature-portrait of Ashton Smith, who is observed winking at us with his left, or sinister, eye!

But it is the second of these two rare negative criticisms that will detain us here, and at some length. Oddly enough (again), this made its appearance just one month after the one in *Diablerie,* and in the second issue of *Tumbrils,* rather well named as it turns out, thus dated June 1945. This overall unfavorable essay concerning Smith and his writing took the form of a brief but penetrating censure entitled "Eblis in Bakelite," by James Blish, a title referring to the Mohammedan concept or image of Satan as physically realized in bakelite, an early form of plastic, or in this case, a synthetic resin, whose uses were like those of celluloid or hard rubber. "Eblis in Bakelite"—it makes an arresting and memorable title, in the same way as is this uncommon piece itself. *Tumbrils* was Blish's own perzine and remains an excellent example of this type of magazine, such as flourished from the middle to later 1930s to the 1940s. Other writers of the same period, who later became famous like Blish, also put out similar publications, sometime regularly, often irregularly, usually mimeographed or hectographed. For example, Fritz and Jonquil Leiber published on a regular basis for half a year or so their own perzine under the title *New Directions*.[1]

In Blish's case, as the title (in the plural) indicates, it provided the writer-editor the opportunity to express critical opinions, if not Olympian judgments, and, it would seem in his case, more unfavorable criticisms than any other type. Tumbrel or tumbril generally refers to the farmer's cart or wagon that during the French Revolution was employed to transport to the guillotine the people condemned to death. In this particular essay, rather unusually for a fantasy and science fiction critic and writer of that general period, Blish concerns himself not just with Smith's prose fictions (as we might expect) but also with some of his best poetry. It remains to this day one of the most vivid and incisive of the very few negative criticisms ever written about Clark Ashton Smith as an overall artist and creative scholar. Let us examine the essay's major points or issues in their order of appearance.

A word of caution. We are not disputing either the opinions held by Blish relative to Smith and his output, or his right to these opinions. To quote the ancient saying: *De gustibus non disputandum est*. There is no disputing in regard to (individual) tastes, or expressed otherwise, there is no arguing about opinions. Nevertheless, it is possible and permissible to suggest other, and possibly more fruitful, approaches to Smith and his oeuvre, and this is that we shall do, using Blish's essay as our criterion of reference.

* * * * *

Surely, if people as diverse as Ambrose Bierce, George Sterling, Edwin Markham, Samuel Loveman, Arthur Machen, Donald Wandrei, H. P. Lovecraft, David Warren Ryder, Benjamin De Casseres, Vachel Lindsay, George Work, David Starr Jordan, and yet still others of similar stature considered Smith "the greatest American poet," or simply a true genius and a great poet, they all must have had excellent reasons for believing as they did, contrary to what Blish somehow suggests that these folk obviously erred in holding such elevated opinions of Smith just as a poet. Blish patently overstates the case when he declares that, apart from a very few brief articles that he managed to find, no true criticism of Smith, especially as poet, has ever made its appearance in print. The official discovery of Smith by the San Francisco press, no less than the reviews accorded to Smith's first three major poetry collections, contain much excellent criticism of Smith, not all of it positive and admiring, and firmly locate him in the poetico-cultural climate and landscape of 1910/11–1925/26. Blish evidently, and not surprisingly, knew nothing of this early critical reaction and acclaim, but even then, had he known of it, he would probably not have reacted positively to the laudatory tone that still is the prevailing one overall.

Personally the present writer feels that, in the case of a little-known but quite exceptional author, it is better to overpraise than to underestimate. At least the former calls attention to itself and the author in question. Some critics will never like or admire certain work of unusual value, no matter what. Today, compared to Smith's period, the cultural scene abounds in excellent poets of every and all schools, whether working in traditional prosody or in free but carefully structured prose. Gifted poets today seem to gain recognition early, receive the benefit of scholarships and fellowships, become teachers and professors, have their collections issued by prestigious publishers in New York City, etc. Almost none of this apparatus existed in the early part of Smith's literary career, and it is unlikely that he could or would have taken advantage of it, given his independent nature. Ironically, and quite contrary to the statement made in "From the Persian," one of Smith's juvenile couplets, Smith as poet received, apart from recognition in California and Great Britain, nothing less than dross for all the gold that he so lavishly purveyed. This early couplet reads: "I read upon a gate in letters bold: / Let him that giveth dross expect not gold." In Smith's case this must be emended as follows: "I read upon a gate in letters bold: / Let him that giveth gold expect but dross."

Contrary to Blish's assertion that "nor did any general anthology include a line of his much-lauded poetry," almost three dozen different poems of Smith's made their appearance in some two dozen anthologies of diverse types in the period between 1914 and 1945 alone, and our list is probably not complete. Also, contrary to Blish's assertion that until 1942 "there was no anthology of Smith's work (i. e., in fiction)," Smith himself had issued six of his best but up-to-then unsalable stories in a single collection during mid-1933 after the press of the *Auburn Journal* had printed some 1000 copies of *The Double Shadow and Other Fantasies*. Although not noted in our reconstituted bibliography following Blish's essay, it is quite possible that Blish may have bought a copy of this now rare first collection for 25¢ and at the same time a copy of *Ebony and Crystal* for $1.00. Smith still had a small remainder of the latter collection from the early 1920s, and he was advertising and selling both books, from the early to the middle 1930s, and probably later. However, *Out of Space and Time* in 1942 and then *Lost Worlds* in 1944 do represent in fact Smith's first two *major* prose collections, and are now, contrary to Blish's negative assessment about *Out of Space and Time*, generally considered excellent collections made from among Smith's best fiction in short-story form.

Blish's original suggestion about assembling a register of typical paragraphs from some of the *best* articles about Smith "with comments appended in the style of the Institute of Propaganda Analysis" is actually quite witty and profitable, and has much to recommend it, inasmuch as it would form an idiosyncratic method for analyzing literature written in praise on behalf of little-known but worthwhile authors. "Does Smith deserve the damnation that his admirers have visited upon him?" Well, a littérateur can react to what seems excessive praise about something unknown but artistic in at least one of two ways: either negatively, if a few typical examples fail to live up to the high praise—or positively, if the characteristic samples more than justify the laudation, thus opening the way to further discovery and exploration.

However, it is anomalous that, after admitting that "Smith at his best is a fine creative scholar," Blish then cites "The Kingdom of the Worm," no less than the special conclusion that Smith provided for "The Third Episode of Vathek," as prime examples of Smith at his best. True, both are worthwhile pieces of (short) prose fiction, perfectly at home in the styles of their respective centuries, the 1400s and the 1700s. Nevertheless, they are not the major efforts represented by "The City of the Singing Flame," "The Dark Eidolon," "The Colossus of Ylourgne," "The Ice-Demon," and "The Voyage of King Euvoran," among others.

As for Smith's poetry being "the product of a pyramid of influences"—such as from Poe, Wilde, Shelley, Milton, James Thomson, no less than other poets but to a lesser extent—S. J. Sackett has already answered this issue. We can do no better than repeat what he states: "It is dangerous to try to find a source for all of Smith; his affinity to certain writers has occasionally led critics to assign to him influences in [i.e., from] other poets whom he has never read" (23). Like other poets before and after him, Smith for profound personal and poetic reasons of his own sometimes treats with all due seriousness certain universal themes first handled in depth by his predecessors. Just as Shakespeare in *The Tempest* and Milton in *Paradise Lost* and *Paradise Regain'd* derived in part out of Spenser and his epic-romance-allegory *The Faerie Queene* (1590–96), and above all out of the *Mutabilitie Cantos* (1609), so did Smith in such pieces of blank verse as "Satan Unrepentant" derive from Milton and his two great epics.

However, in "Satan Unrepentant" and the sonnet "A Vision of Lucifer" Smith introduces a viewpoint strongly opposite to Milton's (at least in a personal sense for the elder poet), and remarkably sympathetic to Satan-Lucifer, no less than undeniably hostile to the usual portrait of the God limned in the Old Testament of the Bible, whom Smith perceives in terms of some Oriental despot, or tyrant-king. In these two poems the Californian poet is clearly continuing, and extrapolating from, selected aspects of the discourse begun by Milton in *Paradise Lost*. With Poe and Wilde, Smith has a genuine personal and poetic affinity, but his "Requiescat" is not just a mere derivative of Wilde's poem of the same name. If Smith uses a concept or theme employed by some predecessor, it is to express something, a creative comment or feeling, of his very own. This brings up the related issue of conscious or unconscious plagiarism, but possibly quotation is the better word. There exists little such in Smith, except what may be perceived as "enrichment," in the sense of the practice favored by Renaissance poets deliberately "imitating" the poets of Graeco-Roman antiquity. The present writer would venture the guess that almost all of Smith's poetry is his own, and that it is technically quite original and not a direct copy of some other poet's lines, despite all the inspiration that Smith may have derived from an intensive study of the work of other poets.

George Sterling, probably more than any other poet, had the greatest influence on Smith, inasmuch as the two poets were contemporaries and particularly close friends during 1911–26. Sterling acted as mentor to the younger poet and encouraged and inspired him. For example, "The Ministers of Law" has nothing to do with "The Massacre at Piedmont," and the title that Blish uses to identify Smith's own sonnet derives from line 13, i.e., "The Constellations of the Law." "The Ministers of

Law" derives indeed from Sterling's epic "rumination" *The Testimony of the Suns* (line 258). The phrase comes from quatrain 65 (lines 257–60), which reads in full:

> What powers throng the pregnant gloom!
> Unseen, the ministers of Law
> Reach from eternity to draw
> The suns to predetermined doom.

Blish apparently knew Smith's poetry only, or primarily, from *Ebony and Crystal* (1922) and *Nero and Other Poems* (1937), in addition to the poems published in *Weird Tales*, but had no knowledge in depth of *The Star-Treader* (1912) and *Sandalwood* (1925). The poetry of Poe and Sterling (e.g., "A Wine of Wizardry"), first experienced and selectively memorized by Smith when he was thirteen and fifteen, respectively, exercised with no doubt about it the greatest influence on Smith and his own subsequent work; but Blish—by not knowing the full range of Smith's early poetry as laid out chronologically in his three major collections—could not thus follow the logical progression of Smith's development first as poet and then as prosateur, and how each major volume of poems led to the next, and then how the prose-poems in *Ebony and Crystal* led to his major (mature) prose fictions, as well as his extended poems in prose, c. 1925/28–1938.

Also, it is perhaps too facile to see Baudelaire's influence on Smith in the genre of the *poème en prose* as greater than what it actually was. The influence of (selected) very short pieces by Poe (such as "Shadow—A Parable," "Silence—A Fable," "Eleanora," and "The Masque of the Red Death") proved undoubtedly greater, inasmuch as it came into operation earlier in Smith's life, and moreover in the English language that perforce both Poe and Smith shared. As far as we are able to discover, Smith first underwent the influence of Baudelaire, his poems both in verse and in prose, thanks to George Sterling and his copy of some translations by Arthur Symons, in the course of his month-long visit with Sterling in Carmel in June 1912. On the other hand, the earliest and possibly strongest influence from the French genre of the poem in prose upon Smith came c. 1910–11, or possibly even earlier, when he first read and studied that rare collection *Pastels in Prose*, translated by Stuart Merrill from the French of thirty-two poet-authors (including Louis Bertrand and Baudelaire, among many others), and published in 1890 by Harper & Brothers. Smith retained a remarkable affection for the book in question all his life, when he would often read and reread this extraordinary anthology. He continued studying the book up to the last years of his life.

Despite Smith's affinities with Poe and Baudelaire among other poets, the mood or effect of the Californian's most serious prose-poems, as for example "The Shadows" and "From the Crypts of Memory," or "The Black Lake" and "The Memnons of the Night," or "The Crystals" and "The Passing of Aphrodite," turns out to be more often than not much more "terrific" or Miltonic than anything else, much of the portentousness of the tone deriving from the strong emphasis not only on fate or destiny but especially on the succinct and vivid cosmic-astronomic element. There is another curious result of Blish's ignorance of the overall corpus of Smith's early (mature) poetry, curious inasmuch as Blish was primarily a science fiction writer, and one might think that he would have made a point of overtly noting this. He not only fails to emphasize the paramount importance of the cosmic-astronomic element or subject matter in Smith's oeuvre, whether positively or negatively (in an artistic sense), but he does not even directly *mention* it in any way, a curious oversight.

Why Blish especially singles out "Medusa," "In November," and "Chant of Autumn," from among so many others, is puzzling because they are not any more noteworthy than most of the other lyrical poems, or pieces in blank verse, but instead are *equally* remarkable. "In November" is only one of not quite a dozen lyrics cast in alexandrines, that is, in iambic hexameter. The alexandrine does not work quite the same in English as in French, and must be handled with great care to avoid the heaviness and monotony often inherent from its use in such a strongly accented language as English, at least for the purposes of the traditional prosody. However, for his greatest and most extended poem cast in non-rhyming verse, Smith chose the traditional iambic pentameter, or expressed otherwise quite genuinely, it chose him. Contrary to his usual practice of slow and careful workmanship, Smith created the roughly 600 lines of blank verse making up *The Hashish-Eater* in about a month and a half, or even somewhat less, literally a fantastic or astonishing achievement. This enormous poem literally came exploding out of his subconscious and remains his most ambitious and exhilarating composition. Most critics or commentators have assessed this amazing exercise in cosmic-astronomic imagination at a high level of accomplishment. Blish stands alone in characterizing this imagery-fraught narrative as "merely the sewage of a plastic-and-chromium Eblis." It is not clear what he means by the phrase "mashed-potato language" whether written by Lovecraft or De Casseres, unless what he purposes by this usage is just "muddled language." Blish's own language is less clear than the phrase that he castigates while criticizing Smith's magnum opus even more severely.

Again, Blish stands alone in his extremely negative stance not only in regard to the carefully cultivated style of Smith's mature prose fictions, c. 1928–38, immediately derived from that of the prose-poems of c. 1914–22 (as gathered into *Ebony and Crystal*), and also from that of those of c. 1925–29—but above all in referring to the style of Sir Thomas Browne in *Hydriotaphia*, or *Urne Buriall*, as "glaucous logorrhea"—although just what Blish means by "yellow-green talkativeness" (or verbosity) is not that clear. *Hydriotaphia, The Garden of Cyrus,* and other masterpieces of baroque prose by the same author are probably the closest things to poetry created in prose before the later experiments in prose style of Thomas De Quincey, Edgar Allan Poe, and others in English, not to mention those of the French poets of the nineteenth century, beginning with Louis Bertrand and continuing through Mallarmé. We would be singularly impoverished if our ultimate preferences in prose style would shrink down only to those favored by admirers of Ernest Hemingway as well as other well-known but serious writers of the twentieth century just past.

While certainly not a novice writer at that time, by mid-1945 James Blish had not yet established himself as one of the leading masters of imaginative narratives or of a rigorously extrapolated scientifiction, such as would later gain for him a richly deserved celebrity. Why then at that stage in his career did he attack an elder scrivener, of little or no wealth, who had no great fame for the most part except among the readers of *Weird Tales* and similar pulp magazines, except among specialists of poetica Californiana, and surely not among the mainstream academic and intellectual communities at large? Such a question might elicit an explanation like the one that follows. There are at least two courses open to an unestablished writer on his way up. He can be pious and reverent in regard to one or more eminent writers in the genre to which he aspires, and he can attach himself to that same writer in some accommodating capacity; or he can call attention to himself by attacking some eminent scrivener in that same genre, and thus make a name for himself by writing one or more stringently critical essays of quite a negative type attacking that established scrivener. Such an individual on the attack can be called or considered a Turk, either a cruel or tyrannical person, or a young Turk, that is, a young dynamic person eager for change, and attempting to bring it about, if necessary, by attacking somebody conspicuous.

Was James Blish during the early to middle 1940s infected or influenced by such a syndrome, the young Turk syndrome? Or was he only expressing some legitimate gripes about a writer whom he sincerely thought was quite overpraised? Well, possibly both, but there can be no doubt that he was absolutely serious in his intention, positive or negative, especially when he states that "the sheer wordage concerning [Ashton Smith] nearly equals that written about Branch Cabell, a truly fantastic numeral if one attempts, as I have, to run most of it down." Although this attempt did not apparently extend to the earliest reviews and critical pieces about Smith, those for the period c. 1911–26, just discovering those for the period c. 1930–43 would have represented a real task. Anyone who goes to such lengths to discover such rare materials must be adjudged utterly sincere and serious. Still, it seems like a great amount of bother to undergo merely to attack a writer at that time but obscurely known, if at all, to the mainstream audience or public.

Blish's no-nonsense condemnation of Smith's prose, with which he concludes his essay "Eblis in Bakelite," came to Smith's attention at some point, as well it might, and it is obvious that he reacted to it. Specifically, noting the challenge implicit in Blish's statement that Smith "has demonstrated conclusively that he has the sensibilities and the sensitivity to handle nearly any prose style that happens to appeal to him, excepting only the very tightest and sparest of modern idioms," he responded by writing one of his briefest stories expressed in some of his sparest prose, "Monsters in the Night," which he composed or finished on 11 April 1953. It first appeared in print as "A Prophecy of Monsters" in the *Magazine of Fantasy and Science Fiction* for October 1954, the only such tale that he ever contributed to that periodical. However, Smith had already responded in general to Blish's austere attack on his characteristic prose, but somewhat earlier, that is, by mid-1950. A gentleman to the last, Smith answered this overt condemnation with his characteristic graciousness, and we shall therefore allow him to have the final word in this debate.

In explanation of the elaborate style characteristic of his poems in prose and of his tales and extended poems in prose—as well as in explanation of his use of rare and exotic words and of word-coinages—Smith commented as follows, in his letter to S. J. Sackett dated 11 July 1950. He also defended, but indirectly, *The Hashish-Eater* and his *modus operandi* in that epic poem:

> As to my employment of an ornate style, using many words of classic origin and exotic color, I can only say that it is designed to produce effects of language and rhythm which could not possibly be achieved by a vocabulary restricted to what is known as "basic English." As [Lytton] Strachey points out [in his essay on Sir Thomas Browne], a style composed largely of words of Anglo-Saxon origin tends to a spondaic rhythm, "which by some mysterious law, reproduces the atmosphere of ordinary life."[2] An atmosphere of remoteness, vastness, mystery and exoticism is more naturally evoked by a style with an admixture of Latinity, lending itself to more varied and sonorous rhythms, as well as to subtler shades, tints and nuances of meaning—all of which, of course, are wasted or worse than wasted on the average reader, even if presumably literate. [. . .]
>
> As to coinages, I have really made few such, apart from proper names of personages, cities, countries, deities, etc., in realms lying "east of the sun and west of the moon." I have used a few words, names of fabulous monsters, etc., drawn from Herodotus, Mandeville, and Flaubert, which I have not been able to find in dictionaries or other works of reference. Some of these occur in "The Hashish-Eater," a much-misunderstood poem, which was intended as a study in the possibilities of cosmic consciousness, drawing heavily on myth and fable for its imagery. It is my own theory that, if the infinite worlds of the cosmos were opened to human vision, the visionary would be overwhelmed by horror in the end, like the hero of this poem.
>
> I hope that I have made it plain that my use of rare and exotic words has been solely in accord with an esthetic theory, or, one might say, a technical theory. (*SL* 365–66)

Notes

1. Quite apart from any real critical or literary value that Blish's essay may possess intrinsically, it may also serve as a pertinent illustration of the difficulties involved in conducting research, bibliographical and otherwise, among materials not collected by, or easily accessible in, academic or other libraries associated with institutions, usually the best homes for uncommon materials. Fanzines, perzines, and semiprozines (i.e.,

semiprofessional magazines) by their very nature did not or do not lend themselves easily to the status of conventional printed collectibles. Although a few college or university libraries may now possess random and meager holdings of the fanzines from the 1930s and 1940s, researchers academic and otherwise have had to rely for the most part on individual collectors for any kind of access to such idiosyncratic publications.

The present writer states this directly from personal experience. While conducting the research for his Clark Ashton Smith bio-bibliography *Emperor of Dreams* (1978), he was fortunate enough to have access to Forrest Ackerman's unparalleled collection of all types of books and magazines dealing with fantasy and science fiction, including what must have amounted (if piled one item on top of another) to a twenty-five- or thirty-foot stack of fanzines of every description, as faithfully amassed by Ackerman from the 1930s on into the early or middle 1960s. This overall collection proved an invaluable resource, even if (as it turned out) Ackerman did not have any copies of *Tumbrils*, and even if we had thought to ask at the time. (We could not have done so because we did not know yet that *Tumbrils* had existed.) It was Fritz Leiber who, following our principal search among Ackerman's archives, let us know of the existence of Blish's essay, of which otherwise we would not have known anything at all. We wrote at once to James Blish himself (address courtesy of Fritz again), then living somewhere on the east coast, requesting of him a copy of his own essay as politely as we could. What better strategy could there be to get a copy than applying directly to the very source himself?

Alas, as the essay's author kindly replied almost at once, his own file of *Tumbrils*, along with many other valuable papers, had undergone such damage in a flood at a previous place of residence near a river that they had emerged from this disaster in a state beyond repair or any further usage. He had no choice except to throw most of them away. Since we had no other clue as to where else to search (nor did Blish himself), we gave up any further quest for the elusive piece, and nobody else appeared to know either.

Many years later, acting on this datum about Blish's essay as reported in our bio-biography, Don Herron finally discovered a copy and bought it at great expense, later sharing it quite generously with others, including Scott Connors, Ronald Scott Hilger, and myself. Otherwise we could not have reproduced Blish's essay here, nor could we deliver our present riposte.

2. In Strachey's essay, the original wording reads: "which seems to produce (by some mysterious rhythmic law) an atmosphere of ordinary life."

The Last Romantic

S. J. Sackett

The late Edwin Markham, author of "The Man with the Hoe" and other poems, once called Clark Ashton Smith "the greatest American poet." Benjamin De Casseres ranked Smith as a poet with Poe, Baudelaire, Shelley, Rimbaud, Keats, and Blake.

And yet, as George Sterling—himself once the leading contender for the laurel in this country, at least in the eyes of H. L. Mencken—has pointed out, "to our everlasting shame, he is entirely neglected and almost unknown."[1]

The busy circles of professional esthetes have never heard of Smith. The not-so-high-brows, who get their introduction to modern poetry through the anthologies of Oscar Williams and Louis Untermeyer, will not find him in the indices to those volumes. At the best, you may get a facetious "Smith? Smith? The name is familiar . . ."

It is clear to those who know Smith's poetry and prose that the reason for his undeserved eclipse is purely a lack of timing. He lived at the wrong time. If he had been born in 1793, instead of a hundred years later, you would have studied him in your undergraduate English survey course. But the currents of his age have passed him by. He never heard about the wasteland; he thought it was a garden all along.

For Clark Ashton Smith is the last of the Romantic poets. There are other writers of traditional verse, but none of them are really Romantics as Smith is. In an anything-but-Romantic age, it is no wonder that his remarkable talents have been too little appreciated. He has refused to conform to the patterns of Pound or the accents of Eliot. He has gone on in the great traditions of poetry no matter what his contemporaries do. He has chosen, deliberately, to be unconfined by his historical period and to write for all time, if not for his age. It is therefore perhaps not wholly surprising that his age ignores him.

The general tone of Smith's poetry can best be described by the words *fin de siècle*. He is a brother-in-arms of Oscar Wilde, Swinburne, D. G. Rossetti, and the other "decadents" of the turn of the twentieth century. He is a translator of Baudelaire and often writes of his own garden of evil in much the same way. Through these Bunthornes of the gay nineties, he looks back also to the Romantics, to Keats and Poe and Coleridge, and through them also to Milton.

He is, of course, derivative. His detractors—who have been surprisingly vocal, considering the little impact Smith has made on the world of letters—have deprecated him as "a creative scholar." And this, in a sense, he is. Surely it is an achievement in itself to be so good a "creative scholar" as Smith is. After all, one could say the same for Eliot.

But Smith is original, too. Or, rather, if not original, neither were Tennyson or Keats or Poe or Coleridge, for they were all derivative poets as well. There is something about Smith's work at best which marks it as distinctive, although it is true that in some poems his influences are incompletely amalgamated. And it is dangerous to try to find a source for all of Smith; his affinity to certain writers has occasionally led critics to assign to him influences in other poets whom he has never read.

Smith does not attempt to mirror the neurosis or frustrations of his age. He does not try to express his reactions to the ills of our world, except in his withdrawal from them. He has no political or psychological axe to grind. All he wants to do is write poetry, write beautiful poetry, write poetry with singing words that will delight the reader. He wants to amuse, in the most noble meaning of the word, just as Poe and Coleridge amused their readers with haunting beauty.

Smith's poetry has appeared in five collected volumes, of which *The Dark Chateau*, published in 1951 by Arkham House, is the most recent and the only one which is readily obtainable. It contains a good sampling of Smith's output; there are the moody and romantic evocations which are his most characteristic utterances, such as "Amithaine," "Averoigne," "Zothique," "The Witch with Eyes of Amber," and "Luna Aeternalis"; there are some examples of his dabblings in Spanish and French poetry, both in his own compositions and in translations from other poets; and there are some of his more ironic pieces, like "Sinbad, It Was Not Well to Brag," "Sonnet for the Psychoanalysts," and "The Twilight of the Gods." From these poems, and the others in this collection, it is possible to get an impression of what Smith can do and what he can do best. It is possible also to decide whether or not one likes him, for this is a matter of individual taste; but, for those who may approach *The Dark Chateau* in order to make this decision, I have one caution. Read the poems aloud, for they have been written with a painstaking attention to sound.

A volume of *Selected Poems* has been advertised for imminent publication ever since *The Dark Chateau* appeared; I have been awaiting its advent but so far have been disappointed.

Smith also writes prose. He does not write short stories so much as short prose tales, more in the vein of Poe than of de Maupassant. The style is the important thing in Smith's fiction; he is concerned with his diction, with getting the exact word in the right place. Character does not interest him at all, and plot is only the framework for style. The best of his stories, however, are very good, once you have made the initial concession to judge Smith's work on its own merits and not to measure him against contemporary followers of Hemingway.

With Smith, as with Poe, the aim of fiction is the creation of a single emotional effect. Also as with Poe, the effect Smith most often aims at is terror. Whether he achieves his effect or not depends on the amount of co-operation he can extort from his reader. You have to approach his fiction with standards different from those by which you would judge most modern writers. You have to be willing to make that suspension of disbelief which constitutes poetic faith. But once you have made that effort of mind, Smith's prose will carry you into lands of long ago and far away where strange and wonderful things happen. It is the music of Smith's language, rather than any empathy with the characters, which most frequently achieves the effect. For this reason, Smith's stories deserve more than any others in English since Poe's to be called "prose poems."

And yet these tales are not all emptiness. There is some substance to them. Smith has things to say about the nature of humanity and of human existence, and he says them in his own way. The vision and the expression are both unique.

They are, frankly, fantasies. In the letter column of *Wonder Stories* for 1932–33, Smith defended fantasy against more realistic forms of literary art. Speaking of realism, Smith said, "The best possibilities lie in the correlation of observed data about life and human problems with inspired speculation as to the unknown forces of cosmic cause and effect. . . .The evil lies in a meaningless Dreiserism, an inartistic heaping of superficial facts or alleged facts which . . . may be erroneous or, at least, too incomplete to permit the safe drawing of dogmatic inferences. . . . It is partly because of this shifting, unstable ground on which the thing called realism stands, that I regard pure, frank fantasy as a more valid and lasting art-expression of the human mind" [*PD* 20–21].

It is, then, his considered judgement that imaginative writing—fantasy—is the only enduring type of art. As he has put it elsewhere, "The animals alone, without having imagination, have no escape from reality. From paretic to psycho-analyst, from poet to rag-picker, we are all in flight from the real. Truth is what we desire it to be, and the facts of life are a masquerade in which we imagine that we have identified the maskers" [*PD* 39]. On epistemological grounds then, because it is impossible to ascertain reality, Smith has written entirely in the fantastic vein.

Smith's prose style has been accused of "verbosity" and of being "Byzantine." It has been called "intolerably arty." In defense of his ornate style, Smith has written that "it is designed to produce effects of language and rhythm which could not possibly be achieved by a vocabulary restricted to what is known as 'basic English'. As Strachey points out (in his essay on Sir Thomas Browne), a style composed largely of words of Anglo-Saxon origin tends to a spondaic rhythm, 'which by some mysterious law reproduces the atmosphere of ordinary life'. An atmosphere of remoteness, mystery, and exoticism is more naturally evoked by a style with an admixture of Latinity, lending itself to more varied and sonorous rhythms, as well as to subtler shades, tints and nuances of meaning" [*SL* 365]. If those are Smith's purposes, certainly it would be a mistake for him to adopt a monosyllabic style. And, in an age dominated by Hemingway, it is difficult for the average reader to see that such a style as Smith's can achieve the effects its author wants. Such, however, is the case; and the styles of Poe and Sir Thomas Browne, which have influenced Smith, are evidences.

Four collections of Smith's short stories have been published; one, by the author himself, *The Double Shadow*, of which I understand that copies are still available; and three more, by Arkham House, of which the first, *Out of Space and Time*, has long been out of print, the second, *Lost Worlds*, is also unobtainable, and the third, *Genius Loci*, may still be available. A fourth Arkham volume, *The Abominations of Yondo*, and a fifth, *Tales of Science and Sorcery*, have for some time been reputed to be in preparation.

I have never seen *Out of Space and Time*, but I can give brief descriptions of the other three published collections. *The Double Shadow* is a paper-bound booklet containing six stories, many of them available by the same or other titles in his other collections. Some of them are purely tales of terror; but two have additional significance. "The Voyage of King Euvoran," for example, teaches that pride can destroy us by driving us to go on when it would be wiser to admit defeat, and "The Maze of the Enchanter" affords a flash of insight into the soul-weariness and disgust with life of a man who can accomplish all things and for whom, therefore, defeat is never possible. As long as he lives, Tiglari, the hero, will have the memory of having dared a brave thing, fully aware of the price he must pay for defeat; Maâl Dweb, however, who does defeat him, lives, by contrast, an empty and unhappy life.

Lost Worlds contains twenty-three stories, fifteen of them set in imaginary worlds created by Smith—Atlantis, Averoigne, Zothique, and Xiccarph. Apart from "The Maze of the Enchanter," which reappears here as "The Maze of Maâl Dweb," my own favorites are "The Tale of Satampra Zeiros," "The Door to Saturn," "The Coming of the White Worm," "The Last Incantation," "The Death of Malygris," "The Holiness of Azédarac," "The Flower-Women," and "The Demon of the Flower." Most of these are tales of terror or of wonder, the other emotion principally exploited by Smith; but "The Door to Saturn" and "The Holiness of Azédarac," at least, display Smith's mastery of a kind of sardonic humor, in both of them directed against the priesthood. In "The Last Incantation" Malygris, the Atlantean philosopher, restores to life Nylissa, his long-dead love, only to find her disappointing; through this situation Smith demonstrates that, as Thomas Wolfe put it, "you can't go home again"—that it is impossible ever to recapture the past.

Smith's most recent collection, *Genius Loci*, contains fifteen stories, only two of which, in my opinion, at all approach the best in *Lost Worlds:* "Vulthoom" and "The Charnel God." Both are terror stories, but the first is particularly interesting because of Smith's effort to combine his customary weirdness and exoticism with some of the trappings of the science-fiction story. Although the combination is not always successful, the result is one of Smith's most suspenseful stories, and the ending is suitably spine-tingling.

Structurally, most of these stories are distinctly "tales" rather than short stories; one turns instinctively to the French word *conte* to describe them. The short story, in our day, is either a smoothly plotted but artificially constructed narrative or a "slice of life" without much plot at all. Smith's *contes* fit neither definition. They have a plot, but it is usually not dominant; it merely provides what one is used to in modern fiction than like folktales or travelers' yarns.

The novice reader of Smith needs one caution: these *contes* need to be read slowly and seldom, Smith needs to be sipped to be enjoyed. You cannot read him hurriedly, or you will lose some of the bouquet. Similarly, if you read him for too long at a sitting, you will probably find that you have lost your taste for him, just as too much sweetness cloys. But read with attention and sympathy, and dipped into occasionally, his stories can be a rewarding experience.

Some day, a long time from now, there may be another Romantic revival. People may be less concerned than at present to find the poet who can most satisfactorily complete fuzzy-minded confusion. They may again turn to poets whose chief interest is in beauty and entertainment.

If so, it will be with considerable interest that the poems of Clark Ashton Smith will be discovered. "Here," they will say, "in the middle of the Age of Naturalism, a man trod on stars and looked beyond the world about him into realms of the imagination. Wholly dissociated from the nervous currents of his period, he had for his only concern the creation of pure poetry. Wholly disregarded by his contemporaries, he can now, with the perspective of history, be recognized as one of the world's fine poets."

With that judgement, the life-long devotion of Clark Ashton Smith to the cause of beauty will be justified and rewarded.

Notes

1. David Warren Ryder, "The Price of Poetry." *Controversy* 1, No. 7 (December 1934): 86; online at http://www.eldritchdark.com/bio/price_of_poetry.html.

Communicable Mysteries:
The Last True Symbolist

Fred Chappell

The publication of *The Last Oblivion* is a singular blessing. Edited by S. T. Joshi and David E. Schultz, the volume is subtitled *Best Fantastic Poems of Clark Ashton Smith*. Hippocampus Press has brought it out in sturdy paper covers, priced it at $15, and reproduced four of Smith's artworks. A bibliography is included, as well as indices of titles and first lines and the editors have contributed a brief but perceptive introduction. There is a helpful glossary of unusual terms like *simorgh, cimar, euphrasy, dolent,* and so forth.

The poems are divided into seven sections, classified under such rubrics as "The Eldritch Dark," "The Refuge of Beauty," and "Medusa and Other Horrors." The editors propose that these categories are to be regarded as "suggestive rather than definitive" and that segregating Smith's more "fantastic" work from the rest "may seem a highly artificial undertaking." The point is worth making; it may be that all poetry, even the dogged "realism" of George Crabbe and Edwin Markham, belongs to a species of discourse that is inherently fabulous. *The Last Oblivion*, then, is a "sheaf" of Smith's verses which contains "a more concentrated dose of the weird than others." The distinction is useful in this application. If one were making a selection of Coleridge's "fantastic" poems, "Christabel" and "Kubla Khan" would be included while "Fears in Solitude" and "France: An Ode" would plausibly be omitted.

But here lies an important difference. The supernatural and fantastic are categories that Coleridge chooses to embrace for specific works, while for Smith they are the usual terms of his literary thought. There are remarkably few of his poems—mostly amatory and satiric—that do not bear some trace of fantasy or some usage of the language of fantasy. For example, "No Stranger Dream" (*S&P* 26) is but a courtly, hyperbolic compliment to a lady's beauty, yet it includes "flying Lemures" and "the silver wraith of Baaltis." It could be argued that a too frequent resort to the terms and tag phrases of fantasy is one of the limitations of Smith's verse.

I should begin to make it clear that I regard Clark Ashton Smith as a very good poet. His pages I often return to with a pleasant assurance of enjoyment. Yet I think that some of the praise I would give his work might not find favor with some of his most ardent partisans. *Expert, solid, reliable, comprehensible, sturdy:* These are perhaps not qualities that we customarily associate with poems titled "Enchanted Mirrors," "The Witch in the Graveyard," "The Nightmare Tarn," and the like. For such productions we might expect such adjectives as *pavonine, bejeweled, cosmic, phantasmagoric,* and, of course, *eldritch.*

But these sets of qualities are not mutually exclusive.

One of the factors that confuses the situation is Smith's continuous exoticism. He loves to pour it on, to "load every rift with ore," as Keats said, and more than that—to go over the top, as far over the top as possible. The acme and avatar of such excess is, of course, *The Hashish-Eater* with its sennet-and-tucket opening ("Bow down: I am the emperor of dreams"), its kaleidoscopic barrage of garish images ("The sacred flower with lips of purple flesh"; "deserts filled with ever-wandering flames"; "wreaths of torpid vipers"), its mythological and faery names (Sabaoth, cockatrice, Enceladus, hippogriff), its resounding Miltonics ("demon tears incessant") and sudden shifts of perspective, place, and vantage—well, all those devices that make it what it is: a showcase of most of the poet's strengths and weaknesses, a curio shop window crowded with valuables and dross alike.

The Hashish-Eater, for all its glut and glitter, for all its sumptuous sonorities and all its fame and favor, is not one of Smith's best works in my judgment and I think that its celebrity may hamper appreciation of some of Smith's other, better productions. The poet himself complained that it was "much-misunderstood"; the visions described and suggested in the lines were not designed to add up to a colorfully jolly experience. "It is my own theory that if the infinite worlds of the cosmos were opened to human vision, the visionary would be overwhelmed by horror in the end, like the hero of this poem" (*SL* 366). The closure is a calculated but still less than fully effective anticlimax and may owe something to the conclusion of Arthur Machen's novel, *The Hill of Dreams.*

The "cosmicism" of Smith's poetry consists of shifting panoramas and it is a method he employs often, in short and longish poems alike. *The Hashish-Eater* only plays out at greater length the techniques that animate "The Star-Treader," "Ode to the Abyss," "The Song of a Comet," "Imagination," "Saturn," and others. Even "Nero," an interior monologue of that dissipated emperor, is in part a "cosmic" panorama in which "dust is loosened into vaporous wings / With soaring wrack of systems ruinous."

This sort of performance at first dazzles but then palls. There is too much of everything—too many cacophonies of Chaos and enraged suns, too many whelmed and reeling worlds, too much gigantic legionry, too much bottomless abyss unvaulted. Reading these poems is like listening to an orchestra that plays nothing but Wagnerian overtures, every note fortissimo. Smith justifies the inchoate nature of *The Hashish-Eater* by saying that his visionary is overwhelmed by horror—but isn't there a possibility that the poet's cosmic vocabulary was simply used up? Maybe he had expended all his images. I find "Nero" the more effective poem because its phantasmagoric elements proceed from the crazed ruler's psychology; they pour from a bizarre but recognizable wellspring. The more famous poem seems to exploit the drug of its title as an excuse to geyser forth a flood of flimsily connected images.

But Smith might defend his poem by saying that psychology—no matter how aberrant—is precisely what he wants to avoid. He complained that the vaunted freedom of commercial science fiction was illusory, asking "why bother about going to other planets," if mere human motives are to be the subject matter (*SL* 134). His ambition seems to have been to create a poetry of vatic vision in which the vision itself is identical with the poet. The poet need have no other motive than to articulate the poem, no other personality than what the poem requires for its articulation, and no other presence than a virtual one in a picturesque universe where, as a seer, he can move about unhindered. This is, at any rate, the role in which the hashish-eater sees himself: "If I will, / I am at once the vision and the seer, / And mingle with my ever-streaming pomps, / And still abide their suzerain" (*LO* 19).

For me the smaller works are more successful than the longer. Many of them, perhaps most, are "cosmic" in the manner of the longer efforts, and that breadth of vision acquires a greater force, is less scattered in effect, in the briefer poems. "In Saturn" offers an example of cosmicism, all the more fantastically suggestive because of its restraint:

> Upon the seas of Saturn I have sailed
> To isles of high primeval amarant,
> Where the flame-tongued, sonorous flowers enchant
> The hanging surf to silence; all engrailed
>
> With ruby-colored pearls, the golden shore
> Allured me; but as one whom spells restrain,
> For blind horizons of the somber main
> And harbors never known, my singing prore
>
> I set forthrightly. Formed of fire and brass,
> And arched with moons, immenser heavens deep
> Were opened—till above the darkling foam,
>
> With dome on cloudless adamantine dome,
> Black peaks no peering seraph deems to pass
> Rose up from realms ineffable as sleep!   (*LO* 40)

This poem does not careen around the zodiac, presenting a travelogue of purple worlds populated by lunar wizards, but still it manages to produce an impression of otherworldliness that lingers like the echo of an English horn berceuse. "In Saturn" contains a number of Smith's customary tropes: mythological blossoms ("amarant"), supernatural beings ("seraph"), and enchantment ("one whom spells restrain"). It also presents his familiar speaker, the poet who is one with his poem in the quest for some ultimate vision.

The figure of the seraph occurs now and again in Smith's lines and there seems no reason to think it connected with the traditional religious symbol, the angel with three pairs of wings as mentioned in Isaiah 6:2. It is only a skyey supernatural being that belongs with Smith's general muster of like creatures: vampires, female giants, Titans, colossi, and, above all, demons. These figures are as customary in the poetry as are certain touchstones of this poet's diction—"gibbous," for instance, and "eldritch," "Cimmerian," "accurst," and "immemorial." We might extend the lists of supernatural figures and frequent adjectives, yet we would still observe that for a poet so reputedly "cosmic" the store of motifs and images is severely limited.

I would not attribute this limitation to lack of imagination. It seems instead a meditated choice, a self-imposed set of boundaries within which Smith plays a subtle, arcane, and continual game. His wyverns, sorcerors, eremites, and paladins—even his gulfs, voids, and abysses—are like pieces on an onyx-and-ivory chessboard to be moved into assigned positions as the separate strategies of the poems dictate. Like certain other poets, Clark Ashton Smith creates a little universe, sufficient unto itself, with each poem he writes. This is not the case with all poets; William Carlos Williams makes a poetry that, being insufficient in its proper self, requires readers to supply its sphere of actuality from their own "realistic" experiences. Williams's poems are often powerful isolated moments, but there is no coherence between them; there is instead a purposeful incoherence. "No ideas but in things."

But Smith's poems do add up to a coherent pattern, a vision that for all its scope and variety is isomorphic in its constituent parts. Taken together, almost all these poems would compose an artificial universe. The ideal of a self-enclosed, hermetic universe purely visionary, impervious to the sordidness and distractions of daily life, was one to which the great French Symbolist writers aspired. Charles Baudelaire, Paul Verlaine, Stéphane Mallarmé, Paul Valéry—these writers and a host of lesser ones strove to contrive a kind of poetry that would draw a reader into a sphere of discourse in which every element was poetry. Whatever was absorbed from the outer, quotidian world would become transfigured—transubstantiated, if you will—into a completely poetic substance. They desired to create a poetry so integral, so complete in its vision, that it would be able to supplant the dull, often seemingly meaningless, world that most of us have been sentenced at birth to endure.

So if the phrase, "a silver trance," and the compound adjective, "dusky-purple," that appear in "The Moonlight Desert" might also plausibly appear in "The City of the Titans" and "Saturn" and "In Slumber" and in a dozen others, it is not because the poet ran short of fresh verbiage. It is because all the poems belong to the same mode of "enchanted" discourse, whatever the occasional and ostensible subjects they undertake separately. Almost any poem by Smith brings us into the whole universe of all his poetry.

It was not whimsy nor his affection for exoticism that led Smith to title his 1958 collection *Spells and Philtres*. I believe that he hoped to cast, as a wizard casts with his magical incantations and concoctions, a more-than-verbal enchantment over his readers, following Symbolist tradition. This volume contains, as did his 1925 *Sandalwood,* a selection of translations from the onlie begetter of French Symbolism, Baudelaire, and there are poems of his own which clearly show strong influence. "Didus Ineptus," for example, is a re-figuration of Baudelaire's "L'Albatros," while "The Pagan" and "The Barrier" take their lineaments from Mallarmé's "L'Après-midi d'un faune." The Symbolists too used certain words and phrases again and again to sustain their enclosed poetic spheres; where in Smith we find "wizardry," "oubliette," and "effulgent," in Baudelaire we find "ennui," in Verlaine "sanglot," in Valéry "azur."

Smith's relationship with French Symbolism seems almost preordained. Although his more learned colleague and admirer, George Sterling, helped to foster his interest and to encourage it, Smith was so taken with the *idea* of Baudelaire that he began to "translate" his work even before he could read the language. In a 1925 letter to Sterling he speaks of diverting himself by "paraphrasing a few of the Baudelaire translations by F. P. Sturm and others." He compares his version of a stanza of "The Remorse of the Dead" with Sturm's and then says, "I've never seen the original; but it seems to me that my version is more *Baudelairean.* B. *might* have written something of the sort" (*SL* 74).

It was cheeky of the young poet to suppose that he might come closer to the spirit of Baudelaire by strength of empathy than might a translator familiar with the language. Yet it is not his lack of familiarity with French that produced such infelicities as "lovely knees enorme" in "La Géante" or the dreadful rendering of the opening of "L'Aube Spirituelle" ("Quand chez les debauches l'aube blanche et vermeille / Entre") as "When comes upon the sot the scarlet-sworded morn" (*S* 40). These errors and some others proceed from a testiness about what he considered a prissy watering-down of Baudelaire by timid translators. This belief could lead him to inventive, overly compensatory excesses, such as supplying to "La Vie Anterieure" "the full bosom of a golden slave" and the suggestion of baroque sexual amusements, "sable queens invented / Fantastic love to tease my weary woe." The original is none so spicy:

> C'est là que j'ai vécu dans les voluptés calmes,
> Au milieu de l'azur, des vagues, des splendeurs
> Et des escalves nus, tout imprégnés d'odeurs,
>
> Qui me refraîchissaient le front avec des palmes,
> Et dont l'unique soin était d'approfondir
> Le secret douloureux qui me faisait languir.

(There I lived within luxurious calmness, / amid azure waves and splendors, / and naked slaves, all bathed with perfumes, // refreshed my forehead with palm fronds; / their only duty was to puzzle out / the unhappy secret that cast me down.)

Even so, most of Smith's versions are at least presentable, usually more graceful (and more accurate!) than those of Arthur Symons. Smith's versions of "Chant d'Automne" and "Le Léthé" can stand with any I have come across, and some of his epigrams capture the true Baudelairean spirit, wry and melancholy: "It is a truism of the mystics that 'as things are above, so are they below.' This raises a speculation as to just how far above, or how far below, the ecstasy of the mystics has carried them" (*S&P* 52).

I have pursued Smith's peculiar relationship with French Symbolism—tenuous but passionate, engaged but spottily informed—in order to point toward a divergence that partly accounts for the place that his poetry occupies today.

The French Symbolist movement was waning by the beginning of the twentieth century, though it still had powerful influence in England, Germany, Switzerland, and in certain Latin American countries. In France it began to metamorphose into surrealism, dada, cubism, "pataphysics," and so forth. These offshoots of the great nineteenth-century movement also had, and still have, strong influence all round the literary world. By reaction as well as by kinship, Symbolism has contributed to the rise of the "language poets" in America and the Oulipo group in Europe. By absorbing influences from psychology, politics, the plastic arts, anthropology, physics, linguistics, and so forth, Symbolism added to its strengths, varied its aims in a thousand ways, and informed not only poetry but our general culture in a manner that its first proponents could hardly have imagined.

In doing so, it largely gave up the purist nature of its hermeticism; to remain dynamic, it had to bid farewell to its artificial paradises, its ingenious and suggestive emblematic systems, its shadows and censers, its twilights and tone poems, its languid voices and lickerish vampires. It could not withstand the onslaught of two world wars without radical change; no more could the rest of society—except for those poets who had become, because of their fast allegiances, reactionaries. They made a carefully deliberated decision. If Symbolism was ever a valid mode, changes of fashion would not invalidate it. "The forms and themes of poetry do not become outworn or exhausted. The exhaustion is in the individual poets" (*S&P* 52). So runs one of Smith's aesthetic apothegms.

There were a number of poets who clung to the Baudelairean tradition and a surprising number of them were Americans. In a recent volume that samples their work (*Decadents, Symbolists, & Aesthetes in America*, ed. Edward Foster [Talisman Press, 2000]), we find such names as Edgar Saltus, James Huneker, Bliss Carman, Stuart Merrill, Francis Viele-Griffin, and George Sterling. The last two English-language poems in the book, "The Eldrich [*sic*] Dark" and "White Death," are by Clark Ashton Smith.

The poets included by Foster in his anthology are no longer names to conjure with. Except for Amy Lowell, E. A Robinson, Conrad Aiken, Sara Teasdale, and maybe Trumbull Stickney, most of them would be unfamiliar even to moderately well read students of our literature. Smith, because of his connection with H. P.

Lovecraft and *Weird Tales*, is probably as well known as all but a few of the others. These writers do not cast shadows upon our contemporary landscape.

But, as the editors remark, literary quality is not determined by contemporaneity. Baudelaire has not diminished as a poet because surrealism, dada, abstractionism, and the other schools supplanted his groundbreaking mode of writing. "L'Invitation au voyage," "Hymne à la beauté," "Sonnet d'automne," and the other great poems remain great. There is, of course, an air of quaintness about some of them, a whiff now and then of musty velour, but lovers of poetry return to his lines and to those of Verlaine, Rimbaud, Mallarmé, and others again and again, as if—well, as if enchanted.

Smith has neither Baudelaire's authority nor his aesthetic judgment. Probably there is no poem in all his work equal to the finest of Symbolist poetry. But his best work can hold its own with almost all the pages of Catulle Mendès, say, and Emile Verhaeren, Henri de Regnier, and the rest. His sonnets are probably his most admirable poetic achievements, better by far than similar efforts by his friends Lovecraft, Samuel Loveman, and Donald Wandrei.

Personal taste is a problematic yardstick, but it is the one that all honest readers are forced to employ in matters of literary judgment. My list of favorite Smith poems is a lengthy one and even after severe pruning it remains too long to set down in toto. But here are some poems I recommend enthusiastically, all of them collected in *The Last Oblivion*:

On Death: "White Death" (90), "The Moonlight Desert" (107), "Retrospect and Forecast" (151);
Eros: "Love Malevolent" (124), "Adventure" (136), "The Sorceror to His Love" (145), "Midnight Beach" (147);
The deserted city: "A Dead City" (90), "The Prophet Speaks" (102), "Forgotten Sorrow" (159);
The "cosmic": "Ode to the Abyss" (33), "The Song of a Comet" (36), "In Saturn" (41);
Antiquity and classical themes: "Nero" (49), "Memnon at Midnight" (98), "Fantaisie d'Antan" (127), "Bacchante" (143), "The Hill of Dionysus" (145);
Apocalypse: "Medusa" (51), "Desert Dweller" (108), "The Last Night" (118), "Dolor of Dreams" (121).

These categories, like those that editors Joshi and Schultz devised to organize the contents of *The Last Oblivion*, are meant to be suggestive, not to establish tight classifications. Many of the poems could be listed comfortably under more than one heading. Two categories I came up with are sometimes nearly indistinguishable—that of *the poet* and that of *exile*.

I noted earlier that in Smith's pages the figure of the poet exists only in order to give voice to the poem. Insofar as this fictive poet possesses definable personal characteristics at all, he is seen as an observer untrammeled by boundaries of time and space and bourgeois morality; his past history, when we are allowed to know it, took place in an area now in ruins or no longer extant. If that place still does exist, he is an exile from it, having been driven away or having left to follow his wandering star. He is grave, melancholy, skeptical, sometimes only nostalgic, but often filled with yearning.

The second stanza of "A Song of Dreams" (119) is perhaps the most explicit portrayal of this figure of the poet, but such pieces as "Pour chercher du nouveau" (83), the allegorical "Necromancy" (176), the chilling "The Refuge of Beauty" (133), "Alienage" (135), "Zothique" (112), and a fair number of others employ this half-vanished bard as speaker. I think my favorite among these might be "Desolation" (155):

> It seems to me that I have lived alone—
> Alone, as one that liveth in a dream:
> As light on coolest marble, or the gleam
> Of moons eternal on a land of stone,
> The days have been to me. I have but known
> The silence of Thulean lands extreme—
> A silence all-attending and supreme
> As is the sea's enormous monotone.
>
> Upon the waste no palmed mirages are,
> But strange chimeras roam the steely light,
> And cold parhelia hang on hill and scaur
> Where flowers of frost alone have bloomed . . . I crave
> The friendly clasp of finite arms, to save
> My spirit from the ravening Infinite.

That last phrase, "the ravening Infinite," is one that Baudelaire himself might have set down if he wrote English. Of all the American poets who are immensely indebted to the great *poète maudit*—T. S. Eliot, Conrad Aiken, Allen Tate, E. A. Robinson, and so many more—Clark Ashton Smith seems to me to come closest in temper of spirit and in tenor of language. Perhaps the scent of quaintness that clings to many of Smith's lines recalls nineteenth-century diction more strongly than does the modernist idiom.

If I knew a young poet who wanted to understand something of Baudelaire but had not had opportunity to study French, I would confidently recommend a list of Smith's poems to communicate a vivid impression of what the Symbolist master had accomplished. This list would include [besides the translations and such homages as "Soliloquy in an Ebon Tower" (171) and "On Re-reading Baudelaire" (167)], "Love Malevolent" (124), "The Tears of Lilith" (132), "The Refuge of Beauty" (133), "The Last Oblivion" (134), "Lamia" (140), and "Selenique" (126). "Ennui" (162) not only borrows Baudelaire's favorite theme, it is cast in that stately Gallic meter, the alexandrine.

One of the most Baudelairean of Smith's poems, and one of his best, speaks obliquely of his own artistic ambitions and, if I surmise correctly, speaks also to the composition of his tales of Hyperborea, Averoigne, and, especially, Poseidonis. It is called "Symbols" (95):

> No more of gold and marble, nor of snow
> And sunlight and vermilion, would I make
> My vision and my symbols, nor would take
> The auroral flame of some prismatic floe.
> Nor iris of the frail and lunar bow,
> Flung on the shafted waterfalls that wake
> The night's blue slumber in a shadowy lake.
> To body forth my fantasies, and show
> Communicable mystery, I would find,
> In adamantine darkness of the earth,
> Metals untouched of any sun; and bring
> Black azures of the nether sea to birth—
> Or fetch the secret, splendid leaves, and blind
> Blue lilies of an Atlantean spring.

What Happens in *The Hashish-Eater?*

S. T. Joshi

The Hashish-Eater is probably Clark Ashton Smith's longest poem, and certainly one of his most complex. As such, it can be read on many levels. The title inclines one to consider it simply the random and chaotic visions of a drug-induced hallucination, and certainly the dense, even crowded imagery of the poem appears to foster this interpretation; but a closer reading may lead one to believe that *The Hashish-Eater* has a definite plot and direction, something perhaps confirmed by a recently published "Argument of 'The Hashish-Eater'" included in the 1989 Necronomicon Press reissue of the poem.

In a letter to Samuel J. Sackett of 11 July 1950 (*SL* 366),[1] Smith refers to *The Hashish-Eater* as "a much-misunderstood poem," and his "Argument" now allows us to have a better idea of what he actually meant by the poem. (Whether he actually accomplished what he meant is something we shall reserve for later discussion.) Even without the "Argument," it can be inferred from the very construction of *The Hashish-Eater* that the poem is something more than a series of unconnected tableaux. Its 582 lines are divided into twelve "paragraphs," and this device—common in epic poetry, although it is rare to find these "paragraph" divisions occurring in the middle of a line, as here—suggests that the poem is meant to be read as some sort of narrative. This suggestion is now confirmed by the "Argument."

In the previously quoted letter to Sackett, Smith says that the poem "was intended as a study in the possibilities of cosmic consciousness," and this suggests that the visions seen by the narrator are just that: "visions" of some actual realm or state of existence, not imaginary vistas spawned by the narrator's imagination. It is true that occasionally the language suggests mere dream-visions: the very opening line, "Bow down: I am the emperor of dreams," hints at it, as does a later passage: "Forgotten splendors, dream by dream, unfold / Like tapestry, and vanish" (155–56);[2] but in this passage, the word "forgotten" seems in context more plausibly to refer not to splendors "forgotten" by the narrator but forgotten by mankind generally because of their existence at some dim, anterior stage of cosmic history.

It is possible to divide *The Hashish-Eater* into four fairly discrete sections, corresponding to the chapters of a story. They are as follows:

> I. A general description of the narrator's visions (in the "Argument" it is said that "By some exaltation and expansion of cosmic consciousness . . . the dreamer is carried to a height [from] which he beholds the strange and multiform scenes of existence in alien worlds") (1–171).

II. The narrator enters his visions and becomes a participant in them (the "Argument" states: "Then, in a state similar to the Buddhic plane, he is able to mingle with them and identify himself with their actors and objects") (171–242).

Ill. The narrator perceives an intruder into his visions (242–83) and is pursued by a series of horrors (283–476), including the monsters in those regions "that knew my trespassing" (417).

IV. Fleeing, the narrator now falls into some strange realm described in the "Argument" as "the verge of a gulf into which falls in cataracts the ruin and rubble of the universe"; from this gulf "the face of infinity itself, in all its awful blankness . . . rises up to confront him" (476–582); the poem ends on a half-line to convey this sense of the narrator's absorption into this realm.

What strikes us about this skeletonic outline is the gradual transformation of the narrator from a position of power to one of helplessness: the figure who at the outset proclaimed himself the "emperor of dreams," and who later refers to himself as a "suzerain" (174), is at the end a small, cowering creature overwhelmed by the chaos and vastness of existence. This transformation can be measured concretely by examining the varying uses of the personal pronoun "I." In the opening sections this pronoun appears not merely with great frequency, but almost always in contexts denoting the strength and vigour of the narrator as master of his visions; in later sections, the use of "I" not only decreases, but when it occurs it is always linked with the narrator's fear of and flight from the scenes and entities he beholds. In the first 113 lines of the poem, "I" occurs fourteen times, three times in the first six lines:

> Bow down: I am the emperor of dreams;
> I crown me with the million-colored sun
> Of secret worlds incredible, and take
> Their trailing skies for vestment when I soar,
> Throned on the mounting zenith, and illume
> The spaceward-flown horizons infinite.

Later instances emphasise the narrator's control: "I convoke" (54), "I behold" (56, 115), "I list" (60), "I see" (66), "I read" (72), "I know" (75, 91, 95), "I lean to read" (85). In an interlude (113–71), to which we shall return later, "I" occurs only twice, and in relatively passive contexts: "I see" (131), "I watch" (141); moreover, these two instances occur at the beginning of the line, whereas the previous instances occurred at the end of the line, where the enjambement creates a dynamic sense of the narrator's power. In what I have deemed the second section of the poem (171–242), "I" occurs twelve times, and once again in positions and contexts of strength:

> If I will,
> I am at once the vision and the seer,
> And mingle with my ever-streaming pomps,
> And still abide their suzerain . . . (171–74)

And later: "It is I" (188), "I fare" (200), "I am page" (216), "I seek" (221), "I hear" (224), "I find" (231, 235).

In the first forty lines of the third section (242f.) "I" appears only twice, both in the same line (246). It is here that the narrator senses an intruding presence in his realm and "Fear is born" (258). Subsequent occurrences of "I" are frequent, but the context is radically shifted, and the narrator is seen stumbling upon horrors ("I find / A corpse the ebbing water will not keep" [288–89]) and fleeing in utter terror:

> But I turn
> To mountains guarding with their horns of snow
> The source of that befouled rill, and seek
> A pinnacle where none but eagles climb,
> And they with falling pennons. But in vain
> I flee . . .   (296–301)

And in the rest of the poem the narrator is more the passive spectator of an apocalypse than an "emperor of dreams."

The suggestion that the narrator has entered into actual realms of entity on other planets (and possibly into past or future epochs) allows for the possibility of a philosophical interpretation of the poem: perhaps we are to see *The Hashish-Eater* as a reflection of Smith's view of human and cosmic existence. Is there any dominant characteristic that can be detected in the narrator's wanderings through space and time? Right from the beginning of the poem we are led to understand that conflict is a ceaseless component of the cosmos. Everything appears hostile and belligerent, as an early passage suggests:

> sorcerers,
> And evil kings, predominantly armed
> With scrolls of fulvous dragon-skin whereon
> Are worm-like runes of ever-twisting flame,
> Would stay me; and the sirens of the stars,
> With foam-like songs from silver fragrance wrought,
> Would lure me to their crystal reefs; and moons
> Where viper-eyed, senescent devils dwell,
> With antic gnomes abominably wise,
> Heave up their icy horns across my way.   (17–26)

Nature itself appears imbued with enmity:

> Like rampant monsters roaring for their glut,
> The fiery-crested oceans rise and rise,
> By jealous moons maleficently urged
> To follow me for ever; mountains horned
> With peaks of sharpest adamant, and mawed

> With sulphur-lit volcanoes lava-langued,
> Usurp the skies with thunder, but in vain,
> And continents of serpent-shapen trees,
> With slimy trunks that lengthen league by league,
> Pursue my light through ages spurned to fire
> By that supreme ascendance . . .   (7–17)

Here, aside from the obvious suggestions of conflict ("monsters roaring for their glut," "maleficently"), we have subtler indications: the mountains are endowed with "peaks of sharpest adamant" for some hostile purpose; and the word "usurp" interjects an explicitly political tone, as if the mountains are intruding upon the domain belonging to the sky.

Nevertheless, it is the narrator's ability to surmount the obstacles of man and Nature that is highlighted in the opening 113 lines; perhaps the most emphatic utterance of this conception occurs at lines 49f.:

> Supreme
> In culminant omniscience manifold,
> And served by senses multitudinous,
> Far-posted on the shifting walls of time,
> With eyes that roam the star-unwinnowed fields
> Of utter night and chaos, I convoke
> The Babel of their visions, and attend
> At once their myriad witness.

The emphasis in these first 113 lines is the narrator's intellectual triumph over hostile forces: he utilises many of his senses and powers of intellect in perceiving the cosmos around him ("behold" [56], "list" [= hear] [60], "know" [71, 91, 95], "read" [72, 85]). One passage here underscores Smith's sense of the tireless conflict that dominates cosmic history:

> I lean to read
> With slant-lipped mages, in an evil star,
> The monstrous archives of a war that ran
> Through wasted eons, and the prophecy
> Of wars renewed, which shall commemorate
> Some enmity of wivern-headed kings
> Even to the brink of time.   (85–91)

The interlude in this first section (113–71) suggests for the first time the limits of the narrator's control over his realm, and foreshadows his reduction to a helpless and inconsequential mote at the end of the poem. In spite of having earlier asserted his "omniscience" (50), the narrator now encounters a "mighty city" (114) whose origin he does not know:

> But whose hands
> Were sculptors of its doors, and columns wrought
> To semblance of prodigious blooms of old,
> No eremite hath lingered there to say,
> And no man comes to learn . . .   (118–22)

By line 152 the narrator attempts to reclaim his omnipotence:

> Surveyed
> From this my throne, as from a central sun,
> The pageantries of worlds and cycles pass . . . (152–54)

And yet there are chinks in his armour even here. He mentions "The face of some averted god" (160), but appears not to know his identity; later, there are "hooded stars inscrutable to God" (168) and also, one supposes, inscrutable to him.

By the beginning of the second section (171f.) the narrator tries to take charge of his visions by bodily entering them:

> I am
> The neophyte who serves a nameless god,
> Within whose fane the fanes of Hecatompylos
> Were arks the Titan worshippers might bear,
> Or flags to pave the threshold; or I am
> The god himself . . .   (174–79)

There is scarcely a greater way of asserting one's power than by claiming godhead, and yet we have already read of those "stars inscrutable to God," which suggests that in this cosmos gods are anything but omniscient; and earlier we read of "plains with no horizon, where a god / Might lose his way for centuries" (147–48): like those of Dunsany, Smith's gods seem all too pathetically fragile in the midst of a vast and unknowable cosmos.

Then, beginning with the third section (242f.), the narrator begins his long descent from emperor to pawn; from pursuer of cosmic visions to pursued:

> Hark!
> What word was whispered in a tongue unknown,
> In crypts of some impenetrable world?
> Whose is the dark, dethroning secrecy
> I cannot share, though I am king of suns,
> And king therewith of strong eternity,
> Whose gnomons with their swords of shadow guard
> My gates, and slay the intruder?   (242–49)

In line 245, "dethroning" is of especial note, explicitly contrasting with the "throne" (153) the narrator earlier claimed as his own. He now confesses that "Fear is born / In crypts below the nadir" (258–59), and his "heart suspends / Its clamor as within the clutch of death" (275–76). At 283f. the narrator strives to reassert his power by calling up visions of beauty, but instead of "meads of shining moly" (284) he finds instead "A corpse the ebbing water will not keep" (289). He flees to a mountaintop, but a huge "silver python" (305) pursues him. He summons a hippogriff to rescue him and take him to a remote planet "where the outwearied wings of time / Might pause and furl for respite" (321–22). Here he finds a castle that appears to be the antithesis of the hostility he has found throughout the cosmos:

> There I find
> A lonely castle, calm, and unbeset
> Save by the purple spears of amaranth,
> And leafing iris tender-sworded. Walls
> of flushed marble, wonderful with rose,
> And domes like golden bubbles, and minarets
> That take the clouds as coronal—these are mine,
> For voiceless looms the peaceful barbican,
> And the heavy-teethed portcullis hangs aloft
> To grin a welcome.   (328–37)

This castle is "unbeset" by enemies; the only weapons are "spears" of delicate and "tender-sworded" flowers. Even the "heavy-teethed" portcullis is rendered harmless in that it "grin[s] a welcome." But the peace is short-lived. A "chuckle sharp as crepitating ice" (353) is heard, and the narrator stumbles into a

> monster-guarded room,
> Where marble apes with wings of griffins crowd
> On walls an evil sculptor wrought, and beasts
> Wherein the sloth and vampire-bat unite,
> Pendulous by their toes, of tarnished bronze,
> Usurp the shadowy interval of lamps
> That hang from ebon arches.   (357–63)

The narrator is again struck with a "fear / That found no name in Babel" (368–69), and he flees from a series of horrors, each worse than the last, including

> a wan, enormous Worm, whose bulk,
> Tumid with all the rottenness of kings,
> Overflows its arms with fold on creased fold
> Obscenely bloating.   (386–89)

Now the narrator hears a mutter "from beyond the horizon's rim" (403) and realises what it is:

> They come,
> The Sabaoth of retribution, drawn

> From all dread spheres that knew my trespassing,
> And led by vengeful fiends and dire alastors
> That owned my sway aforetime!   (415–19)

These may be the most important lines of the poem, and mark the point where the narrator can no longer maintain his pretence of control over the cosmos. Instead, he becomes aware that his previous "sway" was only a sham, and that a paltry human can never have suzerainty over the cosmos. All the monsters of history, legend, and myth arise to pursue the hapless narrator, and his flight is abject:

> In my tenfold fear,
> A monstrous dread unnamed in any hell,
> I rise, and flee with the fleeing wind for wings,
> And in a trice the wizard palace reels,
> And spiring to a single tower of flame,
> Goes out, and leaves nor shard nor ember! Flown
> Beyond the world upon that fleeing wind
> I reach the gulf s irrespirable verge,
> Where fails the strongest storm for breath, and fall,
> Supportless, through the nadir-plunged gloom,
> Beyond the scope and vision of the sun,
> To other skies and systems.   (465–76)

As we begin the fourth section (476f.), we find the narrator in a peculiar realm that the "Argument" terms "a gulf into which falls in cataracts the ruin and rubble of the universe." This description does not seem immediately to apply to the region in which the narrator at first finds himself, for it appears to be simply another exotic world not entirely different in kind from the one he left. But eventually the narrator finds that the lush trees around him fall away, and he sees "an empty desert, all ablaze / With amethysts and rubies, and the dust / Of garnets or carnelians" (499–501). The symbolism appears to suggest the uselessness of these valued gems in this realm of waste and vacancy. Later "the grinding sands give place / To stone or metal" (506–7), and still later:

> A hundred streams of shattered marble run,
> And streams of broken steel, and streams of bronze,
> Like to the ruin of all the wars of time,
> To plunge with clangor of timeless cataracts
> Adown the gulfs eternal.   (514–18)

These substances represent the building materials—and, by an elementary metonymy, the entire civilisations—of all the cultures of earth: primitive man is represented by stone and bronze, classical culture by marble, and the modern age by steel. All have met a similar ignominious fate at the end of time. And when the narrator follows "a river of steel and a river of bronze" (519) whose ripples are "loud and timeless as the clash / Of a million lutes" (520–21), we understand that both the material accomplishments and the aesthetic achievements of mankind, and perhaps the entire cosmos, are no more. The conclusion is now inevitable:

> But when I reach
> The verge, and seek through sun-deafening gloom
> To measure with my gaze the dread descent,
> I see a tiny star within the depths—
> A light that stays me while the wings of doom
> Convene their thickening thousands: for the star
> Increases, taking to its hueless orb,
> With all the speed of horror-changed dreams,
> The light as of a million million moons;
> And floating up through gulfs and glooms eclipsed
> It grows and grows, a huge white eyeless Face
> That fills the void and fills the universe,
> And bloats against the limits of the world
> With lips of flame that open . . .   (568–82)

The universe is finished, and the narrator cannot complete his line because he has perished along with everything else in the cosmos.

Let us now return to the question of how convincing is this portrayal of the rise and fall of the universe in this poem. As stated earlier, the title leads one to suspect merely a farrago of drug-induced delusions; but under this interpretation the subtitle, "The Apocalypse of Evil," could have no coherent meaning. Smith states in the "Argument" that the drug was "used here as a symbol"—or perhaps as a vehicle for the envisioning of the cosmic spectacle. The subtitle clearly points to some cataclysm that will occur at some point in the poem, a cataclysm that will affect not merely the narrator but the world in which he finds himself. In effect, the narrative structure of *The Hashish-Eater* should be evident even without Smith's "Argument": no aesthetic work should require such an external aid to explicate it, and a close reading will establish the direction and purpose of the poem perhaps better than any prose account, whether by Smith or by anyone else.

How much the poem and its symbolism mirror Smith's own philosophy is something that may be left for later study; but the poem may help to shed light on a recent issue in Smith studies. In a provocative article, Steve Behrends queried whether Smith should be regarded as a cosmicist or a misanthrope, and suggests that the latter is closer to Smith's own view. But *The Hashish-Eater* may indicate that Smith's misanthropy (of which his letters offer abundant evidence) was born in part through his cosmicism. In a manner very similar to Lovecraft's, Smith's perception of the vastness of the cosmos could have suggested to him the grotesque puniness of the human puppets who inhabit one tiny corner of it for a twinkling of an eye; and to a man of Smith's keen sensitivity, the spectacle of humanity's ignorance of its own insignificance, or even its pompous claims of actual importance in the cosmos, may have triggered a contempt that ultimately developed into actual misanthropy. Conversely, misanthropy could have led Smith to seek release from petty human concerns and failings in the vastness of the cosmos. Whatever the case, misanthropy and cosmicism need not be perceived as mutually exclusive: one could easily have led to the other. And the "indifference" that Behrends rightly sees as the hallmark of Lovecraft's cosmicism may not be so different from misanthropy as one might think: indifference to human affairs may well be the purest form of misanthropy. In any event, *The Hashish-Eater* may occupy a significant place in Smith's thought as well as his work, as a narrative of cosmic decline and the hubris of the derisive little human insects who are helpless to avert it.

Notes

1. First published in *Klarkash-Ton* No. 1 (June 1988): 22.
2. No recent editions of the poem—the Necronomicon Press edition, the Arkham House edition (*Selected Poems*, 1971), nor the Hippocampus Press edition (*The Last Oblivion*, 2002)—print the line numbers of the poem, but I shall refer to the text in general by line numbers.

Works Cited

Behrends, Steve. "Clark Ashton Smith: Cosmicist or Misanthrope?," *The Dark Eidolon* No. 2 (July 1989): 12–14.

Smith, Clark Ashton. *The Hashish-Eater; or, The Apocalypse of Evil.* West Warwick, RI: Necronomicon Press, 1989.

The Babel of Visions:
The Structuration of Clark Ashton Smith's
The Hashish-Eater

Dan Clore

Clark Ashton Smith's celebrated poem *The Hashish-Eater* derives by expansion from a matrix that can be paraphrased with some such term as *cosmic consciousness* or *mystic attainment*, together with another interwoven matrix of *conflict* in the twin forms of tyranny and rebellion. Every detail of the text derives, directly or indirectly, from these matrices, which technically form a single matrix through the agency of the poem's title. However, before proceeding to a textual explication, some collateral, co-textual evidence seems in order. *Strange Shadows* includes Smith's "Argument of 'The Hashish-Eater'" which also appears in the Necronomicon Press edition of *The Hashish-Eater* and runs as follows:

> By some exaltation and expansion of cosmic consciousness, rather than a mere drug, used here as a symbol, the dreamer is carried to a height from which he beholds the strange and multiform scenes of existence in alien worlds; he maintains control of his visions, evokes and dismisses them at will. Then, in a state similar to the Buddhic plane, he is able to mingle with them and identify himself with their actors and objects. Still later, there is a transition in which the visions, and the monstrous and demonic forces he has evoked, begin to overpower him, to hurry him on helplessly, under circumstances of fright and panic. Armies of fiends and monsters, many drawn from the worlds of myth and fable, muster against him, pursue him through a terrible cosmos, and he is driven at last to the verge of a gulf into which falls in cataracts the ruin and rubble of the universe; a gulf from which the face of infinity itself, in all its awful blankness, beyond stars and worlds, beyond created things, even fiends and monsters, rises up to confront him. (245–46)

Strange Shadows supplements this with a quotation from a letter of Smith's that calls *The Hashish-Eater* "a much misunderstood poem, which was intended as a study in the possibilities of cosmic consciousness, drawing heavily on myth and fable for its imagery. It is my own theory that if the infinite worlds of the cosmos were opened to human vision, the visionary would be overwhelmed by horror in the end, like the hero of this poem" (264).

We need not worry about the "intentional fallacy" of new-critic-speak in quoting such evidence: it merely provides explicit confirmation of the text's own implicit significance. In any case, a text *is not* its author's intentions, and such resort to co-textual evidence constitutes a normal method of interpretation. Indeed, every sign has its significance only by virtue of its placement into a gestalt with other signs; a receiver normally uses other messages emitted by a sender to help infer the correct meaning of a message.

The relationship of the title to the matrices of the poem has become obscured by changes in the culturally determined semantic encyclopedia. The *hashish* sememe that the title alludes to includes semes that differ from the current sememe. The sememe Smith draws on derives from a literary tradition that begins, properly speaking, with De Quincey's *Confessions of an English Opium-Eater*. That work, although dealing with opium rather than hashish or marijuana, set the pattern for the works on hashish that followed it. It emphasizes the dreams or visions created by the drug's influence, the experience's gradual conversion from positive to negative, and the similarity between the drug-state and mystic states as described in eastern religions. Three influential works that follow it, more or less, on these points, come in Théophile Gautier's "The Hashish Club," Charles Baudelaire's *Les Paradis Artificiels* (translated as *The Artificial Paradise*) in a section titled "The Poem of Hashish," and Fitz-Hugh Ludlow's *The Hasheesh Eater*. Even the title of the last clearly shows De Quincey's influence; it and Baudelaire's work had an especial influence on conceptions of the effects of hashish. The third point I listed above, the similarity of the drugs' effects to mystic states, has an even greater relevance to hashish, as a number of Muslim and Hindu sects use the drug specifically to induce mystic states—most notably, the Noble Order of Assassins, a term that popular etymology derived from "hashishin" or hashish-eater (a more likely etymological meaning: "saint" or "holy man")—as does also the Ethiopian Coptic Church (the oldest surviving Christian church, oddly enough). In addition, works that treated mystic experiences, such as William James's *The Varieties of Religious Experience*, which particularly instances ether and other anesthetics as producing mystic experiences.

The title therefore clearly derives from the "mystic attainment" sememe. Further, it provides the motivation for the "cosmic consciousness," for the nature of the mystic state as one of visions, and for the progression from positive to negative over the narrative's course. It motivates the mystic attainment in the first place by providing its cause. The other elements figure as direct consequences. In addition, the title provides, as a metonym of the hashish itself, the hashish-eater, signaling that this character will serve as the poem's speaker, following an oft-used poetic convention that allows a poet to give voice to another person or being (the rhetorical figure *prosopopoeia*), allowing the expression of information not normally available to others—in this case, the description of the hashish-eater's visions and experiences.

In case the main title, together with the text, had not made the matrix sufficiently explicit, the poem also provides a subtitle. This subtitle, "The Apocalypse of Evil," has a number of possible meanings, all of which, however, reinforce the matrix of the text. The first meaning, "revelation" (etymologically, to "uncover" or "disclose"), and specifically a religious revelation in the form of a vision, describes perfectly the content of *The Hashish-Eater*. The second meaning, a (written) description of such a vision, also fits the poem perfectly. The third meaning bears on the content of the vision, specifically of the Apocalypse of Saint John, or the Book of Revelations. This involves a battle, on a cosmic scale, between supernatural forces of good and evil. Such conflict pervades the text (Joshi 17), taking on the twin forms of tyranny and rebellion—drawing heavily on the myths of Prometheus and Satan/Lucifer that formed commonplace topoi of the Romantic-Decadent-Symbolist trajectory from which Smith's aesthetic derives. Well-known biblical intertexts such as the Garden of Eden and Tower of Babel stories provide further topoi. The subtitle's modifier, "of evil," establishes the conversion from positive to negative in the narrative's progression, inverting the usual, implicit, "of good." The conversion again involves an ambiguity, as it could modify either the revelation itself, as if to signal that the hashish-eater himself has an evil nature—supported by his attempts to seize power in the opening sections of the text (a Satanic, rebellious act in a Christian context), or it could modify the cosmic battle's outcome, signaling that evil will win—as it does.

Properly understood, then, the title of the poem establishes the poem's matrix and the overdetermining motivation for many other elements of the text. The "Argument" provides a further clue explaining another of the text's features. The text involves not only the positive-to-negative progression but also many small steps, each greater than the last, on a paradigm set of mystic states. The "Argument" exposes the intertext by its use of the term "Buddhic plane" which derives from Theosophy. Theosophy, in fact, posits a sort of stepladder or paradigm set of progressively greater mystic states. *The Hashish-Eater* more or less follows this sort of progression. Further, the poem takes each of these steps as itself a paradigm set, a number of separate visions in each of them, thus creating the work's "kaleidoscopic" effect.

Before beginning the explication, the chief stylistic feature of the text, noticed by every reader: that of the high proportion of rare words, archaisms, terms from poetic diction, and so on. Michael Riffaterre has dealt with the polarizing, valorizing, hyperbolizing effect of such usages, formulating his rule of "lexical particularization":

> Quite simply, then, any word with conspicuous formal features, such as a technical term or an archaism, a foreign borrowing, a new coinage, any such word, regardless of its own specific meaning, serves as the hyperbole for its more frequent or less peculiar specialized synonym, partial or total. This is the phenomenon I should now like to rephrase as my rule of lexical particularization: *In any lexical paradigm of synonyms (or antonyms), the word with the least collocability or the most morphologically peculiar confers the maximal emphasis upon its metaphorical or metonymic meaning in a given context.* (Riffaterre 1979, 412; emphasis in original)

Each of these categories makes frequent appearances in the poem. One class, neologisms, appear especially in the form of novel compound words, and especially as hyphenated adjectives. Examples include: "million-colored" (2); "spaceward-flown" (6: a double example); "lava-langued" (12: incorporates a rare term as well); "moonquake-throbbing" (another double example); "jewel-builded" (also an archaic form); "storm-possessèd" (also, poetic diction).

The justly famous opening lines establish at once the theme of tyranny and rebellion, introducing as well imagery typical of the poem:

> Bow down, I am the emperor of dreams;
> I crown me with the million-colored sun
> Of secret worlds incredible, and take
> Their trailing skies for vestment when I soar,
> Throned on the mounting zenith, and illume
> The spaceward-flown horizons infinite. (1–6)

The term "emperor" comes from the top of a *royalty* paradigm, while the modifier "of dreams" establishes the nature of the mystic attainment indicated by the title—dreams represent one form of prophetic revelation or apocalypse, and the term also commonly serves to refer to other kinds of vision as well. In the second line the phrase "I crown me" deviates from the norm through its use of a reflexive form of "to crown," as normally another performs the act of crowning a king or emperor, and foregrounds the abnormal usage with the archaic or poetic "me" instead of "myself" as the reflexive object. The modifier "million-colored" applied to "sun" hyperbolizes its normal *light-giving* seme; "million" comes from the top of a *number* scale. The term "vestment" has a specifically religious sense, reinforcing the poem's matrix. "Zenith," through its odd shape and technical use, hyperbolizes its meaning as a highest point, further polarized with the apparently paradoxical modifier "mounting," as this would seem to make an oxymoron when applied to a highest point. The infrequent "illume" hyperbolizes again, through the form's rarity, the *light-giving* seme of "sun," displaced now to the speaker, playing off the matrix as well by the related form "illumination," which has its specifically spiritual-mystical sense (*cf. illuminatus,* "enlightened one"). Whereas the doubly compound neologism "spaceward-flown" and the inverted position of "infinite" (after the modified noun) massively hyperbolize the destruction of normal limits, valorizing the transgressive nature of the rebellion.

The metaphors employed here are traditional; as Carl Jung says, the "crown symbolizes his relation to the sun, sending forth its rays; his bejewelled mantle is the starry firmament; the orb is a replica of the world; the lofty throne exalts him above the crowd" (258).

The next section of the text tells of the attempts of various animated geological features to follow or catch the narrator. "The fiery-crested oceans" (8) invert the usual *water, liquid* seme of the "ocean" sememe, while the "jealous moons" (9) that urge them to follow the narrator serve as the negative of the narrator's own "sun." The "mountains horned / with peaks of sharpest adamant, and mawed / with sulphur-lit volcanoes lava-langued" (10–12) have acquired animal characteristics with their horns and maws; the "adamant" comes from the very top of a *hard-*

ness paradigm scale. They attempt to "Usurp the skies with thunder" (13) wherein "usurp" directly reveals the political nature of the conflict as rebellion or tyranny; the "thunder" appears displaced from the skies, of which it would normally appear as attribute, and indirectly refers to the Romantic theme of the fall of Satan/Lucifer, in which it appears as attribute of both Satan and the tyrant God he rebels against. More Satanic imagery appears in the next line, as "serpent-shapen trees" (14) reflect the Garden of Eden story in which man, tempted by the serpent (Satan) eats of the forbidden tree of knowledge. The continents "Pursue my flight through ages spurned to fire / By that supreme ascendance" (16–17); "spurn" has particular reference to striking with the foot as well as its "reject with disdain" meaning; the "ages" introduce a sequence of reified time periods that appear in the poem as parallels to spatial domains.

The sequence shifts to animate beings proper, as "sorcerors / And evil kings" (17–18) appear armed with "scrolls of fulvous dragon-skin whereon / are worm-like runes of ever-twisting flame" (19–20). Two metonyms of the scrolls here involve the *apocalypse* and *rebellion* matrices: the "dragon" and the "worm," both of which serve as alternative terms for "Satan," the latter as a synonym of serpent or dragon. Next the "sirens of the stars" (21) appear with "star" as a negative sun, as "moon" has already, with the *hostility* seme displaced to the sirens, and a fine use of synaesthetic imagery in the mention of their "foam-like songs of silver fragrance wrought" (22). Moons again appear as negative suns, with their *hostility* seme partially displaced to their inhabitants: "viper-eyed, senescent devils" (24) and "antic gnomes, abominably wise" (25); nevertheless, the moons carry out the rebellious action, as they "Heave up their icy horns across my way" (26) which may, as well, displace the horns of the "devils" already mentioned. (Horns appear frequently in metaphoric descriptions of crescent moons.)

The narrative continues:

> But naught deters me from the goal ordained
> By suns and eons and immortal wars,
> And sung by moons and motes;   (27–29)

The passage underscores again the positive to negative conversion in this passage, as the "suns" find their negative in "moons" and "eons" intrudes a temporal term in an apparently reified, spatial, sense, while "immortal wars" makes explicit the *conflict* matrix, the modifier "immortal" creating an apparent oxymoron as war necessarily occurs in time, therefore making it finite or "mortal." "Motes" has a number of possible meanings; here it occurs in the sense "stars" (cf., for example, Smith's "The Motes" for this sense of the word). The next lines elaborate on the goal:

> the goal whose name
> Is all the secret of forgotten glyphs
> By sinful gods in torrid rubies writ
> For ending of a brazen book; the goal

> Whereat my soaring ecstasy may stand
> In amplest heavens multiplied to hold
> My hordes of thunder-vested avatars,
> And Promethèan armies of my thought
> That brandish claspèd levins.   (29–37)

The secret nature of the goal's name hyperbolizes the narrator's transgression in seeking it; the mysterious "sinful gods" again reiterate the *transgression* seme. The word "writ," here an archaism for "written," also occurs in the terms "holy writ" and "sacred writ," calling in the *mystic attainment* matrix; the "brazen" modifying the "book" involves a similar polysemy, as it literally here means "made of bronze" or perhaps "bronze-hasped" or "bound," but also calls in the "brash, outspoken, over-bold" meaning, actualizing the poem's *conflict* or rebellion semes. As a whole the book image recalls that of mediaeval grimoires and other "forbidden" tomes. Line 33's "ecstasy" again makes explicit the mystic attainment matrix, as its etymological meaning specifically refers to a religious trance, with one "standing out" in an out-of-body experience. The next line's "heavens" provides another dual sign, with its twin meanings of sky and religious otherworld—the appropriate regions for a religious rebel to usurp. "Hordes" and "armies" make explicit the military, combative nature of the narrator's aspirations; the modifiers "thunder-vested" and "that brandish claspèd levins" once again actualizes this seme shared by the rebel Satan and the tyrant God. The term "avatar" refers to an incarnation of a deity, explicitly showing the narrator's pretensions; "Promethèan" refers directly to the myth of Prometheus, foreshadowing the positive to negative narrative conversion.

Having thus established his attainment of this unnamed goal, the narrator calls his memories, "intolerably clad / In light the peaks of paradise may wear" (38–39); emphasizing height with the term "peaks," while the term "paradise," a synonym for the Garden of Eden, again recalls the Biblical story of disobedience and subsequent fall. Having done this, he continues: "And lead the Armageddon of my dreams" (40) which provides a synonym of "apocalypse" in the sense of cosmic battle between forces of good and evil, with the particular modifier "of my dreams" converting it to his own cosmic consciousness. There follows a simile in which we discover that the memories and/or dreams stretch back to "alien epochs" (44) and "their arms / Upraised, are columns potent to exalt / with ease ineffable the countless thrones / of all the gods that are or gods to be, / And bear the seats of Asmodai and Set / Above the seventh paradise" (44–49). Here the narrator explicitly claims more power than "all the gods that are or gods to be," using again "throne" imagery to convey the point. The names "Asmodai" and "Set" both refer to demons in traditional infernal descriptions; the first occurs in the apocryphal Book of Tobit, and more commonly appears as Asmodeus or Chashmodai; the second comes from Egyptian mythology; their odd shape serves to hyperbolize them as metonyms of Satan. "Above the seventh paradise" again explicitly raises the *storming of heaven* intertext and matrix. Thus concludes the poem's first paragraph.

The second paragraph introduces a series of the narrator's visions thus:

> Supreme
> In culminant omniscience manifold,
> And served by senses multitudinous,
> Far-posted on the shifting walls of time,
> With eyes that roam the star-unwinnowed fields
> Of utter night and chaos, I convoke
> The Babel of their visions, and attend
> At once their myriad witness.   (49–51)

Here the hashish-eater usurps the terms "supreme" and "omniscience," both reserved for God in normal theological usage, and further heightens the sense of his power by referring to his "senses" as "serving" him. The phrase "utter night and chaos" invokes classical mythology, in which the personifications of this couple created the universe; "Babel" refers to the biblical myth of ill-fated religious rebellion—many works parallel it with both the Eden myth and the rebellion of Satan; "visions," here literally "sense of sight" (of his "eyes") also involves the religious/spiritual sense of "revelation."

Having established this, the narrator continues with descriptions of many varied scenes, all of which involve the *mystic attainment* or *cosmic consciousness* matrix (at least through the metonymic imageries drawn from "myth and fable" which occur frequently in apocalyptic literature) and the recurrent conflict theme. The first of these concerns the already "fallen Titans" (57) directly evoking the classical myth of tyranny and resultant rebellion; the poem provides them with another set of enemies, in a group of antonymic "dwarves" (59). (One may note that this form was considered incorrect at the time, "dwarfs" serving as the plural until J. R. R. Tolkien popularized the form "dwarves.") The scene shifts to "Some red Antarean garden-world" (66) introducing the poem's first use of an actual star name; "Antares" etymologically means "resembling or rival to" the red war-god Ares or Mars, thus actualizing the conflict theme; the garden imagery of course reintroduces the Eden myth, and indeed we find exactly such a religious rebellion here: the hashish-eater sees:

> The sacred flower with lips of purple flesh,
> And silver-lashed, vermilion lidded eyes
> Of torpid azure; whom his furtive priests
> At moonless eve in terror seek to slay
> With bubbling grails of sacrificial blood
> That hide a hueless poison.   (67–72)

The flower appears shot through with "animal" qualities that violate its normal "plant" nature; the term "grails," with its reference to the Holy Grail, hyperbolizes the religious nature of the transgression.

In the next segment he declares that he reads:

> Upon the tongue of a forgotten sphinx,
> The annulling word a spiteful demon wrote
> In gall of slain chimeras;   (73–75)

He leaves the nature of this vision appropriately enigmatic, but one may note a pervasive "hostility" seme through the passage, together with its sequence of fantastic beasts.

The next vision, that of some wizards capturing a "gulf-returning roc" (77), includes several aleatory details that further connect it to the "apocalypse" matrix: the wizards' "pentacles" (76), typical sorcerors' paraphernalia; the terms "gulf" (77) and "storm" (78), both of frequent occurrence in infernal contexts; the "webs of dragons' gut" (80), *dragon* a common serpent synonym and Satan epithet; the "captive giant" (81) recalling the classical myth of the Giants' rebellion against the gods and subsequent punishment; the "Uranian sapphires" (84) and "amethysts from Mars" (85) both invoke planets named for gods heavily involved in war and rebellion—of the planets, the poem names only Mars, Saturn, and Uranus—the first the god of war, the other two both involved in generational revolutions.

In the next segment, he reads:

> With slant-lipped mages, in an evil star,
> The monstrous archives of a war that ran
> Through wasted eons, and the prophecy
> Of wars renewed, which shall commemorate
> Some enmity of wivern-headed kings
> Even to the brink of time.   (86–91)

The imagery could hardly emphasize the eternal nature of conflict and religious rebellion more clearly than this. Note the term "prophecy." The "kings" (*royalty* seme) have the modifier "wivern-headed," i.e., "dragon-headed," the head normally considered as the center of thought and emotion, and director of action.

The next sentence provides a sequence of three bizarre plant images. The first—"the blooms / of bluish fungi" (91–92) conflates flowers and fungi, which come from opposite ends of a plant paradigm set of *beauty and ugliness,* they grow in "craters of the moon" (93) an inversion of paradisal gardens; and they take as modifier "freaked with mercury" (92) adding a *non-organic* seme in violation of the plants" *organic* seme; perhaps also *poisonous,* and *magical,* as mercury plays a great role in alchemy. The next, "clammy blossoms, blanched and cavern-grown, / Are proffered to their gods in Uranus / by mole-eyed peoples" (96–98) again inverting paradisal gardens, now with infernal caverns. The last involves a Saturnian "black fruit" (99) eaten by some king (Eden myth); from its seed grows a "hellish tree" (102) that takes over the king's throne (*rebellion* seme). The final segment of the paragraph involves corals that "usurp / some harbor of a million-masted sea" (106–7); they lift "up as crowns / the octiremes of perished emperors, / and galleys fraught with royal gems" (110–13). The metaphor makes explicit the *rebellion* matrix. This ends the second paragraph.

The third paragraph begins with the statement that "Swifter and stranger grow / the visions" (113–14) and immediately plunges into descriptions of them. The first describes "a mighty city" (114) destroyed by a "plague of lichens" (124). Even though "whose hands / were sculptors of its doors, and columns wrought / To semblance of prodigious blooms of old, / No eremite hath lingered there to say, / And no man comes to learn" (118–22) the hashish-eater tells us the story of its destruction. Even in its denial the wording invokes the *mystic attainment* seme, with its use of the polarized "eremite" instead of the more common term "hermit." The narrative freely mingles religious and political imagery. "Lichen" comes from a *plant* paradigm set and has the *conquering* seme from its covering trees and stones, both exemplars of hardness. There follows a group of "naked giants" recalling the classical theogony; they blunder into a forest composed of plants animated and endowed with various animal organs. Next he views a war of pygmies—the eternal war between the pygmies and the cranes represented a commonplace topos of classical literature. Many images here recall ones that have appeared earlier in the poem: "plains with no horizon" (147); "wreathèd light and fulgors" (149); "green, enormous moons" (150). So ends the third paragraph.

The fourth paragraph includes many interesting features:

> Surveyed
> From this my throne as from a central sun,
> The pageantries of worlds and cycles pass;
> Forgotten splendors, dream by dream, unfold
> Like tapestry, and vanish; violet suns,
> Or suns of changeful iridescence, bring
> Their rays about me like the colored lights
> Imploring priests might lift to glorify
> The face of some averted god; the songs
> Of mystic poets in a purple world
> Ascend to me in music that is made
> From unconceivèd perfumes and the pulse
> Of love ineffable; the lute-players
> Whose lutes are strung with gold of the utmost moon,
> Call forth delicious languors, never known
> Save to their golden kings; the sorcerers
> Of hooded stars inscrutable to God,
> Surrender me their demon-wrested scrolls,
> Inscribed with lore of monstrous alchemies
> And awful transformations.   (152–71)

Note the reappearance of the sun and throne imagery; the spatialization of "cycles"; the terms drawn from art: "pageantries," "unfold / Like tapestries"; and the "violet suns, / Or suns of changeful iridescence"—cf. the "million-colored sun" of the opening. The simile of the priests connects the passage to the *mystic attainment* matrix; the modifier "mystic" of the poets applies that passage to the same matrix; the "purple" plays off of a polysemy—it may mean "royal," "highly ornate" (as in "purple patch"), or "blood red." Note the recurrence of synaesthetic metaphor in the music's description. The "lute-players" inspire in the hashish-eater "delicious languors, never known / Save to their golden kings" indicating his usurpation; the phrase "inscrutable to God" implies the narrator's supersession of God's powers. The passage as a whole has a sun—moon—star progression.

In the fifth paragraph we encounter a commonplace paradox of mystical literature. The hashish-eater says: "If I will, / I am at once the vision and the seer, / And mingle with my ever-streaming pomps, / And still abide their suzerain" (171–74). Note here the identity of the "vision and the seer," the object and the subject of the action; note as well the term "seer" which may simply mean "one who sees" but could also mean "one who sees visions; diviner; prophet, etc." A parallel example of such a paradox occurs in Algernon Charles Swinburne's "Hertha": "Love or unlove me, / Unknow me or know, / I am that which unloves me and loves; I am stricken and I am the blow" (18–20). Christian theology incorporates the paradox in the form of the simultaneous transcendence and immanence of God.

In the first of these scenes in which he takes part, he describes an enormous fane with "Titan worshippers" (177) recalling classical theogony; the priests give their deity a "monthly hecatomb of gems" (183) "hecatomb" hyperbolizing the sacrifice; these gems come from "realms of hostile serpents" (186) combining political ("realm" = "kingdom") and religious rebellion ("serpent" implies Satan, Eden, etc.) In the next vision he takes the role of a king whose kingdom "the snows / Of hyperborean winter, and their winds" (192–93) have taken over; he seeks "isles of timeless summer" (192). Note that he has "captive kings to urge his serried oars" (197). Next he takes the role of "hero of a quest Achernar lights" (202); the star's etymological meaning of "end of the river" perhaps playing off of his "ever-streaming pomps"; in any case the name recalls the name of the infernal river Acheron, often used as a synecdoche for Hell. He seeks a desert where flames "lick the blenchèd heavens" (207). There, however, resides "A lonely flower by a placid well" (209) which is "Secure as in a garden walled from wind" (208)—the Eden/Paradise image. The flower holds "within / That grail the blossom lifts" (212–13) (note the term "grail" again) "One drop of an incomparable dew / Which heals the parchèd weariness of kings, / And cures the wound of wisdom" (214–16). The next segment inverts his claimed omnipotence and omniscience, as he takes the role of "page / To an emperor who reigns ten-thousand years" (216–17), the polarization of the emperor here serving as polarizer of its negative corollary, page or servant. He seeks through this king's "labyrinthine palace-rooms" (218), "Wherein immensity itself is mazed" (220)—note how this setting reflects upon his own claimed mastery over "immensity" and the "infinite"—for a "golden gorget" (221) which the emperor has lost but instead finds "A sealèd room whose nameless prisoner / Moans with a nameless torture, and would turn / to hell's red rack as to a lilied couch" (232–34) and "Prostrate upon a lotus-painted floor, / The loveliest of all belovèd slaves / My emperor hath, and from her pulseless side / A serpent rises, whiter than the root / Of some venefic bloom in darkness grown" (236–40). Here "venefic" recalls its etymology from Venus as goddess of witches and poisoners.

The sixth paragraph concerns the hashish-eater's temporary overthrow as the emperor of dreams. It begins:

> Hark!
> What word was whispered in a tongue unknown,
> In crypts of some impenetrable world?
> Whose is the dark, dethroning secrecy
> I cannot share, though I am king of suns (242–46)

The passage inverts various earlier assertions of the hashish-eater's power: the "tongue unknown" connects to "The Babel of their visions" (55); the "impenetrable world" and "secrecy" contradict his claim of access to "secret worlds incredible" (3); the "dethroning" contrasts with the pervasive throne imagery of previous paragraphs. Now "all my dreams / Fall … and leave / Spirit and sense unthinkably alone / Above a universe of shrouded stars / And suns that wander, cowled with sullen gloom, / Like witches to a Sabbath" (252–58; ellipses mine). The reversal of former power-building again appears—the simile of "witches to a Sabbath" foregrounds the nature of (religious) rebellion as inversion, as the same term ("Sabbath") refers to both the inverted form of worship and the inverting counter-worship—the "(Black) Sabbath," comprised of parodic rituals; in addition, note the specifically religious sense of "cowled." He continues: "Fear is born / Beneath the nadir, and hath crawled / Reaching the floor of space, and waits for wings / To lift it upward like a hellish worm / Fain for the flesh of cherubim" (258–62). Here "nadir" inverts the "zenith" the narrator claims as throne; "crawled" inverts the narrator's "soaring"; and the "cherubim" provides, as angels, a "heavenly" inversion of the "hellish worm," polarized as vulnerable and weak.

Succeeding passages provide imagery drawn from a *hell* descriptive system; they culminate with a "Thing that crouches, worlds and years remote, / Whose horns a demon sharpens, rasping forth / A note to shatter the donjon-keeps of time, / Or crack the sphere of crystal" (271–74). The "worlds and years remote" again deny the narrator's claim to "omniscience" and knowledge of the most far-flung worlds and epochs. The "Thing," again denies his omniscience, as he must use the vaguest noun that exists to designate it; the capitalization valorizes the creature. After "ages" (275) the hashish-eater regains his powers, as "time / Is mine once more, and armies of its dreams / Rally to that insuperable throne / Firmed on the zenith" (280–83) but the text gives no hint that any action of his own contributed to this restoration to power.

Despite his claim to restored power, the events of the seventh paragraph hardly provide warrant for the alleged reclamation. He begins by searching for "The meads of shining moly I had found / In some anterior vision" (284–85) expanding on an Elysium/Paradise descriptive system; instead he finds a "corpse the ebbing water will not keep" (290) and "all the flowers / About me turn to hooded serpents, swayed / By flutes of devils in lascivious dance / Meet for the nod of Satan, when he reigns / Above the raging Sabbath, and is wooed / By sarabands of witches" (291–96). Note that Satan does not merely preside over the Sabbath but "reigns." Once again the witches dancing at the Sabbath appear as a simile, just as in lines 257–58, with similar significance. The hashish-eater then seeks the rill's source, but finds (hellish) flame instead of snow on the mountain's peak. Looking below he sees "a silver python" (305) "Vast as a river that a fiend hath witched / And forced to flow reverted in its course / To fountains whence it issued" (306–8), another image of religious rebellion. The python surrounds the mountain, and "gapes with a fanged, unfathomable maw / Wherein Great Typhon and Enceladus / Were orts of daily glut" (313–15) recalling the Greek gigantomachy.

To rescue him he summons a hippogriff, which has a number of symbolic meanings derived from its component animals. The horse provides an exemplary steed; the griffon, as combination of eagle and lion, combines the *king* end of *bird* and *land animal* paradigms. Most importantly in the context, the hashish-eater had formerly flown by his own power, "Throned on the mounting zenith" (5). On the other hand, crossbreeding a griffon and a horse—the means of creating a hippogriff—served as a classical exemplar of impossibility (Borges 124). The hippogriff takes him to a planet where "Beauty hath found an avatar of flowers" (325)—again Paradise imagery and the term "avatar."

There he finds "A lonely castle, calm, and unbeset / Save by the purple spears of amaranth / And leafing iris tender-sworded" (329–31). Here the castle appears negativized, as it would normally serve a defensive purpose—we later learn that its "heavy-teethed portcullis hangs aloft / To grin a welcome" (336–37). The flowers, which both have otherworld connotations, appear likewise negativized with ironic "spears" and "swords." He enters the castle's courtyard where the "columns, carved / Of lazuli and amber, mock the palms / Of bright Aidennic forests" (341–43) in which "mock" has a double significance as "imitate" and "deride," whereas "Aidennic" presents a distorted form of "Edenic" as the Garden of Paradise that derives from a specific intertextual source: Edgar Allan Poe. These columns have work that depicts "airy lace / Enfolding drupes that seem as tawny clusters / Of breasts of unknown houris; and convoled / With vines of shut and shadowy-leavèd flowers / Like the dropt lids of women that endure / Some loin-dissolving ecstasy" (344–349). Note here the Paradisal Garden motif imagery; the mention of houris, nymph-like spirits provided to men in the Islamic afterlife; and the double use of "ecstasy" in its sacred and profane meanings—though the latter very frequently appears as a metaphor for the former.

Further details of this scene invert those of the poem's opening. The hashish-eater finds himself "dazed and blinded with the sun" (351) and further "in gloom that changing colors cloud" (352) mocking the "million-colored sun." The following details a room filled with animated sculptures of fantastic monsters and draws heavily on infernal imagery. As he enters a door he hears "A chuckle sharp as crepitating ice / Upheaved and cloven by shoulders of the damned / Who strive in Antenora" (353–55), referring to the frozen river of Dante's *Inferno*, in which the souls of traitors stand neck-deep. Now he feels "a fear / That found no name in Babel" (368–69) and flees to a hall whose curtains "heavier than palls" (372) depict "a weary king / Who fain would cool his jewel-crusted hands / In lakes of emerald evening, or the field / Of dreamless poppies pure with rain" (374–77). Note here the contrast of the "dreamless poppies" (opium) with the dream-producing hashish that the narrator has taken. He moves onward to a room where "caryatides / Carved in the form of voluptuous Titan women" (382–83) recall the classical titanomachy and also the common metaphor of *sensual ecstasy* for *mystical ecstasy*. Here, enthroned, he discovers "a wan, enormous Worm" (386) "Tumid with all the rottenness of kings" (387)—a somewhat unconventional use of a conventional metonymic image of death. With the mention of "phosphorescent slime" we may have a slight pun, Phosphor as well as Lucifer serving as a name for the morning star. He flees unnoticed to a balcony, and so ends the seventh paragraph.

In the next paragraph, an enormous storm immediately arises "from beyond the horizon's rim" (403) and comes sweeping onto the scene, where the hashish-eater recognizes it as "The Sabaoth of retribution, drawn / From all dread spheres that knew my trespassing, / And led by vengeful fiends and dire alastors / That owned my sway aforetime!" (416–19). The term "Sabaoth" represents the Hebrew for "hosts" or "armies"; it serves as a title of God in the Bible, as the Lord of Hosts. The term "alastor" comes from the Greek, in which it served as an epithet for Zeus or another god as an avenging spirit; it could also mean the avenging spirit of one murdered. In mediaeval demonology, it came to represent a personification of Vengeance. Shelley used it in his poem of the title, as "The Spirit of Solitude." Smith provides an impressive catalogue of monsters comprising these hosts:

> Cockatrice,
> Python, tragelaphus, leviathan,
> Chimera, martichoras, behemoth,
> Geryon, and sphinx, and hydra. (419–22)

(For those interested in source-hunting, Donald Sidney-Fryer's introduction to *The Last Incantation* cites a letter of Smith's mentioning Herodotus, Sir John de Mandeville's *Travels*, and Flaubert, presumably *The Temptation of Saint Anthony*, as sources for fabulous monsters which he had not found mentioned elsewhere.) These creatures come upon the narrator in a flash. He further describes: "huge and furnace-hearted beasts / Of hells beyond Rutilicus" (428–29) in which "furnace-hearted" might recall Blake's "The Tyger" and its sources; "Rutilicus," etymologically, may mean either "red" or refer to a sort of weapon. The placement of hells in outer space becomes interesting when compared to the traditional view that places heavenly or celestial regions in the starry spheres, and the hells beneath or inside the earth. The poem's next section describes in great detail the onset of these monsters, adding many more to the list. These include "blue-faced wizards from the world of Saiph. / On whom Titanic scorpions fawn" (446–47); "Saiph" comes from the Arabic *Saif al Jabbar*, the "Sword of the Giant." There also appear "Demogorgons of the outer dark" recalling mediaeval demonology, and Shelley's use of the name in *Prometheus Unbound* as the overthrower and successor to Zeus in the gods' generational war. The hashish-eater, feeling a "tenfold fear / A monstrous dread unnamed in any hell" (465–66) flees, but instead of rising to the zenith again, he falls "through the nadir-plungèd gloom, beyond the scope and vision of the sun, / To other skies and systems" (474–76), once again inverting the imagery of the opening lines.

The brief ninth paragraph describes the world into which he falls "as falls a meteor-stone" (479), a common metaphor for the fall of Lucifer/Satan. Here he wanders through a bizarre forest of fungi whose tops "clamber hour by hour / To touch the suns of iris" (483–84) showing again the contrast between his current position and his former one. Bizarre insect-like and daemonic creatures inhabit this world. This scene may invert a Paradise or Eden topos.

He wanders onward and now discovers "an empty desert, all ablaze / With amethysts and rubies, and the dust / Of garnets or carnelians" (499–501) which recalls the common topos of the Heavenly City made of gemstones, prominent in Apocalyptic literature, most notably the Book of Revelations. He roams onward to an adamantine plain that abuts the very edge of the world, to which "A hundred streams of shattered marble run, / And streams of broken steel, and streams of bronze, / Like to the ruin of all the wars of time, / To plunge with clangor of timeless cataracts / Adown the gulfs eternal" (514–18). Here we see the building materials from the top of a *hardness* and *permanency* paradigm set converted into destructible liquids, running together in a *time vs. timeless* image common to mystic literature, though of course the image has become negativized. The next paragraph further amplifies the image.

In the twelfth and final paragraph (note that epics traditionally have twelve books or sections), the entire rout of ferocious monsters has caught up to the hashish-eater, and they fill the horizon flapping their wings, blowing him to the edge of the ultimate abyss. He looks over it:

> But when I reach
> The verge, and seek through sun-defeating gloom
> To measure with my gaze the dread descent,
> I see a tiny star within the depths—
> A light that stays me while the wings of doom
> Convene their thickening thousands; for the star
> Increases, taking to its hueless orb,
> With all the speed of horror-changèd dreams,

> The light as of a million million moons;
> And floating up through gulfs and glooms eclipsed
> It grows and grows, a huge white eyeless Face
> That fills the void and fills the universe,
> And bloats against the limits of the world
> With lips of flame that open.... (568–81; ellipsis in original)

Once again, we have much imagery that inverts that of the opening lines. Instead of the "million-colored sun" we have "sun-defeating gloom," "a tiny star" with a "hueless orb" and "The light as of a million million moons," which finally eclipses everything else. Instead of the "emperor of dreams," we have nightmarish "horror-changèd dreams." The final image of the "huge white eyeless Face" arises from conversion of typical descriptions of enlightenment, for which the opening of the Third Eye in Europe, or the Eye of Shiva in India, stand as conventional metaphors. In place of a stereotypical symbol of consciousness (the eye), we have a stereotypical symbol of unconsciousness (blindness), arising by inversion. And yet, in another commonplace symbolism, blindness indicates spiritual insight, as compensation for material loss of sight. These two symbolic meanings here combine to form a powerfully ambiguous image, as they interplay to indicate a negative view of cosmic consciousness as unbearable to a mere human. The image has particular significance in light of the hashish-eater's claim as the "emperor of dreams" who convokes the "Babel of their visions."

The "lips of flame" invert the common positive image of lips as moist and luscious, particularly in sexualized descriptions; indirectly, this negativizes the mystic attainment matrix through the common metaphor of sensual ecstasy for mystical ecstasy. The ellipsis at the end of the poem no doubt indicates that the hashish-eater has, in the world of his vision, been devoured by the Face, and, in the fictional real world of the poem, stopped talking as he has gone hopelessly mad.

This close reading should suffice to remove any doubt about the construction of *The Hashish-Eater*. The poem demonstrably derives from a matrix that can be paraphrased as mystic attainment or cosmic consciousness; difficulty in its interpretation derives solely from ignorance of its various intertexts and hypograms, particularly the much-changed culturally defined sememe of the word hashish. Important intertexts for *The Hashish-Eater* and other of Smith's works include the biblical, classical, Hindu, and contemporary occultist mythologies; poets such as Milton, Shelley, Byron, Keats, Poe, Baudelaire, Swinburne, and Sterling; and many more arcane sources. Smith's works presuppose a wide acquaintance with such sources on the part of the reader. Any particular reader may miss some of these references, yet should discover enough of them to realize their significance in the text at hand.

Works Cited or Consulted

Allen, Richard Hinckley. *Star Names: Their Lore and Meaning.* 1899. New York: Dover, 1963.

Borges, Jorge Luis, and Margarita Gerrero. *The Book of Imaginary Beings.* Revised, enlarged, and translated by Norman Thomas di Giovanni in collaboration with the author. New York: Avon, 1969.

Bucke, Richard Maurice. *Cosmic Consciousness: A Study in the Evolution of the Human Mind.* 1901. New York: E. P. Dutton, 1969.

De Quincey, Thomas. *Confessions of an English Opium-Eater and Other Writings.* 1821. New York: New American Library, 1966.

Eco, Umberto. *A Theory of Semiotics.* Bloomington: Indiana University Press, 1976.

Jakobson, Roman. *Language in Literature.* Edited by Krystyna Pomorska and Stephen Rudy. Cambridge, MA: Harvard University Press, 1987.

James, William. *The Varieties of Religious Experience: A Study in Human Nature.* 1902. New York: Macmillan, 1961.

Joshi, S. T. "What Happens in *The Hashish-Eater.*" *The Dark Eidolon* No. 3 (Winter 1993): 16–20.

Jung, C. G. *Mysterium Coniunctionis: An Inquiry into the Separation and Synthesis of Psychic Opposites in Alchemy.* 1963. Princeton: Princeton University Press, 1977.

Regardie, Israel. Editor. *Roll Away the Stone: An Introduction to Aleister Crowley's Essays on the Psychology of Hashish, with the Complete Text of "The Herb Dangerous" by Aleister Crowley.* St. Paul, MN: Llewellyn Publications, 1968. Includes extracts from Ludlow's *Hasheesh Eater* and Crowley's translation of Baudelaire's "The Poem of Hashish." Crowley's essay actually treats more of the nature and typology of mystical experiences than of hashish.

Riffaterre, Michael. *Fictional Truth.* Baltimore: John Hopkins University Press, 1990.

———. "Generating Lautréamont's Text." In *Textual Strategies: Perspectives in Post-Structuralist Criticism.* Edited and introduced by Josué V. Harari. Ithaca, NY: Cornell University Press, 1979.

———. *Semiotics of Poetry.* Bloomington: Indiana University Press, 1978.

Smith, Clark Ashton. *The Last Incantation.* Introduced by Donald Sidney-Fryer. New York: Timescape, 1982.

Solomon, David. Editor. *The Marihuana Papers.* Introduced by Alfred R. Lindesmith. New York: Signet, 1966. Includes Gautier's "The Hashish Club" and extracts from Ludlow's *Hasheesh Eater* and Baudelaire's "Poem of Hashish."

Wilson, Peter Lamborn. *Scandal: Essays in Islamic Heresy.* Brooklyn, NY: Autonomedia, 1988. Information on the Noble Order of Assassins and the use of hashish and other psychotropic drugs in Islamic mysticism.

Clark Ashton Smith's "Nero"

Carl Jay Buchanan

> When someone in a general conversation said: "When I am dead, be earth consumed by fire," he rejoined "Nay, rather while I live," and his action was wholly in accord. For under cover of displeasure at the ugliness of the old buildings and the narrow, crooked streets, he set fire to the city so openly that several ex-consuls did not venture to lay hands on his chamberlains although they caught them on their estates with tow and firebrands, while some granaries near the Golden House, whose room he particularly desired, were demolished by engines of war and then set on fire, because their walls were of stone. For six days and seven nights destruction raged, while the people were driven for shelter to monuments and tombs.... Viewing the conflagration from the tower of Maecenas, and exulting, as he said, "with the beauty of the flames," he sang the whole time the "Sack of Ilium...." Suetonius: *De Vita Caesarum,* "Nero" 38. —Nero, c. C.E. 110. Translated by J. C. Rolfe.

"Nero" (*LO* 49–51), first published in 1912 in *The Star-Treader and Other Poems* (A. M. Robertson), is a poem of paradox and irony. The primary contrasts are established in stanza one, where "my darkling dream" has become, with Rome's burning, the emperor's "effulgency," or "radiant splendor," and the 800-year history and pre-history ("ages piled on ages") of labor to build the Eternal City is contrasted with the "[f]ierce ecstasy of one tremendous hour." From a dream born "darkling" (in darkness), a pyre now burns in a moment separated from all the time that has come before and from all time to come.

The enormity of Nero's opening words in this stanza evokes grandeur, as historic Rome was perceived by Poe, a favorite poet of Smith's.[1] Labor and "the toil of many years" is also contrasted with Nero's dream (his desire to destroy the city) and its fulfillment in relative insouciance. The stance of the opening is clear and even simply delimited, although the lush diction and careful craft of its blank verse is ornate and elegant, like a royal proclamation, or the conversation of a pharaoh. As we observe the carefully reasoned elaboration of Nero's philosophy of supernihilism in succeeding stanzas, we are seduced by him into a momentary agreement with an infinite megalomania, and that is the measure of the poem's success. Smith has used the dramatic monologue and extended its reach beyond that of his poetic forbears, and the poem is a high achievement in that broadening.

Now let us follow the chain of Nero's reasoning. The ironies of a bright dream born from darkness and of an instant obliterating ages are conjoined in the comparison Nero makes of his urban pyre with "any sunset." Nero's sunset is better than the quotidian one because it is destructive of much more than the light of day, and his sunset affects Matter itself on a grand scale, and its redness is more effective, being imbued with "the blood of men." The second complete sentence of stanza two says that the aftereffect that results from an ordinary sunset is that nothing material changes. After the sun's setting, it's simply dark when night has come, and an ordinary night, for Nero, consists of inexpressiveness, a lack. His sunset, however, has changed reality in three significant ways: by creating a great deal of motion, for his fire has rapid motility; by causing a music of screaming (refers also to his harp); and its hue endures, even after the "normal sun" has gone down, as the burned city glares and smolders for days.

Nero considers himself an artist. The historical Nero considered himself a great singer and poet, says the *Catholic Encyclopedia*. After the fire, "the emperor started on a pleasure tour through lower Italy and Greece; as actor, singer, and harp player he gained the scorn of the world." Smith imagines for us Nero's aesthetics of self-conceit, which Smith certainly developed from the Romantic conceptions of Byron and the other English poets he knew well. Their Promethean and Titanic hero-figures were (antedated by Poe and Baudelaire) later abandoned by the turn-of-the-nineteenth century Decadent poets in favor of nihilism, emotional languor, and despair, as well as a repudiation of all traditional values except, in the Symbolist instance, music, and in the Wildean and more popular case, irony derived from simply reversing the traditional. The sheer size of Nero's desire is Byronic, and exemplified throughout the poem, leading to a climax that goes beyond the Romantic poets. We must go back to Milton's Satan to find a poem whose speaker has such evil magnitude:

> Hail, horrors! hail,
> Infernal world! and thou, profoundest Hell,
> Receive thy new possessor—one who brings
> A mind not to be changed by place or time.
> The mind is its own place, and in itself
> Can make a Heaven of Hell, a Hell of Heaven.
> What matter where, if I be still the same,
> And what I should be, all but less than he
> Whom thunder hath made greater?
> *Paradise Lost,* 1.249–57

The poem is highly musical, as was blind Milton's verse. Moreover, music is mentioned prominently in lines 11–15:

> Yet any sunset were as much as this,
> Save for the music forced from tongueless things,
> The rape of Matter's huge, unchorded harp
> By the many-fringed fire—a music pierced
> With the tense voice of Life, more quick to cry
> Its agony . . .

Nero, according to Suetonius, sings/recites the Lay of Troy, presumably Homer's *Iliad,* while Rome burns. He would have accompanied the recitation of this epic poem on the hand-held harp, and we may imagine that the poem we are reading is likewise sung to harp accompaniment.

The essential reversal, the paradox that destruction is, for Nero, creative, is explained beautifully and rigorously, even in the face of our automatic rejection of such a belief, in the third stanza. The first sentence repeats "toil" and "labor" from the poem's first two lines, extending their application from the physical building of Rome to any creative action of great duration and moment. The sheer effort involved in such creation, he opines, must exhaust the creator so that, having given form to his desire, he lacks both "capacity and power" to enjoy its fruits. (One may guess that Nero, perhaps seeing the created universe as having been abandoned by God, refers here to the belief, known long before the Deists, that after having made the world, God no longer acts, but leaves it to his creations to do with as they will.) By contrast, in the latter sentence of stanza two, Nero explains that duration of effort and ability of effort ("faculty") are not requisite for destruction, creation's opposite, and there is no division of purpose in the parts of the thing unmade as opposed to the complex artifact. We cannot disagree, listening to this argument, that a certain purity is nihilism's main attraction, as we generally agree that death levels all men and all things, and one thinks of the refining fire of the Buddhists and of Sati, the Indian rite of bride-burning still extant. Fire purifies, literally and medically, as it destroys. Nero then relates the distinction of the destructive from the creative action back to the artist himself: rather than experiencing a waning of his energies, or post-partum despair, as Coleridge felt in his immemorial "Dejection: An Ode," and as poets have frequently complained (including Catullus), the destroyer "draws a heightened and completer life." Reality may be poorer of some of its created things, but the artist has lost no energy and has remains intact, with the addition of the sensual enjoyment of his pure and nihilistic act. Further, he "both extends and vindicates himself" in that he increases his scope and meaning ("beauty, I suppose, opens the heart, extends the consciousness"—Algernon Blackwood[2]) as well as lays claim to and avenges himself. Nero thus prepares us for his self-aggrandizement into godhood in the remainder of the poem, claims Rome (by destroying it), and avenges himself on creation, which displeases him greatly.

The poem's preamble is over at this point. Stanzas four and five consist of the speaker's frustration: the fundamental paradox of possessing seemingly absolute power as overlord of the Roman Empire at its height, yet feeling that a man's reach should exceed his grasp (ironically twisting Browning's dictum), no matter how great that extension of one's power may be. As only an emperor, with the power to kill others, Nero regrets that he is not god of his own destiny in some sense, for if he were, he would make himself omnipotent.

An extended metaphor on the image of dust follows. Dead kings turn into dust, which may sting and annoy the eyes of those who survive them, as their images may, after their death, vex succeeding kings and emperors. Smith references Shelley's "Ozymandias" here, a poem about two kinds of despair: that of the dead king, whose final works and words must be ironic, as the desert sands conquer his ancient stone image which he thought would endure everlastingly; and the despair of the kings who come after him that they will end as he did, dust to dust, so that Napoleon looking at the Great Sphinx of Giza realized his own mighty works were transitory, and his men opened fire on the face of lion-bodied Rameses.

To break the cycle of creating works to memorialize one's greatness which will only be destroyed in time, one would have to be a god. Now "breath" (l. 51) is the internal rhyming opposite of "death," for the breath is the animating spirit which moved over the waters in Genesis, and which impels matter ("dust") in all forms. Mortality, the dust of death (Psalm 22: "Thou has brought Me into the dust of death") clogs the lungs and prevents the free breath of the body (as metaphor for spirit), the eyeballs of line 49 being abstracted into "perception" in line 54 and clear exercise of will; that is, clear rather than obscured by dust, Nero's material self and its attached limitations to his self-extension into godhood.

The next passage is structured on a dog versus bird image, which is very likely inspired by the Egyptian mythology, in which jackal-headed Anubis, who weighed the heart after one's death, opposes bird-headed Horus, who guided dead souls to the underworld and was the protector of the pharaoh, to some degree. Thoth, inventor of writing and all intellectual pursuits, is also bird-headed, and Wepwawet, assistant to Anubis, also jackal-headed. (The latter's name translates as "Opener of the Ways," a name familiar elsewhere in weird studies.) Lines 55–75 refer to "tongueless dooms which dog the traveling suns" and to "[t]he vampire, Silence, at the breast of worlds," where the heart is kept. It seems that even the suns or stars are weighed up at their death, and their hearts removed; that is, the afterlife judges and condemns all to utter destruction, "crouching at the back of Time." The next-mentioned "[F]ire without light that gnaws [like a jackal or dog] the base of things" may remind us of Milton's "darkness visible" that lights Hell for Satan and his crew in their eternal fiery "afterworld" at the base of the universe. At that base, the spheres or great circles which to both Greeks and Egyptians delimited their differing conceptions of the universe have their fundaments, or bottommost parts and foundations, and the Greek river of forgetfulness in Hades is given tides by Smith, which erosive currents destroy the basis of all creation. (Line 64, a mighty image, may evoke to the reader Yggdrasil and the serpent gnawing at the roots of that World-tree, the Greek kallikanzaroi who do the same, and so on.)

Thus the Egyptian scheme of cosmology is conjoined with and succeeded by the Greek and later by the Hebrew. In this same complex passage, the "dazzled [sun-lit] wings of will" oppose the dark forces of destruction, and the dogged destructiveness and airy potency are renamed the forces of Chaos and Creation. Smith's verse grows more and more Miltonic as he reaches past Keats to the Romantic's master of "things unattempted [previously] in prose or rhyme" in the greatest epic in English, *Paradise Lost*. The "closer war reverseless" alludes to Satan's war against God, an ultimate battle both Smith and his Nero, the latter perforce ignorant of Milton but not of cosmological wars, imagines as parallel to Nero's own war with Rome and reality.

Historically, we know that Nero, according to Suetonius, the contemporary chronicler of the early emperors, sang of Troy's fall while watching Rome burn. That story began with the apple of discord, marked "for the Fairest" being thrown among three goddesses, followed by Paris's choice of Aphrodite, the rape of Helen, Achilles' dogged pursuit of Hector thrice around Troy's walls, and the destruction of that great city. In the *Iliad*, the goddesses of vengeance are described as lame (Oedipus, the name given to Nero's psychological forerunner, means "swollen-foot" or "lame-footed"; see Lévi-Strauss, 206–31) but following inexorably behind offenders; cf. line 93. ("Core" is now obviously a pun.)

Nero concludes this section by identifying himself with the Hebrew hero Sampson (a sun-figure, from the Hebrew Shimshon, "sun-man," thought by some scholars to represent a solar deity[3]). He sets himself above and beyond the dog and god of destruction.[4] Dogs and the final "hound" also evoke Sampson and the fiery foxes he loosed in the fields of the Philistines. References to the greatest Hebraic hero, extended from their original scope, continue.

The sense of this latter half of the great fourth stanza may be paraphrased: If I were a god, I would stand above both principles of Chaos and Creation, I would be above both the greatest deity and his opposer, and they would be as demiurges to me as I initiate a conflict beyond the traditions known to us, and all forces would be redefined under my New Order.

The fifth stanza restates this theme and modifies it somewhat, relating Nero as he watches Rome burn, thinking of Troy's demolition, to a god who plays with the burning suns of the universe. Line 87, "tear out the eyes of light," most likely refers to Oedipus, and Nero's Oedipal relationship with his mother: he supposedly opened her body after having her killed, "to see where I came from." Perhaps this refers also to the blinding of Sampson in Milton's imitation of Greek drama. Line 85 is singularly Miltonic.

The universe is created through the Word, in Genesis, later (much later) identified with God in John 1:1: ". . . and the Word was God." Out of chaos a Word spoke, saying Let There Be Light, and there was light. The poem's climactic stanza develops an antithesis to this, a gospel of destruction to set contrary to and to undo God's creation.

At last, at the height of his egomaniacal euphoria, Nero images himself as a god above gods, having become the godhead itself, what the Hindus call Brahman. The ultimate paradox evolves in the final lines: "casting worlds" as if they were worthless pebbles, so that there is no distinction between the macro- and microcosmic, and finally, "[b]rightening the aspect of Eternity" with suns whose light he himself has extinguished, embodying the notion that darkness and light are no different to his transcendent view, since he is now beyond and above a figure who might speak out of the darkness and say "Let there be Light." Time (93) and eternity are also interchangeable, to one unimaginably beyond both.

This "speech" (91) of godhead is, of course, imagined by Nero, as the entire poem is spoken by him, commenting upon his imperial self as both magnificent and minor. As in many of the best poems ("Ode on a Grecian Urn," for instance), the ironies and cumulative paradoxes enrich our understanding as the rich imagery and well-balanced Miltonic and Keatsian rhythms satisfy our aesthetic natures. One of Smith's strongest efforts, "Nero" bridges realism to cosmic vision as Browning's "Fra Lippo Lippi" spanned a realistic setting with high Renaissance painting's aesthetics, although "I intend to get to God" (line 6, "Johannes Agricola in Meditation") is closer to the speaker Nero in tone.

Tennyson's Ulysses, who speaks of "sail[ing] beyond the sunset" and heroically never yielding, no matter what the challenge, parallels "Nero" in that each speaker shows us the path his desires have taken from the mundane to the extra-human. Both speakers entice us into sympathy with their extreme philosophies through eloquence and chains of reasoning. But though its form has roots in Browning's and Tennyson's dramatic monologues, the imagery of "Nero," it has been said by reviewers, harkens back to Keats, particularly the grandeur of "Hyperion." However, Smith's diction in this poem is more ornate, Latinate, and less casual that Keats's, as a comparison will show in a few moments. Furthermore, to the extent that "Nero" may indeed remind us of "Hyperion," we must be aware that in that poem, Keats was heavily influenced by Milton, consciously and deliberately; see lines 2, 39, 118, 141, 232, and 235–39 from Book 1, for example.

Smith's contemporary, Edwin Arlington Robinson, also employed imaginary speakers, as in "The Man against the Sky" (a poem useful for comparison with "Nero," but which is not as strongly developed, because of Robinson's zeal for ambiguity).

* * * * *

Contemporary reviewers of this poem indicated a generally favorable reaction to the book in which it appeared, *The Star-Treader*, and in each instance where "Nero" was singled out for comment, such commentary was quite favorable. From the column "The Spectator" in *Town Talk* for 16 November 1912: "A strength not boyish [most reviewers alluded to the youth of Smith, nineteen at the time of publication] muscles these lines wherein the last of the Caesars yearns for the godhead which would make his power of mischief infinite. Any poet alive today might well be proud to have written this poem" (12–13). The reviewer declines to specify why.

From the column titled "The Latest Books" in the *Argonaut* for 30 November 1912: "There are no self-searchings, or yearnings, or soul-communions in Mr. Smith's poems, nowhere a trace of the morbid or introspective, and we may expect much from a poet who will at least try to interpret for us the consciousness of nature rather than that of his own personality" (365). Lines 86–91 are then quoted to evidence Smith's "stateliness of diction." (Oddly, the reviewer says the line are from "the opening" of "Nero.") This reviewer does seem to have grasped the notion that a poem need not be autobiographical gushing, as most poetry was in the nineteenth century, and in the twentieth, and as it is published in American periodicals even as you read this.

A third example will suffice to give the range. From "Clark Smith's Poems. Wonderful Lyrics Deserve Recognition With World's Best" in the *San Francisco Bulletin:* "[Smith] will one day be numbered among the world's geniuses. . . . Such poetry as his cannot fail to arouse the admiration of mankind some time. Regarded as the creation of a mature mind, to say nothing of the youth of the poet, what American bard has ever excelled in imaginative splendor or poetic power such lines as the following from Mr. Smith's poem 'Nero'?" (14). The reviewer then quoted lines 38–61 and lines 76–96. I would emphasize imaginative splendor as most important in this review.

Scott Connors sums up for us. The reviews of Smith's first book, *The Star-Treader and Other Poems,* while eager to put forth George Sterling as Smith's "discoverer," also hailed Smith as a poetic genius:

> [They] quoted extensively from Smith's poem "Nero" (the *Bulletin* doing so in its entirety). All expressed amazement that such a genius could hail from so humble a source as an impoverished ranch in the heart of the gold-mining country, especially at so tender an age. All compared him with such past initiates of the poetic muse as Shelley (the *Examiner*), Keats (the *Bulletin*), and (much to Smith's apparent consternation) Milton, Pope, and Dryden (the *Call*)! (28–29)

On the other hand, the self-deprecating Smith himself wrote to George Sterling, his mentor, regarding his poem:

> I am almost afraid to send you "Nero." About four-fifths of it is prose, and not particularly good prose at that. However, I'm sending it. I hope you're not expecting too much of it. It has psychological value, I suppose; pathological might be a better word. The human interest (if it has any of what is usually meant by that term) is sinister and abnormal. It has a few great lines (according to my taste) such as "The vampire Silence of the breast of worlds," but I am not at all hopeful about it. (*SL* 13)

In this self-criticism, Smith picked out the single line which is least "mainstream," least traditional in its diction, and which seems to me to be something of a felicitous sore thumb, diction-wise, in that by its very inappropriateness it makes Nero's speech as a whole seem less planned, hence more human and authentic.

As for whether Smith had a poetic genius, that is a matter for fickle posterity, for in 1912 Ezra Pound was ridiculed whereas Sidney Lanier was exalted. In my lifetime, I've seen Lanier's words dropped entirely from the Norton anthologies that are the standard in American colleges and universities, as I've seen T. S. Eliot's reputation wilt under political attack, and so on. Time will tell us nothing; in fifty years Eliot may ride high on the heap of acclaim, and Smith may rise higher. Perhaps Nero had a point, re Time.

Notes

1. Cf. "To Helen" (1831):
   > On desperate seas long wont to roam,
   > Thy hyacinth hair, thy classic face,
   > Thy Naiad airs have brought me home
   > To the glory that was Greece,
   > And the grandeur that was Rome.

2. *Webster's* 402, an example of how Blackwood is considered by the makers of that most useful dictionary to be an excellent user of words, I suppose; a James Joyce quotation, I've noted in the past, is used for "impinge" in the same dictionary.

3. I thank Dr. Robert Allen of the English Department of the University of Tennessee at Martin for this and several other suggestions.

4. A decade after CAS's present poem, T. S. Eliot used a similar reverse wordplay of great unconscious significance when he wrote "O keep the Dog far hence, that's friend to men, or with his nails he'll dig it up again!" Eliot means both God and the ravager of corpses.

Works Cited

Bashford, Herbert. "Clark Smith's Poems. Wonderful Lyrics Deserve Recognition With World's Best." *San Francisco Bulletin* (30 November 1912): 14.

The Catholic Encyclopedia. Online at http://www.newadvent.org/cathen/.

Connors, Scott. "Who Discovered Clark Ashton Smith?" *Lost Worlds* No. 1 (2004): 25–34.

Eliot, T. S. *The Waste Land and Other Poems*. London: Faber & Faber, 1975.

"The Latest Books." *The Argonaut* (30 November 1912): 365.

Lévi-Strauss, Claude. *Structural Anthropology*. Trans. Claire Jacobson and Brooke Grundfest Schoepf. New York: Basic Books, 1963.

"The Spectator." *Town Talk* No. 1956 (16 November 1912): 12–13.

Webster's New Collegiate Dictionary. Springfield, MA: Merriam, 1981.

Satan Speaks:
A Reading of "Satan Unrepentant"

Phillip A. Ellis

"Satan Unrepentant" (*LO* 60–63) is a fascinating poem for many reasons. It displays a number of features that make it worthy of study independently from other concerns and influences. By so doing, the fullest attention can be placed upon the poem, and such distractions as considerations of a possible Gnosticism can be placed to one side. Further, like others of Clark Ashton Smith's oeuvre, it is a dramatic monologue, illuminating Satan both as a figure and as a Romantic hero. It displays a number of interesting features in its use of speech, to convey both meaning and character. These aspects combine to form what is, certainly, one among many of Smith's interesting and arresting poems. Although not as acclaimed a poem as "Nero," it nonetheless shares and displays many of the same marks of his genius, as well as many of his same concerns. It also displays a fair degree of interest as his interpretation of Satan as a poetic figure, given Satan's importance in Western culture and literature. Overall, then, by looking more closely at this poem and at its various aspects, it is possible to elucidate and illuminate further aspects not only of the poem itself, but also aspects of Smith's creativity and concerns as a poet and human being. But to do such without recourse to its context is clearly and evidently required; it is the poem, not its setting, that must be examined.

Although it is possible and, to some extent, reasonable to examine the poem within its context, such will not be the case here. To do so would divert attention away from the poem itself. It might help to know that its apparent Miltonic grandeur is a reaction against the anti-Miltonic sentiments of Smith's contemporaries, but such, ultimately, has little import for a reading focused solely upon the poem as the origin and measure of its conclusions. Likewise, it is possible to view the figure of Satan within a historical sequence, or milieu, of other Satans, but such denies the fact that what is of interest here is this Satan, this image of God's adversary. If we cannot understand this Satan, how can we place him among others? Further, though it is tempting to place the poem within a definite tradition, I have not done so. I lack the knowledge to do so sufficiently and succinctly, and doing so draws attention away from the poem; it is harder in some ways to look solely at the poem, bringing only one's competence as a reader to it, and that is where this reading must stand or fall. Finally, both the figures of God and Satan may be constructed within a seemingly Gnostic viewpoint of Satan rebelling against the demiurge, yet, clearly, in order to sustain any reading, the principal and sole arbiter of any speculation must be the poem itself, and such, unsupported by the poem, must remain beyond the confines of this essay. As can be seen, it is the poem itself, as an artifact independent of the historical vagaries of its production and of any theological climates that can alter our perception of it, that is of vital and central interest in this analysis. Other views, other considerations, while important and interesting, have no place here at this moment. It is the poem that we must look at, and in doing so it would be well to ask what that poem actually is, what its nature is, its technical aspects and the like, before progressing to the other subjects, such as the nature of Satan.

The poem itself consists of five irregular stanzas, spread over just under three pages of print in Smith's *Selected Poems*. It is written in blank verse, with some variation apparent in the placement of the caesura, evidence of the skill and care placed in the poem's construction. The first stanza introduces the speaker, clearly evident from the poem's title, and also sets the scene: the speaker is "in the doubted dark" (7) away, apparently from the light traditionally associated with God. The second stanza amplifies this sense of place, bringing in, in turn, the stars of the skies and space, as liminal between his and God's place. The third stanza in turn focuses first upon the universe, thence upon God's reign, turning thence to the fourth, which focuses upon the relationship in terms of power of God and Satan. The final stanza looks once again at Satan, waiting, in darkness for the "dreamt, inevitable hour" (78) when he may rise and take God's place. These, then, are the basics of "Satan Unrepentant," both of its nature and structure. It is, of course, much more complex, and therefore further detail, such as its nature as a dramatic monologue, reveals further aspects of interest.

What makes the poem a dramatic monologue, like "Nero" and to some extent *The Hashish-Eater*, is that consists of a speech, spoken by the "I" of the poem. This "I" is, of course, other than the poet. It is Satan who speaks, as evidenced through the title and the poem itself. The poem is evidence that the speaker is unrepentant, according to the poem's title, Satan himself is unrepentant; so therefore the speaker must be Satan. In giving Satan a voice, Smith allows an element of Judaeo-Christian myth a voice, with which to express concerns that reflect in part Satan's own, and in part Smith's. Smith thus speaks about his own concern, but at a remove, through a mouthpiece, so that his concerns become complex, and indistinguishable from the speaker's. This is not to say that the expression and conclusions derived are essentially Smith's; rather, it is an expression about concerns of Smith's as evidenced through another. This enables us to look further, and later, at the speech itself, but first, after some conclusions about the poem as such, it is important to look at the nature and character of Satan, and how Smith allows it to develop through the poem.

By using blank verse as the metrical basis for the poem, Smith utilises a form traditionally associated both with verse dramas and with seriousness. A notable example of this latter aspect is Milton's *Paradise Lost:* again, Satan is a principal figure in that work and the focus of several of its early books, but at greater length and level of complexity than is capable in such a short poem as Smith has written here. The first aspect, the use of blank verse in drama, highlights the dramatic aspect of the poem. It reminds us, subtly, that it is not Smith speaking, but a character, a role or mask as it were. Thus, in being a role, and being in turn Smith's means of speaking about certain concerns, it remains nonetheless a way for Smith to dress the character's concerns, and this duality becomes important later, when the nature and character of Satan is discussed. Overall, this duality sets up a pattern of expectation about the poem, mirrored further in the language and nature of the speech. In this manner, then, is complexity created and maintained, and the central message of the poem conveyed, especially through the nature and character of Satan.

A question must be asked: who is Satan? Left unresolved in the poem is the exact nature of Satan, in relation to God and others of his ilk. He was an archangel, that is certain: the poem starts, after all, with the phrase "Lost from those archangelic thrones" (1). Yet of the angels and fellow demons nothing is mentioned. They are irrelevant, since the poem exists to create and maintain a singular opposition, of Satan and God as two polarities, of evil cast down, and goodness triumphant. Satan is, furthermore, subordinate to God. He has "will not less / Than His, but lesser strength" (43–44), and thus what unites the two is both will and their united nature (see line 50, where he says "I, that am of essence one with His"), whereas what separates them is might. Satan is like God, in essential nature, yet "less in measure" (51). Good and evil, as concepts, are alien to the poem. It is about power, and the power relations between the two central figures. That is what matters, fundamentally, and not moral questions. In a sense, then, this unconcern with morality makes Satan an almost Nietzschean figure, defining his role through power relations, and not through an irrelevant and meaningless set of moralistic terms.

Yet Satan is marked by two key features. He remains unrepentant, and he remains proud. Traditionally, Satan's sin was one of pride: he set out to exalt himself above God. This manifests itself throughout the poem. He is, simply, both "majestic" and "beautiful" (6), he has an "unsubmissive brow" (45), and, finally, he is simply "Confirmed in pride" (76). We know also that Satan is unrepentant, and not just from the title and general tenor of the poem. He states explicitly in line 7 that he is "unregretful." Yet this knowledge of his unrepentancy is largely derived from the tone, the way he speaks. In this way, then, he is content to wait, not directly rising against God, but biding his time for

> That hour of consummation and of doom,
> Of justice, and rebellion justified.   (95–96)

In this, then, he becomes, because he is both speaker and subject, the point of reference whereby we may both assess and approach God. His speech centers upon his position, here where "The shadows of impalpable blank deeps" (13) weigh upon him, and where "Matter [is] tortured into life" (65), and his focus upon God is on his position over him. We also gain a measure of Satan's emotions and perception of God through his language. God is, essentially, a tyrant (as seen in the use of "tyranny" in lines 16, 41 and 70, and "injustice" in line 42; line 49, also, indirectly calls him a tyrant) and despot (62), he has whims, to "rear and mar" (31), his will is "ravenous and insatiable" (34), and he is, finally, unjust, as evidenced in the final line (96). This is not the just, loving God of Christianity, but one hateful, specifically created, as it were, to be hated. As Satan hates God, so he attempts to elicit our sympathies, and tries to persuade us too to hate this figure. This use of language is interesting and leads into further considerations of language, and how the poem utilises it to help create itself.

Language is important to consider in relation to "Satan Unrepentant." As the language encodes and creates the context for the poem's meaning, it embodies facts and assumptions about the poem and the poem's speaker. As the speaker is a fictional character, Satan, it thereby creates and attempts to validate the worldview of that fictional character. Thus, we find that the language reveals aspects of that character's relations with the world, and with the world's architect, God. Therefore, it is important to note how the world and God are referred to, and how these reflect in turn upon the nature and worldview of the speaker.

With regard to the world, the speaker creates a hierarchy, as it were, of existences. At one end is heaven, which is starred by the "archangelic thrones" (1). This is the realm of the angels, and, necessarily, of God. Below this are the deeps, the darkness in which Satan is imprisoned. Between the two are the heavens, the realm of the stars. This is evinced through lines 16–17, where "star after star / Spins endless orbits betwixt [Satan] and heaven." In many ways, the poem is concerned with the heavens, the region between Satan and God. This is because it simultaneously remains God's sphere, yet is made of matter. This we can clearly see where Satan says

> For fain am I to hush the anguished cries
> Of Substance, broken on the racks of change,
> Of Matter tortured into life;   (63–65)

What is important to note here is the language employed. Substance is "broken on the racks," it is referred to as the subject of torture, a reading reinforced by the reference to matter as tortured. Thus, in describing matter as such, the speaker employs emotive and resonant images that convey much not only about matter, but God, who is thereby assumed to be the torturer, given the earlier identification through "God's throne is reared of change" (37). Thus, in creating this hierarchy, the speaker, Satan, refers to each with a language at once emotive and persuasive. The speaker creates a worldview, but one dominated by connotations, not strict denotations, despite the oftentimes precise vocabulary.

This domination is conveyed through a number of means. There is the use of emotion, with implied value judgements. The use of "broken on the racks" and "tortured," as noted earlier, is a clear indication of this. Another is the use of more general connotations. The phrase in line 12 of "ringing moons for cymbals dinned afar" uses the onomatopoeic qualities of the word to help convey an image: though "ringing" has a resonance of clarity of sound, this is compounded by the use of "dinned," conveying a sense of harshness and unregulated strength to create the noise. This is consonant with the overall image of God's might, and his tyranny; he is not gentle, but hateful and harsh, and the use of "dinned" helps convey this impression concisely and with great strength. Other aspects are also utilised. Alliteration, used sparingly, has effect: "discords of the dark" (22) is a telling image, as is "roar of ruin" in the next line. They help convey the difference between the realm of God, and that of Satan. This, the place of Satan's exile, is marked by discord and ruin, and these qualities are highlighted and emphasised through alliterative techniques that combine with the connotative aspects of the actual words used. In these and other ways, the poem seeks to convey an emotional state, an emotional way of looking at the chief situation. God may be dominant, but given time he may fall, and until then Satan waits, ever observant.

What the use of speech does, then, is convey a sense of the world, and the relations of those aspects. The archangelic heaven is remote and of little inherent interest. What is more important is the sphere of matter, in which God is active, which "His tyranny constrains" (26). Though Satan is confined to the deeps, to the darkness and ruin, he is nonetheless ever looking outwards, toward the universe he hopes and seeks to free from change. The relationship between God and Satan is also dwelt upon; it is integral to the poem, and crucial to a close reading of Satan's character. Thus the importance of the phrase "with the hatred born of fear" (57): it reveals much about the relationship between the two actors, and reveals much more about the nature of God. God hates because He fears; God is, therefore, fallible, weak, despite His overwhelming strength. And it is a sense of this weakness that helps maintain the pride and resistance of Satan. In this manner, through the judicious and telling use of language, much is conveyed. The poem establishes a basic cosmology, God and Satan, and it delineates the essentials of the relationships of the actors within that cosmology. In this way, through language, we can begin to understand and appreciate the nature of Satan, and understand and appreciate the poem itself.

"Satan Unrepentant" creates a figure of Satan that is at the same time hero and protagonist of the poem. Through the use of language, a hierarchy is established, as it were, with God at the same time greater and more evil in nature than Satan. Thus the importance of such emotively strong terms as "tyrant," "tyranny," and "injustice" within the poem in relation to God. The poem, given that it is spoken by Satan, and hence has him as the implied standard for comparison, also seeks indirectly to lead the reader toward a sympathy with the speaker. By concentrating upon the evil nature of God, the speaker is implied to be better, almost good in comparison. The poem also conveys aspects of the cause of Satan's plight, in the pride and unrepentant nature of the speaker. Thus the speaker's character is explored and created, particularly through the language used and its emotive nature. Overall, then, what this poem seeks to do is create a picture of Satan as a living, uncaricatured being. It is irrelevant whether he is good or evil, as it is irrelevant whether the poet has sympathy or a sense of identification with his figure. What is relevant is the degree to which the poem, as a dramatic monologue, expresses the nature and worldview of the character, and not of Clark Ashton Smith. This Smith has achieved, with conciseness and economy, in less than a hundred lines. In doing so, it reminds us that the principal source of our understanding should be the poem and what it says, not the poet nor any other external source; it is the poem itself, and the reader's competency in reading it, that determines its meaning, and it is a measure of the poet's skill that the meaning thus conveyed is effectively, and beautifully, done. The principal aim of this essay was to produce such a piece that looked solely at the text analysed, and used that as the focus of a close (as is possible) reading, given what was wanted to be said. Thus all conclusions are drawn from the text as read and not from reference or direct comparison to other texts. To do so would destroy the unity of focus achieved.

Lands Forgotten or Unfound: The Prose Poetry of Clark Ashton Smith

S. T. Joshi

The prose poem, as its name indicates, is a hybrid form that draws equally upon the distinctive qualities of verse and the distinctive qualities of prose. Because it has been practiced relatively rarely in European literature, it has proven difficult to define. William Dean Howells, in the brief essay, "The Prose Poem," prefacing Stuart Merrill's *Pastels in Prose* (1890), noted that the prose poem is "a peculiarly modern invention" but went on to say: "I do not mean that poetical prose has not always been written; it has not been so much written as prosaic poetry; but our language abounds in noble passages of it, and it will always be written as often as a lift of profound feeling gives thinking wings" (Merrill v). Howells observes that the entire Bible, especially the books of Job and Ecclesiastes, could be considered a prose poem, and states:

> In fact, every strain of eloquence is a strain of poetry; every impassioned plea or oration is a poem in prose. At times, at all times, deep emotion takes on movement and cadence, and the curious have often selected rhythmical passages from prose authors, and given them the typographical form of poetry, to show how men might be poets without knowing it. (Merrill v–vi)

Canonically, the prose poem as a concrete genre dates to Aloysius Bertrand's *Gaspard de la nuit* (1842), and it is fitting that Clark Ashton Smith's leading interpreter, Donald Sidney-Fryer, has recently produced a splendid new translation of this esoteric work. Charles Baudelaire claimed direct influence from Bertrand when he wrote his *Petits poèmes en prose,* first published in magazines in 1861–62 and appearing posthumously in book form in 1869. That first word of Baudelaire's title ("small," here meaning "short") may be the most significant; for, apparently in consonance with his great idol Edgar Allan Poe's strictures regarding the impossibility of a long poem to create the desired "unity of effect," Baudelaire regarded brevity as a critical element in the prose poem: its heightened language and compressed expression were evidently meant to duplicate the effect of a short lyric poem. As Francis Scarfe points out, Bertrand consciously modelled his prose poems, even in form, upon poetry:

> Unlike Baudelaire's poems or anyone else's, Bertrand's have their basis in conventional prosody. He equated the paragraph to the poetic strophe or stanza. He instructed his printer to arrange his text in such a way that each prose-poem was clearly divided into four, five, six or seven "alinéas ou couplets" (indentations or versicles) with wide spaces between them. (Baudelaire 14)

I am not certain that Smith was acquainted with Bertrand's work (although one might infer it from his later invention of Gaspard du Nord, protagonist of "The Colossus of Ylourgne"); but he was definitely familiar with Baudelaire's prose poems, as translated by Arthur Symons (1905), as well as the selections from Baudelaire's (and many other French writers') prose poems found in Merrill's scintillating *Pastels in Prose*. Smith refers to both volumes in a letter of 8 April 1918 (*SU* 158), but it seems evident that he had absorbed them well before this date. Smith also refers glancingly to Oscar Wilde's prose poems (*SU* 132), but neither these nor, for that matter, Baudelaire's, can be said to have exercised any significant influence upon Smith's own work.

The first of Smith's prose poems, "The Demon, the Angel, and Beauty," dates to 1913, and is manifestly an outgrowth of his poetry. Indeed, Smith had, with characteristic modesty, said of his splendid poem "Nero" (written in May 1912) that "four-fifths of it is prose" (*SU* 47), suggesting that his prose poems were in some sense extensions of the free-verse odes he was writing at this time. George Sterling, reading an unidentified prose poem sent to him by Smith in November 1913, correctly noted: "It is prose in form only" (*SU* 99). As early as 1916 Smith was envisioning the assembling of "a volume of fantastic prose"—but by this he does not mean the lengthy tales that would later bring him celebrity in the pulp magazines, but rather a succession of shorter works: "fables, allegories, and prose-poems" (*SU* 139), a comment that leads one to conclude that Smith had, like Baudelaire, identified brevity as a central component of the prose poem. The occasion to publish his prose poems in book form did not arise until 1922, when he issued *Ebony and Crystal*, with its significant subtitle "Poems in Verse and Prose." After this, it would be many years before many more of Smith's prose poems appeared in his books: a few were included, almost as afterthoughts, in *Out of Space and Time* (1942) and *The Abominations of Yondo* (1960), but Smith chose to include none in his *Selected Poems*, assembled in 1944–49 and published posthumously in 1971. It required Sidney-Fryer's posthumous assemblage of *Poems in Prose* (1965) for (nearly) all of Smith's prose poems to be collected. At a later date, some unpublished prose poems were discovered in Smith's papers, leading Marc and Susan Michaud to produce a new volume, *Nostalgia of the Unknown* (1988), although whether even this constitutes a complete collection of Smith's prose poems has yet to be determined. Indeed, Sidney-Fryer himself included "Sadastor" in *Poems in Prose* but then categorised it as a short story in his 1978 bibliography.

It is evident that, at least at the outset, Smith used the prose poem as a means of expressing, without even the relatively loose restrictions of free verse, certain moods and conceptions that had also been encompassed in his early poetry. In particular, Smith adopts a quasi-stanzaic structure in a number of his prose poems, whether it be such collections of separately titled works as "Images" or "Vignettes" or such a work as "The Litany of the Seven Kisses," with its seven clearly demarcated sections, each consisting of a single luxurious sentence. It is significant that in "The Flower-

Devil" we actually see Smith affixing the accent to the adjective "ribbèd" (*NU* 2), a transparently poetical device that underscores the importance that Smith placed in the rhythm of his prose poems. This rhythm comes into play in a number of prose poems that utilise *alliteration,* or identical phraseology at identical places in the paragraph. Once again, "The Litany of the Seven Kisses" is noteworthy, each of its seven sections beginning with "I kiss . . ." The later prose poems "Preference" (with its use of the phrase "I would rather . . ." at the beginning of each of its four short paragraphs) and "Offering" (where "Such is my love for thee" or variations thereof appear following each of the four paragraphs) come even closer to verse.

Balance is another element that unites the prose poem with poetry, and Smith uses it in highly ingenious ways. The section of "Images" entitled "Tears" contains a remarkable example. Opening, "Thy tears are not as mine," Smith then contrasts the tears of his beloved ("Thou weepest as a green fountain among palms and roses, with lightly falling drops that bedew the flowery turf") with his own ("My tears are like a rain of marah in the desert, leaving a bitter pool whose waters are fire and poison") (*NU* 2)—only upon reflection do we note that each sentence is 27 syllables (counting "flowery" as a dissyllable, as it would be in verse). "The Days" similarly contrasts a beloved's days with the narrator's, utilising contrasts of both happiness and sadness as well as of brightness and darkness.

One of the chief distinguishing features of poetry, as contrasted with prose (at least, prior to the work of such Modernists as William Carlos Williams, who deliberately chose the language of the common man in their verse), is elevated language. This is, indeed, the most transparent means by which prose poems in general are distinguished from prose, although in Smith's case the distinction was more one of degree than of kind. His use of Biblical diction in such works as "The Traveller" and "Offering" underscore Smith's use of archaism to suggest a removal from present-day concerns and an emphasis on the timelessness of such elements as the quest and the search for love; indeed, "Offering" could be a kind of appendage to the Bible's extraordinary exercise in seduction, the Song of Solomon. The section of "Images" entitled "The Wind and the Garden" encapsulates in a single sentence many of the stylistic elements Smith habitually used in his prose poems:

> To thee my love is something strange and fantastical, and far away, like the vast and desolate sighing of the desert wind to one who dwells in a garden of palm and rose and lotus, filled by no louder sound than the mellow lisp of a breeze of perfume, or the sigh of silvering fountains. (*NU* 3)

Here we find the Biblical "thee"; the unusual and archaic term "fantastical"; the personification of inanimate objects (wind that sighs, a breeze that lisps, fountains that sigh), polysyndeton, or the use of multiple conjunctions ("palm and rose and lotus" instead of merely "palm, rose, and lotus"), and the careful use of rhythm—all elements far more commonly found in verse (at any rate, in Smith's verse) than in prose.

Two prose poems, "The Memnons of the Night" and "The City of Destruction," beg direct comparison with poems Smith had written some time earlier. The first—drawing upon the celebrated image (alluded to by Shelley in "Ozymandias") of the ancient statue of Memnon in Egypt, which purportedly rang out with the first rays of sunrise—was completed in December 1915, about nine months after the sonnet "Memnon at Midnight," on the same theme (see *SU* 131). While it would be difficult to match the sonnet's extraordinarily compressed expression of the crushing weight of years and their obliteration of all things, even the gods, the prose poem retains a vitality of its own, even reversing the thrust of the sonnet by suggesting the power of art to escape the maw of time; for it is those statues, erected "by a race whose towering tombs and cities are one with the dust of their builders," that nonetheless "oppose the black splendour of their porphyritic forms to the sun's insuperable gaze" and "abide to face the terrible latter dawns" (*NU* 8). The fragmentary prose poem "The City of Destruction" was apparently written after the poem "The City of Destruction," labelled by Smith "A Fragment" (*SP* 66). In this case, the prose poem comes off as a feeble and ineffective rewriting of the poem (whose stanzas, each consisting only of two long Alexandrines, are themselves close to prose poetry); the prose poem's use of the phrase "machineries of doom" (*NU* 23) cannot match the piquancy of the poem's "engineries of doom" (*SP* 66), and overall the prose poem conveys a sense of bombast and fustian whereas the poem is endowed with an authentic aura of awe and terror.

The prose poems "The Demon, the Angel, and Beauty" and "The Corpse and the Skeleton" remind us of several dramatic dialogues of Smith's early period, among them "The Masque of Forsaken Gods" (*SP* 27–31), "The Ghoul and the Seraph" (*SP* 137–41), and "The Witch in the Graveyard" (*SP* 156–59). The relation between "The Corpse and the Skeleton" and "The Ghoul and the Seraph" is especially close, for in both works we find a cheerful morbidity and rollicking archaic slang that pungently reflects the all-pervasiveness of death and the absence of any meaningful afterlife. Consider the ghoul's song in the poem—

> Good cheer to thee, white worm of death!
> The priest within the brothel dies,
> The baud hath sickened from his breath!
> In grave half-dug the digger lies:
> Good cheer to thee, white worm of death! (*SP* 138)

with the corpse's opening words in the prose poem: "How now, old bare-bones! What word of the worm? Methinks you have known him well, in your time" (*NU* 26). Both works speak cynically of the inefficacy of religion in the face of dusty oblivion. The ghoul hurls these words in the face of the seraph:

> And who art thou?—some white-faced fool of God,
> With wings that emulate the giddy bird,
> And bloodless mouth for ever filled with psalms
> In lieu of honest victuals? (*SP* 138)

while the skeleton, responding to the corpse's ingenuous query, "Where, then . . . are the heavens of light and hells of fire, promised unto faith by the sybils and hierophants?" states bluntly: "Ask of yonder cadaver, him whose corpulence diminishes momently, for the pampering of worms. He was once a priest, and spoke authentically of these matters, with all the delegated thunder of gods" (*NU* 26–27).

It is in their philosophical messages that Smith's prose poems depart to some degree from the overall thrust of his poems of a contemporaneous period. In particular, the overt cosmicism that we see in such splendid early poems as "The Star-Treader" and "Ode to the Abyss" is generally absent from the prose poems—or, perhaps, expressed in a different way. Possibly Smith had consciously or unconsciously reacted to his mentor George Sterling's repeated warnings to broaden his palette beyond the death of worlds and suns; and although Smith had noted early on that "To my imagination, no other natural event seems half as portentous as the going out of a sun" (*SU* 62), he grudgingly remarked in 1915 that "There'll not be nearly so much of the spacial [*sic*] element in my second book as in the other" (*SU* 122), referring to the overabundance of cosmic verse in *The Star-Treader and Other Poems* (1912). Accordingly, in the prose poems, both early and late, the immensity of space is replaced by the immensity of time—a richly fruitful theme whose multifold ramifications Smith explored in a number of works.

"From the Crypts of Memory" (*NU* 12–13), perhaps Smith's greatest prose poem, is a complex rumination on this conception. Here, the weight of years produces an overwhelming sense of the futility of human effort—a futility underscored by Smith's opening tableau, whereby the star on which his first-person narrator finds himself is known to be destined to plunge into an abyss and thereby "find a dark and disastrous close." The star is one in which "the dead had come to outnumber infinitely the living"—in other words, where the accumulated heritage of the past had so robbed its present-day inhabitants of the initiative to live and create that they come to be like the dead themselves. Even love, otherwise seen by Smith as an affirmation of life, becomes akin to death: "We felt for our women, with their pale and spectral beauty, the same desire that the dead may feel for the phantom lilies of Hadean meads." The imagery of life-in-death is remarkably complete: the people seek "mystic immortelles" (plants that retain their colour even after death), or other flowers that "wept with a sweet and nepenthe-laden dew" (nepenthe being the drug that induces forgetfulness, or the death of memory) "by the flowing silence of Acherontic waters" (Acheron being one of the rivers of the Greek underworld). And the prose poem's conclusion suggests that the distinction between life and death, customarily fraught with immense significance, is itself derisively illusory: "We knew the years as a passing of shadows, and death itself as the yielding of twilight unto night."

"The Garden and the Tomb" (*NU* 9) underscores the same message. The very fact that "in the heart of the garden is a tomb" is itself a metaphor for the intrusion of death into the very fabric of life. At night the garden descends into "slumber" (i.e., a kind of death), and only then do "serpents bred of corruption crawl from the tomb"—symbols of death that come to life and overwhelm the actual life of the garden. In "The Peril That Lurks among Ruins" (*NU* 31–32) a Daemon warns against going too often into ruins, for the shadows that lurk there "have all the sopor of despair" (i.e., they rob the living of the sense of purpose and hope). In a brilliant metaphor, the Daemon notes: "For, heedless of the peril, one may slip on some invisible precipice of the Past and go falling forevermore" to become "a shadow with shadows." Then there is "A Phantasy" (*NU* 13), whose imagery once again so confounds life and death that we scarcely know which is which. Smith uses a succession of paradoxes to convey his message: the "unknown land" of the narrator's dream is "citied"—not by thriving populations, but by "tombs and cenotaphs"; in the air "flit the mysterious wings of seraphim" (traditional inhabitants of heaven) and the "demons of the abyss" (inhabitants of hell); but we also find "black, gigantic angels" (black, associated with death, fusing ill with angels, the symbol of eternal life) who "pause amid the sepulchers to sift from their gloomy and tremendous vans the pale ashes of annihilated stars."

Less cosmic is "The Shadows" (*NU* 15–16), but it is nonetheless a powerful vignette underscoring the motelike ineffectuality of human existence in the wake of accumulated history. The shadows that populate the palace of Augusthes are the "fantastic spectres of doom and desolation," and the throne around which they gather has been "blackened beneath the invisible passing of ages." Augusthes (whose name symbolises the Graeco-Roman past, *Augus-* being a Latin stem and *-thes* a Greek one) rules there alone, "in the intangible dungeon of centuries." Ultimately he dies, becoming a shadow himself. The prose poem ends with an imperishable image of universal obliteration: "And twilight hushed the shadows in the palace of Augusthes, as the world itself swung down toward the long and single shadow of irretrievable oblivion."

If there are any forces that might, for a time, stave off the inexorable doom of time, they are love and art, for these alone appear to offer the only way in which meaning can be lent to life before its engulfment by the glutless worm. A number of Smith's prose poems are nothing more than addresses to a real or imagined beloved. The section of "Vignettes" entitled "The Broken Lute" shows Smith to be a troubadour, seeking the affection of a scornful lover. Here again "The Litany of the Seven Kisses" stands supreme, and one of its segments—"I kiss thy cheeks, where lingers a faint flush, like the reflection of a rose upheld to an urn of alabaster"—contains what is surely one of the most exquisite images in the entire spectrum of English literature. But the work is more than a succession of beautiful images, more even than an artful attempt at seduction; its concluding segment reveals that the two lovers will discover a "secret paradise . . . whence they that come shall *nevermore* depart . . . for . . . the fruit is the fruit of the tree of Life" (*NU* 10; emphasis added)—in other words, love can engender the only kind of immortality that human beings will ever know.

"The Abomination of Desolation" addresses a somewhat similar point. Here the narrator warns us against approaching the desert of Soom, for it contains a horror that no one can precisely specify. But once upon a time two lovers traversed the region: "And they alone . . . have had no tale to relate of any troublous thing, of any horror that followed or lurked before them" (*NU* 18). Love, in effect, produces a kind of visual Lethe, whereby the horrors of existence are forgotten or bypassed. Smith uses Lethe (the river of forgetfulness in Greek myth) to telling effect in several prose poems, generally in the context of lost love. In "A Dream of Lethe" (*NU* 5–6) a man comes to the shores of Lethe "in the quest of her whom I had lost." Finding her, he is distressed to see that she no longer recognises him: she has drunk from the river. He too drinks: "Nor was I able to remember any longer why I had wished to drink of the waters of oblivion." A lost love is best forgotten. This is a message that the protagonist of "The Mirror in the Hall of Ebony" (*NU* 17) would have profited from: although he comes along "the tide of Lethe" to a long hall of ebony, he knows not why he is there; but when he comes upon a mirror and sees his "haggard face" and "the red mark on the cheek where one I loved had struck me in her anger," his recollections return in a flood, and he is "enormously troubled." The slightest of chance occurrences can act as a mnemonic trigger of loss and sorrow.

Smith ingeniously mingles fantasy and eroticism in some of his most delicate prose poems. "In Cocaigne" tells of two lovers who seek the "fabulous and fortunate realm" of Cocaigne, but find it only in a fusion of spiritual and sexual love. "From a Letter" (*NU* 11) has much the same import: in making a plea to his beloved to "join me in Atlantis" or other imaginary lands ("the mountain-vales of Lemuria," "carnelian-built ports beyond Cathay"), the narrator is in reality beseeching her to share a life of love without end. But, as "The Mithridate" (*NU* 21) suggests, love is far from an unalloyed good; it can indeed act as a mithridate (antidote) against all the poisons of the world, but "when you love me not, or love me ill," it itself becomes a poison "that is doubly lethal because it kills so slowly, or does not kill at all."

"The Demon, the Angel, and Beauty" (*NU* 14–15) is a quintessential embodiment of Smith's conception of art as the salvation of humanity. Here the narrator successively queries a Demon and an Angel regarding the existence of Beauty. The Demon thinks he has seen it now and again, but has "fail[ed] to find the thing itself," and therefore, in bitterness, is convinced that Beauty does not exist. The Angel, on the other hand, has also seen only "adumbrations" of Beauty, but these are sufficient to convince her that Beauty does exist, even if it is only "the thing upon which God meditateth." In spite of the religious imagery of the prose poem ("And sometimes there is an echo which fills the empyrean, and hushes the archangelic harps in the midst of their praising God"), the message is a secular one: the Demon is a Demon precisely because, in his refusal to acknowledge the real existence of an entity of which he has seen only fleeting glimpses, he has descended into a cynicism that condemns him to a life bereft of the beauties (fleeting and shadowy as they may be) that existence has to offer. "Chinoiserie," unusual in its Oriental setting, fuses the themes of love and art. Ling Yang, the poet, uses his unrequited love of the Lady Moy as inspiration for his songs; but the Lady Moy, unaware of his affection, envies the Lady Loy, who centuries ago had fulfilled a similar inspirational function for the poet Ling Yung.

Many of Smith's prose poems on art specifically address the art of fantasy, and can thereby serve as anticipations of, and justifications for, the fantastic fiction that Smith would come to write. It is no accident that two of the most powerful of these, "To the Daemon" (16 December 1929; *NU* 17–18) and "The Muse of Hyperborea" (22 December 1929; *NU* 21–22), were both written in the winter of 1929, when Smith commenced the intensive writing of fiction. The narrator of the former, in appealing to a paradoxically "benign maleficent" daemon, urges him to tell him tales, but "none that I have ever heard or have even dreamt of otherwise than obscurely or infrequently." When the narrator beseeches the daemon to "tell me not of anything that lies between the bourns of time or the limits of space," one is reminded of Smith's comment that "I am far happier when I can create *everything* in a story, including the milieu" (*SL* 108). The entire prose poem must be read to see how uncannily it appears to be a kind of manifesto for the fantastic fiction Smith would write over the next six years. "The Muse of Hyperborea," in spite of its title, does not appear to have much to do with the tales of Smith's Hyperborea cycle, even though it was written a month after the first of those tales, "The Tale of Satampra Zeiros." Instead, the muse appears as a more general symbol for cosmic wonder, since as a result of her inspiration the narrator "behold[s] a vision of vast auroras, on continents that are wider than the world, and seas too great for the enterprise of human keels."

The interrelations between Smith's prose poems and his fantastic tales would, indeed, require extensive discussion. Can such works as "From the Crypts of Memory" and "The Peril That Lurks among Ruins" be seen as anticipations of the Zothique cycle, set in the far future on the last inhabited continent of earth? There too the accumulated weight of the centuries has robbed the final denizens of the world of the will to live except as fleeting shadows. "From the Crypts of Memory" actually served as the nucleus of the story "The Planet of the Dead," written on 4 April 1930. In a letter Smith explicitly notes the derivation of the story from the prose poem, but goes on to note that the story "would differ . . . in having an earthly hero, drawn to this planet by his spiritual affinity with the inhabitants" (*SL* 105). In this comment Smith unwittingly points to the central weakness of the story. "From the Crypts of Memory" is almost entirely symbolic; in contrast, "The Planet of the Dead" makes fleeting attempts to be a tale of supernatural realism, but in the process the delicate symbolism of the prose poem is destroyed, substituted by a trite action-adventure scenario whereby one Francis Melchior, melding his consciousness with that of the poet Antarion in the land of Charmalos, must rescue the beauteous Thameera from the clutches of King Haspa, who wishes to possess her before death overtakes the planet with the snuffing out of its sun. "The Planet of the Dead" does not rank high among

Smith's prose tales, and his attempt to adapt his splendid prose poem was a serious error in judgment.

On the other hand, the story "The Demon of the Flower" (begun in 1931 but not completed in 1933) actually improves upon the prose poem "The Flower-Devil" (*NU* 2). Admittedly, the latter is not one of Smith's stellar works, and its narrative of an evil flower inhabited by an "evil demon" and a king who is fearful of destroying the flower lest the demon inhabit some other entity, including that of his own beloved, is marred by a pomposity and purple prose that render it almost comical. Smith has taken the core elements of the prose poem and transformed them into an effective tale that combines beauty and horror in exquisitely balanced proportions.

Other prose poems, while not serving as the basis for later stories, nonetheless come closer to prose narrative than to lyrical verse, although the distinction is really more of emphasis than of genre. Consider "The Black Lake" (*NU* 3–4), one of the more overtly horrific of the prose poems. Although narrated in the first person, the work proves to be little more than a succession of baleful images. "The Princess Almeena" can be considered a narrative of sorts, in which the princess longs for the return of her lover, a commander of a trireme; but the fact that the work is narrated in the present tense, rather than the historical past tense more common in prose tales, suggests that it is meant to be more a frozen image than a narrative of events. "Ennui," although having far more plot in the conventional sense, is surprisingly similar: it too is narrated in the present tense ("In the alcove whose curtains are cloth-of gold . . . reclines the emperor Chan" [*NU* 7]), but it develops a modicum of suspense when the emperor is threatened by an assassin who injures him slightly—an all too fleeting relief from the overwhelming ennui under which he labours.

"The Touch-stone," although plainly a narrative, is almost entirely symbolic. The philosopher Nasiphra, seeking a touchstone that would "reveal the true nature of all things" (*NU* 19), appears to find the object of his quest; but upon his handling it, "the fingers that held the pebble had suddenly become those of a skeleton"—a rather transparent metaphor for the horror that lurks behind the search for truth. Although the most storylike of all Smith's prose poems, "The Touch-stone" is marred by an arch pretentiousness that spoils its message. More successful is "The Forbidden Forest," a delicate tale of a child, Natha, who is repeatedly told by his parents not to venture into the forest near their home, but who on one occasion does so, only to get lost and fall into an everlasting sleep. It is difficult, however, to attach any significant symbolism to the events of this work. Then there is the curious "The Osprey and the Shark," unpublished prior to its appearance in *Nostalgia of the Unknown*. This appears to be not so much a prose poem as a fable, strikingly similar to those included in Ambrose Bierce's *Fantastic Fables* (1899).

We are reaching the stage where the distinction between Smith's prose poems and his fantastic tales is becoming thin to the point of vanishment. Is "Sadastor" a prose poem or a tale? Given that it is substantially longer than any of his other prose poems and contains a more liberal dose of narrative thrust, one would in-cline to categorise it as a tale. But what, then, do we make of "The Abominations of Yondo," written about the same time in 1925? George Sterling, when reading that story, referred to it as "prose-poetry" (*SU* 252), and he was not the only one to come to that opinion. As Smith relates in a letter to Sterling, Farnsworth Wright of *Weird Tales*, in rejecting the story, concluded that it was "more of a prose-poem than a narrative" (*SU* 263). To the extent that nearly all Smith's prose tales employ poetic prose, they could all be classed as prose poems. Recall one of Smith's celebrated discussions of his theory of fantastic fiction:

> My own *conscious* ideal has been to delude the reader into accepting an impossibility, or series of impossibilities, by means of a sort of verbal black magic, in the achievement of which I make use of prose-rhythm, metaphor, simile, tone-color, counter-point, and other stylistic resources, like a sort of incantation. (*SL* 126)

This could serve as a characterisation of his prose poems as well, although in those works he is not striving to convince the reader of the reality of the "impossibilities" expressed in them, since the "events" of the prose poems are (and are understood by the reader to be) metaphors for the philosophical conceptions that underlie them. At the very least, the prose poems can serve, both thematically and chronologically, as a bridge between Smith's poetry and his prose fiction. But, relatively few in number as they are, they deserve consideration in their own right as some of the most flawless and delicate of Smith's literary productions—and as potent embodiments of that "nostalgia of things unknown, of lands forgotten or unfound" (*NU* 4) at the core of Smith's fantastic imagination.

Works Cited

Baudelaire, Charles. *The Poems in Prose, with La Fanfarlo*. Edited, introduced, and translated by Francis Scarfe. London: Anvil Press Poetry, [1986].

Bertrand, Aloysius. *Gaspard de la Nuit*. Translated by Donald Sidney-Fryer. Encino, CA: Black Coat Press, 2004.

Merrill, Stuart. *Pastels in Prose*. New York: Harper & Brothers, 1890.

Sidney-Fryer, Donald, et al. *Emperor of Dreams: A Clark Ashton Smith Bibliography*. West Kingston, RI: Donald M. Grant, 1978.

Wilde, Oscar. *Poems in Prose*. Boston: Brainerd, 1909.

Outside the Human Aquarium: The Fantastic Imagination of Clark Ashton Smith

Brian Stableford

Clark Ashton Smith was born in 1893 and died in 1961, having lived for almost all of his life on the outskirts of Auburn, California. He had three overlapping vocations, working as a poet, as a writer of fantastic short stories, and as a sculptor and graphic artist. These careers brought him relatively little financial reward; he probably made a significant income only from the second-named, and that only for a few brief years in the 1930s, when he wrote fairly prolifically for two pulp magazines, *Weird Tales* and *Wonder Stories*.

The stories which Smith produced during this brief professional phase constitute one of the most remarkable oeuvres in imaginative literature. They were reprinted in a series of collections issued by the specialist publisher Arkham House: *Out of Space and Time* (1942), *Lost Worlds* (1944), *Genius Loci* (1948), *The Abominations of Yondo* (1960); *Tales of Science and Sorcery* (1964), *Poems in Prose* (1964), and *Other Dimensions* (1970). The best of them were rearranged and reprinted in a series of paperbacks in the Ballantine "Adult Fantasy" series: *Zothique* (1970), *Hyperborea* (1971), *Xiccarph* (1972) and *Poseidonis* (1973), which helped to renew interest in Smith's work; various collations of his best works have been issued in more recent years. The last remaining vestiges of his fiction were eventually assembled in *Strange Shadows: The Uncollected Fiction and Essays of Clark Ashton Smith* edited by Steve Behrends with Donald Sidney-Fryer and Rah Hoffman. Many of Smith's highly ornate and sometimes vividly erotic works suffered censorship at the hands of the magazine editors, but for some reason he did not correct the book versions; most of the originals were destroyed by a fire but a few survived to be reconstructed for a series of booklets issued by the Necronomicon Press in 1987–88, whose six volumes are *The Dweller in the Gulf, Mother of Toads, The Vaults of Yoh-Vombis, The Monster of the Prophecy, The Witchcraft of Ulua* and *Xeethra*.

From the viewpoint of modern critics and historians Smith is one of three writers associated with *Weird Tales* in its heyday whose work stands out as being possessed of extraordinary originality. The other two—H. P. Lovecraft and Robert E. Howard—both died in the late thirties, but despite the fact that Smith survived them by a quarter of a century he wrote very little after that period. In a curious sense, Lovecraft's and Howard's deaths did not inhibit the extrapolation of their careers, because other hands took over where they left off, completing story-fragments they left behind and writing pastiches as close as possible in style and spirit to the originals. Lovecraft stands as father-figure to his own sub-genre of weird fiction, his "Cthulhu Mythos" having been used as a background by many other writers, while Howard is one of the key figures in the tradition of "sword and sorcery" fiction, and his violent heroes—most notably Conan the Barbarian—have continued their adventures in the care of other chroniclers. Smith has not been subject to necrophiliac attentions on anything like this scale, partly because he was always the least celebrated of the three writers and partly because his style is virtually inimitable. Although there are certain recurring patterns in his work it has not the kind of homogeneity and stereotypy which would be capable of mass-production.

In terms of popular taste all three of these *Weird Tales* writers were ahead of their time. Their pioneering endeavors appealed in the first instance to a small corps of admirers, whose enthusiasm kept the work alive in the margins of the marketplace until the general evolution of fantastic fiction accustomed a much wider range of readers to the vocabulary of ideas with which they worked. The communicative efficacy of their work had to wait until an audience appeared whose context of understanding could be tuned in to their idiosyncrasies. There are still readers and critics who cannot abide one, two or all three of them and who stigmatize key features of their work as evidences of bad writing. For this reason, Howard is often written off as a hack producer of fast-moving blood-and-thunder narratives; Lovecraft is taken to task for his stilted prose and piled-up adjectives; Smith is criticized for his love of exotic words and his highly-ornamented descriptions.

Such accusations tend to miss the point of the characteristics in question, each of which is a necessary corollary of the particular virtue and virtuosity of the writer's work. The pace and violence of Howard's work, and the adjectival awkwardness of Lovecraft's, are part and parcel of their distinctive moral and existential contexts. Critics out of sympathy with Howard's and Lovecraft's different varieties of quasi-paranoid world-view can hardly be expected to become connoisseurs of their literary development, but it is a pity that this has sometimes prevented the critics from recognizing that what they are seeing is unusual method rather than literary incompetence.

It is particularly necessary to make this point in discussing Smith's work, because although he too was extrapolating in his fiction a quasi-paranoid world-view he was the most unusual of the three writers. Lovecraft was extrapolating a particular kind of anxious consciousness that was already detectable in the works of Edgar Allan Poe, Ambrose Bierce and Robert W. Chambers, while Howard was offering a more hard-bitten version of a species of Romanticism already popularized by Edgar Rice Burroughs. Smith was not without literary forebears, and he was prepared to borrow from both Lovecraft and Howard, but his ambition was to go as far beyond his models as he possibly could. His phantasmagoric Decadent Romanticism was directed to the ultimate purpose of building dream-worlds stranger and more bizarre than had ever been described before. It was not enough for him to escape the mundane world; he wanted also to outdo in imaginative reach all the established mythologies of past and present.

Smith summed up this ambition in a prose-poem, "To the Daemon," where he offered up the following prayer to the fountainhead of his creativity:

> Tell me many tales, O benign maleficent daemon, but tell me none that I have ever heard or have even dreamt of otherwise than obscurely or infrequently. Nay, tell me not of anything that lies within the bourns of time or the limits of space; for I am a little weary of all recorded years and chartered lands....
>
> Tell me many tales, but let them be of things that are past the lore of legend and of which there are no myths in our world or any world adjoining.... Tell me tales of inconceivable fear and unimaginable love, in orbs whereto our sun is a nameless star, or unto which its rays have never reached. (*NU* 17–18)

There is almost nothing in Smith's work of what is usually called "human interest." Those of his characters who live in the mundane world think of it as a drab and desolate place whose tedium is barely tolerable, and they are usually eager to take the opportunities which Smith's imagination offers them: to cross thresholds into worlds where the bizarre and the inexplicable are commonplace. Many of these fantasy-worlds are dangerous in the extreme, but the fascination which they exert on his protagonists is irresistible.

In the jargon popularized by J. R. R. Tolkien, Smith's stories are mostly set in Secondary Worlds which have their own "inner consistency of reality," but the most ambitious of them have do not seem to have the customary relationship with the Primary World that most imaginary worlds in fantasy fiction have. These milieux exhibit neither the heroic permissiveness of Howardesque sword and sorcery fiction, nor the moral crystallization of Tolkienesque fantasy. The excuses offered in Tolkien's famous apologia for fantasy "On Fairy Tales"—that Secondary Worlds provide for Recovery, Escape and Consolation—are effectively scorned by Smith; there is no "eucatastrophe" in any of his most striking and heartfelt stories. His fiction is certainly escapist in its fashion, but the "freedom" which his protagonists win by their escape—and which is set to tantalize, by proxy, the reader—is freedom without security, strangeness without safety, and in many cases leads only to doom or bitter disappointment.

Smith did back up his work with a measure of aesthetic theory. He was prepared to defend, in articulate fashion, the notion that it was entirely proper for a writer to be unconcerned with the human world, or with such issues as careful characterization and the conventions of narrative realism. In a letter to *Amazing Stories* published in the issue for October 1932 he proposed that:

> Literature can be, and does, many things; and one of its most glorious prerogatives is the exercise of imagination on things that lie beyond human experience—the adventuring of fantasy into the awful, sublime and infinite cosmos

outside the human aquarium.... For many people ... imaginative stories offer a welcome and salutary release from the somewhat oppressive tyranny of the homocentric, and help to correct the deeply introverted, ingrowing values that are fostered by present-day "humanism" and realistic literature with its unhealthy materialism and earth-bound trend. Science fiction, at its best, is akin to sublime and exalted poetry, in its evocation of tremendous, non-anthropomorphic imageries. (PD 14–15)

It is not obvious, however, that the kind of escape offered by Smith's fantasies is really all that "salutary and welcome," and its grimness is something which may invite further explanation. If a case is to be made out for there being special merit in Smith's work then his fiction may require an apology more far-reaching than those usually offered for fantastic fictions. Smith's fantasy lies, for the most part, beyond the range of Tolkien's apologia just as its exoticism extends beyond that of more conventional fiction. In order to pave the way for any such explanation and apology, it is necessary to look more closely at the nature, history and sources of inspiration of Smith's work.

What we know of Smith's life, from memoirs penned by people who met him and from short biographies compiled by L. Sprague de Camp and Donald Sidney-Fryer, suggests that it was remarkable for its uneventfulness. Apart from his artwork Smith had no career, though financial necessity drove him to many short periods of casual labor. His parents were relatively elderly when he was born—his father was nearly forty and his mother some years older—and he lived with them until they died, his mother in 1935 and his father in 1937. He did not marry until he was in his sixties, though his biographers suggest that he had earlier love affairs, perhaps with married women. Once the family moved into the small house which his father built on lonely Boulder Ridge in 1907 Smith very rarely left it until he married—visits to friends who lived further away than Auburn seem to have been very few and far between. Although he was highly intelligent, and read voraciously, Smith never attended high school or college, preferring to educate himself.

Despite this virtual isolation, however, there was nothing parochial about Smith's view of the world. In his correspondence he gave every indication that he loathed Auburn, and longed to be elsewhere, and yet he never left it. When he was in his twenties his health broke down, and for eight years between 1913 and 1921 he was unwell, suffering from various aches and pains and from periodic bouts of fever. A local doctor tentatively diagnosed tuberculosis, but de Camp considers this diagnosis to have been unreliable. By the time he had regained his health (and he recovered it sufficiently to undertake some hard manual labors in subsequent years) Smith may have felt that he was bound to Boulder Ridge by the aging of his parents, who needed to be looked after, but it is not easy to say why he did not leave Auburn once they were dead—or, for that matter, why he accomplished almost nothing during the remaining quarter-century of his life. Almost all of his best poetry, and all of his best fiction, was written before 1935.

Smith's interest in the exotic began, it appears, at an early age. He was a precocious child, and records in his brief autobiographical statements (written for the pulp magazines in the thirties) that he began to write in his early teens, producing many oriental fantasies. His interest in the Orient had apparently been provoked by reading the *Thousand and One Nights* at the age of eleven. At the age of thirteen his interest in the exotic was further encouraged by his discovery of Edgar Allan Poe, whose poetry was an important early influence on his own. At fifteen he discovered the work of the California poet George Sterling, who was to become an important influence and eventually a friend.

Though George Sterling is almost forgotten today he published frequently in the popular middlebrow magazines of his day and was a celebrity on the West Coast; his major collections were each reprinted several times during the 1900s. Smith sent some of his poems to Sterling in 1911, at the suggestion of a schoolteacher friend, and began a correspondence which led to a meeting in 1912. At that time Smith stayed with Sterling in Carmel for about a month, and met other admirers who had formed a kind of coterie around him. Shortly afterwards Smith came briefly under the wing of would-be patron of the arts Boutwell Dunlap, who took him to San Francisco and introduced him to the publisher A. M. Robinson, who issued Smith's first book, *The Star-Treader and Other Poems* (1912). This brief venture into the wider world was never repeated, perhaps because of Smith's health troubles. He continued, though, to correspond with Sterling and several other writers, building up a network of pen-friends which was eventually to include H. P. Lovecraft and Robert E. Howard.

George Sterling wrote prefaces for Smith's second and third volumes of poetry, *Odes and Sonnets* (1918) and *Ebony and Crystal* (1922), but he ceased to exercise any direct influence on Smith when he died in 1926, having taken poison—though Smith apparently doubted that he had really committed suicide.

There is a sense in which some of Smith's work takes over where Sterling left off, and Smith was influenced in particular by two of Sterling's poems: "A Wine of Wizardry" and *The Testimony of the Suns*. The former poem, which first drew Smith's attention to Sterling when it was published in *Cosmopolitan* in 1907, describes in a fashion made literal by its mode of presentation a flight of Fancy, which takes her at hectic pace through various mythological scenarios of dark and Satanic character until she quits the earth entirely and sets forth for a distant star. At the end of this peculiar odyssey the poet, despite the fact that his vision has shown him that the world of the imagination is redolent with sinister and malignant figures, declares himself well content to have indulged in its intoxication. *The Testimony of the Suns* had been the title poem of a collection first issued in 1903; it ventures even further into distant realms of the imagination, and Smith wrote that it contained

> lines that evoke the silence of infinitude, verses in which one hears the crash of gliding planets, verses that are clarion-calls in the immemorial war of suns and systems, and others that are like the cadences of some sidereal requiem, chanted by

seraphim over a world that is "stone and night." (*PD* 5)

Though these two poems are exceptional in Sterling's canon they are not entirely without echoes in the work of other California poets. The work of another sometime resident of Carmel, Edwin Markham (a much older man than Sterling, having been born in 1852), includes much religious poetry of a visionary nature, and Markham was ultimately to produce a spectacular supernatural odyssey of his own in "The Ballad of the Gallows Bird," published in the *American Mercury* in 1926. This long poem includes a transit of Hell and is replete with morbid imagery, as when skeletons erupt from their graves. These poems remind us that Smith's work—though undeniably extraordinary—is by no means entirely disconnected from the culture of its place and time.

Sterling knew Markham well (Markham wrote the poem "Sarpedon" in Sterling's memory) and he was also well acquainted with Ambrose Bierce, the most famous of all the Californian writers of the day, to whom he showed some of Smith's poetry. Both Markham and Bierce must be counted among Sterling's influences, and hence among Smith's. Of greater importance, however, in determining the shape of Smith's career as a poet were more distant influences upon "A Wine of Wizardry" which Sterling called to Smith's attention: influences from French literature.

Sterling apparently introduced Smith to Baudelaire's *Fleurs du mal*—in English translation—in 1912, and impressed him sufficiently to inspire him eventually to learn French in order to be able to translate such works for himself. The Arkham House volume of Smith's *Selected Poems* includes along with thirty translations and "paraphrases" of Baudelaire translations from several other writers, including Paul Verlaine, Victor Hugo, José-Maria de Heredia, and Charles Leconte de Lisle (as well as some fake "translations" which are actually Smith's own pseudonymous work). He seems to have discovered a strong affinity with the particular current in nineteenth century French poetry which extended from the lusher products of Romanticism to the morbid extravagances of the Decadent Movement.

Many nineteenth-century French writers had a profound fascination for the Orient, which drove many of them actually to undertake eastward voyages (though few got any further than North Africa). There was also a prolific and potent supernatural element in nineteenth century French literature, where the influence of Poe was supplemented by the influence of such English writers as Edward Young (whose *Night Thoughts*, translated by Letourneur in 1769, had been very popular) and Lord Byron. A "genre macabre" was extrapolated from collections by Théophile Gautier—notably *La Comédie de la mort* (1838)—into the work of Baudelaire, Petrus Borel and Gérard de Nerval's *"supernaturaliste"* poems. The slightly less fevered "Parnassian" poets also made abundant use of mythological material, to which Leconte de Lisle added a broad cosmic perspective strongly influenced by the evolutionist ideas of the day. Many writers of the period, influenced by the fashionable idea that genius was closely akin to madness, were happy to borrow inspiration from delirium, whether it was visited upon them by accidents of fate (like Alfred de Musset and Gérard de Nerval) or whether they had to induce it by means with opium, hashish or even ether (as Baudelaire, Gautier, Rimbaud and Jean Lorrain were interested to do).

All of these concerns are echoed in Smith's work. He presumably came by his interest in Oriental and supernatural exoticism independently, and it is probable that his acquaintance with drugs was limited to those opiates which were used as pain-killers and sleeping-draughts, but he must have found a wonderful coincidence of outlook in the work of the French poets. He probably did not have the opportunity to familiarize himself thoroughly with the abundant short fiction produced by writers associated with the Decadent Movement—most notably Remy de Gourmont, Jean Lorrain, Marcel Schwob and Catulle Mendès—but he would have found common cause with them too, and there is a sense in which Smith may be regarded as the last and most extravagant of the masters of Decadent prose.

Another element of the French literary tradition which may warrant consideration in the light of its influence on Smith's work is its religious context. France was a country very much aware of its Catholic traditions (always under stress after the revolution of 1789) and the atheists among the above-named writers formed their atheism in opposition to Catholic theology. Although reconsideration led some Decadents back from their literary flirtations with evil to a kind of repentance—Verlaine and Joris-Karl Huysmans are the cardinal examples—others remained firmly committed to the flagrant literary Satanism of Baudelaire and Anatole France. The Catholicism whose mythology provided the metaphysical context of all this work—even, and perhaps particularly, that which was moved by a spirit of strident opposition—was a Catholicism heavily influenced (thanks to Pascal, Racine and Alfred de Vigny) by the desolate world-view of Jansenism.

Jansenists believed that man had been abandoned by an indifferent God, so that all that a cosmic voyage of the imagination could possibly reveal was a bleak and impassive universe, empty of any real comfort. Smith had no apparent links with the Catholic faith (although Sterling had; his parents had tried unsuccessfully to bring him up in the faith); he nevertheless acquired and carefully extrapolated a world-view which was in close correspondence with the Romanticized Jansenist pessimism of the French tradition.

In his own poems, Smith sent his Fancy on more extended flights than Sterling's ever took, into the remoter regions of the imagined universe, where it found a multitude of monstrous and baleful apparitions, and an illimitable cold indifference which could offer no comfort to mankind. In "Nero," which led off his first collection, Smith imagines the Roman emperor wishing that he were a god, so that he could supervise the conflict of Chaos and Creation, and play with the stars so as to "tear out the eyes of light." Though such a god is not the quiet, hidden God of the Jansenists he is certainly a deity which offers cold comfort to mankind. In the title-poem of that first collection, "The Star-Treader," the dreaming narrator is given a similar god's-eye view of the universe, and finds a similarly bleak awe in its rapt contemplation. Cosmic perspectives which reduce the earth and its inhabitants to insignificance are offered also in the "Ode on Imagination" and "The Song of the Comet."

In *Ebony and Crystal* this interest in cosmic perspectives—and particularly in the lushness and bizarrerie of the visions available to such perspectives—reaches fuller flower. Its most extended development is to be found in Smith's longest, and perhaps finest, poem: *The Hashish-Eater; or, The Apocalypse of Evil*, which begins with the memorable lines:

> Bow down: I am the emperor of dreams;
> I crown me with the million-colored sun
> Of secret worlds incredible, and take
> Their trailing skies for vestment when I soar,
> Throned on the mountain zenith, and illume
> The spaceward-flown horizon infinite. (*LO* 15)

The intoxicating wine of wizardry which dispatched George Sterling's Fancy clearly had less impetus than the hashish which impelled Smith's emperor of dreams. Sterling's vision is essentially a syncretic amalgam of Earthly myths; to this Smith adds a breadth borrowed from the discoveries of astronomy and speculations of cosmogony, but he adds too a particular viewpoint in which the extremism of the vision is both necessary and inadequate to answer the pangs of imaginative suffocation and stultification. The violent and macabre elements of Smith's vision—its decadent dalliance with satanic imagery—are provocations to an imagination which (it is implied) could not be drawn to awe by any lesser stimulus. For Smith, conventional appeals to the imagination are effete and jejune. This is where Smith found his intellectual kinship with Baudelaire and Rimbaud: for them too the ultimate enemy of the human soul was not evil but ennui, and they too sought release from spiritual anaesthesia in magniloquence of vision and cultivation of mordant exoticism.

The influence of Baudelaire is most clearly seen in the twenty-nine poems in prose which Smith published in *Ebony and Crystal*. Indeed, the first of these to be published (in *The Smart Set* in 1918) is entitled "Ennui"; like "Nero" it features an emperor for whom earthly pleasures are inadequate to secure any spiritual release. Here, though, the emperor is brought to momentary sensation not by dreams of godhood but by a close brush with death.

These poems in prose contain the seeds of much of Smith's later fantastic fiction. It is not just that some of his stories are built around images recapitulated from the prose-poems ("The Demon of the Flower" around "The Flower-Devil" and "The Planet of the Dead" around "From the Crypts of Memory") but that it was in the prose-poems that he cultivated the tone and world-view of so much of his later prose fiction.

The way in which Smith developed his poetry in prose has both significant similarities and important contrasts to the way that French prose-poetry developed from Aloysius Bertrand's *Gaspard de la Nuit* through Baudelaire's *Petits poèmes en prose* to Rimbaud's *Illuminations*. Bertrand's medievalism gave way to the more varied exoticism of Baudelaire, and Baudelaire also began to produce more extended prose-poems, notably "L'Invitation au voyage," whose theme is recapitulated by Smith in "In Cocaigne." Rimbaud was not much concerned with the further development of Baudelaire's exoticism, but he did import a special kind of fervor into the form, seen especially in some of the most memorable passages of the patchwork prose-poem *Une Saison en enfer*—a kind of horrified rage which ultimately comes to delight in delirium and celebrate "the alchemy of the word."

The manner in which Smith's work sets off in a different direction is to do with his adoption of a rather different mythos, which draws upon the fantasies of science. It was not simply the largeness of the cosmic perspective which impressed him, but also the detachment and clinicality of the scientific outlook, and its calmness in confrontation with the alien and unimaginable. In this respect he is a distinctly twentieth century writer, and though the work he did for the science fiction pulps is mostly weak by comparison with his *Weird Tales* stories he nevertheless drew something important from the scientific world-view. For most pulp science fiction writers (and, for that matter, most scientists) the modern world-view simply invalidated all the fabulous beings of ancient mythology, and so science fiction writers developed their own distinct vocabulary of ideas; for Smith, though, it was only the attitude of mind which one adopted to demons, sorcerers, satyrs and the like which needed to be transformed: he could achieve a remarkable synthesis of scepticism and credulity, which is one of the unique features of his work.

In discovering this new direction, Smith was of course aided by one of his American literary heroes, Edgar Allan Poe, whose own poems in prose presumably influenced Baudelaire. Like Smith, Poe had also imbibed something of the scientific world-view, and was himself given to cosmic visions, but in Poe there is no synthesis—such works as "Mesmeric Revelation" and *Eureka* remain quite distinct from his tales of the supernatural. Only in the extended prose-poem "The Masque of the Red Death" do we find in Poe's work a real precursor of Smith's fiction.

What Smith shares most intimately with the French tradition is his notion of the goad which drives the imagination to construct rhapsodies in prose, one of whose facets is ennui, another spleen. One may borrow (taking it, admittedly, out of context) Rimbaud's reference to the "alchemy of the word" to describe Smith's method, because he was a great exponent of the alchemy of words. He used his vocabulary to transform descriptions into incantations directly evoking a sense of the strange, a distortion of attitude and feeling. Smith's prose is geared to apply to the reader an experiential wrench or jolt, to permit the relief of "seeing" worlds of the imagination—which might otherwise have gone stale along with the hopeless world of *mundanity*—through a new linguistic lens. This is what his best prose fiction intends to accomplish.

* * * * *

Smith's earliest ventures in the marketing of prose fiction were tales of the orient written in his late teens. Four were published in *The Black Cat* and *The Overland Monthly* during 1910–12. Some ten years later Smith began writing light contemporary fiction aimed at "sophisticated" magazines, but the only one known to have sold was "Something New" in *10 Story Book* in 1924. His earliest experiments with extended poems in prose, the brief but highly ornate fantasies "Sadastor" and "The Abominations of Yondo," were produced soon afterwards, in 1925. Both were submitted to *Weird Tales* but rejected by editor Farnsworth Wright. "The Abominations of Yondo" appeared in *The Overland Monthly* in 1926. Smith did try his hand at material in a more orthodox *Weird Tales* vein, selling "The Ninth Skeleton" to Wright in 1928, but it was not until 1929 that he established a better working relationship with the editor, which encouraged him to produce more adventurous material. In 1930 Smith had five stories in *Weird Tales* (including "Sadastor"), and also placed two stories with Hugo Gernsback's pulps. Thus began Smith's prolific phase, which lasted from the autumn of 1929 until the spring of 1934 (although the stories continued to appear in print for some years thereafter).

"Sadastor" and "The Abominations of Yondo" both prefigure clearly the direction in which Smith's work would develop. The first begins as an Oriental tale, with a demon telling a story to amuse a fretful lamia, but the story concerns a "forgotten and dying planet" set "among the remoter galaxies." The same ambition is confirmed in the opening lines of "The Abominations of Yondo":

> The sand of the desert of Yondo is not as the sand of other deserts; for Yondo lies nearest of all to the world's rim; and strange winds, blowing from a gulf no astronomer may hope to fathom, have sown its ruinous fields with the gray dust of corroding planets, the black ashes of extinguished suns. The dark orblike mountains which rise from its wrinkled and pitted plain are not all its own, for some are fallen asteroids half-buried in that abysmal sand. Things have crept in from nether space, whose incursion is forbid by the gods of all proper and well-ordered lands; but there are no such gods in Yondo, where live the hoary genii of stars abolished, and decrepit demons left homeless by the destruction of antiquated hells. (*AY* 55)

This passage might serve as an introduction to Smith's work in general, promising as it does a blending of the notions of the satanic and the alien.

The location of Yondo in space and time is vague, and in his early days Smith had some difficulty finding an appropriate milieu for his fiction. "The End of the Story" (1930) was the first of numerous stories which Smith set in the imaginary French province of Averoigne. It is a standardized story of a young man's seduction by a lamia, and of his determination to return to her embraces even after he has been "saved" from her attentions by an older and wiser man. It echoes the theme of Keats's "Lamia" and several stories by Théophile Gautier (especially "Clarimonde" and "Arria Marcella"), and has a similar outlook to Gautier's tales, which celebrate the superiority of deliciously dangerous supernatural consorts over mere mundane women.

In his subsequent tales of Averoigne Smith was able to recapitulate his enthusiasm for French Romanticism, sometimes coming close to pastiche. He is frequently close to the spirit of Anatole France's tales in *The Well of St. Clare*—especially "San Satiro"—and "The Disinterment of Venus" seems to have been inspired by Prosper Mérimée's "The Venus of Ille." An imaginary French province was, however, too close to home to accommodate Smith's wilder imaginings, even when he imported an alien invader (in "The Beast of Averoigne," 1933). Only in "The Colossus of Ylourgne" (1934) was his taste for the bizarre allowed full rein, though "The Holiness of Azédarac" (1933) shows off his sense of irony to good advantage in a tale which borrows from Robert W. Chambers's "The Demoiselle d'Ys" and from H. P. Lovecraft.

The other scenario used in an early tale which was to be further explored was Atlantis, featured in "The Last Incantation" (1930). This is another extended poem in prose, in which the sorcerer Malygris, suffering from ennui, conjures up an image of a lost love, but cannot recover the innocence of viewpoint which made the girl so beautiful in the sight of his earlier self. "The Uncharted Isle" (1930) is a timeslip story which also seems to feature a fragment of an Atlantean civilization, though this is not stated. "A Voyage to Sfanomoë" (1931) is an interplanetary story which begins in Atlantis, but the exoticism of Atlantean sorcery is only displayed to its fullest advantage in "The Double Shadow" (1933) and "The Death of Malygris" (1934), which are both stories in which curious supernatural dooms claim the main characters—a favorite Smith formula.

In order to find more open imaginative territory Smith borrowed another mythical civilization from Greek mythology: Hyperborea, which he first featured in "The Tale of Satampra Zeiros" in 1931. This is the story of two thieves who attempt to plunder a shrine erected to the dark god Tsathoggua in a city which now lies in ruins; they are unwisely undaunted by the evil reputation which the place has. The protagonist escapes, though not intact, after seeing his companion horribly killed.

The characterization of the evil god in this story owes something to H. P. Lovecraft, to whose Cthulhu Mythos Tsathoggua is sometimes attached. The formula of following the fortunes of characters who invite awful supernatural judgment with their recklessness is here rendered in a sarcastic vein, and this appears to reflect the fact that—as in many of the Averoigne stories—wherever Smith consciously borrowed from other writers his tone tended to become more ironic, and sometimes rather flippant, his auctorial voice being distanced from the substance of the tale.

The irony of the Hyperborean tales (in the first of his Arkham House collections, *Out of Space and Time*, they are aptly dubbed "Hyperborean Grotesques") was something which Smith chose to conserve and exaggerate when he used the setting further. "The Door to Saturn" (1932) describes how the priest Morghi pursues the sorcerer Eibon through a doorway to another world, where they combine forces in order to explore until they find a place to settle down. This is one of the least violent and most sardonic of all Smith's stories. It also includes some of his most tongue-wrenching nomenclature—a trend continued in "The Weird of Avoosl Wuthoqquan" (1932), which follows the familiar pattern of reckless greed leading to macabre extinction, as do "The Ice-Demon" (1933) and the magnificently bizarre "The Coming of the White Worm" (1941).

Less irony is to be found in "Ubbo-Sathla" (1933), the most Lovecraftian of the Hyperborean stories, in which a modern occultist finds a magic lens which unites him with the personality of its wizard owner, and allows him to share that owner's visionary quest to find the parent of all Earthly life, in which is incarnate Smith's typical blend of the evil and the alien:

> There, in the gray beginning of Earth, the formless mass that was Ubbo-Sathla reposed amid the slime and the vapors. Headless, without organs or members, it sloughed from its oozy sides, in a slow, ceaseless wave, the amebic forms that were the archetypes of earthly life. Horrible it was, if there had been aught to apprehend the horror; and loathsome, if there had been any to feel loathing. About it, prone or tilted in the mire, there lay the mighty tablets of star-quarried stone that were writ with the inconceivable wisdom of the premundane gods. (OST 299)

By contrast, the most savagely ironic of the Hyperborean tales is "The Testament of Athammaus" (1932), told by a hapless headsman who is called upon to execute a demonic bandit. Each time the task is complete the bandit miraculously rises from the dead, and each time his head is struck from his shoulders he becomes more loathsome, until his hideousness forbids further interference. Like "Ubbo-Sathla" this is essentially a tale of devolution—a regression from order toward chaos (a devolution which is, in a sense, implicit in the very nature of the stories as they use a modern viewpoint to look back at a more disturbed and rough-hewn era).

All these chief elements of the Hyperborean tales are combined in the best of them all: "The Seven Geases" (1934). Here the vainglorious magistrate Ralibar Vooz goes hunting for extraordinary prey but falls prey himself to the wrath of the sorcerer Ezdagor after venturing into a strange underworld. Ezdagor places him under a geas which requires him to descend further into the Tartarean realm to present himself as a blood-offering to Tsathoggua. But Tsathoggua has no need of him, and so sends him further on, and the pattern repeats. In the company of the bird-demon Raphtontis, Ralibar Vooz delivers himself in turn to the web of the spider-god Atlach-Natha, to the palace of the "antehuman sorcerer" Haon-Dor, to the Cavern of the Archetypes, and to the slimy gulf of Abhoth, "father and mother of all cosmic uncleanliness":

Here, it seemed, was the ultimate source of all miscreation and abomination. For the gray mass quobbed and quivered, and swelled perpetually; and from it, in manifold fission, were spawned the anatomies that crept away on every side through the grotto. There were things like bodiless legs or arms that flailed in the slime, or heads that rolled, or floundering bellies with fishes' fins; and all manner of things malformed and monstrous, that grew in size as they departed from the neighborhood of Abhoth. And those that swam not swiftly ashore when they fell into the pool from Abhoth, were devoured by mouths that gaped in the parent bulk. (*OST* 63)

By this time, though, the magistrate is in a realm so remote that his own ordered world is known only by vile rumor, so Abhoth can think of no more awful place to send him than home. Alas, the journey back is fraught with far too many dangers for it to be safely made, so Ralibar Vooz, who is too puerile even to be worth devouring, cannot capitalize on the good fortune of his insignificance.

Here, despite the ironic voice with which the story opens, Smith is clearly carried away by the impetus of his constructed nightmare, and this is a key story in his oeuvre. The descent into the underworld is a fine representation of the metempirical reality in which Smith embeds his fantastic tales. The revelation that the ultimate reality is utterly loathsome is, of course, something which Smith echoes from Lovecraft's tales, but Smith's version is far more elaborate and far more colorful. Lovecraft is essentially a monochrome writer, but Smith's imagination is lush and fecund—his universe is not simply a horrific one, but a multitudinously populous one, in which there are not merely more things than are dreamt of in the Lovecraftian philosophy, but more things than are dreamt if in any philosophy.

This can be seen well enough in Smith's work for the sf pulps. It is surprising, in a way, that Gernsback made room in his magazines for a writer so ill-fitted to his declared manifesto (to the effect that sf was a futurological species of fiction which would anticipate technological developments), but Smith did have an imaginative verve which enlivened the pages of *Wonder Stories* quite considerably. His first story there, "Marooned in Andromeda" (1930), set the pattern for many others, featuring an odyssey across an alien landscape replete with strange life-forms.

Some of these stories of strange alien life-forms are hard to distinguish from his horror stories of vile godlings and devolved protoplasmic entities—"The Immeasurable Horror" (1931) and "The Vaults of Yoh-Vombis" (1932) both appeared in *Weird Tales* despite being notionally science fiction, and "The Dweller in the Gulf" (published as "The Dweller in Martian Depths" in *Wonder Stories* [1933]) might have been better suited to *Weird Tales*—but others are content to rejoice in their representations of the exotic. The best are those which deal with radical transfigurations of space and time, particularly "The Eternal World" (1932) and "The Dimension of Chance" (1932).

It is clear that Smith found some of these science-fictional tales impossible to take seriously, and some—like "The Letter from Mohaun Los" (1932) and "The

Monster of the Prophecy" (1932)—decay into uneasy satire. The seductive attraction of the exotic, however, was something which Smith was capable of taking very seriously indeed, and his best sf stories are pure celebrations of that allure. The most famous of them is "The City of the Singing Flame" (1931), which is combined in most book versions with its sequel "Beyond the Singing Flame" (1931).

The narrator of this story discovers on a lonely Californian ridge (effectively identical to the one where Smith lived) a gateway to a parallel world, where an assortment of alien creatures trek in pilgrimage to a fabulous city in order to achieve ecstatic immolation in a fountain of flame which attracts them with mesmeric music. Like some of the stories of A. Merritt (especially "The Moon Pool") this story presents an archetypal image of the irresistible temptations of the imagination.

"Beyond the Singing Flame" is a much weaker story, and does the original no favors when combined with it, because the passage through the flame (which turns out to be a multidimensional gateway to other modes of existence) cannot help but be a de-mystification, and hence an anti-climax. The science-fictional imagination is inextricably involved with such de-mystifications and dis-enchantments, because it must deal in pretended possibilities. For this reason Smith could not find sf a satisfactory genre in which to work—the problem is just as obvious in "The Light from Beyond" (1934) as it is in "Beyond the Singing Flame"—but he was enthusiastic to borrow some elements of the science-fictional imagination, in order to add a more grandiose sweep to his fantasies. Two of his most gaudy and fanciful fantasies, "The Maze of the Enchanter" (1933) and "The Flower-Women" (1935) take advantage of an extraterrestrial setting to increase their exoticism.

It is hardly surprising, therefore, that Smith developed the most dramatically appropriate of all his imaginary milieux by placing it not in the remote past but in the farthest imaginable future. This was Zothique, "the world's last continent," in which decadence could be allowed unchallenged sway. The name may be derived from Rimbaud's *Album dit "Zutique,"* which title involves a fanciful piece of wordplay on the French expletive *zut!*—which might be paralleled (appropriately, if this is indeed where Smith got the name Zothique from) by some such English expression as "to hell with you!"

Because Hyperborea existed in earth's past, the viewpoint of stories set there had to accept the implication that Order would ultimately oust Chaos, but in Zothique the implied future is empty; science and civilization are gone and utterly forgotten, and all that happens there is but part of a prelude to annihilation.

The first Zothique story was "The Empire of the Necromancers" (1932), a marvelous extravaganza in which two magicians conjure themselves an empire out of the dust of the ages and the corpses of the ancient dead, but then reap a just reward after the rebellion of their subjects. This is one of the most graphic of all Smith's horror stories, and its tone is pure nightmare:

> All that night, and during the blood-dark day that followed, by wavering torches or the light of the failing sun, an endless army of plague-eaten liches, of tattered

skeletons, poured in a ghastly torrent through the streets of Yethlyreom and along the palace-hall where Hestaiyon stood guard above the slain necromancers. Unpausing, with vague, fixed eyes, they went on like driven shadows, to seek the subterranean vaults below the palace, to pass through the open door where Illeiro waited in the last vault, and then to wend downwards by a thousand steps to the verge of that gulf in which boiled the ebbing fires of earth. There, from the verge, they flung themselves to a second death and the clean annihilation of the bottomless flames. (*RA* 324–25)

Not all the Zothique stories have this intensity of feeling. Some are ironic in the vein of the Hyperborean grotesques, most notably the excellent "The Voyage of King Euvoran" (1933), whose eponymous hero offends a necromancer and is punished by the loss of his remarkable crown, which is carried away by the reanimated fabulous bird that topped it. Misled by an apparently-favorable oracle the king goes in quest of his lost crown, but finds instead a peculiarly apt humiliation.

Nor are all the Zothique stories entirely original—"The Isle of the Torturers" (1933) has echoes of Poe's "Masque of the Red Death" and Villiers de l'Isle-Adam's "Torture of Hope" embedded in its account of a sadistic orgy whose victim eventually wins a Pyrrhic victory over his tormentors. In general, though, the best of the Zothique stories are each possessed of an unparalleled dramatic surge which carries them helter-skelter through a mass of bizarre detail to a devastating conclusion.

The Zothique stories frequently contain erotic elements, but consummation is usually denied, and the seductive sorceresses who feature in "The Witchcraft of Ulua" (1934) and "The Death of Ilalotha" (1937) are certainly not treated with the same sentimental affection as the sorceresses and lamias of the tales of Averoigne—the Gautieresque touches of "The End of the Story," "The Holiness of Azédarac" and "The Enchantress of Sylaire" (1941)—are nowhere to be seen. Necrophilia is a theme which crops up several times, most strikingly in "The Death of Ilalotha" and "The Charnel God" (1934).

This repellent eroticism exists side-by-side with savage cruelty—torture is a commonplace in Zothique and sadism is the norm. These quasi-pornographic features are not evidences of any depravity on the part of the author, but rather represent a determined effort to confront and make manageable the most nightmarish products of the imagination. Here, the most awful and terrifying creations of delirium and anxiety are submitted to the command of a rigorous literary imagination. The characters usually move in quasi-ritual step toward their predestined dooms, sometimes taking entire cities with them, as in "The Witchcraft of Ulua" and the very violent "The Dark Eidolon" (1935). The latter story, concerning a sorcerer who defies his supernatural protector in order to carry forward his vendetta against a king who abused him in his youth, features a literal feast of horrors:

In the wide intervals between the tables, the familiars of Namirrha and his other servants went to and fro incessantly, as if a phantasmagoria of ill dreams were embodied before the emperor. Kingly cadavers in robes of time-rotten brocade, with worms seething in their eye-pits, poured a blood-like wine into cups of the opalescent horn of unicorns. Lamias, trident-tailed, and four-breasted chimeras, came in with fuming platters lifted high by their brazen claws. Dog-headed devils, tongued with lolling flames, ran forward to offer themselves as ushers for the company. And before Zotulla and Obexah, there appeared a curious being with the full-fleshed lower limbs and hips of a great black woman and the clean-picked bones of some titanic ape from there upward. And this monster signified by certain indescribable becks of its finger-bones that the emperor and his odalisque were to follow it. (RA 381)

The background against which these stories are set is described in terms as far from naturalistic as the mechanics of their plots. Idiosyncrasy is displayed with unashamed extravagance, as in the opening paragraph of "The Witchcraft of Ulua":

Sabmon the anchorite was famed no less for his piety than for his prophetic wisdom and knowledge of the dark art of sorcery. He had dwelt alone for two generations in a curious house on the rim of the northern desert of Tasuun: a house whose floor and walls were built from the large bones of dromedaries, and whose roof was a wattling composed of the smaller bones of wild dogs and men and hyenas. These ossuary relics, chosen for their whiteness and symmetry, were bound securely together with well-tanned thongs, and were joined and fitted with marvelous closeness, leaving no space for the blown sand to penetrate. This house was the pride of Sabmon, who swept it daily with a besom of mummy's hair, till it shone immaculate as polished ivory both within and without. (AY 21)

In stories such as these the possibility of a happy ending is simply out of the question. For this reason they cannot be considered tragedies, or even simple horror stories, for no fate can really be considered tragic or horrific if it cannot possibly be avoided. Indeed, such is the inversion of values permitted by these stories that it is the echoes of affection and success which resound therein which seem in the end to be the most awful things of all. This can be seen in what are perhaps the finest of the tales of Zothique, "Necromancy in Naat" (1936) and "Xeethra" (1934).

In "Necromancy in Naat" a ship carrying a prince who is searching for his lost love (who has been carried off by slavers) is caught by a black current and wrecked near the island of Naat. The prince is the sole survivor, but finds himself reunited with the drowned crew of the ship—and with his loved one, also dead but reanimated—in the service of a family of necromancers, whose intention is to feed him to their vampiric familiar. He avoids this fate by joining in a plot to help the two sons murder their father, but in the hideous conflict which follows (in which the intended victim will not be still despite mortal wounds) he is killed. The sole surviving necromancer commits suicide, leaving the resurrected servants to find a "ghostly comfort" in their liberation: "The quick despair that had racked him aforetime, and the long torments of desire and separation, were as things faded and forgot; and he shared with Dalili a shadowy love and a dim contentment" (*RA* 436).

In "Xeethra" a goat-boy strays into the underworld realm of the dark god Thasaidon, where he eats fruit which recall to him consciousness of a former existence as a king. He sets off to find his kingdom, but after a long journey finds it desolate and inhabited by lepers. He sells his soul to enter a dream in which the kingdom's lost glory is restored to him, agreeing to surrender it if ever he regrets his estate. Thasaidon eventually sends a dark piper to him in a time of strife, to seduce that all-important moment of regret. Xeethra becomes a goat-boy again, but the real horror of his fate is that Thasaidon does not need to snatch him away into some infernal region, because the anguish of his loss is hell enough for him, and the "dark empire" of Thasaidon is now within his soul.

It is in these images of special suffering, of death-in-life or hell-in-life, that Smith reaches the true culmination of all his trafficking with nightmares. In these two denouements more than in any of his myriad tales which end with ugly death, he achieves a true moment of climax. If his quest into the farthest and strangest reaches of the imagination can be said to have reached a destination, this was surely it.

"Necromancy in Naat" was published two years after Smith's major phase of writing activity had petered out. Three more Zothique stories—"The Death of Ilalotha," "The Garden of Adompha" (1938) and "The Master of the Crabs" (1948)—were yet to appear, and a handful of other stories left over from the prolific phase filtered into print over the years, but Smith was never able to get back into the writing of prose on any significant scale. Those stories which seem to have been written at a much later date—"Schizoid Creator" (1953), "A Prophecy of Monsters" (1954) and "The Symposium of the Gorgon" (1958)—are brief literary jokes, manifesting none of the author's earlier fascinations.

This abrupt draining away of inspiration is in its way as remarkable as what his inspiration produced while Smith was possessed by it. It implies some essential change in Smith, whether in his personality or his environment. He offered no explanation himself, and was presumably unconscious of any reason.

One can only speculate about the possible psychodynamics of his literary endeavors and their frustrating conclusion, and such speculations are inevitably hazardous. Any conjecture remains untestable. There is, however, evidence in Smith's work of the motive force which carried him away to such far-flung fantasy worlds, and contemplation of this motive force does encourage certain hypotheses regarding possible reasons for its decline.

None of Smith's stories are in any straightforward sense autobiographical, but they do contain several pen-portraits of characters imbued with an escapist fervor which bears metaphorical comparison with his own. The writer Philip Hastane is a character who appears in several stories. He relays the manuscript which forms the story of "The City of the Singing Flame," and then becomes the protagonist of "Beyond the Singing Flame." He is also the narrator of two Lovecraftian tales: "The Hunters from Beyond" (1932), which is strongly reminiscent of Lovecraft's story "Pickman's Model," and "The Devotee of Evil" (1933).

In these stories it is not Hastane who is the focus of interest but the characters to whom things happen: the writer Giles Angarth, the sculptor Cyprian Sincaul and the occultist Jean Averaud. Each of these three is seduced by the allure of the extraordinary into an encounter which destroys them (Angarth actually survives, but expresses the wish that he were dead). Averaud's fate is the most graphic—he builds a machine to put himself in touch with the ultimate evil, whose emanations apparently extend through all Creation, and is petrified by the possessive force of that evil. Although he is only a witness, Hastane too is touched and changed by this exposure:

> Vainly, through delirious months and madness-ridden years, I have tried to shake off the infrangible obsession of my memories. But there is a fatal numbness in my brain, as if it too had been charred and blackened a little in that moment of overpowering nearness to the dark ray that came from pits beyond the universe. On my mind, as upon the face of the black statue that was Jean Averaud, the impress of awful and forbidden things has been set like an everlasting seal. (*AY* 42)

To some extent, this must be seen simply as the kind of conclusion which a Lovecraftian story demands—the genre is characterized by its emphasis of the awfulness of moments of revelation which reveal the hideousness of the hidden order of the universe. But the lessons which Hastane learns from these encounters with men similar to himself seem to be accepted with real feeling.

Even in Smith's most romantic and sentimental stories, though there is nothing in their formula which demands it, there is nothing really to be gained from visionary experience. Among the least horrific of all Smith's stories is "The Planet of the Dead" (1932), which features a much more kindly vision, and a much more gentle visionary:

> By profession, Francis Melchior was a dealer in antiques; by avocation, he was an astronomer. Thus he contrived to placate, if not to satisfy, two needs of a somewhat complex and unusual temperament. Through his occupation, he gratified in a measure his craving for all things that have been steeped in the mortuary shadows of dead ages, in the dusky amber flames of long-sunken suns; all things that have about them the irresoluble mystery of departed time. And through his avocation, he found a ready path to exotic realms in further space, to the only spheres where his fancy could dwell in freedom and his dreams could know contentment. For Melchior was one of those who were born with an immedicable distaste for all that is present or near at hand; one of those who have drunk too lightly of oblivion and have not wholly forgotten the transcendent glories of other eons, and the worlds from which they were exiled into human birth; so that their furtive, restless

thoughts and dim, unquenchable longings return obscurely toward the vanishing shores of a lost heritage. The earth is too narrow for such, and the compass of mortal time is too brief; and paucity and barrenness are everywhere; and in all places their lot is a never-ending weariness. (*RA* 287)

Melchior—whose situation is surely a fanciful transfiguration of Smith's own—shares for a while the consciousness of the poet Antarion, and his idyllic love-affair with the lovely Thameera—a love-affair brought to its conclusion by the death of the sun which lit their world. Though it is something to be treasured, Melchior's vision leaves him unhappier than ever, possessed by a "dull regret that he should ever have awakened."

These stories exemplify the most constant and oft-repeated pattern in Smith's work. No good ever really comes of dalliance with the supernatural. Very rarely is a character invigorated by it, and the exceptions belong to works in the flippant and satirical vein. The metempirical order of things is always either hostile or pregnant with doom. In most of his horror stories Smith's assumptions are very like those of H. P. Lovecraft or William Hope Hodgson, both of whom supposed that anything godlike must be implacably opposed to man, essentially evil. But Smith's version of this world-view does not concentrate on the evil nature of these hypothetical forces—even when, as in "The Devotee of Evil" such a case is made explicitly. His emphasis is on the utter irrelevance and insignificance of man, and the sheer helplessness of human ambition in the face of cosmic processes which render human efforts meaningless and absurd. Thus, in "The Planet of the Dead" human affection is impotent in the face of cosmic catastrophe, just as in the Zothique stories everything is overshadowed by the impending end of earth. This sensibility is what links Smith to the Jansenist-influenced aspects of French Romanticism. Where can it have come from?

All Smith's notable fiction was written before the spring of 1934. His parents were then in their eighties, and both were soon to die. It seems highly probable that the problem of caring for them (in a lonely cabin with no electricity and no running water) became increasingly difficult, and that Smith was ultimately forced to stop writing largely because of the necessity of devoting his attention wholly to his parents' needs. His mother eventually died in September 1935 and his father in December 1937. One might expect that this would have freed him to begin writing again, but it did not, and this must surely make us wonder whether it was actually the situation of living with his aged parents, and the continually escalating strain which that situation put upon him, which is distortively reflected in his fantasies. The preoccupation with the inevitability of extinction, the idea that such inevitability made the longings of human affection impotent and absurd, and the constant emphasis on the sheer claustrophobia of real-world experience could all be linked in this way. If this is true, then the culmination of Smith's wilder stories in images of hell-in-life reflects no mere ennui or spleen, but rather a terrible anguish.

The memoirs written of Smith suggest that he was a very devoted son, and that he loved his parents dearly. If he was imprisoned on Boulder Ridge it was by honest affection rather than by force. It is surely not too difficult to understand how the paradoxical character of such an imprisonment might lend itself well to expression in such paradoxical fantasies as Smith's. If the escapism of his fiction is to be seen as the "escape of the prisoner" rather than "the desertion of the soldier," then it was an escape which brought him very little in the way of consolation, perhaps because he was never quite able to see it that way himself. It might make more sense to see his creative burst of the early thirties not so much as an escape but as an expulsion—in which case his fantasy worlds were not so much places for him to visit as places into which he could pour the constructed phantoms of his resentments, his frustrations, and his fears—none of which would have been easy to accommodate or express in any other way. If one sees the creative period as a special purgation, then it may no longer be puzzling to ask why, once it was finished, it was finished for good.

To read and appreciate the work of Clark Ashton Smith requires more than a broad vocabulary and a sympathy for stylistic ornamentation. It requires the possibility of identifying with the curious world-view enshrined in that work: with a determination to get as far away from mundanity as language and the imagination can take one, and yet be content to discover there a universe utterly alien and inhumane, and to find in that revelation a sense of propriety which outweighs in value any mere comfort or pleasure. This may make Smith a difficult writer to enjoy, but it should not detract at all from the respect to which he is entitled.

An imagination which is bound by the aim of wish-fulfilment (as in so much romantic and heroic fantasy) could not begin to match Smith's achievement. Nor could an imagination narrowly directed to the production of the thrill of horror or disgust (as displayed in most horror stories). Smith's work is more exploratory in character, though it would not be confined, either, by the boundaries of scientific possibility which the science-fictional imagination respects. No other writer has been able to match him (including his own later self), not because none could master such an esoteric vocabulary or equal his teratological ingenuity, but because none has ever found that same combination of motive force and attitude, that same determined "alchemy of the word."

As with all true experiments in alchemy, Smith's literary work remains unique.

Clark Ashton Smith: Master of the Macabre

John Kipling Hitz

The short stories and poems of Clark Ashton Smith display a freshness of conception and a coincidence of thematic treatment that establish him as the one author who reflects, most nearly, the versatile genius of Edgar Allan Poe. Even more overtly than his famous correspondent H. P. Lovecraft, Smith, who for most of his life was a native of Auburn, California, pays homage to Poe. The fact that he translated the rather outré verses of Charles Pierre Baudelaire, the great Poe enthusiast, is pertinent. Smith was indebted to Baudelaire and Stéphane Mallarmé for poetical inspiration just as these Symbolists were inspired by the bard of Richmond. In prose, his other noteworthy influences were his friend Lovecraft, William Beckford's arabesque novel *Vathek,* and Ambrose Bierce, the San Franciscan satirist and short story writer.

The title of Smith's first major volume, *Out of Space and Time* (1942), derives from Poe's "Dream-Land." Both Poe and Smith began writing poetry in their early teens, and each regarded himself as primarily a poet. However, this article comprises only a modest overview of Smith's fiction, and those tales that bear especial reference to the works of Edgar Allan Poe.

The most compelling feature of Smith's weird fiction, which represents the lion's share of his output, is an initially overwhelming stylistic virtuosity, "a sort of verbal black magic," as one of his letters describes it (*SL* 126). His painstaking attention to phonetic pattern, often fashioned to the point of ostentation, is combined with an abundance of visual detail and figurative language. It is a very rhythmical and ornate style, comparable to Poe, yet embodying also the influence of Lafcadio Hearn, whose colorful early writings included landmark translations of Gustave Flaubert and Théophile Gautier. The following exemplary passage is from the original version of "The Double Shadow":

> Stern and white as a tomb, older than the memory of the dead, and built by men or devils beyond the recording of myth, is the mansion wherein we dwell. Far below, on black, naked reefs, the northern sea climbs and roars indomitably, or ebbs with a ceaseless murmur as of armies of baffled demons; and the house is filled evermore, like a hollow-sounding sepulcher, with the drear echo of its tumultuous voices; and the winds wail in dismal wrath around the high towers, but shake them not. (*DS* 18)

Smith's rich vocabulary, regarded as "too flowery" by those who, perhaps, are reacting against his innate romanticism, was garnered through a deliberate study of the dictionary, with emphasis on Latin and French origins, and nouns pertaining to natural forms. By and large, the wide vocabulary is used very expressively and is a fundamental asset to the prose style. Coinages include prefix and suffix variations as practiced by Poe, and forced plurals like "lamiae" and others. The range of vocabulary is even more amazing when one considers that his publishing prospects were limited to pulp magazines like *Weird Tales* and *Wonder Stories*. While most of his fiction was written in a prolific eight-year span, from "The Last Incantation" in 1929 to "The Garden of Adompha" in 1937, he generally abhorred the commercial attitude toward writing. Words such as "plenilune" and "fulgor" (in "An Offering to the Moon") are resonant facets of a careful method of revision, adding to the sense of remoteness from the mainstream, or of a disruption in the continuous fabric of space and time.

For example, "sea-lost littorals of Mu" (*OST* 103) is a lyrical phrase associating a legendary lost continent with the ocean depths surrounding Mark Irwin, stranded narrator of "The Uncharted Isle." This tale was cited by the author as a personal favorite. Its central situation is drawn from Poe's "Ms. Found in a Bottle." Placed by the vicissitude of sea-faring fate on an island which should not exist, Irwin is unable to make his presence known to the strange, ancient persons who are its forlorn inhabitants:

> None of them appeared to notice me; and I went up to a group of three who were studying one of the long scrolls I have mentioned, and addressed them. For all answer, they bent closer above the scroll; and even when I plucked one of them by the sleeve, it was evident that he did not observe me. Much amazed, I peered into their faces, and was struck by the mingling of supreme perplexity and monomaniacal intentness which their expression displayed. (*OST* 106)

The outcasts are forever bewildered by the vanishment of the sunken continent of Mu, according to Irwin's description of their maps. He wanders the island, noting the same expression on every face. Entering their temple one evening, he watches as they prepare to sacrifice a boy, the only child among them, to a monstrous half-human idol. A cloud of horror paralyzes Irwin's memory, and he awakens at sea, to be rescued after several days of rowing. The story reflects Smith's perception of life as paradox, for he stated that "it can be read as an allegory of human disorientation" (*PD* 73).

Irwin's wandering of the island discloses the crux of the predicament, a generic plot-device. Based on a nightmare of Smith's youth, "The Primal City" describes an untrodden mountain region where architectural remnants of unearthly origin attract a party of explorers. The mammoth-sized ruins are guarded by vast, sentient, and forbidding clouds, which rout the trespassers, "their voices calling like clarions in the sky, with ominous, world-shaking syllables that the ear can never seize" (*GL* 109). The title character of "Xeethra" is a young goatherd who strays into an ominous cavern, then descends to the mythical Underworld of

Thasaidon (improvisations of Hades and Satan).

Smith's own "perambulations" in the Sierra foothills near his parents' cabin, where he would remain alone for many years after their deaths until his marriage to Carol Dorman, are alluded to in his letters, and in the amusingly autobiographical story "The Light from Beyond": "My name is Dorian Weirmoth. My series of illustrative paintings, based on the poems of Poe, will perhaps be familiar to some of my readers" (*LW* 366–67). Weirmoth has withdrawn to the seclusion of his cabin in the Sierras, to gain artistic inspiration from the same mountain vistas that Smith knew so intimately. Like his brilliantly imaginative fantasy, "The City of the Singing Flame," this story of beings from another dimension impinging upon our world was successful with readers because of Smith's clinical skill in the involvement of all the senses (not just the visionary sensations) through the evocative descriptions of his artistic narrator:

> the wheel of rays began once more to revolve slowly. It swiftened, and presently I could no longer distinguish the separate beams. All I could see was a whirling disk, like a moon that spun dizzily but maintained the same position relative to the rocks and junipers. Then, without apparent recession, it grew dim and faded on the sapphire darkness. I heard no longer the remote and flute-like murmur; and the perfume ebbed from the valley like an outgoing tide, leaving but elusive wraiths of unknown spicery. (*LW* 369)

A similar setting near the Smith cabin was described in a letter to H. P. Lovecraft, almost three years earlier. In August 1930, Smith said that he had composed "The Red World of Polaris" "beneath the thousand-year-old junipers on granite crags; and the giant firs and hemlocks by the margin of sapphire tarns" (Behrends, "Chronology" 18). Its main idea, of an alien race "who had their brains implanted into indestructible metal bodies, and who are going to perform the same office for the humans who visit their world" (Behrends, "Hieroglyphs" 9), is roughly similar to Lovecraft's "The Whisperer in Darkness," begun in February of that same year, but not finalized until 26 September, just over a month after the date of Smith's letter (*Dagon* 447). This is doubly ironic because Lovecraft's letter to Smith of 21 January 1927 had told him that the similarity between Donald Wandrei's prose-poem "The Messengers" and Smith's poem "The Envoys" demonstrated "the essential parallelism of the fantastic imagination in different individuals—a circumstance strongly arguing the existence of a natural & definite (though rare) mental world of the weird" (*Selected Letters* 2.98–99).

In his essay, "The Song of the Necromancer: 'Loss' in Clark Ashton Smith's Fiction," Steve Behrends distinguishes two sources of poetic melancholy: the loss of love and the loss of the past. In their development of mood, Smith's tales were habitually an outgrowth of these themes. Among the many contributors to the fantasy Mecca that was *Weird Tales* in the 1930s, only he and Robert E. Howard developed, in convincing detail, several imaginary-world scenarios for their works. Settings such as prehistoric Hyperborea, Poseidonis (Atlantis), or the medieval French province of Averoigne helped Smith capture that sense of "lostness," which for him was, personally and artistically, of paramount significance. No less lost or time-eaten is the far-future continent of Zothique, the setting of sixteen tales and a one-act play, *The Dead Will Cuckold You*. This poetic melancholy, as metaphor, lends its luster to stories that are otherwise exercises in pure macabre, like "The Garden of Adompha," in which human body parts sprout from plants that have been nourished by the corpses of murdered concubines. Sages, sorcerers, and kings, though they summon "spirits from the vasty deep," are themselves subject to regret and ennui. This is why we find only a slight treatment of the contemporary life of people in Smith's fictional worlds; they are overshadowed by the subject at hand, be it the death of a beautiful woman or the imaginatively dramatized struggle to overcome personal unhappiness. His opinion of literary realism is clear-cut:

> My distaste for the literature of quotidian detail is doubtless the result of a sort of personal disenchantment with the social world . . . With me, though, there is no conscious desire to go back in time—only a wild aspiration toward the unknown, the uncharted, the exotic, the utterly strange and extra-terrestrial. (*SL* 126)

Leaving few stones unturned, Smith revelled in tales of revenge, eldritch horror, supernal happenings, and time-space voyages. "The Dark Eidolon," "The Vaults of Yoh-Vombis," "Xeethra," "The Double Shadow," and "The Chain of Aforgomon" belong on the short list of permanent classics in the genre. Although he dealt with all manner of fantasies, he is often thought of as being preoccupied with morbid themes. However, some of his more gruesome works use psychological detail sparingly but tellingly, as they reach pinnacles of descriptive ghastliness; the finality of death is more of an afterthought than a focal point. Marvin R. Hiemstra called this "an intense concern with the precise psychological state" (*EOD* 265), and it evinces a masterful exposition of the macabre.

Superficially, Smith shares Poe's interest in the disintegration of personality, but his sardonic sense of humor is frequently the Venus flytrap to our instinctive sympathy for the characters. "The Empire of the Necromancers" combines mordant humor with pull-out-the-stops supernaturalism. Two outcast wizards, Mmatmuor and Sodosma, create a desert-kingdom for themselves, by resurrecting the skeletal remains of a people whose land had been visited by the plague in a bygone age. A triumph of style over substance, Smith's cadent phrasing turns a facile juxtaposition of the dead and living into a bizarre portrait of greed:

> Tribute was borne to them by fleshless porters from outlying realms; and plague-eaten corpses, and tall mummies scented with mortuary balsams, went to and fro upon their errands in Yethlyreom, or heaped before their greedy eyes, from inexhaustible vaults, the cobweb-blackened gold and dusty gems of antique time. (*LW* 163)

Such danse-macabre atmosphere evokes a peculiar mood. It could even be interpreted as a muted satire on the poetry of T. S. Eliot (1885–1965), where "the present fades into the past and the past into the present" (Altick 1586). Raised from the dead by the necromancers, the former emperor Ileiro makes observations that merge with Smith's putative reaction to the disdaining of Romantic "excess" by Imagist poets:

> He saw their caprices of cruelty and lust, their growing drunkenness and gluttony. He watched them wallow in their necromantic luxury, and become lax with indolence, gross with indulgence. They neglected the study of their art, they forgot many of their spells. (*LW* 165)

Ileiro had been a boy-king, so his indignation at being torn with unutterable violence from the sleep of death is horrifying and amusing at the same time. Mmatmuor and Sodosma are fittingly beheaded in their sleep, their blood "adding a deeper red to the rose and a brighter hue to the sad purple of their couches" (*LW* 168).

"A Night in Malnéant" is nearer in spirit to Poe than anything else from Smith's pen, excepting his prose poems. He referred to it as "one of my best atmospherics" (Behrends, "Chronology" 17), and indeed it is a small masterpiece of sustained centrality of effect. It begins as follows:

> My sojourn in the city of Malnéant occurred during a period of my life no less dim and dubious than that city itself and the misty regions lying thereabout. I have no precise recollection of its locality, nor can I remember exactly when and how I came to visit it. But I had heard vaguely that such a place was situated along my route; and when I came to the fog-enfolded river that flows beside its walls, and heard beyond the river the mortuary tolling of many bells, I surmised that I was approaching Malnéant. (*OST* 43)

The narrator has been wandering, not out of curiosity, but to assuage a deep remorse and sense of guilt regarding the death of the lady Mariel from "the anodyne of a lethal poison" (*OST* 43). The allusive tone recalls Poe's last poem, "Annabel Lee": "For she had loved me with an affection deeper and purer and more stable than mine; and my changeable temper, my fits of cruel indifference or ferocious irritability, had broken her gentle heart" (*OST* 43).

The bereaved man asks direction from two scurrying women, who cryptically reply that they cannot tell, because they are shroud-weavers and have been fashioning a shroud for Mariel. It appears that the entire community is involved in the preparations for her funeral, to the exclusion of all other activities. And so at last he ventures into the cathedral, where he is directed to walk down the aisle to behold her corpse:

> The tides of time were frozen in their flowing; and all that was or had been or could be, all of the world that existed apart from her, became as fading shadows;

and even as once before (was it eons or instants ago?) my soul was locked in the marble hell of its supreme grief and regret. (*OST* 49)

In the same fashion as "The Uncharted Isle," the narrator's circular movements, and the surface imagery of the seemingly illogical behavior he observes, create a dreamlike mutability of incident. The sentence just quoted, though it only confirms what we have come to expect, is strangely riveting and clinches the story.

"The Second Interment" is based on Poe's "The Premature Burial," and its protagonist is "Sir Uther Magbane." Impelled by a premonition that he will be buried alive, he installs a push-button alarm in his casket. Mentally confined by his obsessive fear and psychosomatic illness, he fails to realize that the real threat is posed by his avaricious brother. Like Roderick Usher, he is inevitably "a victim to the terrors he had anticipated." Nightmarish images, preceded by a dreamscape vision of his former fiancée, race through his mind as he suffocates: "He was climbing eternal stairs, bearing in his arms the burden of some gigantic corpse, only to have the stairs crumble beneath him at each step, and to fall back with the corpse lying upon him and swelling to macrocosmic proportions" (*OST* 127–28). This ending, with its implicit criticism of a self-deluded response to feminine beauty, is similar in tone to Smith's poem "The Nightmare Tarn."

"Sadastor" wakes the echoes of Poe's "Silence—A Fable." Both are tales first told by a demon, then anonymously related to us. Each begins with the verb "listen," and each presents stark, otherworldly scenery surrounding a mysterious figure wrapped in gloom and sorrow. The conversation of the demon Charnadis with the siren Lyspial elicits a sense of pathos. Lyspial is the last member of her race, abiding by the dwindling waters of a briny pool that once was a vast ocean. Her speech is rendered as a kind of lilting lament, contrasting "the barrenness of the present" (Altick 1585) with the glories of the past.

"The Isle of the Torturers" recapitulates the opening story-line of "The Masque of the Red Death." The newly ascended king Fulbra of Yoros sets sail in a vain attempt to "seek shelter in the southern isle of Cyntrom" (*LW* 174) from the swift advent of the "Silver Death." Drifting off course, his barge is approached by another vessel, and a tempest ensues, driving both ships to shore on the sinister isle of Uccastrog. The forms of torture perpetrated on the abducted king and his retinue are ended only when Fulbra, in despair, removes a red metal ring, given to him as a magical protection from the lethal plague. This dooms them all, for the contagion is immediately released: "And oblivion claimed the Isle of Uccastrog; and the torturers were one with the tortured" (*LW* 189).

Agitating features like torture, suicide, murder, or eroticism are never at center stage, nor are they simply sidelights. They are blended in "to achieve a more varied sensation of weirdness" (*SL* 219). Smith objected to *Weird Tales* editor Farnsworth Wright's suggestion that that he was catering to prurient interest. Rather, as with the art lover of "The Willow Landscape," who, forced to part with his treasures, is magically transported into a delicate landscape painting of a bamboo bridge with an Oriental maiden walking on it, Smith was "fond of plunging his readers into an unreal world which is not necessarily opposed to the reassuring world of everyday reality" (Marigny 7).

Then again, some stories do hinge upon the rejection of mundane aspects of daily life. A young protagonist in "The Witchcraft of Ulua" is cautioned about "the true nature of carnal desire" (*AY* 30), while "The Holiness of Azédarac," on the other hand, finds the monk Ambrose traveling back in time by the agency of green and red philters, to exchange his chaste existence for sexual fulfillment. And in "Morthylla," the poet Valzain is dispirited by the hollowness of pleasure and investigates the rumor of a beautiful lamia, said to haunt the local necropolis. But when he finds that the mesmerizing Morthylla is really only a similarly disillusioned woman named Beldith, Valzain kills himself in despair. His shade then returns to reenact their meeting, as the narrative circles back on itself to repeat the description of his first approach of the abandoned cemetery. Like Ambrose, Valzain chooses a dangerous escape from the safe tedium of "reality."

Tales relying on familiar Gothic elements are always reinvigorated by Smith's intense imagination. His first published tales were several arabesque fantasies dating from his teenage years, but he made his breakthrough with popular fiction readers by using the vampire myth in "The End of the Story" and "A Rendezvous in Averoigne." The medieval province, named after the Old French province of Auvergne, provides the ideal milieu for an encounter with the Undead. The "ruinous and haunted Château des Faussesflammes," and the "double tomb" of "Sieur Hugh du Malinbois and his chatelaine" (*OST* 26), are situated in the mazes of a thick forest, to entrap nocturnal wayfarers. As Charles M. Collins wrote in 1965:

> Smith's vampires occupy a weird, Kafka-like castle in which illusion and reality are inextricably joined. They are of obscure noble lineage, obnoxious in the company of men, and retain the charnel odor of the grave. . . . It is as if Smith restored the image to its rightful position; to a proper historical perspective wherein the image may exist against its heraldic tapestry of legend and myth. (Collins 16–17)

Smith's werewolf fable, "The Beast of Averoigne," exists in two strikingly different versions. It originally began with "The Deposition of Brother Gerome," who gave an account of a sighting of the beast, but is later found dead, a mangled corpse, in his cell. This was followed by "The Letter of Theophile to Sister Therese," relating how the fiendish attacks have occurred even within the hallowed grounds of the abbey of Perigon, and relinquishing all hope: "Pray for me, Therese, in my bewitchment and my despair: for God has abandoned me, and the yoke of hell has somehow fallen upon me, and naught can I do to protect the abbey from this evil" (quoted in Dziemianowicz 8). The abbot is himself the werewolf, his body invaded by a demon from a passing comet. The standard version, being told from a single point of view, omits both accounts. Longest and most wildly impressive of the Averoigne chronicles is "The Colossus of Ylourgne," concerning the dire form of vengeance taken on the citizens of Vyones by the dwarfish necromancer, Nathaire. He puts together a titanic corpse, "formed from the bones and flesh of dead men unlawfully raised up" (*GL* 151) and "energized" by the passing of his soul into it when his body dies. A rampage of devastation is ended by the countering magic of Gaspard du Nord, and the colossus, its many constituent parts seeking return to earth, lays down in "a monstrous and self-made grave" (*GL* 155) by the river Isoile.

A few of the Averoigne stories benefit from touches of Zola-esque realism. "The Maker of Gargoyles" is a grim study of jealousy and unclean passion as motivating factors. Blaise Reynard, a stone-cutter, is responsible for two of the gargoyles "that frowned or leered from the roof of the new-built cathedral of Vyones" (*TSS* 168). Rebuffed by Nicolette Villom, the taverner's daughter, he resorts to the occult. The gargoyles become animate and terrorize the town, imbued with the same lust and anger as their creator. As Nicolette's father and two of his cronies are slain, one of the monsters seizes her, its brushing wing knocking the petrified Reynard senseless. Nicolette is crushed in the embrace of the incubus. Staggering to the roof of the cathedral, the distraught and repentant Reynard raises a hammer to strike one of the gargoyles when he is caught from behind by the other one, which glares down at him as he lies with his head and shoulders over the edge of the precipice. After he falls to his death, his body is found by the archbishop, who also observes that one paw of the gargoyle (returned to stone) "was stiffly outthrust and elongated, as if, like the paw of a living limb, it had reached for something, or had dragged a heavy burden with its ferine talons" (*TSS* 184).

In "The Mandrakes," a disputatious witch named Sabine gains revenge on the husband who murdered her and buried her body in a meadow. The mandrakes grow in unnatural profusion over the site, but the love potions made from them are reversed in their effect: they incite violent hatred instead of amorous passion. The outcome recalls Poe's "The Black Cat," as one of the uncanny mandrake roots, "cloven in the very likeness of a woman's body and legs" (*OD* 258), emits audible words, telling the constabulary where to dig with their shovels.

Smith once said that he was compelled to believe that evil exists in some absolute sense because of its manifestations. If horror, as a mode of artistic expression, is validated when the images it presents point a finger of blame at the course of human existence, then the horror in Smith's fiction derives from the human center in evil. Replete with the imagery of death—of moldering skulls and "mausoleums sinking slowly in the dunes" (*OD* 315), his best macabre stories convey an ineffable sadness for diminished rather than perished lives, often dealing with the theme of self-division in a manner that breaks with Poe by stressing mankind's insignificance in the cosmic scheme of things, instead of the idea of tragic choice.

A marvelous exception is "The Chain of Aforgomon," wherein Calaspa, a priest of the titular god of Time, is a well-developed tragic figure. When his betrothed dies just prior to their wedding date, he performs a blasphemous ritual that enables him to reexperience one stolen hour from the past with her. The vain hour of reunion ends at a symbolic moment of dissension between the lovers, and Calaspa is brought back to face the desolation and doom wrought by his folly. The cleverly inverted plot begins in modern San Francisco with the hideous death of writer John Milwarp, whose body is branded with "blinding coils of pure white fire, in the form of linked chains" (*OST* 145). A manuscript he had been writing at the time of his death, under the influence of the drug "souvara," contains the very thoughts of Calaspa, whose execution by "fiery chains" (ordered by Aforgomon in the body of the high priest) occurred in an incalculably remote epoch. Calaspa's soul is reincarnated throughout all the cycles of earth-time, forever debarred from uniting with the various incarnations of his beloved until, remembering his crime at last, he must "perish out of time" (*OST* 162). Milwarp's published writings mysteriously disappear from the bookstalls, and all memory that he ever existed fades away, implying that the story itself, like all our hours stolen from time, will be swallowed in oblivion.

"Necromancy in Naat," with its walking dead, patricide, and necrophilia, is probably the best of a half-dozen excellent horror tales written between 1935 and 1937, when the pace of Smith's production had slackened. During this period he became very frustrated with the restrictions placed upon him by editors, as well as delays in payment for his work. Farnsworth Wright had insisted that Smith soften the unremittingly bleak ending; consequently, the story has a slightly upbeat tone in the final paragraph, as in one of Robert E. Howard's popular sword-and-sorcery melodramas. Smith followed it up with "The Black Abbot of Puthuum," which is even more reminiscent of Howard's work, but a signed typescript of that story, now in the John Hay Library collection, is inscribed, "First Version Rejected by Weird Tales."

Many earlier works had also met with editorial interference. Smith trimmed about 1700 words from "The Vaults of Yoh-Vombis" (1931) to satisfy Wright. In so doing, what had been intended as a preface to "The Narrative of Rodney Severn" (a suggestive name) became a "postscript." This preface, by an unnamed medical interne who took Severn's account by dictation, tells of a self-destructive mania, exhibited by this lone survivor of the Octave expedition to the ancient ruins of Yoh-Vombis, on the planet Mars. The harrowing doom that befalls the expedition is related with a consummate economy of prose. Unfortunately, the most chilling aspect of the story (a suicidal mania dooming the already traumatized victims) is undercut by the relocation of the preface. Smith's condensation of the text also lessens the cumulative atmosphere; the reader feels more detached from the horror than was intended. He surely compromised his idea of having a concentrated build-up of weird atmosphere for an interplanetary setting by cutting such a sentence as this: "The stark, eroded stones were things that might have been reared by the toil of the dead, to house the monstrous ghouls and demons of primal desolation" (*Vaults* 2).

The plots of two stories with modern settings follow a Poe-like progression of obsession leading to madness and the "shock" ending. "The Devotee of Evil" is minor, but has the same premise as an unfinished novel, *The Infernal Star*. Occultist Jean

Averaud, after years of study, postulates a metaphysical basis for evil: the extragalactic radiation of a black sun. Determining that some locations are more naturally receptive, he buys the dilapidated, reputedly haunted Larcom house in Auburn, converting one room into a triangular structure suitable for magnifying the baleful emanation. The grounds of the property have "the charm of rampancy and ruin" (*AY* 33) for novelist Philip Hastane, an autobiographical character who also narrates "Beyond the Singing Flame" and "The Hunters from Beyond." He becomes the unfortunate witness of Averaud's immersion in the cosmic rays:

> There was a sickness inexpressible, a vertigo of redeemless descent, a pandemonium of ghoulish phantoms that reeled and swayed about the column of malign omnipotent force which presided over all. Averaud was only one more phantom in this delirium, when with arms outstretched in his perverse adoration, he stepped toward the inner column and passed into it till he was lost to view. (*AY* 41)

Smith waggishly echoes a line from "The Fall of the House of Usher" ("From that chamber, and from that mansion, I fled aghast"), by writing, "I went forth for the last time from that chamber and from that mansion" (*AY* 42).

"Genius Loci" is the title story in the third of six volumes published by Arkham House. Essentially in the tradition of Algernon Blackwood and M. R. James, it is original in its treatment of the main idea. It opens with a landscape artist named Amberville nervously describing to his writer-friend a place he found while walking in a hilly area near a deserted ranch:

> There is nothing but a sedgy meadow, surrounded on three sides by slopes of yellow pine. A dreary little stream flows in from the open end, to lose itself in a *cul-de-sac* of cat-tails and boggy ground. The stream, running slowly and more slowly, forms a stagnant pool of some extent, from which several sickly-looking alders seem to fling themselves backward, as if unwilling to approach it. A dead willow leans above the pool, tangling its wan, skeleton-like reflection with the green scum that mottles the water. (*RA* 231)

With an air of compulsion, he shows the two sketches he's made of the dismal scene. After Murray scrutinizes them, Amberville says that he also had a peripheral vision of a sinister old man watching him as he was drawing, who vanished when the artist looked at him directly. The narrator comments on the artwork: "fantastic as this will seem—the meadow had the air of a vampire, grown old and hideous with unutterable infamies. Subtly, indefinably, it thirsted for other things than the sluggish trickle by which it was fed" (*RA* 233). Amberville's speech and mannerisms soon give evidence of an insidious obsession, prompting Murray to contact Avis Olcott, a close friend of the artist. She is caught "in the same phantasmal web" (*RA* 244), and in a catastrophic conclusion, they are both found dead, with Avis held and dragged in the arms of Amberville, her face covered by the scum of the pool, and Amberville's hidden under her shoulder. Simultaneously, Murray sees what caused their deaths:

The true horror lay in the thing, which, from a little distance, I had taken for the coils of a slowly moving and rising mist. It was not vapor, nor anything else that could conceivably exist—that malign, luminous, pallid emanation that enfolded the entire scene before me like a restless and hungrily wavering extension of its outlines—a phantom projection of the pale and death-like willow, the dying alders, the reeds, the stagnant pool and its suicidal victims. The landscape was visible through it, as through a film; but it seemed to curdle and thicken gradually in places, with some unholy, terrifying activity. Out of these curdlings, as if disgorged by the ambient exhalation, I saw the emergence of three human faces that partook of the same nebulous matter, neither mist nor plasm. One of these faces seemed to detach itself from the bole of the ghostly willow; the second and third swirled upward from the seething of the phantom pool, with their bodies trailing formlessly among the tenuous boughs. (RA 245–6)

The interplay of imagery here is a characteristic technique; the pool becomes a wellspring of unnaturally coalescent images. Seldom is Smith content to merely suggest what he can so vividly describe. It is in what Lovecraft called his "fertility of conception" (*Dagon* 412), or sheer imaginative genius, that Smith surpasses other weird-fantasy authors. Such central or climactic passages strive for an effect combining a sense of beauty with the sensation of horror. The sound of certain repeated consonants tends to act in concert with what is being delineated, to underscore the image like a musical background. "The Gorgon," a run-of-the-mill effort in which a despondent man is led through the foggy streets of London to a viewing of the head of Medusa, has these lines of Shelley's as a preface:

> Yet it is less the horror than the grace
> Which turns the gazer's spirit into stone.

It may easily be inferred, from Smith's persistent fascination with archaic settings and the lore of antiquity, that the ancient world was aesthetically preferable to the modern. A rejection of an advancing machine-age culture was intrinsic to some writers of his generation, and the perished beauty and wonder of ancient Greek and Roman civilization engaged him as deeply as all but a few of them. In 1932, he replied to a criticism of science fiction with the statement that "The intolerable conditions of modern life and mechanistic civilization, will, one thinks, be more and more conducive to the development of a literature of imaginative 'escape'" (*PD* 16). This attitude underlies the mockery of tone in such humorously absurd fantasies as "The Weird of Avoosl Wuthoqquan" and "The Seven Geases." He fitfully expressed the disquieting idea that our search for significance, our bland assurance of self-importance or self-control, is an illusion: an uneasy truth, but a common experience in realistic American novels of that era.

Given the facts of Smith's strong preference for poetry, the failure to finish his only novel, and his rationalizing complicity in the continual misprinting of some of his best fiction, it seems unreasonable to say that his prose is as good as his verse.

It is better to assert their unity; the rest is a matter of taste. Smith's adherence to the aesthetic principle, declared by Coleridge and Poe, that exalts imaginative thinking above what is merely fanciful, humorous, or critical, relates his fiction to his poetry. In the words of Shelley:

> Poetry enlarges the circumference of the imagination by replenishing it with thoughts . . . which have the power of attracting and assimilating to their own nature all other thoughts, and which form new intervals and interstices whose void forever craves fresh food. (Shelley 606)

This intersection of poetical themes with weird fantasy is Smith's greatest virtue as a storyteller. His musical style, exotic vocabulary, and genre-spanning variety of story ideas are attributes that contribute, unevenly, to "a literature of imaginative escape." And, as Edgar Allan Poe said of Imagination: "Its materials extend throughout the universe. Even out of deformities it fabricates that beauty which is at once its sole object and its inevitable test."

Works Cited

Altick, Richard D., et al. *A Literary History of England.* 2nd ed. Englewood Cliffs, NJ: Prentice-Hall, 1965.

Behrends, Steve. "An Annotated Chronology of Smith's Fiction." *Crypt of Cthulhu* No. 26 (Hallowmas 1984): 17–23.

———. "The Last Hieroglyphs: Smith's Lost or Unpublished Fiction." *Crypt of Cthulhu* No. 26 (Hallowmas 1984): 9–12.

———. "The Song of the Necromancer: 'Loss' in Clark Ashton Smith's Fiction." *Studies in Weird Fiction* No. 1 (Summer 1986): 3–12.

Collins, Charles M. "Introduction." In *A Feast of Blood.* Ed. Charles M. Collins. New York: Avon, 1965. 9–17.

Dziemianowicz, Stefan. "Into the Woods: The Human Geography of Clark Ashton Smith's Averoigne." *Dark Eidolon* No. 3 (Winter 1993): 2–9.

Lovecraft, H. P. "Supernatural Horror in Literature." In *Dagon and Other Macabre Tales.* Sauk City, WI: Arkham House, 1986.

———. *Selected Letters.* Sauk City, WI: Arkham House, 1965–76. 5 vols.

Marigny, Jean. "Clark Ashton Smith and his World of Fantasy." Trans. S. T. Joshi. *Crypt of Cthulhu* No. 26 (Hallowmas 1984): 3–8.

Shelley, Percy Bysshe. *The Poetical Works of Shelley.* Boston: Houghton Mifflin, 1974.

Smith, Clark Ashton. *The Vaults of Yoh-Vombis.* Edited by Steve Behrends. The Unexpurgated Clark Ashton Smith. West Warwick, RI: Necronomicon Press, 1988.

Gesturing Toward the Infinite: Clark Ashton Smith and Modernism

Scott Connors

When *Current Opinion* reviewed Clark Ashton Smith's first book of poetry, *The Star-Treader and Other Poems* (1912), it began by noting that "The appearance of a new poet ought to be of at least equal importance with the discovery of a new comet. For what have the comets ever done except to frighten us out of our wits in the past with their portents of disaster?" (150). Although Smith's collection was both a critical and financial success, these words were ominously prophetic. When his next major collection appeared, the reviewer for the *San Francisco Examiner* wrote that "A volume more at variance with the spirit of the poetry of today would be hard to conceive of" (20). During the ten-year period between *The Star-Treader* and *Ebony and Crystal* (1922), there occurred changes in American poetry that would greatly affect the artistic and personal fortunes of both Smith and his mentor, George Sterling.

American poetry at the turn of the century was in the grip of what George Santayana called "the genteel tradition," which referred to a perceived split in the nation's psyche:

> America is . . . a country with two mentalities, one a survival of the beliefs and standards of the fathers, the other an expression of the instincts, practice, and discoveries of the younger generations. In all the higher things of the mind—in religion, in literature, in the moral emotions—it is the hereditary spirit that still prevails. . . . The truth is that one-half of the American mind, that not occupied intensely in practical affairs, has remained, I will not say high-and-dry, but slightly becalmed . . . while, alongside in invention and industry and social organization the other half was leaping down a sort of Niagara Rapids. This division may be found symbolized in American architecture . . . The American Will inhabits the skyscraper, the American intellect inhabits the colonial mansion. The one is the sphere of the American man; the other, at least predominantly, of the American woman. The one is all aggressive enterprise; the other is all genteel tradition. ("The Genteel Tradition in American Philosophy" 39–40)

This split, which Santayana attributed to our Calvinist heritage, resulted in a situation where "culture was something reserved and refined for the Sunday people: women, ministers, university professors and the readers of genteel magazines" (Cowley ii). Of these latter, Thomas Benediktsson observed that while the great literary periodicals of the nineteenth century were still regarded as sanctuaries of culture, the editors of these magazines exercised their role as a literary priesthood in a largely proscriptive manner, refusing to publish "anything that could not be read by the women of the family circle" (62). Magazine poetry of the best sort was

> characterized by traditional Romantic motifs of escape, antiquarianism, primitivism, and the supremacy of Beauty. But almost universally Romanticism supplied merely a stance or a choice of subject, because it was subordinated to genteel requirements of refinement, good manners, pleasant didacticism, and sentimentality.... The poets of the close of the century display generous quantities of optimism, conventional piety, and sentiment, but not, unfortunately, of originality or skill. (Benediktsson 62–63)

The most popular poets of this period included the so-called "Fireside Poets:" Henry Wadsworth Longfellow, John Greenleaf Whittier, and James Russell Lowell. Two poets now thought of as among America's best from the nineteenth century, Edgar Poe and Walt Whitman, were not part of the canon, the former being considered too morbid and the latter too earthy.

This is not to say that poetry which did not fit the description outlined in the preceding paragraph was not being written. There is certainly no way in which these lines from Stephen Crane's *War Is Kind* can be termed "optimistic" or "sentimental":

> A man said to the universe:
> "Sir, I exist!"
> "However," replied the universe,
> "The fact has not created in me
> A sense of obligation." (480)

Unfortunately, editors responded in a similar manner when poets not willing to yield to their demands that poetry be uplifting and entertaining submitted work. While naturalist writers such as Frank Norris and Theodore Dreiser might challenge its tenets in prose, the economic facts of life dictated that genteelism would exert a stifling influence over American poetry. This led H. L. Mencken to "sound a revolt against that puerile kittenishness which marks so much of latter day English poetry. Nine-tenths of our living makers and singers it would seem are women, and fully two-thirds of these women are ladies.... Our poets are afraid of passion; the realities of life alarm them..." (166).

In this "twilight interval" one of the few poets to challenge the status quo was George Sterling. Inspired by the critical principles of his friend and mentor, Ambrose Bierce, Sterling would assault the optimistic piety of the times in large part by making use of the discoveries of nineteenth-century science that were both a cause and a by-product of the great change in the nation's character from agrarian republic to industrial democracy. Among the lessons learned from Bierce were a disdain for didacticism, which reduced the poem to a mere moral commonplace, and a belief that while it was the task of the poet to make the reader feel, an excess of sentiment detracted from the sublimity of the poem by making it "too human." When coupled with the scientific materialism of Ernst Haeckel's *The Riddle of the Universe,* which denied the concepts of free will, a personal deity, and the existence of an immortal human soul, Sterling became one of the first practitioners of a literary school later called "Cosmicism" by a writer whose early stories he would later read with some bewilderment, H. P. Lovecraft. This was first evident in *The Testimony of the Suns* (written in 1901–02), but combined with a Schopenhauerian pessimism it would remain with Sterling to some degree until his death in 1926. Consider, for example, the sonnet "To Science," which Sterling apparently never collected:

> And if thou slay Him, shall the ghost not rise?
> Yea! if thou conquer Him thy enemy,
> His specter from the dark shall visit thee—
> Invincible, necessitous and wise,
> The tyrant and mirage of human eyes,
> Exhaled upon the spirit's darkened sea,
> Shares He thy moment of Eternity,
> Thy truth confronted ever with His lies.
>
> Thy banners gleam a little, and are furled;
> Against thy turrets surge His phantoms tow'rs;
> Drugged with His opiates the nations nod,
> Refusing still the beauty of thine hours;
> And fragile is thy tenure of this world
> Still haunted by the monstrous ghost of God.

When Sterling's "A Wine of Wizardry" was published in the Hearst *Cosmopolitan,* among his readers was a youngster from Auburn, California (the subject of Bierce's satire "The Perverted Village") named Clark Ashton Smith. In Smith's words, "In the ruck of magazine verse it was a fire-opal of the Titans in a potato-bin; and, after finding it, I ransacked all available contemporary periodicals for verse by George Sterling, to be rewarded, not too frequently, with some marmoreal sonnet or 'molten golden' lyric" (*SU* 294). Smith soon began to write his own poetry, some of which found professional publication in the *Overland Monthly.* A schoolteacher friend of Clark was personally acquainted with Sterling, and at her encouragement he began a correspondence and a friendship which would last until Sterling's death some fifteen years later.

Sterling soon was acting as Smith's mentor, dropping his name into assorted magazine interviews, arranging for stipends from wealthy friends to assist the penurious Smith family, assisting in the preparation of the manuscript for *The Star-Treader,* and in general extending the favor that Bierce did for him. When Sterling received a request for contributions from a proposed magazine in Chicago, he urged Smith to submit some of his work. Thus it happened that Smith was one of the first contributors to Harriet Monroe's *Poetry: A Magazine of Verse*.

There had been attempts to start a magazine completely devoted to poetry before Monroe launched her magazine, but her success in obtaining financial support from the Chicago business community ensured that *Poetry* would not be reliant upon its subscriptions for its continuance. In her flyer, she outlined three principles that would guide her policy. The first was an assurance that the restrictions imposed upon poets by popular periodicals would not apply, as the assumption was that *Poetry*'s readers actually *wanted* to read poetry! The second was that *Poetry* would publish good poetry regardless of length, character, or style; all schools were welcome. The last, and by no means the least, was that contributors would be paid for their work—only ten dollars a page, but still they would be paid. The December 1912 issue of *Poetry* contained three poems by Sterling, including his sonnets "At the Grand Cañon" and "Kindred," both of which contained elements of Cosmicism, as well as two poems by Smith, "Remembered Light" and "Sorrowing of Winds," both later collected in *Ebony and Crystal*. In the "Notes and Announcements" section of the issue, Monroe described her contributors thus:

> Mr. George Sterling, of Carmel-by-the-Sea, California, is well known to American readers of poetry through his two books of verse, *Wine of Wizardry* and *The House of Orchids*.
> Mr. Clark Ashton Smith, also of California, is a youth whose talent has been acclaimed quite recently by a few newspapers of his own state, and recognized by one or two eastern publications. (99)

The April 1913 issue contained a brief review of *The Star-Treader* in which Monroe found in the young poet "a rare spirit and the promise of poetic art," although she qualified this by observing that it would be "idle to complain that his subjects are chiefly astronomic" and that "Life will bring him down to earth, no doubt, in her usual brusque manner" (31–32). This period of acceptance by the *avant garde* was, however, short-lived. Smith wrote to Sterling that "Miss Monroe of 'Poetry' has just returned a bunch of my late things with a gentle intimation that she doesn't think much of 'em. What do *you* think of that editor and that magazine, by the way? 'Poetry' seems to be getting badder and badder, what with the Whitmanesque Hasidu in the last number" (*SU* 92). Sterling's response was "As to 'Poetry,' I agree with you that it keeps getting worse. Miss Monro [*sic*] has been 'infected' by Ezra Pound, who is rabid for a 'new form,' and she is letting *poetry* go by the board.... If 'Poetry' were not subsidized, it would cease publication in a very few months, as it represents only a clique of no-poets *now*" (Sterling to CAS, 30 July 1913; *SU* 93).

Despite the stated intention that all schools would be welcome in *Poetry*, by 1913 it was obvious that the magazine had been largely taken over by the followers of its London correspondent, Ezra Pound, who called themselves the Imagists. Although Monroe would deny this, in a review of the anthology *Some Imagist Poets* she pointedly mentions that "the finest entries of its six poets ... appeared in this magazine," and notes that "It is pleasing to see so honorable a house as the great Boston firm [Houghton Mifflin] falling into line behind us" (150). Imagism was defined by two essays, by F. S. Flint and Pound, in the March 1913 issue. In the first, Flint admitted that the Imagists were contemporaries of the Post-Impressionists and the Futurists, but denied any common ground with these schools, and insisted that their work drew upon the best classical traditions of Sappho, Catullus, and François Villon. He listed three rules, which Pound went on at length to explain. These were:

1. Direct treatment of the "thing," whether subjective or objective.
2. To use absolutely no word that did not contribute to the presentation.
3. As regarding rhythm: to compose in sequence of the musical phrase, not in sequence of a metronome. (Flint 199)

Pound expounded upon these points, defining an "Image" as "that which presents an intellectual and emotional complex in an instant of time" (200). Elsewhere Pound would differentiate between an "Image" and a "Symbol," holding that the latter was inferior because

> it fixes an existential value in a word and replaces a physical with an intellectual (or mystical) value; the Symbolist then proceeds ... to circulate the substitution term as poetic currency. "The imagiste's images," on the other hand, "have a variable significance, like the signs *a*, *b*, and *c* in algebra," Pound said. The resilience of the image was its ability to resist capture by whatever rhetoric a greedy politician or an incompetent poet might dream up to exploit it. (Barbarese 288–89)

Of course, the "semi-mystical doctrine of the symbol" was "at the centre of the aesthetic theory" of Romanticism, for "within it, a whole set of conflicts which were felt to be insoluble in ordinary life" became reconcilable (Eagleton 19).

Although Smith has often been called a Romantic poet—sometimes even "The last of the great Romantic poets"—he at first resisted the label, feeling perhaps that he was called that more for what he *wasn't* than for what he *was*. He wrote that "I don't think much of Cale Young Rice's classification of modern poets. I'm sick of classification, anyway. . . . He'd call me a 'romanticist,' I suppose. Well, at a pinch, I'd rather be called that than a 'realist'" (*SL* 49). He would later reluctantly accept the label, writing that it was not worth even submitting the manuscript for *Ebony and Crystal* to Henry Holt and Company "if [Robert] Frost is their [poetry] advisor. He would doubtless live up to his name, in respect to romantic poets like myself" (CAS to Sterling, 16 March 1922; *SU* 204).

Unfortunately for Smith and Sterling, Pound's attitude was representative of an emerging intellectual trend that disparaged Romanticism. Besides Pound and the Imagists, other critics of Romanticism included Pound's protégé, T. S. Eliot;

one of Eliot's Harvard professors, Irving Babbitt, who would later be a leader in the New Humanist movement; and the followers of F. R. Leavis and the English critical journal *Scrutiny*, who were also heavily influenced by Eliot's thought. Eliot, perhaps influenced by Babbitt, identified Romanticism with "excess":

> Romanticism stands for *excess* in any direction. It splits up into two directions: escape from the world of fact, and devotion to brute fact. The two great currents of the nineteenth-century—vague emotionalism and the apotheosis of science (realism)—alike spring from Rousseau. (Eliot, *Syllabus of a Course of Six Lectures on Modern French Language*, quoted in Rabate 217)

In "The Function of Criticism," Eliot further equated Romanticism with emotionalism and individualism. He looked back with approval on the time of the Metaphysical poets, such as John Donne, in whom Eliot perceived thought and emotion as existing hand in hand, while blaming on the Romantics a "disassociation of sensibility" which separated thinking and feeling, leading to language being set adrift from experience. In his Harvard doctoral dissertation, *Knowledge and Experience in the Philosophy of F. H. Bradley*, Eliot asserted that "experience comes to us most directly through sensations, which then become associated with feelings and are subsequently worked up into complex emotions. Poetry should affect the reader as directly as a physical sensation" (Materer 53). In "Hamlet and His Problems," Eliot described how this should occur:

> The only way of expressing emotion in the form of art is by finding an "objective correlative"; in other words, a set of objects, a situation, a chain of events which shall be the formula of that *particular* emotion; such that when the external facts, which must terminate in sensory experience, are given, the emotion is immediately evoked. (124–25)

Thus for Eliot a test of how "authentic" a poem was involved "how vividly a poetic emotion seems to arise out of physical sensations or images linked to these sensations" (Materer 53). Smith disputed the reliability of our sensory experiences, writing to H. P. Lovecraft that "the bare truth about the nature of things may be more fantastic than anything any of us have yet cooked up.... Five senses and three dimensions hardly scratch the hither surface of infinitude" (*SL* 229). In a story unpublished in his lifetime, Smith wrote that

> The fact that all so-called sane and normal people, possessed of sight, hearing and the other senses, agreed substantially in their impressions of outward phenomena, might prove only the existence of common flaws or limitations in the sensory apparatus of the species. The thing called reality, perhaps, was merely a communal hallucination; and certainly, as science itself had tended to prove, man could lay claim to no finality of perception. (*SS* 8)

Another story, "A Star-Change," dealt with the revelation of "the conditional nature of our perception of reality" when he is transported to another world where his senses are altered by the inhabitants to withstand local conditions (*SL* 128). Upon his return to his own world, he experiences the earth through his new senses and finds it unbearable. Smith's most famous poem, *The Hashish-Eater*, dealt with what would happen "if the infinite worlds of the cosmos were opened to human vision . . . the visionary would be overwhelmed by horror in the end" (*SL* 366). Smith's position was by no means unique; philosophers such as Descartes, Locke, and Hume all had expressed similar reservations. Hugh Elliot is perhaps the best such example; in *Modern Science and Materialism,* he wrote: "Not only are our senses few, but they are extremely limited in their range" (quoted in Joshi 84). In a letter to the magazine *Wonder Stories,* Smith wrote: "it is partly because of this shifting, unstable ground on which the thing called realism stands, that I regard pure, frank fantasy as a more valid and lasting art-expression of the human mind" (*PD* 21).

Eliot also based his theory of language upon sense perception. His early criticism extolled the "superiority of the precise, clear, and definite" over the "vague, general, and indefinite." Eliot attended Bertrand Russell's course on symbolic logic while a graduate student at Harvard and was tremendously impressed by Russell's theories of language. These were referential theories "where words get their meaning from the objects they refer to and where the primary objects were sensations or 'sense-data'" (Shusterman 36–37). Therefore, language was ultimately related to experience. But, the English language had become "abstract and anemic":

> In really "English" writing, however, language "concretely enacted" such felt experience. . . . This whole notion of language rested upon a naive mimeticism: the theory was that words are somehow healthiest when they approach the condition of things, and thus cease to be words at all. Language is alienated or degenerate unless it is crammed with the physical textures of actual experience, plumped with the rank juices of real life. Armed with this trust in essential Englishness, latinate or verbally disembodied writers (Milton, Shelley) could be shown the door, and pride of place assigned to the "dramatically concrete" . . . (Eagleton 32)

It was for this reason that Harriet Monroe wrote of Sterling's "shameless rhetoric. . . . Already the young poet's brilliant but too facile craftsmanship was tempted by the worse excesses of the Tennysonian tradition: he never *thinks*—he *deems*; he does not *ask*, but *crave*; he is *fain* for this and that; he deals in *emperies* and *auguries* and *antiphons,* in *causal throes* and *lethal voids* . . ." (309). This is also the reason why Marjorie Farber said of Smith's prose style (in a review of *Lost Worlds*): "Another feature of this style is its use of two words in place of one: 'consider or conjecture,' 'speed and celerity of motion.' Why Mr. Smith failed to say a 'mouth of amazing and astounding capacity' I don't know; perhaps he was in a hurry" (26). Smith's response to this was as follows:

> I too was rather amused by the N. Y. Times review; especially by the complacency with which the lady displays her ignorance of the finer shades of meaning in English

words. One might well 'consider' without conjecturing at all; and vice versa. Even her attempt at sarcasm falls down, since 'amazing' is far from synonymous with 'astounding,' the first meaning to perplex or confuse with fear, terror, wonder, etc., and the latter to overwhelm or stun with awe, etc. But of course such nuances are lost on the average reader . . . (CAS to August Derleth, 13 December 1944)

It was in statements such as this that Smith's debt to Ambrose Bierce is most evident. Cathy N. Davidson points out parallels between Bierce's theories and those of another Harvard philosopher, C. S. Peirce, the founder of semiotics. Consider this assessment by Bierce of William Dean Howells:

> The other day in fulfillment of a promise, I took a random page of [Howells's] work and in twenty minutes had marked forty solecisms—instances of the use of words without a sense of their importance or a knowledge of their meaning—the substitution of a word that he did not want for a word that he did not think of. (quoted in Davidson 7–8)

Peirce took an organicist approach to language, as opposed to the referential approach Eliot derived from Russell: he "located meaning in the perceiver and insisted that signs could be understood only with reference to other signs (interpretants) previously held by the perceiver. A whole web of prior signs gives meaning to the new sign and, in addition, becomes the self which interprets new signs" (Davidson 9). Smith told Donald Wandrei about his first reading of Sterling's "A Wine of Wizardry": "I first read it when it appeared in the old 'Cosmopolitan,' about 1907, with an accompanying eulogy by Ambrose Bierce, who ranked it among the greatest imaginative poems in literature" (*SL* 97). Shortly thereafter Bierce published a rebuttal to criticism of Sterling's poem and his own praises of it, "An Insurrection of the Peasantry." One of the criticisms directed against Sterling was his use of "strange, unfamiliar words." Bierce ridiculed these "critics" for their ignorance, because "there are not a half-dozen words in the poem that are not in common use by good authors, and none that any should man should not blush to say that he does not understand" (201). He particularly signaled out for attack those who objected to the lines

> Infernal rubrics, sung to Satan's might,
> Or chanted to the Dragon in his gyre.

After pointing out that it is not the poet's fault if the reader has never heard of a "gyre," Bierce points out that "Gyre means, not a gyration, but the path of a gyration, an orbit. And has the poor man no knowledge of a dragon in the heavens?—the constellation Draco, to which, as to other stars, the magicians of old chanted incantations?" (203). It is not surprising that when Smith quit school his self-education consisted in large part of reading through *Webster's Unabridged Dictionary* and making a study of the meaning of each word and their etymologies.

Smith had an understanding of language which paralleled certain theories held by the Poststructuralists: "Language is far more unstable and mysterious, far more given to radical undecidability, far more elusive than has previously been thought" (Burleson 3). Smith wrote to the poetry journal *Epos* concerning his work that "My prime requisites in poetry are music and magic" (27). As to how he achieved this, he wrote Lovecraft "my own conscious ideal has been to delude the reader into accepting an impossibility, or series of impossibilities, by means of a sort of verbal black magic, in the achievement of which I make use of prose-rhythm, metaphor, simile, tone-color, counter-point, and other stylistic resources, like a sort of incantation" (*SL* 126). A deconstructionist could make much of the fact that an incantation implies both magic and music, ultimately deriving from the Latin *cantare*, to sing. It is precisely for this reason that Smith embraced the use of a Romantic language:

> As to my own employment of an ornate style, using many words of classic origin and exotic color, I can only say that [it] is designed to produce effects of language and rhythm which could not possible be achieved by a vocabulary restricted to what is known as "basic English." As Strachey points out, a style composed largely of words of Anglo-Saxon origin tends to a spondaic rhythm, "which by some mysterious law, reproduces the atmosphere of ordinary life." An atmosphere of remoteness, vastness, mystery and exoticism is more naturally evoked by a style with an admixture of Latinity, lending itself to more varied and sonorous rhythms, as well as to subtler shades, tints and nuances of meaning—all of which, of course, are wasted or worse on the average reader, even if presumably literate. (*SL* 365)

Smith's use of language, in direct opposition to Pound's Imagist aesthetics, is related by Brian Stableford to the French Symbolists, harkening back to Rimbaud:

> [Smith] was a great exponent of the alchemy of words. He used his vocabulary to transform descriptions into incantations directly evoking a sense of the strange, a distortion of attitude and feeling. Smith's prose [and his poetry] is geared to apply to the reader, an experiential wrench or jolt, to permit the relief of 'seeing' words of the imagination—which might have gone stale along with the hopeless world of mundanity—through a new linguistic lens. (239)

In other words, Smith bypassed totally a language grounded in the experience of the senses in favor of one grounded in the imagination.

Eliot's stance on Romanticism was similar to that of his mentor, Irving Babbitt, who came to lead a critical movement called the New Humanists. This movement took Matthew Arnold as its model and attempted to uphold human dignity and moral rectitude, and stressed the human elements of experience over supernatural. The New Humanists attacked Romanticism for its embrace of individualism and emotionalism, and stressed reason and respect for authority. They regarded man as a moral creature, and emphasized the importance of ethics in literature. Babbitt called for writers to "combine ethical insight" with "excellence of form, or . . . high seriousness of substance," and stressed what he called the "ethical imagination—the imagination that has accepted the veto power" as opposed to the limitless imagination of a Shelley or a Sterling (274). To Babbitt literature was most "vital" that was subordinate to the affirmation of "a general nature, a core of normal experience" that was open to most normal people (27)

As can be imagined, Clark Ashton Smith was not at all in agreement with any of the tenets of the New Humanism. He wrote in *The Black Book*, following Bierce, that "Poetry, though its proper concerns are not primarily intellectual, is none the worse for having behind it a keen and firm intelligence. But intelligence alone does not make poetry, as glaringly exemplified by the latter works of T. S. Eliot, which while no doubt profound from a philosophical standpoint, has little or nothing of the bardic magic and mystery; all such elements have been ruthlessly sacrificed, leaving an obscurity which, unlike that of Gérard de Nerval, is devoid of color, glamor, and the allurement of new *imaginative* meanings and analogies which would justify obscurity" (*BB* item 164, emphasis added). We find this reflected in two of his finest stories. "The Double Shadow," the title story of his first short story collection, deals with what Peter Goodrich called "the mutual logocentrism of sorcery and literary art" (220). The sorcerer Avyctes, once the pupil of the Atlantean archmage Malygris, has eschewed the temporal path of his master in favor of a sterile scholasticism. When confronted by an ancient tablet washed ashore after a great storm, they were unable to divine its meaning through their scholarship, resorting to the spirit of a dead shaman to provide "the key to the meaning of the letters" (*OST* 133), although "the symbols and ideas [were] alien" to men (134). The ritual apparently fails, although later they discover a grotesque shadow trailing each of them in turn that remains speechless until it merges with their own shadow, at which time they are in turn absorbed into something rather unpleasant. The story ends with the narrator observing that the shadow is separated from his own by a space "no wider than the thickness of a wizard's pen." The sorcerers failed because ironically they failed to respect the magic inherent in the language: they understood the words, but not the symbols or thoughts behind the words. Even experience fails to provide meaning to the doomed wizards, for after they and the shadow merge the newly formed hybrid remains just as speechless as before. Likewise, in "The City of the Singing Flame," Giles Angarth writes of his experiences in the new dimension he has discovered that "Words are futile to express what I have beheld and experienced" (*RA* 194), except through the intervention of the reader's own imagination, as both Ray Bradbury and Harlan Ellison have testified. In her review of *The Star-Treader* Harriet Monroe said of Smith that "he shows an unusual imaginative power of visualizing these remote splendours until they have the concrete definiteness of a *personal experience* [emphasis added]" (31–32). From a Modernist perspective there was no greater praise.

Surprisingly, George Sterling appeared somewhat receptive to portions of the New Humanist program toward the end of his life, telling Smith "As one grows older, one takes pleasure in writing things that have a vital value, a human relationship, as apart from 'the literature of escape'" (Sterling to CAS, 16 October 1925; *SU* 260). Smith rankled at the charge that imaginative poetry was somehow inferior, replying "I think the current definition or delimitation of what constitutes life is worse than ridiculous. Anything that the human imagination can conceive of becomes thereby a part of life, and poetry such as mine, properly considered, is not an 'escape' but an extension" (*SL* 94). He confessed to Wandrei on 11 November 1926 his frustration with these developments, but clung to the belief that "Romanticism is revolt, the Promethean spirit ever seeking to overthrow the gods of the commonplace—and the marketplace. The latest ruse of the forces of Law and Order is to throw the Romantic-fantastic type of imagery out of court as being 'non-vital.' Even G. S. seems to be 'falling' for this."

After Sterling's death, Smith began to write the great body of his short stories, and found himself under attack in the letter columns of *Wonder Stories* and *Amazing Stories* by readers who objected to the ultra-human nature of his fiction. Smith responded in a series of letters which were really self-contained essays, in which he defended his belief "that there is absolutely no justification for literature unless it serves to release the imagination from the bounds of every-day life" (*SL* 123). When a reader stated that the proper intent of a science fiction story was "to show a cross-section of a man's life, at a point where he is faced with some problem" and to portray "the breakdown or building up of his character, or the way he reacts to the test" (notes to *PD* 81), Smith replied that this definition of literature was "rather narrow and limited," and offered the opposing opinion that "imaginative stories offer a welcome and salutary release from the somewhat oppressive tyranny of the homocentric, and help to correct the deeply introverted, ingrowing values that are fostered by present-day 'humanism' and realistic literature with its unhealthy materialism and earth-bound trend" (*PD* 14). Smith argued that because of the limitations of our sensory apparatus "fantasy of one kind or another is about all that is possible for us" (*PD* 21), and that even so-called "realistic" writers were in fact writing a type of fantasy, since "it is axiomatic that in thought or art we deal not with things themselves, but with concepts of things. . . . The animals alone, being without imagination, have no escape from reality" (*PD* 38–39). By discounting the powers of the imagination, modern writers were in danger of perpetuating a "meaningless Dreiserism, an inartistic heaping of superficial facts or alleged facts, which, after all, through our perceptual limitations, may be erroneous, or, at least, too incomplete to permit the safe drawing of dogmatic inference" (*PD* 21) by "abnegating the one gift that raises man above the other animals" (*PD* 23). Smith saw the role of fantastic literature as leading "the human imagination *outward*, to take it into the vast external cosmos, and *away* from all that introversion and introspection, that morbidly exaggerated prying into one's own vitals—and the vitals of others—which Robinson Jeffers has so aptly symbolized as 'incest'" (*PD* 12). The danger existed that such exaggerated introversion and introspection could lead to a type of hubris or cosmic ethnocentrism, since "it [is] only the damnable, preposterous and pernicious egomania of the race, which refuses to admit anything but man's own feelings, desires, aims and actions as worthy of consideration" (*PD* 16). Because of the anthropocentrism of modern literature, Smith felt that it was desirable "for one genre, at least, to maintain what one might call a centrifugal impetus, to make 'a gesture toward the infinite' rather than toward the human intestines" (*PD* 19). Far from offering an escape from reality, Smith saw ultra-imaginative works of art resulting from "an impulse to penetrate the verities which lie beneath the surface of things; to grapple with, and to dominate, the awful mysteries of mortal existence" (*PD* 33).

Smith was not alone in scorning the lack of cosmic perspective in Modernism. Conrad Aiken took Harriet Monroe and *Poetry* to task for being a traditionalist "ethically and emotionally," and in fact for not being *avant garde* at all:

> The only answer is that Miss Monroe, if she is really a radical at all, is chiefly so as regards form; as regards the material of poetry (and to any genuine well-wisher of poetry this is the important thing), she suffers from many of the curious inhibitions, for the most part moral, which played havoc with the Victorians. The truth must not be told when it is disagreeable or subversive. One's outlook on life must accord with the proprieties. Above all, one should be a somewhat sentimental idealist—anthropocentric, deist, panpsychist, or what not, but never, by any chance, a detached or fearless observer. (390)

When Smith condemned Babbittism and "the 'vital' theory" for being "the old didacticism in a new disguise" (CAS to Wandrei, 13 November 1926), he found himself unknowingly echoing no less a philosopher than George Santayana. In "The Genteel Tradition at Bay," Santayana argued that the program of the New Humanists was nothing more than the old genteel tradition in new dress. In discussing the "appeal to the supernatural" which he saw as forming the ultimate basis for their ethical position, Santayana used language remarkably similar to that used by Smith: "I am far from wishing to deny that the infra-natural exists; that below the superficial order which our senses and science find in the world, or impose upon it, there may not be an intractable region of incalculable accident, chance novelties, or inexplicable collapses." He even recognized that an interest in the "infra-natural . . . positively fascinates some ultra-romantic minds, that detest to be caged even in an indefinite world, if there is any order in it" (171). Ultimately Santayana concluded that Babbitt and the entire New Humanist movement were, to use Lovecraft's description of August Derleth, "self-blinded little earth gazers," because "how shall any detached philosopher believe that the whole universe, which may be infinite, is nothing but an enlarged edition, or an expurgated edition, of human life?" (180).

This desire to transcend the bounds of human existence, more than his use of traditional prosody or Latinate vocabulary, is probably the main reason for Smith's lack of recognition. Other poets such as Edwin Arlington Robinson and Robert Frost employed traditional forms, and Edna St. Vincent Millay also used a difficult Latinate vocabulary. However, none of these poets had any desire to tread the stars. "I am astonished to find how few really grasp the sublimity and vastness of the stars and star-spaces," Smith told Sterling early in their friendship. "One acquaintance did not think such things suitable for poetic treatment, and from the indifference or bewilderment with which most who have seen it regard my cosmic work, I must regard those fitted to understand such things as being very rare" (*SL* 5). Consider the comments of the poet Wittner Bynner on the cosmic elements of Sterling and Smith's poetry: "It is too stellar for me . . . There's too much Aldebaran in it. It gives me cosmic indigestion. Someone at the Bohemian jinks called Sterling and this young poet Clark Ashton Smith the Star Dust Twins" (O'Day 7). Robert Frost's lines concluding "Desert Places" states eloquently the Modernist objection to Cosmicism:

> They cannot scare me with their empty spaces
> Between stars—on stars where no human race is.
> I have it in me so much nearer home
> To scare myself with my own desert places. (296)

As D. W. Harding put it, "For what is unintelligible, the judgment of 'abnormal' is available, serving to insulate the deviant behaviour or opinion, denying it social relevance and excluding it from the network of mutual support and mutual contact that makes up society" (33). The verdict of "deviant" was handed down by those poets and critics who still thought of man in pre-Copernician terms. Nonetheless, Smith refused to bow to fashion: "perhaps I am merely one of those unfortunate and perverse individuals who are constitutionally 'agin the Government.' When fantasy is acclaimed by Irving Babbitt . . . I may take refuge in the writing of case histories!" (*PD* 22) As he so well put it in the title poem of his first collection,

> Who rides a dream, what hand shall stay! (*SP* 11)

Works Cited

Aiken, Conrad. "The Monroe Doctrine in Poetry." *Dial* 62 (3 May 1917): 389–90.

Babbitt, Irving. *Rousseau and Romanticism*. 1919. New York: Meridian, 1955.

Barbarese, J. T. "Ezra Pound's Imagist Aesthetics." In *The Columbia History of American Poetry*, ed. Jay Parini and Brett C. Millier. New York: Columbia University Press, 1993.

Benediktsson, Thomas E. *George Sterling*. Boston: Twayne, 1980.

Bierce, Ambrose. "An Insurrection of the Peasantry." In *The Collected Works of Ambrose Bierce*, Vol. 10. 1912. New York: Gordian Press, 1966

"Boy Publishes More Poems." *San Francisco Examiner* (17 December 1922): 20.

Burleson, Donald R. *Lovecraft: Disturbing the Universe*. Lexington: University Press of Kentucky, 1990.

Cowley, Malcolm. *After the Genteel Tradition*. Carbondale: Southern Illinois University Press, 1964.

Crane, Stephen. Excerpt from *War Is Kind*. In *Three Centuries of American Poetry*, ed. Allen Mandelbaum and Robert D. Richardson, Jr. New York: Bantam, 1999.

Davidson, Cathy N. *The Experimental Fictions of Ambrose Bierce*. Lincoln: University of Nebraska Press, 1984.

Eagleton, Terry. *Literary Theory: An Introduction*. 2nd ed. Minneapolis: University of Minnesota Press, 1996.

Elliot, T. S. *Selected Essays*. New York: Harcourt, Brace, 1950.

Farber, Marjorie. "Atlantis, Xiccarph." *New York Times Book Review* (19 November 1944). Rpt. in *Klarkash-Ton* No. 1 (June 1988): 26–27.

Flint, F. S. "Imagisme." *Poetry* 9 (March 1917): 198–200.

Frost, Robert. *The Poetry of Robert Frost*. Ed. Edward Connery Lathem. New York: Holt, Rinehart & Winston, 1969.

Goodrich, Peter H. "Sorcerous Style: Clark Ashton Smith's *The Double Shadow and Other Fantasies*." *Paradoxa* Nos. 13–14 (1999–2000): 213–25.

Harding, D. W. "The Character of Literature from Blake to Byron." In *From Blake to Byron*, ed. Boris Ford. (The New Pelican Guide to English Literature 5.) London: Penguin, 1976.

Joshi, S. T. *H. P. Lovecraft: The Decline of the West*. Mercer Island: Starmont House, 1990.

Materer, Timothy. "T. S. Eliot's Critical Program." In *The Cambridge Companion to T. S. Eliot*, ed. A. David Moody. Cambridge: Cambridge University Press, 1994.

Mencken, H. L. "The Merediths of Tomorrow." *Smart Set* 33 (April 1911): 161–64.

Monroe, Harriet. "Notes and Announcements." *Poetry* 1 (December 1912): 99.

———. "The Poetry of George Sterling." *Poetry* 7 (March 1916): 307–13.

———. [Review of *The Star-Treader and Other Poems* by Clark Ashton Smith.] *Poetry* 2 (April 1913): 31–32.

———. [Review of *Some Imagist Poets—An Anthology*.] *Poetry* 6 (June 1915): 150–53.

O'Day, Edward F. "Varied Types—XC: Witter Bynner." *Town Talk* (7 September 1912): 7.

Pound, Ezra. "A Few Don't by an Imagiste." *Poetry* 1 (March 1913): 200–206.

Rabate, Jean-Michel. "Tradition and T. S. Eliot." In *The Cambridge Companion to T. S. Eliot*, ed. A. David Moody. Cambridge: Cambridge University Press, 1994.

"Recent Poetry" [review of *The Star-Treader and Other Poems*]. *Current Opinion* 54 (February 1913): 150.

Santayana, George. *The Genteel Tradition*. Ed. Douglas L. Wilson. 1967. Lincoln: University of Nebraska Press, 1998.

Shusterman, Richard. "Eliot as Philosopher." In *The Cambridge Companion to T. S. Eliot*, ed. A. David Moody. Cambridge: Cambridge University Press, 1994.

Smith, Clark Ashton. Letter to August Derleth, 13 December 1944. Ms., August Derleth Papers, State Historical Society of Wisconsin.

———. Letter to "The Poet Speaks." *Epos* 8, No. 1 (Fall 1956): 27.

———. Letter to Donald Wandrei, 11 November 1926. Ms., Donald Wandrei Papers, Minnesota Historical Society.

Stableford, Brian. "Outside the Human Aquarium: The Fantastic Imagination of Clark Ashton Smith." In *American Supernatural Fiction*, ed. Douglas Roillard. New York: Garland, 1996.

Sterling, George. "To Science." In *The Thirst of Satan*. Ed. S. T. Joshi. New York: Hippocampus Press, 2003.

Clark Ashton Smith:
A Note on the Aesthetics of Fantasy

Charles K. Wolfe

Clark Ashton Smith was one of our foremost practitioners of fantasy, but he was also a writer very much aware of exactly what he was doing and why he was doing it. Unlike some of his contemporaries, who all too often saw themselves as entertainers rather than artists, Smith from the very beginning of his writing career saw himself as a serious artist, and saw his work as the realization of a cogent and well-formed aesthetic theory. This essay is an attempt to partially define that aesthetic, at least as it existed for Smith's fiction, and to relate it to the mainstream literary tradition.

During his lifetime Smith wrote well over thirty nonfictional essays of varying lengths. Unlike his friend, H. P. Lovecraft, Smith seldom wrote essays on topics of "general interest," such as cats or geographical locales; nearly every one of Smith's essays deals directly with literature or literary influences. Included among these essays are assessments of George Sterling, Lovecraft, M. R. James, Ambrose Bierce, Poe, William Hope Hodgson, and Donald Wandrei. But the most interesting essays are those in which Smith talks about his own art. Significantly, he never talks much about his poetry in these public essays (though he did frequently in his private letters); his attention is directed almost exclusively to his stories. A possible reason for this is that his short stories were much more public than his poetry; they were being exposed to all manner of reader in the pages of mass circulation magazines like *Wonder Stories* and *Amazing Stories*. With such a wide and occasionally hostile audience, Smith was more inclined to explain his intentions and defend his art.

Since over half of Smith's stories were written and published in the early to mid-1930s, it is not surprising that most of his important critical statements also date from that time. Especially interesting are a series of public debates Smith engaged in through the letter columns of *Wonder Stories, Amazing Stories, Strange Tales,* and the *Fantasy Fan* in 1932–33. Smith came under attack from those who were insisting upon more "realism" in science fiction; psychological realism was in vogue in mainstream literature in the 1930s (with Anderson, Dreiser, and Hemingway setting the pace), and various writers and fans of speculative fiction insisted that the only way by which speculative fiction would ever be accepted as "serious" literature would be for it to adopt more "realistic" modes. Smith perceived that realism was only one tradition, and that romanticism was an equally valid tradition. He rejected the definition that literature was a study of human reactions and character development; he called such a definition "narrow and limited." In the August 1932 issue of *Wonder Stories,* Smith wrote:

> To me, the best, if not the only function of imaginative writing, is to lead the human imagination outward, to take it into the vast external cosmos, and away from all that introversion and introspection, that morbidly exaggerated prying into one's own vitals—and the vitals of others—which Robinson Jeffers has so aptly symbolised as "incest." What we need is less "human interest," in the narrow sense of the term—not more. Physiological—and even psychological analysis—can be largely left to the writers of scientific monographs on such themes. (*PD* 12)

Smith saw the folly of people who equated "realism" with quality in literature; only in the last decade has literature begun to recover from the tyranny of the realism criterion, the assumption that the only function of literature is to tell it "how it is." Smith fought his lonely battle during the height of the realistic movement, in the 1930s; only today is the literary mainstream beginning to appreciate the fact that some writers are not trying to be "realistic," and that reading them requires a different set of standards. Oddly enough, Smith today is quite at home in a contemporary literature in which the most respected writers are neo-romantics like Barth, Borges, Vonnegut, and Hawkes. (The only concession to "realism" Smith made was in regard to writing ability as opposed to intention; he repeatedly insisted on the all-important distinction between realism as a literary school and simple writing ability; he suggests that much of the criticism of speculative fiction launched in the 1930s would be eliminated if writers would simply write better, not in a different mode.)

But to simply say Smith is a "romantic" is hardly enough; the term is hopelessly broad and inclusive, and means a dozen different things. In what specific ways is Smith romantic and not romantic, and according to what standards? We must deal with these questions before we can really come to terms with what Smith was doing in his fiction.

Of course, no one can deny that Smith's prose style is romantic by any definition of the word; the texture, color, sentence structure, and, especially, the vocabulary is in the best tradition of the self-conscious story-teller, always reminding us that we are in the hands of an artist, and what we are reading is indeed art, and reminding us of the difference between the world of art and the everyday world. The recent textual work of Lin Carter and others is showing us just how rich Smith's prose style was; it was richer even than we had imagined, for the editors of the time apparently were quite ruthless in editing his stories. One could, indeed, make a good argument for style being the most important aspect of Smith's art, and that his style is frequently an end in itself. But for the sake of argument, let us artificially divide style from content, and look at some of the structural patterns in Smith's stories: how are they romantic?

If any basic structural pattern emerges from Smith's various stories, it is one of the journey by the hero into some other world, some sort of magic world; it may be via a space voyage, via dimension, via the past, or via a mystic experience. But frequently Smith's heroes must make this journey; they must cross the threshold into some sort of alternative reality. (This term seems better than the term "fantasy world," since "fantasy world" implies an unfair distinction; it implies that the "real" world—the common, recognizable world—is more basic or more important than the other world; Smith would have insisted that both worlds were equally important, were equally "real.") Stories of this sort are multifold; the titles of two Smith collections, *Lost Worlds* and *Other Dimensions,* testify to the pervasiveness of this theme in his work. Perhaps the most centrally significant of these threshold stories is "The City of the Singing Flame," which suggests multiple alternative realities.

In many stories Smith goes out of his way to stress the significance of this threshold; he does this by creating in his readers a feeling of incredible *remoteness* from these alternate realities. A reader is hardly impressed by a threshold to a world very much like his own; thus a successful fantasy, like *Alice in Wonderland,* will strive to make the alternative reality as different as possible from the "control," everyday reality. Smith was fond of manipulating his readers by attempting, through various devices, to "distance" the events of his story from the reader's world. For example, "The End of the Story" is presented through the manuscript of a law student found sometime after 1789; the real plot of the story thus is distanced from us, first, by the fact that it is second-hand, coming in a manuscript, and second, by the fact that the manuscript is removed from us by history. In "The Testament of Athammaus," we have the obviously ancient narrative of a chief headsman in Commoriom, who then tells the story of *his* youth of how Commoriom fell; again, we have two stages of distancing. The story of Commoriom has already become a misty legend to the narrator; and yet the narrator is already remote to us because he is from Hyperborea; the actual story of Commoriom is thus infinitely more remote to us. But Smith did not need to rely on the past in creating a sense of remoteness; he just as easily used space travel and the future. For instance, "The Dweller in the Gulf" contains no less than four "distancing" elements: (1) the Martian setting; (2) the time setting (obviously the future); (3) the antiquity of the cavern into which the party wanders and the antiquity of the Martian surface; and (4) the bizarre descent into the sub-world of Mars. In short, we have an alternative reality within an alternative reality, et al., like a series of Chinese boxes, one within the other. Of course, these distancing devices have been used since the time of Irving and Hawthorne to try to lend an aura of antiquity to relatively recent and commonplace events; but Smith's imagination allowed him to develop this art of distancing to striking perfection. And when it works, his readers are made acutely aware of the alien quality of Smith's other worlds. This is perhaps what Smith meant when he said the function of imaginative literature was to lead the imagination *outward.* (Smith admitted in a 1940 essay, "Planets and Dimensions," published in *Tales of Wonder,* No. 11, that among his science fiction tales, "the majority have dealt either with worlds remote in space or worlds hidden from human perception" [*PD* 56]. This would seem to indicate that Smith used his science fiction stories to illustrate the same basic themes as he developed in his stories of antiquity.)

But what happens to characters who encounter these remote alternative realities? And what is the nature of these realities: are they hostile, beneficent, or what? These complicated questions need longer answers than we can provide here, but one or two points are obvious. We might first note that Smith's basic plot—the hero crossing the threshold into an alternative reality—is closely related to the classic hero myth as traced throughout the ages from primitive myth to folk legend to literature. Joseph Campbell, in *The Hero with a Thousand Faces,* has defined this basic structural pattern or monomyth, as follows: "A hero ventures forth from the world of common day into a region of *supernatural wonder* (italics mine): fabulous forces are there encountered and a decisive victory is won: the hero comes back from this mysterious adventure with the power to bestow boons on his fellow man" (30). Now the first part of this structure fits the stories of Smith well; the hero does go, frequently, from a recognizable world into a world of wonder: the past, a remote planet, another dimension, or even occasionally a dream. But here the pattern breaks down, for in many of Smith's stories, the heroes do not return from their alternative realities. Some of them strive to return, but fail; witness stories like "The Dweller in the Gulf," "The Weird of Avoosl Wuthoqquan," "The Weaver in the Vault," "The Second Interment," or "Master of the Asteroid." Others, like Giles Angarth in "City of the Singing Flame," make it back but are shattered by the experience. A few, like the law student in "The End of the Story," prefer to stay in the alternative reality; the speaker in the poem "Amithaine" says, "who has seen the towers of Amithaine / Shall sleep, and dream of them again" and, in the end, chooses to remain in the romantic dream world, the "fallen kingdoms of romance" (*LO* 109).

Now exactly how romantic is this pattern? On one level, readers of extremely popular writers like Burroughs expect and receive their heroes' return from the alternative reality to the "natural" world; here Smith is writing a different sort of fiction, to be sure. But on a literary level, even with a more abstract definition of romance, it would seem Smith is writing something different. One of the keystones of romanticism as a philosophy is the ability of man to triumph over his environment; Smith's characters seem defeated by their environments, even though the environments are alternative environments created by Smith. In one respect, there's not much difference between Stephen Crane's Maggie being crushed by social and economic forces—a hostile environment—and Smith's heroes being destroyed by the Dweller in the Gulf; in both cases, attempts of the heroes to assert themselves and to escape are futile. (The editors of *Wonder Stories,* incidentally, found the ending of "Dweller" so bitter that they changed it; Smith wrote to a friend, "In the tale as I submitted it, no escape was possible for any of the three earth-men, since the Dweller was filling the whole of the narrow path ahead of them. Bellman met the same fate as the others. . . . The tale is hopelessly ruined . . ., and I am writing a letter of protest to the editor."[1]) Nor is this pessimism simply apparent in Smith's fiction: he often seems quite naturalistic in certain aspects of his critical statements. In a letter he published in *Amazing Stories,* October 1932, Smith protested the view that saw man as the center of the universe; the real thrill of properly done fantastic fiction, he said, "comes from the description of the *ultrahuman* events, forces and scenes, which properly dwarf the terrene actors to comparative insignificance" (*PD* 14). Fantasy should emphasize the non-human or extra-human; "isn't it only the damnable, preposterous and pernicious egomania of the race" (*PD* 16) that insists on realistic fiction? In "The Tale of Macrocosmic Horror," in *Strange Tales,* January 1933, Smith said that in the "tale of highest imaginative horror," "the real actors are the terrible arcanic forces, the esoteric cosmic malignities" (*PD* 18). Thus most of Smith's characters are hopeless pawns in the face of some alternative reality; they seldom assert themselves, and all too often pay the ultimate price for crossing the threshold.

In this respect, then, we can hardly call Smith a romantic. This side of Smith certainly has affinities with someone like Ambrose Bierce (who was a major influence on Smith, though Smith made perfectly clear in private letters—especially one to R. H. Barlow, 19 September 1933—that he never met Bierce), or Kurt Vonnegut, whose notion of human civilization in *Sirens of Titan* would surely have appealed to Smith. The point is that, like most serious writers, Clark Ashton Smith was too complex to be pigeonholed by a single term. He was uniquely himself, and, for me at least, his appeal lies in this uniqueness. But I hope this discussion has shown us that "fantasy' and "romance" are not necessarily synonymous terms, that Smith knew this, articulated it, and illustrated it in his fiction.

Notes

1. CAS to R. H. Barlow, 8 February 1933; ms., JHL.

Works Cited

Campbell, Joseph. *The Hero with a Thousand Faces.* 2nd ed. 1968. Rpt. Princeton: Princeton University Press, 1972.

Fantasy and Decadence in the Work of Clark Ashton Smith

Lauric Guillaud

According to literary critics (Rancy 3), the aesthetic and decadent literary periods extends from 1880 to 1900. We should ask, however, whether this *"fin-de-siècle"* period does not spill over into the twentieth century, blurring the dividing line between them and the next literary movement. While some critics view the decadent period as the end of an era (see Buckley, Houghton), others perceive it as the beginning of the next (see Kermode), or at least as a transitional period (see Gerber). If we consider the evolution of fantastic literature as it continued at the beginning of the twentieth century, we see that the pursuit of escapist literature, with all its usual themes—the unknown, modernity, the "call of the abyss," "elsewhere"—continued well beyond the decadent period. The weariness of modern humankind, and despair at the apparent decline of Western nations, all began to coalesce as the prospect of world conflict loomed on the horizon. The degeneration of the human race was to become a topical literary theme.

The "call of the abyss" is so often present in the genre of fantasy that we may legitimately ask whether fantastic literature is not inherently haunted by the theme of decadence: "pre-decadent" in the case of Edgar Allan Poe and Nathaniel Hawthorne, and "post-decadent" with respect to H. P. Lovecraft, Clark Ashton Smith, and R. E. Howard? What characterizes the "call of the abyss"? A pessimistic conception of existence, an idealization of the past, an exploration of the beyond, a predilection for the macabre, a mythical renewal, the "fatal" nature of women, refined surroundings, and an obsession with snakes ("ophidianism"), are all customary elements in the *fin-de-siècle* decadent literature. Indeed, all these tropes and themes can be found, with variations, in the literature of the 1830s as well as in that of the 1930s; the fantastic is well and truly at home within the decadent literary period.

Lovecraft, Smith, and Howard have several points in common. All three were scholars; even though they were mostly self-taught, they demonstrated precocious talent. They were recluses who hardly ever traveled, and they were contemptuous of the literary set. They all had difficult, often short lives (Howard committed suicide at thirty) and went through depression or serious illness. They had eccentric imaginations, and they delighted in transposing their nightmares onto paper. They were, above all, poets who favored the short story. They were fatalists haunted by the past, who turned to the future, to science fiction, but their panoramic vision of the future was pessimistic. They shared a sensibility for strange, exotic, and macabre things, especially a fascination for the "beyond" in all its spatial and temporal shapes and forms. Finally, all three men were united by a similar intellectual and ludic complicity that led them to elaborate and consolidate Lovecraft's Cthulhu Mythos; ten "Cthulhian" short stories were written by Smith, four by Howard.

Where should we place Clark Ashton Smith in this continuum? And within the genre of fantasy, what is his relationship within the decadent literary movement?

Smith and Howard are often labelled authors of *heroic fantasy*. In the years 1920–30, they created never-never lands; fabulous and wonderful places which owed more to their creators' imaginations than to geographers, more to the Middle Ages than to expansionism, and more to fantasy than to reason. The "lost" continents of Zothique, Commoriom, Cimmeria, and Aquilonia belong to a lost historical period somewhere off the modern map. Science and verisimilitude were abandoned in favor of myth, legend and the impossible; in their work, the imaginary was given free rein.

According to some critics (van Herp 240; de Camp 14), *heroic fantasy* was officially launched in 1880 by William Morris. Morris was fascinated by the Middle Ages, so it is especially in this historical epoch that one must look for the exact source of the genre. Morris led the way with three novels that form the very foundations of heroic fantasy: *The Wood Beyond the World* (1894), *The Well at the World's End* (1896), and *The Water of the Wondrous Isles* (1897), all novels that bridge the gap between medieval courtly novels and the beginnings of the modern heroic fantasy genre (as exemplified in Tolkien's work). The great epics of heroic fantasy grew out of medieval *chansons de geste*, out of Arthurian legend, out of the courtly novel, out of the eighteenth century's *A Thousand and One Nights*. In England, during the Romantic period, diverse currents merged and gave life to the Gothic novel (Walpole's *The Castle of Otranto*, 1764), and the historical novel (Sir Walter Scott's *Waverly*, 1814). Fantastic novels, then, under the influence of the romanticized medieval atmosphere, gave birth to heroic fantasy.

Subsequently, Lord Dunsany's mythology, his use of kingdoms and cities set in an improbable past, appealed to a wider cultural obsession with an imaginary world that offered perspectives on a breathtaking and infinite void. Dunsany's works—*The Gods of Pegāna* (1905), *Time and the Gods* (1906), *The Sword of Welleran* (1908), *A Dreamer's Tales* (1910), *The Book of Wonder* (1912), *The King of Efland's Daughter* (1924)—greatly influenced both Lovecraft and Smith. Among other important precursors to Smith and Lovecraft, we must also cite E. R. Eddison (*The Worm Ouroboros*, 1922) and James Branch Cabell (*Figures of the Earth*, 1921; *The Silver Stallion*, 1926).

From 1919 to 1927, Lovecraft had his own "Dunsanian period" (Burleson 24), during which he created a fantastic, almost Oriental, universe of kingdoms and allegorical or dreamlike cities ("Polaris," "The White Ship," "The Doom That Came to Sarnath"). Such stories as "The Cats of Ulthar," "Celephaïs," "The Quest of Iranon," "The Other Gods," and "The Silver Key" led naturally to *The Dream-Quest of Unknown Kadath* (1926–27), in which he sketched a world of demons inhabiting a land of somnolence.

Smith's and Howard's use of the fantastic also stems from a romantic and lyrical Dunsanian tradition, but the "heroic" dimension emerges from a dark vision of the world, a world doomed to inevitable and contagious degradation. In Smith's oeuvre, as we shall see, the theme of contagion is expressed through an attraction to the macabre, whereas in Howard, the theme of contagion is manifest in an attraction to violence. Like all decadent writers, including Poe, they did not hesitate to shock their readers, and they employed a vision which, in Smith's case, included the darkest, most disgusting views of the world, a world in which the beauty inherent in horror was exposed.

Smith spent practically all his life in Auburn, California. Despite his fierce loyalty to Lovecraft (which was reciprocal; on several occasions Lovecraft voiced his admiration for Smith's work) and Howard, and an obvious inspirational connection with them, Smith distinguished himself from the others through his unique imaginative skills and style. He had a rich range of artistic talents: he wrote several collections of poetry, which the critics compared to those of Chatterton, Rossetti, and Bryant; his paintings shared the same imaginative sources as the symbolist Odilon Redon; and he took up sculpture, drawing his inspiration both from pre-Colombian art and Lovecraft's creations.

Smith's Poetry

After publishing his first collection of poetry, *The Star-Treader* (1912), and following an attack of tuberculosis, Smith developed a nervous depression. The fever during his illness made him delirious and provoked nightmares that the author would later incorporate into his poems and tales, in a manner similar to Lovecraft's.

While Smith's fiction is moderately well known, his poetry (1911–28) is more or less unknown, even in North America. No fewer than twelve collections of his poetry were published in the U.S., seven during his lifetime. Indeed, the man called the "Keats of the Pacific Coast" (Rickard 5) or the "last great Romantic poet" (Sidney-Fryer 1) was the best-known figure of the "West Coast Romantics," a poetry circle that included Ambrose Bierce, George Sterling, and Nora May French. Lovecraft greeted the publication of *Ebony and Crystal* (1922) with much acclaim. In response to one of Smith's poems, he said, "The Hashish-Eater is the greatest imaginative poem in English literature" (Sidney-Fryer 4).

In his collection *Selected Poems* Smith published an English translation of Gérard de Nerval's poem, "El Desdichado":

> The star upon my scutcheon long hath fled,
> A black sun on my luth doth yet remain.[1]

This "black sun" became an obsessive figure of cosmic decline in Smith's work and set the general tone of his poetry. Smith felt he was a "disconsolate prophet," out of place in his own country. He felt that his literary heritage went back as far as the twelfth century, where he found inspiring examples of epic and romance novels, the *chansons de geste*, historical songs, the novels of antiquity, and the *romans de la rose*, not to mention Spenser's *The Faerie Queene*. Smith, like Spenser before him, created works that fused different elements, although it was Smith who created a link between the courtly age and the space age. This synthesis of genres, which led among other things to the creation of the romance genre, was used by Poe (Smith first encountered Poe in 1907), by Swinburne, and by the other practitioners within the decadent period, including George Sterling, whose poetry already presaged the "discovery" of *Zothique:*

> Then, wave to wave in deeper anthems roared,
> And realm by realm, the belted sunset soared,
> As tho' a city of the Titans burned
> In lands below the sea-line, undiscerned,
> Till desolation touched it, zone by zone,
> Its splendors gone, like jewels turned to stone,
> And sad with evening sang the ocean-choirs,
> Doomed by the stars' imperishable fires.
> (George Sterling, "Duandon," 135)

The image of the decline of the "city of the Titans" was taken up by Smith in his sonnet "The City of the Titans," in which he developed Sterling's ideas in a more metaphysical manner, with a melancholy figure that prefigured the author's future lost continents:

> I saw a city in a lonely land:
> Foursquare, it fronted upon gulfs of fire;
> Behind, the night of Erebus hung entire;
> And deserts gloomed or glimmered on each hand.
>
> Sunken it seemed, past any star or sun,
> Yet strong with bastion, proud with tower and dome:
> An archetypal, Titan-builded Rome,
> Dread, thunder-named, the seat of gods foredone.
>
> Outreaching time, beyond destruction based,
> Immensely piled upon the prostrate waste
> And cinctured with insuperable deeps,
>
> The city dreamed in darkness evermore,
> Pregnant with crypts of terrible strange lore
> And doom-fraught arsenals in lampless keeps.
> ("The City of the Titans," 1911, *SP* 58–59)

Smith's later collection, *Ebony and Crystal* (1922), marked a new creative phase. The "romance" previously to be found in his earlier work was gradually transposed from the medieval world to futuristic worlds, in which we encounter evidence of an inability to live in the present, but as a consequence, a diffuse feeling of fascination and fear when faced with cosmic otherness.

> Beyond the far Cathayan wall,
> A thousand leagues athwart the sky,
> The scarlet stars and morning die,
> The gilded moons and sunsets fall. [. . .]
>
> Ere love and beauty both grew old
> And wonder and romance were flown
> On irised wings to worlds unknown,
> To stars of undiscovered gold.
>
> And I their alien worlds would know,
> And follow past the lonely wall
> Where gilded moons and sunsets fall,
> As in a song of long ago.
> ("Beyond the Great Wall," *LO* 93)

In the context of his hyperawareness of and fascination with entropy, Smith sought desperately to find once more the lost world of his youth, of love, and of beauty.

> Voices of love and the autumn sun,
> In my heart ye are one!
> Fairer the petals that fall,
> Dearer the beauty that dies
> And the pyres of autumn burning,
> Than a thousand springs returning . . .
> O, perishing love that call
> In my heart and the hollow skies!
> ("Chant of Autumn," *SP* 126)

The "cosmic troubadour," as Sidney-Fryer calls him (13), attempted to rediscover fragments of worlds and beauty that lay outside the ineluctable decay of the universe. Adventure remained possible, but paradoxically, only where the quest was without hope. An infinity of worlds remained to be discovered, yet the heavens seemed hollow. Faced with decay and destruction, the poet must attempt to restore a lost sense of wonder by fusing tradition with modernity, the classic with the futuristic, the sublime with the horrific.

> Whatever alien fruits and changeling faces
> And pleasures of mutable perfume

> The flambeaux of the senses shall illume
> Amid the night-furled labyrinthine spaces, [. . .]
>
> Yea, for the lover of lost pagan things,
> No vintage grown in islands unascended
> Shall quite supplant the old Bacchantic urn,
> No mouth that new, Canopic suns make splendid
> Content the mouth of sealed rememberings
> Where still the nymph's uncleaving kisses burn.
> ("Avowal," 1938, *SP* 403)

In his poetry, Smith can be seen as the depository of the sacred flame of romanticism and as a prophet of the apocalypse, as a seeker after purity and as the bard of degradation. Admittedly these contradictions would seem to place him close to *fin-de-siècle* aesthetics, if alongside these contradictions we did not find another Clark Ashton Smith. But we do find another. And this second side can be seen most clearly in his use of the extravagant and archaic worlds of heroic fantasy; moreover, his pessimistic future-oriented cosmology underscores Smith's creative originality.

His fantastic poems paved the way for his lyrical tales, which we may regard as authentic prose poems. The end of "The Memnons of the Night" (1915) can be read as a genuine poem:

> Only at eve, when the west is like a brazen furnace, and the faroff mountains smoulder like ruddy gold in the depth of the heated heavens—only at eve, when the east grows infinite and vague, and the shadows of the waste are one with the increasing shadow of the night—then, and then only, from the sullen throats of stone, a music rings to the bronze horizon, a strong, sombre music, strange and sonorous, like the singing of black stars, or a litany of gods that invoke oblivion; a music that thrills the desert to its heart of stone, and trembles in the granite of forgotten tombs, till the last echoes of its jubilation, terrible as the trumpets of doom, are one with the black silence of infinity. (*NU* 8–9)

These prose poems, in which we see the influence of Baudelaire, Gautier, and other French Symbolists, draw to a close, more often than not, upon themes of irreversible decline and tragic oblivion ("the black silence of infinity") and with the recurrent images of the sands of time and the twilight sun (cf. "From the Crypts of Memory" and "The Shadows").

The spectacular and visual side of Smith's art[2] also surfaced in two other forms of expression, namely sculpture and painting. In Smith's mind, the three art forms were complementary and responded synesthetically to one another; a sonnet was able to inspire a sculpture, a painting could act as the source of a story. Insofar as it was poetic and wild, extravagant and refined, Smith's art reflected the contradictions which lay inside him.

Smith's Tales

In their own way, Lovecraft and Smith conform to the principles of "aesthetic fiction" set out by Oscar Wilde in "The Decay of Lying,"[3] while at the same time adding a note of cosmic horror to such principles. For Smith, literature had to strive toward transcendence and the sublime.

During an eight-year period (1929–37), Smith wrote more than a hundred of the one hundred and forty tales he eventually produced. The majority were published in *Weird Tales*. They were probably published on Lovecraft's recommendation, to whom Smith felt so close that he christened certain of his tales with titles that are resolutely Lovecraftian: "The Hunters from Beyond," "The Treader of the Dust," "The Light from Beyond," "From the Crypts of Memory," and "The Dweller in the Gulf."

"Evaluating" both the short stories and the author is a challenge (Bleiler, *Science Fiction Writers* 1.458). Certain tales are set in the past, others in the future, certain take place on earth, others are set on a variety of planets. Throughout his tales, the author favors exoticism and esoteric milieux and situations, and a quest for forgotten worlds. Above all, he strove to be original:

> Tell me many tales, O benign maleficent daemon, but tell me none that I have ever heard or have even dreamt of otherwise than obscurely or infrequently. . . . Tell me many tales, but let them be of things that are past the lore of legend and of which there are no myths in our world or any adjoining. . . . Tell me tales of inconceivable fear and unimaginable love, in orbs whereto our sun is a nameless star, or unto which its rays have never reached. ("To the Daemon," *NU* 17–18)

This desire to cut himself free from external supports says a great deal about the author's fundamental creativity, and it also reveals Smith's profound knowledge of mythology and of literature in general.

The decadent aspects of Smith's universe, found especially in the universe of "Zothique," the importance of the *femme fatale*, of mythology, of lost civilizations, as well as an unflagging interest in the archaic in all its forms can be connected with a *fin-de-siècle* aesthetic vision. Moreover, as a reflection of his "onomastic curiosity" (the "science" of proper nouns, especially the names of people, an obsession worthy of Lord Dunsany and Flaubert), Smith also possessed his *gueuloir*—his collection of rare names of incantatory and exotic charm—Xeethra, Morthylla, Maâl Dweb, Naat, Ylourgne, etc.

Smith's tales provide in themselves an anthology of decadent themes: black magic ("The Last Incantation," "A Rendezvous in Averoigne"), the theme of body doubles ("The Double Shadow"), fascination with ruins ("The Primal City"), Faustian pacts ("Xeethra"), cursed love potions ("A Vintage from Atlantis"), a taste for jewels ("The Weird of Avoosl Wuthoqquan"), the theme of despoilment ("The Tale of Satampra Zeiros"), metamorphosis ("The Maze of the Enchanter"), threatening vegetation ("A Voyage to Sfanomoë"), the cult of antiquity ("The Satyr," "The Gorgon"), *femmes fatales* ("The Ghoul," "Morthylla," "Sadastor"), vampires ("The Flower-Women"), and the omnipresence of snakes: snake-men in "The Double Shadow" or in "The Seven Geases," and snake-women in "The End of the Story" or "The Gorgon," and giant worms found in "A Tale of Sir John Maundeville" and in "The Coming of the White Worm."

The macabre, the first stage of all decadent literature, dominates Smith's literary production. At the heart of this output shines the obscure star of death which is associated with the obsessive metaphor of physical decomposition. Decay in general is linked to the past, which recalls Henry James's famous phrase, "the monstrous heritage of antiquity" (James 115). Paradoxically, Smith's obsession with death was expressed, as in Poe, through ideas of a physical afterlife (the Poe-like theme of premature burial: "The Second Interment"), and through the idea of fatal return ("The Resurrection of the Rattlesnake"), themes that opened the door to the fantastic genre. Black magic enabled Smith's characters to struggle against death and presented the reader with a profusion of "live contamination," examples of supernatural milieux as well.

As with a number of other decadent authors, Smith's fantasy production, which allied life and death, depicted the existence of an autonomous life-form in the midst of decomposition. Mummies shake off their lethargy in "The Double Shadow" or in "Necromancy in Naat," gods or witches from the past are brought back to life in "The Charnel God" or in "The Witchcraft of Ulua," and corpses refuse to die or to decompose in "The Testament of Athammaus" or in "The Supernumerary Corpse."

Occasionally, the art of illusion enables the author to play with death. In "The Death of Malygris" (1934), two magicians come across the corpse of Malygris. Just when they decide to steal his magic ring, they are attacked by a viper, which is suddenly transformed into a gigantic python; from beyond the grave, Malygris continues to exercise his magic. When his rival creates an exact replica of the archmagus in order to be able to decompose a kind of protoplasmic golem, the two thieves are eaten alive.

In the tradition of Stevenson, Poe, and Wilde, the concept of body doubles is resolutely attached to the themes of dissolution and decomposition. In "The Double Shadow" (c. 1933), for example, some necromancers send the shadow of a corpse back into the past in order to unravel the enigma of a "primitive continent" populated by snake-men. The consequences of their acts, however, are tragic. One of the magi suddenly finds himself wearing a second shadow that eventually contaminates him. There then follows an elaboration of putrescence and decay that rivals Poe. As in the previous story, the complete identification of the shadow with the magician's flesh causes the dissolution of the magician's body. The terrified narrator entrusts the last anguished message of a doomed continent to drift away on a wave. This example is typical of the contagion which links the dissolution of the individual with the contagion of a city or continent.

Smith's *Hyperborean* world became the favored site to the threat of perpetual falling and being swallowed. Such a threat was expressed in various isomorphic forms. In "The Seven Geases" (1934), Lord Ralibar, who is the victim of a curse, has to sacrifice himself to the terrible god Tsathoggua. He has to venture into the center of the earth in order to go through seven stages which correspond to seven curses. A classic *regressus ad uterum* leads him to relive the world's past inside an extinct volcano which is home to the "Cave of Archetypes."

Smith's imagination creates an underground universe of infernal creatures straight out of Bosch's paintings, such as "monstrous one-legged toads," "huge worms with multiple segments," and "deformed lizards." Hell is depicted in its medieval form, in the manner adopted by Gustave Doré in his illustrations for Dante's *Inferno*: "a sort of pool with a margin of mud that was marled with obscene offal," "the ultimate source of all miscreation and abomination" (*RA* 147). The final phase of the quest—the seventh stage—proves to be fatal for Ralibar Vooz, who succumbs to the Queen spider's web and falls into a bottomless void.

The same tragic end awaits Avoosl, "the richest and most avaricious moneylender in all Commoriom," in "The Weird of Avoosl Wuthoqquan" (1932). In a grotto which has a "muddy and foul-smelling floor," the usurer discovers a deep well full of jewels to which he is irresistibly drawn. He is terrified as he realizes that he is sinking into his treasure, as if he were in "treacherous sinking sands." At the same time, from the depths of the well a toad-like monster surges up and swallows him (*RA* 130). The usurer's punishment takes on an ironic and unusual dimension as the author uses a grotesque monster, evocative of the most repulsive pagan divinity, to convey a moralistic, almost Christian, message.

The most horrible of punishments cannot be avoided, yet death can sometimes play tricks on us. In "The Testament of Athammaus" (1932), the narrator recounts the successive transformations of someone sentenced to death, who nevertheless survives all of the execution attempts inflicted upon him, and who changes his appearance and embarks on a series of monstrous adventures. After various decapitations, the man's body becomes snakelike and swells disproportionately. The mass starts "frothing as with the venomous foam of a million serpents," becomes a "round, blackish ball" and eventually changes into a "python-shaped mass of frothing and hissing matter" (*OST* 275–76)—a gigantic creature reminiscent of the shoggoths found in Lovecraft's *At the Mountains of Madness*.

In "The Tale of Satampra Zeiros" (1929), two thieves penetrate the temple that houses the tomb of the Cthulhian god Tsathoggua. Suddenly, a "viscous and semi-liquescent substance" gushes out from the base of the statue giving off putrid flames which form a misshapen creature with an "immense mouth" and a sort of "tapering tail." The thing devours one of the thieves and severs the other's hand with one of its tentacles (*RA* 163).

Smith was obsessed with the image of "devouring evil" which is linked to the theme of darkness. Following G. Durand's analysis, it would be easy to highlight a "mutilation complex" in Smith's work which is linked to symbols of the abyss and the mouth, which, in turn, reveals "terror before the change and before the devouring death."[4] The grotesque figure of the batrachian god Tsathoggua, a lunar animal *par excellence,* and the various spiderlike and octopuslike creatures, refer to the image of the "Terrible Mother, an ogre that sexual taboos have strengthened."[5] The frequent images of swallowing and of biting reinforce the cannibalistic terror linked to femininity. Hyperborea is likened to a kind of feminoid mouth, a *vagina dentata* which threatens to swallow everything, even to gobble herself up. The *femme fatale* could thus be associated with the image of the "fatal continent": the "White Sybil" predicts the unavoidable advent of the "white death" that devours the mythic lands in an ultimate mutilation.

Alongside this morbid chain of events could be added the sadistic theme of torture. Indeed, in "The Isle of the Torturers" or in "The Chain of Aforgomon," we are given a detailed catalogue of various types of tortures, which equal those created by Poe or Kafka: red-hot chains, bodies flayed alive, brainwashing, asphyxia, acid burns, snake bites, eyelids torn away. In "The Empire of the Necromancers" (1932), one of the most original forms of torture consists in coupling with a corpse. Eros gets married with Thanatos in an atmosphere of clinical and grotesque horror, as in "The Ninth Skeleton," where we witness the birth of a "baby skeleton." Indeed, to attempt to resuscitate one's beloved or to bring back from the grave an exquisite divinity is a fatal transgression. In "The Last Incantation," the necromancer, Malygris, wishes to recover his beloved from the dead in order to contemplate her original beauty. When the ghost appears, the magician fails to recognize the young girl who has haunted his memories. His "evanescent hopes" are dashed. All that remains is "shadow, dullness and dust" and the burden of a sense of "torment that nothing would ever cure." Malygris thus utters his "last incantation," which serves to send the spectre back into the void from whence it came. He becomes aware of the limits of his own magical powers: he is incapable of recovering his lost youth or the distant yearnings of his heart.

Smith, ever faithful to the first principles of decadence, sometimes created a mixture of drugs, sex, and oriental mysticism that produced an orgiastic atmosphere. His vampiric tales were said to be "the most erotic of fantastic literature" (*Cahier Zothique,* 7). Smith salted some of his tales with scenes of necrophilia ("The Death of Ilalotha," "The Epiphany of Death"), and he delighted in evoking the portrait of *femmes fatales* ("The Disinterment of Venus"), and of fascinating pagan goddesses who are ghouls, lamias, or gorgons ("The End of the Story," "Sadastor," "Morthylla"), ready to swallow their prey; the "Muse of Hyperborea" was a kind of mermaid who drew the narrator irresistibly to his death in a last fatal union with her.

This fatal intertwining reflects images of vegetal growth, whose characteristic snakelike movements convey the threat of a lethal embrace. The themes of vegetal invasion, of the decay and proliferation of the "green darkness" lay at the center of

Ella d'Arcy's short story "The Villa Lucienne": "The ground was covered with lichens, deathstool, and a spongy moss exuding water beneath the foot, and one had the consciousness that the whole place, floor, wall and roof, must creep with the repulsive, slimy, running life which pullulates in dark and solitary places" (d'Arcy 265). We might also refer to "The Moonslave" (1901) by Oscar Wilde, where sprawling vegetation was synonymous with latent horror, or to Lord Dunsany's tales, "The Dream of King Karna-Vootra" (1915) and *The Blessing of Pan* (1927), which evoked the silent threat represented by proliferating plants that were transformed into snake-shaped arabesques. These references, which stem from the decadent movement, highlighted a source of inspiration which Smith preserved.

In "A Voyage to Sfanomoë" (1931), two brothers from Atlantis are impotent witnesses to the geological process which pulls Atlantis down to the depths of the ocean. After having flown forward several decades, they discover on Sfanomoë (Venus) an extraterrestrial floral world composed of "virgin primeval landscapes." However, this paradise quickly becomes hellish when the two brothers are absorbed by Sfanomoë's luxuriant flora. Thus, the last two inhabitants of Atlantis meet their end, and are "the first (and last) humans to have set foot on Sfanomoë's soil" (*RA* 119). Likewise, the "Venus of Azombeii" (c. 1931) turns out to be fatal for its discoverer and gives the impression that the Venusian star shines with malefic properties. The apparent intoxication and voluptuousness, which were deceptive signs of a "springtime feast for the intoxication of the senses," give way to the "lady of destinies" and to the "queen of spells," who are figures which evoke cannibalistic femininity.

Extraterrestrial feminoid vegetation was continuously associated with death in Smith's work, whether in "The Flower-Women" (1935), or in "The Demon of the Flower" (1933), in which Smith transformed the image of a delicious garden into a demon's lair.

All these *fin-de-siècle* themes are energized by an author whose ambition transcended time and space. Smith was a poet of the past and the future, he transformed the genre of heroic fantasy by situating the romantic tradition in science fiction, and, in the process, produced a variation that provoked a sense of sublime disorientation and a feeling that humanity had been surpassed. Admittedly, the omnipresence of the macabre makes the tagging of the label of "decadent fantasy" seem more appropriate when applied to Smith's work, whereas the expression "heroic fantasy" finds its full embodiment in, for example, the work of Howard.

Compared to Howard's "Hyborian" world, however, Smith's universe appears to be more personal. It is composed of enclosed, impenetrable worlds, which are organized according to their own internal sense of coherence, their individual cultures, their unique gods. Smith's lost continents, located outside any particular historical perspective, are governed by the most extreme sense of "otherness." The human race seems insignificant and appears to be doomed to collapse, beneath the gaze of indifferent gods. The theme of decadence henceforth becomes universal.

Smith's Cycles

Whether Smith sought exoticism in a city, a country, or a planet, each quest was followed by a period of delusion, which, in turn, led to a period of decline in his work. The shadow of the dying sun was emblematic of Smith's extraterrestrial cycle ("Sfanomoë," "The Dweller in the Gulf," "The Plutonian Drug," etc.). Smith's dreamlike cities were symbols of beauty and of disenchantment. The evocation of the "jewel-city" in Lord Dunsany's "The City on Mallington Moor" (1916) prefigured the quest found in "Xeethra," which ended in "dust and dearth" (*RA* 364). While the dreamlike city only belongs to the select few, for other people, a sense of loss produces a taste of ash.

In Smith's "The City of the Singing Flame" (1931), everything became insignificant, and even "literature was nothing more than shadow" (*RA* 194)—a perception that probably represented the climax of terror for Smith. The conclusion of this "trans-dimensional" voyage takes place in the ruins of a mysterious city. The protagonists are left with the option of returning to our world, but their souls have been contaminated by death's breath and their hearts are laden with a feeling of eternal regret. Death is imminent for one of the protagonists, who is about to be crushed by a monolith, and the quest terminates in dire misfortune, while the reader is left to wonder if the chaos and devastation that have swept down upon Ydmos will not soon strike his own world.

This short story provides a useful example of Smith's tormented tone, which he perhaps borrowed from Dunsany's "decorative nightmares." For each person's individual mystic experience, there corresponds the cosmic threat of "universal night." In "Where the Tides Ebb and Flow," Dunsany referred to the "glamour of calamity" (Rancy 129), a tale in which we can identify the essence of the decadent movement, and yet a tale in which the sombre romanticism of "dead cities"—Zaccarath, Babbulkund, Perdóndaris, Bethmoora, etc.—was exalted. Feelings of ecstasy provoked by contemplating flight gives way to feelings of impending cataclysm; and the quest for the "center" leads to the discovery of the apocalypse. Smith's protagonists observe a world encircled by darkness, an image which reflects the agony of the sun in the futuristic world of Zothique.

In "The City of the Singing Flame" we are shown a future war which takes place in the "rubble of destroyed worlds," or we are shown a "hideous wave" which rises up from a "wall of darkness," or we are told about "acts of self-sacrifice" by the inhabitants of Ydmos whose bodies are "burnt to cinders." When we add Smith's repeated references to the city of "Babel"—a symbol of tyranny and confusion, a city associated with the idea of punishment for a collective fault—to this parallel world, this distant world suddenly becomes more real (*RA* 187).

The doors that lead to infinity do indeed conceal certain threats. The hallucinating traveler in "The Light from Beyond" (1933) attains "spheres ulterior and superior," apprehends "the colossal, shadowy god that still towered above the stars" and skims over "the utmost heavens and nether gulfs beyond the suns" (*LW* 387), but he is finally threatened with destruction. The hero of "The Eternal World" (c. 1930), who was likewise projected "beyond time," discovers the Babel-like world of the "Immortals" which is soon menaced by a reign of chaos. As Jean Marigny says, "the lands of dream become very soon lands of nightmare" (Marigny 10). In "The Primal City" (1934), the explorers are literally plucked from the ground by monstrous clouds which are the guardians of this cursed Babel.

The three concepts of transgression, punishment and fatality can be mapped onto the idea of inexorable cycles which consign the human world to inescapable decay. The cycle of transgression, punishment and fatality explain the gloomy tone of certain prose-poems such as "The Passing of Aphrodite" and "The Memnons of the Night," all of which depict decadent worlds wherein resounds the "litany of gods that invoke oblivion" (*NU* 9). In such universes, humankind is alone, nostalgic and lost in a lost world. The land is in agony while the sun grows dark, "as if it has been shielded by a huge, invisible mass." The world rushes headlong into oblivion, an image that concludes the poem "The Shadows" (1922).

All this points naturally to "The Dark Age" (1938), a tale which is set in the distant future after the disappearance of civilization. A laboratory that serves as the stronghold of knowledge is isolated in the midst of lands that have returned to barbaric practices.[6] The bastions of civilization are besieged by monsters. The world will become lost in the "cosmic night."

Smith's pessimism is unabashedly unfurled throughout his literary cycles (Poseidonis, Hyperborea, Zothique), where the author emphasizes the downward and decadent part of the cyclic journey. He is clearly less interested in the historical apogee than in the return to nothingness. The Poseidonis tales hinge on the idea of an implacable punishment that must be inflicted upon Atlantis. This idea gave rise to the following observations: Poseidonis is the "last" Atlantis; and the "last" magician, who will utter the "last" invocation, lives on this island. This "primal" land, which will be home to the elaboration of a forbidden science, is doomed to be the "last" land, a land with no hope of salvation.

Fatality permeates Smith's tales. Indeed, in "A Vintage of Atlantis" (1933), the inhabitants of the world are "ghosts," a "black night" floats above the sea, and the city vanishes into thin air. When the narrator eventually comes to his senses, his companions have all disappeared, having been snatched up by the past.

The slightest transgression of the laws of the past results in extreme punishment, namely, liquefaction, decay or disappearance. In "An Offering to the Moon" (c. 1930), two archeologists' "bodies and souls" vanish into the past. Smith's waning Atlantean worlds are closely associated with the concepts of decomposition and disintegration. In them we see that Smith recapitulates Plato's morally decadent universe. In Plato's *Critias*, the people of Atlantis have gradually lost the love of wisdom and virtue; their divine nature is diluted; they have become greedy, corrupt, and domineering.[7]

Smith's tormenting obsession with deterioration is not only moral but physical and clinical to the point of necrophilia. This morbid tendency could be perceived as a sign of despair in Smith's work if we did not also see in it the desire to emphasize the immortality of lost knowledge, knowledge that continues to flourish even though continents have been swallowed up; nothing ever dies entirely, a concept illustrated symbolically through the recurrent ophidian figure (Malygris's snake, the snake-men of Mu, lunar goddesses), which is metamorphic and therefore immortal. Yet is this reminder sufficient to erase the impression of uneasiness that stems from Smith's Atlantean worlds? Nothing is less certain. The author does not manage to eclipse the feeling of morbidity that prevails in his work. Smith's imagination is too firmly anchored in a world of darkness, as is the case for his friends and fellow authors Howard and Lovecraft.

Contrary to the positive Greek version of Hyperborea, Smith's version conjures up a genuine dreamlike *topos* in which we find a teeming species of threatening creatures, and where fearsome and extremely knowledgeable magicians hatch evil plots. The "White Sybil" predicts that Hyperborea and Commoriom, whose capitals are linked to the polar ice sheets, will meet with disastrous consequences. Two plagues will devour the land; the first scourge, depicted in "The Testament of Athammaus," will force the population of Commoriom to flee their land in anticipation of a huge iceslide that threatens the whole continent with destruction in "The Ice-Demon."

The color white, which is associated both with the dying world of Hyperborea and with the priestess who announces the catastrophe, takes on the negative value of that color. The "White Sybil" is in fact a "divine illusion," and behind the virginal whiteness lies the piercing bite of a fatal frost. After having seduced her prey, however, she transforms herself into an ice demon ("a frozen corpse," "a leper-white mummy") and disintegrates (*AY* 70).

This image of the lethal bite lies at the heart of Smith's imagination. In "The Coming of the White Worm" (1941), the feeling of repulsion at the idea of the cold takes on an ophidian nature, and we find close associations between the theme of the giant worm, the all-engulfing ice, and the threatening nature of whiteness. The same idea is developed in "The Ice-Demon" (1933): a mountain of ice is assimilated to a monster who tears apart its victims and then swallows them. Once more, the "whiteness of death" is tainted black, as a gigantic, "prickly" mass engulfs the horizon and floats toward us in a threatening fashion.

Zothique, the "continent of the end of time," is set in a hypothetical future, eons distant. Smith depicts an enclosed world in which the enchanter has got the better of enchantment, where death takes precedence over life. If we take exoticism (ex-zothique) to mean the exterior expression of an interior ritual, an expression fueled by memory, then we must invent another word, following the author's lead, that will exemplify the decadent and obsessive otherness of the dreamlike future world of Zothique, which is threatened by a veritable apocalypse. If we consider that the "lost world" is often synonymous with the "last world," then Zothique represents the last terrestrial continent. Zothique, which is enclosed on itself, in a non-historical and non-chronological space and time, also represents an eschatological dimension associated with the image of the dying sun. Indeed, Smith articulates a poetic unity of lost, evanescent lands that languish under the rays of a dying sun.

From the first verse of his poem "Zothique," Smith throws the reader into the dark beyond and announces the general melancholic tone which pervades his cycle:

> He who has trod the shadows of Zothique
> And looked upon the coal-red sun oblique,
> Henceforth returns to no anterior land,
> But haunts a latter coast
> Where cities crumble in the black sea-sand
> And dead gods drink the brine. (*LO* 112)

It is clear that this world has only been given a brief reprieve, a world where the sun is about to die, where kingdoms are decadent and gods perish. The expression "sea-sand" refers to two plagues which eat slowly away at Zothique, namely that of the pitiless sea that has already swallowed up all the other continents, and the desert sand that progressively covers the populated lands like an hourglass, an image that conveys the fatal passing of time and marks the end of a cycle. This movement is accentuated by the darkness of the universe, a darkness linked to the magic and sorcery that are prevalent in a declining world.

The necromancer's magic, which attempts to curb, at least temporarily, the natural balance of things, is the sole recourse against this decline. But is this powerful magic illusory? "The Empire of the Necromancers" (1932) would seem to indicate "yes." A general wind of decrepitude is exhaled over this world, both as concerns the characters individually (death of the protagonists), and the universe itself (progressive extinction of the continent). Two necromancers run off into the desert of Cincor, which is an arid, leprous, and grey region burned by a sun of glowing embers, home to the devastated city of Yethlyreom, a city whose inhabitants are skeletons and mummies.

The only empire possible is the empire of the dead. Consequently, sorcerers set about the blasphemous job of bringing the forgotten city's population back to life in order to have the city thereafter at their mercy. However, in accordance with an ancient prophecy, one of the living dead, Illeiro, discovers in one of the city's underground passages the key that opens the gates of hell. Passing through these gates will allow the dead to return to the obliterating depths that death offers. As for the mutilated corpses of Mmatmuor and Sodosma, they will seek "vainly through the black maze of nether vaults the door that was locked by Illeiro" (*RA* 325). In this dark universe, the only glimmer of hope is to find a second liberating death.

Death is always on the horizon, and because it is feared and imagined so intensely, in the end it is almost welcomed as a comforting alternative. In "The Isle of the Torturers" (1933), the "silver death" which sweeps over the population living in the south of Zothique, is reminiscent of the tragic effects of the "white death" (icy cold, instantaneous rigidity, whitening of bodies) found in Hyperborea.

Thanks to necromancy, the worlds of the living and the dead are no longer in opposition; however, the fusing of the two worlds is only artificial, and death always triumphs, as in "Necromancy in Naat" (1935). The possibility of securing happiness on Zothique turns out to be illusory, all the more so since the gods multiply the number of traps that are set in order to thwart humankind's vigilance. Indeed, the short story "Xeethra" (1934) serves as proof. In a world without landmarks, one can only become lost. Yet is it correct to assume that Smith's universe is really barren of any hope?

The Eternal Return

The best way of bringing a cycle to a close is to lead the reader to believe in the eternal recurrence of things. "A Vintage from Atlantis" or "An Offering to the Moon" show that the pasts of lost continents continue to contaminate both the present and the future, wreaking havoc and spreading evil, to such an extent that the mythical lands threaten to swallow up reckless travelers in a sort of "posthistoric" vengeance.

The esoteric dimension of Smith's obsession with cycles is demonstrated in at least two of his short stories written during the 1930s—"Ubbo-Sathla" and "The Last Hieroglyph." In the epigraph to "Ubbo-Sathla," we find an excerpt from the *Book of Eibon*, which serves to set the terrifying and solemn tone to the tale:

> For Ubbo-Sathla is *the source and the end*. Before the coming of Zothaqquah or Yok-Zothoth or Kthulhut from the stars, Ubbo-Sathla dwelt in the steaming fens of the new-made Earth: a mass without head or members, spawning the gray, formless efts of the prime and the grisly prototypes of terrene life.... And all of earthly life, it is told, shall go back at last through *the great circle of time* to Ubbo-Sathla. (*OST* 291; italics added)

Smith's pantheon swells to the point of incorporating the "Cthulhoid" divinities penned by Lovecraft. This act of homage to the master of the genre also serves to underline the cosmic and threatening nature of forgotten gods, whether they be found among the stars or in the depths of the Earth. What matters above all is the periodicity of these divine apparitions, as it symbolizes another decadent theme, namely the notion of cyclical time (Rancy 185).

Paul Tregardis, the hero of "Ubbo-Sathla," who is attracted by the mysterious light given off from a crystal heart, undergoes a process of "duality" and then reidentification, which leads him to embark on a regressive quest in search of his origins. He ends up returning, in the same vein as a character from Arthur Machen, to the alluvium from whence he came.⁸ He has the impression of having decayed beyond space and time and of having voyaged through the successive cycles which separate him from the "Beginning." He relives countless lives and dies a "myriad of deaths." In a process which can be called "monstrous degeneration," he travels back in time, over several eras of Hyperborea's long cycles. "Death becomes birth and birth becomes death." Tregardis is subjected to a variety of involutions common to the ophidian trope (pterodactyl→behemoth→snake-man) before he rejoins the original marshy mire in which lies the shapeless mass of Ubbo-Sathla, the sire of "archetypes of earthly life" and the guardian of supreme knowledge. The hero has disappeared into the "grey beginnings of the Earth," but his "forgotten search" has revealed to him the ultimate mystery of the origins of the Earth. "Becoming a shapeless eft of the prime, it crawled sluggishly and obliviously across the fallen tablets of the gods"—this recalls the extraterrestrial monolith in Clarke's and Kubrick's *2001: A Space Odyssey*—before becoming once again what he was in 1933. In this way, the eternal circumference of the evolution of humankind is recapitulated.

In the same way that the "Cave of Archetypes" (cf. "The Seven Geases") lies at the center of the Earth, so do we find "Ubbo-Sathla" the shapeless creative mass of the "archetypes of terrestrial life" at the center of time and space. In "The Light from Beyond," we find "superior spheres" and "bottomless abysses," and in "The Eternal World," we witness the presence of "Immortal beings." These fantastic visions of the eternal return do not correspond to the disparaged contemplation of the Wheel of Time that can be seen to emanate from King Kull in R. E. Howard's short story "The Mirrors of Tuzun Thune," for instance. Hyperborea takes on the garb of Kronos, an ogre who devours humanity, which serves to explain the reason for the numerous images of swallowing that occur in this cycle where the author's morbid poetry runs rampant.

The author's irony culminates in "The Last Hieroglyph" (1935), unveiling the ultimate aim of existence. This aim consists of being made into hieroglyphics and thus being tidied and filed in the great book belonging to the gods, a supreme indication of universal memory or a form of oblivion. Thus, we could conclude, by referring to the familiar pessimistic tone of Smith's work, that everything is reduced to death and emptiness, had the author not himself given his short story a significant epigraph. In the end, the world itself will be designated by a "circular monogramme." Hence, Zothique's ancient prophecy casts a different light on the cycle, for the "circular monogramme," which symbolizes the world in agony, plots the familiar curve of the great periodic return. The author's emphasis on astrology in this tale is not accidental, for it serves to remind us of Smith's cyclical conception of things and stresses the disappearance and reappearance of humanity.⁹

This esoteric short story enables us to better understand the concept of fate (which permeates some science fiction tales, such as "The Letter from Mohaun Los," c. 1935). For at the end of a journey through time, the hero of the aforementioned short story concludes that "Perhaps we shall follow the *great circle of time*, till the years and aeons without number have returned upon themselves once more, and *the past is made a sequel to the future!*" (*LW* 365; italics added).

This futuristic cycle of events can be put into perspective by considering the apocalyptic works that treated the theme of "empty lands" at the end of the nineteenth century and the beginning of the twentieth. Zothique's ailing sun is a reference to the decaying sun found in *Fragment d'histoire future* (1896) by Gabriel Tarde, or a reference to the reddish sun depicted in Wells's story *The Time Machine* (1895). Despite the cyclical turn taken by the "Last Hieroglyph," the dark and pessimistic tone that envelopes the kingdom of Zothique enables us to liken Smith's world vision to the tragic vision of the universe that pervades Wells's work. We could suggest that, following the example of Howard and Lovecraft, Smith plots the graph of eternal return in an anguished and tormented style. The unhappy continents of Poseidonis and Hyperborea have been swallowed up by the same cyclical destiny that gnaws away at Zothique's condemned shores. Despite the initial inscription in the book of the gods, once the "last continent" has yielded to the biting effect of time, a "last hieroglyph," burnt by the sun, will remain, and will one day be discovered by a new human race. Thus the theme of oblivion, which genuinely seems to torment the artist, will relinquish its place to the memory of the writing, which remains the only pathetic hope available for life here below.

Conclusion

Smith's unique exotic and poetic vision, the notion of a universe "queerer than we can imagine," contributed a new mythological framework to modern fantasy. In Smith's world, the amoral flourish and the good are the victims of ironic fates. In "The Maze of Maâl Dweb" and "The Demon in the Flower," the protagonists ultimately fail to rescue their lovers. Smith's fatalistic vision can only generate a decadent sort of fantasy—*unheroic* fantasy?—in which gloom, tomb, and doom prevail.

Smith's fascination with morbidity must be analyzed within the context of the entire body of his work, which reveals, as it does in Howard's and Lovecraft's work, a constant obsession with portraying the struggle against time. People as well as continents appear to be threatened with extinction in Smith's universe. His art, which portrays quasi-surrealistic worlds reminiscent of the work of Bosch or Dali, can thus be located on the boundaries of time and space. Smith can be considered one of the great demiurges of the imaginary, equaling the fantastic production of writers at the end of the previous century. But throughout his work, even when the nadir of horror had been plumbed, the beauty of the poetry remains. One of his last tales, "Phoenix" (1954), expresses both the notions of the sublime and despair, in which humanity strives to reignite a dying sun. Since Smith can be situated in the tradition of "phantasmagorical romantic" writers (Bleiler, *Science Fiction Writers*

2.139), we are better able to understand Lovecraft's tribute to Smith, written two months before Lovecraft's death:

> . . . here, apart, dwells one whose hands have wrought
> Whose graven runes in tones of dread have taught
> What things beyond the star-gulfs lurk and leer.
> Dark Lord of Averoigne whose windows stare
> On pits of dream no other gaze could bear! (Lovecraft 81)

The artist's individual combat against time also corresponds to the *Zeitgeist* of a world that, since Paul Valéry, had been aware of the fact of the "mortality of our civilizations." Even though Smith's sombre romantic tendencies were rooted in the remote past, he used the *fin-de-siècle* themes as a pretext for renewing the fantastic genre and expressing a general fear of decline. Smith, on the eve of the outbreak of the second world war, realized, in much the same way that W. H. Hodgson did while lying in the bottom of a trench in 1918, that civilization had fatally transformed itself into a "Night Land."

Notes

1. "Je suis le Tenebreux,—le Veuf,—l'Inconsolè, / Le prince d'Aquitaine à la Tour abolie: / Ma seule Etoile est morte,—et mon luth constelle / Porte le *Soleil noir de la Mélancolie.*" (Gérard de Nerval 177.)

2. See especially the work of Dennis Rickard (*Fantastic Art of Clark Ashton Smith*).

3. Wilde concluded his essay on "The Decay of Lying" with a pathetic appeal to aesthetic invention: "Out of the sea will rise Behemoth and Leviathan, and sail around the high-pooped galleys, as they do in the delightful maps of those ages when books on geography were actually readable. Dragons will wander about waste places, and the phoenix will soar from her nest of fire. We shall lay our hands on the basilisk, and see the jewel in the toad's head. Champing his gilded oats, the Hippogriff will stand in our stalls, and over our heads will float the Blue Bird, singing of beautiful and impossible things, that are not and that should be" (Wilde 930).

4. "La terreur devant le changement et devant la mort dévorante" (Durand 95).

5. "Mère Terrible, ogresse que vient fortifier l'interdit sexuel" (Durand 113).

6. This allegory might refer to Hodgson's apocalyptic novel, *The Night Land* (1912).

7. "Zeus, the god of gods, who rules by law, and is able to see into such things, perceiving that an honorable race was in a most wretched state, wanted to punish them that they might be chastened and improve" (Plato, quoted in Stemman 18).

8. "By the power of that Sabbath wine, a few grains of white powder thrown into a glass of water, the house of life was driven asunder and the human trinity dissolved, and the worm which never dies, that which lies sleeping within us all, was made tangible and an external thing, and clothed with a garment of flesh" (Machen 228).

9. Mircea Eliade provides us with some historical examples in his book *Le Mythe de l'éternel retour.*

Works Cited

Bleiler, E. F. *The Guide to Supernatural Fiction*. Kent, OH: Kent State University Press, 1983.

———, ed. *Science Fiction Writers*. New York: Charles Scribner's Sons, 1982.

Buckley, J. H. *The Victorian Temper*. New York: Vintage, 1964.

Burleson, Donald R. *H. P. Lovecraft: A Critical Study*. Westport, CT: Greenwood Press, 1983.

d'Arcy, Ella. "Two Stories." *Yellow Book* 10 (July 1896).

de Camp, L. Sprague. *Literary Swordsmen and Sorcerers*. Sauk City, WI: Arkham House, 1976.

Dunsany, Lord. "The Dream of King Karna-Vootra." In *Fifty-one Tales*. London: Elkin Mathews, 1915.

———. *The Blessing of Pan*. London: Putnam, 1927.

Durand, G. *Les Structures anthropologiques de l'imaginaire*. Paris: Bordas, 1979.

Eliade, Mircea. *Le Mythe de l'éternel retour*. Paris: Gallimard, 1969.

Gérard de Nerval. "El Desdichado." *Les Chimères*, in *Aurelia*. Paris: Livre de Poche, 1990.

Gerber, Helmut E. "The Nineties: Beginning, End or Transition?" In *Edwardians and Late Victorians*, ed. Richard Ellmann. New York: Columbia University Press, 1960.

———. *The English Short Story in Transition 1880–1920*. New York: Pegasus, 1967.

Hodgson, William Hope. *The House on the Borderland*. 1908. New York: Carroll & Graf, 1983.

Houghton, Walter Edwards. *The Victorian Frame of Mind*. New Haven: Yale University Press, 1957.

James, Henry. "The Last of the Valerii." In *The Complete Tales of Henry James*. Ed. Leon Edel. Philadelphia: J. B. Lippincott Co., 1962, 89–122.

Kermode, Frank. *Romantic Image*. London: Routledge & Kegan Paul, 1957.

Lovecraft, H. P. *The Ancient Track: Complete Poetical Works*. Ed. S. T. Joshi. San Francisco: Night Shade, 2001.

Machen, Arthur. "The Novel of the White Powder." In *Tales of Horror and the Supernatural*. New York: Pinnacle, 1983.

Marigny, Jean. "L'Univers Fantastique de C. A. Smith." *Cahier-Zothique*, ed. Jean-Luc Buard. Maurepas: Presses d'Ananké, 1985.

Rancy, Catherine. *Fantastique et Décadence en Angleterre, 1890–1914*. Paris: Editions du CNRS, 1982.

Rickard, Dennis. *The Fantastic Art of Clark Ashton Smith*. Baltimore: Mirage Press, 1973.

Stemman, Roy. *Atlantis and the Lost Lands*. Garden City, NY: Doubleday, 1977.

Sidney-Fryer, Donald. *The Last of the Great Romantic Poets*. Albuquerque, NM: Silver Scarab Press, 1973.

Van Herp, Jacques. *Panorama de la science-fiction.* Verviers, Belgium: Gérard, 1973.
Wilde, Oscar. *Works.* London: Collins, 1948.

Humor in Hyperspace:
Smith's Uses of Satire

John Kipling Hitz

Satire, in my opinion, contrary to that of my friend Benj. De Casseres, is far from being the highest form of art. As Lovecraft once remarked in a letter, if one laughs too persistently at things, it might come to seem that they were worth laughing at. (*SL* 222)

Many of Clark Ashton Smith's finest stories were essentially evocations of cosmic fantasy with a bent for the macabre, but at least an equal number of them are powerful treatments of the supernatural with a highly stylized development of weird atmosphere. To varying degrees, these "straight weirds" also rely upon ironic contrast, the grotesque, and mordant humor to intensify mood, although the limited use of humor is more overt in the imaginative flights through space and time for which he is best known.

One of the most remarkable aspects of his long-lost novelette, "The Red World of Polaris," is its satire. The characterization of Captain Volmar as a vainglorious space-jock lends a mock-epic tone to this mingling of science-fiction and horror concepts. Distinctly better than the two previous entries in a short-lived series of tongue-in-cheek space exploration fantasies, it mixes satirical humor with the usual light banter between Volmar and the crew of the spaceship *Alcyone* (the name refers to the daughter of *Aeolus*, guardian of the winds, who aroused the wrath of Zeus by her audacity). There is some question as to whether this humor was also, as I believe, meant to soften the horror element, or if it is solely an expression of Smith's contempt for the social conformity fostered by a machine-age culture, as represented by the alien *Tloong* race, which has thwarted death by transferring their brains *en masse* into artificial bodies of perdurable metal. Without question, social criticism is a salient feature. Witness the scene just prior to the imaginative *tour-de-force* detailing the cataclysmic destruction of the red world, when Volmar's crew is told of their captor's decision to surgically dispose of their bodies:

> The Koum (said the Tloong) had decreed that incorruptible metal bodies should be made for the visitors, that their brains should be transferred to these bodies, and that they should remain permanently in the red world. In time, it was hoped, by virtue of their ensuing immortality and long contact with the supremely civilized people of this world, they might develop into beings of a high order of intelligence. Through motives of benignity, as well as curiosity regarding the biological result, the Koum

had decided upon this experiment when he first beheld the earthlings (*RWP* 101).

The humorous confusion apparent in each race's perception of the other, particularly the reference to the Tloongs as "people," serves to emphasize imagery loosely associated with the *grotesque*, a term defined as "a decorative style in which animal, human, and vegetable forms are interwoven and deformed to the point of absurdity" (*EOL* 495). The "half-vegetable, half-animal" *Murms* that eventually annihilate the Tloongs represent Smith's ultimate mockery of the kind of formulaic interplanetary fiction offered by pulps like *Wonder Stories*, which rejected the story on the basis of an editorial policy that insisted upon "a play of human motives, with alien worlds for a background" (*SL* 134). Introducing the book that incredibly featured its premiere appearance, seventy-three years after it was written, Ronald S. Hilger and Scott Connors quoted from a letter to Donald Wandrei, in which Smith eccentrically declared his disdain for the sci-fi pulps: "If I proffer any 'sops to Mammon and hoi polloi,' they'll have a squirt of hydrocyanic acid concealed in them, in the form of satire. It would delight me to 'put over' that sort of thing" (*RWP* 2). Since the Murms are subterranean creatures, "whose life-habit was one of perpetual feeding and pullulation" (100), Smith's pride in the tale's apocalyptic imagery, a sort of one-upmanship of repetitious pulp-fiction scenarios, is proof both of his satirical intentions and what Connors and Hilger referred to as his "higher aspirations for the series" (2). The Tloongs' scientific culture and "the infinite grotesqueries which they devised and created" (98) are the central attributes of the fantasy, but my concern here is with its melding of satire and *humor noir*, a term I first want to discuss in a more general context.

Eliciting smirks and grimaces rather than smiles and grins, *humor noir* (black humor) is "marked by the use of morbid, ironic, or grotesquely comic episodes that ridicule human folly" (*EOL* 144). Neither Poe nor Bierce used such humor in quite the same way that Smith uses it. Two unique features of his work are the cosmic point of view with which it is informed and the eclectic vocabulary that characterizes his prose style. Rather than following the burlesque mode as Poe did, or mounting an aggressive satirical attack like Bierce, his satirical forays are more closely related to his cosmicism. Whether he subscribed to the view of Poe as "a misunderstood writer creating twisted and bizarre humorous pieces" in order to reconcile "his two opposing visions of the world" (Stauffer 1) is a question of peripheral interest to Smith studies, just as Baudelaire's suggestion that Poe's death was a suicide is of only marginal relevance to Poe studies . But we can see the use of *humor noir* as integral to Smith's satirical or semi-satirical pieces, as well as his somewhat atrabilious dramatization of sexual contretemps in "The Holiness of Azédarac," "The Witchcraft of Ulua," "The Satyr," and several other tales. Smith also enjoyed tipping his hat to Poe, and to a lesser extent, Lovecraft. A close reading of even so minor a story as "The Supernumerary Corpse" will disclose that the romantically frustrated narrator (Felton Margrave) is a parody of Montresor, the narrator of Poe's "The Cask of Amontillado," and the central situation, involving two identical corpses of a murder victim—the one buried, the other supernaturally defying Margrave's attempt to get rid of it—is bleakly comical. However, Smith's sardonic sense of humor is apt to make us think not of Poe, but of his fellow Californian, Ambrose Bierce. "The Ninth Skeleton" and "The Phantoms of the Fire" suggest an early influence, but perhaps only "The Resurrection of the Rattlesnake," as Smith put it, "owes something to Bierce" (*SL* 109).

What is striking about the passage quoted from "The Red World of Polaris" is the clear implication that the Koum, like other potentates in Smith's fantasies, is vain and delusional, like so many of our career politicians and their supporters. The Koum's edict supposedly confers the boon of "incorruptible metal bodies" upon the humans, yet previously the narrative relates that "the tower of the Koum was invaded throughout its underground vaults; and some of the Murms had almost reached the royal presence before they were destroyed" (*RWP* 99). Here Smith is injecting the narrative with a dose of pathos, to show the inevitable result of the Tloongs' technology-dependent existence. Their demise is caused by their own obsession with biological research. Some of the Tloong scientists toy with death, creating strange hybrids that rapidly reproduce, and then eradicating them, until the fatal creation of those "half-vegetable, half-animal" Murms by one biologist whose zeal for experimentation exceeds all rational limits, like H. G. Wells's Dr. Moreau. In a conclusion that fulfills Smith's vow to Wandrei about concealing the "hydrocyanic acid" of satire in his science fiction, these products of deranged science kill their creators by eating through their metallic craniums and devouring their huge brains.

Smith's satirizing of the Tloongs' pride in their science and technology showcases his keen sense of irony, with word-play that simultaneously blurs the very distinctions being made while dropping hints of the aliens' appalling fate. The bodyguards of the magisterial Koum are "cyclopean-headed" (102), signifying not only a greater fund of knowledge, but also a narrowness of vision. The adjectives "Babelian" and "Atlantean" describe the sky-cleaving towers and vast terraces of Tloong architecture, and on one of his guided tours, Volmar sees the construction of a tower from desert sands integrated into "ever rising walls and floors, like Ilion rising to the music of Apollo" (100). These allusions to mythical and historical sites where architectural marvels were brought to nothing anticipate the tale's superb climax, in which "planetary paroxysms of doom and destruction" (106), are described with a panoramic intensity rivalling Smith's best science-fiction story, "The City of the Singing Flame." The Tloongs have evaded death psychologically and physically by becoming literally wrapped up in themselves. When an alarm warns of the deadly recrudescence of the ravenous Murms, their "four-eyed" surgeons, clutching "formidable knives and saws" are sent into a panic reminiscent of the doomed revelers in "The Masque of the Red Death." We are left with a rear-view mirror vision of the dying planet, and the reflection that, as beings housed in robes of flesh, humans may be less vulnerable to the creeping insanity that overtakes the intellectual Tloongs, but in our ignorance we are no less dangerous to ourselves.

A Freudian interpretation of Smith's humor as a form of displaced aggression is certainly plausible, especially considering the scorn heaped upon authoritarian figures (or the self-blinded values they represent) in wildly imaginative works such as "The Last Hieroglyph," "The Seven Geases," "The Door to Saturn," and "The Planet Entity"—the latter a being whose relation to mankind is "like a god in comparison with insects" (*TSS* 149). Of course, it is hard to see how else humanity could be regarded from the vantage of the omniscient consciousness portrayed in that story. Smith's lighter moments are more often than not a blending of Balzacian drollery with black humor, presumably because a sustained approach to satire wasn't market-friendly in the 1930s. Consider what happens when Domitian Malgraff and Li Wong, his housekeeper and valet, "escape from the machine-ridden era" (*LW* 329) of the twentieth century in Malgraff's time-machine, in "The Letter From Mohaun Los." Reaching the surface of a planet, their senses are assaulted by an astonishing variety of weirdly commingled plant, vegetable, insect, and animal forms, some of the latter "in varying stages of decomposition," and spawning "huge, pale, flabby leaves with violet veinings in which I seemed to detect the arterial throb of sluggish pulses" (*LW* 336). Other disturbing visions follow, yet after this surrealistic rendering of grotesque horror, Smith indulges in levity:

> "Me no likee this." He shook his head gravely as he spoke. "Can't say that I care much for it, either," I returned. "Considered as a hiding place, this particular planet leaves a good deal to be desired. I fear we'll have to go on for a few more million or trillion years, and try our luck elsewhere." (*LW* 338)

Here both fantasy and satire are sublimated by mere frivolity; nevertheless, the satire and the cosmic imagery are mutually supportive. Cosmicism involves a deliberate suggestion of "concepts vast and mysterious" and an emphasis on "startling, unearthly imagery" (Behrends 12). Smith's tales so frequently aim for this effect (as do his paintings and stone carvings) that astute readers will discern why Bierce wasn't cited as an influence in a 1949 autobiographical letter to Samuel J. Sackett (*SL* 359–62). He theorized that weird fiction properly deals with "man's relationship—past, present, and future—to the unknown and infinite" (*BB* 82). A manifesto, stressing the artistic vitality of cosmicism and proving that the poet did not regard the art of prose composition as less challenging than verse. In this he was affirmed by Lovecraft, whose first letter to Smith enthused about his ability to conjure "abysses of infinity and elder time" in the 1922 poetry collection *Ebony and Crystal*. The aesthetics of the weird tale is very relevant to the subject at hand because it accounts for the Juvenalian humor in the Hyperborea series—fantasies set in a mythical prehistoric realm of the far north, doomed by the coming of the Ice Age (this generally refers to the Pleistocene Epoch though there were other ice ages even more remote in time). Naturally, we find humor to a greater or lesser extent depending on the setting, but it would be a mistake to view the Hyperborean tales as less serious or effective weird fiction than the tales of Zothique on this basis alone. While the sardonic tone of the Hyperborea series is suited to the time-lost setting for the tales, that setting itself is grounded in Smith's pessimistic *Weltanschauung*, and the series as a whole represents his most cogent indictment of the coarseness, stupidity, and credulous vanity of the human animal. The "Rabelaisian rogues and scoundrels" within these tales, most of which, as he told August Derleth, "were written in a vein of grotesque humor" (Murray 8) have names like "Veezi Phenquor," "Hoom Feethos," "Ralibar Vooz," and "Avoosl Wuthoqquan," all suggestive of the unctuous sleaziness of their possessors. Driven by greed or the desire for notoriety, they receive their comeuppance through encounters with forces "vast and mysterious," which do not submit to man's attempts to know them. The attitude conveyed, albeit obliquely, accords with the sad but true observations of de Tocqueville:

> In Europe, people talk a great deal about the wilds of America, but the Americans themselves never talk about them; they are insensible to the wonders of inanimate nature and they may be said not to perceive the mighty forests that surround them till they fall beneath the hatchet. Their eyes are fixed upon another sight . . . they . . . march across these wilds, draining swamps, turning the course of rivers, peopling solitudes, and subduing nature. (557)

Smith bemoans this mindless consumerism in a few of his letters, even wistfully expressing a desire to move to the East Indies (*SL* 292). Distanced from the mainstream and contemporary movements in art and culture at-large, he used humor at strategic moments in his stories to manipulate the sense of distance between his fantasy worlds and the familiar world of the reader's experience. In the macabre fiction that he preferred writing, *verisimilitude*, defined as "the semblance of reality in dramatic or nondramatic fiction" (*EOL* 1162) must be established. Smith pushed the envelope by asking readers to accept temporarily the idea of an *alternative reality*, instead of the *extension of reality* sought by Lovecraft. In other words, he encourages us to adopt an aesthetic attitude. That is one reason why he "unleashes his wide and esoteric vocabulary without restraint" (Joshi 504), for as Terry Heller observed, "In order to be pleased by terror, they [readers] must exercise . . . all those faculties which are necessary for the arts of reading and understanding" (47). Heller quotes Edward Bullough on the necessity of reducing *narrative distance* in fiction: "What is, therefore, both in appreciation and production most desirable is the *utmost decrease of distance without its disappearance*" (43).

"Mother of Toads," from the series placed in the imaginary medieval French province of Averoigne, exemplifies how *humor noir*, which basically attempts to disorient and upset the reader, may also serve to *reduce* narrative distance. The controversial temptation scene describing the grossly fat body of the witch, Antoinette, is unsettling because it forces us into a receptive attitude, even as the narrative switches from the sensual to the psychological at that point ("This time he did not draw away. . . ."). We would feel disgusted with ourselves if we were much titillated by its explicit eroticism because of the earlier description of her voice, eyes, throat, breasts and hands as hideously "batrachian" (*MOT* 9). So we reestablish our distance, our uneasiness negotiating the tension between the real and the unreal, making Pierre Baudin's dramatic drowning in marshy waters by a crushing multitude of frogs more terrifying—especially the final sentence's confirmation of our fear that the witch is not merely a repulsively fat woman, but an inhuman changeling as well.

The best of Smith's purely comical stories are "The Weird of Avoosl Wuthoqquan," wherein a deceitful money-lender is served his just desserts by a cave-dwelling monster hoarding a mountainous pile of gems, and "The Great God Awto," a very clever piece of satire that envisages how the architectural relics of our car-loving culture could be misinterpreted by sixtieth-century anthropologists. A few others, notably "Schizoid Creator" and "Symposium of the Gorgon," are slight farces. The former toys with Gnosticism's concept of the *demiurge*, a secondary deity who originated evil and was sometimes identified with the Jehovah of the Bible. It may have been conceived as a jocular tribute to his friend E. Hoffmann Price's story, "The Stranger from Kurdistan" (*Weird Tales*, July 1925). Each focuses on the personification of good and evil. Smith's ill-fated protagonist, Dr. Carlos Moreno, is obsessed with the idea that God and Satan are the twin personas of one and the same deity. Standing in an occult protective circle robed in black, ritualistic knife and specially modified hazelwood staff in hand, with metallic sigils attached to his chest and forehead, he determines to conjure and cure the schizophrenic godhead, or die trying. But psychiatrists make delusional demonologists, for Moreno only manages to capture the demon Bifrons, and compounds his error by assuming that Bifrons is the real deal (Satan). The demon, piqued at the interruption of an "amorous dalliance with the she-imp Foti" (*TSS* 215), pretends to be cured after enduring an elaborate form of shock therapy: "You have restored Me to My Divinity, O wise and beneficent doctor. Pronounce the formula of release and let Me go. Hell is henceforth abolished, together with all evil, sin and disease. The Devil is dead. God alone exists. And God is good" (218). Overconfident of success, Moreno complies, whereupon Bifrons trashes his makeshift laboratory, leaving the human in a state of gibbering lunacy. Predictably, the ending confirms Moreno's theory, as Satan, exiting by "the small postern door of Hell," transforms into his holy alter ego and steps "across the sill into Heaven" (221).

The first-person narrator of "Symposium of the Gorgon" is transported to the ancient palace of the Gorgons after a night of heavy drinking. Written late in the author's life, its best moment is a speech by the mythological winged horse, Pegasus, who, "neighing in excellent Greek," refuses to carry the drunkard back to his point of origin, the New York of the twentieth century:

> I cannot visit the century, and, in particular, the country, that you name. Any

poets who are born there must do without me—must hoist themselves to inspiration by their own bootstraps, rather than the steed of the Muses. If I ventured to land there, I should be impounded at once and my wings clipped. Later they would sell me for horse meat. (*TSS* 225–26)

Smith is simply reaffirming his disgust with the drabness of most modern poetry, and reflecting upon his youthful disappointment with the changing tastes of the literary establishment. This attitude found its clearest expression in his satirical masterpiece, "The Monster of the Prophecy." The plot is an allegory of Smith's writing career, with many amusing points of departure. Everything from astrology to furniture fabric to unfair labor laws is touched upon. The protagonist is Theophilus Alvor, a "country-bred" poet with "lodgings so humble as almost to constitute the proverbial poetic garret" (*OST* 303).

He is dissuaded from jumping off the Brooklyn Bridge by a clairvoyant stranger who takes him to his lodgings. The stranger's ability to read thought waves is proven by his knowledge of the friendless poet's unpublished writings, and he compliments Alvor on his "Ode to Antares," which he ominously says was written "with an inspiration more prophetic than you dream" (*OST* 306). Identifying himself as Vizaphmal, an intergalactic sojourner from the planet Sattabor in the Antares system, and a scientist whom "the more ignorant classes" regard as a wizard (*OST* 307), he reveals his true appearance as a seven-foot tall being with an incredible morphology of five arms, three legs, and an elongated, curved neck supporting a red-crested head with three eyes that give forth a "green phosphorescence." In addition, "the head, the limbs and the whole body were mottled with interchanging lunes and moons of opalescent colors, never the same for a moment in their unresting flux and reflux" (*OST* 309). This extravagance of description is typical of Smith's humor—his bemused way of seeing Alvor's fixation with his financial problems, and his willingness to compromise his art for money—through an imaginative lens. When Alvor returns to Sattabor with the alien, he is employed in a scheme to gain political control of Ulphalor, a realm covering the northern part of the planet. Exploiting the weakness of a populace hopelessly steeped in "religious sentiment and the veneration of the past," they stage a quasi-fulfillment of an ancient prediction by the revered prophet Abbolechiolor, who foretold the coming of a great wizard and "a most unique and unheard-of monster with two arms, two legs, two eyes and a white skin," which would result in the deposing of the king before noon (*OST* 324). The hyper-religious Sattaborians do indeed revolt when Vizaphmal and the "monster" make their appearance, timed in conjunction with the lunar phases of Sattabor's three moons as detailed by the "long-winded" prophet. An amusing coda to the spoof is supplied by the triumphant Vizaphmal's glib statement to Alvor: "You must agree with me that the great Abbolechiolor was happily inspired" (*OST* 331).

Eventually the deception wears thin, and a counter-revolution forces Vizaphmal's Dr. Who–like decampment to points unknown in the cosmos. Alvor is captured and tortured by a priestly class, on the pretext that his ugliness is an insult to "Cunthamosi, the Cosmic Mother" (*OST* 335), but he escapes to Omanorion, a southern realm free of religious strife, and becomes the paramour of the empress, Ambiala. By an absurd coincidence, she is also a poetess who wrote an ode to our own sun, known to her as Atana. Smith clearly implies that Ambiala's ode, "replete with poetic fancies of a high order" (*OST* 345) is superior to the one by Alvor, whose thoughts about his own sexual reorientation to Ambiala's anatomy are contrasted with her more respectable conviction that they are truly compatible. Even in a rare happy ending, Smith cannot resist a jest at the expense of human dignity. We can only respond by echoing the sentiments of Domitian Malgraff, who after precipitating himself into the Void, would say, "Even in the bleak abyss that yawns unbridgeable between the stars, I was not allured by the thought of the stale and commonplace world I had left" (*LW* 346).

Works Cited

Behrends, Steve. "Clark Ashton Smith: Cosmicist or Misanthrope." *Dark Eidolon* 2 (1989): 12–14.

Bullough, Edward. "Psychical Distance as a Factor in Art and an Aesthetic Principle." In *Critical Theory Since Plato,* ed. Hazard Adams. New York: Harcourt, 1971.

De Tocqueville, Alexis. *Democracy in America.* Trans. Arthur Goldhammer. New York: Library of America, 2004.

Heller, Terry. "Poe's *Ligeia* and the Pleasures of Terror." *Gothic* 2, No. 2 (December 1980): 39–48

Hilger, Ronald S., and Scott Connors. "The Magellan of the Constellations: An Introduction." In *Red World of Polaris.* By Clark Ashton Smith. San Francisco: Night Shade, 2003.

Joshi, S. T. *H.P. Lovecraft: A Life.* West Warwick: Necronomicon Press, 1996.

Merriam Webster's Encyclopedia of Literature. Springfield, MA, 1995. [*EOL*]

Murray, Will. "Introduction." In *The Book of Hyperborea.* By Clark Ashton Smith. West Warwick, RI: Necronomicon Press, 1996.

Smith, Clark Ashton. *Mother of Toads.* The Unexpurgated Clark Ashton Smith. Ed. Steve Behrends. West Warwick, RI: Necronomicon Press, 1988. [*MOT*]

Stauffer, Donald Barlow. *The Merry Mood: Poe's Uses of Humor.* Baltimore, MD: The Enoch Pratt Free Library and The Edgar Allan Poe Society, 1982.

Song of the Necromancer:
"Loss" in Clark Ashton Smith's Fiction

Steve Behrends

The writings of Clark Ashton Smith display a continuity of idea and image that can only be described as remarkable. Fantastic settings and happenings from his early poems crop up twenty years later as the bases for short stories; prose-poems written in Smith's mid-twenties were fleshed into the elaborate fictions of his forties; he would write of Medusa in 1911, in his verse masterpiece "Medusa," and in 1957, four years before his death, in the ironic tale "The Symposium of the Gorgon." Evidence for the interconnectedness of Smith's literary output is discernible in nearly every poem and story. The endurance of this imaginative vision should give us all pause. Equally impressive is the tenacity with which Smith clung to certain emotional themes throughout his work, and of these, he returned most frequently to "loss."

Perhaps a quarter of Smith's fantastic stories (25 or 30 out of some 110) deal in a basic fashion with the subject of loss, and in this essay we shall concern ourselves with the most prominent of these; but nearly every Smith tale and many of his poems make some reference to loss, or use an image of loss metaphorically to set an emotional tone.

In this article attention will be paid to the types of loss we find in Smith's fiction (with some discussion as to why he chose to present those types), and to his attitude toward attempts to regain whatever was lost. The structure of the essay has been inspired by "Song of the Necromancer," a poem in Smith's jotting notebook, *The Black Book*, that seems to encapsulate nearly all the major aspects of his relationship to loss. The poem strikes me as a piece of some importance for an understanding of Smith's work in fiction:

> I would recall a forfeit woe,
> A buried bliss; my heart is fain
> Ever to seek and find again
> The lips whereon my lips have lain
> In rose-red twilights long ago.
>
> Lost are the lands of my desire,
> Long fled, the hours of my delight,
> The darkling splendor, fallen might:
> In aeons past, the bournless night
> Was rolled upon my rubied pyre.

* * *

> In far oblivion blows the desert
> Which was the lovely world I knew.
> Quenched are the suns of gold and blue. . . .
> Into the nadir darkness thrust,
> My world has gone as meteors go. . . . (BB 23)

Coming from a man whose tales abound with mages and wizards, and who had a poetic image of himself as a solitary sorcerer (an entire cycle of his personal love-poems was to have been called "Wizard's Love"), the poem's title is a very suggestive one. In fact, "The Song of the Necromancer" is Smith's own "song."

Like any writer who has ever had to scramble to provide motivation for some character, Smith used loss as a plot-element in several of his tales, including "The Ghoul," in which a man's despair over the death of his wife drives him to bargain with a demon; "The Flower-Women," wherein Maâl Dweb's yearning for his action-filled youth leads him to challenge the denizens of an untamed world; and "Thirteen Phantasms," whose main character is plagued by bizarre hallucinations of his lost beloved. But for Smith there was an importance to loss that went far beyond plot: his real interest was not in what loss could make his characters do, but in how it could make them feel.

Smith created scores of situations in which individuals lose the things closest to their hearts and live on only to regret their loss and to contrast their fallen state with the glory they once knew. He gave his characters the capacity to realize the extent of their loss, and to express the pain they felt; and he used their scrutiny—their comparisons of "now" and "then," of "what once had been" and "what is no more"—to spotlight the emotions he wished to convey to his readers.

These emotions, attendant to "falls from grace" of one sort or another, were very special to Smith, and he worked all their shadings and manifestations into his literary output: regret, nostalgia, homesickness, alienation, grief, ennui, loss of innocence, age, death, decay. Certain verbs and adjectives literally ring in our ears after a session with his stories or poems, so often do we encounter them: "sunken," "faded," "fallen," "lost," "irretrievable," "longing," "yearning," "seeking."

Having just argued for such a central role for "loss" in Smith's fiction, permit me a brief aside. You have in your hands, to the best of my knowledge, the very first essay to discuss Smith's profound fixation with "loss"; I have never encountered this word linked to Smith in any forum whatsoever. How, then, is it possible that the overarching concern of Smith's literary life has gone entirely unnoticed by generations of his critics? Why has this "Pattern in Smith's Carpet," so to speak, not been recognized before now? Good questions; but for all that I might speculate on their answers, my most honest reply really boils down to "Beats me."

But having said that . . . perhaps it's partly been a case of mistaken identity. This has been true, I believe, for those critics who have viewed Smith as an individual preoccupied with Death. Fritz Leiber, for instance, wrote that "Death in all its phases—from maggot-banquets to mere forgetting, erasing forever from all tables of memory—seems to be [Smith's] chief inspiration and theme" (72). But this is a misdiagnosis, an oversimplification, a mistaking of the symptom for the disease. It may well be true, as L. Sprague de Camp once said, that "no one since Poe has so loved a well-rotted corpse" (65), but Death in itself never obsessed Smith. Rather, Death opened a doorway; and through it would come Death's handmaidens, Yearning and Loss. These were the real objects of Clark Ashton Smith's obsession, the groundnotes to his emotional life. We hear them sounding clearly in the voice of John Milwarp, writer of imaginative fiction and hero of Smith's "The Chain of Aforgomon": "In the background of my mind there has lurked a sentiment of formless, melancholy desire, for some nameless beauty long perished out of time" (*RA* 216).

Taking "Song of the Necromancer" as our guidebook to "loss" in Smith, we note that the Necromancer of the poem recites a litany of his greatest losses: love, youth and vigor and power, a world of impossible splendor—all have vanished. These three varieties of loss will be discussed in turn. While it is true that the sources for his characters' feelings of loss were of lesser interest to Smith than the feelings themselves, this choice of organization provides us a ghoulish opportunity for some biographical muckraking. We will look for significant events and circumstances in Smith's own life, the echoes and shadows of which may represent the different kinds of loss we find in his fiction.

We conclude the essay by discussing the fates of those who choose "to seek and find again" what they have lost.

"*. . . the lips whereon my lips have lain . . .*"

As might be expected of a poet, Smith was greatly attracted to the strength of the emotion of love, and the fervor with which we cling to it and to our lovers. (Note that his love-poems certainly outnumber his more famous "fantastic" or "horrific" poems.) Since it looms so large in our lives, Smith found love an ideal thing for the characters of his stories to lose.

And as it happens, Smith himself had suffered such a loss. Facts are scanty at present, but Smith is known to have fallen in love with "Iris," a "nymph of . . . harvest-colored hair" (as he said of her in an unpublished poem, "For Iris"), perhaps in the early 1920s. His eventual wife, Carol Jones Dorman, wrote that "he lavished his love upon his first, hopelessly ill beloved, who died of consumption before she was thirty. . . . And always, after the first tragedy of love for the beautiful blonde separated from her husband . . . [Smith] chose brunettes for his deepest loves." And among the poems Smith wrote to or for his Iris, we find the following item, untitled and unpublished, from February 1923:

> Your hair, a memory of gold
> Alone remains from buried years:
> What love was ours, what grief, or happy tears,
> Is now a tale untold.

But Smith would tell the tale of this lost love, veiled and fictionalized perhaps, in many poems and stories.

The textbook example of such a "loss of love" story is "The Venus of Azombeii." The central character of this tale, Julius Marsden, has felt throughout his life "the ineffable nostalgia of the far-off and the unknown" (compare this against Smith's own "wild aspiration toward the unknown, the uncharted, the exotic, the utterly strange and ultra-terrestrial," as he stated it to Lovecraft in October 1930 [*SL* 127]), which compels him to make a journey to dark and mysterious Africa. In a wilderness region he meets a beautiful black woman, Mybaloë, whom he comes to love. Marsden experiences a time of wild happiness: "A powerful fever exalted all my senses, a deep indolence bedrugged my brain. I lived, as never before, *and never again,* to the full capacity of my corporeal being. . . . The world and its fullness were ours" (*OD* 229, 231; emphasis added).

As Smith would have it, though, their life together is soon shattered through the treachery of a rival suitor to Mybaloë. Both lovers are poisoned with a slow-killing brew, by which, please note, Smith gives them plenty of time to realize the sadness of their fate and the fullness of their loss. "Dead was all our former joy and happiness. . . . Love, it was true, was still ours, but love that already seemed to have entered the hideous gloom and nothingness of the grave. . . . The leaden lapse of funereal days, beneath heavens from which for us the very azure had departed" (*OD* 236–37). Smith shows us the high peak of their love, and in contrast the low ebb of their fallen state.

Identical in its emotions but with a slight twist to its development is the extended prose-poem "Told in the Desert." A young traveler loses his way while crossing a desert expanse. He eventually stumbles upon a cool and fertile oasis where dwells a beautiful girl, Neria. We are told that the young man's sojourn with Neria, like that of Marsden and Mybaloë in "Azombeii," was "a life remote from all the fevers of the world, and pure from every soilure; it was infinitely sweet and secure" (*OD* 327).

Unlike Marsden in "Azombeii," however, the hero of "Desert" abandons his idyllic love-nest, his "irretrievable Aidann," rather than having it taken away from him. But Smith does not end the story there. The man comes to yearn for his "bygone year . . . of happiness"; and seeking in later years the splendor of the oasis, he is doomed to wander in vain, and all his days thereafter are filled with "only the fading visions of memory, the tortures and despairs and illusions of the quested miles, the waste whereon there falls no lightest shadow of any leaf, and the wells whose taste is fire and madness" (*OD* 329).

The next two stories to be discussed, "The Chain of Aforgomon" and "The Last Incantation," have necromancers as their main characters rather than adventurous young men, and possess some other common features to which we will return later.

In "Aforgomon" the sorcerer Calaspa invokes the powers of an evil god to win back a flown hour with his dead beloved, Belthoris. The past is temporarily regained through this necromancy, and in typical fashion Smith presents their resurrected love in the grandest of terms. "We dwelt alone in a universe of light, in a blossomed heaven. Exalted by love in the high harmony of those moments, we seemed to touch eternity" (*RA* 224). We are left to contrast this with Calaspa's mood after the hour has passed: "Sorrow and desolation choked my heart as ashes fill some urn consecrated to the dead; and all the hues and perfumes of the garden about me were redolent only of the bitterness of death" (*RA* 218).

"The Last Incantation" contains some of Smith's finest descriptions of the emotions of loss, and the story also serves as a bridge between the "loss of love" and "loss of the past" tales.

At the height of his powers as the mightiest sorcerer of Poseidonis, Malgyris the Mage sees only the empty, unchallenging years ahead of him, and the barren moments of the present, and takes but a cold and hollow joy from his exalted position. Smith's description of this state of mind is worth quoting in full:

> ... and turning from the greyness of the present, from the darkness that seemed to close in upon the future, he groped among the shadows of memory, even as a blind man who has lost the sun and seeks it everywhere in vain. And all the vistas of time that had been so full of gold and splendor, the days of triumph that were colored like a soaring flame, the crimson and purple of the rich imperial years of his prime, all these were chill and dim and strangely faded now, and the remembrance thereof was no more than the stirring of dead embers.... There was nothing left but shadow and greyness and dust, nothing but the empty dark and the cold, and a clutching weight of insufferable weariness, of immedicable anguish. (*RA* 94, 97)

Amid this desolation, Malgyris is sustained only by a gentle memory from his innocent youth which "like an alien star ... still burned with unfailing luster—the memory of the girl Nylissa whom he had loved in days ere the lust of unpermitted knowledge and necromantic dominion had ever entered his soul" (*RA* 94).

Like the male protagonists of the other stories discussed, Malgyris aches for his lost love. Unlike the others, however, his mind also dwells upon the passing of his former, untarnished self, the "fervent and guileless heart" of his youth, and the glorious, sun-filled days of his past. This sentiment leads us to a group of stories featuring Smith's second method for bringing loss and regret into the lives of his characters.

"... the darkling splendor, fallen might..."

Smith set his most famous cycle of stories, the tales of Zothique, in a "fallen" world where the past infinitely outweighs the future. "On Zothique, the last continent, the sun no longer shone with the whiteness of its prime, but was dim and tarnished as if with a vapor of blood" (*RA* 365). There are constant reminders of age and decay, of a glory withered away by Time: vast deserts of tombs and buried cities, frequent references to the greater potency of potions and spells of elder wizards, etc.

On the level of the individual, Smith dishes out the same bitter meal. His fiction is filled with characters haunted by memories of a more desirable past, from whom Time has stolen precious years. Depending on the character in question—again, Smith's focus is on loss itself, not the object lost—they may desire the power and glory they once knew, the simplicity and vigor of the years of youth, a lost innocence, some splendorous state of being, or the vanished beauty and grandeur of incomparable cultures and beloved worlds. (Here, of course, one notes the title of Smith's second collection of short stories, *Lost Worlds*, originally *The Book of Lost Worlds*.)

Just why Smith was so obsessed with the notion of "a fall from a past of grace" is a matter for speculation, and we should bear in mind that "armchair psychoanalysis" is a dubious profession. Still, it is possible that at the time he wrote the bulk of his stories, Smith felt that he had suffered a profound "fall from grace." Smith's late teens and early twenties had certainly been a heady period: he'd been taken under the wing of a personal idol, the poet George Sterling, and his first book of poetry had brought him comparisons to Keats and Shelley. This notoriety must surely have raised his standing in his small hometown, not to mention his own expectations for the future. And yet the Depression found Smith without a job or viable occupation, unable to eke out a living as a poet, with girlfriends berating him for his lack of ambition. And while his switch to writing fiction for the pulps did put bread on the table, he found it a very distasteful business at times—he once said to Sterling that writing prose was "a hateful task, for a poet, and [one which] wouldn't be necessary in any true civilization" (*SU* 283). In short, it may be that Smith suffered that variety of "letdown" or loss peculiar to child prodigies.

As a simple example of this yearning for the past, consider the following paragraph from "The Testament of Athammaus," a story that details the desertion of the Hyperborean capital Commoriom as seen through the eyes of the one-time public executioner.

> Forgive an aged man if he seem to dwell, as is the habit of the old, among the youthful recollections that have gathered to themselves the kingly purple of removed horizons and the strange glory that illumes irretrievable things. Lo! I am made young again when I recall Commoriom, when in this grey city of the sunken years I behold in retrospect her walls that looked mountainously down upon the jungle . . . (*OST* 257–58)

Note that the years after Commoriom are "sunken," and its glory is "irretrievable." Also note that Athammaus is alone in his suffering: "And though others forget, or haply deem her no more than a vain and dubitable tale, I shall never cease to lament Commoriom" (*OST* 258). Though others are healed, Smith chose to center his tale on a man whose feelings of regret have remained strong and vivid.

In "Xeethra," perhaps his most famous tale of Zothique, Smith presents multifold loss alongside monstrous irony. A young goatherd, Xeethra, eats an enchanted fruit and is henceforth tormented by the memories of a past life wherein he was Prince Amero, ruler of the fair kingdom of Calyz. The bewildered and newly awakened king is repelled by the rude and simple life of Xeethra; he longs for a dimly recalled life of opulence. He journeys in search of Calyz, but discovers that the land has become a parched desert. Xeethra/Amero is "whelmed by utter loss and despair" at the sight of his ruined and crumbled homeland.

At this point in the story an emissary from Thasaidon, the Satan of the future, appears and offers him a strange deal. At the price of his soul, the life Amero once knew will be returned to him—but it will remain only so long as he wishes it to. Not really understanding this clause, the young man accepts the bond; and suddenly the past lives again for him, and he is the king of a bountiful land. But in time he succumbs to ennui, and finds himself wishing for the simple life of a goatherd. In an instant he is back once more in the leper-peopled desert of Calyz.

> His heart was a black chill of desolation, and he seemed to himself as one who had known . . . the loss of high splendor; and who stood now amid the extremity of age and decay. . . . Anguish choked the heart of Xeethra as if with the ashes of burnt-out pyres and the shards of heaped ruin. . . . In the end, there was only dust and dearth; and he, the doubly accursed, must remember and repent for evermore all that he had forfeited. (*RA* 363, 364)

Xeethra can never return to either the powerful life of a monarch, or the carefree and uncluttered life of a shepherd.

An even grander scale of suffering arising from "the loss of the past" is displayed in the prose-poem "Sadastor." On a distant planet, "dim and grey beneath a waning sun . . . a token of doom to fairer and younger worlds" (*OST* 219), the demon Chamadis discovers the mermaid Lyspial wallowing in a small briny pool that had once been a far-flung ocean. She has witnessed the slow desiccation of the sea and the destruction of the glorious world of her past; she is tortured with the knowledge of her present state, and of all she has lost.

> "Of the seas wherein I swam and sported at leisure . . . there remains only this fallen pool. Alas! my lovely seas, with their mingled perfumes of brine and weed . . . Alas! the quinquiremes of cycle-ended wars, and the heavy-laden argosies with sails of cordage and byssus. . . . Alas! the dead captains, the beautiful dead sailors that were borne by the ebbing tide to my couches of amber seaweed. . . . Alas! the kisses that I laid on their cold and hueless lips . . ." (*OST* 220, 221)

Another fallen world is presented in the prose-poem, "From the Crypts of Memory." The setting is a shadowy planet orbiting "a star whose course [was] decadent from the high, irremeable heavens of the past" (*NU* 12). The people of this world are unspeakably ancient and have fallen far from their golden past. Only in memories can they haltingly recapture "an epoch whose marvelous worlds have crumbled, and whose mighty suns are less than shadow" (*NU* 12). But such memories only add to the burden of age and sorrow, and by contrast their lives are made to seem even more pale and ghostly: "Vaguely we lived, and loved as in dreams—the dim and mystic dreams that hover upon the verge of fathomless sleep. We felt for our women . . . the same desire that the dead may feel" (*NU* 13).

And it doesn't stop there—for Smith's characters, not even death is an end to yearning and despair. On the contrary: while "a living death" was used in "From the Crypts of Memory" as a metaphor for a great suffering, a literal "life in death" is employed in "The Empire of the Necromancers" as a tool for generating feelings of loss. The legions of the dead, drawn forth from their tombs to serve as slaves to a pair of necromancers, find themselves living a sort of half-life: "the state to which they were summoned was empty and troublous and shadow-like. They knew no passion or desire, or delight." We hear of their longings through the resurrected Prince of the people, who "knew that he had come back to a faded sun, to a hollow and spectral world. Like something lost and irretrievable, beyond prodigious gulfs, he recalled the pomp of his reign . . . and the golden pride and exultation that had been his in youth. . . . Darkly he began to grieve for his fallen state" (*RA* 321). Smith tormented the poor souls of this story with the loss of their glorious pasts, their very lives, and even the peace of oblivion.

". . . Quenched are the suns of gold and blue. . . ."

Now how do I top that? Smith must have asked himself. We find his answer in a handful of stories in which individuals lose not simply the past, nor even life itself, but a glory beyond life, some "unnatural" state or condition. In every case the "unnatural state of being" is an ecstatic and desired one, and of course this makes perfect sense: Smith wanted his characters to long for the splendor they had experienced, beside which everyday life is wan and inadequate. And given such glorious experiences, they would naturally make the contrasts and comparisons of "then" and "now" that Smith liked to use, and feel the kind of regret and empty despair that so fascinated him.

The visions presented to these hapless characters are often so completely strange and wondrous that they can only be seen or understood in part. They are too far beyond the mundane sphere of human experience, like the image of incarnate Beauty glimpsed in Smith's poem "A Dream of Beauty": "Her face the light of fallen planets wore, / But as I gazed, in doubt and wonderment, / Mine eyes were dazzled, and I saw no more" (*LO* 153). This itself is a technique Smith used to intensify and magnify the contrast of the inconceivable state of being, and the return to commonplace reality.

Stories in this category include "The City of the Singing Flame," "The End of the Story," "The Light from Beyond," and "The White Sybil." There is no need to describe the distinct wonders found in each of these tales. We need only note the similarity of their characters attitudes as they "come off the high" of their unique experiences:

> Words are futile to express what I have beheld and experienced. . . . Literature is nothing more than a shadow. Life, with its drawn-out length of monotonous, reit-

erative days, is unreal and without meaning, now. ("The City of the Singing Flame" [*RA* 194])

I have forgotten much of the delirium that ensued.... There were things too vast for memory to retain. And much that I remember could only be told in the language of Olympus.... Infinities were rolled before me.... I peered down upon the utmost heavens.... I am a mere remnant of my former self. ("The Light from Beyond" [*LW* 386, 387, 388])

Of all that followed, much was forgotten afterwards by Tortha. It was like a light too radiant to be endured ... ever afterward there was a cloudy dimness in his mind, a blur of unresolving shadow, like the dazzlement in eyes that have looked on some insupportable light. ("The White Sybil" [*AY* 69, 71])

For the heroes of these stories this past glory shall always be more resplendent and desirable than either the present or the future, a time always to be longed for. And for some it is a thing they must try to regain, whatever the cost.

"... *I would recall ... a buried bliss ...*"

"Song of the Necromancer" has been our general guidebook to Smith's relationship to loss, and we take note that it begins with a declaration of intent: the unhappy sorcerer (we learn of his unhappiness in the subsequent stanzas) would seek to resummon his lost past, and to draw back his dead love from the tomb. As we have seen, the same is true of several of the characters we find in Smith's short stories.

Why Smith should have them strive to recapture what they have lost is obvious—such striving serves to underscore their unhappiness, and the depths of their dissatisfaction. That all these attempts either fail or end in self-destruction reflects Smith's generally pessimistic outlook. "You can never go home again," he's telling us, "it's no longer there." Or if it is still there, and somehow you succeed in making it back, the achievement will amount to a very mixed blessing.

In a story like "Told in the Desert" what is sought after is literally unattainable, for though he may search the desert for the rest of his life, that young man will never again find the fertile oasis in which he lived so happily with Neria.

What Malgyris seeks in "The Last Incantation" is just as unattainable, though more figuratively so. Believing that he would be content to have his lost Nylissa beside him again, he summons her specter from the grave. Once she has materialized, however, he begins to find fault with her manner and appearance. Dissatisfied and unsettled, he dismisses the phantom, at which point his familiar explains the true nature of his yearning and its predestined failure: "No necromantic spell could recall for you your own lost youth or the fervent and guileless heart that loved Nylissa, or the ardent eyes that beheld her then" (*RA* 97).

This same lesson is learned in Smith's unfinished tale "Mnemoka." Space-Alley Jon, a drifter of the space-lanes, purchases an illicit Martian drug which brings back memories with all the strength of real experiences. Jon intends to relive his first sexual experience, back in his innocent adolescence, with a girl named Sophia: "[R]emoved in time by years spent on half the solar worlds . . . [t]he thrill of that yielding . . . remained poignant in memory" (*SS* 137–38). But after downing the drug, he is haunted instead by visions of a brutal murder he recently committed. His life has become too soiled to allow retrieval of the moment he longed for. The boy who had lain with Sophia no longer existed. Jon, like Malygris, has learned that the same river can never be crossed twice.

Calaspa's quest in "The Chain of Aforgomon" is also unsatisfying, and is self-destructive as well. His conjured hour with Belthoris vanishes back into the past just as a temporary spat develops between the two lovers. Ending on such a sour note, he proclaims that "vain, like all other hours, was the resummoned hour; doubly irredeemable was my loss" (*RA* 225). Equally tragic is the price Calaspa pays, as he knew he must, for casting the time-distorting spell: he is tortured and killed by the local priesthood, and his soul is cursed to travel from body to body into the future, until in some other incarnation he shall die again for his crime.

Indeed, even when the acknowledged price is their own destruction, Smith's men go forward unhaltingly to retrieve what they have lost, so great is their despair. The narrator of "The City of the Singing Flame" ends the tale by saying that he will return to the City and immolate himself in the Flame, that he might merge with the unearthly beauty and music that he had sampled and lost; and the hero of "The End of the Story" makes the same resolution, to die on the couch of a deadly lamia, from which he had been taken by force, rather than live out his years without her love:

> I lamented the beautiful dream of which [I had been] deprived. . . . Never before had I experienced a passion of such intensity, such all-consuming ardor, as the one I conceived for [the lamia Nycea] . . . and I know that whatever she was, woman or demon or serpent, there was no one in all the world who could ever rouse in me the same love and the same delight. (*RA* 75)

But whether they seek to regain their loss, or choose to suffer through a life of torment and regret, the characters in the stories we've discussed are all made to feel "the loss of high splendor," to live through "sunken years," and to long for the return of "a buried bliss"; and as each is the puppet-creation of Clark Ashton Smith, their songs of woe should be seen as those of the Necromancer himself.

Works Cited

de Camp, L. Sprague. "The Prose Tales of Clark Ashton Smith." In *In Memoriam: Clark Ashton Smith*, ed. Jack L. Chalker. Baltimore: Anthem/Jack L. Chalker and Associates, 1963, pp. 65–68.

Leiber, Fritz. "Clark Ashton Smith: An Appreciation." In *In Memoriam: Clark Ashton Smith*, pp. 71–73.

Smith, Carol Jones Dorman. "The Man Who Walks the Stars." Ms., Clark Ashton Smith Papers. John Hay Library, Brown University.

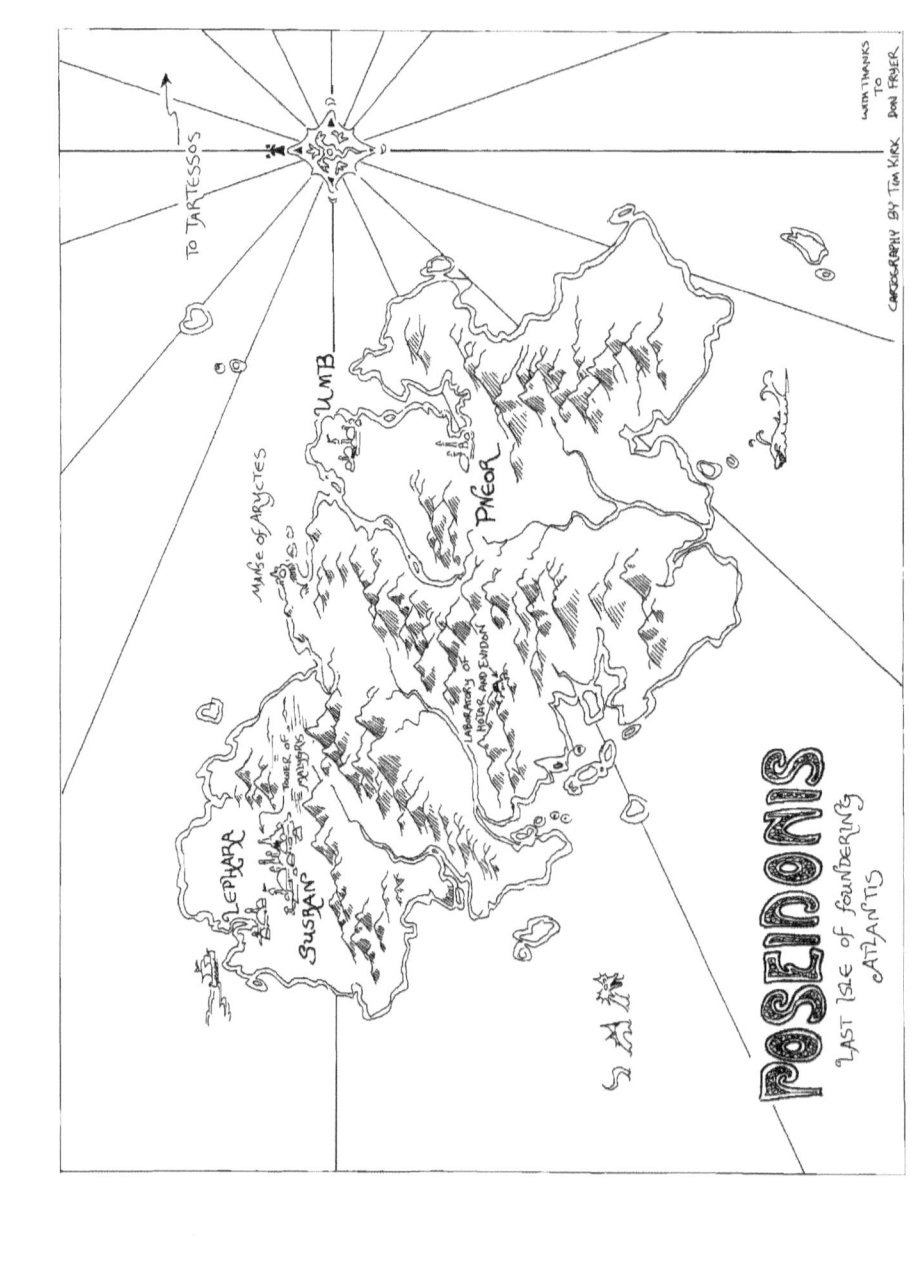

Brave World Old and New:
The Atlantis Theme in the Poetry and Fiction of Clark Ashton Smith

Donald Sidney-Fryer

One of the themes pivotal to the oeuvre of the late Clark Ashton Smith is that which may be identified, specifically and generically, as the Atlantis theme, whether it assumes the name of Atlantis or that of some other Atlantis-like locale, such as Mu or Lemuria, or Hyperborea or Zothique for that matter. It is a theme or background that runs through the tapestry of a lifetime in word-weaving from virtually his first published work to literally his last. Of all the writers who have used, or extrapolated from, Plato's "quaint conceit," the Atlantis myth (as detailed in the two dialogues, the *Timaeus* and the *Critias*), few have done so with the taste, invention, and seriousness that Smith has demonstrated in his handling of this theme and/or background.

This is probably because Smith—of all such writers—is the closest to Plato in the quality of sheer poetic imagination. Just as much as Plato who created the Atlantis myth for didactic purposes, Smith has utilized it for his own serious ends, whether in verse or in prose. And Smith is undeniably the only major poet in English who has to date featured it in his own poetry and prose on a comparatively important scale, all discussion of novels by romancers of hackneyed imagination swept aside. This is odd when one considers the rare possibilities for splendor and "glamour" that this Platonic near-utopia proffers to the original poet.

Whatever the reasons for its neglect as a source of poetry, Smith in his literary output overall is the first and foremost poet in English to achieve, radiating from this theme, a sizeable body of poetry that possesses genuine substance and beauty. However, Smith's great patron and poetic mentor George Sterling had included in his magisterial narrative in verse "A Wine of Wizardry" (first published in the *Cosmopolitan* for September 1907, in which issue the young Smith first read the poem) an implicitly Atlantean passage, as follows:

> Shapes of men that were
> Point, weeping, at tremendous dooms to be,
> When pillared pomps and thrones supreme shall stir,
> Unstable as the foam-dreams of the sea. (150)

This especial passage, among others from the same source, would fructify the younger poet's imagination and haunt it, long after he had first read and conned Sterling's poem, not only in Smith's own early but first mature poetry but just as much in his later tales of Atlantis, or (in his own employment of the fabled background) its embodiment as a good-sized final fragment, "Poseidonis," a concept that Smith apparently derived from the Theosophist writings of Helena Blavatsky.

The most salient examples in which Smith gives expression to the Atlantis theme are found for the most part not so much in his miscellaneously published poetry as in his collections of poetry, whether appearing early or late in his career. The first examples characteristically occur in Smith's first volume of verse, *The Star-Treader and Other Poems* (1912). And the very first example, proto-Atlantean, is contained in the first stanza of the poem "The Cloud-Islands."

> What islands marvellous are these,
> That gem the sunset's tides of light—
> Opals aglow in saffron seas?
> How beautiful they lie, and bright,
> Like some new-found Hesperides! (*LO* 91)

In Greek mythology, the Hesperides were those islands in the extreme west (i.e., as such appeared to the ancient Greeks living in Greece itself), and which contained the gardens wherein grew the golden apples guarded by nymphs (also called Hesperides) with the aid of a dragon. Presumably these islands lay somewhere in the Atlantic Ocean. Atlantis, according to Plato, lay somewhere in the North Atlantic and west of the Pillars of Heracles or Hercules (the Straits of Gibraltar), and hence was undoubtedly a hesperian island continent. The Hesperides prefigure Atlantis and possibly may have served, together with other islands, as a model for the Atlantis of Plato, an island empery remarkable for its wealth, extent, and antiquity, as well as for its almost utopian justice and order.

The next example, the sonnet "Atlantis" (*LO* 89), gives us an impressive submarine tableau of the sunken capital of the empire of Atlantis:

> Above its domes the gulfs accumulate
> To where the sea-winds trumpet forth their screed;
> But here the buried waters take no heed—
> Deaf, and with closed lips from press of weight
> Imposed by ocean. Dim, inanimate,
> On temples of an unremembered creed
> Involved in long, slow tentacles of weed,
> The dead tide lies immovable as Fate.
>
> From out the ponderous-vaulted ocean-dome,
> A clouded light is questionably shed
> On altars of a goddess garlanded

> With blossoms of some weird and hueless vine;
>   And wingèd, fleet, through skies beneath the foam,
> Like silent birds the sea-things dart and shine.

In particular, amongst many other things, we might note what a subtle visual effect is achieved by line 10: "A clouded light is questionably shed"—but the sonnet is a highly creditable achievement throughout.

Smith's third volume of verse—and his second major collection of poetry—*Ebony and Crystal: Poems in Verse and Prose* (published by Smith himself in 1922), contains some half-dozen references to Atlantis or Atlantis-like places. While these references may for the most part be but peripheral, they hint at a proto-historic world of unimaginable glamour and beauty.

> The secret rose we vainly dream to find,
> Was blown in grey Atlantis long ago,
> Or in old summers of the realms of snow,
> Its attar lulled the pole-arisen wind;
> Or once its broad and breathless petals pined
> In gardens of Persepolis, aglow
> With desert sunlight, and the fiery, slow
> Red waves of sand, invincible and blind.
>
> On orient isles, or isles hesperian,
> Through mythic days ere mortal time began,
> It flowered above the ever-flowering foam;
> Or, legendless, in lands of yesteryear,
> It flamed among the violets—near, how near,
> To unenchanted fields and hills of home! (*"Rosa Mystica," LO* 94–95)

Note that the Atlantis mentioned above is "grey"—thus obliquely indicating that this is the post-cataclysmic Atlantis lying beneath the ocean, and evidently mantled with the grey of the deep-sea silt.

The second reference is to that Atlantis of the Pacific, the Mu postulated by James Churchward, or sometimes rendered as Lemuria (as in the present case), also postulated as extant in the Indian Ocean, stretching between Madagascar and the Indian subcontinent once upon a time. This reference appears in the sonnet "Mirrors," which Smith has cast in that metre somewhat rare in English (but not in French, where it serves as the basic line in classical prosody), the alexandrine, a metre he handles characteristically with incomparable dexterity.

> Mirrors of steel or silver, gold or glass antique!
> Whether in melancholy marble palaces
> In some long trance you drew the dreamy loveliness
> Of Roman queens, or queens barbarical, or Greek;
> Or, further than the bright and sun-pursuing beak

> Of argosy might fare, beheld the empresses
> Of lost Lemuria, or behind the lattices
> Alhambran, have returned forbidden smiles oblique
> Of wan, mysterious women!—Mirrors, mirrors old,
> Mirrors immutable, impassible as Fate,
> Your bosoms held the perished beauty of the past
> Nearer than straining love might ever hope to hold;
> And fleeing faces, lips too phantom-frail to last,
> Found in your magic depth a life re-duplicate. (*SP* 83)

Note the hyper-subtle effect the poet achieves by the enjambement in lines 6 through 9, an effect tantalizing in its half-palpable quality, as of images that disappear before they are fully formed in our minds but that hint at an extraordinary beauty just beyond our powers to imagine.

The third reference is to Lemuria and Atlantis both, and is found in lines 40–53 of Smith's elegy "To Nora May French."[1]

> If thy voice
> In any wise return, and word of thee,
> It is a lost, incognizable sigh,
> Upon the wind's oblivious woe, or blown,
> Antiphonal, from wave to plangent wave
> In the vast, unhuman sorrow of the main,
> On tides that lave the city-laden shores
> Of lands wherein the eternal vanities
> Are served at many altars; tides that wash
> Lemuria's unfathomable walls,
> And idly sway the weed-involvèd oars
> At wharves of lost Atlantis; tides that rise
> From coral-coffered bones of all the drowned,
> And sunless tombs of pearl that krakens guard. (*LO* 166)

The reader will have noted how naturally the references to Lemuria and Atlantis occur within the context of the given passage (with its imagery of sea-wind and sea-tide).

The fourth reference—or (rather) in this case, example—is the entire sonnet "In Lemuria," a masterpiece of compression and subtle suggestiveness. This otherworldly sonnet narrates its tale through a succession of exotic scenes or images, a succession that culminates in the hyper-exotic reference, the "jaspers from the moon."

> Rememberest thou? Enormous gongs of stone
> Were stricken, and the storming trumpeteers
> Acclaimed my deed to answering tides of spears,

> And spoke the names of monsters overthrown—
> Griffins whose angry gold, and fervid store
> Of sapphires wrenched from marble-plungèd mines—
> Carnelians, opals, agates, almandines,
> I brought to thee some scarlet eve of yore.
>
> In the wide fane that shrined thee, Venus-wise,
> The fallen clamours died. . . . I heard the tune
> Of tiny bells of pearl and melanite,
> Hung at thy knees, and arms of dreamt delight;
> And placed my wealth before thy fabled eyes,
> Pallid and pure as jaspers from the moon. (*LO* 60)

Is it to a goddess or empress, statue or living woman, that the warrior-prince-narrator proffers the booty of conquest? It is a tribute to the author's adroitness that we do not definitely know. The only clue that we have is the tinkling of the "tiny bells of pearl and melanite," which might indicate a living person making the natural slight movements that a sitting person makes. Yet the tinkling could be caused by the wind or by some artificial means, as of a priest stirring those bells by hand or by some hidden mechanism in the statue, if the object in question is indeed a statue.

The fifth Atlantean reference occurs in the sonnet "Symbols." In this lyric the poet abjures his already quite exotic style of imagery for one even more exotic, if possible. (The poem immediately precedes, in the original *Ebony and Crystal*, Smith's greatest and most imaginative effort, *The Hashish-Eater; or, The Apocalypse of Evil.*)

> No more of gold and marble, nor of snow,
> And sunlight, and vermilion, would I make
> My vision and my symbols, nor would take
> The auroral flame of some prismatic floe,
> Nor iris of the frail and lunar bow,
> Flung on the shafted waterfalls that wake
> The night's blue slumber in a shadowy lake. . . .
> To body forth my fantasies, and show
> Communicable mystery, I would find,
> In adamantine darkness of the earth,
> Metals untouched of any sun; and bring
> Black azures of the nether sea to birth—
> Or fetch the secret, splendid leaves, and blind,
> Blue lilies of an Atlantean spring. (*LO* 95)

It seems clear from the context (lines 13–14) that the springtime to which Smith refers is not so much specifically that of Plato's lost continent as it is, more generally, a springtime indescribably primal. Observe the original way in which the poet indicates the fact that these "Blue lilies of an Atlantean spring" are buds—through the subtle epithet "blind."

The sixth reference, or example, is only implicitly Atlantean, and occurs in lines 105–13 of *The Hashish-Eater*. This is the vision or episode that closes the second of the overall ten sections (as originally published in 1922) that make up this compressed epic, sections two, three, and four consist of a relentless piling-up of one vision on top of another.

> I beheld
> The slowly-thronging corals that usurp
> Some harbor of a million-masted sea
> And sun them on the league-long wharves of gold
> Bulks of enormous crimson, kraken-limbed
> And kraken-headed, lifting up as crowns
> The octiremes of perished emperors,
> And galleys fraught with royal gems, that sailed
> From a sea-deserted haven. (*EC* 51–52)

This vision suggests an ultramundane Atlantis which is in process of being overwhelmed, not by one great catastrophe of earthquake and tsunami but by a stranger doom requiring aeons of time.

The seventh and last Atlantean reference in *Ebony and Crystal* is to Atlantis and Lemuria both, and is found in the first and shorter of the two sections of the poem in prose "From a Letter":

> Will you not join me in Atlantis, where we will go down through streets of blue and yellow marble to the wharves of orichalch, and choose us a galley with a golden Eros for figurehead, and sails of Tyrian sendal? With mariners that knew Odysseus, and beautiful amber-breasted slaves from the mountain-vales of Lemuria, we will lift anchor for the unknown fortunate isles of the outer sea; and, sailing in the wake of an opal sunset, will lose that ancient land in the glaucous twilight, and see from our couch of ivory and satin the rising of unknown stars and perished planets. (*NU* 11)

The above is one of the rare instances wherein the poet gives us a palpable envisioning of Plato's fabled city, complete with a mention of that fabulous alloy of copper and gold (mixed-in with some silver) called orichalch, or orichalcum, evidently a bright or pale flame-gold. Note in particular the magisterial handling of the rhythm in the second period, a rhythm which seems to lift anchor for us, and to rise and fall with the waves of the ocean herself—a rise and fall first stated in the two subordinate phrases opening the sentence, and then echoed or repeated in the last part of the last phrase, "the rising of unknown stars and perished planets."

Smith's fourth volume of verse—and his third major collection of poetry—*Sandalwood* (published by Smith himself in 1925), contains only two specifically Atlantean references. These occur in two sonnets, the first cast in alexandrines, the second in the usual decasyllabics.

The first sonnet, "Forgotten Sorrow," is one of the most delicate and subtle tasks that Smith ever assigned to himself, to give embodiment to a theme which threatens to disappear during the handling of it, due to its utter filmy character, or to be destroyed if the given embodiment prove too heavy. The razor-thin terrain wherein such manifestation can take place, the poet just achieves, no more and no less. The Atlantean allusion occurs in the final image, which contains both visual and aural clues. The final image occupies the entire fourteenth line, thus logically capping the rest of the sonnet. Smith is ever the master of style and form, discovering the perfect expression for his poetic substance.

> A stranger grief than any grief by music told
> Is mine: regret for unremembered loves, and faces
> Veiled by the night of some unknown farewell, or places
> Lost in the dusty ebb and lapse of kingdoms old
> On the slow desert, rises vague and manifold
> Within my heart at summer twilight. Through the spaces
> Of all oblivion, voidly then my soul retraces
> Her dead lives given to the marbles and the mould
> In dim Palmyra, or some pink, enormous city
> Whose falling columns now the boles of mightier trees
> Support in far Siam. . . . All grievous love and pity,
> All loveliness unheld for long, and long estranged,
> Appeals with voices indistinguishably changed,
> Like bells in deep Atlantis, tolled by summer seas. (LO 159)

The second sonnet wherein we find an Atlantean reference is "Enchanted Mirrors." The entire piece possesses an abundance of those peculiarly Smithian elements of poetic magic, but the reference to Atlantis especially seems to possess, if possible, an even greater amount of this magical quality. We must call particular attention to the final lines of both the octet and the sestet which, although differing as to where the pauses or semi-pauses fall (in the vocal delivery of the lines), manage to achieve an almost similar rhythm or rhythmical effect, but with this one major distinction: the pauses in the last line of the sestet reverse those in the last line of the octet.

> These are enchanted mirrors that I bring—
> By daemons wrought from metals of the moon
> To burnished forms of lune or plenilune;
> Therein are faery faces vanishing,
> And warm Pompeiian phantoms lovelier
> Than mortal flesh or marble; and the gleam
> Of Atlantean suns that rose in dream
> And sank on golden worlds that never were.

* * * * *

> Therein you shall behold unshapen dooms,
> And ghoul-astounding shadows of the tombs;
> Oblivion, with eyes like poppy-buds,
> Or love, with blossoms plucked in Devachan,
> In stillness of the lily-pillared woods—
> But nevermore the moiling world of man.[2] (*LO* 125–26)

Created at about the same time as the poems included in the original *Sandalwood* and, like those poems, first published in the *Auburn Journal*, are two quatrains that contain Atlantean or peripherally Atlantean references, and which are both similar in form, rhetoric, and effect. (Smith included both "Dissidence" and "Lemurienne" in his collection of collections, *Selected Poems,* in the section "Sandalwood.") The first quatrain, "Dissidence" (first entitled "Diversity"), contains the peripherally Atlantean reference:

> Within your voice the boughs of Eden sigh
> In scented winds blown from the summer foam;
> But in your gaze the lulling hills of home
> Accept the silence of an autumn sky.[3] (*SP* 169)

The equation of Eden to the almost utopian, semi-paradisiacal world of Plato's Atlantis is borne out by one possible interpretation of lines 1–2. Restricting our examination to these two lines only, we may evolve two different interpretations of what exactly is the physical image that Smith intends within the context. The first reading is that the boughs of Eden sigh because of the scented winds blown from the summer foam (i.e., at the edge of the ocean littoral). The second reading is that, within the scented winds blown from the summer foam, we can hear the boughs of Eden sigh, and that the summer foam causes this sound as a memory, as an auditory resurrection, of an Eden lost or sunk, Atlantis-wise, beneath the sea. Which reading is the correct one, is impossible to tell due to the word-arrangement dictated by the exigencies of verse-rhetoric.

The second quatrain, "Lemurienne" (first entitled "The Lemurienne"), has a directly generical Atlantean reference, apart from the title (which apparently indicates a female inhabitant of that Atlantis of the Indian Ocean, or of the Pacific, Lemuria).

> From dawn to dawn your eyes of graven spar
> For ever change, with chill forgotten runes;
> But all the while your spirit lies afar,
> A sphinx that peers on prediluvian moons.[4] (*SP* 169)

Also created at approximately the same time (1923–25) as the poems in *Sandalwood* (including the pieces quoted above among others) is an extensive series of epigrams and pensées first published in the *Auburn Journal*. This is one of the few places in his overall creativity where Smith makes a number of overt references to a narrow contemporaneity. Most of these epigrams might be characterized as up-to-date, smart, topical; and these have predictably dated the most. Some of them are still amusing, and some still possess genuine interest. In the *Auburn Journal* for Thursday, 15 November 1923, four items appear under the title "Points for the Pious." The second of these four items, one of the most perceptive of the real pensées, contains an unexpected reference to Atlantis:

> The terror of Lilith, the fear of beauty and its destructive potentialities, lies at the heart of all puritanism. Humanity has always been divided into those who loved beauty and those who were afraid of it. Doubtless there were witch-burners in ancient Atlantis. (*DN* 53)

These same years also saw Smith writing his first play, *The Fugitives*, which he failed to complete. This was a romantic drama composed in blank verse interspersed with songs. All the songs that Smith wrote for the play, he included in *Sandalwood*: "Song" or "The Fugitive"; "The Song of Aviol"; "The Love-Potion"; and "The Song of Cartha." In his letter to R. H. Barlow dated 23 November 1936, Smith described the plot, one surprisingly dealing with Atlantis, as follows:

> The plot was a simple and quite romantic one: it began with the mutual dawning of love in an Atlantean boy and girl, soon to be separated. Later, they were to meet again: the boy a wandering poet of recognized genius, the girl a king's concubine. Their old love reawakens, they flee from the Atlantean court and capital, to perish in the wilderness after several days and nights of mad happiness. (*SL* 275)

Such a play, developed in several acts and various tableaux, would have made a notable addition to the one play that he did complete, but evidently much later, *The Dead Will Cuckold You*.

In the summer of 1928, following the death of George Sterling in November 1926 (an event of great consequence for Smith as one of Sterling's closest friends), Smith began writing his mature fiction, a development marked by the brief prose fantasy "The Ninth Skeleton." Between 1928 and 1938 he was to write over one hundred and forty short stories and novelettes. In December 1929 he created some ten poems in prose later designated as "prose pastels"—and in one of them, "To the Daemon," composed on the 16th, the poet addresses his tutelary daemon, or genius, asking this entity, suitably enough, to tell him "many tales" but not necessarily of Atlantis, among other esoteric locations.

> Tell me many tales, O benign maleficent daemon, but tell me none that I have ever heard or have even dreamt of otherwise than obscurely or infrequently. Nay, tell me not of anything that lies between the bourns of time or the limits of space; for I am a little weary of all recorded years and chartered lands; and the isles that are westward of Cathay, and the sunset realms of Ind, are not remote enough to be made the abiding-place of my conceptions; and Atlantis is over-new for my thoughts

to sojourn there, and Mu itself has gazed upon the sun in aeons that are too recent.

Tell me many tales, but let them be of things that are past the lore of legend and of which there are no myths in our world or any world adjoining. [...] Tell me tales of inconceivable fear and unimaginable love, in orbs whereto our sun is a nameless star, or unto which its rays have never reached. (*NU* 17–18)

However, be his request as it may have been, the daemon did tell him something of Plato's lost world, for included in Smith's prose fictions of 1928–38 are five tales of Atlantis, or (more correctly) "the last isle of foundering Atlantis"—to wit, Poseidonis. These tales comprise "The Last Incantation," "The Death of Malygris," "The Double Shadow," "A Voyage to Sfanomoë" (the last word Smith pronounced with the accent on the second syllable), and "A Vintage from Atlantis." These must be ranked among Smith's finest efforts in prose. It is very difficult to classify these tales, as it is most of Smith's fiction. In form they are poems in prose; but conceptually and symbolically they may be generally considered as fables, parables, allegories.

An important point to remember is that, while only five of his tales concern Atlantis, or Poseidonis, precisely, Smith's other lost worlds, especially his other continents of Earth—which he has used or created as a background for some of his other stories—are implicitly Atlantean in concept-principle: Hyperborea, the first inhabited continent of Earth, a sort of proto-Atlantis; and Zothique, the last continent of Earth, a sort of infinitely latter-day Atlantis arisen out of the sea, while all the other former continents have subsided beneath the globe-wide oceans.

In one of the specifically Atlantean tales the poet vouchsafes us a full-scale vision of Plato's ancient capital of Atlantis. This occurs in "A Vintage from Atlantis," a tale that Smith created in November 1931. This vision is one of the great set-pieces of typically Smithian description, comparable to any of the same engineered by Edmund Spenser for his epic-romance-allegory *The Faerie Queene*.

> The air about me seemed to brighten, with a redness of ghostly blood that was everywhere; a light that came not from the fire nor from the nocturnal heavens. I beheld the faces and forms of the drinkers [the fellow crew-members of the narrator], standing without shadow, as if mantled with a rosy phosphorescence. And beyond them, where they stared in troubled and restless wonder, the darkness was illumed with a strange light.
>
> Mad and unholy was the vision that I saw: for the harbour waves no longer lapped on the sand, and the sea had wholly vanished. The *Black Falcon* was gone, and where the reefs had been, great marble walls ascended, flushed as if with the ruby of lost sunsets. Above them were haughty domes of heathen temples, and spires of pagan palaces; and beneath were mighty streets and causeys where people passed in a never-ending throng. I thought that I gazed upon some immemorial city, such as had flourished in Earth's prime; and I saw the trees of its terraced gardens, fairer than the palms of Eden. Listening, I heard the sound of dulcimers that were sweet as the moaning of women; and the cry of horns that told forgot-

ten glorious things; and the wild sweet singing of people who passed to some hidden, sacred festival within the walls.

I saw that the light poured upward from the city, and was born of its streets and buildings. It blinded the heavens above; and the horizon beyond was lost in a shining mist. One building there was, a high fane above the rest, from which the light streamed in a ruddier flood; and from its open portals music came, sorcerous and beguiling as the far voices of bygone years. And the revellers passed gayly into its portals, but none came forth. The weird music seemed to call me and entice me; and I longed to tread the streets of the alien city, and a deep desire was upon me to mingle with its people and pass into the glowing Lane.

Verily I knew why the drinkers had stared at the darkness and had muttered among themselves in wonder. I knew that they also longed to descend into the city. And I saw that a great causey, built of marble and gleaming with the red luster, ran downward from their very feet over meadows of unknown blossoms to the foremost buildings.

Then, as I watched and listened, the singing grew sweeter, the music stranger, and the rosy luster brightened. Then, with no backward glance, no word or gesture of injunction to his men, Captain Dwale went slowly forward, treading the marble causey like a dreamer who walks in his dream. And after him, one by one, Roger Aglone and the crew followed in the same manner, going toward the city.

Haply I too should have followed, drawn by the witching music. For truly it seemed that I had trod the ways of that city in former time, and had known the things whereof the music told and the voices sang. Well did I remember why the people passed eternally into the Lane, and why they came not forth; and there, it seemed, I should meet familiar and beloved faces, and take part in mysteries recalled from the foundered years.

All this, which the wine had remembered through its sleep in the ocean depths, was mine to behold and conceive for a moment. And well it was that I had drunk less of that evil and pagan vintage than the others, and was less besotted than they with its luring vision. For even as Captain Dwale and his crew went toward the city, it appeared to me that the rosy glow began to fade a little. The walls took on a wavering thinness, and the domes grew insubstantial. The rose departed, the light was pale as a phosphor of the tomb; and the people went to and fro like phantoms, with a thin crying of ghostly horns and a ghostly singing. Dimly above the sunken causey the harbor waves returned; and Red Barnaby and his men walked down beneath them. Slowly the waters darkened above the Lading spires and walls; and the midnight blackened upon the sea; and the city was lost like the vanished bubbles of wine. (*AY* 52–54)

It is of interest to note—among the abundance of many other details in this overall vision—that, toward the end of the second paragraph quoted, we have a repeat or echo of "the palms of Eden" from the original version of "Dissidence"—"and I saw the trees of its terraced gardens, fairer than the palms of Eden."

After 1938, Smith virtually gave up the writing of prose fiction, at least in any real amount, and had returned to his first love, the creation of poetry in verse. In some of this later lyric poetry we find some scattered Atlantean references, and even a few full-scale Atlantean poems. Smith's new, rejuvenated poetic drive or impulsion would last almost up until the time of his death, fueled as it was by two remarkable and lasting love affairs.

In 1951, Arkham House, after bringing out three collections of Smith's highly imaginative fiction (in 1942, 1944, and 1948), published its first collection of poetry by the same author, *The Dark Chateau*, three of whose pieces contain Atlantean references. In the sixth and seventh stanzas of *"Dominium in Excelsis"* we note "the fabled Atlantean doom," but now coupled with a resurrection out of the condition of such a catastrophic death.

> Thou shalt respire the flame and fume
> Of Beltis' altars drowned in gloom
> Under her sharded fanes; or share
> The fabled Atlantean doom,
>
> And rise unharmed to light and air
> Out of old death, once more to dare
> With antinomian deed and thought
> The planet of thy slain despair— (*DC* 17–18)

In the second and third stanzas of "Malediction" there occurs a reference to Atlantis but the Atlantis in question is imaged as being "accurst." (We also quote the sixth stanza as well as the final single line that follows it for an easier syntactical comprehension by the reader.)

> While the worms, apart from light,
> Eat the page where magians pored;
> While the kraken, blind and white,
>
> Guards the greening books abhorred
> Where the evil oghams rust—
> In accurst Atlantis stored;
>
> [...]
>
> Never shall the spell be done
> And the curse be lifted never
> That shall find and leave you one
>
> With forgotten things for ever. (*DC* 26)

And in the final lines (47–54) of "Revenant" we note an allusion to "atlantean fanes" but clearly intended by the poet in a generic rather than a specific usage, as clearly demonstrated by his abandonment of the upper-case *a* at the start of the adjective "atlantean."

> Mummied and ceremented,
> I sit in councils of the kingly dead,
> And oftentimes for vestiture I wear
> The granite of great idols looming darkly
> In atlantean fanes;
> Or closely now and starkly,
> I cling as clings the attenuating air
> Above the ruins bare. (*DC* 54)

In 1958, Arkham House published its second collection of poetry by Smith, *Spells and Philtres*, which has two Atlantean references. Our first example Atlantean is the entire poem of "Tolometh," detailing as it does a major god of Poseidonis, the large island that Smith presents as the last major fragment of foundering Atlantis, evidently taking a clue from the Theosophist writings of Helena Blavatsky:

> In billow-lost Poseidonis
> I was the black god of the abyss;
> My three horns were of similor
> Above my double diadem;
> My one eye was a moon-bright gem
> Found in a monstrous meteor.
>
> Incredible far peoples came,
> Called by the thunders of my fame,
> And passed below my terraced throne
> Where titan pards and lions stood,
> As pours a never-lapsing flood
> Before the wind of winter blown.
>
> Below my glooming architraves
> One brown eternal file of slaves
> Came in from mines of chalcedon,
> And camels from the long plateaus
> Laid down their sard and peridoz,
> Their incense and their cinnamon.
>
> The star-born evil that I brought
> Through all that ancient land was wrought;
> All women took my yoke of shame;
> I reared, through sunless centuries,
> The thrones of hell-black wizardries,
> The hecatombs of blood and flame.

> But now, within my sunken walls,
> The slow blind ocean-serpent crawls,
> And sea-worms are my ministers,
> And wandering fishes pass me now
> Or press before mine eyeless brow
> As once the thronging worshippers. . . .
>
> And yet, in ways outpassing thought,
> Men worship me that know me not.
> They work my will. I shall arise
> In that last dawn of atom-fire,
> To stand upon the planet's pyre
> And cast my shadow on the skies. (*SP* 274–75)

Our second example Atlantean occurs in "The Prophet Speaks," which devotes its full second stanza to an Atlantean allusion but, as in the case of "Malediction" included in *The Dark Chateau*, the Atlantis in question the poet views through a glass darkly. (We quote the first full stanza as well on behalf of the reader's easier comprehension.)

> City forbanned by seer and god and devil!
> In glory less than Tyre or fabled Ys,
> But more than they in mere, surpassing evil!
>
> Yea, black Atlantis, fallen beneath dim seas
> For sinful lore and rites to demons done,
> Bore not the weight of such iniquities. (*LO* 102)

For our final examples of Atlanteana from Smith's overall corpus of published poetry, we turn to the final section of his final and finally published collection of collections, *Selected Poems*, brought out by Arkham House in late 1971. This final section embodies the cycle of love poems *The Hill of Dionysus*, which evolved out of the great friendship or deep love that Smith shared with the younger poet Eric Barker and his wife, the dancer Madelynne Greene.[5] Their friendship began in early 1938 and did not end until Smith's death in August 1961, but waxed at its strongest in the period 1938–55, the poems themselves apparently coming into being in the years 1939–47.

Smith's mother Fanny, or Frances, Gaylord Smith, had passed on in early September 1935, and his father in late December 1937. The family had lived together since the poet's birth, and just as his parents had nurtured him both as person and as poet, so their son had nurtured and nursed the parents, both of them in turn, through their final phase of old age or terminal ill health. Thus the family had always been very close, that is, had lived as almost constant companions for over four full decades, from the early 1890s on into the mid-1930s. By early 1938 Smith found himself not only very much alone but also very lonely. Into this real void the

Barkers arrived, and their friendship filled and fulfilled a true need in Smith's life. The three of them would visit back and forth between Auburn and the California coast (mostly San Rafael, San Francisco, and the Monterey, Carmel, and Big Sur area) during the next twenty years. They would share many pleasant hours of companionship, not to mention a number of whimsical adventures. How much this love meant to Smith, and in particular the love that he consummated with Madelynne, the poet reveals in "Wizard's Love," one of the earliest poems in the cycle *The Hill of Dionysus,* a favorite hill in San Rafael covered with giant oak trees where they loved to have picnics and similar outings.

> O perfect love, unhoped-for, past despair!
> I had not thought to find
> Your face betwixt the terrene earth and air:
> But deemed you lost in fabulous old lands
> And rose-lit years to darkness long resigned.
> O child, you cannot know
> What magic and what miracles you bring
> Within your tender hands;
> What griefs are lulled to blissful slumbering,
> Cushioned upon your deep and fragrant hair;
> What gall-black bitterness of long ago,
> Within my bosom sealed,
> Ebbs gradually as might some desert well
> Under your beauty's heaven warm and fair,
> And the green suns of your vertumnal eyes.
>
> O beauty wrought of rapture and surprise,
> Too dear for heart to know, or tongue to tell! (*SP* 366–67)

The lucid statement of profound emotion in "Wizard's Love" informs us without equivocation just how much value Smith placed on the supreme adventure of love, a value also borne out emphatically by the two final paragraphs from "The Enchantress of Sylaire," one of Smith's Averoigne chronicles. The two main characters are the poet Anselme and the enchantress herself:

> Again the clinging deliciousness of Sephora was in his arms, and her fruit-soft mouth was crushed beneath his hungry lips.
> The strongest of all enchantments held them in its golden circle. (*AY* 140)

As we know from her letter to Donald Sidney-Fryer, written in the spring of 1967 (*EOD* 154), the love that bound Ashton, Eric, and Madelynne together, and that Madelynne fully shared, inspired the three of them in so many different ways. However, as Madelynne made it clear to Sidney-Fryer in the course of their friendship (from late 1966 until her death at the age of fifty-eight in the early or middle 1970s), Smith had often wanted Eric and herself to move to Auburn so that they could all reside together or close by each other. Nevertheless, Madelynne as dancer and as teacher of dance needed the conveniences and advantages of a big city like San Francisco. She confided that, as much as she loved Ashton, and loved spending long sojourns with him near Auburn or on the coast, she could never have lived with him on a regular basis. As Madelynne expressed this, and with real regret, she found Smith such a melancholy man that she found it much too depressing to stay with him indefinitely. She and Eric later introduced Smith to Carol Jones Dorman sometime during latter 1954. Eric was living at that time as a caretaker on some property in Little Sur (not far from Big Sur), and Smith had come to visit on an occasion when Carol also happened to be there as a friend to both Eric and Madelynne. Smith and Carol fell in love almost immediately, and were married in mid-November 1954.

Too many readers or critics, at least those of male gender, have underestimated or have simply ignored the specific love poems by Smith, beginning with those included in *Ebony and Crystal* and *Sandalwood*, continuing through *The Jasmine Girdle,* and concluding with *The Hill of Dionysus* (which remains Smith's last major cycle of poems of any description). Such poems unequivocally make us intimate with the hope and even optimism that Smith reveals in this one area of experience, even in the face of unavoidable doom. *Maître de conférence* and specialist in highly imaginative literature in the English department at the University of Nantes (the major city in northwest France at the mouth of the river Loire, just southeast of Brittany), Lauric Guillaud has asked in a recent and excellent critical evaluation of Smith's oeuvre the following question: "Yet is it correct to assume that Smith's universe is really barren of any hope?" (207). In answering his own question, Guillaud typically neglects or overlooks the evidence to be found in Smith's overt love poetry.

The final stanza of "Resurrection" embodies our first specific Atlantean reference from *The Hill of Dionysus:*

> Witch belovèd from of old
> When upon Atlantis rolled
> All the dire and wrathful deep,
> You had kissed mine eyes asleep.
> On my lids shall fall your lips
> In the final sun's eclipse;
> And your hand shall take my hand
> In the last and utmost land. (*LO* 144–45)

Our next Atlantean reference we find in the opening and closing of "Bond," with its poignant statement of love's eternal return with the same lovers reincarnating from century to century:

> By the red seal redoubled of that kiss
> When thy lips parted softly to my own
> Ere the sun sank from doomed Poseidonis;

> [. . .]
> By the sealed ways no prophet has foreshown,
> Whereon our lips shall meet, our footsteps go:—
> By these, by these I claim thee for mine own. . . .
>
> Even as I have claimed thee long ago. (*SP* 378)

Some especially poignant Atlantean references feature in the opening and closing of *"Amor Hesternalis."* The opening stanza is particularly haunting:

> Our blood is swayed by sunken moons
> And lulled by midnights long foredone;
> We waken to a foundered sun
> In Atlantean afternoons:
> Our blood is swayed by sunken moons.
> [. . .]
> We are the specters of past years:
> But soon Atlantis from the main
> Shall lift; and Sappho bring again,
> Risen from ancient brine and tears,
> The living Lesbos of past years. (*SP* 387)

The entire lyric that is "Sea Cycle" adumbrates, but only implicitly, an Atlantean content as the opening and closing of the poem in question clearly demonstrate:

> Below the cliff, before the granite stair,
> The foam-crests curl and feather in blue air,
> Numberless as the helmet-plumes of hosts
> Resurgent from millennium-foundered coasts.
> [. . .]
> Though prayer be vain, this thing shall come to pass,
> For still the solemn cycles wane and flow,
> Bringing again the lost and long ago.
> All that the sea has taken, the sea restores:
> Somehow, somewhere, on ocean-winnowed shores,
> Again we two shall wander, and shall not stay,
> Finding the golden wrack of yesterday. (*SP* 399–400)

Another example of a lyric doing so implicitly, the very final poem in the entire cycle, the sonnet "Avowal," adumbrates many an Atlantis arising out of the far future—deep in "the cosmic sea sublime"—but all of which shall arise in vain, if it does not restore to us the pristine beauty, wonder, love, and mystery from our collective past, immeasurable and immemorial:

> Whatever alien fruits and changeling faces
> And pleasances of mutable perfume
> The flambeaux of the senses shall illume
> Amid the night-filled labyrinthine spaces,
> In lives to be, in unestablished places,
> All, all were vain as the rock-raveled spume
> If no strange close restore the Paphian bloom,
> No path return the moon-shod maenad's paces.
>
> Yea, for the lover of lost pagan things,
> No vintage grown in islands unascended
> Shall quite supplant the old Bacchantic urn,
> No mouth that new Canopic suns make splendid
> Content the mouth of sealed rememberings
> Where still the nymph's uncleaving kisses burn. (*SP* 403)

The last completed poem that Smith created (insofar as our present information allows us to state) is the sonnet in alexandrines, "Cycles," written on 4 June 1961, a little more than two months before his death on 14 August 1961. Donald Sidney-Fryer commissioned this lyric expressly for his *Emperor of Dreams: A Clark Ashton Smith Bibliography*, omitted therefrom by happenstance. This thus contains Smith's very last reference to Atlantis in print:

> The sorcerer departs . . . and his high tower is drowned
> Slowly by low flat communal seas that level all . . .
> While crowding centuries retreat, return and fall
> Into the cyclic gulf that girds the cosmos round,
> Widening, deepening ever outward without bound . . .
> Till the oft-rerisen bells from young Atlantis call;
> And again the wizard-mortised tower upbuilds its wall
> Above a re-beginning cycle, turret-crowned.
>
> New-born, the mage re-summons stronger spells, and spirits
> With dazzling darkness clad about, and fierier flame
> Renewed by aeon-curtained slumber. All the powers
> Of genii and Solomon the sage inherits;
> And there, to blaze with blinding glory the bored hours,
> He calls upon Shem-hamphorash, the nameless Name. (*LO* 174)

The love specifically taking place between Smith and Madelynne, which waxed at its strongest, it would seem, during 1939–47 (approximately), had enabled Smith to discover a late-blossoming period of intensely poetic activity and creativity. During the middle to latter 1940s the poet was concurrently preparing the enormous typescript of his *Selected Poems*, a task that represented a huge challenge for him in terms of collating manuscripts, and of rethinking and retyping a vast amount of material. The whole task became hampered and complicated by the fact that during much of the process Smith was experiencing serious eye trouble.

Nevertheless, despite such problems, out of this enormously fruitful period, like some unexpected Atlantis arising out from the ocean of time and memory, there came into palpable being his last major cycle of new poetry, and of new love poems at that. This new corpus of pure but accessible lyricism presents a remarkable efflorescence of creativity, indeed, for a poet at the half-century mark of his lifetime, when some commentators might have considered him already to be past his most fruitful prime. As formulated elsewhere, "Phoenix-like, the poet had been reborn out of the ashes of the fiction-writer" (Sidney-Fryer, 19).

Acknowledgments

Together with other materials by other authors, this essay was originally prepared for a special issue (No. 5) of the then promising semi-prozine *Anubis*. The issue was projected to appear sometime during the late 1960s (or the early 1970s). Most of the contents were written or compiled c. 1966 or 1967. For a variety of reasons not quite explained or made clear, the number in question has never made its appearance, nor has any other issue of *Anubis*, for that matter.

When a photocopy of this essay (as laid out on sheets readied for photopublishing), together with a copy of a map of Poseidonis by Tim Kirk, found their way back into the hands of the present author (courtesy of Don Herron and Ronald S. Hilger) in May 2002, the original conclusion was completely missing (i.e., following the first mention of the 1958 Arkham House collection of poems *Spells and Philtres*). The present author perforce had to re-create it from a re-reading of the cycle of love poems *The Hill of Dionysus* and other materials, with a discussion of which he had originally finished the essay. To this he has added some biographical details never before vouchsafed concerning the relationship among the poet Eric Barker, the dancer Madelynne Greene, and Clark Ashton Smith himself.

Otherwise, during the latter half of September 2002, the present author has also revised this essay in ways both major and minor. In particular he would like to thank his personal friends Don Herron, Ronald Hilger, and Rah Hoffman for verifying information or for the use of books and other materials.

Notes

1. Nora May French, a remarkably gifted poet, was born at Aurora, New York, in 1881 and died by her own hand at Carmel-by-the-Sea, California, in late 1907 while residing there as a guest of George and Carrie Sterling. (GS was the unofficial poet laureate of the west coast from about 1903 until his death in 1926.) Nora May's body was cremated, and a group of friends in a special ceremony scattered her ashes into the Pacific Ocean from Point Lobos just south of Carmel. Posthumously gathered and edited by Henry Anderson Lafler (with the help of GS and critic Porter Garnett), her one and

only collection *Poems* appeared in 1910, as published by the Strange Company, San Francisco. (Porter Garnett himself did the actual printing of the volume.)

2. CAS eliminated the reference to Atlantis when he revised this poem for *SP*. In the first published version of this poem, "the boughs of Eden" reads "the palm of Eden."

3. In the first published version of the poem above, l. 4 reads: "A sphinx that peers on lost Lemuric moons."

4. The original version of this poem was republished in the *Arkham Collector* for Summer 1968.

5. The young Madelynne Greene was a strikingly beautiful woman of Irish descent with dark auburn hair, green eyes, and well-shaped body, which she kept supple, strong, and well-toned by means of her daily dance exercises.

Works Cited

Greene, Madelynne. Letter. In *EOD,* p. 154.

Guillard, Lauric. "Fantasy and Decadence in the Work of Clark Ashton Smith." *Paradoxa* 5 (1999–2000): 189–212.

Sidney-Fryer, Donald. *The Sorcerer Departs*. 1963. West Hills, CA: Tsathoggua Press, 1997.

Sterling, George. *The Thirst of Satan: Poems of Fantasy and Terror*. Ed. S. T. Joshi. New York: Hippocampus Press, 2003.

Coming In from the Cold:
Incursions of "Outsideness" in Hyperborea

Steven Tompkins

This primal continent seems to have been particularly subject to incursions of "outsideness"—more so, in fact, than any of the other continents and terrene realms that lie behind us in the time stream.
—Clark Ashton Smith, Letter to H. P. Lovecraft, February 1931

Humanism: a sort of cosmic provincialism; the egomania of the species; the jingoism of earthlings; the religion of Lilliput.
—*The Devil's Notebook*

> All things that move between the quiet poles
> Shall be at my command. Emperors and kings
> Are but obeyed in their several provinces.
> Nor can they raise the wind or rend the clouds.
> But his dominion that exceeds in this
> Stretcheth as far as doth the mind of man:
> A sound magician is a demi-god.
> —Christopher Marlowe
> *The Tragical History of Doctor Faustus*

Clark Ashton Smith's Hyperborea is usually just a flyover on the nonstop trillion-year flight to Zothique. Critical attention has for the most part followed the migratory route of the gazolba-bird in "The Voyage of King Euvoran"; before leading that monarch on the end-times equivalent of a wild-goose chase to "the archipelagoes of wonder" and "far coasts of dawn" in the finalized story, the fowl in question first had to wing its way from the Hyperborean setting of Smith's initial inspiration across sundering series-seas to the Last Continent.

Even the distinction Smith confers upon Hyperborea in the letter to H. P. Lovecraft that yielded this article's first epigraph endures for only one sentence, and then, as so often, the last shall be first:

> But I have heard it hinted in certain obscure and arcanic prophecies that the far-future continent called Gnydron by some and Zothique by others, which will rise millions of years hence in what is now the South Atlantic, will surpass even Hy-

perborea in . . . incursions of "outsideness" . . . and will witness the intrusion of Things from galaxies not yet visible; and worse than this, a hideously chaotic breaking-down of dimensional barriers which will leave parts of our world in other dimensions and vice-versa. (*CAS* 24)

Steve Behrends has pointed out that the Hyperborean cycle "acts in some ways as a foil to the Zothique series" (*CAS* 38), and the Last Continent, which would be a tough act to follow were it not for the fact that nothing *will* follow, is certainly a tough act for Hyperborea to precede. The earlier landmass, "at the opposite extreme of Earth's habitability" (*CAS* 38), lacks the necrotic appeal of Zothique, the stories about which can be read in the dark by the light of their own ghastly viridescence. As the *ne plus ultra* of "terrene realms," Zothique has going for it "the black weariness of a dying race, grown hopeless of all but oblivion." Constituting as it does a definitive refutation of Andrew Marvell's assertion in "To His Coy Mistress" that *The grave's a fine and private place / But none, I think, do there embrace*, the Last Continent offers a modicum of carrion comfort to the reader and more than that to the author, deemed by Donald Sidney-Fryer to be "one of death's most lyrical celebrators" (Sidney-Fryer 22). The consensus on this subject choruses from commentators like L. Sprague de Camp ("Nobody since Poe has so loved a well-rotted corpse" [de Camp 206]), James Cawthorn and Michael Moorcock ("If Death had ever decided to hire a good PR man, Smith would have filled the bill" [Cawthorn and Moorcock 95]), and Fritz Leiber ("Death in all its phases—from maggot-banquets to mere forgetting (erasing forever from all tables of memory)—seems to be his chief inspiration and theme" [Leiber 72]). Theodore Sturgeon suggested that the attraction was mutual: "Death always loved and wooed you, Klarkash-Ton" (Sturgeon xiv).

Zothique at its most Zothiquean, as a congeries of death's other kingdom[s]," could be the "last of meeting places" in T. S. Eliot's "The Hollow Men":

> This is the dead land
> This is the cactus land
> Here the stone images
> Are raised, here they receive
> The supplication of a dead man's hand
> Under the twinkle of a fading star. . . .
>
> There are no eyes here
> In this valley of dying stars
> In this hollow valley
> This broken jaw of our lost kingdoms.

Hyperborea by comparison is aglow by the dawn's early light; "the world is new and fresh . . . and humanity is a relative newcomer" (*CAS* 38). But humanity's tomb would turn out to be a livelier place than humanity's womb. The Hyperboreans are not the last of any, but merely the first of many, to be damned or doomed. The quick and the dead of Zothique model their cerements on their doom-black runway with the glamour of the lost and the last, while the inhabitants of the earlier landmass seem afflicted with rigor mortis. They come to bad ends without having come to life first; they are often consumed but never by doubts, and their egos dwarf even the still-abundant local megafauna. The stories of the Primal Continent are a bonfire of the vanities over which Smith roasts his not-so-grand inquisitors, and although his indebtedness to Lord Dunsany has been disputed, the stratospheric altitude of the Hyperborean cycle, the sense of some eyrie from which Smith looks down upon even the toploftiest tip of what would be considered high tragedy from a less elevated perspective, is very much in the tradition of the Dunsanian agenda cited by S. T. Joshi in his introduction to *The Complete Pegāna*: "One of the most chilling lines in all literature, perhaps, is the simple utterance of the gods in 'Of How Imbaun Met Zodrak': 'Let Us call up a man before Us that We may laugh in Pegāna'" (Joshi x).

And yet the theme of these weird fiction stories is not just *Oh, what fools these mortals be*, but also *Oh, how mortal these mortals be*. Mindful of Smith's strictures in his "Macrocosmic Horror" essay, we need to look at how weird things get in Hyperborea, and how they get weird:

> the main object is the creation of a supernatural, extra-human atmosphere; the real actors are the terrible arcanic forces, the esoteric cosmic malignities; and the element of human character, if one is to achieve the highest, most objective artistry, is properly somewhat subordinated. . . . One is depicting things, powers and conditions that are beyond humanity; therefore, artistically speaking, the main accent is on these things, powers and conditions. (*PD* 18)

As "the proper focus of interest," the "terrible arcanic forces" and "esoteric cosmic malignities" that are "the real actors" on the Hyperborean stage deserve our consideration.

It is a pleasant departure from the ridicule that the late Lin Carter was so assiduous in bringing upon himself to be able to note that Steve Behrends and Will Murray have complimented his "conjectural ordering" of the Hyperborean stories as "an ingenious job" (*CAS* 43) and "quite sound" (Murray, *BH* 14). This article will mostly review Hyperborea's "incursions of outsideness" in the Carter-dated sequence, so as to avoid the chronological rewinds and fast-forwards cheerfully acknowledged by Murray:

> The reader coming to Clark Ashton Smith's Hyperborea for the first time will find that the story sequence skips back and forth through Hyperborean eras, with cities rising up and falling back into ruin at random, and doomful hints and portents bearing cold fruit in later tales while older dooms are explained long after the fact. (Murray, *BH* 14)

In "The Seven Geases" with none of Murray's cold fruit in the offing as of yet we meet Hyperborean hubris incarnate in the person of Lord Ralibar Vooz, "High magistrate of Commoriom and third cousin to King Homquat" and a Nimrod in more ways than one, with the blue-blood's passion for bloodsports. He disdains "the great sloths and vampire-bats of the intermediate jungle, as well as the small but noxious dinosauria" in favor of the peak experience of hunting the most dangerous, because most nearly human, game on Mount Voormithadreth in "the black Eiglophian mountains"—the Voormis, autochthonous hominids known for "the uses to which their captives were put before death and after it," as a spare but unsparing Smith disclosure tells us (*BH* 126).

The hunting party is divided against itself—lordling on one side, retainers on the other—when it comes to the origin of the Voormis. Conventional wisdom has it that they are

> the offspring of women and certain atrocious creatures that had come forth in primal days from a tenebrous cavern-world in the bowels of Voormithadreth. Somewhere beneath that four-coned mountain, the sluggish and baleful god Tsathoggua, who had come down from Saturn in years immediately following the Earth's creation, was fabled to reside; and during the rites of worship at his black altars, the devotees were always careful to orient themselves toward Voormithadreth. (*BH* 126)

Ralibar Vooz prides himself on being a freethinker, or at least sees no reason to worship anything but his own ancestors:

> He swore with many ribald blasphemies that there were no gods anywhere, either above or below Voormithadreth. As for the Voormis themselves, they were indeed a misbegotten species; but it was hardly necessary, in explaining their generation, to go beyond the familiar laws of nature. They were merely the remnant of a low and degraded tribe of aborigines, who, sinking further into brutehood, had sought refuge in those volcanic fastnesses after the coming of the true Hyperboreans. (*BH* 126)

So it would seem that the Hyperboreans were trespassers long before they ever set foot in the Eiglophians. They accordingly tote crossbows and long-handled bills for engaging in meaningful dialogue with the Voormis at a safe, or at least safer, distance. Forewarned is forearmed—forearmed to the teeth:

> The whole party was variously studded with auxiliary knives, throwing-darts, two-handed scimitars, maces, bodkins, and saw-toothed axes. The men were all clad in jerkins and hose of dinosaur-leather, and were shod with brazen-spiked buskins. Ralibar Vooz himself wore a light suiting of copper chain-mail, which, flexible as cloth, in no wise impeded his movements. In addition he carried a buckler of mammoth-hide with a long bronze spike in its center that could be used as a thrusting-sword; and, being a man of huge stature and strength, his shoulders and baldric were hung with a whole arsenal of weaponries. (*BH* 125)

The marshalling of so much martial paraphernalia, that "huge stature and strength"—how many *Weird Tales* readers fell for Smith's feint in the direction of the sword-and-sorcery Robert E. Howard had made so popular by 1934? After he is separated from his men-at-arms, circumstances force Ralibar Vooz to serve as his own herald, trumpeting his significance to the sorcerer Ezdagor, but the latter, disturbed in mid-ritual, snaps "I care not if you are the magistrate of all swinedom or a cousin to the king of dogs" (*BH* 129)—a retort of such brio as to reinforce what we already knew from *The Dead Will Cuckold You*, that Smith could have been a dramatist of some notoriety in any century save the twentieth.

Ezdagor proceeds to chastise the Hyperborean with a geas that compels him to fight his weaponless way past the Voormis and deliver himself to none other than Tsathoggua, the Primal Continent's paramount toad-in-the-hole. For a psychopomps he is loaned Rapthontis, the mage's familiar, proof that the loss of the gazolba-bird to Zothique did not leave Hyperborea ornithologically bereft: "A lizard-tailed and sooty-feathered bird, which seemed to belong to some night-flying species of archaeopteryx, began to snap its toothed beak and flap its digited wings on the objectionably shapen stela that served it for a perch" (*BH* 129). What follows reads like a Howardian means to a Smithian end:

> Weaponless he fought them in obedience to his geas, striking down their hideous faces with his mailed fists in a veritable madness that was not akin to the madness of a huntsman. He felt their nails and teeth break on the close-woven links as he hurled them loose; but others took their place when he won onward a little into the murky cavern; and their females struck at his legs like darting serpents; and their young beslavered his ankles with mouths wherein the fangs were as yet ungrown. (*BH* 132)

As "The Seven Geases" spelunks its way through caverns measureless to man, it becomes clear that man is not the measure of all things. Ralibar Vooz is no Heracles, Odysseus, or Aeneas in the underworld, but merely an interruption and an irritant. He survives repeated rejections by various entities and phantasmal phyla even if his *amour-propre* does not; among those he encounters is the "antehuman sorcerer" Haon-Dor, whose thousand-columned palace might have rivaled Gaznak's Fortress Unvanquishable or Tsotha-lanti's Scarlet Citadel had we been permitted to revisit in a completed "The House of Haon-Dor": "A chill spirit of evil, ancient beyond all conception of man, was abroad in those halls; and horror and fear crept through them like invisible serpents, unknotted from sleep" (*BH* 135). Ultimately redirected to "the bleak and drear and dreadful limbo known as the Outer World," Ralibar Vooz is digesting not only humble pie but the sushi Rapthontis shares with him when he loses his footing as he has lost his place in the hierarchy of being. Pride goeth before a fall, but it goeth so many geases before *this* fall that current readers may be inclined to think, as does Ryan Harvey, of "the written equivalent of a rim-shot punctuating a stand-up comedian's bad joke" (Harvey, "Fantasy Cycles" Part II). "The Seven Geases" is not a throwaway, but its protagonist is.

J. R. R. Tolkien said of the saurian whose hot pursuit of a single item thieved from his hoard draws Beowulf into one last man-versus-monster confrontation that "Nowhere does a dragon come in so precisely where he should" (Tolkien, "Beowulf" 31). Similarly, nowhere does a monster for whom the arrival of a "plump and well-fed" moneylender guarantees that he, too, will feed well come in so precisely where he should as in "The Weird of Avoosl Wutthoqquan":

> The entity was wholly and outrageously unhuman; and neither did it resemble any species of animal, or any known god or demon of Hyperborea. Its aspect was not such as to lessen the alarm and panic of the moneylender; for it was very large and pale and squat, with a toad-like face and a swollen, squidgy body and numerous cuttlefish limbs or appendages. It lay flat on the shelf, with its chinless head and long slit-like mouth overhanging the pit, and its cold, lidless eyes peering obliquely at Avoosl Wuthoqquan. (*BH* 69)

The usurer's comeuppance is richly deserved (and richly encumbered as he flounders in a "treacherous quicksand" of wealth). His pursuit of profit leads him to the discovery that the story's creature is itself a moneylender or speculator of sorts, one that suffered two of its emeralds to be borne away into the outside world, confident that it need not bestir itself like the *Beowulf*-dragon—that there would be a return on its investment. Best of all, it gloats over Avoosl Wuthoqquan "in a thick and loathsome voice, like the molten tallow of corpses dripping from a wizard's kettle" (*BH* 69). The monsters of the Hyperborean stories are never misunderstood; they are dependably, forthrightly-or-wrongly, *monstrous*. Smith abhorred modernism as a crawling chaos, and yet to read some of his stories is to experience the distinctly modern sensation of crossing a razor-edged bridge from the *conte cruel* to the *acte gratuit*.

As we have it Hyperborea contains fewer "facts on the ground" than its coevals the Attluma of David C. Smith or Theem'Ohrdra the Primal Land of Brian Lumley; although had Farnsworth Wright not been so discouraging with his rejections and reconsiderations the continent might be better endowed cartographically and chronologically. "The White Sybil" is an exception; a cup that overrunneth with createdness as for the first time we see the First Continent through a poet's eyes—or, more accurately, the poet outside the story allows us to see it through the eyes of the poet inside:

> Tortha, the poet, with strange austral songs in his heart, and the umber of high and heavy suns on his face, had come back to his native city of Cerngoth, in Mhu Thulan, by the Hyperborean sea. Far had he wandered in the quest of that alien beauty which had always fled before him like the horizon. Beyond Commoriom of the white, numberless spires, and beyond the marsh-grown jungles to the south of Commoriom, he had floated on nameless rivers, and had crossed the half-legendary realm of Tscho Vulpanomi, upon whose diamond-sanded, ruby-gravelled shore an ignescent ocean was said to beat forever with fiery spume. He

had beheld many marvels, and things incredible to relate: the uncouthly carven gods of the South, to whom blood was split on sun-approaching towers; the plumes of the *huusim*, which were many ells in length and were colored like pure flame; the mailed monsters of the austral swamps; the proud argosies of Mu and Antillia, which moved by enchantment, without oar or sail; the fuming peaks that were shaken perpetually by the struggles of imprisoned demons. (*BH* 94)

Now Tortha is back in Cerngoth, where he is be-Mused by the White Sybil, a *belle dame sans merci* as well as a poetic inspiration:

> No human lover had aspired to the Sybil, whose beauty was a perilous brightness, akin to meteor and fireball; a fatal and lethal beauty, born of trans-arctic gulfs, and somehow one with the far doom of worlds. Like the brand of frost or flame, her memory burned in Tortha. Musing among his neglected books, or walking abroad in reverie on which no external thing could intrude, he saw always before him the pale radiance of the Sybil. He seemed to hear a whisper from boreal solitudes: a murmur of ethereal sweetness, poignant as ice-born air, vocal with high, unearthly words, that sang of inviolate horizons and the chill glory of lunar auroras above continents impregnable to man. (*BH* 96)

The poet-protagonist's eventual tryst with all of that pale radiance and chill glory carries Smith's prose even deeper into poetry:

> It was real beyond all that men deem reality: and yet it seemed to Tortha, at moments, that he, the Sybil, and all that surrounded them, were part of an aftermirage on the icy deserts of time; that he was poised insecurely above life and death in some bright, fragile bower of dreams. (*BH* 100)

Both insecurity and fragility are cruelly confirmed, for Tortha cannot help himself; as a man he seeks to possess what as an artist he yearns merely to express:

> Dreadfully, unutterably, she seemed to change in his arms as he sought to embrace her—to become a frozen corpse that had lain for ages in a floe-built tomb—a leper-white mummy in whose frosted eyes he read the horror of the ultimate void. Then she was a thing that had no form or name—a dark corruption that flowed and eddied in his arms—a hueless dust, a flight of gleaming atoms, that rose between his evaded fingers. Then there was nothing—and the faery-tinted flowers about him were changing also, were crumbling swiftly, were falling beneath flurries of white snow. The vast and violet heaven, the tall slim trees, the magic, unreflecting stream—the very ground under him—all had vanished amid the universal, whirling flakes. (*BH* 100)

Tortha's fall is very different from that of Ralibar Vooz, and is paralleled by the fall of Clark Ashton Smith into the story through identification with his fellow poet. The denouement is for once rueful rather than ruthless as Tortha is nursed back to health by a Sybil-substitute named Ilara among the "half-savage people of the mountains" (*BH* 102). Barbarism borders several of the Hyperborean stories, quietly subverting the civilizational claims of the First Continent's annalists; here we might think not only of Ilara's folk but also "the savage robbers of uncouth outland tribes" mentioned in "Athammaus" (*BH* 47) and the fact that one of Eibon's offenses in "The Door to Saturn" is his collection of tribal art and artifacts. Backwardness in many fantasy stories signifies not just primitivism, but an eminently justified orientation.

As accounts of poets whose artistic reach exceeds their human grasp, "The White Sybil" and Karl Edward Wagner's "The Dark Muse" are a matched set carved from ebony and ivory. Wagner's Klinure, the muse of dream, is a figurine sculpted by one Amderin of Carsultyal: "Black as the starless night of sleep, the night she dwells within, the night from which she calls . . . the shadow of unfinished dreams" (Wagner 109). During "The Dark Muse" we learn that Amderin had been found "crushed and broken as if he had fallen from a very great height"—which of course he did (Wagner 108). Smith is both more and less merciful to Tortha.

The White Sybil had promised "a strange doom" for Commoriom "long before the encroachment of the ice" (*BH* 95), and in "The Testament of Athammaus" a survivor of that doom, the eponymous lord high executioner, looks back from a "grey city of the sunken years" upon the receding reverie of the lost capital:

> Opulent among cities, and superb and magnificent, and paramount over all was Commoriom, to whom tribute was given from the shores of the Atlantean sea to that sea in which is the immense continent of Mu; to whom the traders came from utmost Thulan that is walled on the north with unknown ice, and from the southern realm of Tscho Vulpanomi which ends in a lake of boiling asphaltum. (*BH* 46)

But what follows is not an elegy; there is a perceptible lightness at work, or at play, in the story. "I raised the sword of justice high in air and smote with heroic might," Athammaus assures us (*BH* 55), but heroic might does him no more good than do "huge stature and strength" Ralibar Vooz. The power vested in him by his hereditary office and headsman's prowess is powerless against Smith's delight at having set something much more panic-inducing than a cat among his Hyperborean pigeons:

> I guess you won't wonder that Commoriom was deserted when you read this explanation of the raison d'etre. In my more civic moods I sometimes think of the clean-up which an entity like Knygathin Zhaum would make in a modern town. I really think that he (or it) is about my best monster to date. (Murray, *BH* 12)

Knygathin Zhaum loses his head repeatedly, but never his focus, and cleans up the town by clearing it out. Smith sketched a sequel to R. H. Barlow in September 1934:

> Knygathin Zhaum, the half-breed Voormi, reverted to the most primitive ancestral characteristics following the stress of his numerous decapitations. I have yet to translate the dire and abominable legend telling how a certain doughty denizen of Commoriom (not Athammaus) returned to the city after its public evacuation and found that it was peopled most execrably and innumerably by the fissional spawn of Knygathin Zhaum, which retained no vestige of anything earthly. (Murray, *BH* 169)

Note the slyness of that verb "peopled"—the war against the Voormis has come home to those who launched it. Hyperborean justice in "The Testament of Athammaus" is blind, blind to the handwriting on the city walls.

The incursion of outsideness in "The Tale of Satampra Zeiros" is that of the would-be desecrators Satampra and Tirouv Ompallios into Commoriom, which has been a Forbidden City to humans since "The Testament of Athammaus." Vegetation is frequently animalistic in Smith's work, and the rotting riot of jungle fecundity in this story, the "oppressive odors of lush growth and vegetable corruption" (*BH* 18), are all the more noticeable when contrasted with the icy sterility elsewhere in the series, an overabundance as opposed to an absence of life. The story does not so much feature a monster as it does acquire monstrous elasticity and ulteriority itself, as when its larcenous narrator becomes aware of "a night that clung to us and clogged us like an evil toad, like the toils of a monstrous web" (*BH* 23). The trespassers are hounded "with an effortless glide, with a surety of motion and intention too horrible, too cynical to be borne" (*BH* 24), and the word "cynical" jumps out at the reader; if not necessarily strange bedfellows, cynicism and horror are also not necessarily compatible ones.

From White Sybil to White Worm: the events of "The Coming of the White Worm," with their "weird whisper of voices from realms of perennial winter" (*BH* 107), are so chilling as to induce readers to huddle next to a Jack London story or Robert W. Service poem for warmth. Discussing the Hyberborean tales where Smith's bonfire of the vanities becomes a freezer-burn for Howard Jones's Sword & Sorcery website, Ryan Harvey proposes "a link to the grim gods of the Norsemen" (Harvey, "Fantasy Cycles Part II"), but Smith was after something behind or beneath the Norse elements of Leiber's *Rime Isle* and Greg Bear's "Thor Meets Captain America," behind or beneath Fimbelwinter and Niflheim, something even older and colder than "the fiendish spirit of ice and frost and darkness that the sons of the North deified as Odin" in Howard's "The Cairn on the Headland." That something is personified, or vermified, in Rlim Shaikorth:

> Something he had of the semblance of a fat white worm; but his bulk was beyond that of a sea-elephant. His half-coiled tail was as thick as the middle folds of his body; and his front reared upward from the dais in the form of a white round disk and upon it were imprinted vague lineaments. Amid the visage a mouth curved uncleanly from side to side of the disk, opening and shutting incessantly on a pale

and tongueless and toothless maw. Two eye sockets lay close together above the shallow nostrils, but the sockets were eyeless, and in them appeared from moment to moment globules of a blood-colored matter having the form of eyeballs; and ever the globules broke and dripped down before the dais. And from the ice-floor there ascended two masses like stalagmites, purple and dark as frozen gore, which had been made by this ceaseless dripping of the globules. (*BH* 114)

Unusually for the Hyperborean cycle, all this story's grotesquerie is concentrated in the White Worm. A brilliant *coup de theatre* sees to it that the bodily fluid that gushes from his wound is "hotter by far than blood, and smoking with strange steam-like vapours" (*BH* 121), a detail that links the wound-inflicting warlock Evagh to Sigurd Fafnirsbane and northern dragonslaying lore. But although he is an exceptionally unprepossessing Muse, it cannot be gainsaid that Rlim Shaikorth provokes a poetry "pale and frigid as fire of ice" (*BH* 110) from Smith:

> But Evagh was uneasy at heart, and rebelled in secret against his thralldom to Rlim Shaikorth; and he beheld with revulsion the doom that went forth from Yikilth upon lovely cities and fruitful ocean-shore. Ruthfully he saw the blasting of flower-girdled Cerngoth, and the boreal stillness that descended on the thronged streets of Leqquan, and the frost that seared with sudden whiteness the garths and orchards of the sea-fronting valley of Aquil. (*BH* 116)

Evagh, commended by Smith as "a man of much hardihood and resolution" (*BH* 121), is a noteworthy figure in the Hyperborean cycle. There seems to be neither praying nor preying involved in his relationship with his fisher-folk neighbors; we might deem him a white magician save for the fact that white now becomes the color of death in Mhu Thulan. In a heart-freezing story, Evagh's organ is fully functional: "And sorrow was in his heart for the fishing-coracles and the biremes of trade and warfare that floated manless after they had met Yikilith" (*BH* 116). By his hero's death, by his overriding of Rlim Shaikorth's insistence on "the repudiation of all bonds that had linked [his servants] to mankind" (*BH* 113), the warlock makes "The Coming of the White Worm" a rare Smithian example of heroic, rather than anti-heroic or heroism-precluding, fantasy.

To tamper with a John McPhee title, "Ubbo-Sathla" is as close as we come to annals of this former world, to a sort of "Hyperborean Age" essay. Londoner Paul Tregardis impulsively buys a milky curio from the Miocene strata of Greenland (Mhu Thulan when the White Worm got through with it) and reverts or regresses to a previous life as the sorcerer Zon Mezzamalech—an identity which fails to break his fall. He plummets past even the promising reference in "The Testament of Athammaus" to "the mythic generations of the primal kings" (*BH* 46):

> He fought as a warrior in half-legendary battles; he was a child playing in the ruins of some olden city of Mhu Thulan; he was the king who had reigned when the city was in its prime, the prophet who had foretold its building and its doom.

A woman, he wept for the bygone dead in necropoli long-crumbled; an antique wizard, he muttered the rude spells of earlier sorcery; a priest of some pre-human god, he wielded the sacrificial knife in cave-temples of pillared basalt. Life by life, he retraced the long and groping cycles through which Hyperborea had risen from savagery to a high civilization. He became a barbarian of some troglodytic tribe, fleeing from the slow, turreted ice of a former ice age into lands illumed by the ruddy flare of perpetual volcanoes. Then, after incomparable years, he was no longer man but a man-like beast, roving in forests of giant fern and calamite, or building an uncouth nest in the boughs of mighty cycads. Through eons of anterior sensation, of crude lust and hunger, of aboriginal terror and madness, there was someone—or something—that went ever backward in time. (BH 76)

In "The Seven Geases" Smith's serpent-men hiss not revanchist threats but "formulae" before spurning Ralibar Vooz because their "economy" holds no place for him. The ophidians of "Ubbo-Sathla" are less of a deliberate departure from the shapeshifting string-pullers of Howard's "The Shadow Kingdom," but preoccupying Hyperborea as they do, they have no reason to be preoccupied by arisen apes:

At length, after eons of immemorial brutehood, it became one of the lost serpent-men who reared their cities of black gneiss and fought their venomous wars in the world's first continent. It walked undulously in ante-human streets, in strange crooked vaults; it peered at primeval stars from high, Babelian towers; it bowed with hissing litanies to great serpent-idols. Through years and ages of the ophidian era it returned, and was a thing that crawled in the ooze, that had not yet learned to think and dream and build. And the time came when there was no longer a continent, but only a vast chaotic marsh, a sea of slime, without limit or horizon, that seethed with a blind writhing of amorphous vapors. (BH 77)

Reverse-ontogeny repeals phylogeny, and Ubbo-Sathla turns out to be "headless, without organs or members," but progenitive as it spawns "from its oozy sides, in a slow ceaseless wave, the amebic forms that were the archetypes of earthly life. Horrible it was, if there had been aught to apprehend the horror; and loathsome, if there had been any to feel loathing" (BH 77). That horror was apprehended and that loathing was felt throughout the pulp era, as writers like Lovecraft, Howard, C. L. Moore in "Black Thirst," and Leigh Brackett in "The Beast-Jewel of Mars," gave way to the impulse to return to the womb of all biotica and shudder while splashing around in the amniotic fluid.

"The Door to Saturn" offers not an incursion of outsideness but rather an excursion into that outsideness, a Saturnian travelogue somewhere between Sir John Mandeville, to whom Smith once devoted a story, and Baron von Munchhausen. It features Smith's reliably Rabelaisian respect for men of the cloth, who hotfoot it to the house of their prey toting "a formidable writ of arrest, with symbolic flame-etched runes on a scroll of human skin," only to be crestfallen when Eibon's escape leaves them "no early prospect of trying out the ingenious agonies, the intricately harrowing ordeals" they have brainstormed (*BH* 28). At story's end, too, the transplanted high-priest Morghi must make do with fungus-wine and faux-females: "Though the Ydheems were religious, they did not carry their devotional fervor to the point of bigotry or intolerance; and it was quite impossible to start an inquisition among them" (*BH* 44).

"The Door to Saturn" occurs during "the last century before the onset of the great Ice Age." Smith first chronicled that Ice Age in July 1932 with "The Ice-Demon" before finishing "The Coming of the White Worm" in September 1933. He put effect on paper before cause, and as we read "The Ice-Demon" we must assume that what Rlim Shaikorth set in motion continued on without him. By this point "the glacier itself [is] a live, malignant entity with powers of unknown bale":

> Men fled before the ever-advancing glaciations; and strange legends were told of how people had been overtaken or cut off in lonely valleys by sudden, diabolic shiftings of the ice, as if it had stretched out a living hand. And legends there were, of awful crevasses that yawned abruptly and closed like monstrous mouths upon them that dared the frozen waste; of winds like the breath of boreal demons, that blasted men's flesh with instant, utter cold and turned them into statues hard as granite. (*BH* 80)

But the tomb-robbers of this story think they know better, think they know *later*:

> Ice—even though it had conquered half of a continent—was merely ice, and its workings conformed invariably to certain natural laws. Iluac had said that the ice-sheet was a great demon, cruel, greedy, and loath to give up that which it had taken. But such beliefs were crude and primitive superstitions, not to be entertained by enlightened minds of the Pleistocene age. (*BH* 84)

A Smith aphorism has it that "The commonest and gravest error of modernity lies in believing that antiquity is dead" (*DN* 73), and said error gets one treasure hunter an icicle through the skull and another crunched between the frozen teeth of a cave-mouth. Quanga, whose name and "iron thews inured to protracted marches" suggest that he is a barbarian, lasts longer. En route to the plunder-site, his plans for the thawed swag had run along lines we might associate with a certain Cimmerian: "He could drink to his full content the costly wines, redder than the rubies, that came from far Uzuldaroum in the south. The tawny, slant-eyed girls of Iqqua would dance at his bidding; and he could gamble for high stakes" (*BH* 85).

His last stand is also Conan-esque: "With a mad momentary defiance, he unslung his bow and discharged arrow after arrow, emptying his quiver at the huge and bleak and formless shadow that seemed to impend before him on the sky" (*BH* 92), but this is *a* Hyperborean age rather than *the* Hyborian Age.

Conan's creator confided to Lovecraft that, despite being a native of the American Southwest, the majority of his dreams were "laid in cold, giant lands of icy wastes and gloomy skies, and of wild, wind-swept fens and wilderness over which sweep great sea-winds, and which are inhabited by shock-headed savages with light fierce eyes." To a remarkable extent modern fantasy as a whole is similarly Nord-centric or North-fixated, as the Australian fantasist Sara Douglass notes in her essay "Creating the Modern Romance Epic":

> January and February are cold and snowy, and June and July are hot. Why? I am often asked. . . . Well, mostly because we're forced to by the expectations of our readership. We might live in the great hot southern land, but our culture, and our mythic imaginations, are mostly European. And the northern European landscape (both geographic and mythological) is still where most fantasy writers choose to set their grand tale. (Douglass, "Creating")

Across that landscape *Winter is the season that haunts and hunts the other seasons, and the North is Winter's lair.* If we all came from an African womb, then the cold and the dark of the Uttermost North symbolize some black negation of nativity, a realm suggestive of both the most pessimistic possibilities for an afterlife and the unimaginable aeons before life was kindled. As Michael Scott Rohan planned his *Winter of the World* trilogy, "The Ice seemed to be so much the enemy, vast and lowering and implacable, that I almost unconsciously began to cast it as an intelligence in itself, *the* intelligence"—an intellect even colder and more unsympathetic than those of Wells's Martians:

> What kind of mind would prefer an Ice-world, beautiful but bleak and sterile? A mind that hearkened back to the world as it had been, perhaps, in the long aeons before life appeared, a mind, or minds, whose reason for existence had been that lifeless world, and now felt it had been usurped. (Rohan, "Welcome to My Worlds")

Smith conjures up the "looming, crenelated wall of the realm-wide glaciation" in "The Ice-Demon," but the frisson that wall affords us has become genre-wide (*BH* 83). W. H. Auden, who devised the shorthand-concept "the Northern thing" and acquitted himself doughtily in early critical tourneys upholding the merit of *The Lord of the Rings*, discerned an especial northwardness or northerliness in Tolkien's work. Which earned him this response in February 1967:

> Auden has asserted that for me 'the North is a sacred direction.' That is not true. The North-west of Europe, where I (and most of my ancestors) have lived, has my affection, as a man's home should. I love its atmosphere, and know more of its histories and languages than I do of other parts; but it is not 'sacred,' nor does it exhaust my affections. . . . That it is untrue for my story, a mere reading of the synopses should show. The North was the seat of the fortresses of the Devil. (Tolkien, *Letters* 376)

By "the Devil," Tolkien meant his original Dark Lord, of whom Sauron was merely a lieutenant: Morgoth, whose ramparted strong place the North is in *The*

Silmarillion and many of the *Lost Tales*. Paul H. Kocher argues that "Tolkien gives the realm of Morgoth an extra level of allusiveness by describing it as so bitterly cold that after its destruction 'those colds linger still in that region, though they lie hardly more than a hundred leagues north of the Shire' . . . Add the fact that the Witch-king of Angmar, Morgoth's henchman, has powers that wane in summer and wax in winter and it becomes hard not to associate Morgoth in some way with a glacial epoch" (Kocher 48). Cold lingering with intent to injure, winter as a ghost that stalks the memory of entire landmasses, these are elements almost as crucial as the more narrowly Germanic "Northern thing" to modern fantasy. Even before Tolkien created Melko (the forerunner of Morgoth), in one of his earliest poems, "Kortirion among the Trees" (1915), he visualized "Winter and his blue-tipped spears / Marching unconquerable upon the sun" (Tolkien, "Kortirion" 109). In *The Book of the Damned* Tanith Lee's Winter "[rides] through Paradys on a grey horse, a lord in mail and armour, with a vizored helm and his train behind him" (Lee 135).

The genre lacks a countervailing Southern orientation to offset North-looking post-Tolkien heavyweights like Guy Gavriel Kay, Tad Williams, and George R. R. Martin; the golden grasslands in the Nyumbani stories of Charles R. Saunders notwithstanding. Like Morgoth, Rakoth Maugrim, the Dark Lord of Kay's *The Fionavar Tapestry*, seeks out "the wind-blasted north" for his power base: "Here he had set his feet upon the Ice, and so made the northland the place of his power, and here he had raised up jagged Starkadh. And when it was full-wrought, a claw, a cancer in the north, he had risen to the topmost tower and screamed his name that the wind might bear it to the tamed gods whom he feared not, being stronger by far than any of them." The reconstructed Starkadh is "a brutally superimposed black upon the white plateaus of the glaciers" (Kay 309).

The doom of Smith's Quanga—"Dimly he heard a sound as of clashing icicles, a grinding as of heavy floes, in the blue-green gloom that tightened and thickened around him. It was as if the soul of the glacier, malign and implacable, had overtaken him in his flight" (*BH* 92)—is also that of "earlier civilizations of men, whose traces had largely been obliterated by time and the Ice" in Michael Scott Rohan's *The Winter of the World*. Rohan's glaciers are the chief beauty and the chief peril of a winter wonderland as sentient as Smith's:

> Far out into the distance below him stretched the glacier, infinitely far along the widening valley between dwindling peaks and out onto a vast expanse of softly glowing gray-white. The eastern walls of the mountains sank into it as if into a sea, overwhelmed; here and there, as if in mockery of former majesties, a remote peak protruded, blunted and crumbling like a slighted fortress. Beyond these pathetic remnants it stretched out into an infinite distance so featureless that the eye strained to focus on it and blurred painfully, finding no hold or reference. . . . Whatever the truth of it, the sight filled Elof with the sudden chill feeling that he, that the whole warmly living world of earth and flowers and beasts and men and

women were nothing but very thin crust of dirt upon an infinity of cool sterile whiteness, a smear of filth on the chill beauty of a gem, at the mercy of its slightest movement or disturbance, utterly insignificant. (Rohan, *Anvil* 177)

In Tad Williams's *Memory, Sorrow and Thorn*, blizzards and icestorms are the outriders of Ineluki the Storm King, undead heart of Faerie's irredentist vendetta against mortal men. Ineluki's ally the Norn Queen rules the subarctic portion of Osten Ard and commands the White Foxes of *Sturmrspeik* Mountain, around which "guttering, sickly flares" play. The North of George R. R. Martin's *A Song of Ice and Fire* is a cold mother who nurses only the strongest and strangest of her children— wildlings "from the northernmost reaches of the haunted forest, the hidden valleys of the Frostfangs, and even queerer places: the men of the Frozen Shore who rode in chariots made of walrus bones pulled along by packs of savage dogs, the terrible ice-river clans who were said to feast on human flesh, the cave dwellers with their faces dyed blue and purple and green" (Martin, *Storm* 172). Beyond even the wildlings there begins the Land of Always Winter haunted by the Others, wights shaped by cold and darkness whose language is "like the cracking of ice on a winter lake" (Martin, *Game* 8).

Even as Martin's rival houses of Stark and Lannister (the resemblance to York and Lancaster is no coincidence) dance a murderous sarabande in the southlands, the North is poised overhead like a frost-forged Sword of Damocles. Against the Others there stands only a Wall, Hadrianesque in ambition but hewn from the ice itself and maintained not on behalf of the *pax Romana* but against forces that would extinguish all hearths and stop all hearts forever. That Wall is manned by the Night Watch, the brothers of which, mostly gallows-bait and gaol-sweepings, swear an oath that defines them by defying all prior feudal loyalties while also daring to defy the cold and the dark. The Night Watch's green recruits are said to "smell of summer," and after an era in which too many fantasy series smelled of summer shiftlessness and the sticky sentimentality of pseudo-Shires, Martin's arrived with a wintry charisma.

Even if Tolkien denied that the North was for him a sacred direction, modern fantasy has witnessed a snowblinded sacralization of the Arctic and sub-Arctic regions, a conviction that the North must somehow be propitiated. The Canadian poet Gwendolyn MacEwen captures something of this in her "Terror and Erebus," which imagines a lost Arctic explorer not dead but rather "somewhere walking between / The icons of ice, pensively / Like a priest / Wrapped in the cold holiness of snow." From Smith's Hyperborean icecapping and "the Frost Giant's Daughter" through Fritz Leiber, Poul Anderson, and recent work like George R. R. Martin's, fantastic fiction has venerated its own icons of ice and attributed a deadly holiness to snow. It is depressing, if we quit fantasy for reality even briefly, to reflect that if the Ultimate North has been a threat to our species since before human history began, it is now human history's turn to threaten the Ultimate North. In any event, decades before the seasonal affective disorders of Kay, Williams, or Martin, Clark Ashton Smith called down the cold upon the hapless characters of "The Coming of the White Worm" and "The Ice-Demon." Where the later fantasists disposed of hundreds, or thousands, of pages in their bibliobehemoths, the Hyperborean tales continue to impress us with what we might pilfer from Satampra Zeiros and term "the unbelievable speed and celerity" of Smith's storytelling. He is the poet laureate of any permafrost Parnassus.

Conscripted by the White Worm, Evagh swears "the threefold vow of unspeakable alienation" (*BH* 115), but of course his creator swore it first. The rock critic Robert Christgau once provided the crucial insight into the Rolling Stones when he characterized Mick Jagger as being "obsessed with distance," the co-creator of music defined by its compulsion to gaze "across (and down) the generation gap and the money gap and the feeling gap and the meaning gap . . . [The Stones'] following will never be as huge as that of the high-spirited Beatles (or of a techno-cosmic doomshow like Led Zeppelin)" (Christgau, "The Rolling Stones").

To adopt Christgau's phrasing, Smith's following will never be as huge as that of the high-spirited Howard (whose darkness is always fire-shot with defiance) or of a techno-cosmic doomshow like H. P. Lovecraft. Many readers keep their distance because of Smith's insistence upon keeping his. The notorious vocabulary is a contributing factor here, and he is remarkably unfazed by the prospect of creating and communicating from his defining distance. Fritz Leiber comments on that disengagement in "Clark Ashton Smith: An Appreciation":

> And certainly Smith didn't seem to have been much interested—for literary purposes—in "the little things that are so dear to civilized men and women. He was concerned only with the naked fundamentals of life. . . . The warm intricacies of small, kindly things, the sentiments and delicious trivialities that make up so much of civilized men's lives were meaningless to him." This quote, which seems to me at the moment to fit Smith's writing, is—perhaps quite oddly—from a description of Conan the Cimmerian by Robert E. Howard in "Beyond the Black River." Not—Crom forbid!—to suggest any particular connection between their writings, but simply to point out that the Smith of the writings fits very well the role of the lone-wolf artist, standing apart, seeing precious little in human behavior but fear and desire, looking upon his own culture as a rather grotesque and tasteless show . . . with hardly an atom of loyalty to the human adventure. (Leiber 72)

This passage would be an embarrassment of riches—one fantasy grandmaster quoting another to explain a third—were it not for Leiber's critical acumen. He offers the Smith student not hype but Hyperborea: *precious little in human behavior but fear and desire; a rather grotesque and tasteless show*—into our minds "with boneless ease" there slides the "wholly and outrageously unhuman" entity of "The Weird of Avoosl Wuthoqquan, still "grinning sardonically." And as for *hardly an atom of loyalty to the human adventure,* recall the whim of Dunsany's pantheon: *Let Us call up a man before Us, that We may laugh* . . . Smith calls up Ralibar Vooz, and Avoosl Wuthoqquan, and Athammaus, and Morghi, and Quanga, and Satampra Zeiros and Tirouv Ompallios, before us, that we may laugh and perhaps flinch at the sound of our own laughter. We have met the incursions of outsideness, and they is, well, us, if only for a moment.

But Smith *stays* outside. Writing to him in March 1934, Robert E. Howard professed to be fascinated by his fellow *Weird Tales* regular's "comments on the forces that play upon the earth," and speculated that "human life" might be "affected vastly more than we guess by electrons or emanations from outside" (Howard 62). Did it occur to the Texan that at least insofar as his fictioneering was concerned, Smith knew whereof he spoke? One of the most perceptive if regrettably unpublished students of Howard, Larry Richter, is wont to refer to him as the god of Hyboria; if Smith is the god of Hyperborea, his characters are sinners in the hands of a sardonic rather than an angry god.

The sorcerer may depart, but the pantocrator remains, more demiurge than thaumaturge: Donald Sidney-Fryer sees Smith "in an ideal sense as a literary Man-God creating and peopling many worlds of his imagination" (Sidney-Fryer 27). Leiber, too, espies something extra, or something extraterrestrial: "It's as if Smith looked at the world and then, instead of concentrating on or falling in love with this or that part of it, simply looked toward the sky and with the materials on hand and a keen silver poetic knife carved all manner of strange other worlds" (Leiber 72).

Don Herron also implies a particular positioning in his observation that "When CAS sets out artistically to evoke a mood or create a doom, he enters the story without any personal or artistic reservations as to whether or not he should be coy or straightforward" (Herron 101).

He enters the story; one can only enter something from outside. If Smith is usually without empathy, mercy, or compassion; that is only to be expected from someone who is, after all, *without*. The Hyberborean stories are not so much emotionally stunted as they are perspectively enhanced. Most stories of heroes are campfire tales told to fend off the surrounding cold and dark, and perhaps Smith's work approximates other tales told, or even enacted, by the cold and the dark as those Forces wait for the campfire to go out. The "incursions of outsideness" which beset Mhu Thulan and Commoriom are authorial; just as the single most perceptive comment on Howard's stories remains that of his pen pal/sparring partner Lovecraft, that the Texan himself was in every single one, of Smith's stories we might observe that *he himself is external to every one of them*. To accept his invitation to Hyperborea is to accept an invitation to step outside.

Works Cited

Cawthorn, James, and Michael Moorcock. *Fantasy: The 100 Best Books.* New York: Carroll & Graf, 1988.

Christgau, Robert. "The Rolling Stones." http://www.robertchristgau.com/xg/music/stones-76.php.

de Camp, L. Sprague. *Literary Swordsmen and Sorcerers: The Makers of Heroic Fantasy*. Sauk City, WI: Arkham House, 1976.

Douglass, Sara. "Creating the Modern Romance Epic." http://www.saradouglass.com/epic.html

Harvey, Ryan. "The Fantasy Cycles of Clark Ashton Smith, Part II: The Book of Hyperborea." http://www.swordandsorcery.org/cas1.asp.

Herron, Don. "The Double Shadow: The Influence of Clark Ashton Smith." In *Jack Vance*, ed. Tim Underwood and Chuck Miller. New York: Taplinger, 1980.

Howard, Robert E. *Selected Letters: 1931–1936*. Ed. Glenn Lord et al. West Warwick, RI: Necronomicon Press, 1991.

Joshi, S. T. "Introduction." In *The Complete Pegāna*. By Lord Dunsany. Oakland, CA: Chaosium, 1998.

Lee, Tanith. *The Book of the Damned*. London: Unwin Hyman, 1988.

Leiber, Fritz. "Clark Ashton Smith: An Appreciation." In *In Memoriam: Clark Ashton Smith*, ed. Jack L. Chalker. Baltimore: Jack L. Chalker & Associates, 1963.

Martin, George R. R. *A Game of Thrones*. New York: Bantam, 1996.

———. *A Storm of Swords*. London: HarperCollins, 2000.

Rodgers, Alan. "Introduction." In *The Throne of Bones*. By Brian McNaughton. Black River, NY: Terminal Fright Publications, 1997.

Rohan, Michael Scott. *The Winter of the World, Volume One: The Anvil of Ice*. New York: Avon, 1995.

———. "Welcome to My Worlds, *The Winter of the World*: The Ice." http://www.users.zetnet.co.uk/mike.scott.rohan/first_page.htm.

Sidney-Fryer, Donald. *Clark Ashton Smith: The Sorcerer Departs*. West Hills, CA: Tsathoggua Press, 1997.

Sturgeon, Theodore. "Clark Ashton Smith 1893–1963." In *In Memoriam: Clark Ashton Smith*, ed. Jack L. Chalker. Baltimore: Jack L. Chalker & Associates, 1963.

Tolkien, J. R. R. "Beowulf: The Monsters and the Critics." In *The Monsters and the Critics and Other Essays*. Boston: Houghton Mifflin, 1984.

———. "Kortirion among the Trees." In *Tolkien and the Great War: The Threshold of Middle-Earth*. By John Garth. Boston: Houghton Mifflin, 2003.

———. *The Letters of J. R. R. Tolkien*. Ed. Humphrey Carpenter. Boston: Houghton Mifflin, 1981.

———. *Unfinished Tales of Númenor and Middle-Earth*. Ed. Christopher Tolkien. Boston: Houghton Mifflin, 1980.

Wagner, Karl Edward. "The Dark Muse." In *Night Winds*. New York: Warner Books, 1978.

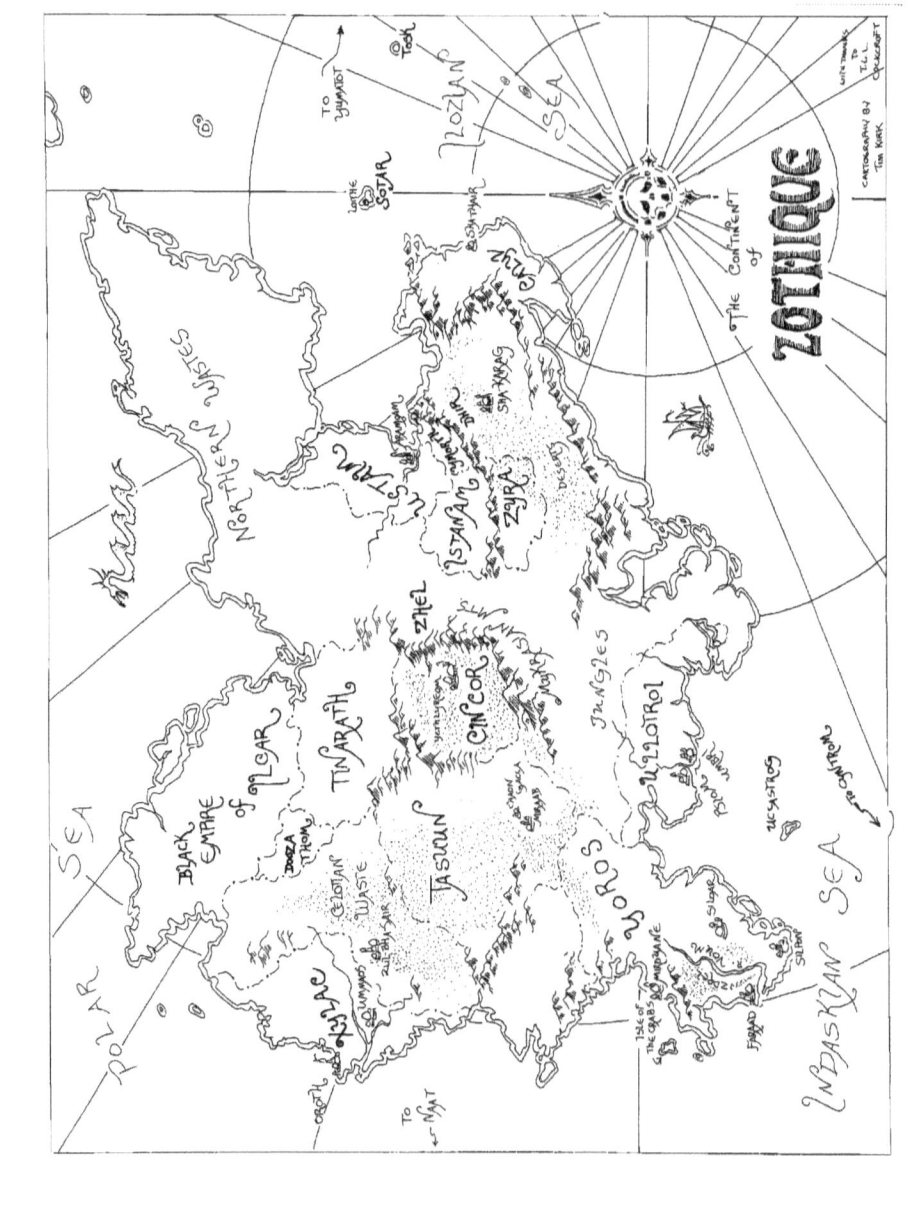

As Shadows Wait upon the Sun: Clark Ashton Smith's Zothique

Jim Rockhill

> Courts adieu, and all delights,
> All bewitching appetites;
> Sweetest breath and clearest eye,
> Like perfumes go out and die;
> And consequently this is done.
> As shadows wait upon the sun.
> Vain the ambition of kings,
> Who seek by trophies and dead things,
> To leave a living name behind,
> And weave but nets to catch the wind.
> —John Webster, *The Devil's Law Case* (1620), 5.4.122–31

Over a period of twenty-five years, Clark Ashton Smith completed one poem, one verse drama, and sixteen stories set on Earth's last continent. The Zothique cycle represents its author's most sustained contribution to created-world fantasy literature and has been one of his most popular conceptions since "The Empire of the Necromancers" first appeared in the September 1932 issue of *Weird Tales*. British fantasist and genre scholar Brian Stableford has aptly termed this series, set during the last epoch of mankind reveling in its decadence beneath a dying sun, "the most dramatically appropriate of all his imaginary milieux" (Stableford 245). The first attempt to gather all the works in this cycle, the 1970 paperback *Zothique*, issued as part of the popular Ballantine Adult Fantasy series under the editorship of Lin Carter, was also the first collection of Smith's work to reach a mass market. That book received a warm welcome from the master fantasist and science fiction writer Fritz Leiber, has been included among James Cawthorn and Michael Moorcock's *Fantasy: The 100 Best Books*, and is still eagerly sought by fantasy readers. *Tales of Zothique*, a small-press trade paperback, which adds the play *The Dead Will Cuckold You* and utilizes all the unexpurgated texts available at that time, appeared twenty-five years later and is even more highly prized.

The sources of inspiration for Zothique and its development from the early eschatological sonnet "The Last Night" in 1911 to the synopsis for an unwritten story titled "A Tale of Gnydron" in 1931 have been covered in depth by Steve Behrends in *Clark Ashton Smith* and Will Murray's introduction to the *Tales of Zothique*. The series owes many of its most salient characteristics to the author's childhood love for the *Arabian Nights* and William Beckford's Arabian Gothic *Vathek* (1786), H. P. Blavatsky's Theosophist vision of the final race of men in *The Secret Doctrine* (1888), and the peculiarly dry climate and desolate terrain of the author's native California. The potent effect of this last is suggested in a letter to H. P. Lovecraft dated 11 November 1929, in which Smith writes of atmospheric phenomena around his cabin in terms that forecast later manifestations in Zothique:

> Our dry fall is becoming a drouth. I hear that conditions will become serious if there is not rain before long. The atmospheric conditions here strike me as being genuinely abnormal: among other things, our sky (though the stars are very bright) has a peculiar iron blackness at night which I have never seen before. And a woman-friend of mine tells me that she saw the noon sky actually whiten the other day, as if there were some intense momentary radiation. That sort of things sets one's imagination to working. (*SL* 104)

Smith's fullest description of the geography, population, and language of this ultimate continent appears in his letter to L. Sprague de Camp of 3 November 1953:

> Zothique, vaguely suggested by Theosophic theories about past and future continents, is the last inhabited continent of earth. The continents of our present cycle have sunk, perhaps several times. Some have remained submerged; others have re-risen, partially, and re-arranged themselves. Zothique, as I conceive it, comprises Asia Minor, Arabia, Persia, India, parts of Northern and eastern Africa, and much of the Indonesian archipelago. A new Australia exists somewhere to the south. To the west, there are only a few known islands, such as Naat, in which the black cannibals survive. To the north are immense unexplored deserts; to the east, an immense unvoyaged sea. The peoples are mainly of Aryan or Semitic descent, but there is a negro kingdom (Ilcar) in the north-west; and scattered blacks are found throughout the other countries, mainly in palace-harems. In the southern islands survive vestiges of Indonesian or Malayan races.
>
> The science and machinery of our present civilization have long been forgotten, together with our present religions. But many gods are worshipped; and sorcery and demonism prevail again as in ancient days. Oars and sails alone are used by mariners. There are no fire-arms—only the bows, arrows, swords, javelins, etc., of antiquity. The chief language spoken (for which I have provided examples in an unpublished drama) is based on Indo-European roots and is highly inflected, like Sanskrit, Greek and Latin. (*SL* 374)

It "lies at the other end of the time-cycle from Hyperborea, Mu, etc." and its mores would give pause to those like the Theosophists who deem man a perfectible species, "since the Zothiqueans as I have depicted them are a rather sinful and iniquitous lot, showing little sign of the spiritual evolution promised for humanity in its final cycles" (*SL* 367).

*

It is characteristic of Clark Ashton Smith's aesthetic aims that the description he offers to H. P. Lovecraft in his description of "A Tale of Gnydron" dated February 1931—

> This primal continent seems to have been particularly subject to incursions of "outsideness"—more so, in fact, than any of the other continents and terrene realms that lie behind us in the time stream. But I have heard it hinted in certain obscure and arcanic prophecies that the far-future continent called Gnydron by some and Zothique by others, which is to rise millions of years hence in what is now the South Atlantic, will surpass even Hyperborea in this regard and will witness the intrusion of Things from galaxies not yet visible; and, worse than this, a hideously chaotic *breaking-down* of dimensional barriers which will leave *parts* of our world in other dimensions, and vice versa. When things get to that stage, there will be no telling where even the briefest journey or morning stroll might end. The conditions will shift, too; so there will be no possibility of charting them and thus knowing when or where one might step off into the unknown. (*SL* 149)

—not only marks the inception of what would become his most extensive series of fantasy tales, but that it should also create, in a discussion of his prose fiction, an echo of a desire he had expressed to George Sterling five years earlier concerning his poetry: "Indeed, my fondest dream is to find a *Hyperborea beyond Hyperborea*, in the realm of imaginative poetry. I have the feeling that my best and most original work is still to be done" (*SL* 94).

Zothique, even more than the fantasy worlds he had fashioned from the variously distant past, such as Hyperborea, Poseidonis, and Averoigne, offers the author an exemplary location for the creation of what he perceived as an ideal fantasy literature—

> I, too, am capable of observation; but I am far happier when I can create *everything* in a story, including the milieu. This is why I do best in work like "Satampra Zeiros." Maybe I haven't enough love for, or interest in, real places, to invest them with the atmosphere that I achieve in something purely imaginary. (*SL* 108)

—conceived not as an excuse for wallowing in "the sentimental, erotic bog in which Occidental literature is floundering" (*SL* 91), but as an extension of life through the renunciation of his age's "supreme superstition, Reality" (*SL* 95):

> I've no quarrel with the slogan of "art for life's sake," but I think the current definition or delimitation of what constitutes life is worse than ridiculous. Anything that the human imagination can conceive of becomes thereby a part of life, and poetry such as mine, properly considered, is not an "escape," but an extension. I have the courage to think that I am rendering as much "service" by it (damn the piss-pot word!) as I would by psycho-analyzing the male and female adolescents or senescents of a city slum in the kind of verse that slops all over the page and makes you feel as if somebody had puked on you. (*SL* 93–94)

> As for the problem of phantasy, my own standpoint is that there is absolutely no justification for literature unless it serves to release the imagination from the bounds of every-day life. (*SL* 123)

The creation of a future world in Zothique with no future of its own and the concomitant removal of all the crutches that bolster "the current literary humanism" and "general gross materialism of the times" (*SL* 95) provides Smith with the perfect platform from which to divorce his blinkered readers from the mundane, and confront them anew with the concepts of eternity, mystery, and the sublime:

> When the novelty of modern discoveries, etc., has worn off, it seems to me that people must go back to a realization of the environing, undissipated mystery, which will make for a restoration of the imaginative. Science, philosophy, psychology, humanism, after all, are only candle-flares in the face of the eternal night with its infinite reserves of strangeness, terror, sublimity. (*SL* 123)

What continues to make this group of works fascinating, however, is how Smith achieved these aesthetic aims and the themes he chose to explore in this milieu.

Rhetoric is always an important consideration when discussing this author's work, and Smith makes clear his intent in two letters written to H. P. Lovecraft in the fall of 1930:

> My own *conscious* ideal has been to delude the reader into accepting an impossibility, or series of impossibilities, by means of a sort of verbal black magic, in the achievement of which I make use of prose-rhythm, metaphor, simile, tone-color, counterpoint, and other stylistic resources, like a sort of incantation. (*SL* 126)

> The problem of "style" in writing is certainly fascinating and profound. I find it highly important, when I begin a tale, to establish at once what might be called the appropriate "tone." If this is clearly determined at the start I seldom have much difficulty in maintaining it; but if it isn't, there is likely to be trouble. Obviously, the style of "Mohammed's Tomb" wouldn't do for "The Ghoul"; and one of my chief preoccupations in writing this last story was to *exclude* images, ideas and locutions which I would have used freely in a modern story. (*SL* 137)

In acknowledgment of this level of conscientious craftsmanship, Donald Sidney-Fryer has referred to Smith as "The Lyricist of Lost Worlds," pointing out that Smith had "deployed his poetical genius" to transmute the realm of imaginative poetry "into the realm of imaginative or fantastic prose" to produce "fantastic narratives which must rank with some of the best and most original work that he accomplished" (Sidney-Fryer 9). Despite surface resemblances to the work of Dunsany, Poe, and others, this transmutation results in an incredibly rich and varied body of work, which demonstrates an even greater affinity with the malleable dramatic verse of Shakespeare's contemporaries through a successful fusion of the utility of prose with the range of rhetorical effects available to the poet.

Only the simple substitution of the words "tale" for "drama" and "prose" for "verse" in these descriptions by M. C. Bradbrook of the conventions of speech in Elizabethan verse drama are necessary to make them apply equally to Smith's "imaginative and fantastic prose," both in intent and practice:

> The essential structure of Elizabethan drama lies not in the narrative or the characters but in the words. (Bradbrook 5)
>
> Patterned speech may be defined as verse which, by an elaborate use of alliteration, assonance, balance of epithets and clauses, parallelism and repetition or the use of rhyme stands out from the rest . . . (97)
>
> Patterned speech thus played a part in determining the degree of dramatic intensity or attachment . . . also how far an action was of symbolic weight and significance . . . (103)

Nor is Bradbrook's statement, "The greatest poets are also the greatest dramatists" (5) inapplicable to Clark Ashton Smith or supernatural fiction in general if one agrees with Robert Aickman's dictum, "The true ghost story is akin to poetry" (Aickman, "Essay" 65).[1]

Although rhymed verse does not appear frequently in the Zothique cycle outside the poem bearing that continent's name (*The Dark Chateau*, 1951) and the posthumously published verse drama *The Dead Will Cuckold You*, Smith uses it to preface several of the tales in order either to forecast a portion of the plot or to reinforce its theme. The most spell-binding displays of rhetoric appear in the speeches and descriptive passages.

The opening paragraph to "Xeethra" is an object-lesson in the infusion of prose with poetic rhetoric in the service of narrative:

> Long had the wasting summer pastured its suns, like fiery stallions, on the dun hills that crouched before the Mykrasian Mountains in wild easternmost Cincor. The peak-fed torrents were become tenuous threads or far-sundered, fallen pools; the granite boulders were shaled by the heat; the bare earth was cracked and creviced; and the low, meager grasses were seared even to the roots. (*RA* 347)

Smith employs a variety of devices in this splendid passage, including alliteration and consonance ("wa*s*ting *s*ummer pa*s*tured it*s s*uns like fiery *s*tallions," "*c*ra*ck*ed and *c*reviced," "gra*ss*es were *s*eared even to the root*s*"—with the repetitive hissing sound in the first and third groups and the hard *kay* in the second each producing an onomatopoetic effect), assonance ("s*u*mmer . . . s*u*ns . . . d*u*n," "f*a*r . . . f*a*llen"), metaphor ("pastured its suns, like fiery stallions"), and the pathetic fallacy (the prior example and "summer . . . crouched"). Parallelism appears in many forms: the alliterative *esses* that dominate the beginning and end of the paragraph; the two pairs of hyphenated words with their *ef*s flipped on either side of the hyphen and a third *ef* added as alliterative reinforcement; and a cunning pattern formed when the third-person past indicative of the verb "be" is yoked to verbs in the passive voice four times in succession (three plural usages interrupted by one singular), each embedded in a distinct rhythmic accompaniment of nouns, adjectives, conjunctions, and prepositions. By a miracle of rare device, these and other rhetorical devices utilized by Smith in this passage combine to ease rather than hinder the flow of the prose, and in setting the scene so memorably increase the reader's expectations for what is to follow.

With the appearance of *The Star-Treader and Other Poems* in 1912, Smith had already demonstrated an unusual facility for absorbing anything he found useful in the work of earlier writers, and adapting it toward the expression of his own ideas. Even though he admits with some shame in a 1933 letter to H. P. Lovecraft that he has not "looked into any of the old dramatists for ages" (*SL* 230), it is clear that he was familiar with at least a portion of their work from his having read all of the books in the local Carnegie library, and the references he makes to Cyril Tourneur and John Webster in his letters. Nor, as Donald Sidney-Fryer observes, were these the only Elizabethans Smith had encountered or admired: one phrase from Sir Thomas Browne's celebrated *Hydriotaphia* (1658) stirs echoes in both "From the Crypts of Memory" and "The Planet of the Dead," two of Smith's works that anticipate the creation of Zothique (Sidney-Fryer, *Sorcerer* 31). If he prefers the Elizabethan pastiches of Thomas Lovell Beddoes for what he perceives as "a superadded subtlety and atmosphere which none of the old dramatists seem to have had" (*SL* 246), this does not diminish the lessons he learned in the shaping of lyric poetry into dramatic prose from them—whether at first hand or through the second-hand examples of Beddoes or Samuel Loveman.

These tales are also not dissimilar to the work of the Elizabethan and Jacobean dramatists in their focus on titanic figures, earth-shattering events, and victories that engulf the vanquished, the victor, and innocent victims alike. If comets foretell disaster and accompany the deaths of princes; entire kingdoms falter over a single murder or adulterous act; Faustus suffers damnation for seeking wisdom; Tamburlaine strides through mountains of corpses in monstrous glory, with an emperor as his slave; and all manner of supernatural creatures clamor on the stage or merely fester in the verse of English Renaissance drama, Smith's world makes use of like prodigies and magnifies them. In Zothique, astrology and other arts of divination summon the gods themselves, while the sun foretells its own demise; Xeethra is damned and damned again "at all times and in all places" for striving after what he perceives to be a better life. A pair of necromancers enslave the very bones and mummies of past empire to create an empire of their own; and no nightmare creature appears in metaphor that is not also perilously present in the flesh.

Nor do the puissant figures in Smith fare any better than their counterparts in Renaissance drama. The Book of Samuel's refrain "How are the mighty fallen" would find a ready echo in this world, because power in Zothique is rarely wielded without hubris. Emblematic of this tendency is King Euvoran who, after losing every last shred of his power and dignity in a quest to restore his crown, is left figuratively eating crow while dining on the bird that had once symbolized his authority. Related to this, the concept of futility is felt even during the few moments of victory. Those like Xeethra, and Namirrha in "The Dark Eidolon," who gain their heart's desire almost invariably live to regret it. And over all hangs the clotted, bloated, dimming specter of the sun, inescapable and ultimately fatal reminder of what Juvenal and Samuel Johnson term "the vanity of human wishes."

The preponderance of larger than life figures and events in conjunction with the removal of mankind from the comforts of humanism, science, and technology could be considered alienating, which is precisely the point. The dying of the sun has resulted in a withering of the human heart. Pity, lust, and passion may be present, but very little love, and that invariably either unhappy or pathetic. Ilalotha's belief in love lasting beyond death takes him into the clutches of a lamia, just as Morthylla's lover rejects human love in favor of death and the dream of necrophilia. Predation and exploitation are more common than friendship. Vast deserts and turbulent seas separate one nation from another, leading to the development of island nations like those of Naat in "Necromancy in Naat" and Uccastrog in "The Isle of the Torturers"—separated from each other and the mainland by what Matthew Arnold had ruefully referred to as "the unplumb'd, salt, estranging sea"—which consider all foreigners nonpersons to be enslaved as corpses or subjected to the fine art of torture. Similarly, the king of Sotar in "The Garden of Adompha" decorates his unusual garden with grafts selected from those among his subjects whose entire persons no longer amuse him. It is not just the incursions of "outsideness" that have no legitimate place in this world, but many of Zothique's most notable human denizens. Namirrha is first rejected and abused by his countrymen as a child, then by his patron demon as an adult. Xeethra the doubly damned finds no peace as king or shepherd, in the past, the present, or the future. "The Charnel God" welcomes the dead but rejects the living. In "The Empire of the Necromancers," the founder of a dynasty awakens after millennia of peaceful death to an unfamiliar land, a distant era, and the toils of a slave. And beyond all these, it is Nushain the astrologer's fate, in "The Last Hieroglyph," to seek meaning and pattern from the stars only to find himself no more than a cipher in a book.

Will Murray has observed that "the original concept of Zothique as a platform for extraterrestrial visitations never quite jelled. Instead, Smith focused on two themes that filled his own poetic soul—doom and loss" (Murray 9). The cycle's most memorable tales suggest there is some truth to this statement, as does Steve Behrends's essay "The Song of the Necromancer: 'Loss' in Clark Ashton Smith's Fiction," and the same author's chapter on Zothique in *Clark Ashton Smith*. Nonetheless, a powerful if intermittent thread related to "incursions of 'outsideness'" appears throughout the cycle, which goes far toward reinforcing its author's original concept. "The Dark Eidolon," "The Voyage of King Euvoran," "The Weaver in the Vault," "The Tomb-Spawn," and even the star-sent plague that destroys Yoros in "The Isle of the Torturers" all involve a variety of ultramundane phenomena that are no less outré than those witnessed in Hyperborea. In like measure, the prodigies that appear in "The Last Hieroglyph," "The Black Abbot of Puthuum," and other tales, if less clearly extraterrestrial in origin, are no less novel and not a whit less astounding.

*

The first tale in the series, "The Empire of the Necromancers" (written 17 January 1932; first published *Weird Tales,* September 1932), offers an ideal introduction to the world of Zothique, outlining the differences in geography between the twentieth century and the distant future; distancing the reader from events through a multilayered network of references not only to the reader's own time, but also three distinct eras within the story's past spread over two thousand years; introducing three of the continent's nations; providing several vivid images of the dying sun at dawn, day, and sunset; and contrasting its own grim story, which may "serve to beguile for a little the black weariness of a dying race, grown hopeless of all but oblivion" with the "glad legends of the prime" (*RA* 315), just as it contrasts the "illimitable weariness" and hazily remembered nobility of the dead called back to "the bitterness of mortal being" (*RA* 321) with the lazy and hedonistic necromancers who have left their native Naat to enslave them. Its nation's fate long since "ordained and predicted from the first" (*RA* 325), its planet's doom clearly manifest in the "darkening stagnant blood of ominous sunset" (*RA* 317), and the last of its citizens long ago fallen victim to pestilence, the tale is filled with images of dry decay, embers, and drying blood. Smith infuses the tale so thoroughly with desuetude that his readers sympathize not with the living but with the dead, "stirred like autumn leaves in a sudden wind" (*RA* 324).

Prophecy and pestilence also figure prominently in the second tale, "The Isle of the Torturers" (written 31 July 1932; first published *Weird Tales,* March 1933). Again the young ruler of a dead race, like Hestaiyon in the preceding tale, must contend with the evil machinations of the denizens of an island nation intent upon practicing their dark art upon any non-native they encounter, except that King Fulbra's hosts, though not unskilled in sorcery and necromancy, are not interested, as are the necromancers of Naat and Sotar, in blind obedience, but in the total destruction of their prey, mind, body, and soul. Anyone tossed onto the beaches of this land finds himself in the clutches of a vicious race possessed of "a dire longing that they could assuage only through the pain of their fellow-men" (*RA* 462), who use "cunning and subtle" (*RA* 458) gradations of pain, fear, confusion, anticipation, revulsion, and humiliation against their guests. Smith even develops a variation on Villiers de l'Isle-Adam's "La Torture par l'espérance" (*Nouveaux Contes cruels*, 1888) so that hope and "brief, piteous love" appear in the story only to be replaced by "ashes steeped in gall" (*RA* 461). Images of light shining out of darkness appear throughout the tale, but in keeping with the cruel direction toward which all symbols of life trend in this story, they are most often associated with pain and death:

> The plague passed like an eerie, glittering light from countenance to countenance

under the golden lamps; and the victims fell where they were stricken; and the deathly brightness remained upon them. (*RA* 449–50)

This would appear to be the antithesis of the Judeo-Christian interpretation of such imagery—"The people that walked in darkness have seen a great light, and they that dwell in the land of the shadow of death, upon them hath the light shined" (Isaiah 9:2)—until the very end, when Prince Fulbra's final desperate attempt to save his soul from "a long pilgrimage through monstrous and infamous hells" results in an ironic and literal recreation of Isaiah's metaphor—"his face shone brightly with the coming of the Death . . . and the pestilence remained like a glittering light on the faces and shone forth from the nude bodies of the women" (*RA* 462–63).

Irony, dissolution, and contrasts between darkness and light, life and death are also on display in "The Charnel God" (written 15 November 1932; first published *Weird Tales*, March 1934). Here, the necrophagous god and his priesthood, despite their fearsome appearance and grisly activities, are viewed as "utilitarian," and it is those with carnal rather than charnel interests who are to be despised. Smith handles the manifold significance of shadows, a motif that appears frequently in this series (note especially the direct interplay between shadow and substance in "The Black Abbot of Puthuum"), with exceptional deftness in this tale, thereby undermining the significance of the human characters and their actions. Thus, Phariom searching for his cataleptic bride in the charnel fane, moves "like a shadow among shadows" (*RA* 338), and once reunited feels that "he and Elaith were but faint shadows in the presence of embodied death and dissolution" (*RA* 345). The god Mordiggian, on the other hand, though first perceived as "a colossal shadow that was not wrought by anything in the room" (*RA* 344) and less stable in appearance than its human quarry, dwarfs everything around it, like the omnipresent specter of the planet's faltering star; it is "more than a shadow: it was a bulk of darkness, black and opaque" that gleams "with eddying hues of somber iris, like the spectrum of a sable sun" (*RA* 345).

"The Dark Eidolon" (written 23 December 1932; first published *Weird Tales*, January 1935) is the first of the Zothique tales Smith is known to have shortened or otherwise revised prior to its acceptance by the editor of *Weird Tales;* unfortunately it is the only one of those expurgated tales of Zothique whose original manuscript continues to elude Smith scholars. Comparison of other texts revised for publication with Smith's first versions reveal some clarification of action in the revision with a considerable loss of the original's finesse, atmosphere, pacing, and precision in language, though "The Dark Eidolon" appears, like "Xeethra," to have suffered less from expurgation than such extreme examples as "The Maze of Maâl Dweb" and "The Beast of Averoigne." If, as with other tales known to have been shortened for publication, some descriptive passages have been lost, those that remain possess a sullen splendor; the language is as gorgeously grim as that in Shakespeare's *Macbeth*, Webster's *The Duchess of Malfi*, and Tourneur's *The Revenger's*

Tragedy at their most morose; and the pacing is perfectly gauged, like a great crescendo that begins with murmurs of disquiet and builds steadily, horror upon horror, with each more impressive than the last.

James Cawthorn and Michael Moorcock have praised this work as "the apex of incarnadined horror . . . the tale of a childhood injury avenged on a scale which would tax the visual resources of a major studio" (Cawthorn and Moorcock 96). Curiously, Universal had considered both this story and "The Colossus of Ylourgne" from the Averoigne cycle as vehicles for horror films before the studio was sold, though it is doubtful that even current cinematic artistry could equal the work's full range of shocking effects, which encompass every gradation of horror from the multitudinous grotesqueries of the charnel house to the sublimity of the scene in which the macrocosmic stallions of Thamagorgos take shape from the clouds and spread their shadows for miles "like the evil gloom of eclipse," their eyes "half-way between earth and zenith, like baleful suns that glare down from soaring cumuli" (*RA* 386). Each of these, let alone such intermediate individual horrors as Namirrha's congress with demons and the powers of the outer spheres, an increasingly intrusive haunting by ghostly hooves, soul exchange, transformation, and the battle between splintered portions of the same psyche would provide sufficient material for most fantasists; but Smith aims at, and achieves a cumulative effect based on the interweaving of two major themes. His rich vocabulary, command of rhetoric, and use of striking visual and auditory imagery ensure that each of the components making up these patterns is thrilling in its own right as well as contributing to the awe-inspiring potency of the whole. The haunting of Zotulla's palace, the murderous banquet, the trampling of the city of Ummaos, and the branding of Zotulla's concubine are all expressions of Namirrha's obsession with the trampling and scarring he suffered from Zotulla's horse as a boy. Less obvious is the notion of those bitter enemies—the emperor Zotulla and the sorcerer Namirrha—being metaphorical twins or incomplete portions of a greater whole:[2] Zotulla's luxuries and turpitudes are referred to as "a twin marvel to the bruited necromancies of Namirrha" (*RA* 367); his palace and that which Namirrha builds beside it are at the same level; the people of Ummaos, grown used to the presence of the sorcerer's palace, brags of the infamies of both men; Zotulla is equally in thrall to the demon lord Thasaidon as Namirrha, though he serves him unwittingly and Namirrha rejects his own "fatal fealty" (*RA* 375); Namirrha briefly usurps the body of Zotulla; and in the end Namirrha battles furiously against his mirror-image, alternately deeming himself a sorcerer warring against an emperor, an emperor smiting a sorcerer, and a third man fighting an unknown foe.

Even more crammed with incident, but completely different in tone is "The Voyage of King Euvoran" (written January 1933; first published in *The Double Shadow*, 1933), originally intended as part of the cycle set at the opposite end of man's tenancy of earth. The tale's grotesquerie and humor continues to lend it a flavor much closer to that of Hyperborea than to Zothique, but also makes for a welcome respite from the unrelievedly grim tales that had preceded it. Over several episodes, its titular king encounters a necromancer, ape-men, griffins, hordes of winged voracious vampires so numerous as to sink ships through their very weight, man-sized intelligent birds, and other prodigies; reacts with overweening pride and unthinking brutality at every turn; and suffers repeated losses in personnel, possessions, and dignity as a result. Deflationary jabs aimed at the king are frequent and amusing:

> It was a tedious journey, and Euvoran was much annoyed by the huge and vicious gnats of Sotar, which were no respecters of royalty, and were always insinuating themselves under his turban. (*AY* 95)
>
> Indeed, methinks that a stuffed king (since even the vermin have kings) will serve to enhance my collection. (*AY* 103)
>
> And the skin [of the bird he had slain] fit him well enough because of his pigeon-breast and his potbelly . . . (*AY* 105)

Smith fills the tale with effective scenes of suspense and horror, but never leaves the wry, Swiftian smirk of satire far behind, as when Euvoran's fleet limps away after a horrendous battle with the vampires, its decks covered with blood, corpses, and vast quantities of malodorous guano.

Unlike the tales that had preceded it, neither "The Weaver in the Vault" (written 14 March 1935; first published *Weird Tales*, January 1934) nor "The Tomb-Spawn" (begun July 1933; first published *Weird Tales*, May 1934) is strong in plot or characterization. Both could be said to fall into what has been jokingly referred to as the "Here is an old legend . . . aargh, it got me!" school of weird fiction construction. Nonetheless, each of the tales is atmospheric and well-paced—once the need for a perfunctory exposition has been met—takes place amid surroundings of decaying grandeur, and introduces a fabulous and unique monstrosity. The grim and magnificent climax of "The Weaver in the Vault," featuring a beautiful, prismatic lattice spun from carrion, could also be viewed as a metaphor for the artist's use of materials associated with death and decay to create works attaining to the dark sublime.

"The Witchcraft of Ulua" (written 22 August 1933; first published *Weird Tales*, February 1934) is a more ambitious tale of sorcery in which "erotic imagery was employed . . . to achieve a more varied sensation of weirdness" (*SL* 219). Although "the net result" was intended to be "macabre rather than risqué," the story was rejected as "a sex story and therefore unsuitable for *W.T.*" (*SL* 219), making it necessary for Smith to create a "slightly subtilized version" for publication (*SL* 233). Although the expurgations forced upon Smith are not as extensive as they are for several of his other works, the fusion of macabre and erotic elements in the restored version make for a more consistently atmospheric and potent tale than the version commonly reprinted. Even the expurgated version, however, retains the catastrophic climax and such delightfully morbid conceits as this description of a sorcerer's dwelling on the rim of the desert:

> a house whose floor and walls were built of the large bones of dromedaries, and whose roof was a wattling composed of the smaller bones of wild dogs and men and hyenas. These ossuary relics, chosen for their whiteness and symmetry, were bound securely together with well-tanned thongs, and were joined and fitted with marvellous closeness, leaving no space for the blown sand to penetrate. The house was the pride of Sabmon, who swept it daily with a besom of mummy's hair, till it shone immaculate as ivory both within and without. (*AY* 21)

Among the tales of Zothique, only the "The Dark Eidolon" rivals "Xeethra" (written 21 March 1934; published *Weird Tales*, December 1934) in the dark magnificence of its conception and the mastery of its execution. Elements from Genesis, the Faust legend, the *Arabian Nights*, *Vathek*, and even H. P. Lovecraft's stylish but self-pitying fable "The Quest of Iranon" (1921) all combine in a work remarkable for its pathos, and a range of effects vividly evocative of youth and decay, hope and despair, growth and ruin, the pastoral and the diabolical, the regal and the squalid, the mundane and the terrifying. Ultimately, Xeethra's plight, unlike Iranon's, is not merely pitiful, it is tragic. The essence of tragedy as understood by the ancients is not the destruction of innocents by forces beyond their control, but the flaws or errors that lead the individual toward his own destruction; and it is these, just as much as the subtle temptations of the demon Thasaidon, that lead the tale's hero again and again to "dust and dearth" (*RA* 364). Much of the tale's power resides in its author's careful attention to verbal felicities which equal and are responsible for heightening its manifold wonders and threats. For instance, throughout Xeethra's visit and flight from the mysterious cavern, Smith produces a cunning progression in his use of simile, which suggests an unwelcome truth behind the sights and sounds that greet the young man ("his torch was extinguished by a hot gust that blew upon him like the expelled breath of some prankish demon" [*RA* 349]; "There was no sound other than the sighing of leaves in the perfume-burdened wind: a sound like the hissing of many small hidden serpents" [*RA* 349]), then focuses away from matters of similarity to those of probability ("Before him he heard a long rumbling as of summer thunder . . . or the laughter of colossi" [*RA* 351]) as Xeethra tastes of the hellish fruit and begins to sense things he had never before even suspected.

If "The Empire of the Necromancers," "The Isle of the Torturers," and "Xeethra" all concern themselves on some level with prophecies and foreordination, the *ne plus ultra* in the depiction of inexorable fate is "The Last Hieroglyph" (written March–May 1934; first published *Weird Tales*, April 1935). Nushain's horoscope forecasts a journey led by three guides through three of the four elements—earth, water, and fire—before a final encounter with the fourth element in the presence of "the most powerful and mysterious of the genii" (*RA* 404). Smith ingeniously combines the concepts of the logos and astrology before carrying them to their logical extreme, with individual symbols not only representing but also briefly incarnating every thing that ever existed on earth and in the heavens. One source for this tale appears amid the "marvellous illustrations" (*SL* 138) Sidney Sime had created for Lord Dunsany's *The Gods of Pegāna* (1905). Although he admitted he "never could work up much enthusiasm over Lord Dunsany's work" in the book (*SL* 138), it is not difficult to note resemblances between the final scene in Smith's tale and Sidney Sime's depiction of "the Thing that is neither god nor beast" (Dunsany 50), sitting upon the Rim of the Worlds, "whose book is the Scheme of Things" (Dunsany 51) in which all beings and objects exist until the turning of the last page where their names are written.

This tale has, as Will Murray has so aptly put it, a "culminating resonance" (11), and nearly a year passed before Smith completed another work in the cycle. "Necromancy in Naat" (written 6 February 1935; first published *Weird Tales,* July 1936) is a fine amalgam of adventure, supernatural horror, and bittersweet love story, full of unusual characters and odd events, which ranks among the best works in this series. Unfortunately, *Weird Tales* rejected the first version of the story, causing Smith to lament that he had been forced to "mutilate the ending" (*SL* 289) in order to ensure publication. A perusal of the typed manuscript, recently recovered by Scott Connors and Ron Hilger, reveals much more extensive revision than Smith suggests: one 500-word passage describing the initial stages of Yadar's search for his beloved has been reduced to a few lines, descriptive passages and those focusing on the characters' mental states have been removed or pared to the bone, much detail near the conclusion has been discarded in order to limit the action to one viewpoint; and throughout, atmosphere has been sacrificed to speed of narration, and nuance to action. Ever the craftsman, Smith is careful even in the truncated text to change word order and alter syntax in order the rebalance the rhythm of his prose. Curiously, however, the sad, sweet line that concludes the tale originated not with Smith's first submission, but in the revision.

Further stories appeared at irregular intervals over the next twenty years, all good, but only a few capturing the height of astonishment and depth of pathos seen in the series up to this time.

"The Black Abbot of Puthuum" (written before April 1935; first published *Weird Tales,* March 1936), "The Death of Ilalotha" (written 16 March 1937; first published *Weird Tales,* September 1937), and "The Garden of Adompha" (written 31 July 1937; first published *Weird Tales,* June 1938), are all fine weird tales, full of novel phenomena, vividly evoked locales, carefully modulated suspense, and an effective denouement, with each story focused on a distinct mixture of horrific, grotesque, and adventurous elements, with a leavening of eroticism. The same could be said of "The Master of the Crabs" (written 3 August 1947; first published *Weird Tales,* March 1948), minus the erotic element.

It is Smith's free deployment of eroticism in the cycle's final tale and verse drama that restore the cycle to the level it had reached at its peak.

Steeped in the same dour beauty as John Keats's "Ode to a Nightingale" and "Ode on Melancholy" (both 1819), as well as making free use of imagery from poems such as Charles Baudelaire's "La Géante" (*Les Fleurs du mal*, 1857, which Smith had translated as "The Giantess"), "Morthylla" (written September or October 1952; first published *Weird Tales*, May 1953) is one of its author's most melancholy and moving tales. The poet Valzain longs for a world more satisfying than the sensuality into which his fellows have abandoned themselves, and travels to a necropolis where "dim, lengthened, and attenuate, his shadow went before him like a ghostly guide" (*RA* 467). He fancies that the cemetery is "the gently sloping bosom of a giantess, studded afar with pale gems that were tombstones and mausoleums" (*RA* 467), and is all too prone to "a dreamer's acceptance of things fantastic elsewhere than in sleep" (*RA* 469). As one might suspect, once he convinces himself the mysterious woman he has met beside the mausoleum has "turned all else to shadow" (*RA* 470), then fails to heed her warnings to not "risk awakening from the dream" (*RA* 469), he invites disillusionment, and gives way to despair. Smith then introduces a subtly varied recapitulation of Valzain's initial encounter in the necropolis, turning dream into reality, and rewarding "one who, without positive belief, had longed vainly for visions from beyond mortality" (*RA* 467, 472).

Smith's final work in the cycle, one among "a few unpublished masterpieces" (*SL* 373) of his final years, the short play entitled *The Dead Will Cuckold You* (written 1951/52, revised 1956; first published *In Memoriam: Clark Ashton Smith*, August 1963). It is in six brief scenes and written in blank verse with short passages of rhymed song and incantation. In language it is akin to the more morbid specimens of Renaissance revenge tragedy, but its structure owes at least as much to Lord Dunsany's early fantasy plays. The play makes much use of a double-horned motif shared by the cuckold, the demon lord Thaisadon, and the fertility goddess Ililot, each of which confers a different curse, or blessing, upon those who evoke it. Whereas the queen, who has no reason to fear the other two more than her murderous husband and seeks a means of escape from

> This palace where my feet forever pace
> From shades of evil to a baleful sun (*SS* 236)

successfully evokes the third, her husband, whose soul has been made "a cavern where close-knotted serpents nest" through pride, jealousy, fear, brutality, and insecurity, dreads them all, without fully comprehending any of them—

> In all my kingdom, or in Thasaidon's
> Deep tortuous maze of torments multi-circled,
> There is no darker gulf than this shut room
> Which reason cannot fathom, being shunted
> From the blank walls of madness. (*SS* 241)

At the locked door to his wife's chamber wherein he has been told is the reanimated corpse of the man he had slain for fear of cuckoldry, he seeks only the most immediate means of ingress, choosing death by flame over a thwarted will or the possibility of embarrassment. He lacks the insight to recognize that

> Hell hath no limits, nor is circumscribed
> In one safe place; for where we are is hell,
> And where hell is there must we ever be.
> (Christopher Marlowe, *Dr. Faustus*, v. 121–23)

*

In a letter dated 22 May 1926, Smith praised his friend Benjamin De Casseres in lavish terms that could readily be applied to the imagination and level of accomplishment evinced by his own tales of Zothique:

> You have a tremendous vision of the phantom-flux of time and matter, the masques and mummeries of the infinite, and the ineluctable trans-substantiation of suns and monads ... You break the bottles of the Djinns, you tear the swaddlings of Ialdabaoth and the mummy-cloths of Maya. You are a cosmic eagle who can carry worlds aloft and let them drop in the carapace of God. (*SL* 87)

Smith had planned on a broader reception and more widespread appreciation of his story cycles than has yet materialized: "Printed on good paper and decently bound, I think that all of these tales would show up as fine literature, in no wise inferior to Dunsany or Cabell" (*SL* 219). Scholarship, diligence, and renewed attention to the texts Smith intended to publish, rather than those forced upon him by the marketplace, are proving the truth of this statement to an ever wider audience. His vision is a unique one, which has been ill-served for decades by those interested only in the contrasts his work bears to that of his contemporaries H. P. Lovecraft and Robert E. Howard. His long-held position as a shadow figure to two titans is undeserved. The author's Zothique cycle, the largest, most varied, most exotic, and most deeply felt of his works is the ideal place for the reader to gain the acquaintance of one of the most conscientious and imaginative of fantasists ever to take up a pen under this or any sun.

Notes

1. Aickman's definition of the "ghost story" is astonishingly broad. In his introduction to the first *Fontana Book of Great Ghost Stories*, he writes "The majority of ghost stories, however, have no actual ghost.... The technique, like the subject is fragile but with a grip of iron. And a vital ingredient is beauty." (Aickman, "Introduction," 7, 9).
2. This theme deserves to be explored in the context of the mythic hero archetype.

Works Cited

Aickman, Robert. "An Essay." In *First World Fantasy Awards,* ed. Gahan Wilson. Garden City, NY: Doubleday, 1977. 63–65.

———. "Introduction." In *The Fontana Book of Great Ghost Stories,* ed. Robert Aickman. London: Fontana, 1964. 7–10.

Behrends, Steve. "The Song of the Necromancer: 'Loss' in Clark Ashton Smith's Fiction." *Studies in Weird Fiction* No. 1 (Summer 1986): 3–12.

Bradbrook, M. C. *Themes and Conventions of Elizabethan Tragedy.* Cambridge: Cambridge University Press, 1935.

Burleson, Donald R. "The Mythic Hero Archetype in 'The Dunwich Horror.'" In *A Century Less a Dream,* ed. Scott Connors. Holicong, PA: Wildside Press, 2002. 206–13.

Cawthorn, James, and Michael Moorcock. *Fantasy: The 100 Best Books.* New York: Carroll & Graf, 1988. 95–96.

Dunsany, Lord. *The Gods of Pegāna.* 1905. Boston: John W. Luce, 1916.

Murray, Will. "Introduction." In *Tales of Zothique.* By Clark Ashton Smith. West Warwick, RI: Necronomicon Press, 1995.

Rockhill, Jim. "The Poetics of Morbidity: The Original Text to Clark Ashton Smith's 'The Maze of Maal Dweb' and Other Works First Published in *The Double Shadow and Other Fantasies." Lost Worlds* No. 1 (2004): 20–25.

Sidney-Fryer, Donald. *Clark Ashton Smith: The Sorcerer Departs.* West Hills, CA: Tsathoggua Press, 1997.

———. "Introduction: Lyricist of Lost Worlds." In *The Monster of the Prophecy.* By Clark Ashton Smith. New York: Timescape, 1983. 7–10.

Stableford, Brian. "Outside the Human Aquarium: The Fantastic Imagination of Clark Ashton Smith." In *American Supernatural Fiction: From Edith Wharton to the* Weird Tales *Writers,* ed. Douglas Robillard. New York: Garland, 1996. 229–52.

Into the Woods:
The Human Geography of Averoigne

Stefan Dziemianowicz

Writing to H. P. Lovecraft in 1930, Clark Ashton Smith referred to his recently written "A Rendezvous in Averoigne" as a tale of "the *purely* fantastic" (*LL* 15). Only when given its proper context—Smith was juxtaposing this superior tale of the supernatural to the second-rate science fantasies he was churning out for Hugo Gernsback's *Wonder Stories*—does his description make any sense, for Smith's story of two lovers waylaid in the woods of medieval France by a vampire lord and lady reads like an exercise in the sort of literary realism he so abhorred, when compared to more otherworldly (and as-yet-unwritten) fantasies such as "Xeethra" (of his Zothique story cycle), "The Coming of the White Worm" (of his Hyperborea cycle), "The Last Incantation" (of his Poseidonis cycle),, and numerous others.

Although Smith believed "that there is absolutely no justification for literature unless it serves to release the imagination from the bounds of everyday life" (*SL* 123), the eleven stories of his Averoigne cycle are a distinct exception: they are remarkable, if anything, for their realistic insights into human nature and their evocation of a mundane world in which supernatural machinations seem all the more exotic. As Steve Behrends has noted, it was in his Averoigne tales that "Smith came closest to producing a series with a non-fabulous backdrop" (*CAS* 49). More to the point, these stories temper Behrends's otherwise astute observation that Smith "revelled in exoticism and the ultra-human, in coined names, in descriptions of unearthly flora and strange, vapor-hung sunsets" (*CAS* 12). Smith did indeed strive to make the "ultra-human" the focus of all his stories, but the sympathy for humanity that permeates his tales of Averoigne gives them a psychological and philosophical substance too often lacking in the rest of his fiction. As a result, these stories can be read both as links between Smith's horror and fantasy stories and at the same time fiction that transcends the limitations of Smith's aesthetic of the purely fantastic.

The template for all the Averoigne stories can be found in the first published story in the series, "The End of the Story." The tale is presented as the written narrative of Christophe Morand, a young law student from Tours who has disappeared following a journey through the province of Averoigne in 1798. Christophe's manuscript recounts his overnight stay at the abbey of Périgon, wherein resides a sect of Benedictine monks headed by the liberal abbot Hilaire.

Hilaire recognizes in Christophe a fellow scholar and delights in showing him some of the abbey's rare manuscripts. Among these is an account of one Gérard de Venteillon, who on the eve of his wedding centuries before was lured by a satyr to the nearby Château des Faussesflammes and never seen again. Despite discouragement by Hilaire, Christophe finds himself irresistibly drawn to the château whose ruins sit on a hill just above the abbey. He visits there the next day and upon entering a grove finds himself transported to a glorious pastoral landscape presided over by the seductive Nycea. Christophe's idyll is abruptly ended by the appearance of Hilaire, who dispatches Nycea with holy water and explains to the crestfallen young man that she is a lamia who has used her sorcery to beguile him. The story ends with Christophe so smitten by Nycea's enchantments that he vows nevertheless to return and seek her company.

Although the most recent story of the Averoigne cycle by internal chronology—it takes place later than eight other stories for which Behrends has been able to date events (*CAS* 54)—"The End of the Story" exhibits most of the characteristics that make the series so compelling. Primary among these is Smith's evocation of the landscape. The story opens in the forest of Averoigne, which surrounds the principle towns of Ximes and Vyones and plays a crucial role in, if not serving as the actual site for, the marvels related in nine of the tales. Smith's delineation of the interrelationship between this dense and often impenetrable forest and the local towns lays the foundation for the fantastic in these stories much the same way rural settings do in contemporary horror fiction: it creates a sense of isolation and removal from the rest of the world. Although there are allusions in several of the stories to the larger world beyond the woods of Averoigne, for the most part this remote sector of the Provence region seems untouched by time or world events. A perfect example is the *mise en scène* of "The End of the Story," which takes place nine years after a political and social revolution that convulsed not only France but also much of Western civilization, yet still unfolds as though it were taking place in the medieval times of the earliest stories in the cycle.

In addition to having a literal presence, the woods of Averoigne also have a symbolic weight. As Smith tells us in the sixth published tale, "A Rendezvous in Averoigne":

> [T]he gnarled and immemorial wood possessed an ill-repute among the peasantry. Somewhere in this wood there was the ruinous and haunted Château des Faussesflammes; and also there was a double tomb, within which Sieur Hugh du Malinbois and his chatelaine, who were notorious for sorcery in their time, had lain unconsecrated for more than two hundred years. Of these, and their phantoms, there were grisly tales; and there were stories of loup garous and goblins, of fays and devils and vampires that infested Averoigne. (*RA* 77)

In the seventh published tale, "The Satyr," Smith reinforces this image of the woods as a wellspring of local superstition:

> Here, some of the huge oaks were said to date back to pagan days. Few people ever passed beneath them; and queer beliefs and legends concerning them had been prevalent among the local peasantry for ages. Things had been seen within these precincts, whose very existence was an affront to science and a blasphemy to religion; and evil influences were said to attend those who dared to intrude upon the sullen umbrage of the immemorial glades and thickets. (GL 157–58)

Untamed and imbued with a sense of antiquity that dwarfs the age of the towns it surrounds—we are informed in "The Holiness of Azédarac" that the woods was once the site of Druidic worship in 475 A.D., and in "The Enchantress of Sylaire" that the moor the forest gives way to "was studded with Druidic monoliths, dating from ages prior to the Roman occupation" (AY 130)—the forest of Averoigne is a locus of mystery upon which the townspeople project their primitive (and not entirely unfounded) fears. Thus, it does not take much of an interpretative leap to view the interrelationship of the towns and woods of Averoigne as an externalization of the psyches of the inhabitants of Averoigne: the civilized self, threatened on all sides by the primal fears it has pushed to the periphery of its consciousness but not entirely dispelled.

It is surely no coincidence, then, that Smith's favorite symbol of the horrors that lurk in the forest is the werewolf. Although werewolves appear in only three of the Averoigne stories—"The Beast of Averoigne," "The Enchantress of Sylaire," and (by implication) "The Mandrakes"—they are omnipresent in the background of all the stories. Smith repeatedly describes the woods as "haunted" or "infested" with werewolves, a subtle evocation of the rational self overwhelmed by the primitive side of its nature.

If the forests of Averoigne represent the irrational side of human nature, then the Church can be viewed as embodying the rational side. Although the religious authority of the Benedictine monks and Catholic clergy is woven into the social background of all the Averoigne stories, in six—"The End of the Story," "The Maker of Gargoyles," "The Beast of Averoigne," "The Holiness of Azédarac," "The Colossus of Ylourgne," and "The Disinterment of Venus"—Smith specifically uses the godliness represented by either the cathedral of Vyones or the abbey of Périgon as the standard against which the ungodliness of the supernatural is measured.

Like the forest, the Church occupies both a literal and a symbolic space in the stories: the cathedral of Vyones is the largest building in the town, and thus a symbol for the pinnacle of civilization, serving to remind us of the role the Church played in preserving western culture during the Dark Ages (which have just about ended by the time of the events in "The Maker of Gargoyles," the first story in the cycle by internal chronology). When the supernatural occurs in these stories, it represents not only an affront to the teachings of the Church, but by extension a threat to the values that define the humanity of the characters.

Smith broadens the human dimension of this part of the backdrop to the Averoigne cycle by showing that the separation between the forest and the town, the irrational and rational sides of human nature, is far from clear-cut. When Hilaire invokes the power of Christ to save Christophe from the lamia in "The End of the Story," Smith portrays the event not so much as a triumph of good over evil, but of religious faith over pagan belief. This distinction is important for understanding the world-view of the citizens of the province. Averoigne, as Smith sketches it, is a region where paganism still exerts a strong hold on the imagination and where religious faith and superstition coexist restlessly in the minds of the people. Smith reminds us of this by several means in the "The End of the Story": symbolically, through the physical proximity of the abbey of Périgon to the ruins of the Château des Faussesflammes (they are separated by only a half-hour's walk), and literally, through the speech of the satyr to Gérard de Venteillon:

> "The power of Christ has prevailed like a black frost on all the woods, the fields, the rivers, the mountains, where abode in their felicity the glad, immortal goddesses and nymphs of yore. But still, in the cryptic caverns of earth, in places far underground, like the hell your priests have fabled, there dwells the pagan loveliness, there cry the pagan ecstasies." (*RA* 64)

As is evident from the history of the ruins told to Christophe by a young monk, not even the clergy are immune to the influence of the pagan beliefs they struggle to supplant with their religious faith:

> "For untold years, men say, they have been the haunt of unholy spirits, or witches and demons . . . Some say that the demons are abominable hags whose bodies terminate in serpentine coils; others that they are women of more than mortal beauty, whose kisses are a diabolic delight that consumes men with the fierceness of hell-fire . . . As for me, I know not whether such tales are true; but I should not care to venture within the walls of Faussesflammes." (*RA* 66)

In Averoigne, it would appear that Christianity is a relatively recent, and sometimes temporary, affectation of the populace. The most devout are forever in danger of falling back upon their primitive superstitions, and in moments of moral weakness, such as "the suffocating burden of superstitious terror" that grips the townsfolk of Vyones in "The Maker of Gargoyles," some are capable of reverting to ungodly practices:

> Everyone now felt a truly formidable assault was being made by the powers of Evil on the Christian probity of Vyones. In the condition of abject terror, or extreme disorder, and demoralization that followed upon this new atrocity, there was a deplorable outbreak of human crime, or murder and rapine and thievery, together with covert manifestations of Satanism, and celebrations of the Black Mass attended by many neophytes. (*TSS* 175)

The Averoigne stories are nothing if not studies of such moments of human fallibility. In virtually every one, the supernatural gets the upper hand only after human characters succumb to their passions or give in to illicit desires; in fact, "The Colossus of Ylourgne" and "The Beast of Averoigne" are the only tales in the cycle in which romantic passion, or lust, are not the catalyst for the weird events that follow. Although Smith divides these episodes of human frailty evenly between men and women, he relies on a favorite emblem of flawed humanity to make his point: the monks of Périgon. Regardless of whether he portrays them as too ascetic for their own good, as in "The Disinterment of Venus," or as holy hypocrites in "The Holiness of Azédarac," Smith achieves some his most poignant and satiric moments as a writer by showing his monks to be the perfect embodiment of the contradictions of the human condition, people with divine aspirations but feet of clay.

A fine example is the abbot Hilaire in "The End of the Story." Smith treats Hilaire more kindly than any other clergyman in his stories, portraying him as both holy and enlightened when he introduces himself to Christophe:

> "We are a Benedictine order, who live in amity with God and with all men, and we do not hold that the spirit is to be enriched by the mortification or impoverishment of the body. We have in our butteries an abundance of wholesome fare, in our cellars the best and oldest vintage of the district of Averoigne. And, if such things interest you, as mayhap they do, we have a library that is stocked with rare tomes, with precious manuscripts, with the finest works of heathendom and Christendom, even to certain unique writings that survived the holocaust of Alexandria." (*RA* 59)

Nevertheless, Hilaire's openmindedness has its price, for it leads to Christophe's introduction to the manuscript of Gérard de Venteillon and thus indirectly implicates the abbot in Christophe's temptation and eventual destruction.

More often, Smith presents his monks in a less flattering light as men who use their holy station as a cloak for their inadequacies as human beings. In two stories, there is actual collusion between the clergy and the sorcerers who cater to the pagan beliefs of the people. This collusion is indirect and almost benign in "The Mandrakes," in which we learn that because of the number of honest marriages promoted by the philtres of a husband and wife team of sorcerers, "the local clergy were content to disregard the many illicit amours that had to come to a successful issue through the same agency" (*OD* 253). But in "The Beast of Averoigne," when the abbot of Périgon and the marshal of Ximes engage the wizard Luc le Chaudronnier to use whatever means necessary to destroy a legendary monster beyond the control of the Church and state, the collaboration is direct and a testimony to the limits of religious faith:

> "[I]n dealing with this devil, it may be that you shall succeed where all others have failed. Not willingly do we employ you in the matter, since it is not seemly for the church and the law to ally themselves with wizardry. But the need is desperate lest the demon should take other victims. In return for your aid we can

promise you a goodly reward of gold and a guarantee of lifelong immunity from all inquisition which your doings might otherwise invite. The Bishop of Ximes, and the Archbishop of Vyones, are privy to this offer, which must be kept a secret." (*LW* 150–51)

The seriousness of the stories mentioned above prevents Smith from attempting more than a few wry observations regarding the duplicity of the clergy. But in "The Holiness of Azédarac," the one overtly humorous tale of Averoigne, he is at his satiric best. Azédarac is the Bishop of Ximes, but secretly a sorcerer who has adopted the guise of holiness to put himself above suspicion. As he observes to a subordinate, "'the chief difference between myself and many other ecclesiastics is, that I serve the Devil wittingly and of my own free will, while they do the same in sanctimonious blindness'" (*RA* 5). The monk who bears evidence of Azédarac's blasphemies to Vyones, the likeable Brother Ambrose, exemplifies Azédarac's insight: when sent back in time 700 years by a potion concocted by Azédarac's henchman, he indulges in a sexual relationship with the Lady Moriamis and rationalizes away its sinfulness, because theoretically he has yet to be born. Smith ends the tale with Ambrose discovering that fifty years hence Azédarac will be canonized and his transmigration from the earthly plane by means of black magic mistaken for an assumption into Heaven. This final ironic touch leaves the reader with an image of Averoigne as a place where deceivers and the self-deceived lived in perfect harmony.

In light of the foregoing discussion, it is hardly surprising that when the supernatural erupts through the plain veneer of everyday life in Averoigne, it takes on a decidedly human cast. In this regard, the Averoigne stories resemble Smith's fantasy fiction, in which the marvels that occur are consistent with the otherworldliness of their setting, more than straight horror stories like "Genius Loci," "The Return of the Sorcerer," and "The Nameless Offspring," which depend for their effect on abominations horrifyingly inconsistent with the natural world. To be sure, the Averoigne stories are stocked with the monsters of supernatural horror fiction—vampires, werewolves, the reanimated dead, satyrs, and gargoyles, just to name a few. In each one, though, Smith not only emphasizes the human aspects of these creatures but uses them as mirrors to reflect on the behavior of his all-too-human characters.

For example, the Sieur du Malinbois and his wife Agathe, the vampire couple of "A Rendezvous in Averoigne," can be viewed as a demonic exaggerations of the troubadour Gérard de l'Automne and Fleurette Cochin, their mutual thirst for blood mirroring the obsessive passion that has forced the pair of lovers to rendezvous in the shunned forest of Averoigne. The satyr who spirits away the lady Adèle in "The Satyr" is an expression not only of the bestial urges of lust and territoriality that motivate Adèle's lover Olivier du Montoir and her husband, Raoul, Comte de la Frenaie (respectively), but also of Adèle's own desires. In "The Mandrakes," sorcerer Gilles Grenier discovers that the roots of the mandrake plants growing out of his wife Sabine's grave both resemble her in physical shape, and mock the murderous rage that drove him to kill her, when those who drink love potions made from them are afflicted with "a woeful and Satanic madness, irresistibly impelling them to harm or even slay the persons who had sought to attract their love" (*OD* 257). In "The Maker of Gargoyles," the town of Vyones is terrorized by a pair of animated gargoyles, one of whom wreaks random destruction upon the townspeople while the other molests the womenfolk, as a result of stonecarver Blaise Reynard investing one with "all his festering rancor, all his answering spleen and hatred toward the people of Vyones, who had always hated him," and the other with "his own dour satyrlike passion" for a local barmaid. And "Mother of Toads" tells of the toadlike witch woman, Mère Antoinette, who seduces apothecary apprentice Pierre Baudin and, in a scene redolent with Freudian implications, sends an army of toads to smother the boy when he flees in disgust.

It probably would be inaccurate to give the impression that Smith consciously contrived these stories as a sort of roadmap to the human soul, or used the threads of common humanity they share to weave a more deliberate unity of setting or spirit than found in his Zothique, Hyperborea, or Poseidonis stories. Both "The Holiness of Azédarac" and "The Satyr," for example, are obviously meant as light entertainments, and several of the other stories might as easily have been transplanted to one of Smith's otherworldly realms just as "Mother of Toads" and "The Mandrakes" could have been told as straight horror stories. Nevertheless, in the best tales of the Averoigne cycle, one finds Smith grappling with ideas so fundamental to human psychology that they could probably never have been executed outside of the unpretentious environs of this homely and familiar milieu.

"The End of the Story" is more than just a vampire tale. It is, in fact, a recapitulation of the biblical story of the Fall of Man, in which Smith substitutes a forbidden text for the traditional apple as the object of temptation. It is not stretching the analogy too far to say that, for the scholarly Christophe, the library of Périgon represents a sort of Eden that eventually tests his free will. The abbot Hilaire gives the student free access to the manuscripts except for that of Gérard de Venteillon, forbidding him to think of it—although not making it entirely inaccessible to him-in a warning laden with biblical portents:

> "Christophe, there are things beyond your understanding, things that it were not well for you to know. The might of Satan is manifestable in devious modes, in diverse manners; there are other temptations than those of the world and the flesh, there are evils no less subtle than irresistable, there are hidden heresies, and necromancies other than those which sorcerers practice." (*RA* 61)

If Hilaire's is the voice of divine authority, then the satyr who has promised to tell Gérard de Venteillon "'a secret, knowing which, you will forget the worship of Christ, and forget your beautiful bride of tomorrow, and turn your back on the world and the very sun itself with no reluctance and no regret'" (*RA* 65) is surely the devil, tempting men like Gérard and Christophe to their downfall. Although Hilaire appears to have saved Christophe from doom, we know by the end of the story that he is lost. He has tasted the forbidden fruit of Nycea's world and found the certain death it holds in store preferable to the pleasant but limited existence he has known before:

> Soon, I shall return, to visit again the ruins of the Château des Faussesflammes, and redescend into the vaults below the triangular flagstone. But, in spite of the nearness of Périgon to Faussesflammes, in spite of my esteem for the abbot, my gratitutde for his hospitality, and my admiration for his incomparable library, I shall not care to visit my friend Hilaire. (*RA* 75)

Smith leaves ambiguous in this story whether Christophe is acting under his own free will or the influence of Nycea through a spell placed upon de Venteillon's manuscript. In "The Enchantress of Sylaire," though he resolves this question. As Behrends notes, this story is essentially "an unintentional remake" of "The End of the Story." Once more Smith presents us with a young man, Anselme, tempted by a sorceress, Sephora, who is "the essence of all the beauty and romance that he had ever craved." Salvation intervenes in the form of Malachie du Marais, a wolf who turns back into a man long enough to warn Anselme that Sephora will subject him to the same feral transformation once she grows tired of his love, and to present him with a "mirror of Reality" in which he can view her true corruption. Anselme briefly weighs his options before turning his back on his mortal lover, killing du Marais, and throwing out the mirror, assuring Sephora, "'I am content with what my eyes tell me, without the aid of any mirror'" (*AY* 140). It is worth noting that this study of willful self-deception is the last-written tale in the Averoigne cycle. Thus, consciously or not, Smith begins and ends the series with treatments of the fall, the supreme moment of human fallibility from which all others flow.

"The Colossus of Ylourgne," with its series of increasingly bizarre events culminating in the rampage of the most awesome monster to appear in Smith's fiction, comes the closest of any of the Averoigne tales to evoking the sense of wonder in Smith's otherworldly fantasies. Here again, though, the plot is one concerned with human ambitiousness that results in overreaching and downfall. The story tells of the Nathaire, an ugly and deformed sorcerer of "minikin stature" reviled by the citizens of Vyones. Hounded from the city, he takes up residence in nearby Ylourgne where he fashions a simulacrum as tall as the cathedral out of the skin and tissues of corpses into which he projects his soul. When the creature begins to ransack the countryside, the people of Averoigne discover one final surprise: *"the face of the stupendous monster . . . was the face of the Satanic dwarf, Nathaire—remagnified a hundred times, but the same in its implacable madness and malevolence!"* (*GL* 144). Although Nathaire possesses the power of God in his ability to create a being in his own image, his handiwork is revealed here to be no more than a desperate act of psychological overcompensation by which he hopes to achieve the stature (literally) he was denied in life. Smith appears to be saying that even the sorcerers of Averoigne are unable to transcend their flawed humanity, a point he drives home symbolically in the final image of the monster dispatched by a sorcery that compels it to dig its own grave, lie down in it, and rot to pieces, even as Nathaire, now powerless to stop the process of natural corruption, protests vehemently.

In contrast to the grotesque excesses of "The Colossus of Ylourgne," "The Disinterment of Venus" is one of Smith's most subtly understated stories, a human comedy that is as gentle in its satire as "The Holiness of Azédarac" is unrelenting. While digging in the garden of the abbey of Périgon one day, three monks uncover a replica of the Roman Venus, yet another reminder of the pagan history underlying the region. The statue exerts a curious effect upon them:

> During the course of their excavations, the brothers had felt a strange, powerful excitement, whose cause they could hardly have explained, but which seemed to arise, like some obscure contagion, from the long-buried arms and bosom of the image. Mingled with a pious horror due to the infamous pagantry and nudity of the statue, there was an unacknowledged pleasure which the three would have rebuked in themselves as vile and shameful if they had recognized it. (GL 111)

In essence, the statue appears to have reminded these holy men that they are not only holy, but also *men,* and have repressed the same appetites and desires that laymen enjoy freely. The statue begins to disrupt monastic life throughout the abbey, spurring the monks on to indiscretions forbidden by their vows of poverty and chastity, after which they blame the statue, "saying that a pagan witchcraft had come upon them from its flesh-white marble" (GL 114). One hears this excuse enough to begin suspecting that, in the statue, the monks have found a convenient excuse for indulging their unspoken vices. Only at the climax of the tale does Smith shift the burden of blame from the passions of the monks to a supernatural agency, when the fanatical Brother Louis leaves in the middle of the night to take a hammer to the statue and is found the next day crushed in the embrace of marble arms that have shifted position to hold him. "The iron hammer, lying beside the hole, was proof of the righteous intention with which Louis had gone forth; but it was all too plain that he had succumbed to the hellish charms of the statue" (GL 117). This is as good a symbol as any of the adage that those who would enforce morality the most strenuously are those most insecure about themselves, and Smith reinforces it by having Louis interred still wrapped in the arms of the statue.[1]

Of all the tales of Averoigne, the one which best expresses the human dimension of the cycle is "The Beast of Averoigne," although one would not guess this from the version published in *Weird Tales* in 1933. The story is presented as sorcerer Luc le Chaudronnier's account of the events of 1369, when a series of bestial murders throughout the region leads to the engagement of his services by the authorities of Averoigne. Le Chaudronnier consults a demon and is told that the slaughter is the handiwork of a demon from a passing comet, which can only manifest itself by infesting a human form. He lies in wait for the beast one night, and after killing it watches it turn into the abbot Theophile of Périgon, one of the same men who hired him.

This unremarkable variation on the traditional werewolf tale was not the story that Smith originally submitted to editor Farnsworth Wright. In its first full incarnation, "The Beast of Averoigne" was 1400 words longer and told in what Smith referred to as "the documentary mode of presentation" (*SS* 254): three different accounts from three different people of the story's events. By merging these three viewpoints into the single perspective of le Chaudronnier, Smith created a story that appealed more to Wright (who initially had rejected it), but wound up purging it of the elements that make it one of his most extraordinary pieces of writing.

In the original version, the first third of the narrative is "The Deposition of Brother Gerome." Gerome is the first person to catch a glimpse of the beast, and in his innocence blames this unfortunate honor on his having "broken the rule of St. Benedict which forbids eating during a one-day's errand away from the monastery" (*SS* 52). Gerome has been charged by the abbot Theophile with the task of writing down everything that is known about the beast, and before he is found slaughtered in his cell he records an important observation that differs markedly between the two versions of the story (the original of which is presented first):

> Our good abbot was greatly exercised over this evil, which had chosen to manifest itself in the neighborhood of the abbey, and whose depredations were all committed within a five hours' journey of Périgon. Pale from his over-strict austerities and vigils, with hollow cheeks and burning eyes, Theophile called me before him and made me tell my story over and over, *listening as one who flagellates himself for a fancied sin* [italics mine]. And though I, like all others, was deeply sensible of this hellish horror and the scandal of its presence, I marvelled somewhat at the godly wrath and indignation of our abbot, in whom blazed a martial ardor against the minions of Asmodai. (*SS* 54)

> Theophile, the abbot of Périgon, was much exercised over this evil that had chosen to manifest itself in the neighborhood and whose depredations were all committed within a few hours' journey of the abbey. Pale from overstrict austerities and vigils, he called the monks before him in assembly, and a martial ardor against the minions of Asmodai blazed in his hollowed eyes as he spoke. (*LW* 147)

In the second part of the original version, "The Letter of Theophile to Sister Therese," Theophile writes to a niece in the Benedictine convent of Ximes that the beast has struck several times within the abbey itself, leading him to despair that "exorcisms and the sprinkling of holy water at all doors and windows have failed to prevent the intrusion of the Beast; and God and Christ and all the holy Saints are deaf to our prayers" (*SS* 56). In addition to his crisis of faith, Theophile confesses how he frequently finds himself passed out on the floor after his prayer vigils, oblivious to the horrors that have swept through the abbey. His final plea to his sister, steeped in his belief that he has somehow failed both God and his fellow man, is one of the most poignant passages to be found in all Smith's writing: "Pray for me, Therese, in my bewitchment and my despair: for God has abandoned me, and the yoke of hell has somehow fallen upon me; and naught can I do to defend the abbey from this evil" (*SS* 57).

In the revised, published version of the story this section, like the first, does not exist. The events recounted by Theophile are delivered purely as facts by le Chaudronnier, and mention of the abbot's letter is condensed into a single *sentence* regarding Therese's own death at the hands of the beast that fails to do justice to Theophile's painful soul-searching in the original version: "In her dead hands, it was told, the pious Therese tightly clasped a letter from Theophile in which he had spoken at some length of the dire happening at the monastery, and had confessed his grief and despair at being unable to cope with the Satanic horror" (*LW* 149).

Not surprisingly, the final third of the original version, "The Story of Luc le Chaudronnier," is the one part that most faithfully echoes the published version of the story. Coming after the first two parts of the story, though, it treats le Chaudronnier as a mere participant in the final slaying of the beast, rather than the central character in the published version. Smith clearly thought his man-slays-werewolf plot of subordinate importance to the meditation on the limits of human understanding developed through his portrayal of the naive ignorance of Brother Gerome in the first part and Theophile's tortured lack of self-awareness in the second part. Thus, the parts of le Chaudronnier's story that he retained for the published version take on an added significance when read in the context of the original version. For le Chaudronnier is wise enough to know that, even though the abbot is not responsible for the murders he has committed while under the influence of the comet demon, "the good renown of the holy Theophile" is in jeopardy unless the monk can be made out a martyr to thereby reinforce his holy image in the eyes of the citizens. This imparts an intriguing ambiguity to the final passage of the story, which can be read as something of an epigraph for the entire series:

> [T]hose who read this record in future ages will believe it not, saying that no demon or malign spirit could ever have prevailed upon true holiness. Indeed, it were well that none should believe the story: for strange abominations pass evermore between earth and moon and athwart the galaxies; and the gulf is haunted by that which were madness for man to know. Unnameable things have come to us in alien horror, and shall come again. And the evil of the stars is not as the evil of earth. (*SS* 62)

The evil of the stars is, indeed, not as the evil of earth. For as Smith shows repeatedly throughout the Averoigne stories, the human heart and mind hold in their unexplored recesses truths that are in some ways more awesome and terrifying than the secrets of the cosmos.

In his correspondence with Lovecraft and other writers, Smith has little to say about his Averoigne stories. Indeed, it appears that he did not think of them any differently from the other sorts of fiction he wrote, save for his science fantasies. It is left for readers to surmise why this series distinguishes itself so noticeably from the rest of Smith's work. It could be that, because the stories constitute his second largest integrated series, after the tales of Zothique, Smith was able to develop their background with a coherence lacking in the shorter story cycles. It also could be that Smith's choice of a more realistic, earthbound milieu in the Averoigne stories enforced upon his writing a stricter set of guidelines from those used in his more fanciful works of fantasy. But such distinctions are beside the point. It is enough that Averoigne stories reveal a side of Smith's writing more serious and engaging than many of his best and worst critics have given him credit for, and that even those works that have been deemed the ephemera of his oeuvre continue to yield up deeper meaning upon re-examination.

Notes

1. In his original synopsis for the story, CAS expressed no intention to explain the story in terms of the supernatural (*SS* 166–67). Furthermore, the original victims of the statue's influence were to be peasants working in a turnip field; the shift of setting to the abbey of Périgon was clearly intended to exploit the incongruity of the *events* that follow, and better render the "moral" of the story.

Bibliography

There are eleven full stories and three fragments in the Averoigne cycle. All but one story, "The Satyr," first appeared in *Weird Tales*. Steve Behrends has established the year in which the stories are set for nine (*CAS* 54). The list below presents the Averoigne stories as they were published, followed by the year in which they are set, their magazine appearance date, and the collection in which they were first published.

The End of the Story [1798] (May 1930; *OST*)
A Rendezvous in Averoigne [ca. 1550] (April–May 1931; *OST*)
The Satyr [1575] (*La Paree Stories*, July 1931; *GL*)
The Maker of Gargoyles [1138] (August 1932; *TSS*)
The Mandrakes [ca. 1400] (February 1933; *OD*)
The Beast of Averoigne [1369] (May 1933; *LW*)
The Holiness of Azédarac [1175] (November 1933; *LW*)
The Colossus of Ylourgne [1281] (June 1934; *GL*)
The Disinterment of Venus [1550] (July 1934; *GL*)
Mother of Toads (July 1934; *TSS*)
The Enchantress of Sylaire (July 1941; *AY*)

Sorcerous Style: Clark Ashton Smith's *The Double Shadow and Other Fantasies*

Peter H. Goodrich

Explanations are neither necessary, desirable, nor possible. (*BB* 57)

The Californian poet, short fiction writer, and artist Clark Ashton Smith was described by his friend and frequent correspondent H. P. Lovecraft in terms that created the model for subsequent Smith criticism: "In sheer daemonic strangeness and fertility of conception, Mr. Smith is perhaps unexcelled by any other writer dead or living. Who else has seen such gorgeous, luxuriant, and feverishly distorted visions of infinite spheres and multiple dimensions and lived to tell the tale? His short stories deal powerfully with other galaxies, worlds, and dimensions, as well as with strange regions and aeons on the earth.... Some of Mr. Smith's best work can be found in the brochure entitled *The Double Shadow and Other Fantasies*" (74–75). Due to a voluminous correspondence, the memoirs of his friends, and the invaluable spade work of independent scholars like Donald Sidney-Fryer, Steve Behrends, and Scott Connors, we know a good deal about Smith's life and work. But Smith has remained a writer more eulogized than interpreted. His symbolist poetry and fictional art, typified by the short story collection so praised by Lovecraft, deserve more study than they have received.

Lovecraft's hyperbole calls into question Smith's own acknowledged influences, which include such "feverishly distorted" stylists as William Beckford, Edgar Allan Poe, and Charles Baudelaire. Did these writers not see such extraordinary visions and live to tell the tale? Or is there some gift peculiar to Smith that sets him apart from them? As a romantic mannerist in his art, Smith does stand out as a rococo among the baroque practitioners of weird fiction. His literary art at least is analogous to the gorgeously decorative Art Nouveau drawings and sculptures of Erté that enjoyed a modest revival near the end of the twentieth century. As Smith himself observed, "In art or literature, it is better to err on the side of overflamboyance or exuberance than to prune everything down to a drab, dead and flat level. The former vice is at least on the side of growth; the latter represses or even tends to extirpate all growth" (*BB* 55). Despite a certain similarity between the logos-destroying horror of Hemingway's *nada* and Smith's *mal-néant*, it seems unlikely that Smith would have approved the extreme spareness of a modernist short story like Hemingway's "A Clean, Well-Lighted Place." Unlike Hemingway's

BY CLARK ASHTON SMITH

The Double Shadow and Other Fantasies

Tales of glamor, sorcery, terror and exotic beauty, written in atmospheric prose. Unpublished in any American periodical. Printed in large magazine format, on smooth paper.

CONTENTS

THE WILLOW LANDSCAPE: A fanciful Chinese tale, about an impoverished scholar and the old landscape painting with which he was loath to part.

THE DOUBLE SHADOW: A strange tale of two Atlantean sorcerers, who made use of a dreadful antehuman spell, without knowing what would come in answer to their evocation.

THE VOYAGE OF KING EUVORAN: A droll and richly hued narrative telling how the sacred gazolba-crown of Ustaim was reft by necromancy from the brow of Euvoran, its ninth wearer, and how Euvoran sought to recover the crown in a fantastic odyssey among the Isles of Wonder.

THE DEVOTEE OF EVIL: The story of a man who sought to evoke the ultra-cosmic radiation of Evil in its absolute purity—and succeeded.

A NIGHT IN MALNÉANT: The tale of a bereaved lover who sought oblivion in far wanderings, but found the phantom of his dead love awaiting him in a spectral city.

THE MAZE OF THE ENCHANTER: An account of the bizarre and curious perils faced by a barbaric hero and his princess in the fearful mesa-builded labyrinth of the sorcerer Maal Dweb.

Send 25c (coin) to Clark Ashton Smith, Auburn, California, for a postpaid copy.

ALSO

EBONY AND CRYSTAL

Poems and prose-poems. Lyrical, romantic, imaginative, fantastic. Contains one hundred and fourteen items, including The Hashish-Eater, which has been called the greatest poem in the literature of the grotesque. Bound in cloth. Published at $2.00.

The small remainder of the edition is for sale at $1.00 per copy, postpaid. Send check, coin, bill or money order to Clark Ashton Smith, Auburn, California.

Clark Ashton Smith's original advertising flyer for *The Double Shadow and Other Fantasies* aesthetic, Smith's ornateness did not become famous or dominate literary culture, although it has continued to attract adherents with a taste for exotic worlds and rhetoric. Smith was well aware of, and perhaps even relished this marginalization—never anticipating that his own voice would become appropriate to a millennial postmodern period which has revived interest in profusion and marginalized discourses of all kinds.

Curiously, none of the six stories in *The Double Shadow and Other Fantasies* pamphlet that Lovecraft admired so much is included in the recent "best of" collection, *A Rendezvous in Averoigne* (1988), published by Arkham House. However, *The Double Shadow* remains particularly significant because it was selected and published by Smith himself using the stock and press of his local newspaper, the *Auburn Journal*. It provides a cross-section of Smith's fictional subjects and settings and gives us a personal perspective on his work that no second-party collection can.

One thousand copies were printed at a frightening expense ($125) to the impecunious Smith. Produced between February and June 1933, it was termed "ill-omened and disastrous" by Smith in a letter to Lovecraft a year later. By 1937 fewer than 400 copies had been sold, many of which had been given away by Smith—despite the reasonable asking price of twenty-five cents (*CAS* 8, 21). Perhaps Lovecraft was in his way trying to boost sales by praising his friend, but it does not appear to have helped. My second-hand, somewhat battered, but autographed copy purchased in 1964 from bookseller Gerry de la Ree cost less than seven dollars. However, according to a source at the Dawn Treader bookstore in Ann Arbor, Michigan, the pamphlet sold at auction a decade later for fifty dollars and by the turn of the century was probably worth "between fifty and one hundred dollars." According to Scott Connors, more than 700 copies may have survived, mostly in libraries and the hands of Smith friends and collectors.

The primary motivation for the collection appears to have been Smith's problems getting his work published, untampered with, by the science fiction pulps. The first draft of his advertising flyer for the pamphlet reads rather defensively: "The Devotee of Evil & six other tales unpublishable in magazines. For lovers of weird atmosphere & arabesque fantasy.... Poetic rather than plotty. Will not appeal to devotees of action" (*BB* 4–5). However, in the second draft of the flyer the word "unpublishable" was wisely changed to "unpublished" and the total number of stories was reduced from seven to six, along with a price reduction from thirty to twenty-five cents (*BB* 5). Although these changes may have been as much coincidental as politic or cost-related, it appears likely that in the meantime one of the intended (but apart from "The Devotee of Evil" unnamed) stories had indeed been published and consequently omitted for copyright reasons. The remaining, published tales each represented a different setting selected from Smith's emerging work: Zothique in "The Voyage of King Euvoran," Xiccarph in "The Maze of the Enchanter," Poseidonis, the remnant of Atlantis in "The Double Shadow," neo-medieval Europe (possibly Averoigne) in "A Night in Malnéant,"[1] Smith's home town in "The Devotee of Evil," and Mandarin China in "The Willow Landscape." The settings not included were Hyperborea and Mars. Hyperborea is mentioned in "The Double Shadow," but most of the fantasies set in that primeval continent were already finding publication in *Weird Tales*, where Smith was one of the favorite authors. Stories set on Mars, however, which he had been writing since 1931, are not even mentioned in the pamphlet and are therefore the group most likely to have furnished the omitted tale. This likelihood is increased by the red-penciling misfortunes they had been suffering at the pulps.

Smith's first Martian story, "The Vaults of Yoh-Vombis," had been substantially edited for publication in *Weird Tales*, and his second Martian story was even more ill-starred. Its original 1932 version, titled "The Eidolon of the Blind," had been rejected by *Weird Tales* as too dismal; retitled "The Dweller in the Gulf," it was accepted by *Wonder Stories* only on condition that Smith include more "scientific motivation" (Ashley 6, *CAS* 63). Smith wrote in a new character to satisfy Hugo Gernsback, but didn't hear back until the revised story appeared in the March issue with its ending and many descriptive passages cut out, under Gernsback's title "Dweller in Martian Depths." Smith was furious at this "hog-butcher[y]" (Ashley 6) and even mailed uncut versions to many of his friends (*CAS* 63). With its motifs of blindness, perverse worship, and ironic reversal, this story would have been thematically well suited for *The Double Shadow* pamphlet Smith was planning. For these reasons it is the most likely tale for Smith to have wished to include with the other six—although "Vulthoom," written but unpublished about this time, is also a strong possibility. Partly in response to the editorial treatment of his Martian stories, Smith's original publicity specifically deplores plottiness and action. Most pulp editors demanded these propulsive qualities, yet Smith considered them the qualities least essential for his craft.

The other important change in the revised flyer is the shift from "The Devotee of Evil" to "The Double Shadow" as featured story. Perhaps Smith thought the initial title might seem too autobiographical, but more likely, he recognized "The Double Shadow" as the better story and the more central to his artistic conception. The flyer that eventually appeared stresses the qualities "of glamor, sorcery, terror and exotic beauty, written in atmospheric prose." Despite the listed order of contents, Smith revised the actual order of the stories in the pamphlet to make better transitions and conceptual sense. In doing so, he created a pattern that reveals his mannerist poetics of fantasy as preeminently a conjuration of the Other.

For Smith, whose first vocation was poetry under the tutelage of Californian Symbolist poet George Sterling, language is the lever that shifts reality. As he observed in *The Black Book*, his personal *grimoire* or writer's journal, "All things conceivable exist, have existed, or will exist somewhere, sometime" (47). Since "all things conceivable" require language in order to be shaped and represented, Smith believed that both the actual and the imaginary are linguistically equivalent, whether or not they ever exist in any humanly verifiable form. In his "Philosophy of the Weird Tale," a manifesto from *The Black Book* printed in the *Acolyte* for Spring 1944, he applied this logocentric idea to his preferred fictional genre and to human consciousness:

> The weird tale is an adumbration or foreshadowing of man's relationship—past, present, and future—to the unknown and infinite, and also an implication of his mental and sensory evolution. Further insight into basic mysteries is only possible through future development of higher faculties than the known senses. Interest in the weird, unknown, and supernormal is a signpost of such development and not merely a psychic residuum from the age of superstition. (*BB* 82)

Smith would scarcely be surprised by the agreement among literacy theorists like Walter Ong, futurists like Ray Kurzweil, and science/culture synthesizers like Leonard Shlain that technologies of the word change and develop human consciousness.[2] Moreover, he would probably feel thoroughly at home with New Age esotericism and neopaganism. What is surprising is that the New Age market has not yet discovered and revived Smith's work. Perhaps that is because Smith's work has never been widely known or available, or because esotericists have never been very conscientious or systematic about crediting sources; more likely, it is because his stories do not push any mental or social agenda but exist for their own sake.

The magical roots of words, then—their ability to evoke correspondences between matter, spirit and human perception—are at the core of Smith's aesthetic. Rhetorically, Smith's diction favors exotic coinages and archaic words; along with these, the evocative devices of hyperbole, synaesthesia, oxymoron, and onomatopoeia characterize his fantasies in *The Double Shadow* pamphlet. In compiling these tales, he was not only striking a blow against the technocratic and commercial bias of his publishers, but delineating his prose as a form of sorcerous incantation that replaces and controls reality by images—signs that conjure not only semiotic absences that hold power because they continually escape language, but the Inconceivable itself. And such a thaumaturgic art aims at growing a text that will ultimately absorb both its producer and its perceiver into the remade image. For Smith sequences the stories in his pamphlet to induce in the reader growing doubts about the rigidity of perceptual boundaries and the nature of selfhood.

The first of these stories, "The Voyage of King Euvoran," immediately establishes as the existing state of its far-future alternate world the excessive selfishness and materialism that Smith so deplored in twentieth-century American culture. It begins by describing in detail the magnificent, gazolba-bird-surmounted crown worn by King Euvoran of Ustaim. Euvoran's name is etymologically significant: the prefix "eu-" meaning alternatively that which is good and that which is not or non-existent, and the root word "-vor" meaning greedy, insatiable, lacking, vain, and finally containing the Indo-European root "-or" meaning "large bird." He had ascended the throne after his father expired "from a surfeit of stuffed eels and jellied salamanders' eggs" (5). Habituated to the royal "we," this absolute monarch of a tame and subservient "us" is diverted from a boring session of law-giving by the arrival of an outlandish wild man, whose somersaulting appearance between two constables is described as simultaneously goat- and bird-like. Identifying himself as a necromancer, the strange figure is condemned to the rack where, "to the stupefaction of all present, it became plain that the elasticity of his arms, legs, and body was beyond the extensibility of the rack itself" (6). Calling "a foreign word that was shrill and eldritch as the crying of migrant fowl that pass over toward unknown shores in the night" (6), the necromancer reanimates the stuffed gazolba-bird on Euvoran's crown, which flaps seaward as the magician also departs. Since the rare bird represents the kingship itself, Euvoran has effectively been deposed and must recapture it. The remainder of the story relates his seafaring quest—modeled on the Irish genre of marvelous *immrama* like the voyages of Bran, Maelduin, and Saint Brendan[3]—to regain his lost kingship by finding and slaying another gazolba. As Euvoran sails eastward toward the land of origins, his fleet is progressively stripped of ships and crews by flying vampires and birds that ironically reverse the selfish indifference and abuse of power that Euvoran has been accustomed to. Finally he is shipwrecked and cast alone upon an uncharted island abounding in gazolbas. There he subsists upon the birds, unkinged, with his sole companion a shipwrecked commoner, until they both die of old age.

The elastic, unnamed necromancer is the first of the implied author figures that inhabit each story, and the fate that he imposes upon the antiheroical Euvoran typifies the fate that Smith's fictional heroes frequently meet. Charles K. Wolfe and others have identified the "basic structural pattern" of Smith's fiction as "the journey by the hero into some otherworld, some sort of magic world" (10). This magical voyage metaphor becomes a leitmotif of the remaining stories just as the necromancer becomes the metaphor of the artist-creator. Smith's own published opinion confirms these metaphors: "To me, the best, if not the only function of imaginative writing, is to lead the human imagination *outward*, to take it into the vast external cosmos, and *away* from all that introversion and introspection, that morbidly exaggerated prying into one's own vitals"—symbolized in the story by stuffed eels and jellied salamanders' eggs (Wolfe 9; Smith's italics). Thus his purpose is often cautionary, and the voyage motif is elaborated in the remaining five stories by additional devices of distancing and estrangement, such as settings remote in time and space from the present, or the summoning of cosmic forces that overwhelm the temporal, spatial, and sense-related limitations of the present.

Although the ending of the first and longest story in the pamphlet suffers from anticlimax after all the marvels the tale has traversed, the next story picks up these motifs in another quest. "The Maze of the Enchanter" commences with a barbarian hunter, Tiglari, tigerishly invading the mountain-top domain of the sorcerer Maâl Dweb to rescue his beloved, Athlé, from being "eternalized." However, the protagonist roles are again reversed as the enchanter is here an absolute monarch like Euvoran, and Tiglari a supple challenger like the necromantic trickster.

The results are also reversed: Tiglari proves no match for Maâl Dweb's superhuman foresightedness and power. However, the hunter is a far more sympathetic figure than the sorcerer, who not only exercises seignioral rights over the loveliest maidens of the planet Xiccarph but also apparently makes no better use of their beauty than freezing them into art-objects by exposure to his "mirror of Eternity." Maâl Dweb's aesthetic yet flatly sexist stereotyping of the female form extends also to their disenfranchised lovers, like Tiglari and his rival Mocair. Despite their stalking skills and animal cunning, they are transformed into shambling hairy apes from the neck down by the flowers of "primordial life" in his arboreal maze. But the wizard, although remaining absolute master of his planet, suffers at the end of the story from a fate similar to Euvoran's: repetition compulsion and ennui. We are left with the conviction that he has so isolated himself from humans and human emotions that despite his lip-service to diversity in his future enchantments, hollowly repeated by his inhuman iron servitor Mong Lut, he has become too much like his sword-handed automatons and statuesque women—deadly and petrified.

In this way, the estrangement motif associated with the hero's quest is extended to the sorcerer and author-creator. As the French anthropologist Marcel Mauss observed, "Isolation and secrecy are two almost perfect signs of the intimate character of a magical rite" (23). However, imaginations that become intimate with infinitude—like those of Smith's tricksters and enchanters—can also become bored and misogynistic when language is used for necromantic purposes that deny life and suppress dissent. The resulting rite dooms its practitioner as well as any against whom the rite may be directed; its isolation and intimacy becomes self-reflexive and immobilizing. In Smith's aesthetic the exotic atmosphere evoked by luxuriant images predominates, and the tale often admonishes as much as celebrates both the creators and the consumers of art. Deconstructing the *Double Shadow* pamphlet's tales suggests that the sensuous aesthetic appreciation championed by Smith becomes arrested development rather than revitalizing epiphany. In short, it constitutes an implicit and perhaps unintentionally reflexive critique of Smith's own rhetorical art.

The pamphlet's key third story confirms and extends this self-replicating and self-canceling turn of art-as-sorcery. "The Double Shadow," one of Smith's most famous and effective tales, reveals the wizards as the victims of their own enchantment. The narrator is Pharpetron, the pupil of Avyctes (who is himself the pupil of Malygris in a link to other stories of Smith's Atlantean cycle). Pharpetron discovers a glittering triangular tablet cast upon the shore after a storm. The tablet is inscribed with strange characters that neither Avyctes nor his acolyte can read. A sorcerer in the proper sense of summoning spirits to enact his magic, Avyctes finally sends the ghost of a prehistoric wizard into the abyss of an even more distant past to learn that the tablet contains a conjuration of long-vanished serpent-men. Possessed of the key, the two decipher the tablet and Avyctes insists upon enacting the ritual, even though its result is not named by the tablet. The sorcerers station themselves at the corners of a triangular design simulating the tablet, employing a magically animated mummy named Oigos at the third corner, and recite the spell. But nothing appears to happen. The wizards think they have failed until much later, when Pharpetron sees an indescribably noisome shadow trailing behind Avyctes, "a distorted loathly blot, having a pestilent unnamable hue," and "a streaming ooze of charnel pollution, a foulness beyond the black leprosies of hell" (20). Despite their efforts to conjure this repulsive undulating shadow into speech, it remains unresponsive and slowly nears Avyctes, until it and the hapless sorcerer coalesce into a single ghastly being, all the more terrifying for its continued speechlessness. The sorcerer's castle also takes on the fluid characteristics of the monster, like a bad dream, so that the terrified Pharpetron is unable "to reach the topmost outer stair; for at every step the marble flowed beneath me, fleeing like a pale horizon before the seeker" (21). The stalking shadow makes no distinction between the living and the dead: Oigos is stalked and engulfed next. Despairing, the trapped Pharpetron throws the alien tablet back into the sea and seals his tale in a bottle before the double shadow takes him. The ages-old message-in-a-bottle motif that frames the narrative artfully doubles the finding of the tablet, just as the act of reading Pharpetron's story cautions us against the unknown and indecipherable. The cylinder's enclosure echoes the captivity of the helpless wizards within the unforeseen consequences of their own spell. And the final lines of the message, "the space is no wider than the thickness of a wizard's pen" (22), also inscribe the mutual logocentrism of sorcery and literary art, and their nearness to the absent and unspeakable Other that is their object.

It is a logocentrism, however, with literally nothing at its core. In the weird tale, nothingness *is* the ultimate horror. It is horrible precisely because it is palpable yet anonymous, incommunicable, and therefore uncontrollable. Similarly, it may be that we are so enclosed by and dependent upon the language of signs that we cannot ever master or get "outside" it. The summoners' power is negated and consumed by the power summoned. The serpentlike horror doubles and personifies the sorcerers' own consuming ignorance, a silent and inexpressible other, "the sign of an entity" (21) that implacably represents the very absence of the signified.

In this way, Smith implicitly questions the sorcerer's fundamental mode of operation: the replacement of reality by images. As Mauss writes, "A magician does nothing, or almost nothing, but makes everyone believe that he is doing everything, and all the more so because he puts to work collective forces and ideas to help the individual imagination in its beliefs" (141–42). However, it is not the magical power of language that Smith is interrogating, but the appropriateness of its uses. At first Avyctes and Pharpetron think they have done nothing, that their conjuration, rather than defining an absence to be made present, is defined only by the absence of results. After all, the "collective forces and ideas" they have put to work are not their own or even comprehended by them. When they realize their error, it is too late to save themselves from absorption by the alien belief system for which they have no language, so horribly manifested in its otherness that Pharpetron can only describe it in terms of his own hysterical revulsion. And the sorcerer's duel implicit in the tale is not only metalinguistic, but made concrete. As Daniel O'Keefe describes it, dueling and paranoia are at the heart of sorcery, which "fears reflect the hostile action of *rivals* . . . Sorcery itself is already magic—*your rival's magic*" (420; his emphasis).

If magic is so double-edged in this story, it remains nearly as much so in "A Night in Malnéant." After the terrifying indeterminacy of the spell that swallows Avyctes and Pharpetron, the lack of a name for the following story's narrator appears all the more self-absorbed (as it is in Poe's "The Raven" and "The Fall of the House of Usher," narratives with a similar theme). The narrator's apparently random and indefinite journeying to "old-world city to city" (22) and "old-world realms of fog and mist" (24) suggest Smith's mythical realm of Averoigne, yet that realm is never mentioned and the narrator never tells us how he has heard of Malnéant itself. He is literally in a fog, and the city becomes for him a labyrinth of self-pity and guilt in which everyone is preparing for the funeral of Mariel, whom he claims poisoned herself because "my changeable temper, my fits of cruel indifference or ferocious irritability, had broken her gentle heart" (22). As lugubrious as the previous story was brilliant, the narrative suits the narrator. Yet no one there recognizes him, suggesting his own lack of self-knowledge. *Malnéant* itself translates as "evil nothingness or unknowing," and it is a mortuary limbo. It may also serve as an architectural metaphor for magic. Again according to Mauss, "Magic is a living mass, formless and inorganic, and its vital parts have neither a fixed position nor a fixed function" (88). If this is so, then Malnéant with its clammy fog and tolling bells not only externalizes the narrator's descent into the solipsistic maelstrom of his "belated remorse," but symbolizes the disappearing distinction between rite and representation that constitutes magic. Like the doom that consumes the Atlantean sorcerers, the narrator's obsessive confrontation with the object of his grief does not absolve him. Instead, it brings only the conviction that "this one event, the death of the lady Mariel, had drawn apart from all other happenings, had broken away from the sequence of time and found for itself a setting of appropriate gloom and solemnity; or perhaps had even built around itself the whole enormous maze of that spectral city" (24).

Smith's fixation on compulsive repetition, possession and dispossession, and the ways in which the magician loses control of his rite—becoming trapped within his own representations—therefore corresponds to the theme of the implied author-creator or reader losing control of the work as it absorbs them and grows into text. Smith states in *The Black Book:*

> Whether the poet deals with nearby and familiar things, or with the remote and fabulous is, in the last analysis, immaterial; since, in either case, he is dealing with concepts and mental figments rather than ultimate reality. The world itself is quite possibly a mere superstition of the senses—and no less so because the superstition

is universally shared by beings with the same sense-equipment. (56)

The implied equivalence of rite and representation also breaks down the distinction between primary and secondary worlds.

In the next tale, the dark nothingness of the self is materially transformed into the cosmic nothingness of absolute evil—a nothingness in which there may or may not be a center. "The Devotee of Evil" brings Smith's time-space spiral right into his fictionalized hometown of Auburn, California, where the haunted Larcom house is purchased by a New Orleans creole named Jean Averaud. Smith himself takes on the fictional mask of Philip Hastane, novelist (although Smith never wrote one). Averaud is attended by a single servant, a striking, mute mulatto named Fifine who is also reputed to be his mistress. Links with the preceding story are created by carrying over the enclosing architectural metaphor from city to house, by the trait of obsessiveness that Averaud shares with the unnamed visitor to Malnéant, and by the simile with which Hastane likens the devotee to a "medieval alchemist, who believed himself to be on the point of obtaining his objective after years of unrelenting research" (24).

The alchemical search for the means to transmute base matter into gold and mortal into eternal life is once again signified by writing. Like any magician's library, Averaud's is remarkable. It contains "an ungodly jumble of tomes that dealt with anthropology, ancient religions, demonology, modern science, history, psychoanalysis, and ethics. Interspersed with these, were a few romances and volumes of poetry. Beausobre's monograph on Manichaeism was flanked with Byron and Poe; and 'Les Fleurs du Mal' jostled a late treatise on chemistry" (25)—all collected for the study of evil. The library's apparent incoherence is another analogue to the formless mass of magic with which the sorcerer models reality, and whose evil source he desires to summon. Averaud's model-building is not expressed through linguistic analysis, evocation, or incantation, however, but in a curious machine designed to "receive" a "monistic evil, which is the source of all death, deterioration, imperfection, pain, sorrow, madness, and disease" (25). The mechanism itself repeats a triangular geometry of evil that we have already seen in the serpent-men's tablet and conjuration; it is a tripod structure of gongs and hammers placed in a triangular room. After an inconclusive but frightening demonstration while the machine is still incomplete, Hastane stays away in a neurotic funk, only to return at the moment when Averaud completes and activates it. Before Fifine rushes in to switch it off, Hastane is incurably scarred by madness and Averaud, stepping into the "double column of triangular shadow" (28), is permanently petrified into an icy black image of the evil he has summoned.

The mechanistic analogy to Pharpetron's fate signifies the inorganic conceptual nature of what Averaud worships. Thus, despite the tale's Lovecraftian intimation of absolute, even sentient evil, we are left to wonder if he has summoned the independent cosmic force that he had postulated, or merely focused some formless mass of black magic created by his own obsessive imagining. Averaud's machine replaces a linguistic system of signs as the mystical invocation of infinitude, suggesting that technology is merely modern magic that begins as a tool and ends by consuming its creator. Typically for Smith, its effects upon the characters are described especially through the rhetoric of oxymoron ("the agonizing rapture of his perverse adoration" [28]) and synaesthesia ("chill awe," "sable fire," "black cold" [28]); devices he inherited from Symbolist poetry to connote quasi-religious ecstasy, the confusion of categories and manifestation of transcendence.

Still, whether mechanistic or animistic, human imagination and writerly devices cannot long sustain the effect. And if we may choose any imaginary world to be our home, why should it not be a more pleasant one than our primary one or a Dantean Malebolge? Sorcery is not only coercive and combative, but medical in its application, potentially healing the split between matter and spirit. So Smith ends his pamphlet of alternate realities with a parable in which the protagonist achieves, finally, a blissful heart's desire instead of an eternal dark night of the soul. "The Willow Landscape" redeems the theme of loss and estrangement through its protagonist's passage into the idyllic alternative world of an ancient landscape painting. The tale does not start hopefully, however. Shih Liang, "a scholar, a poet, and a lover of both art and nature" (28), is progressively stripped of his health, his position as court secretary, and his ancestor's art treasures which he must sell to support himself and finance his younger brother's education. This decline in wealth, power, and available actions parallels Euvoran's experience in the first story, although Shih Liang's admirable character is more akin to Haldane than Euvoran. The pattern of reversal culminates in the sale of Liang's last treasure, the willow landscape, to an avid collector. Before surrendering it, Liang requests one more day to contemplate it.

At this point, however, the sorcery that in other stories resided within the characters and was externalized through their summonings finds a different locus: the realm of art itself. "Somehow the picture was more than a painting, was more than a veritable scene: it possessed the enchantment of far-off things for which the heart has longed in vain, of years and of places that are lost beyond recall. Surely the artist had mingled with its hues the diviner iris of dream or of retrospect, and wine-sweet tears of a nostalgia long denied" (28). As Liang watches, the landscape grows, deepens, and assumes "the illusion of an actual place" (28). And as it does so, it speaks, inviting Liang to enter it "because your heart is native here but alien to all the world beside" (29). Stripped of all his other possessions, he finds release in this last, most treasured one. Because of words like "nostalgia" and "illusion" we might suspect that this is the voice of the artist's narcissism, but Smith clearly intends more than a mere escapist fantasy. As he wrote to Donald Wandrei in 1926, "Poetry such as mine, properly considered, is not an 'escape,' but an extension [of life]" (Sidney-Fryer 20). The concluding lines of the story reject the blindness of the so-called primary world and celebrate the fleshly vitality of the secondary one with a directness bordering on crudity: had the painting's new owner look at it more often, he "might have found that the peony maiden and the person who resembled Shih Liang were sometimes engaged in other diversions than that of merely passing the time of day on the bamboo bridge!" (30) This final fantastic reversal of the ground rules for art transfers the quality of illusion from the secondary world to the primary one, making it clear that the implied author prefers Liang's perspective. In this transaction the painting's sentience heals the "double shadow" or split between art and nature, as the sentence simultaneously confirms and disenchants the text by intimating sexual relations and the return from aesthetic to bodily functions. This "sign of an entity" does not become a avatar of or portal to nothingness, but a more encompassing and satisfying form of human experience.

Or so Smith would have us believe. His pervasive nostalgia for a mythic connectedness between aesthetic and worldly experience rejects realism in favor of the essential unity—the double-shadowed unity—of the symbol. The arc of these stories moves from exotic and grotesque worlds gradually into our own fictionalized world and through it to the "healthier" environment of the heart's desire in an art that outlives life. His is a backward-journeying glance, toward an incipience expressed by a fondness for magical technology, the medieval, and the oriental. Like his contemporary Mauss, Smith regards magic and the imagination as essentially non-intellectual, as a form of *mana*, a fluid quality of wealth or force that can be represented but not captured by the texts and substances that are its vehicles. From such a perspective, the *mana* that informs or inhabits the text does not derive from human "experience, from analogical reasoning, or from scientific error" but constitutes a "milieu" that "avoids these rigid and abstract categories, which our language and reasoning impose" (Mauss 108).

This fluid, undulating perspective is what makes Smith a romantic symbolist and liberates him to concentrate his art in mannerist high fantasy. His subject and style should thus be read as a conjuration not so much of aesthetic decadence as of *mana*, which is in Mauss' words, "something mysterious and separate . . . a spiritual action that works at a distance and between sympathetic beings . . . a kind of internal, special world where everything happens as if mana alone were involved. . . . It is produced in a closed circuit, in which everything is mana and which is itself mana" (112). In other words, symbol is a form of solipsism, both communal and individual, as well as a bridge to the transcendent Other. Smith cautions us against the solipsism, yet asserts the transcendence of this magical milieu and indulges it as a totality of being-in-the-world. Symbolist magic is a form of essentialism that moves through the text and—for better or worse—aspires to some scarcely perceived, tangible but inexpressible reality beyond mundane living. In this way, Smith also exhibits the New-Age or neopagan "turn" before it became possible for society to acknowledge and appropriate these philosophies by the commercialism that he so abhorred. Reading *The Double Shadow and Other Fantasies* is to be provoked and ensorcelled by *mana*.

Notes

1. The *Auburn Journal* apparently lacked a typeface with foreign characters or accent marks, although CAS intended them. I have restored the accents.

2. See Ong's ground-breaking *Orality and Literacy: The Technologizing of the Word* (London: Methuen, 1982); Kurzweil's *The Age of Intelligent Machines* (Cambridge, MA: MIT Press, 1992); and Shlain's *The Alphabet Versus the Goddess: The Conflict Between Word and Image* (New York: Viking, 1998).

3. See especially H. P. A. Oskamp, *The Voyage of Máel Dúin: A Study in Early Irish Voyage Literature* (Groningen: Wolters-Noordhoff, 1970), for details about the *immrama*. These voyages were generally marvel-filled island-hopping searches for the Celtic otherworld.

Works Cited

Ashley, Mike. "The Perils of Wonder: Clark Ashton Smith's Experiences with *Wonder Stories*." *Dark Eidolon* No. 2 (July 1989): 2–8.

Connors, Scott. Telephone interview. 4 June 2005.

Lovecraft, H. P. *Supernatural Horror in Literature*. New York: Ben Abramson, 1945.

Mauss, Marcel. *A General Theory of Magic*. Trans. Robert Brain. New York: W. W. Norton, 1975.

O'Keefe, Daniel Lawrence. *Stolen Lightning: The Social Theory of Magic*. New York: Vintage, 1983.

Sidney-Fryer, Donald. "A Statement for Imagination: George Sterling and Clark Ashton Smith." *Romantist* 6–8 (1982–84): 13–23.

Wolfe, Charles K. "CAS, A Note on the Aesthetics of Fantasy." *Dark Eidolon* No. 2 (July 1989): 9–11.

Loss and Recuperation: A Model for Reading Clark Ashton Smith's "Xeethra"

Dan Clore

In his *Structuralist Poetics* Jonathan Culler describes a notion of "literary competence"—the ability to decipher a work of literature as such (113–30). This involves various processes of "naturalization" by which the reader fits a text into an understandable framework, and thereby "recuperates" the work (described in some detail on 131–60). Just as grammar makes explicit the way the linguistic competence of a native speaker allows her to understand an utterance, so criticism, Culler argues, should make explicit the literary competence used by effective readers. Using this idea, we can see how some critics and periods have devalued various kinds of literature because their dominant processes of recuperation and naturalization did not adequately deal with the works and genres at issue, just as using the grammar or vocabulary of the wrong language or dialect would lead to the misunderstanding of a linguistic utterance.

In this way the "new" critics, who used "ambiguity" or "irony" as their dominant method of recuperation, gave the metaphysical poets a high place because of their emphasis on the conceit, but devalued the poetry of the romantics, who worked in a different vein. The new method proved useful where older models had failed, but failed where the same older models had succeeded. In just such a way have many modern critics devalued works of fantasy and weird fiction, because their primary methods of naturalization do not do justice to these kinds of text. These methods involve concentration on a work as a depiction of the "real" world, and a focus on character drawing as supreme value. Since fantasy and weird fiction does not depict the real world and its focus lies elsewhere than on character drawing, these methods can only show their works as "false" and "one-dimensional."

Edmund Wilson, called the "Dean of American critics," gives an excellent example of this trend. He could not recoup Tolkien's *Lord of the Rings;* it lacked proper characterization, did not develop its episodes correctly, and so on (see "Oo, Those Awful Orcs!" in Wilson). Likewise, the entire horror story genre excited his wrath. He did attempt to recoup Lovecraft by comparing the effects of the meteorite in "The Colour out of Space" with that of the atomic bomb (in Joshi 49), but that effort dooms itself to failure. Only by reading them as allegorical or psychological studies were fantasy or weird works ever sufficiently naturalized for Wilson. He cited Poe's "Fall of the House of Usher" as an allegory of a man going insane, held firmly to the view that the ghosts in James's *Turn of the Screw* existed only in the mind of the governess-narrator, and even championed Cabell's elegant fantasies as expressions of the social attitudes of the South after the Civil War (see "The James Branch Cabell Case Reopened" in Wilson).

I believe that structural and semiotic analysis will help show the methods of naturalization necessary to recuperate works of fantasy and the weird. Here I will use the method of Roland Barthes in his *S/Z*. While Barthes does not create a systematic theory, one can deduce a clear methodology from the exhaustive example he gives, together with the applications of it by Scholes (99–104) and Anderson (17–21). With this method I will analyze Clark Ashton Smith's poignant story of loss, "Xeethra," placing emphasis on those elements which distinguish the sort of analysis necessary to a fantastic text from that of a realistic work.

Barthes analyzes Balzac's short story "Sarrasine" by breaking it down into units of reading, or *lexias*, which vary from a few words to over a paragraph in length. Each of these lexias he examines as carrying meaning through any of several codes. The majority of lexias, in fact, belong to more than one code.

Barthes distinguishes five codes in his analysis of "Sarrasine," as follows:

The Proairetic Code or code of actions. This code includes all the actions that the various characters perform. It has great usefulness in describing plot. Adventure stories and heroic fantasies emphasize the proairetic code.

The Hermeneutic Code or code of enigmas. This includes all the various puzzles that a story poses for the reader. Barthes distinguishes eight stages of delay between the posing and solution of an enigma. Mystery stories emphasize this code; weird fiction often includes a strong element of the hermeneutic code as well.

The Semic Code or code of connotations. This includes connotations in general, and several subcodes as well. One, the code of character, occupies an especially important place in realist works. Barthes also mentions, but does little to describe, codes of the object and of atmosphere, which have a greater importance for fantastic literature.

The Referential Code or code of culture. In a sense, all the codes could belong here, as all ideas exist as cultural constructs. However, those things traditionally thought of as "cultural" belong to their own level of discourse. Barthes mentions, as subcodes of the cultural code, a Gnomic code of proverbs, codes of Medicine and Psychology, codes of Art, of History, and others. A writer can use these either to reinforce his work's verisimilitude by drawing on them to establish its "reality," or he can use them to question the accepted ideas of his culture.

The Symbolic Code or code of symbols. This works through oppositions and mediations. Two opposite images can symbolize almost any opposition. The sun and moon, for example, appear in different traditions representing male and female, sister and brother, husband and wife, they may take the same sex and illustrate some other kind of opposition, and soon. Either of them can take either place; the sheer opposition of the two has more importance than any inherent similarity to the symbolized ideas (Culler 52). Most works including opposing symbols will also include a symbol that mediates between the two. Two kinds of mediatory images can occur: first, one which mediates by lacking the distinctive qualities of both opposites—in "Sarrasine," Barthes argues, a castrato mediates between the two sexes. The other kind of mediation involves combination of both opposites—an hermaphrodite would serve as example. Symbolic codes loom especially large in allegorical works.

Let us now see how these codes apply to the text of "Xeethra."

The Proairetic Code. The major actions of both the protagonist and antagonist (Thasaidon, largely through his unnamed emissary) both concentrate on the tale's theme of loss. Xeethra's main actions all involve seeking. First, he sets out in search of pasture for his goats. He then stumbles across the mouth of a cave, and seeks inside for what he might find. Having taken the fruit, he remembers his life as King Amero of Calyz and sets out to find his lost kingdom. When he does find it, only a leper colony remains of it. The emissary of Thasaidon reappears and offers to make him king again, on the condition that he never regret it. He accepts, but when misfortunes befall his kingdom, he does regret his kingship and seeks out the life of a goatherd. He then returns to his life as Xeethra. He has now lost both the contentment he formerly knew as a goatherd and the splendor of his kingship and thus remains in the kingdom of Thasaidon.

The major actions of Thasaidon all involve the temptations that lead Xeethra to his loss. He leads the goatherd to the opening of his domain with an illusory oasis, and, inside the cavern, tempts him with the dark fruit. The fruit, by making Xeethra remember his former life as King Amero, makes him lose the contentment of his life as goatherd and seek the city of Shathair. Finding the city proves a further loss. Finally, Thasaidon allows him to regain his kingship, on terms that cause him to lose the kingship, through the temptation of the Demon's emissary as a shepherd luring him to a rural life. The actions of "Xeethra" show a remarkable unity that centers on the theme of loss.

The Hermeneutic Code. "Xeethra" includes a strong enigmatic element. The enigmas begin with the quotation that heads the story, posing the question of what "subtle and manifold" snares the "Demon" will employ, and how he will follow his chosen victim "from birth to death and from death to birth." Further enigmas pose themselves as Xeethra discovers the newly opened cavern and smells the strange odors wafting out of it. Inside it, the strange light, the unnatural vegetation, all pose further enigmas. The two beings who appear after he has eaten the fruit, and the odd memories he begins to experience both heighten the enigmatic nature of the narrative.

Once he has regained his identity as Amero, the responses of others in reply to his questions as to its whereabouts add a further enigma. Through his search, the minor actions of others, who mock him, laugh at him because of his quest, or merely eye him strangely, provide a strong counterpoint of enigma to the action of seeking. Finally, when he discovers Shathair, the Demon resolves the major enigmas of the story.

The Semic Code, in "Xeethra," works most strongly on the codes of object and atmosphere, unlike realist works, which emphasize the codes of character. On the level of object, its importance begins inside the cavern that Xeethra discovers. Here, the unnatural light that shines in the place and its station underground connote <supernatural>. (Angle brackets indicate reference to the word's meaning, the signified, rather than to the word itself, the signifier plus the signified.) The vegetation of the place all combines animal qualities with its plant qualities. The grasses coil with "verminous writhings," the flowers resemble eyes that stare at him, the trees palpate as if "a sanguine ichor flowed" in them rather than sap, and the wind makes a noise like hissing snakes as it passes through the leaves. All of which imply <supernatural>.

The code of objects has further importance when Xeethra reaches Shathair. He discovers a statue of a lion, now fallen into disrepair, connoting <decay, loss>. The ruins of the city and the lepers that inhabit the place further add to the connotations of <decay, loss>.

The code of atmosphere pervades the entire tale. The proper names fall into several groups of connotation. Some of them, such as Pornos, Carnamagos ("The Treader of the Dust" mentions that a manuscript of his Testament surfaced in a Graeco-Bactrian tomb), Thasaidon (cf. Poseidon), and Mykrasian, have a Greek feel that connotes <mythological, poetic, sublime> in contemporary associations. Others, such as Calyz, Shathair, Sha-Karag, and Dhir, have a Semitico-Arabic feel that associates them with the *Arabian Nights* or *Vathek*, giving the connotation <fantastic>. Yet others have wholly unfamiliar sound combinations, as Xeethra, Zhel, Ongath, and Ymorth, connoting thereby <strange, exotic>.

Smith also employs a style that heavily emphasizes the code of connotations to create atmosphere. The first paragraph of the tale provides an excellent example of his use of rhetorical devices:

> Long had the wasting summer pastured its suns, like fiery red stallions, on the dun hills that crouched before the Mykrasian Mountains in wild easternmost Cincor. The peak-fed torrents were become tenuous threads or far-sundered, fallen pools; the granite boulders were shaled by the heat; the bare earth was cracked and creviced; and the low, meager grasses were seared even to the roots.

This paragraph includes a flurry of rhetorical devices. The entire passage shows inversion of word order. The first sentence combines a metaphor and a simile, in its description of the sun as horses pasturing, and another metaphor in its description of hills as "crouching." Another figure, the conversion of a singular to a plural ("suns"), occurs as well. The second sentence includes alliteration ("torrents," "tenuous," "far-sundered," "fallen," "cracked and creviced") and an extreme grammatical parallelism. All these rhetorical devices connote <poetic, sublime>.

Individual word-choice carries a heavy load of connotation in this story as well. Smith often uses archaic words or word-forms such as "levin," "whelmed," "wonderment," and "goodly," which, through their usage conventions, carry connotations of <poetic, sublime>. Rare words, including "coigns," "appetence," "unceremented," and "postern" carry connotations of <exotic, strange>. Many of the words used by Smith could fall into either or both of these two groups. In addition, a large number of the words used throughout the story carry atmospheric connotations through conventions of poetic diction. A notable number of the uncommon words Smith uses have familiar roots combined with different terminations than their more common congeners, as "verdurous," "colossean," and others. This serves to convey the sense of strangeness while simultaneously preserving the sense for ordinary readers.

The Referential Code. On the level of the cultural codes, Smith includes items that help thematize the work for its reader, such as the comparison of the cave with the garden of Eden, and the hissing "as of serpents" that Xeethra hears therein, which lead directly to the "forbidden fruit" imagery. Others, which include the word "Stygian" and the comparison of Thasaidon's emissary to a "Terminus reared in hell," give connotations of <mythological, poetic, sublime>. They help to familiarize these elements of the story by referring to our own culture's mythic archetypes, while at the same time carrying connotations of <sublime, fantastic> because of their mythological provenance.

By far the greatest use of referential coding, however, involves the creation of Zothique's imaginary culture. They have religious scripture (the Testament of Carnamagos) and well-defined social stations for the various characters, ranging from goatherd to king, and from merchant to leper. Smith creates the world of Zothique with its geography, its flora and fauna, and so on, by the use of this code in its creative aspect. On this level, "Xeethra" works largely by references to contemporary cultural ideas. The mention of "spires," "turrets," "odalisques," "mummers," and so on, gives the tale an *Arabian Nights* or *Vathek*-like setting and mood, with perhaps a flavor of mediaeval Europe as well.

The Symbolic Code. Here the two opposed images appear clearly: that of the goatherd and the king. These in turn define themselves by contrary negative and positive attributes. The goatherd has a contentment that arises from his relative lack of care, and a counter-balancing lack of power and wealth. The king, contrariwise, has great power and wealth, but lacks contentment because of the great responsibilities that come with them. (These refer, as well, easily enough to our cultural stereotypes of the referential code, with its literary model of pastoral shepherds and rustics leading an idyllic life, and the "crown that sits heavy on the head" of him who wears it. Almost all elements work through more than one of these codes.)

Appropriately for a tale of loss, each of these defines itself for Xeethra by what it lacks. The mediation that appears further reinforces and in effect totally finalizes the sense of loss. The "dark empire of Thasaidon" mediates between the two in the same way that the castrato in "Sarrasine" mediates the opposite sexes: by its lack of the positive features of both. Having lost the power and wealth of kingship, Xeethra cannot regain them; and having had them, he cannot regain the contentment that comes from life as a goatherd. This represents the absolute loss of both extremes.

We have now seen how an application of Barthes's methodology helps to lay bare the kind of activity necessary to read "Xeethra" successfully. By carrying this out overtly and explicitly, we see the process that enabled adolescent readers of pulp magazines to recuperate stories that literary critics of the day could not recoup. More specifically, we see that the operations of naturalization differ primarily on, first, the weird tale's code of connotations, which emphasizes codes of the object and codes of atmosphere over the codes of character that realist works emphasize, and second, we see that the fantasy genre's use of the referential code in its creative aspect differs very widely from the realist genre's primary uses. (Tolkien's *Lord of the Rings* started a trend toward very heavy emphasis on the creative aspect of this code in fantasy works; many science fiction writers, such as Jack Vance, utilize it heavily as well.) In addition, the hermeneutic and symbolic codes take on an additional importance.

In conclusion, the structuralist and semiotic methods of analysis employed here can help make apparent the operations needed to appreciate the genius of a writer like Smith. They show us not only how his texts work, but equally important, how certain methods of reading have failed to give them their proper estimation. As Northrop Frye, speaking of another noted fantasist, says, "a great romancer should be examined in terms of the conventions he chose. William Morris should not be left on the side lines of prose fiction merely because the critic has not learned to take the romance form seriously" (305).

Works Cited

Anderson, James. "'Pickman's Model': H. P. Lovecraft's Model of Terror." *Lovecraft Studies* Nos. 22/23 (Fall 1990): 15–21.

Barthes, Roland. *S/Z: An Essay*. Trans. Richard Miller. Pref. Richard Howard. New York: Noonday Press/Farrar, Straus & Giroux, 1974.

Culler, Jonathan. *Structuralist Poetics: Structuralism, Linguistics and the Study of Literature*. Ithaca: Cornell University Press, 1975.

Frye, Northrop. *Anatomy of Criticism: Four Essays*. Princeton: Princeton University Press, 1957.

Joshi, S. T., ed. *H. P. Lovecraft: Four Decades of Criticism*. Athens: Ohio University Press, 1980.

Scholes, Robert. *Semiotics and Interpretation*. New Haven: Yale University Press, 1982.

Smith, Clark Ashton. *Xeethra*. The Unexpurgated Clark Ashton Smith. Ed. Steve Behrends. West Warwick, RI: Necronomicon Press, 1988.

Wilson, Edmund. *The Bit Between My Teeth: A Literary Chronicle of 1950–1965*. New York: Farrar, Straus & Giroux, 1965.

"Life, Love, and the Clemency of Death": A Reexamination of Clark Ashton Smith's "The Isle of the Torturers"

Scott Connors

The tales of Zothique, the last continent of an earth dimly lit by a dying red sun, are among the finest fantasies to emerge from the imagination of Clark Ashton Smith. However, the second story in the series, "The Isle of the Torturers," is often dismissed even by Smith enthusiasts as inferior and derivative, or perhaps we should say inferior *because* it is derivative. However, the perceptive reader who examines closely Smith's poem "Zothique" may infer that there is more to the story than may appear at first. The last stanza reads:

> He who has sailed in galleys of Zothique
> And seen the looming of strange spire and peak,
> Must face again the sorcerer-sent typhoon,
> And take the steerer's post on far-poured oceans
> By the shifted moon or the re-shapen Sign. (*LO* 113)

Stephen Posey recently provided a masterful explication of this stanza in an Internet discussion group dedicated to Smith. He posted the following comments:

> CAS set Zothique in the far future, he surely knew (or intended) that the orbit of the moon ("the shifted moon") and the arrangements of the constellations ("re-shapen Sign") would alter over time. So, someone from our age wanting to navigate in the age of Zothique would be confronted with a sky altered from its present configuration. By implication then, the reader must find different touchstones than familiar literary ideas and symbols to properly read and appreciate ("navigate") the poems and stories of Zothique.

The old gods and devils may have returned to Zothique under new names, but the same cannot be said of the old chestnuts about literature. Smith warns us that his work cannot be judged by what we have read before, but that it requires the reader to judge its on its own terms, just as we should approach any work of art.

Brian Stableford describes Zothique as "the most dramatically appropriate" of Smith's "imaginary milieux," but warns that "Isle" is not "entirely original" due to "echoes of Poe's 'Masque of the Red Death' and Villiers de l'Isle-Adam's 'Torture of Hope'" (245–46). However, in "The Masque of the Red Death," the titular plague is omnipresent throughout the plot and the atmosphere. The story is, in Hervey Allen's description, an ecstatic evocation of "the ruthlessness of nature" (415), whereas in Smith's story the "Silver Death" is what Alfred Hitchcock called the "maguffin": it is merely an excuse to set the plot in action.

Villier de l'Isle-Adam's "The Torture of Hope" was first published in his collection *Contes cruels*, and as the title implies it is indeed a story where the cruelty that human beings inflict on their fellows is the theme. A prisoner of the inquisition who is due to be immolated at the *auto da fé* attempts to escape, only to discover that the seemingly open path was deliberately left open to him so that his despair upon recapture might be all the greater. Smith's story likewise involves a similar psychological game of cat and mouse, yet it is the tortured prisoner whose deception resolves the plot, not the actions of the torturers.

In this story, Smith tells how the Silver Death has descended upon Yoros, causing all in its capital city, Faraad, to perish, except for its young king, Fulbra. His survival is due to a ring given to him by Vemdeez, the court astrologer, because the king's horoscope shows that he will not die in Yoros. The magician warns his king that he bears the contagion of the Silver Death, and that should the ring be removed it would immediately resume its former virulence.

Fulbra is overpowered with grief by the loss of his people, so he sets off on an ebon barge across the seas to an island-tributary, Cyntrom, to the south. The barge is blown off course by an uncanny storm, running aground on an "unknown shore" (*RA* 453) that turns out to be the ill-famed island of Uccastrog, of whose hospitality mariners did not speak well. Fulbra believes that the king of the island would not mistreat a brother king, but this hope is soon dashed.

King Ildrac is a sinister figure whose invitation to partake of the sundry diversions offered by his people accepts no refusal, and Fulbra is imprisoned in a deep dungeon cell bordered on one side with thick glass overlooking a submarine scene of horror. While being escorted to his cell, Fulbra meets a young girl, "fairer and less sullen of aspect" (*RA* 456) than her sisters, who urges him in his own language to endure bravely his ordeals and assures him that he is not friendless. Fulbra takes much comfort from this over the next few days, as he is subjected to a variety of novel tortures. One night the girl, Ilvaa, comes to him in secret and confides to him that an escape has been arranged. The next day he is bound to the wheel and it is revealed that Ilvaa's ministrations are part of his torment. Now that he is without hope, a drugged wine will be forced upon him that will evoke a series of hellish visions robbing him of all memories of his royal status.

Seeing no other escape, Fulbra pleads with Ildrac to do anything to him but not to take away his ring. Ildrac of course takes the ring, freeing the Silver Death: Fulbra dies immediately, and the courtiers and torturers seconds later. Ildrac, who is unaware that the ring is his protection, throws the ring away thinking that it is the cause of what has happened. He dies, and Smith ends the story: "And oblivion claimed the Isle of Uccastrog; and the Torturers were one with the tortured" (*RA* 463).

A close reading of the text of "The Isle of the Torturers" may surprise the reader who does not expect to encounter its sophisticated imagery and classical construction. The opening tells how the Silver Death descended "from the great star, Archernar," which evokes an association with the river Acheron, the river in the Greek underworld across which Charon ferries the souls of the dead. "Borne by the dim currents of ether" to the land of Yoros, it smites all "with an icy, freezing cold, an instant rigor, as if the outermost gulf had breathed upon them" (*RA* 449).

As we reflect on the opening paragraph, we realize that Smith is saying more than his words' obvious meaning. The fate that has befallen Yoros is nothing less than the fate that will eventually claim the whole earth once the red sun of Zothique sets for the last time, leaving our world helpless before the cold of space. Smith tells us in the first paragraph of the first story of the cycle, "The Empire of the Necromancers," that these stories were meant to "beguile for a little the black weariness of a dying race, grown hopeless of all but oblivion" (*RA* 316). When Fulbra mourns the loss of his people, he is in fact mourning the impending doom of all humanity as the interstellar cold inches ever closer.

Fulbra is supposedly a king, the establisher of justice and peace who ensures the prosperity of his people (Chevalier 567, 568), but he now stands apart from his people by virtue of the ring that provided him the protection that he could not give to his subjects. The ring symbolizes both Fulbra's isolation from his people as well as his ultimate bondage to their fate. Despite his royal status, Fulbra's freedom of action is inferior to that of the reader, as shown by his naive faith that Ildrac would not harm a fellow monarch or his unresisting surrender of personal weapons. Combined with Smith's detached point of view, "The Isle of the Torturers" clearly belongs to that fictional mode which Northrop Frye describes as *ironic*.

Irony is a subtle word whose meaning can be elusive, but which describes Smith's fiction very well indeed, especially when employed in its near-synonym "sardonic," which means "bitter irony." Smith often employs the detached viewpoint of the objective observer who is merely reciting the events as he watches them unfold, but there is a second level of meaning to his words that subverts the obvious. An excellent example occurs in Smith's "The Weird of Avoosl Wuthoqquan." A beggar whom the titular moneylender has refused alms predicts that

> "The hidden opulence of earth shall allure you and ensnare you; and earth itself shall devour you at the last."
>
> "Begone," said Avoosl Wuthoqquan. "The weird is more than a trifle cryptic in its earlier clauses; and the final clause is somewhat platitudinous. I do not need a beggar to tell me the common fate of mortality." (*RA* 124)

The prophecy turns out to be quite accurate, although in a manner that a concrete reading of the prophecy could not foresee. Likewise, when Smith writes of the devastation wrought in Faraad by the Silver Death, he tells how "Diggers died in the half-completed graves they had dug for others; but no one came to dispute their possession" (*RA* 450) These lines bring a smile to the reader, but it is a *risus sardonicus*, a death's-head grin, as we realize the immensity of the literal disaster which befell the land, besides which mere questions of land tenure are inconsequential.

Fulbra's story is tragic in that tragedy deals with the separation of the individual from society: first he is separated by his failure to share the fate of his people, and second by his imprisonment and torture by the inhabitants of Uccastrog. Frye distinguishes this type of tragic irony from other, more familiar types where a leader is brought down by a "tragic flaw" by removing any responsibility for his fate from the hero. His fate is out of proportion with anything he has done. Fulbra has become the scapegoat chosen solely by fate (his horoscope) to undergo terrible torments at the hands of the Torturers, and as such his fate is as terrible and as undeserved as that of Job.

Frye points out that "the incongruous and the inevitable . . . separate into opposite poles of irony" (42). At one pole is the inevitable, whose archetype is Adam, "human nature under sentence of death," justifying Fulbra's fate not by what he has done but by what he is, a human being as guilty as any other of belonging to a corrupt race. At the other pole is the archetype of the incongruous, Christ, "the perfectly innocent victim excluded from human society" whose innocence transforms all attempts at transferring guilt onto him into dignity (42). Fulbra falls between these poles, attaining through his suffering something of a heroic nature. Frye describes his archetype as that of Prometheus, the Titan who gave man fire and suffered terribly for that.

Irony is one of five fictional modes that Frye describes, each one set apart by the nature of the hero. The highest of these modes is myth, where the hero is superior to other men and to his environment by kind. They descend in a cyclical progression through romantic and high and low mimetic modes until in the ironic mode the central character is inferior to the reader in power, intelligence, and understanding (33-34). Each of these modes has enjoyed a period of ascendancy, gradually metamorphosing into its successor. We see especially in the tragic ironic mode a tendency to evoke the mythic, especially in suggestions of dying gods. Charles K. Wolfe was one of the first to note that "Smith's basic plot—the hero crossing the threshold into an alternative reality—is closely related to the classic hero myth as traced throughout the ages from primitive myth to folk legend to literature" (21). He quotes Joseph Campbell ("A hero ventures forth from the world of common day into a region of supernatural wonder: fabulous forces are there encountered and a decisive victory is won: the hero comes back from this mysterious adventure with the power to bestow boons upon his fellow man" [30]), noting that in Smith the second half of the structure (where the hero returns with the boon for his fellow man) breaks down. However, this structure survives more intact in "The Isle of the Torturers" than it does in other Smith stories.

Regardless of his failure or inability to fulfill his royal duties, Fulbra remains a king, and as such is a being removed from ordinary humanity by an order of magnitude. Although protected by the ring, Fulbra has been contaminated by the Silver Death and will immediately show its effects if the ring is removed. Later on, Fulbra is tormented by "a mirror of strange wizardry, wherein his own face was reflected as if seen after death" (*RA* 460). He sees therein also his fellow prisoners, their faces "dead, swollen, lidless and flayed, that seemed to approach from behind" (*RA* 460). Upon turning, he discovers that the mirror had reflected these figures accurately, raising a question about the veracity of his own image. In "The Enchantress of Sylaire," a similar mirror reveals to the coquette Dorothée her true nature. The hero, Anselme, declines to view the true visage of the lamia Sephora in the same mirror, casting it from him with the declaration that "'I am content with what my eyes tell me, without the aid of any mirror'" (*AY* 140). The poem "Enchanted Mirrors" warns that therein one "shall behold unshapen dooms / And ghoul-astounding shadows of the tombs; . . . But nevermore the moiling world of man" (*LO* 126). Based upon Smith's other uses of enchanted mirrors, it is not incredible that the self-image beheld by Fulbra in the mirror was indeed emblematic of his status of having transcended death.

This suggestion is strengthened when we consider that he departed Yoros by sea on an ebon barge, *ebon* suggesting funerary associations. Frye notes that "Water . . . traditionally belongs to a realm of existence below human life, the state of chaos or dissolution which follows ordinary death, or the reduction to the inorganic" (146). The sea voyage to Cyntrom is analogous to crossing the river Acheron (evoked earlier by the "great star Achernar"), but instead of arriving at an Elysian Fields, Fulbra is instead delivered to "an unknown shore" (so suggestive of Shakespeare's "undiscovered country") redolent with demonic imagery: the people are clad in garments of "blood red and vulturine black" (*RA* 454), their voices are "high and shrill and somehow evil" (*RA* 454), ruled by a monarch at whose side stood "a tall, brazen statue, with cruel and demonic visage, like some implacable god of the underworld" (*RA* 457) presiding over a court strewn with instruments of torture. Fulbra is imprisoned in a cell "after descending many steps," one side of which is walled with thick glass. The submarine imagery revealed, of tentacled devil-fish and flayed corpses, reinforces the infernal imagery, and also suggests some intriguing possibilities. For instance, during his quest the hero often slays a dragon or other monster, which represents the fallen world of sin and death. A variation on this is the leviathan, a sea monster sometimes depicted as a squid or octopus similar to the kraken or Lovecraft's Cthulhu. Inasmuch as Uccastrog is a terror of seamen and is intimately associated with death, perhaps Uccastrog is the Leviathan and all who dwell therein are trapped in the belly of the beast, waiting for a redeemer (see Frye 190).

It should not be forgotten that the inhabitants of Uccastrog are just as doomed as the other inhabitants of Zothique, and their sadistic pastimes are perhaps the means by which they lessen their own fear and ennui. In the film *Tombstone,* Wyatt Earp asks Doc Holliday what the matter is with men like opposition gunslinger

Johnny Ringo, and is told that he is seeking revenge. "For what?" asks the lawman, to which his friend replies, "For being born." Racial stereotypes of the cruel Oriental aside, Uccastrog could not be a pleasant place even for its inhabitants. It is hard to credit that its torture devices would remain idle under a tyrant such as Ildrac if there were no distressed mariners at hand. Perhaps some of their merriment at the suffering of Fulbra and his companions derives from the same impulses that cause Winston Smith to urge his captors in George Orwell's novel *1984* to put the rat cage on the face of his lover instead of him.

Ildrac (whose name evokes associations with Dracula, although Smith would have meant the vampire and not the actual Wallachian prince who was terrifyingly close to Ildrac come to life) is a demonic double or Shadow of Fulbra, representing the fallen world. Frye describes their character-types as opposite ends of the same pole: "In the sinister human world one individual pole is the tyrant-leader, inscrutable, ruthless, melancholy, and with an insatiable will, who commands loyalty only if he is egocentric enough to represent the collective ego of his followers. The other pole is represented by the *pharmakos* or sacrificed victim, who has to be killed to strengthen the others" (148). It is Ildrac that Fulbra must overcome in order to save himself, thereby saving the world around him. Ildrac is like Satan guarding the gates of Hell, trying to prevent the escape of his charges when Christ descended into the underworld after the crucifixion. In many ways Fulbra's suffering is reminiscent of the Passion, since both are essentially accounts of dying gods whose suffering redeems their worlds.

Ildrac is assisted in his harrowing of Fulbra by a young girl, Ilvaa. She differs from her sisters outwardly because her mother came from Yoros and because, upon being shipwrecked, she chose marriage over the alternative. By providing encouragement to Fulbra, she tricks him into prolonging his own suffering:

> And through his clouding terror and sorrow, he seemed to see the comely face of the girl who had smiled upon him compassionately, and who, alone of all that he had met in Uccastrog, had spoken to him with words of kindness. The face returned ever and anon, with a soft haunting, a gentle sorcery; and Fulbra felt, for the first time in many suns, the dim stirring of his buried youth and the vague, obscure desire of life. So, after a while, he slept; and the face of the girl came still before him in his dreams. (*RA* 456–57)

This passion is not to be consummated, but "frustrates the one who possesses it" (Frye 149). Ilvaa is revealed later to be not the innocent she pretends, but is instead the "harlot, witch, siren or other tantalizing female, a physical object of desire" that goads men on with promises of pleasures never kept (Frye 149).

It is at this point that we stumble upon an example of where Smith actually was influenced by another writer, to the point where he borrows a motif or idea from another's work and develops it further, making it his own. Smith's great mentor was the California poet George Sterling. Sterling's greatest work was perhaps the dramatic poem *Lilith* (1919, rev. ed. 1926). This drama tells how Tancrede was driven by his love for the temptress Lilith to commit terrible crimes, only to have her disappear after their commission. She appears to him a total of three times, each time driving him to forsake loved ones by promising him her body, but each time denying it to him. Many years later, we discover, Tancrede is an ascetic monk at the royal court, and the ageless Lilith is the mistress of the king. Tancrede's wanderings have given him a certain wisdom, but he remains an idealist who rebukes the king for squandering the taxes of his peasants on feasts. Lilith tricks him into attacking both church and state, whose representatives demand his death. The *femme fatale* appears to him in the dungeon, where she reveals that he is to be tortured to death over several hours, but Tancrede clings to his ideals. Lilith grants him a cosmic vision:

> Nothingness . . . Nay—I see a drop of blood
> Far down, yet visible. Beside it now
> A drop of dew appears, touched by a sun,
> Unseen, to many hues. And now from each
> Rise vapors, ever denser and more bright.
> They soar, they robe us in magnificence.
> Great chambers open in the splendor, rooms
> Of changing opalescence. Phantom shapes
> Are dwellers there, that woo and wed and war,
> Mingling in shadow. (101)

Lilith reveals to him that only the two drops are real:

> All is illusion, born of those twin drops
> Alone found real. See! The mists subside,
> Thou gazing in relentlessness, and now
> That orb of Pain glows redly, and the orb
> Of Pleasure gleams in subtle iris-flame.
> Of those thy dreams are born, and every thought
> Of good or evil. There is naught beside. (101)

Shaken, Tancrede clings to his illusions despite his horror at his impending fate, but resolves to remain steadfast and accept his pain and his pleasure as all the meaning that there is in this world.

Smith thought highly of the poem, writing in a letter published in Edward F. O'Day's *Oakland Enquirer* column that it was "certainly the best dramatic poem in English since the days of Swinburne and Browning. . . . The last scene—to mention nothing else—is unforgettable in its perfect beauty and terror—a complete symbol of life." The last scene depicts the assignation of Raoul the Troubadour with Jehanne the servant girl in the garden, where their tryst is disturbed by the sounds echoing from the dungeon where Tancrede is being flayed alive. Raoul overcomes her disquiet by stuffing her ears with rose petals, and their sighs echo antiphonally with his groans. Benediktsson observes quite correctly that Lilith is "herself Pleasure and Pain" personified (143). He quotes Sterling's description of the ending of the play: "I ended it with a contrast between pleasure and pain as indicative of that strangest and most awful of human faculties, our ability to be happy when we know others are in agony. I can never forgive myself nor humanity for that" (142).

Sterling asserts the philosophy behind *Lilith* in an essay called variously "Life," "The Implications of Infinity," and finally "Pleasure and Pain." A thorough exploration of its argument is beyond our current discussion. What is relevant is Sterling's pronouncement that, Schopenhauer to the contrary, "we exist not to escape pain but to embrace pleasure" (242). Good, evil, mercy, truth, beauty, and all other abstractions are just synonyms for the two opposing realities of pleasure and pain. "It is from our sensations, painful or otherwise, that we have derived what we are pleased to call our souls. Our very term 'the riddle of the universe' is meaningless in the Absolute, and has significance relative to us alone. The universe *is*. It is the Absolute" (242).

Viewed in the light of Sterling's essay, Uccastrog is revealed as a metaphor for the World itself: Fulbra's tenacious hold on life is renewed by the illusion of love to endure the most abominable tortures, just as we suffer the pangs of hunger because of the pleasures of food. When the Torturers explode this illusion, revealing Ilvaa's complicity and his own status as a fool, this is intended to intensify his emotional suffering. It has the desired effect: "The brief, piteous love that had been born amid sorrow and agony perished within him, leaving but ashes steeped in gall." In a Christ-like manner, he forgives his tormenters: "Yet, gazing at Ilvaa with sad eyes, he uttered no word of reproach" (*RA* 461).

By playing Brer Rabbit to Ildrac's Brer Fox, Fulbra tricks the demonic king into removing the ring, which like the ring of Polykrates symbolizes the fate which man cannot escape. No sooner is it removed than Fulbra meets the yearned-for death, and soon the entire court save the king is dead. We have come full circle, once more the king is isolated from all around him. Yet although he is dead, Fulbra is the one who is victorious, since not only does he escape the death that the Torturers had outlined to him, but he also puts an end to the abominable civilization founded on pain, despair, and *Schadenfreude* that was Uccastrog. This is an example of what Philip Wheelwright describes as paralogical dimensionality. Don Herron is probably the first critic to apply this to weird fiction, and I follow here his discussion of the concept.

Paralogical dimensionality refers to the ability of a symbol to transcend its concrete or universal meanings and express something "for which there is no publicly accepted word, formula or symbol already available" (30). The aspect of paralogical dimensionality which Herron applies, and which is applicable to our present discussion, is "the ability of literature successfully to convey the feeling of victory-in-defeat" (31). He cites as examples the manner in which Lear and Othello regain their dignity after enduring much suffering. By renouncing pleasure and love as illusions binding us to the pain of this world, Fulbra succeeds in tricking Ildrac into removing the ring and thus uniting their fates, thereby achieving a type of victory-in-defeat. Fulbra succeeds in liberating not only himself but also the inhabitants of Uccastrog from the wheel of destiny to which they were all bound together, as stated so eloquently in the last sentence of the story. Fulbra becomes an ironic inversion of Christ, a nihilistic Messiah who delivers mankind out of a life of pain to merciful oblivion, the only salvation possible in the insentient and uncaring universe visualized by Smith.

While conventional critics of Smith's work have overplayed the influences of Poe and Villiers de l'Isle-Adam on "The Isle of the Torturers," they have missed completely the strong influence exerted on the story by Sterling. Smith was familiar with this sort of critical myopia, writing to a fan that "the bane of every new creative artist . . . [is] people who can see nothing but resemblances either real or fancied (usually the latter) and who can always be depended upon to miss or ignore the essential *differences* between a new talent and its predecessors" (*SL* 365; italics in original).

Viewed in light of this and other critical approaches, we can appreciate Smith's achievement in recasting the work of his mentor into his own artistic image. "The Isle of the Torturers" illustrates Smith's quintessentially ironic detachment at the same time that it presents his most hellish portrait of the individual isolated from his society. The story is not just a *conte cruel*, but a parable about man rejecting the traps of this world and achieving a rough kind of transcendence. It is in this manner that the achievement of Clark Ashton Smith in this and other works needs to be reexamined and reappreciated.

Works Cited

Allen, Hervey. *Israfel: The Life and Times of Edgar Allan Poe*. New York: George H. Doran, 1926.

Benediktsson, Thomas E. *George Sterling*. Boston: Twayne, 1980.

Campbell, Joseph. *The Hero with a Thousand Faces*. 2nd ed. 1968. Princeton: Princeton University Press, 1972.

Chevalier, Jean, and Alain Gheerbrant. *The Penguin Dictionary of Symbols*. Trans. John Buchanan-Brown. 2nd ed. London: Penguin, 1996.

Frye, Northrop. *Anatomy of Criticism: Four Essays*. 1957. Princeton: Princeton University Press, 1971.

Herron, Don. "'The Red Brain': A Study in Absolute Doom." *Studies in Weird Fiction* No. 2 (Summer 1987): 30–35.

O'Day, Edward F. (as "The Clubman"). "Men and Women in the Mirror." *Oakland Enquirer* (10 January 1920): 8.

Posey, Stephen. "Meaning of 'Zothique's' Last Line." Online posting. 25 June 2003. Zothique Nights. http://groups.yahoo.com/group/ZothiqueNights/message/11031.

Stableford, Brian. "Outside the Human Aquarium: The Fantastic Imagination of Clark Ashton Smith." In *American Supernatural Fiction from Edith Wharton to the* Weird Tales *Writers*, ed. Douglas Robillard. New York: Garland, 1996. 229–52.

Sterling, George. *Lilith: A Dramatic Poem.* New York: Macmillan, 1926.

———. "The Testament of an American Schopenhauer: George Sterling's 'Pain and Pleasure.'" Ed. Joseph W. Slade. *Resources for American Literary Study* 3 (1973): 230–48.

Tombstone. Screenplay by Kevin Jarre. Dir. George P. Cosmatos. Perf. Kurt Russell, Val Kilmer. Touchstone Studios, 1993.

Villiers de l'Isle-Adam, Philippe-Auguste. "The Torture of Hope." *Magazine of Horror* 10 (August 1965): 19–23.

Wolfe, Charles K. "CAS, A Note on the Aesthetics of Fantasy." *CAS-Nyctalops.* Ed. Harry O. Morris. Special issue of *Nyctalops* 7 (1972): 20–22.

Regarding the Providence Point of View

Ronald S. Hilger

In 1996, Necronomicon Press published *The Book of Hyperborea* by Clark Ashton Smith, as edited by Will Murray. I have read the book with mixed impressions of interest and confusion. The book itself appears well made, the cover art by Robert Knox is striking, and the title is very appropriate. Will Murray's introduction is informative and exhaustive in its research of completion dates of the tales, as well as dates of magazine submissions, rejections, and publications. While all this is well and good, and I applaud every effort to publish the work of a neglected master of horror and fantasy, I still must disagree with his assertion that H. P. Lovecraft was somehow responsible for Smith's Hyperborean tales. Will Murray states in his introduction: "If Clark Ashton Smith had not come into contact with H. P. Lovecraft and fallen under his mesmeric literary influence, he would probably not have written his legendary *Weird Tales* stories. And he would certainly never have written the Hyperborean tales that comprise this volume" (*BH* 7).

Perhaps Murray has some information that I am unaware of, but even so, he does not explain how he came to his astonishing conclusion. I have researched the five volumes of Lovecraft's *Selected Letters*, and also Steve Behrends's collection of Smith's letters to Lovecraft, but see little to support this statement. In fact, a careful study of the letters Lovecraft wrote to Smith shows very little actual encouragement regarding Smith's fiction, especially when compared to Smith's constant praise of Lovecraft's stories and frequent suggestions that Lovecraft spend less time on revisory work and more on writing fiction.

Frankly, I am more than a little tired with this narrow-minded "Providence point of view" in which all weird horror seems to emanate outward from the sunlike Howard Phillips Lovecraft, influencing, inspiring, overshadowing all other writers in the field, his contemporaries as well as subsequent writers, who are too often viewed as diminutive satellites basking in the light of his glory and success. It's not that I don't appreciate the writings of Lovecraft. I do. I've read all his stories (several times, in fact), and I enjoy them very much and recommend them highly. But I don't see why Lovecraft's success should detract from the achievements and recognition of Smith.

Even more inaccurate and misleading is Murray's suggestion that Clark Ashton Smith would probably not have written any of his legendary stories had he not come into contact with Lovecraft. On the contrary, Smith received his main impetus toward entering the pulp fiction market from the urgent suggestion of his great friend Genevieve Sully during the well-documented camping trip of August 1927 to the Donner Summit/Castle Peak region of the Sierra Nevada. Shortly thereafter, this "prodding" led Smith to begin plotting, writing, and turning out weird fiction in earnest, beginning with "The Ninth Skeleton" in March 1928. Mrs. Sully wrote of this occasion in *Emperor of Dreams*, the bibliography by Donald Sidney-Fryer:

> ... we proposed a longer walk—to Crater Ridge—where we had gone many times in the past, but now we were going with a companion who came under a spell of strange thought, transforming the scene into a foreboding and grotesque landscape, which Clark later used in his now famous story, "The City of the Singing Flame." ... Later in the afternoon while Clark was still feeling a strange influence, ... I suddenly suggested that he use his powers of writing for fiction, which would be more remunerative than poetry. His financial situation at the time was critical, and some practical advice seemed in order. This prodding led to Clark's writing of weird fiction and, thus, the walk to Crater Ridge started the flow of work which has made Clark the well-known writer that he is. (190)

As Mrs. Sully points out, Smith's financial situation was indeed a major factor that led to his writing fiction for the pulp magazines. Smith's parents were then in their mid-seventies and totally dependent on their only son. With the onset of the Depression, Smith desperately needed extra money to support them. Smith himself supports Mrs. Sully's assertion in a letter to Lovecraft in January 1931:

> As to my appalling prolificality, there are doubtless several reasons and explanations. About eighteen months ago, I was taken to task for idleness by a woman-friend, and pledged myself to industry. ... Other reasons are, that it is necessary for me to make a little money; also, that I need an imaginative escape from the human aquarium—and, moreover, a "safety-valve" to keep from blowing up and disrupting the whole countryside. And, beyond all this, I am finding a pleasure in fiction-writing, and deriving a mental "kick" from it which I seldom got from poetry. (*SL* 145)

Obviously many factors contributed to Smith's advent as a fictioneer other than Lovecraft's influence.

Of course, Smith deeply admired Lovecraft's stories, just as Lovecraft likewise admired Smith's poetry, prose-poems, and paintings. I would not argue the point that Lovecraft was instrumental in getting Smith's tales published in *Weird Tales*, where he enjoyed a good deal of popularity with the readers and hence, with the editor. Murray also credits Lovecraft with introducing Smith to *Weird Tales* without offering any evidence. Since Murray advanced his theory, a letter has come to light that contradicts this: Lovecraft wrote F. Lee Baldwin on 27 March 1934 that it was actually Smith who was the first to direct his attention to the magazine (*Lord of a Visible World* 255). Therefore, to suggest that Smith would never have written his legendary stories at all had he not fallen under the "mesmeric literary influence" of Lovecraft is simply ludicrous and has more to do with Murray's "Providential" opinion than with reality.

Rather than being "heavily influenced" by the emerging Cthulhu Mythos, Smith's Hyperborean tales owe nothing in concept or in content to Lovecraft, aside from once or twice mentioning the *Necronomicon* and a few gods created by Lovecraft. To the contrary, these tales merely continue the themes Smith had already developed in his poetry, as indicated by this excerpt from *The Hashish-Eater:* "For the snows / Of hyperborean winter, and their winds, / Sleep in his jewel-builded capital, / Nor any charm of flame-wrought wizardry, / Nor conjured suns, may rout them." This quotation is an obvious precursor to the Hyperborean sequence and to "The Coming of the White Worm" in particular, written before Smith ever corresponded with Lovecraft. As Lin Carter points out in his introduction to the Ballantine edition of *Hyperborea,* and as Murray also mentions, Smith elaborates on the intriguing ideas of the ancient Greeks and the contemporary Madame Blavatsky, as he mentions to Lovecraft in a letter dated 1 March 1933, in which he states: "One can disregard the theosophy, and make good use of the stuff about elder continents, etc. I got my own ideas about Hyperborea, Poseidonis, etc. from such sources, then turned my imagination loose" (*SL* 203).

Smith told George Wetzel that, "As to the Cthulhu Mythos, I believe I added as much to it as I borrowed. Tsathoggua and The Book of Eibon were my own inventions, and were promptly utilized by Lovecraft. In turn, I borrowed the *Necronomicon*" (*PD* 75). If Smith was so influenced by Lovecraft, why did he not emulate Lovecraft's style and concept of the emerging Mythos instead of simply mentioning a few of Lovecraft's creations such as Abdul Alhazred and his *Necronomicon* here and there throughout his Hyperborean sequence?

Why then must Smith be considered an acolyte of Lovecraft? Or merely as one of the "Lovecraft circle"? When Lovecraft first wrote to Smith on 12 August 1922, he wrote as a humble admirer addressing an inspired, successful writer who had already published two books of poetry, and his third, *Ebony and Crystal* (which contained twenty-nine prose-poems as well as the monumental *The Hashish-Eater*) was only a few months away from publication. Lovecraft wrote in his first letter, "I should deem it a great honour to hear from you if you have the leisure & inclination to address an obscurity . . . That I have not work of even approximately equal genius to exhibit in reciprocation, is the fault of my mediocre ability & not of my inclination" (*Selected Letters* 1.194). And again, after reading *Ebony and Crystal,* he wrote on 25 March 1923: "My card sent from Salem last month attempted in a feeble way to express the delirious delight & unboundedly enthusiastic admiration which *Ebony and Crystal* aroused in me. . . . It is genius, if genius ever existed! . . . The magnificence of 'The Hashish-Eater' is beyond description . . . I delight in your use of the cosmos instead of merely the world as a background" (*Selected Letters* 1.213–14). Apparently it was Smith's poetry that influenced Lovecraft in this direction toward cosmicism, quite possibly inspiring Lovecraft's extraterrestrial Old Ones. When examined in this light, it could well be argued that Smith influenced Lovecraft more than the other way around. But is it not more likely that the two kindred spirits equally encouraged and inspired the other?

Murray himself points out, and I wholeheartedly agree, "But Clark Ashton Smith was not Howard Phillips Lovecraft" (*BH* 8). In fact, the two writers utilize completely different methods to their writing. Lovecraft, the realist, carefully plotted a documentary approach to his Cthulhu Mythos stories, constructing a firm foundation of scientific fact to support his fiction, cleverly incorporating invented research and journalistic records along with existing books and actual events. Smith, the imaginative artist, utilized an artistic approach, describing in great detail the sights and sounds and emotions he wished to convey. Smith developed a luxurious, evocative prose style in which he meticulously painted a complete mental picture and atmosphere in which to immerse the reader in order to achieve the illusion of reality.

A careful study of Smith's poems, prose-poems, and tales will reveal many recurrent themes: humanity's insignificance in the greater cosmic arena, loss, love, journeys through space and time, omnipotence, ennui, mortality, to name just a few. These recurrent themes detail a gradual evolution from poetry to prose-poems to tales, a process that began before Lovecraft wrote his first letter to Smith and culminated with his amazing burst of stories written and published 1928 to 1936. After this period, Smith once again concentrated on poetry, painting, and his newest medium of self-expression, sculpting.

Another major flaw in *The Book of Hyperborea* is the overstressing of scholarly value at the expense of aesthetics and the cohesiveness of the collection as a whole. Once again, I must agree with Murray when he states that his listing of the tales by completion dates can be a "bewildering" experience for the reader. Also, the inclusion of "The House of Haon-Dor" (a fragment of a rough draft only peripherally related to Hyperborea) in the middle of the sequence markedly detracts from the general reading experience.

For my money, I would much rather take my chances in the used book market, searching out Lin Carter's *Hyperborea*, which boasts a smooth narrative sequence, several additional prose poems, and a primitive map of Hyperborea.

Works Cited

Lovecraft, H. P. *Lord of a Visible World.* Ed. S. T. Joshi and David E. Schultz. Athens: Ohio University Press, 2000.

———. *Selected Letters.* Ed. August Derleth, Donald Wandrei, and James Turner. Sauk City, WI: Arkham House, 1965–76. 5 vols.

Sully, Genevieve K. Letter. In *Emperor of Dreams: A Clark Ashton Smith Bio-Bibliography* by Donald Sidney-Fryer and Divers Hands. West Kingston, RI: Donald M. Grant, 1978.

An Annotated Chronology of the Fiction of Clark Ashton Smith

Steve Behrends

Chronologies are dull affairs. Of course they can come in handy at times, but how often have you curled up with one before a crackling fire? It would be much more interesting, say, to have a list of the stories that the author himself considered his finest. Smith never gave us such a list; and while he did select his best work for inclusion in *Out of Space and Time,* he commented at the time that the "Choice seems pretty difficult, since, after a few outstanding items such as 'The Double Shadow' and 'A Night in Malnéant,' I seem to find dozens or scores of fairly equal merit" (*SL* 333).

Although he may not have put them down in one place, Smith did have opinions about his stories and frequently expressed them to his pen-pals. In an effort to bridge the gap between arid scholarship and light entertainment, some of these comments have been gathered together, along with other informational tidbits, and appear below the pertinent title in the following Smith chronology.

A date in brackets indicates a date of completion, unless noted, and a number in parentheses before a title gives that story's place in the Completed Stories log. This ordering has been followed as much as possible, despite minor disagreements with dates from other sources. Only when a tale's completion was considerably delayed with respect to its inclusion in the log has the ordering been changed. Unfinished works are marked with an asterisk.

"The Abominations of Yondo" [1925] "I think it was mainly Lovecraft's interest and encouragement that led me to ['Yondo'], which appeared in *The Overland Monthly*" and "evok[ed], I was told, many protests from the readers."

(1) "Sadastor" [1925]

(2) "The Ninth Skeleton" [after 4/28 and before 8/28]

(3) "The Last Incantation" [9/23/29]

"The End of the Story" [10/1/29] "It's a good tale—especially from the sales-angle."

(4) "The Phantoms of the Fire" [10/6/29] "I prefer nearly all my other tales."

(5) "A Night in Malnéant" [10/15/29] "One of my best atmospherics."

(6) "The Resurrection of the Rattlesnake" [10/10/29] "Pretty punk, except for the touch of genuine horror at the end." "There isn't much to it."

(7) "Thirteen Phantasms" [10/11/29]

(8) "The Venus of Azombeii" [11/11/29] "A weird mixture of poetry and melodrama."

(9) "The Tale of Satampra Zeiros" [11/16/29] "One of my best."

(10) "The Monster of the Prophecy" [12/3/29] "One of my favorite yarns." "Absolutely novel in inter-planetary fiction." "The result of a definite inspiration." "The plot . . . was good from any angle; and I am willing to bet that the satiric implications will be missed by a lot of readers." "I'm sure it's the first interplanetary story on record, where the hero doesn't return to earth at the end!"

(11) "The Metamorphosis of Earth" [late 1929] "Based on a far from bad idea." "Probably the best element is the satire." ". . . am now engaged in killing off an odious bunch of scientists . . ."

(12) "The Epiphany of Death" [1/25/30] "Inspired by [Lovecraft's] '[The Statement of] Randolph Carter' and . . . written in about three hours."

(13) "A Murder in the Fourth Dimension" [1/30/30]

(14) "The Parrot in the Pawn-Shop" [2/5/30]

(15) "A Copy of Burns" [2/27/30]

(16) "The Devotee of Evil" [3/9/30]

(17) "The Satyr" [3/31/30]

(18) "The Planet of the Dead" [4/6/30]

(19) "The Uncharted Isle" [4/21/30]

* "Vizaphmal in Ophiuchus" [plotted 4/30]

(20) "Marooned in Andromeda" [3/14/30, begun 1/24/30] "An excellent peg for a lot of fantasy, horror, grotesquery and satire."

(21) "The Root of Ampoi" [5/28/30] "A dud."

(22) "The Necromantic Tale" [6/23/30]

(23) "The Immeasurable Horror" [7/13/30]

(24) "A Voyage to Sfanomoë" [7/17/30] "A sort of favorite with me." Smith listed it among his best pseudo-scientific yarns.

(25) "The Door to Saturn" [7/26/30] "This tale is one of my favorites, partly on account of its literary style." "I take out the ms. and read it over, when I am too bored to read anything in my book-cases!"

(26) "The Red World of Polaris" [late 8/30] "Passably written, but suffer[ing] from triteness of plot." "It was written on several mountain-tops, beneath the thousand-year-old junipers on granite crags; and the giant firs and hemlocks by the margin of sapphire tarns." "Mere words didn't seem to stand up in the presence of those peaks and cliffs. But now, amid the perspective of familiar surroundings, 'The Red World' doesn't seem so bad."

(27) "Told in the Desert" [?]

(28) "The Willow Landscape" [9/8/30]

- (29) "A Rendezvous in Averoigne" [9/13/30] "One of my own favorites—in fact, I like it much better than the celebrated 'End of the Story.'"
- * "The Eggs From Saturn" [begun late 9/30] "[will feature] a realistic local setting for its interplanetary mysteries and horrors."
- * "The Ocean-World of Alioth" [plotted and begun late 9/30]
- (30) "The Gorgon" [10/2/30]
- (31) "An Offering to the Moon" [10/30] "No great favorite of mine." "Maybe I tried too much for character-study and contrast, to the detriment of the weird atmosphere and the 'action.'"
- (32) "The Kiss of Zoraida" [10/15/30] "An ungodly piece of pseudo-Oriental junk. " "Well enough done, with some touches of terrific irony."
- (33) "The Face by the River" [10/30]
- (34) "Like Mohammed's Tomb" [10/30]
- * "The Sorceress of Averoigne" [plotted late 10/30]
- (35) "Checkmate" [11/7/30]
- (36) "The Ghoul" [11/12/30] "The legend is so hideous, that I would not be surprised if there were some mention of it in the *Necronomicon*."
- (37) "A Tale of Sir John Maundeville" [11/16/30] "A good short." "['Sir John' and 'The Ghoul'] pleased me for their archaism." "The kingdom of Antchar, which I have invented for this tale, is even more unwholesome, if possible, than Averoigne."
- (38) "An Adventure in Futurity" [12/27/30] "An awful piece of junk."
- (39) "The Justice of the Elephant" [12/29/30]
- (40) "The Return of the Sorcerer" [1/6/31] An "original plot; but it seems to need some additional atmospheric development."
- (41) "The City of the Singing Flame" [1/15/31] "Some day I must look for those two boulders . . . If you and other correspondents cease to hear from me, you can surmise what has happened!"
- * "A Tale of Gnydron" [plotted 2/31] Note: Zothique conceived.
- (42) "A Good Embalmer" [2/7/31] "Have spent three days over a six-page horror . . . It is not in my natural genre, and may not even have the dubious merit of being salable." "[It] should take the palm for macabre grotesquery."
- (43) "The Testament of Athammaus" [1/22/31, plotted 4/30] "I shall feel rather peeved if Wright turns it down; since it is about as good as I can do in the line of unearthly horror." "I really think he (or it) is about my best monster to date."
- (44) "The Amazing Planet (A Captivity in Serpens)" [3/31, begun 11/30] "I'll give them their 'action' this time!!!"
- (45) "The Letter from Mohaun Los" [4/9/31]
- (46) "The Hunters from Beyond" [4/28/31] "I'm none too fond of the story." "Doesn't please me very well—the integral mood seems a little second-rate,

probably because the modern treatment is rather uncongenial for me."
(47) "The Holiness of Azédarac" [5/21/31] "The plot maketh rather a merrie tale, methinks."
(48) "The Maker of Gargoyles" [6/16/31]
(49) "Beyond the Singing Flame" [6/30/31] "Strikes me as the best thing I have done recently."
(50) "Seedling of Mars (The Martian)" [7/20/31] "A pretty fair scientifictional opus."
* "The Master of Destruction" [plotted 8/31] "It ought to make a thriller."
(51) "The Vaults of Yoh-Vombis" [9/12/31] "A rather ambitious hunk of extra-planetary weirdness." "The interplanetary angle . . . adds considerably to the interest." In October 1932 Smith submitted "Yoh-Vombis" (and "Empire of the Necromancers") to an anthologist, as examples of his best work.
* "The Rebirth of the Flame" [plotted before 9/22/31]
(52) "The Eternal World" [9/27/31] "The best and most original of my super-scientific tales, so far." "The toughest job I have ever attempted." "Gernsback took 'The Eternal World,' but advised me to put 'more realism' into my future stories, saying that the late ones were 'verging dangerously on the weird.' That's really quite a josh—as well as a compliment."
(53) "The Demon of the Flower" [10/17/31] Smith had considered including this in *The Double Shadow,* as one of his best stories not sold to magazines.
* "Slaves of the Black Pillar" [plotted and begun 10/31]
(54) "The Nameless Offspring" [11/12/31, plotted 1/31] "The plot is about as diabolic as anything I am ever likely to devise." This work was inspired by Machen's "The Great God Pan."
(55) "A Vintage from Atlantis" [11/31] "It is far from bad."
(56) "The Weird of Avoosl Wuthoqquan" [11/25/31]
(57) "The Invisible City" [12/15/31] "A hunk of tripe . . . Not enough atmosphere to make it good—and too many unexplained mysteries for the scientifiction readers, who simply must have their formulae . . . am pretty thoroughly disgusted by it." "So punk that I don't want to show it to anyone."
(58) "The Immortals of Mercury" [1/19/32] "A lot of tripe, I'm afraid; but if it brings me a 200.00 dollar check, will have served its purpose."
(59) "The Empire of the Necromancers" [1/7/32] "A tale which pleased me considerably." "There is a queer mood in this little tale . . . it is much over-greened with what H. P. once referred to as the 'verdigris of decadence.'"
(60) "The Seed from the Sepulcher" [2/32] "[I like it] for its imaginative touches, but am going to chuck the malignant plant idea after this. I don't want to run it into the ground!"
(61) "The Second Interment" [1/29/32]

(62) "Ubbo-Sathla" [2/15/32]
(63) "The Double Shadow" [3/14/32]
(64) "The Plutonian Drug" [4/5/32] "Among my best in the field of science-fiction." "It was certainly tough writing, and I'm still a little groggy." "Hellishly hard to do."
(65) "The Supernumerary Corpse" [4/10/32, plotted 11/30]
(66) "The Master of the Asteroid" [6/9/32]
(67) "The Colossus of Ylourgne" [5/1/32] "Others have commended the tale, so I begin to think that perhaps I have under-estimated it." "[It has a] striking plot."
(68) "The Mandrakes" [5/15/32] "Not a very important item."
(69) "The Beast of Averoigne" [6/18/32] "Rather good—terse, grim, and devilishly horrible." "I think that I have done better tales, but few that are technically superior."
(70) "A Star-Change" [6/32, plotted 10/30] "A whale of an idea." "A high-grade science-fiction tale." "'A Star-Change' is more realistic [than 'The Light from Beyond'], but, in my estimation, is equally good. As far as I know it is the only attempt to convey the profound disturbance of function and sensation that would inevitably be experienced by a human being on an alien world."
(71) "The Disinterment of Venus" [7/32, plotted 6/31] "A rather unimportant piece." "This, of all my recent tales, will be hardest to sell, since it combines the risque and the ghastly." "Rather a wicked story."
(72) "The White Sybil" [7/14/32]
(73) "The Ice-Demon" [7/22/32] "Well written. But I had to work it over so much that it went stale on me, somehow."
(74) "The Isle of the Torturers" [7/31/32] "The best of the summer's crop . . . a strange mixture of eeriness, grotesquery, bright color, cruelty, and stark human tragedy." "One of my own favorites."
(75) "The Dimension of Chance" [8/32] "Probably better as a satire than anything else."
(76) "The Dweller in the Gulf" [8/32] Smith had bad luck with this story. He considered it "a first-rate interplanetary horror, sans the hokum of pseudo-explanation," and yet to sell it on second submission he was forced to add a character (John Chalmers) to provide just such hokum. "The tale has a magnificent Dantesque ending," which was hacked apart by Hugo Gernsback himself when it appeared in *Wonder Stories*.
(77) "The Maze of Maâl Dweb" [9/32] "Ultra-fantastic, full-hued and ingenious, with an extra twist or two in the tail for luck." The title was originally "The Maze of Mool Dweb," but Smith felt that "Maal Dweb—two syllables—would be preferable perhaps, for tone-color, etc." After finalizing this title, he indulged in a bit of self-praise: "I think it should be admitted that some

(78) "The Third Episode of Vathek" [9/16/32] "I really think the ending is one of the best pieces of work I have done lately."

(79) "Genius Loci" [9/26/32] "An experiment for me . . . It was damnably hard to do, and I am not certain of my success. I am even less certain of being able to sell it to any editor—it will be too subtle for the pulps, and the highbrows won't like the supernatural element."

(80) "The Light from Beyond" [10/31/32, plotted 8/31] "First-rate."

(81) "The Charnel God" [11/15/32] "A devil of a yarn—necromancy, invultuation, necrophilism and necrophagy—but strictly moral at the end, since the foul necromancers get it in the neck." "For my taste, it has a little too much plot and not enough atmosphere."

(82) "The Dark Eidolon" [12/23/32] "A devil of a story, and if Wright knows his mandrakes, he certainly ought to take it on. If the thing could ever be filmed . . . it might be a winner for diabolic drama and infernal spectacles." "Contains some of my best imaginative writing."

(83) "The Voyage of King Euvoran" [1/33]

(84) "Vulthoom" [2/14/33, begun 10/32] "Fails to please me." "[It] seems to have pleased [Wright] for some ungodly reason; but after all it's a cut or two above Edmond Hamilton."

(85) "The Weaver in the Vault" [3/14/33] "I like the tale myself, particularly some of the atmospheric touches."

*(90) *The Infernal Star* [begun early 3/33]

(86) "The Flower-Women" [3/33, begun 10/32]

(87) "The Dark Age" [4/33] "My lousiest in many moons, largely no doubt, because of the non-fantastic plot, which failed to engage my interest at any point. The one redeeming feature is the final paragraph, which takes a sly, underhanded crack at the benefits (?) of science."

(89) "The Death of Malygris" [4/33]

(91) "The Tomb-Spawn" [begun 7/33]

* "The House of Haon-Dor" [begun 7/33]

(92) "The Witchcraft of Ulua" [8/22/33] "I feel that it is well-written; and it gives a certain variant note to my series of tales dealing with Zothique." "Erotic imagery was employed in the tale merely to achieve a more varied sensation of weirdness." "I wouldn't have had the originality to write it a few years back."

(93) "The Coming of the White Worm" [9/15/33] "A tale that I am inclined to favour in my own estimation." "It [was] hard to do, like most of my tales, because of the peculiar and carefully maintained style and tone-colour, which involves rejection of many words, images and locutions that might ordinarily be employed in writing."

(94) "The Seven Geases" [10/1/33] "Outrageously grotesque, sardonic and satiric." "I am rather partial to that opus. These grotesque and elaborate ironies come all too naturally to me, I fear."
(88) "The Chain of Aforgomon" [1/34, begun 4/33] "A devilishly hard yarn to write ... a most infernal chore, since the original inspiration seems to have gone cold, leaving the tale as immalleable as chilled iron."
(95) "The Primal City" [1/34]
* "The Scarlet Egg" [begun 3/34]
(96) "Xeethra" [3/21/34, plotted 8/33 or before]
(97) "The Last Heiroglyph" [4/7/34] "A whale of a weird notion."
*(98) "Shapes of Adamant" [?]
(99) "Necromancy in Naat" [2/6/35] "Seems the best of my more recently published weirds; though Wright forced me to mutilate the ending . . ."
(100) "The Treader of the Dust" [2/15/35]
(101) "The Black Abbot of Puthuum" [before 4/35]
(102) "The Death of Ilalotha" [3/16/37] "Quite good, I believe, especially in style and atmosphere. It is unusually poisonous and exotic." "I seem to have slipped something over on the PTA."
(103) "Mother of Toads" [3/20/37, begun ca. 5/35] "A passable weird, with a sufficiently horrific ending."
(104) "The Garden of Adompha" [7/31/37] "A tale which I am inclined to like."
(105) "The Great God Awto" [begun 9/37? (published 2/40)]
(106) "Strange Shadows" [begun 3/40?] A later version, "I Am Your Shadow," may have been completed 11/41.
(107) "The Enchantress of Sylaire" [? (published 7/41)]
(108) "Double Cosmos" [3/24/40 (penultimate version), begun 3/34]
(109) "Dawn of Discord" [? (E. H. Price's rewrite published 1939 or 1940)]
(110) "House of the Monoceros" [? (Price's rewrite published 2/41)]
* "The Painter in Darkness" [begun 7/46]
"Nemesis of the Unfinished" [7/30/47 (first version)]
(111) "The Master of the Crabs" [8/3/47]
*(112) "Eviction by Night" [?]
"Morthylla" [(9 or 10)/52]
"Schizoid Creator" [(9 or 10)/52]
"Monsters in the Night" [4/11/53]
"Phoenix" [1953 (published 11/53)]
"The Theft of Thirty-nine Girdles" [4/57, begun 10/52]
"The Symposium of the Gorgon" [8/5/57]
"The Dart of Rasasfa" [7/21/61]

Addendum

The following synopses or incomplete stories are "major," but either cannot be dated, or have only very unrestrictive bounds on date of composition:

* "In a Hashish-Dream"/"A Tale of Hashish-Land" [begun in 1920s]
* "Asharia: A Tale of the Lost Planet" [plotted before 1/32] "Has great possibilities, I feel."
* "The Minotaur's Brother" [plotted after 5/26/35]
* "Offspring of the Grave" [plotted after 5/26/35]
* "I Am a Witch" [plotted after 3/16/37]
* "Mandor's Enemy" [begun in early 1950s]
* "The Wink and the Chuckle" [begun before 4/53]
* "Chincharerro" [begun after "The Wink and the Chuckle"]
* "Mnemoka" [begun in 1950s]
* "Unquiet Boundary" [begun in 1950s]
* "Djinn without a Bottle" [begun in 1950s]
* "Beyond the Rose-Arbor" [?]
* "Maker of Prodigies" [?]
* "Music of Death" [?]
* "Queen of the Sabbath" [?]

Bibliography

I. Primary Sources

A. Poetry

The Star-Treader and Other Poems. San Francisco: A. M. Robertson, 1912.
Odes and Sonnets. San Francisco: Book Club of California, 1918.
Ebony and Crystal: Poems in Verse and Prose. Auburn, CA: Printed by The Auburn Journal Press, 1922.
Sandalwood. Auburn, CA: Printed by The Auburn Journal Press, 1925.
Nero and Other Poems. Lakeport, CA: The Futile Press, 1937.
Selected Poems. Sauk City, WI: Arkham House, 1971. [Prepared 1944–49.] Includes "Clark Ashton Smith: Emperor of Shadows" by Benjamin De Casseres (foreword).
The Dark Chateau and Other Poems. Sauk City, WI: Arkham House, 1951.
Spells and Philtres. Sauk City, WI: Arkham House, 1958.
The Hills of Dionysus: A Selection. Pacific Grove, CA: Roy A. Squires and Clyde Beck, 1962.
¿Donde Duermes, el Dorado? y Otros Poemas. As by "Clerigo Herrero." Glendale, CA: 1964. [La Imprenta de Rojo Escuderos.]
Poems in Prose. Sauk City, WI: Arkham House, 1965. Contains "Clark Ashton Smith: Poet in Prose" by Donald S. Fryer.
The Fugitive Poems of Clark Ashton Smith. Zothique edition. Glendale, CA: Roy A. Squires.
    The Tartarus of the Suns. First fascicle. 1970.
    The Palace of Jewels. Second fascicle. 1970.
    In the Ultimate Valleys. Third fascicle. 1970.
    To George Sterling: Five Poems. Fourth fascicle. 1970.
The Fugitive Poems of Clark Ashton Smith. Xiccarph edition. Glendale, CA: Roy A. Squires.
    The Titans in Tartarus. First volume. 1974.
    A Song from Hell. Second volume. 1975.
    The Potion of Dreams. Third volume. 1975.
    The Fanes of Dawn. Fourth volume. 1976.
    Seer of the Cycles. Fifth volume. 1976.
    The Burden of the Suns. Sixth volume. 1977.
Grotesques and Fantastiques. Saddle River, NJ: Gerry de La Ree. 1973.
Klarkash-Ton and Monstro Ligriv. Saddle River, NJ: Gerry de la Ree, 1974.

The Hashish-Eater; or, The Apocalypse of Evil. West Warwick, RI: Necronomicon Press, 1989.

The Hashish Eater; or, The Apocalypse of Evil. Ed. Donald Sidney-Fryer. [Sacramento, CA: Donald Sidney-Fryer, 1990.] Rev. ed. New York: Hippocampus Press, forthcoming.

Nostalgia of the Unknown: The Complete Prose Poetry of Clark Ashton Smith. Ed. Marc Michaud, Susan Michaud, Steve Behrends, and S. T. Joshi. West Warwick, Rhode Island: Necronomicon Press, 1988.

The Last Oblivion: Best Fantastic Poetry of Clark Ashton Smith. Ed. S. T. Joshi and David E. Schultz. New York: Hippocampus Press, 2002.

Complete Poems and Translations. Edited by David E. Schultz and S. T. Joshi. New York: Hippocampus Press, 2006–07. 3 vols.

B. Fiction

The Double Shadow and Other Fantasies. [Auburn, CA: Clark Ashton Smith, 1933.] *Contains:* The Voyage of King Euvoran; The Maze of the Enchanter; The Double Shadow; A Night in Malnéant; The Devotee of Evil; The Willow Landscape.

Out of Space and Time. Sauk City, WI: Arkham House, 1942; rpt. London: Neville Spearman, 1971, and Lincoln, NE: University of Nebraska Press, forthcoming, introduction by Jeff Vander Meer. *Contains:* "Clark Ashton Smith: Master of Fantasy" by August Derleth and Donald Wandrei. *Contains:* The End of the Story; A Rendezvous in Averoigne; A Night in Malnéant; The City of the Singing Flame (includes sequel, Beyond the Singing Flame); The Uncharted Isle; The Second Interment; The Double Shadow; The Chain of Aforgomon; The Dark Eidolon; The Last Hieroglyph; Sadastor; The Death of Ilalotha; The Return of the Sorcerer; The Testament of Athammaus; The Weird of Avoosl Wuthoqquan; Ubbo-Sathla; The Monster of the Prophecy; The Vaults of Yoh-Vombis; From the Crypts of Memory; The Shadows.

Lost Worlds. Sauk City, WI: Arkham House, 1944; rpt. London: Neville Spearman, 1971, and Lincoln, NE: University of Nebraska Press, forthcoming, introduction by Jeff Vander Meer. *Contains:* The Tale of Satampra Zeiros; The Door to Saturn; The Seven Geases; The Coming of the White Worm; The Last Incantation; A Voyage to Sfanomoë; The Death of Malygris; The Holiness of Azédarac; The Beast of Averoigne; The Empire of the Necromancers; The Isle of the Torturers; Necromancy in Naat; Xeethra; The Maze of Maâl Dweb; The Flower-Women; The Demon of the Flower; The Plutonian Drug; The Planet of the Dead; The Gorgon; The Letter from Mohaun Los; The Light from Beyond; The Hunters from Beyond; The Treader from the Dust.

Genius Loci and Other Tales. Sauk City, WI: Arkham House, 1948; rpt. London: Neville Spearman, 1972. *Contains:* Genius Loci; The Willow Landscape; The Ninth Skeleton; The Phantoms of the Fire; The Eternal World; Vulthoom; A

Star-Change; The Primal City; The Disinterment of Venus; The Colossus of Ylourgne; The Satyr; The Garden of Adompha; The Charnel God; The Black Abbot of Puthuum; The Weaver in the Vault.

The Abominations of Yondo. Sauk City, WI: Arkham House, 1960; rpt. London: Neville Spearman, 1972. *Contains:* The Nameless Offspring; The Witchcraft of Ulua; The Devotee of Evil; The Epiphany of Death; A Vintage from Atlantis; The Abominations of Yondo; The White Sybil; The Ice-Demon; The Voyage of King Euvoran; The Master of the Crabs; The Enchantress of Sylaire; The Dweller in the Gulf; The Dark Age; The Third Episode of Vathek; Chinoiserie; The Mirror in the Hall of Ebony; The Passing of Aphrodite.

Tales of Science and Sorcery. Sauk City, WI: Arkham House, 1964. *Contains:* Master of the Asteroid; The Seed from the Sepulcher; The Root of Ampoi; The Immortals of Mercury; Murder in the Fourth Dimension; Seedling of Mars; The Maker of Gargoyles; The Great God Awto; Mother of Toads; The Tomb-Spawn; Schizoid Creator; Symposium of the Gorgon; The Theft of the Thirty-nine Girdles; Morthylla. Contains memoir by E. Hoffmann Price.

Other Dimensions. Sauk City, WI: Arkham House, 1970. *Contains:* Marooned in Andromeda; The Amazing Planet; An Adventure in Futurity; The Immeasurable Horror; The Invisible City; The Dimension of Chance; The Metamorphosis of Earth; Phoenix; The Necromantic Tale; The Venus of Azombeii; The Resurrection of the Rattlesnake; The Supernumerary Corpse; The Mandrakes; Thirteen Phantasms; An Offering to the Moon; Monsters in the Night; The Malay Krise; The Ghost of Mohammed Din; The Mahout; The Raja and the Tiger; Something New; The Justice of the Elephant; The Kiss of Zoraida; A Tale of Sir John Maundeville; The Ghoul; Told in the Desert.

The Unexpurgated Clark Ashton Smith. Series editor, Steve Behrends. West Warwick, RI: Necronomicon Press. *Comprises:* The Dweller in the Gulf (1987); The Monster of the Prophecy (1988); Mother of Toads (1987); The Vaults of Yoh-Vombis (1988); The Witchcraft of Ulua (1988); Xeethra (1988).

A Rendezvous in Averoigne. Introduction by Ray Bradbury. Sauk City, WI: Arkham House, 1988. *Contains:* The Sorcerer Departs (poem); The Holiness of Azédarac; The Colossus of Ylourgne; The End of the Story; A Rendevous in Averoigne; The Last Incantation; The Death of Malygris; A Voyage to Sfanomoë; The Weird of Avoosl Wuthoqquan; The Seven Geases; The Tale of Satampra Zeiros; The Coming of the White Worm; The City of the Singing Flame (restored text); The Dweller in the Gulf; The Chain of Aforgomon; Genius Loci; The Maze of Maâl Dweb; The Vaults of Yoh-Vombis; The Uncharted Isle; The Planet of the Dead; Master of the Asteroid; The Empire of the Necromancers; The Charnel God; Xeethra; The Dark Eidolon; The Death of Ilalotha; The Last Hieroglyph; Necromancy in Naat; The Garden of Adompha; The Isle of the Torturers; Morthylla.

Strange Shadows: The Uncollected Fiction and Essays of Clark Ashton Smith. Ed. Steve Behrends with Donald Sidney-Fryer and Rah Hoffman. New York: Greenwood Press, 1989.

Tales of Zothique. Ed. Will Murray with Steve Behrends. West Warwick, RI: Necronomicon Press, 1995. *Contains:* "Introduction" by Will Murray; The Empire of the Necromancers; The Isle of the Torturers; The Charnel God; The Dark Eidolon; The Voyage of King Euvoran; The Weaver in the Vault; The Tomb-Spawn; The Witchcraft of Ulua; Xeethra; In the Book of Vergama; The Last Hieroglyph; Shapes of Adamant (fragment); Necromancy in Naat; The Black Abbot of Puthuum; The Death of Ilalotha; The Garden of Adompha; Zothique (poem); The Master of the Crabs; Mandor's Enemy (fragment); Morthylla; The Dead Will Cuckold You (play); "Postscript" by Will Murray.

The Book of Hyperborea. Ed. Will Murray. West Warwick, RI: Necronomicon Press, 1996. *Contains:* "Introduction" by Will Murray; The Tale of Satampra Zeiros; The Muse of Hyperborea (prose-poem); The Door to Saturn; The Testament of Athammaus; The Weird of Avoosl Wuthoqquan; Ubbo-Sathla; The Ice-Demon; The White Sybil; The House of Haon-Dor; The Coming of the White Worm; The Seven Geases; Lament for Vixella (poem); The Theft of the Thirty-nine Girdles; Appendix: The Coming of the White Worm (abridged); "Postscript" by Will Murray.

The Black Diamonds. Ed. S. T. Joshi. New York: Hippocampus Press, 2002. A juvenile novel written c. 1907.

Red World of Polaris: The Adventures of Captain Volmar. Ed. Ronald S. Hilger and Scott Connors. San Francisco: Night Shade, 2003. *Contains:* "The Magellan of the Constellations: An Introduction" by Ronald S. Hilger and Scott Connors; Marooned in Andromeda; The Red World of Polaris; A Captivity in Serpens; The Ocean-World of Alioth (fragment). Afterword by Donald Sidney-Fryer.

The Sword of Zagan and Other Writings. Ed. Dr. W. C. Farmer. New York: Hippocampus Press, 2004. Introduction by S. T. Joshi. A collection of mainly juvenile writings, including a 39,000-word novella, nine completed short stories, several fragments, and a number of poems written over Smith's entire lifetime, all taken from papers entrusted by Smith to his friend Dr. William C. Farmer, who also provides an invaluable memoir.

Star Changes. Ed. Scott Connors and Ronald S. Hilger. Seattle: Darkside Press, 2005. *Contains:* "Introduction: The Non-Human Equation" by Scott Connors and Ronald S. Hilger; The Monster of the Prophecy; The Letter from Mohaun Los; The Plutonian Drug; The Immortals of Mercury; The Eternal World; The Demon of the Flower; A Star-Change; The Secret of the Cairn; The Vaults of Yoh-Vombis; The Dweller in the Gulf; Vulthoom; Phoenix.

The Collected Fantasies of Clark Ashton Smith. Edited by Scott Connors and Ronald S. Hilger. San Francisco: Night Shade, 2006f. 5 vols.

C. Nonfiction and Miscellany

The Black Book of Clark Ashton Smith. Sauk City, WI: Arkham House, 1979. Also contains two memoirs by George Haas, "As I Remember Klarkash-Ton" (from Chalker, 1963) and "Memories of Klarkash-Ton" (from Morris, August 1972).

The Devil's Notebook: Collected Epigrams and Pensées of Clark Ashton Smith. Compiled by Donald Sidney-Fryer. Ed. Don Herron. Mercer Island, WA: Starmont House, 1990.

Letters to H. P. Lovecraft. Ed. Steve Behrends. West Warwick, RI: Necronomicon Press, 1987.

Planets and Dimensions: Collected Essays of Clark Ashton Smith. Ed. Charles K. Wolfe. Baltimore: Mirage Press, 1973.

Selected Letters of Clark Ashton Smith. Ed. David E. Schultz and Scott Connors. Sauk City, WI: Arkham House, 2003.

The Shadow of the Unattained: The Letters of George Sterling and Clark Ashton Smith. Ed. S. T. Joshi and David E. Schultz. New York: Hippocampus Press, 2005. Includes a letter about Smith by Ambrose Bierce as well as writings by Sterling and Smith about each other.

II. Secondary Sources

In addition to articles cited in the notes, the following books and articles are useful to the student of Clark Ashton Smith (the most accessible source is usually cited). Many of these pieces, as well as many stories, poems, and other works by Smith may be found at www.eldritchdark.com, Boyd Pearson's Website devoted to Smith. Additional items may be found in Sidney-Fryer's *Emperor of Dreams.*

Ambrose, Michael E. "The Poetry of Clark Ashton Smith: An Introduction." *Dragonbane* 1 (Spring 1978): 48–51. Brief but cogent general essay on Smith as a poet.

Ashley, Mike. "The Perils of Wonder: Clark Ashton Smith's Experiences with *Wonder Stories.*" *Dark Eidolon* No. 2 (July 1989): 2–8.

———, and Robert A. W. Lowndes. *The Gernsback Days.* Holicong, PA: Wildside Press, 2004.

Behrends, Steve. "CAS and Diverse Hands." *Crypt of Cthulhu* No. 26 (Hallowmas 1984): 30–31. Rpt. *The Horror of It All.* Ed. Robert M. Price. Mercer Island, WA: Starmont, 1990. 65–67.

———. *Clark Ashton Smith.* Starmont Reader's Guide 49. Mercer Island, WA: Starmont House, 1990. Only full-length study to date.

———. "Clark Ashton Smith: Cosmicist or Misanthrope?" *Dark Eidolon* No. 2 (July 1989): 12–14.

———, ed. *Klarkash-Ton: The Journal of Smith Studies* No. 1 (June 1988); as *The Dark Eidolon: The Journal of Smith Studies* No. 2 (July 1989) and No. 3 (Winter, 1993).

Originally published by Robert M. Price's Cryptic Publications, then by Necronomicon Press, this regrettably defunct journal provided a forum for both new articles on Smith as well as a source for reprinting important material from the past.

Bell, Joseph, and Roy A. Squires. *The Books of Clark Ashton Smith.* Toronto: Soft Books, 1987. Updates Sidney-Fryer et al. (1978).

Brandenberger, Mary Ann. "Poetic Devices in 'The Empire of the Necromancers.'" *Niekas* No. 45 (1998): 87–89.

Chalker, Jack, ed. *In Memoriam: Clark Ashton Smith.* Baltimore: Anthem, 1963. Contains important articles and tributes by Fritz Leiber, Ethel Heiple, George Haas, Ray Bradbury, Theodore Sturgeon, L. Sprague de Camp, and others.

"Clark Ashton Smith." In *Contemporary Literary Criticism.* Vol. 43. Detroit: Gale Research, 1987. pp. 416–25. Contains excerpts from essays and reviews by Lovecraft, Lin Carter, Benjamin De Casseres, Gahan Wilson, Harlan Ellison, Sam Moskowitz, Charles K. Wolfe, and Steve Behrends.

"Clark Ashton Smith." In *Modern Fantasy Writers.* Ed. Harold Bloom. New York: Chelsea House, 1995. pp. 151–64. Contains excerpts from works by Bierce, Sterling, Donald Wandrei, Lovecraft, Francis T. Laney, Fritz Leiber, Jean Marigny, Ray Bradbury, and others.

Cockcroft, T. G. "The Reader Speaks: Reaction to Clark Ashton Smith in the Pulps." *Dark Eidolon* No. 2 (July 1989): 15–20.

Connors, Scott. "An Arthur Machen Review of Clark Ashton Smith." *Faunus: The Journal of the Friends of Arthur Machen* No. 6 (Autumn 2000): 31–38.

———. "Who Discovered Clark Ashton Smith?" *Lost Worlds* No. 1 (2004): 25–34.

———, and Arinn Dembo. "The Last Continent: An Exchange." *New York Review of Science Fiction* No. 157 (September 2001): 18–19.

———, ed. *Lost Worlds: The Journal of Clark Ashton Smith Studies.* New York: Seele-Brennt Publications. Nos. 1, 2 (2004); No. 3 (forthcoming). Picks up where Klarkash-Ton/Dark Eidolon left off. Covers feature color reproductions of Smith's paintings.

de Camp, L. Sprague. "Sierra Shaman." In *Literary Swordsmen and Sorcerers: The Makers of Heroic Fantasy.* Sauk City, WI: Arkham House, 1976. pp. 195–214.

Ellison, Harlan. "Out of Space and Time by Clark Ashton Smith." In *Horror: 100 Best Books.* Ed. Stephen Jones and Kim Newman. New York: Carroll & Graf, 1998. pp. 135–39.

Galpin, Alfred. "Echoes from Beyond Space." *United Amateur* 24, No. 1 (January 1921): 3–4. Rpt. *Letters to Alfred Galpin* by H. P. Lovecraft. Ed. S. T. Joshi and David E. Schultz. New York: Hippocampus Press, 2003. pp. 273–75.

Hall, Mark. "Clark Ashton Smith Collections in the San Francisco Bay Area, Pt. 1: Letters to Samuel Loveman." *Lost Worlds* No. 2 (2004): 31–38.

Herron, Don. "Collecting Clark Ashton Smith." *Firsts* (October 2000): 26–37.

———. "The Double Shadow: The Influence of Clark Ashton Smith." In *Jack Vance*. Ed. Tim Underwood and Chuck Miller. New York: Taplinger, 1980. pp. 87–102.

Hilger, Ronald S. *One Hundred Years of Klarkash-Ton: The Clark Ashton Smith Centennial Conference*. n.p.: Averon Press, 1996. Record of a conference held in Auburn to commemorate the 100th anniversary of Smith's birth. Includes color reproduction of paintings and carvings by Smith. Also includes memoirs by Violet Nelson Heyer and Robert B. Elder.

———, and Donald Sidney-Fryer. "The Phospor Lamps of Clark Ashton Smith." *Chronicles of the Cthulhu Codex* No. 17 (Winter 2000): 43–51.

Hillman, Arthur F. "The Poet of Science Fiction." *Fantasy Review* No. 14 (April–May 1949). Rpt. *Yawning Vortex* No. 9 (1996): 35–37.

Hussey, Derrick. "Clark Ashton Smith and the Bohemian Club." *Underworlds* No. 1 (December 2002): 91–92.

Joshi, S. T., and Marc A. Michaud. "The Prose and Poetry of Clark Ashton Smith." *Books at Brown* 27 (1979): 81–87.

Leiber, Fritz, "On Fantasy: Lost Fantasies." *Fantasy Newsletter* 5, No. 8 (September 1982): 7–9.

Lovecraft, H. P. *The Annotated Supernatural Horror in Literature*. Ed. S. T. Joshi. New York: Hippocampus Press, 2000. pp. 54–55.

———. Review of *Ebony and Crystal*. *L'Alouette* 1, No. 1 (January 1924): 20–21. In *Collected Essays*. Ed. S. T. Joshi. Vol. 2. New York: Hippocampus Press, 2004. pp. 73–74.

Luserke, Uwe. "Klarkash-Ton: Poet des Monströsen: Leben und Werk des Clark Ashton Smith." *Science Fiction Times* (Germany) 27, No. 3 (March 1985): 4–7.

Lyman, William Whittingham. "Clark Ashton Smith." Unpublished ms., Lyman Family Papers, Bancroft Library, University of California at Berkeley. Brief memoir of Smith and his family in the late 1920s by a friend not associated with fantasy fandom.

Marigny, Jean. "L'Univers fantastique de Clark Ashton Smith." *Caliban* 15, No. 1 (Publications de l'Université de Toulouse-le-Mirail, 1979). Rpt. *Cahier Zothique*. Ed. Jean-Luc Buard. Maurepas, France: Les Presses d'Ananké, 1985. As "Clark Ashton Smith and His World of Fantasy." Trans. S. T. Joshi. *Crypt of Cthulhu* No. 26 (Hallowmas 1984): 3–12.

———. *Les Mondes perdus de Clark Ashton Smith*. Dole, France: La Clef d'Argent, 2004.

Mayer, F. J. "Clark Ashton Smith, Artist and Sculptor." *Fantasy: A Forum for Science Fiction and Fantasy Artists* 2, No. 4 (Winter 1980): 8–11.

Mitchell, Steve. "Secret Worlds Incredible: The Weird Fiction of Clark Ashton Smith." *Paperback Parade* No. 34 (June 1993): 65–84.

———. "The Weird Corner." *Echoes* (December 1991): 20–25.

Morris, Harry, ed. *CAS-Nyctalops*. Albuquerque, NM: Silver Scarab Press, August 1972. Special issue (number 7) of this important and long-running fanzine, with contributions by Robert Bloch, Marvin K. Hiemstra, Frank Belknap Long, George Haas, Dennis Rickard, Charles K. Wolfe, S. J. Sackett, T. G. L. Cockcroft, and many others.

Mullen, Stanley. "Cartouche (Clark Ashton Smith)." *Gorgon* No. 3 (July 1947): 54–58.

Parker, Robert Allerton. "Such Pulps as Dreams Are Made On." *VVV* (1943). Rpt. *Radical America* (January 1970): 70–77. Early positive notice from a surrealist perspective.

Petaja, Emil. "The Man in the Mist." *Mirage* No. 10 (1971): 21–25. Memoir.

Price, E. Hoffmann. *Book of the Dead: Friends of Yesteryear: Fictioneers & Others*. Ed. Peter Ruber. Sauk City, WI: Arkham House, 2001. Contains expanded version of Price's memoir from *TSS*. pp. 94–125.

Rickard, Dennis. *The Fantastic Art of Clark Ashton Smith*. Foreword by Gahan Wilson. Baltimore: Mirage Press, 1973. Contains many photos (unfortunately, black and white) of Smith's paintings and carvings.

Robillard, Douglas. "Clark Ashton Smith." In *Supernatural Fiction Writers*. Ed. E. F. Bleiler New York: Scribner's, 1985. pp. 875–82.

Rockhill, Jim. "The Poetics of Morbidity: The Original Text to Clark Ashton Smith's 'The Maze of Maal Dweb' and Other Works First Published in *The Double Shadow and Other Fantasies*." *Lost Worlds* No. 1 (2004): 20–25.

Ruber, Peter. "Clark Ashton Smith." In *Arkham's Masters of Horror*. Sauk City, WI: Arkham House, 2000. pp. 53–61.

Rubin, Hal. "Clark Ashton Smith: Ill-Fated Master of Fantasy." *Sierra Heritage* 5, No. 1 (June 1985): 34–38. Written by an acquaintance of Smith's, it nonetheless contains several major errors amidst some invaluable contemporary accounts.

Schwartz, Robert. "Clark Ashton Smith: Dunsanian Temporality, Visions and Literary Concepts." *Tales of Horror and Damnation* No. 6 (January 1985): 6–13, 17.

Schweitzer, Darrell. "Clark Ashton Smith: Master of Fantastic Worlds and Muddy Prose." *Space and Time* No. 18 (May 1973): 28–31.

———. "Klarkash-Ton, Sorcerer-Poet." In *The Maker of Gargoyles and Other Stories*. By Clark Ashton Smith. Holicong, PA: Wildside Press, 2004. pp. 7–9.

Sidney-Fryer, Donald. *Clark Ashton Smith: The Sorcerer Departs*. West Hills, CA: Tsathoggua Press, 1997. Reprint of biographical-critical article from Chalker, 1963.

———. "Klarkash-Ton & Ech-Pi El: Or the Alleged Influence of H. P. Lovecraft on Clark Ashton Smith." *Mirage* 1, No. 6 (Winter 1963–64): 30–33.

———. *The Last of the Great Romantic Poets*. Albuquerque, NM: Silver Scarab Press, 1973. Essay-review of Smith's *Selected Poems*.

———. "A Memoir of Timeus Gaylord: Reminiscences of Two Visits with Clark Ashton Smith, &c." *Romantist* 2 (1978): 1–19.

———. "O Amor atque Realitas! Clark Ashton Smith's First Adult Fiction." *Dark Eidolon* No. 3 (Winter 1993): 22–25.

———. "On the Alleged Influence of Lord Dunsany on Clark Ashton Smith." *Amra* No. 23 (January 1963); rpt. *Klarkash-Ton* No. 1 (June 1988): 9–13, 15.

———. "A Statement for Imagination: George Sterling and Clark Ashton Smith." *Romantist* 6–7–8 (1982–83–84): 13–23.

———, and Divers Hands. *Emperor of Dreams: A Clark Ashton Smith Bibliography.* West Kingston, RI: Donald M. Grant, 1978. Also contains memoir-letters by Eric Greene, Rah Hoffman, Genevieve K. Sully, and Ethel Heiple, plus letters of appreciation by such writers as Harlan Ellison, Ray Bradbury, Fritz Leiber, Avram Davidson, and others. The foundation upon which all Smith scholarship rests.

Smith, Andrew. "The Dead Will Cuckold You, in Print and Manuscript, and an Additional Observation." *Dark Eidolon* No. 3 (1993): 20–22.

Smith, Eldred. "The Short Stories of Clark Ashton Smith." *Alien Culture* No. 2 (April 1949): 3–6.

Stableford, Brian, "Clark Ashton Smith." In *Science Fiction Writers*. Ed. E. F. Bleiler. New York: Scribner's, 1982. pp. 139–144.

———. "The Short Fiction of Smith." In *Survey of Modern Fantasy Literature.* Ed. Frank N. Magill. Vol 4. Englewood Cliffs, NJ: Salem Press, 1983. pp. 1692–97.

Stockton, Richard. "Appreciation of the Prose Works of Clark Ashton Smith." *Acolyte* No. 14 (Spring 1946): 6–7. Rpt. *Klarkash-Ton* No. 1 (June 1988): 14–15.

Van Hise, James, ed. *The Fantastic Worlds of Clark Ashton Smith.* Yucca Valley, CA: The Editor, forthcoming. A collection of reprint and original material.

Wandrei, Donald. "Emperor of Dreams." *Overland Monthly* 84 (December 1926): 380–81, 407, 409. Rpt. *Klarkash-Ton* No. 1 (June 1988): 3–8.

Weinberg, Robert. *The Weird Tales Story.* West Linn, OR: FAX Collector's Editions, 1997. Rpt. Holicong, PA: Wildside Press, 1999.

Whitechapel, Simon. "Clark Ashton Smith: Fantasiste or Science Fictioneer?" *Chronicles of the Cthulhu Codex* No. 17 (Winter 2000): 27–36.

Contributors

Steve Behrends discovered Clark Ashton Smith during the Fantasy Boom of the 1970s. Several trips to inspect the Smith Papers at Brown University's John Hay Library eventually led to several projects, culminating in *Strange Shadows* (1989). The *Reader's Guide* was originally to be written with Douglas A. Anderson (*The Annotated Hobbit*), but circumstances necessitated a solo performance; it was written alongside a Ph.D. thesis in experimental particle physics. A pioneer in Clark Ashton Smith studies, he is most proud of the "Unexpurgated Clark Ashton Smith" series, and is grateful to Necronomicon Press's Marc Michaud and artist Bob Knox, his "Athos and Porthos," for their encouragement. He has also written studies of Donald Wandrei and Darrell Schweitzer. He currently works as a Research Fellow in High Energy Physics.

James Blish (1921–1975), while best known as an author of seminal science fiction novels (*A Case of Conscience, Cities in Flight, Black Easter, The Day After Judgment*), was also a scholar of classical literature, scientist (degree in biology), musicologist, historical novelist (*Dr. Mirabilis*), playwright, critic, and poet. During the decade when he was at the top of his creative form, roughly 1949 to 1959, Blish produced a remarkable body of work that contributed a great deal to the definition of American magazine science fiction. Under the pseudonym William Atheling, Jr., he wrote two volumes of seminal science fiction criticism, *The Issue at Hand* (1964) and *More Issues at Hand* (1970).

Carl Jay Buchanan was Associate Editor of English at the University of Tennessee at Martin, and also taught at schools in Dubai, Turkey, and Cyprus. He was the author of a book of poems, *Ripper* (University of South Carolina Press, 1999), and a contributor to such publications as *Lovecraft Studies, Ghost & Scholars Newsletter,* and *Extrapolation*. He passed away suddenly in 2003.

Fred Chappell teaches advanced composition, poetry, and fiction at the University of North Carolina–Greensboro, and also writes about poetry every month as a *News & Observer* book columnist. He has written fourteen books of verse, two volumes of stories, one of criticism and eight novels. In December 1997, Governor Jim Hunt appointed Chappell to the post of Poet Laureate of North Carolina. He was awarded the World Fantasy Award for Best Short Story in 1994 for "The Lodger."

Dan Clore has appeared in such publications as *Lovecraft Studies, Studies in Weird Fiction,* and *Necrofile*, and is the author of a collection of short stories, *The Unspeakable and Others* (2001).

Scott Connors received his B.A. in English and History from Washington and Jefferson College and also studied at the University of Salzburg. He has written for such publications as *Nyctalops, Fantasy Crossroads, Lovecraft Studies, Studies in Weird Fiction, Faunus, Wormwood, The Explicator, Publishers Weekly, Weird Tales,* the anthology *The Barbaric Triumph,* and *Supernatural Literature of the World: An Encyclopedia.* He is the editor of H. P. Lovecraft's *Science Versus Charlatanry* (with S. T. Joshi) and *A Century Less a Dream: Selected Criticism on H. P. Lovecraft.* With Ronald S. Hilger, he is editing a new edition of Smith's short fiction, and is also writing a critical biography of Smith.

Stefan Dziemianowicz is the author of the definitive study of *Unknown Worlds.* He has edited numerous anthologies, including *The Rivals of Weird Tales* and *Weird Tales: 32 Unearthed Terrors,* and was coeditor of *Necrofile: The Review of Horror Fiction.* His articles and reviews have appeared in *Lovecraft Studies, Studies in Weird Fiction, Crypt of Cthulhu, Publishers Weekly,* and S. T. Joshi and David E. Schultz's critical anthology *An Epicure in the Terrible: A Centennial Anthology of Essays in Honor of H. P. Lovecraft* (Fairleigh Dickinson University Presses, 1991). He and Joshi also edited the monumental *Supernatural Literature of the World: An Encyclopedia.*

Phillip A. Ellis is a poet and scholar who is working on a concordance of Clark Ashton Smith's poetry. He is currently involved in bibliographic projects relating to Arthur Machen and Christopher Brennan. He is a citizen of Australia and is studying English, concentrating upon poetry, as an external student.

John Kipling Hitz teaches English in Kentucky. His articles have appeared in *Lovecraft Studies* and *Studies in Weird Fiction.*

Peter H. Goodrich is professor of English and assistant department head at the University of Northern Michigan. He specializes in Arthurian romances and is the author of *The Romance of Merlin* (Garland, 1991) and is editor of *Merlin: A Casebook* (Garland, forthcoming).

Lauric Guillard teaches American literature and civilization at the University of Nantes, France. His Ph.D. dissertation was on *Le Thème du monde perdu dans la littérature de langue anglaise, 1864–1933.* His books include *L'Aventure mysterieuse de Poe à Merritt* (Liege 1993), *Mondes perdus* (Paris, 1993), *Atlantides: Les Iles englouties* (Paris, 1995), and *L'Eternel Deluge: Voyage dans les littératures atlantidiennes* (Paris, 2001).

Ronald S. Hilger lives in Grass Valley, California, not far from Smith's home in Auburn. A longtime admirer of Smith's work, he was largely responsible for the dedication of a plaque honoring Smith at Auburn's Centennial Park, and organized a conference in 1993 devoted to the Smith Centennial Celebration. He edited *The Averoigne Chronicles* (forthcoming from Donald M. Grant) and recovered the manuscript for Smith's story "The Red World of Polaris," long believed to have been lost. With Scott Connors he edited Smith's collections *Red World of Polaris* and *Star Changes,* and is at work on a new edition of Smith's fiction for Night Shade. He is coeditor of the journal *Lost Worlds.*

S. T. Joshi received his A.B. and A.M. degrees from Brown University and is former senior editor of the literary criticism division at Chelsea House Publishers. He is currently a freelance editor and author. Best known for his groundbreaking work on H. P. Lovecraft, he has also edited collections of the work of Ambrose Bierce and H. L. Mencken and is the author of *The Weird Tale* (1990), *H. P. Lovecraft: A Life* (1996), and *God's Defenders: What They Believe and Why They Are Wrong* (2003). With Stefan Dziemianowicz, he edited the three-volume *Supernatural Literature of the World: An Encyclopedia*, published by Greenwood Press in 2005. He has edited or coedited several collections of Smith's work, including *Nostalgia of the Unknown*, the juvenile novel *The Black Diamonds*, *The Last Oblivion*, and *Shadow of the Unattained* (Smith's correspondence with George Sterling), as well as Sterling's *The Thirst of Satan* and *From Baltimore to Bohemia*, the collected correspondence between Sterling and Mencken..

Jim Rockhill has been an avid reader of supernatural fiction since the age of eleven. He has edited the complete supernatural fiction of Joseph Sheridan Le Fanu for Ash-Tree Press (2002–04) and Bob Leman for Midnight House (2002), served as coeditor to Jane Rice's collected weird tales for Midnight House (2003), and assisted with many other volumes, including Battered Silicon Dispatch Box's compilation of the complete adventures of Seabury Quinn's occult detective, Jules de Grandin (2001). His reviews and articles appear in *Supernatural Fiction of the World: An Encyclopedia*, the journals *All Hallows* and *Lost Worlds*, and on the websites "Robert Aickman—An Appreciation" and "The Weird Review." His fiction has begun to appear in the journal *Supernatural Tales* and the *Darkside* anthology series from Roc.

S. J. Sackett was Professor of English at Fort Hays University, Hays, Kansas. A longtime science fiction fan and writer, he visited Smith in the late 1940s. He currently enjoys retirement in Thailand.

Donald Sidney-Fryer, poet and performing artist, is the last in the great line of Californian Romantics (Ambrose Bierce, George Sterling, Nora May French, and Clark Ashton Smith). A pupil of Clark Ashton Smith, Sidney-Fryer has edited *The Selected Poems of Clark Ashton Smith* as well as the Smith story collections *Other Dimensions*, *The City of the Singing Flame*, *The Monster of the Prophecy*, and *The Last Incantation*. Sidney-Fryer also assembled the mordant horror and fantasy poetry of Ambrose Bierce under the title *A Vision of Doom*. He compiled the first full-length bibliography of Clark Ashton Smith, *Emperor of Dreams*, and his own first collection of verse, *Songs and Sonnets Atlantean*, was the final book to appear from Arkham House under the personal supervision of August Derleth, one of the cofounders.

Brian Stableford teaches creative writing at University College, Winchester, and has also lectured in sociology at Reading University. He has published more than 50 novels and 200 short stories as well as numerous nonfiction books and translations from the French. Stableford has completed postgraduate work in biology and sociology and received a Ph.D. for his thesis "The Sociology of Science Fiction." He is the author of *Scientific Romance in Britain 1890–1950* (1985), and he is currently working on a 400,000-word volume for Routledge entitled *Science Fact and Fiction: An Encyclopedia*. His scholarship has been recognized by the J. Lloyd Eaton Award (1987), the Distinguished Scholarship Award of the International Association for the Fantastic in the Arts (1987), the Science Fiction Research Association's Pioneer Award (1996), and the SFRA's Science Fiction Research Association's Pilgrim Award (1999).

Steven Tompkins grew up in West Hartford, Connecticut, and now lives in New York City. He contributed to Wandering Star's *The Illustrated Worlds of Robert E. Howard* and Don Herron's critical anthology *The Barbaric Triumph*, both 2004 publications. He edited *The Black Stranger and Other American Tales*, a collection of Robert E. Howard's New World heroic fantasy and horror stories published in 2005 by Bison Books, an imprint of The University of Nebraska Press.

Charles K. Wolfe was Professor of English at Middle Tennessee State University in Murfreesboro. He edited *Planets and Dimensions: Collected Essays on Clark Ashton Smith* in 1973. He was the author of numerous books on American folk and popular music and had written more than a hundred articles, published in such collections as *The Encyclopedia of Southern Culture*, *Journal of American Folklore*, and *The New Grove Dictionary of American Music*. He was nominated three times for a Grammy Award for his album liner notes and twice won the ASCAP–Deems Taylor Award. He passed away early in 2006.

Acknowledgements

"The Centaur" copyright © 1958 by Clark Ashton Smith for *Spells and Philtres* (Arkham House). Reprinted by permission of Arkham House Publishers Inc. and CASiana Literary Enterprises.

Vachel Lindsay's letter to Clark Ashton Smith is courtesy of the manuscript proprietor, Special Collections of the University of Iowa Library.

Edwin Markham's letter to Clark Ashton Smith is courtesy of John Hay Library, Brown University.

The excerpt of Lovecraft's letter to F. Lee Baldwin is courtesy of the estate of H. P. Lovecraft and John Hay Library, Brown University.

"Klarkash-Ton and 'Greek'" is original to this collection and is copyright © 2006 by Donald Sidney-Fryer.

"Eblis in Bakelite" first appeared in *Tumbrils* 2 (June 1945), and is provided by courtesy of Don Herron.

"James Blish Versus Clark Ashton Smith" copyright © 2004 by Seele Brennt Publications for *Lost Worlds* 1. Reprinted by permission of Donald Sidney-Fryer.

"The Last Romantic" first appeared in *Fantasy Sampler* (June 1956). Reprinted by permission of S. J. Sackett.

"Communicable Mysteries" copyright © 2005 by Seele Brennt Publications for *Lost Worlds* 2. Reprinted by permission of Fred Chappell.

"What Happens in *The Hashish-Eater*?" copyright © 1993 by Necronomicon Press for *The Dark Eidolon* no. 3 (Winter 1993). Reprinted by permission of S. T. Joshi.

"The Babel of Visions" copyright © 1996 by Necronomicon Press for *Studies in Weird Fiction* 18 (Winter 1996). Reprinted by permission of Dan Clore.

"Clark Ashton Smith's 'Nero'" copyright © 2001 by Carl Jay Buchanan. Reprinted by permission of the late Carl Jay Buchanan.

"Satan Speaks: A Reading of 'Satan Unrepentant'" is original to this collection and is copyright © 2006 by Phillip A. Ellis.

"Lands Forgotten or Unfound" is original to this collection and is copyright © 2006 by S. T. Joshi.

"Outside the Human Aquarium" copyright © 1996 by Douglas Robillard for *American Supernatural Fiction From Edith Wharton to the* Weird Tales *Writers* (Garland Publishing, Inc.). Reprinted by permission of Brian Stableford.

"Master of the Macabre" copyright © 1996 by Necronomicon Press for *Studies in Weird Fiction* 19 (Summer 1996). Reprinted by permission of John Kipling Hitz, who revised it for this appearance.

"Gesturing Toward the Infinite" copyright © 2001 by Hippocampus Press for *Studies in Weird Fiction* 25 (Summer 2001). Reprinted by permission of Scott Connors, who revised it for this appearance.

"A Note on the Aesthetics of Fantasy" copyright © 1972 by Harry O. Morris and Edward P. Berglund for *Nyctalops* 7 (August 1972). Reprinted by permission of the late Charles K. Wolfe.

"Fantasy and Decadence" copyright © 2000 by *Paradoxa* 5, No. 13–14. Reprinted by permission of Lauric Guillaud.

"Humor in Hyperspace" is original to this collection and is copyright © 2006 by John Kipling Hitz.

"The Song of the Necromancer" copyright © 1986 by Necronomicon Press for *Studies in Weird Fiction* 1 (Summer 1986). Reprinted by permission of Steve Behrends.

"Brave World Old and New" copyright © 2004 by Seele Brennt Publications for *Lost Worlds* 2. Reprinted by permission of Donald Sidney-Fryer.

"Coming In from the Cold" copyright © 2004 by Seele Brennt Publications for *Studies in Fantasy Literature* 1. Reprinted by permission of Steven Tompkins, who revised it for this appearance.

"As Shadows Wait Upon the Sun" is original to this collection and is copyright © 2006 by Jim Rockhill.

"Sorcerous Style" copyright © 2000 by *Paradoxa* 5, No. 13–14. Reprinted by permission of Peter H. Goodrich.

"Loss and Recuperation" copyright © 1993 by Necronomicon Press for *Studies in Weird Fiction* 13 (Summer 1993). Reprinted by permission of Dan Clore.

"Life, Love and the Clemency of Death" copyright © 2004 by Tartarus Press for *Wormwood* 2 (Spring 2004). Reprinted by permission of Scott Connors.

"Regarding the Providence Point of View" copyright © 1999 by Mythos Books for *Crypt of Cthulhu* 102 (Lammas 1999). Reprinted by permission of Ronald S. Hilger.

"An Annotated Chronology" copyright © 1984 by Cryptic Publications for *Crypt of Cthulhu* 26 (Hallowmas 1984). Reprinted by permission of Steve Behrends.

Index

"Abomination of Desolation, The" 144
"Abominations of Yondo, The" 20, 67, 147, 157, 338
Abominations of Yondo, The 74, 88, 139, 148
Ackerman, Forrest J. 76, 84n1
Acolyte 309
"Adventure in Futurity, An" 340
After Sunset (Sterling) 17
Aickman, Robrt 281
Aiken, Conrad 95, 97, 191
"Albatros, L'" (Baudelaire) 94
Album dit "Zutique" (Rimbaud) 161
Alice in Wonderland (Carroll) 197
"Alienage" 97
Allen, Hervey 325
Allen, Robert 131n3
"Amazing Planet, The" 340
Amazing Stories 150, 190, 195, 199
American Mercury 153
"Amithaine" 86, 198
"Amor Hesternalis" 255
Anderson, Sherwood 195
"Annabel Lee" (Poe) 53, 172
Anubis 257
"Après-midi d'un faune, L'" (Mallarmé) 94
Arabian Nights 32, 57, 152, 201, 278, 288, 321, 322
Argonaut 53, 60, 129–30
"Argument of 'The Hashish-Eater'" 99, 100, 105, 108, 110
Arkham Collector 258n4
Arkham House 8, 9, 32, 61, 72, 74, 86, 88, 148, 153, 177, 250, 251, 252, 257, 307
Arnold, Matthew 188, 283
"Arria Marcella" (Gautier) 158
Arts and Decoration 27
"Asharia: A Tale of the Lost Planet" 345
Ashley, Mike 308
"At the Grand Cañon" (Sterling) 183
At the Mountains of Madness (Lovecraft) 208
Atlantis 88, 158, 171, 210, 212, 239–58,
307, 311
"Atlantis" 240–41
Auburn Journal 24, 27–28, 58, 64, 66, 70n20, 74, 78, 246, 247, 307
Auden, W. H. 271
Averoigne 7, 61, 69n18, 72, 88, 98, 157, 158, 162, 171, 174, 225, 279, 286, 293–304, 307, 313, 340
"Averoigne" 86
"Avowal" 255–56

Babbitt, Irving 185, 188–89, 191, 192
Baird, Edwin 67
Baldwin, F. Lee 335
"Ballad of the Gallows Bird, The" (Markham) 153
Ballantine Books 9, 148, 277, 336
Balzac, Honoré de 224, 319
Barbarese, J. T. 184
Barker, Eric 252–54, 257
Barlow, R. H. 72, 199, 266
"Barrier, The" 94
Barth, John 196
Barthes, Roland 319–20, 323
Baudelaire, Charles 27, 28, 29, 60, 61, 66–67, 73, 80, 85, 93, 94–95, 96, 97, 98, 109, 122, 125, 138, 139, 153, 154, 155, 156, 168, 205, 222, 290, 305
Bear, Greg 267
"Beast-Jewel of Mars, The" (Brackett) 269
"Beast of Averoigne, The" 158, 174, 285, 295, 297, 301–3, 342
Beatles, The 274
Beckford, William 72, 168, 278, 305
Beddoes, Thomas Lovell 282
Behrends, Steve 9, 106–7, 148, 170, 172, 224, 260, 261, 277, 283, 293, 294, 300, 304, 305, 334
Bender, Albert 25–26, 64
Benediktsson, Thomas 20, 180–81, 331
Benét, William Rose 8, 57, 61
Beowulf 264

Bertrand, Aloysius 80, 81, 138, 139, 156
"Beyond the Black River" (Howard) 274
Beyond the Breakers and Other Poems (Sterling) 16, 23, 33
"Beyond the Great Wall" 56, 204
"Beyond the Rose-Arbor" 345
"Beyond the Singing Flame" 161, 165, 177, 341
Bierce, Ambrose 8, 13, 14, 15, 20, 21, 24, 26, 28, 61, 70n19, 77, 146, 149, 153, 168, 181, 182, 187, 189, 195, 199, 202, 222, 223
Binding of the Beast and Other War Verse, The (Sterling) 16
Björkman, Edwin 38
"Black Abbot of Puthuum, The" 176, 284, 285, 289, 344
Black Book, The 189, 308, 309, 313–14
Black Cat 157
"Black Cat, The" (Poe) 175
"Black Lake, The" 80, 146
"Black Thirst" (Moore) 269
Blackwood, Algernon 126, 177
Blake, William 85, 120
Blavatsky, Helena P. 240, 251, 278, 336
Bleiler, E. F. 206, 217
Blessing of Pan, The (Dunsany) 210
Blish, James 76–84
Bloch, Robert 7
Bohemian Club 16, 17, 24
"Bond" 254–55
Bonnet, Theodore 22
Book Club of California 16, 24
Book of Eibon 215, 336
Book of the Damned, The (Lee) 272
Book of Hyperborea, The 334, 337
Book of Wonder, The (Dunsany) 201
Borel, Petrus 153
Borges, Jorge Luis 119, 196
Bosch, Hieronymus 208, 217
Boston Evening Transcript 51
Boucher, Anthony 61
Brackett, Leigh 269
Bradbrook, M. C. 281
Bradbury, Ray 189
Braithwaite, William Stanley 51
Bridges, Robert 38
Browne, Sir Thomas 73, 81, 83, 87, 282

Browning, Robert 38, 41, 129, 330
Bryant, William Cullen 202
Bullough, Edward 225
Burleson, Donald R. 188, 201
Burroughs, Edgar Rice 149, 198
"Butterfly, The" 37, 42
Bynner, Witter 8, 22–23, 38, 192
Byron, George Gordon, Lord 39, 41, 122, 125, 153, 314

Cabell, James Branch 71, 82, 201, 291, 319
Caged Eagle and Other Poems, The (Sterling) 16
"Cairn on the Headland, The" (Howard) 267
California the Wonderful (Markham) 63
Campbell, Joseph 198, 327
Cantos, The (Pound) 30, 73
Carman, Bliss 57, 95
Carroll, Lewis 43
Carter, Lin 196, 261, 277, 336, 337
"Cask of Amontillado, The" (Poe) 223
Cassidy, B. A. 27
Castle of Otranto, The (Walpole) 201
Catholic Encyclopedia 125
Catholicism 154
"Cats of Ulthar, The" (Lovecraft) 201
Catullus, C. Valerius 184
Cawthorn, James 260, 277, 286
"Celephaïs" (Lovecraft) 201
"Chain of Aforgomon, The" 171, 175–76, 209, 231, 232–33, 238, 344
Chambers, Robert W. 149, 158
"Chant d'Automne" (Baudelaire) 95
"Chant of Autumn" 73, 81, 204
"Charnel God, The" 88, 162, 207, 283, 285, 343
Chatterton, Thomas 41, 202
"Checkmate" 340
Chevalier, Jean 326
"Chincharerro" 345
"Chinoiserie" 144–45
"Christabel" (Coleridge) 90
Christgau, Robert 274
Christianity 51, 109, 110, 117, 132–37, 285, 295–96, 297–98
Churchward, James 241

"City of Destruction, The" (poem) 141
"City of Destruction, The" (prose poem) 140–41
"City of the Singing Flame, The" 66, 69n18, 79, 161, 165, 170, 189, 198, 211, 223, 236–37, 238, 335, 340
"City of the Titans, The" 93, 203
"City on Mallington Moor, The" (Dunsany) 211
"Clarimonde" (Gautier) 158
Clark Ashton Smith (Behrends) 277, 283
"Clark Ashton Smith: An Appreciation" (Leiber) 274
"Clark Ashton Smith: Emperor of Shadows" (De Casseres) 74
"Clark Ashton Smith's Column" 27
Clarke, Arthur C. 216
"Clean, Well-Lighted Place, A" (Hemingway) 305
Cline, Leonard 9
"Cloud-Islands, The" 34–35, 37, 67n2, 240
Coleridge, Samuel Taylor 15, 53, 85, 86, 90, 126, 179
Collins, Charles M. 174
"Colossus of Ylourgne, The" 62, 79, 139, 158, 174–75, 286, 295, 297, 300–301, 342
"Colour out of Space, The" (Lovecraft) 318
Comédie de la mort, La (Gautier) 153
"Coming of the White Worm, The" 88, 159, 207, 213, 267–68, 270, 274, 293, 336, 343
"Coming Singer, The" (Sterling) 33
Complete Pegāna, The (Dunsany) 261
Confessions of an English Opium-Eater (De Quincey) 109
Connors, Scott 84n1, 130, 222, 289, 305, 307
"Constellations of the Law, The." *See* "Ministers of the Law, The"
Contes cruels (Villiers de l'Isle-Adam) 325
Coolbrith, Ida Donna 13, 18
"Copy of Burns, A" 339
"Corpse and the Skeleton, The" 141–42
Cosmopolitan 15, 21, 152, 182, 187, 239
Cowley, Malcolm 180

Crabbe, George 90
Crane, Stephen 181, 198
"Creating the Modern Romance Epic" (Douglass) 271
Critias (Plato) 212, 239
Crocker, Templeton 25
Cross, Thomas 71
"Crystals, The" 80
Culler, Jonathan 318, 319
Current Opinion 180
"Cycles" 256

Dali, Salvador 217
Dante Alighieri 120, 208, 315, 342
d'Arcy, Ella 209–10
"Dark Age, The" 212, 343
Dark Chateau, The 86, 250, 252, 281
"Dark Eidolon, The" 70n18, 79, 162–63, 171, 283, 285–86, 288, 343
"Dark Muse, The" (Wagner) 266
"Dart of Rasasfa, The" 344
Davidson, Cathy N. 187
Davidson, John 38
"Dawn of Discord" 344
"Days, The" 140
Dead Will Cuckold You, The 171, 247, 263, 277, 281, 290
"Death of Ilalotha, The" 162, 164, 209, 283, 289, 344
"Death of Malygris, The" 88, 158, 207, 248, 343
Decadents, Symbolists, and Aesthetes in America (Foster) 95
de Camp, L. Sprague 7, 69n18, 151, 231, 260, 278
De Casseres, Benjamin 7, 27, 71, 74, 75, 77, 81, 85, 221, 291
"Decay of Lying, The" (Wilde) 206
"Dejection: An Ode" (Coleridge) 126
de la Ree, Gerry 307
"Demoiselle d'Ys, The" (Chambers) 158
"Demon, the Angel, and Beauty, The" 139, 141, 144
"Demon of the Flower, The" 88, 146, 155, 210, 217, 341
De Quincey, Thomas 81, 109
Derleth, August 8, 61, 73, 74, 191, 225
Descartes, René 186

"Desdichado, El" (Gérard de Nerval) 202
"Desert Places" (Frost) 192
"Desolation" 97
Devil's Dictionary, The (Bierce) 28
Devil's Law Case, The (Webster) 277
Devil's Notebook, The 28, 259
"Devotee of Evil, The" 165, 166, 176, 307, 308, 314–15, 339
Diablerie 76
"Didus Ineptus" 94
"Dimension of Chance, The" 160, 342
"Disinterment of Venus, The" 62, 158, 209, 295, 297, 301, 342
"Dissidence" 246, 249
"Diversity" 246
"Djinn without a Bottle" 345
"Dominium in Excelsis" 250
Donne, John 185
"Doom That Came to Sarnath, The" (Lovecraft) 201
"Door to Saturn, The" 88, 159, 224, 266, 269–70, 339
Doré, Gustave 208
Dorman, Carol Jones 170, 231, 254
"Double Cosmos" 344
"Double Shadow, The" 158, 168, 171, 189, 206, 207, 248, 307, 308, 311–13, 338, 342
Double Shadow and Other Fantasies, The 78, 88, 286, 305–17, 341
Douglass, Sara 271
Dowson, Ernest 38
"Dream Bridge, The" 35
"Dream-Land" (Poe) 168
"Dream of Beauty, A" 38–39
"Dream of King Karna-Vootra, The" (Dunsany) 210
"Dream of Beauty, A" 236
"Dream of Lethe, A" 144
Dream-Quest of Unknown Kadath, The (Lovecraft) 201
Dreamer's Tales, A (Dunsany) 201
Dreiser, Theodore 87, 181, 190, 195
Dryden, John 130
Duchess of Malfi, The (Webster) 285
Du Maurier, George 40
Duncan, Isadora 18

Dunlap, Boutwell 22, 152
Dunsany, Lord 62, 69n18, 103, 201, 202, 206, 210, 211, 261, 274, 280, 289, 291
Durand, G. 208
"Dweller in the Gulf, The" 160, 197, 198, 206, 211, 308, 342
Dziemianowicz, Stefan 174

Eagleton, Terry 184, 186
"Eblis in Bakelite" (Blish) 76–84
Ebony and Crystal 20, 22, 24, 26, 27, 28, 29, 32, 53–60, 74, 78, 80, 81, 139, 152, 155, 180, 183, 184, 202, 203, 224, 241, 243, 254, 336
Eddison, E. R. 201
"Eggs from Saturn, The" 340
"Eidolon of the Blind, The" 308
"Eldritch Dark, The" 95
"Eleanora" (Poe) 80
Eliot, T. S. 30, 85, 86, 97, 131, 172, 184–86, 187, 188, 189, 260
Elliot, Hugh 186
Elliott, William Foster 58
Ellison, Ralph 189
"Empire of the Necromancers, The" 161, 171, 209, 214, 236, 277, 283, 284, 288, 326, 341
Emperor of Dreams: A Clark Ashton Smith Bibliography (Sidney-Fryer) 9, 74, 84n1, 256, 335
"Enchanted Mirrors" 90, 245–46, 328
"Enchantress of Sylaire, The" 162, 253, 295, 300, 344
"End of the Story, The" 157, 162, 174, 197, 198, 207, 209, 238, 293–94, 295, 296, 297, 299–300, 338, 340
"Ennui" (poem) 97
"Ennui" (prose poem) 146, 155
"Envoys, The" 170
"Epiphany of Death, The" 209, 339
"Eternal World, The" 62, 160, 212, 216, 341
Eureka (Poe) 156
Evanescent City, The (Sterling) 16
"Eviction by Night" 344
Experiments in Haiku 32

"Face by the River, The" 340

Faerie Queene, The (Spenser) 79, 203, 248
Fait, Eleanor 70n22
"Fall of the House of Usher, The" (Poe) 173, 177, 313, 318
Fantastic Fables (Bierce) 146
Fantasy: The 100 Best Books (Cawthorn-Moorcock) 277
Fantasy Fan 72, 195
Fantasy Fiction 31
Fantasy Review 62
Farber, Marjorie 186
"Father Coyote" (Sterling) 23
"Fears in Solitude" (Coleridge) 90
Figures of Earth (Cabell) 201
Fionavar Tapestry, The (Kay) 272
FitzGerald, Edward 29, 40
"Flamingoes" 55
Flaubert, Gustave 83, 120, 168, 206
Fleurs du mal, Les (Baudelaire) 29, 153, 314
Flint, F. S. 184
"Flower-Devil, The" 139–40, 146, 155, 230
"Flower-Women, The" 88, 161, 207, 210, 343
"For Annie" (Poe) 53
"For Iris" 231
"Forbidden Forest, The" 146
"Forgotten Sorrow" 245
Foster, Edward 95
"Fra Lippo Lippi" (Browning) 129
"Fragment, A" 55–56
France, Anatole 154, 158
"France: An Ode" (Coleridge) 90
French, Nora May 13, 202, 257n1
Fresno Bee 69n17
"From a Letter" 144, 244
"From the Crypts of Memory" 80, 142, 145, 155, 205, 206, 235–36, 282
"From the Persian" 78
Frost, Robert 184, 192
Frye, Northrop 323, 326, 327, 328, 329
Fugitives, The 247
"Function of Criticism, The" (Eliot) 185

"Garden and the Tomb, The" 142–43
"Garden of Adompha, The" 164, 169, 171, 283, 289, 344

Garden of Cyrus, The (Browne) 81
Garnett, Porter 34, 258n1
Gaspard de la nuit (Bertrand) 138, 156
Gaspard du Nord 139, 175
Gautier, Théophile 109, 153, 154, 158, 205
"Géante, La" (Baudelaire) 94, 290
"Genius Loci" 177–78, 298, 343
Genius Loci and Other Tales 62–63, 88, 148
George Sterling (Benediktsson) 20
"George Sterling—An Appreciation" 21
Gérard de Nerval 153, 154, 189, 202
Gernsback, Hugo 160, 293, 308, 341, 342
"Ghoul, The" 207, 230, 280, 340
"Ghoul and the Seraph, The" 141
Gladstone, William Ewart 40
Gods of Pegāna, The (Dunsany) 201, 289
Golden Whales of California (Lindsay) 70n22
"Good Embalmer, A" 340
Goodrich, Peter 189
"Gorgon, The" 178, 207, 340
Gourmont, Remy de 154
"Great God Awto, The" 226, 344
"Great God Pan, The" (Machen) 341
Greene, Madelynne 252–54, 256, 257
Gross, Dalton 68n5
Guillaud, Lauric 254

Haeckel, Ernst 182
"Hamlet and His Problems" (Eliot) 185
Harding, D. W. 192
Harte, Bret 13
Harvey, Ryan 263, 267
Hasheesh Eater, The (Ludlow) 109
"Hashish Club, The" (Gautier) 109
Hashish-Eater, The 8, 21, 25, 26, 29, 31, 57, 73, 81, 83, 91, 99–123, 133, 155, 186, 202, 243, 244, 336
Havens, Frank C. 13
Havens, Mrs. Frank C. 15
Hawkes, John 196
Hawthorne, Nathaniel 197, 200
Hearn, Lafcadio 168
Hearst, William Randolph 71, 182
Heller, Terry 225
Hemingway, Ernest 82, 86, 87, 195, 305
Henley, W. E. 38

Heredia, José-Maria de 153
Hermaphrodite and Other Poems, The (Loveman) 74
Hero with a Thousand Faces, The (Campbell) 198
Herodotus 83
Herron, Don 28, 84n1, 257, 275, 331–32
"Hertha" (Swinburne) 117
Hesperides 240
Hiemstra, Marvin R. 9, 171
Hilger, Ronald Scott 84n1, 222, 257, 289
Hill of Dionysus, The 32, 252, 253, 254, 257
Hill of Dreams, The (Machen) 91
Hillman, Arthur F. 62
Hippocampus Press 90
Hitchcock, Alfred 325
Hodgson, William Hope 166, 195, 218
Hoffman, Rah 148, 257
"Holiness of Azédarac, The" 88, 158, 162, 174, 222, 295, 297, 298, 299, 301, 341
"Hollow Men, The" (Eliot) 260
Holt, Henry 27, 184
Homer 126
"House of Haon-Dor, The" 263, 337, 343
"House of the Monoceros" 344
House of Orchids, The (Sterling) 16, 21, 183
Housman, A. E. 38
Howard, Robert E. 7, 148, 149, 150, 152, 170, 176, 200, 201, 202, 210, 216, 217, 263, 267, 269, 274, 275, 291
Howells, William Dean 138, 187
Hugo, Victor 153
Hume, David 186
Huneker, James 95
"Hunters from Beyond, The" 165, 177, 206, 340
Huysmans, Joris-Karl 154
Hydriotaphia (Browne) 73, 81, 282
"Hymne à la beauté" (Baudelaire) 96
Hyperborea 7, 30, 61, 70n18, 98, 158–59, 161, 162, 171, 197, 208, 212, 213, 215, 216, 217, 225, 234, 239, 248, 259–76, 278, 279, 284, 286, 293, 299, 308, 334, 336, 337
Hyperborea 148, 336, 337
"Hyperion" (Keats) 129

"I Am a Witch" 345
"Ice-Demon, The" 79, 159, 213, 270, 271, 274, 342
Iliad (Homer) 126, 128
Illuminations (Rimbaud) 156
"Images" 139, 140
"Imagination" 91
"Immeasurable Horror, The" 160, 339
"Immortals of Mercury, The" 341
"In a Hashish-Dream" 345
"In Cocaigne" 144, 156
"In Lemuria" 242–43
"In November" 73, 81
"In Saturn" 92
"In Slumber" 93
Incantations 32
Infernal Star, The 176, 343
Inferno (Dante) 120, 208
Ingersoll, Robert G. 57
"Insurrection of the Peasantry, An" (Bierce) 187
"Invisible City, The" 341
"Invitation au voyage, L'" (Baudelaire) 96, 156
Irving, Washington 197
"Isle of the Torturers, The" 162, 173, 209, 214–15, 283, 284–85, 288, 324–33, 342
Ives, Charles 70n22

Jagger, Mick 274
James, E. Olon 70n22
James, Henry 207, 318
James, M. R. 177, 195
James, William 109
Jasmine Girdle, The 32, 254
Jeffers, Robinson 17, 19, 190, 196
Jesus Christ 327, 329, 331, 332
Johnson, Samuel 283
Jones, Howard 267
Jordan, David Starr 77
Joshi, S. T. 68n5, 90, 96, 110, 186, 225, 261
Joyce, James 131n2
Juday, Chauncey 64
Jung, Carl 111
Jury, John 46

"Justice of the Elephant, The" 340
Juvenal (D. Junius Juvenalis) 283

Kafka, Franz 209
Kay, Guy Gavriel 272, 273
Keats, John 41, 43, 53, 54, 57, 85, 86, 91, 122, 127, 129, 130, 158, 234, 290
Khayyam, Omar 29
"Kindred" (Sterling) 183
King of Elfland's Daughter, The (Dunsany) 201
"Kingdom of the Worm, The" 72, 74, 78
Kipling, Rudyard 53
Kirk, George 67
Kirk, Tim 257
"Kiss of Zoraida, The" 340
Knopf, Alfred A. 26
Knowledge and Experience in the Philosophy of F. H. Bradley (Eliot) 185
Kocher, Paul H. 272
"Kortirion among the Trees" (Tolkien) 272
"Kubla Khan" (Coleridge) 15, 57, 90
Kubrick, Stanley 216
Kurzweil, Ray 309

Lafler, Harry Anderson 23, 258n1
"Lament of the Stars, The" 43
"Lamia" (Keats) 97, 158
Lanier, Sidney 73, 130
"Last Hieroglyph, The" 215, 216, 217, 224, 283, 284, 288–89, 344
"Last Incantation, The" 88, 158, 169, 206, 209, 232, 233, 237, 247, 293, 338
Last Incantation, The 120
"Last Night, The" 277
"Last Oblivion, The" 97
Last Oblivion, The 90
Leaves 72
Leavis, F. R. 185
Leconte de Lisle, Charles Marie René 153
Led Zeppelin 274
Lee, Tanith 272
Leiber, Fritz 77, 84n1, 230–31, 260, 267, 274, 275
Leiber, Jonquil 77
Lemuria 241–42, 246
"Lemurienne" 246

"Léthé, La" (Baudelaire) 95
"Letter from Mohaun Los, The" 160, 216, 224, 340
Lévi-Strauss, Claude 128
"Light from Beyond, The" 161, 170, 206, 211–12, 216, 236, 237, 342, 343
"Like Mohammed's Tomb" 340
Lilith (Sterling) 17, 20, 330–31
Lindsay, Vachel 8, 65, 77
"Litany of the Seven Kisses, The" 139, 140, 143
Literary Review (New York Evening Post) 64
"Live Oak Leaf, A" 35
Locke, John 186
London, Jack 13, 14, 18, 20, 267
Longfellow, Henry Wadsworth 181
Lord of the Rings, The (Tolkien) 271, 318, 323
Lorrain, Jean 154
Lost Tales (Tolkien) 272
Lost Worlds 74, 78, 88, 148, 186, 197, 234
"Love Malevolent" 97
"Love-Potion, The" 247
Lovecraft, H. P. 8, 61, 72, 74, 81, 148–49, 191, 200, 201, 269, 274, 318, 328, 341; on CAS, 65–67, 71, 77, 178, 217–18, 305; CAS's relation's with, 7, 96–96, 107, 152, 166, 195, 291; correspondence with CAS, 9, 14, 70n22, 168, 170, 185, 224, 232, 259, 278, 279, 280, 282, 303, 307; influence on CAS, 62, 69n18, 158, 159, 160, 165, 182, 208, 215, 222, 288, 293, 334–37, 338, 339
Loveman, Samuel 65, 71, 74, 77, 96, 282
Lowell, Amy 95
Lowell, James Russell 181
Ludlow, Fitz-Hugh 109
Lumley, Brian 264
"Luna Aeternalis" 86
Lundborg, Florence 24
Lusitania 16
Lyric Year 68n5

Macbeth (Shakespeare) 285
MacEwan, Gwendolyn 273
Machen, Arthur 61, 77, 91, 215, 341
"Macrocosmic Horror" 261

Magazine of Fantasy and Science Fiction 82–83
"Maker of Gargoyles, The" 175, 295, 296, 299, 341
"Maker of Prodigies" 345
"Malediction" 250, 252
Maliano 76
Mallarmé, Stéphane 81, 93, 94, 96, 168
"Man against the Sky, The" (Robinson) 129
"Man with the Hoe, The" (Markham) 71, 85
"Mandor's Enemy" 345
Mandeville, Sir John 72, 83, 120, 269
"Mandrakes, The" 175, 295, 297, 298–99
Marigny, Jean 174, 212
Markham, Edwin 8, 63–65, 70n22, 71, 77, 85, 90, 153
Marlowe, Christopher 259
"Marooned on Andromeda" 160, 339
Mars 308
Martin, George R. R. 272, 273–74
Martin, John 64
Martin Eden (London) 14
Marvell, Andrew 260
"Masque of Forsaken Gods, The" 43–44, 47, 51, 141
"Masque of the Red Death, The" (Poe) 80, 156, 162, 173, 223, 324–25
"Massacre at Piedmont, The" (Milton) 72, 79
"Master of the Asteroid, The" 198, 342
"Master of the Crabs, The" 164, 289, 344
Masters, Edgar Lee 57
Materer, Timothy 185
Maupassant, Guy de 86
Mauss, Marcel 311, 312, 316
"Maze of Maâl Dweb, The" 88, 217, 285, 342–43
"Maze of the Enchanter, The" 88, 161, 206, 307, 310–11
"Medusa" 42, 73, 74–75, 81, 229
"Medusa of Despair, The" 75
"Memnon at Midnight" 141
"Memnons of the Night, The" 80, 140, 141, 205, 212
Memory, Sorrow and Thorn (Williams) 273
Mencken, H. L. 20, 26–27, 85, 181

Mendès, Catulle 96, 154
Meredith, George 38
Mérimée, Prosper 158
Merrill, Stuart 80, 95, 138, 139
Merritt, A. 161
"Mesmeric Revelation" (Poe) 156
"Messengers, The" 170
"Metamorphosis of Earth, The" 339
Michaud, Marc A. 139
Michaud, Susan 139
Middleton, Richard 38
Millay, Edna St. Vincent 192
Miller, Joaquin 13, 14
Milton, John 41, 53, 72, 79, 80, 85, 91, 122, 125, 127, 128, 129, 130, 132, 186
"Ministers of the Law, The" 72n, 79–80
"Minotaur's Brother, The" 345
"Mirror in the Hall of Ebony, The" 144
"Mirrors" 241–42
"Mirrors of Tuzun Thune, The" (Howard) 216
"Mithridate, The" 144
"Mnemoka" 237–38, 345
Modern Science and Materialism (Elliot) 186
"Mohammed's Tomb" 280
Monroe, Harriet 52, 70n22, 183–84, 186, 189, 191
"Monster of the Prophecy, The" 62, 69n18, 160–61, 227–28, 339
"Monsters in the Night." *See* "Prophecy of Monsters, A"
"Moon Pool, The" (Merritt) 161
"Moonlight Desert, The" 93
"Moonslave, The" (Wilde) 210
Moorcock, Michael 260, 277, 286
Moore, C. L. 269
Morris, William 201, 323
"Morthylla" 174, 207, 209, 283, 290, 344
"Motes, The" 112
"Mother of Toads" 225–26, 299, 344
"Ms. Found in a Bottle" (Poe) 169
Mu 241, 278
Mullen, Stanley 8
Munchhausen, Baron von 269
"Murder in the Fourth Dimension, A" 339
Murray, Will 225, 261, 277, 283, 289, 334, 335–36, 337

"Muse of Hyperborea, The" 145
"Music of Death" 345
Musset, Alfred de 154
Mutabilitie Cantos (Spenser) 79
"Mystic Meaning, The" 43

"Nameless Offspring, The" 298, 341
Nathan, George Jean 27
"Necromancy" 97
"Necromancy in Naat" 163–64, 176, 207, 215, 283, 289, 344
"Necromantic Tale, The" 339
Necronomicon (Alhazred) 336, 340
Necronomicon Press 139, 148, 334
"Nemesis of the Unfinished" 344
"Nero" 36, 39, 42, 48, 58, 91, 124–31, 132, 133, 139, 154, 155
Nero and Other Poems 74, 75, 80
New Directions 77
New York Times Book Review 50, 186
New Yorker 27
"Night in Malnéant, A" 172, 307, 313, 338
Night Land, The (Hodgson) 218n6
Night Thoughts (Young) 42, 153
"Nightmare Tarn, The" 90, 173
1984 (Orwell) 329
"Ninth Skeleton, The" 157, 209, 223, 247, 335, 338
"Nirvana" 40, 51
"No Stranger Dream" 90
Norris, Frank 181
Nostalgia of the Unknown 139, 146

Oakland Enquirer 330
"Ocean-World of Alioth, The" 340
O'Day, Edward F. 22, 330
"Ode on a Grecian Urn" (Keats) 129
"Ode on Imagination" 36–37, 68n11, 155
"Ode on Melancholy" (Keats) 290
"Ode on the Centenary of the Birth of Robert Browning" (Sterling) 68n5
Ode on the Opening of the Panama-Pacific International Exposition (Sterling) 16
"Ode to a Nightingale" (Keats) 290
"Ode to Music" 68nn10, 13
"Ode to the Abyss" 38, 43, 51, 91, 142

Odes and Sonnets 24, 25, 64, 74, 75, 152
"Of Corsets and Flea-Traps" (Maliano) 76
"Offering" 140
"Offering to the Moon, An" 169, 212, 215, 340
"Offspring of the Grave" 345
O'Keefe, Daniel 313
"On Fairy Stories" (Tolkien) 150
"On Re-reading Baudelaire" 97
Ong, Walter 309
Orwell, George 329
O'Sheel, Shamus 50
"Osprey and the Shark, The" 146
Other Dimensions 74, 148, 197
"Other Gods, The" (Lovecraft) 201
Out of Space and Time 61–62, 74, 78, 88, 139, 148, 158, 168, 338
Outsider and Others, The (Lovecraft) 8
Overland Monthly 19, 21, 157, 182, 338
"Ozymandias" (Shelley) 127, 141

"Pagan, The" 94
"Painter in Darkness, The" 344
Palmer, Frederic 51
Palmer, Mary 51
Panama-Pacific International Exposition 16, 17, 24
Paradis Artificiels, Les (Baudelaire) 109
Paradise Lost (Milton) 64, 79, 125, 128, 133–34
Paradise Regain'd (Milton) 79
Parker, Robert Allerton 8
"Parrot in the Pawn-Shop, The" 339
Partch, Virgil 76
Pascal, Blaise 154
"Passing of Aphrodite, The" 80, 212
Pastels in Prose (Merrill) 80, 139
Peirce, C. S. 187
"Peril That Lurks among Ruins, The" 143, 145
"Perverted Village, The" (Bierce) 182
Petits poèmes en prose (Baudelaire) 138, 156
"Phantasy, A" 143
"Phantoms of the Fire, The" 223, 338
Phelan, James Duvall 25, 26
"Philosophy of the Weird Tale" 308–9
"Phoenix" 217, 344

"Pickman's Model" (Lovecraft) 165
"Pine Needles" 35–36, 44
"Planet Entity, The" 224
"Planet of the Dead, The" 145, 155, 165–66, 282, 339
"Planets and Dimensions" 197
Plato 212, 239, 240, 243, 244, 246, 248
"Pleasure and Pain" (Sterling) 331
"Plutonian Drug, The" 211, 342
Poe, Edgar Allan 21, 29, 53, 58, 61, 72, 73, 79, 80, 81, 85, 86, 87, 119, 122, 124, 125, 138, 149, 152, 153, 156, 162, 168, 170, 171, 172, 173, 175, 176, 179, 181, 195, 200, 202, 203, 207, 209, 222, 223, 231, 280, 305, 313, 314, 318, 324, 332
"Poem of Hashish, The" (Baudelaire) 109
Poems (Palmer-Palmer) 51
Poems in Prose 139, 148
Poems to Vera (Sterling) 17
Poetry: A Magazine of Verse 52, 70n22, 183, 191
"Poets of the Pacific Coast, The" (Sterling) 68n5
"Polaris" (Lovecraft) 201
Pope, Alexander 130
Poseidonis 98, 171, 212, 248, 251, 257, 279, 293, 299, 307, 336
"Poseidonis" 240
Poseidonis 148
Posey, Stephen 324
Pound, Ezra 30, 85, 130, 183, 184, 188
"Pour chercher du nouveau" 97
"Precept, A" 54
"Preference" 140
"Premature Burial, The" (Poe) 173
Price, E. Hoffmann 226, 344
"Price, The" 36
"Price of Poetry, The" (Ryder) 74, 89n1
"Primal City, The" 169, 206, 212, 344
"Princess Almeena, The" 146
Prometheus Unbound (Shelley) 121
"Prophecy of Monsters, A" 82, 164, 344
"Prophet Speaks, The" 252

"Queen of the Sabbath" 345
"Quest of Iranon, The" (Lovecraft) 201, 288

Rabelais, François 269
Racine, Jean 154
Rancy, Catherine 200, 211, 215
"Raven, The" (Poe) 313
"Rebirth of the Flame, The" 341
"Red World of Polaris, The" 170, 221–22, 223, 339
Redon, Odilon 202
"Refuge of Beauty, The" 97
Regnier, Henri de 96
"Remembered Light" 183
"Remorse of the Dead, The" 94
"Rendezvous in Averoigne, A" 174, 206, 293, 294, 298, 340
Rendezvous in Averoigne, A 307
"Requiescat" 72, 79
"Resurrection" 254
"Resurrection of the Rattlesnake, The" 207, 223, 338
"Retrospect and Forecast" 35, 48
"Return of the Sorcerer, The" 9, 298, 340
"Revenant" 250–51
Revenger's Tragedy, The (Tourneur) 285–86
Rice, Cale Young 184
Rice, Jane 69n18
Richter, Larry 275
Rickard, Dennis 9, 202
Riddle of the Universe, The (Haeckel) 182
Riffaterre, Michael 110
Rimbaud, Arthur 85, 96, 154, 155, 156, 161, 188
Rime Isle (Leiber) 267
Robertson, A. M. 16, 17, 25, 26, 34, 39, 41, 44, 46, 152
Robinson, Edwin Arlington 95, 97, 129, 192
Robinson Jeffers: The Man and the Artist (Sterling) 17
"Rod Serling's Night Gallery" 9
Rohan, Michael Scott 271, 272–73
Rolling Stones, The 274
"Root of Ampoi, The" 339
"Rosa Mystica" 241
Rosamund (Sterling) 17, 20
Rossetti, Dante Gabriel 85, 202
Rubaiyat (Khayyam) 29
Ruskin, John 40

Russell, Bertrand 186, 187
Ryder, David Warren 71, 74, 77, 89n1

S/Z (Barthes) 319
Sackett, Samuel J. 79, 83, 99, 224
Sacramento Bee 58
Sacramento Union 70n22
"Sadastor" 20, 67, 139, 146, 157, 173, 207, 209, 235, 338
Sails and Mirage (Sterling) 17
Saison en enfer, Une (Rimbaud) 145
Saltus, Edgar 95
San Francisco Bulletin 130
San Francisco Call 34, 130
San Francisco Chronicle 61
San Francisco Examiner 180
San Francisco Evening Post 43
San Jose Mercury and Herald 46
"San Satiro" (France) 158
Sandalwood 28, 29, 60–61, 80, 94, 244, 246, 247, 254
Santayana, George 180, 191
Sappho 184
Saroyan, William 61
"Sarpedon" (Markham) 153
"Sarrasine" (Balzac) 319–20
"Satan Unrepentant" 72, 79, 132–37
Saturday Evening Post 61
Saturay Review of Literature 8
"Saturn" 91, 93
"Satyr, The" 206–7, 222, 294–95, 298, 299, 304, 339
Saunders, Charles R. 272
Scarfe, Francis 138
"Scarlet Egg, The" 344
"Schizoid Creator" 21, 31, 164, 226, 344
Scholes, Robert 319
Schultz, David E. 90, 96
Schwob, Marcel 154
Scott, Sir Walter 201
Scrutiny 185
"Sea Cycle" 255
"Sea-Memory" 22
"Second Interment, The" 173, 198, 207, 341
Secret Doctrine, The (Blavatsky) 278
"Seed from the Sepulcher, The" 341
"Seedling of Mars" 341

Selected Poems 32, 86, 133, 139, 153, 202, 246, 252, 257
Selected Poems (Sterling) 17, 25, 27, 32
"Selenique" 97
Service, Robert W. 267
"Seven Geases, The" 159, 178, 207, 208, 216, 224, 261–63, 269, 344
"Shadow—A Parable" (Poe) 80
"Shadow Kingdom, The" (Howard) 269
"Shadow of Nightmare, The" 43
"Shadows, The" 80, 143, 205, 212
Shakespeare, William 79, 280, 285
"Shapes of Adamant" 344
Shelley, Percy Bysshe 53, 72, 79, 85, 120, 121, 122, 127, 130, 141, 186, 189, 234
Shlain, Leonard 309
Shusterman, Richard 186
Sidney-Fryer, Donald 9, 28, 71, 120, 138, 139, 148, 151, 202, 204, 253, 254, 256, 257, 260, 275, 280, 282, 305, 315, 335
"Silence—A Fable" (Poe) 80, 173
Silmarillion, The (Tolkien) 271–72
"Silver Key, The" (Lovecraft) 201
Silver Stallion, The (Cabell) 201
Sime, Sidney 289
"Sinbad, It Was Not Well to Brag" 86
Sirens of Titan, The (Vonnegut) 199
"Slaves of the Black Pillar" 341
Smart Set 26, 27, 155
Smith, Clark Ashton: as columnist, 27–28, 246–47; cosmicism of, 7–8, 190–91; criticism of, 8–9, 3470, 71, 76–84, 129–30; as essayist, 195–96; as fiction writer, 8–9, 31–32, 61–63, 66–67, 72, 73, 78–78, 81–83, 86–89, 145–50, 156–79, 196–99, 206–18, 221–38, 247–50, 259–345; life of, 65–66, 151, 170, 202, 252–54, 335; as Modernist, 180–94; philosophy of, 85–89, 106–7, 148–51, 180–99, 225, 293; as poet, 8, 19–31, 32–33, 34–61, 63–65, 66–67, 71–73, 77–78, 79–81, 86, 90–137, 152, 154–55, 183–84, 188, 202–5, 214, 229–30, 231, 239–46, 250–57, 290–91; as prose poet, 138–47, 155–56, 235–36, 244; prose style of, 87, 168–69, 189–90, 196; as satirist, 221–28; as Symbolist, 90–98, 188

Smith, Frances Gaylord 252
"Soliloquy in an Ebon Tower" 97
"Solution" 59
Some Imagist Poets 184
"Something New" 157
"Song" 247
"Song of Aviol, The" 247
"Song of Cartha, The" 247
"Song of Dreams, A" 97
Song of Ice and Fire, A (Martin) 273
"Song of the Comet, The" 38, 91, 155
"Song of the Necromancer" 229–30, 231
"Song to Oblivion" 44, 51
"Sonnet d'automne" (Baudelaire) 96
"Sonnet for the Psychoanalysts" 86
Sonnets to Craig (Sterling) 17
"Sorceress of Averoigne, The" 340
"Sorrowing of Winds" 183
"Soul of the Sea, The" 68n12
Spells and Philtres 93, 257
Spencer, Herbert 53
Spenser, Edmund 79, 203, 248
"Spirit of Solitude, The" (Shelley) 120
Stableford, Brian 277, 324
"Star-Change, A" 62, 185–86, 342
"Star-Treader, The" 36, 37, 46–47, 68nn6–9, 91, 142, 154–55
Star-Treader and Other Poems, The 22, 24, 25, 26, 29, 34–53, 58, 65, 66, 75, 80, 124, 129, 130, 142, 152, 180, 182, 183, 189, 202, 240, 282
"Statement of Randolph Carter, The" (Lovecraft) 65, 339
Stauffer, Donald Barlow 222
Sterling, Carrie 18, 257n1
Sterling, George 70nn19, 22, 75, 94, 202, 257n1; CAS on, 21, 195; on CAS, 25, 33, 71, 74, 77, 85, 139, 147; correspondence with CAS, 68nn5, 15, 69nn16, 17, 70n21, 130, 183, 184, 189–90, 192, 279; influence on CAS, 7, 8, 19–33, 50, 53, 58, 60, 79, 80, 130, 142, 152, 155, 180, 234, 239–40, 308, 329–31, 332; life of, 13–14, 247; as poet, 14–19, 24, 95, 122, 152, 153, 181–82, 183, 186, 187, 203, 329–31
Stevenson, Robert Louis 13, 207
Stickney, Trumbull 95

Stockton, Richard 8
Strachey, Lytton 83, 84n1, 87
"Strange Shadows" 344
Strange Shadows 108, 148
Strange Tales 195, 199
"Stranger from Kurdistan, The" (Price) 226
Structuralist Poetics (Culler) 318
Sturgeon, Theodore 69n18, 260
Sturm, F. P. 94
Suetonius (C. Suetonius Tranquillus) 124, 126, 128
Sully, Genevieve K. 30, 335
"Supernumerary Corpse, The" 207, 222, 342
Swinburne, Algernon Charles 73, 85, 117, 122, 330
Sword of Welleran, The (Dunsany) 201
"Symbols" 98, 243
Symons, Arthur 38, 80, 95, 139
"Symposium of the Gorgon, The" 164, 226–27, 229, 344

"Tale of Gnydron, A" 277, 279, 340
"Tale of Macrocosmic Horror, The" 199
"Tale of Satampra Zeiros, The" 88, 145, 158, 206, 208, 267, 279, 339
"Tale of Sir John Maundeville, A" 74, 207, 340
Tales of Science and Sorcery 88, 148
Tales of Zothique 277
Tate, Allen 97
"Tears of Lilith, The" 97
Teasdale, Sara 95
Tempest, The (Shakespeare) 79
Temptation of Saint Anthony, The (Flaubert) 120
10 Story Book 157
Tennyson, Alfred, Lord 86, 129, 186
"Terror and Erebus" (MacEwen) 273
"Testament of Athammaus, The" 69n18, 159, 197, 207, 208, 213, 234, 266, 267, 268, 340
Testimony of the Suns, The (Sterling) 14–15, 19, 21, 23, 80, 152, 182
Theodore, Brother 8
"Theft of the Thirty-nine Girdles, The" 344

"Third Episode of Vathek, The" (Beckford-Smith) 74, 78, 343
"Thirteen Phantasms" 230, 338
Thirty-five Sonnets (Sterling) 16, 24
Thomson, James 72, 79
"Thor Meets Captain America" (Bear) 267
Thousand and One Nights. *See Arabian Nights*
Timaeus (Plato) 239
Time and the Gods (Dunsany) 201
Time Machine, The (Wells) 217
"To Annie" (Poe). *See* "For Annie"
"To Helen" (Poe) 131n1
"To His Coy Mistress" (Marvell) 260
"To Nora May French" 242
"To Science" (Sterling) 182
"To the Daemon" 145, 150, 206, 247–48
"To the Darkness" 49–50
"To the Sun" 52–53
Todd, Frank Morton 53, 60
"Told in the Desert" 232, 237, 339
Tolkien, J. R. R. 114, 150, 151, 201, 264, 271–72, 273, 318, 323
"Tolometh" 251–52
"Tomb-Spawn, The" 283, 287, 343
Tombstone (film) 328–39
Toqueville, Alexis de 225
"Torture of Hope, The" (Villiers de l'Isle-Adam). *See* "Torture par l'espérance, La"
"Torture par l'espérance, La" (Villiers de l'Isle-Adam) 162, 284, 324, 325
"Touch-stone, The" 146
Tourneur, Cyril 282, 285
Town Talk 22, 129
Tragical History of Doctor Faustus, The (Marlowe) 259
"Transcendence" 54
"Traveller, The" 140
"Treader of the Dust, The" 206, 321, 344
Treadwell, Sophie 43
Triumph of Bohemia, The (Sterling) 15, 17
Truth (Sterling) 17, 20
Tsathoggua 208, 209, 263, 336
Tumbrils 76, 84n1
Turn of the Screw, The (James) 318
Twain, Mark 13
"Twilight of the Gods" 86

2001: A Space Odyssey (Clarke-Kubrick) 216
"Tyger, The" (Blake) 120

"Ubbo-Sathla" 159, 215–16, 268–69, 342
"Ulalume" (Poe) 53
"Uncharted Isle, The" 158, 169, 173, 339
Unknown Worlds 61, 69n18
"Unquiet Boundary" 345
"Unrevealed, The" 43
Untermeyer, Louis 64, 85

"Valediction to George Sterling, A" 20
Valéry, Paul 93, 94, 218
Vance, Jack 323
"Varied Types" (O'Day) 22
Varieties of Religious Experience, The (James) 109
Vathek (Beckford) 57, 72, 168, 278, 288, 321, 322
"Vaults of Yoh-Vombis, The" 70n18, 160, 171, 176, 308, 341
"Venus of Azombeii, The" 210, 232, 339
"Venus of Ille, The" (Mérimée) 158
Verhaeren, Emile 96
Verlaine, Paul 93, 94, 96, 153, 154
"Vie Anterieure, La" (Baudelaire) 94
Viele-Griffin, Francis 95
"Vignettes" 139, 143
Vigny, Alfred de 154
"Villa Lucienne, The" (d'Arcy) 209–10
Villiers de l'Isle-Adam, Jean-Marie-Mathias-Philippe-Auguste, comte de 162, 284, 324, 325, 332
Villon, François 184
"Vintage from Atlantis, A" 206, 248–49, 341
"Vision of Lucifer, A" 79
"Visitors from Mlok, The" 62
"Vizaphmal in Ophiuchus" 339
Vonnegut, Kurt 196, 199
Voyage and Travel of Sir John Mandeville, The 72
"Voyage of King Euvoran, The" 79, 88, 162, 259, 282–83, 286–87, 307, 309–10, 343
"Voyage to Sfanomoë, A" 206, 210, 211, 247, 339

"Vulthoom" 62, 88, 308, 343

Wagner, Karl Edward 266
Walpole, Horace 201
Wandrei, Donald 74, 77, 96, 170, 187, 190, 195, 222, 315
War Is Kind (Crane) 181
Wasp 39
Waste Land, The (Eliot) 30, 73
Water of the Wondrous Isles, The (Morris) 201
Watson, William 41
Waverly (Scott) 201
"Weaver in the Vault, The" 198, 283, 287, 343
Webster, John 277, 282, 285
Webster's Unabridged Dictionary 187
"Weird of Avoosl Wuthoqquan, The" 70n18, 159, 178, 198, 206, 208, 226, 264, 274, 326, 341
Weird Tales 7, 8, 20, 61, 67, 72, 80, 82, 96, 147, 148, 149, 156, 157, 160, 169, 170, 173, 176, 206, 263, 275, 277, 284, 285, 287, 288, 289, 290, 301, 304, 308, 334, 335
Well at the World's End, The (Morris) 201
Well of St. Clare, The (France) 158
Wells, H. G. 217, 223, 271
Wetzel, Geoerge 336
Wheelwright, Philip 331
"Where the Tides Ebb and Flow" (Dunsany) 211
"Whisperer in Darkness, The" (Lovecraft) 170
Whistler, James A. McNeill 40
"White Death" 95
"White Ship, The" (Lovecraft) 201, 213
"White Sybil, The" 209, 236, 237, 264–66, 342
Whitman, Walt 181
Whittier, John Greenleaf 181
Wilde, Oscar 72, 74, 79, 85, 125, 139, 206, 207, 210
Williams, Oscar 85
Williams, Tad 272, 273–74
Williams, William Carlos 93, 140
"Willow Landscape, The" 173, 308, 315–16, 339

Wilson, Edmund 318–19
"Wine of Wizardry, A" (Sterling) 15, 16, 18, 19, 21, 29, 31, 32, 50, 57, 80, 152, 153, 182, 187, 239–40
Wine of Wizardry and Other Poems, A (Sterling) 16, 21, 183
"Wink and the Chuckle, The" 345
Winter of the World trilogy (Rohan) 271, 272–73
"Witch in the Graveyard, The" 90, 141
"Witch with Eyes of Amber, The" 86
"Witchcraft of Ulua, The" 162, 163, 174, 207, 222, 287–88, 343
"Wizard's Love" 230, 253
Wolfe, Charles K. 9, 310, 327
Wolfe, Thomas 88
Wonder Stories 20, 62, 87, 148, 160, 169, 186, 190, 195, 196, 198, 222, 293, 308, 342
Wood, W. E. 14
Wood Beyond the World, The (Morris) 201
Wordsworth, William 52
Work, George 77
World War I 16, 30
Worm Ouroboros, The (Eddison) 201
Wright, Farnsworth 67, 147, 157, 173, 176, 302, 343

"Xeethra" 163, 164, 169, 171, 206, 211, 215, 234–35, 281, 282, 283, 285, 288, 293, 318–23, 344
Xiccarph 88, 307, 311
Xiccarph 148

Y., G. R. 40
Yosemite: An Ode (Sterling) 16
Young, Edward 42, 153
"Young Poet and True, A" (Garnett) 34

Zola, Emile 175
Zothique 7, 61, 69n18, 72, 88, 145, 161–63, 166, 171, 203, 206, 211, 212, 213–14, 216, 217, 225, 233, 234, 239, 248, 259, 260, 261, 277–92, 293, 299, 304, 307, 322, 324, 326, 328, 340, 343
"Zothique" 86, 97, 214, 324
Zothique 148, 277

www.ingramcontent.com/pod-product-compliance
Lightning Source LLC
Chambersburg PA
CBHW020938180426
43194CB00038B/221